Veröffentlichungen des Europa Zentrums Tübingen
Kulturwissenschaftliche Reihe

Herausgegeben von
Michael Bosch und Gerd Schulten

Irland und Europa
Ireland and Europe

Die Kirche im Frühmittelalter
The Early Church

Herausgegeben von
Próinséas Ní Chatháin
und Michael Richter

Klett-Cotta

Gedruckt mit Unterstützung des Ministeriums für Wissenschaft und Kunst des Landes Baden-Württemberg, des Stifterverbandes für die Deutsche Wissenschaft und der National University of Ireland.

Das Bildmotiv auf dem Schutzumschlag entstammt dem "Book of Dimma" (ca. 750 n. Chr.) fol. 104 v, Symbol des Evangelisten Johannes. Der Abdruck erfolgt mit freundlicher Genehmigung der Trinity College Library, Dublin.

CIP-Kurztitelaufnahme der Deutschen Bibliothek

Irland und Europa, die Kirche im Frühmittelalter =
Ireland and Europe, the early church / hrsg. von
Próinséas Ni Chatháin u. Michael Richter. —
Stuttgart : Klett-Cotta, 1984.
(Veröffentlichungen des Europa-Zentrums Tübingen :
Kulturwiss. Reihe)
ISBN 3-608-91549-4
NE: Ni Chatháin, Próinséas [Hrsg.]; PT

Vorwort

Von
Gerd Schulten

Irland, die Insel vor einer Insel, hat im Bewußtsein der Europäer immer nur eine untergeordnete Rolle gespielt. Dies widerspricht allerdings ganz eklatant der wirklichen Bedeutung, die Irland für den Kontinent besessen hat. Denn nach dem treffenden Urteil des 1981 in Dublin verstorbenen großen Gelehrten Ludwig Bieler war Irland ein „Wegbereiter des Mittelalters"[1]. Die Grundlagen und Anfänge der abendländischen Kultur sind also nicht nur in Antike und Christentum, sondern auch auf der keltischen Insel am Westrand Europas zu suchen. Hier entfaltete sich nämlich unberührt von den Wirren der Völkerwanderung seit dem 5. Jahrhundert eine Kunst und Bildung pflegende Klosterkirche, die klassische, keltische und christliche Traditionen miteinander verband und an die noch wenig zivilisierten Völker der Britischen Insel und des Festlands weitervermittelte: ex occidente lux – das Licht aus dem Westen[2].

Dieser Tatsachen beginnt man sich erst langsam wieder zu erinnern[3]. Die Iren selbst machen auf die glanzvolle Epoche ihrer Geschichte aufmerksam, indem sie die beeindruckendsten Schätze keltisch-christlicher Kunst auf kulturpolitisch äußerst wirksame Ausstellungen nach Europa und Übersee schicken. Man braucht hier nur auf die „Treasures of Early Irish Art" hinzuweisen, die von Oktober 1982 bis Juni 1984 in Paris, Köln, Berlin, Amsterdam und Kopenhagen zu bewundern waren[4]. Aber auch von europäischer Seite wird einiges getan, um die historische Leistung der Mönche von der grünen Insel im werdenden Abendland angemessen zu würdigen. So veranstaltete das Europa Zentrum Tübingen bereits zwei internationale Kolloquien zum hier behandelten Thema, und zwar zunächst

---

1 *Ludwig Bieler*, Irland – Wegbereiter des Mittelalters, Olten/Lausanne/Freiburg i. Br. 1961.

2 So der englischsprachige Titel des Buches von *William H. Marnell*, Light from the West: the Irish mission and the emergence of modern Europe, New York 1978.

3 Zwar waren schon vor mehr als einhundert Jahren grundlegende Werke zu diesem Themenbereich erschienen, doch verfolgte *J. H. A. Ebrard*, Die iroschottische Missionskirche des 6., 7. und 8. Jahrhunderts, Gütersloh 1873, ND Hildesheim/New York 1971, so sehr konfessionalistische Ziele, daß ihm die eigentlich angemessene Wirkung versagt blieb. In einer Art Gegenreaktion neigte man dazu, die Bedeutung der irischen Mission und Kultur zu unterschätzen, zu stark waren die Urteile „von der Parteien Gunst und Haß verwirrt". Vgl. dazu *Johannes Duft*, Iromanie – Irophobie. Fragen um die frühmittelalterliche Irenmission, exemplifiziert an St. Gallen und Alemannien, Zeitschrift für Schweizerische Kirchengeschichte 50 (1956), S. 241–262.

4 Die Ausstellung wurde zunächst in New York, San Francisco, Pittsburgh, Boston und Philadelphia gezeigt. (Gleichlautender Katalog, hg. vom Metropolitan Museum of Art, New York 1977). Der deutsche Katalog erschien unter dem Titel: Irische Kunst aus drei Jahrtausenden – Thesaurus Hiberniae. Mainz 1983.

1979 in Tübingen und dann gemeinsam mit dem Board of Medieval Studies 1981 am University College in Dublin[5]. Die Dubliner Vorträge sind – zum Teil erweitert und überarbeitet – in dem vorliegenden Band zusammengefaßt.

Die Durchführung des Kolloquiums 1981 und die Drucklegung seiner Ergebnisse wurden erst ermöglicht durch eine große Anzahl namhafter Spenden. Folgenden Personen und Institutionen sei deshalb auch an dieser Stelle nochmals ausdrücklich gedankt:

Prof. Kurt A. Koppenhöfer, Stuttgart

Bischof Dr. Ernst Tewes, Erzbistum München und Freising

Bischöfliches Ordinariat Rottenburg

Evangelischer Oberkirchenrat Karlsruhe

Ministerium für Wissenschaft und Kunst des Landes Baden-Württemberg

Stifterverband für die Deutsche Wissenschaft

Gustav Schickedanz KG, Fürth

Motoren- und Turbinen-Union, Friedrichshafen

Deutsch-Irischer Freundeskreis in Baden-Württemberg e.V.

Bank of Ireland

University College Dublin

European Cultural Foundation, Amsterdam

Besonderer Dank aber gebührt dem Initiator der gesamten Kolloquiumsreihe, dem Stuttgarter Architekten Professor Kurt A. Koppenhöfer, denn unser Wissen über Irland wäre, wie in Dublin formuliert wurde, ohne seine Generosität und Ingeniosität sehr viel geringer, als es inzwischen tatsächlich ist.

Die Ergebnisse des Tübinger Kolloquiums, auf die nun im folgenden eingegangen werden soll, sind unter dem Titel „Die Iren und Europa im früheren Mittelalter" veröffentlicht worden. In diesem rund 1100 Seiten umfassenden Standardwerk zeichnen über vierzig Wissenschaftler aus fast allen Ländern, in denen irische Missionare tätig waren, ein facettenreiches Bild der alten irischen Kultur und vor allem ihrer Ausstrahlung auf den frühmittelalterlichen Kontinent[6].

Da die Insel Hibernia von den Römern niemals erobert worden war, bewahrte sie ihren eigenständigen keltischen Charakter. Daran änderte sich auch nichts, als der hl. Patrick 431 die rasche und erfolgreiche Christianisierung des Landes einleitete. Die Kirche zeigte vielmehr eine erstaunliche Offenheit gegenüber den alten, heidnischen Lebensgewohnheiten und Ausdrucksformen, so daß es in Kunst, Literatur und Rechtsprechung, aber auch in Religion und Theologie zu einer Verschränkung und Überlagerung von keltischen und christlichen Elementen

---

5 Im August 1984 findet ein weiteres Kolloquium in Dublin statt über „Irland und Europa im Frühmittelalter III: Bibelstudien und Glaubensvermittlung in den nicht-romanischen Ländern, ca. 550–ca. 800".

6 *Heinz Löwe* (Hg.), Die Iren und Europa im früheren Mittelalter, 2 Teilbände, Stuttgart 1982. = Veröffentlichungen des Europa Zentrums Tübingen.

kam. Als Beispiel dafür sei angeführt, daß selbst noch die späten Hochkreuze des 10. und 11. Jahrhunderts biblische und mythologische Szenen einträchtig nebeneinander stellten.

Das frühchristliche Irland unterschied sich vor allem darin vom Festland, daß es in einer Mönchskirche organisiert war, die den Bischof dem Abt unterordnete. In jurisdiktioneller und kultureller Hinsicht dominierten ganz eindeutig die Klöster, deren engmaschiges Netz die gesamte Insel überzog. Auch heute noch spürt der Besucher von Glendalough, Monasterboice und Clonmacnois, daß diese Orte die geistigen und geistlichen Zentren des Landes waren. Von hier aus brachen die Mönche zur Mission der Picten, Angelsachsen, Franken, Alemannen und Langobarden auf, oder um es mit modernen Begriffen zu sagen: der Schotten, Engländer, Deutschen, Franzosen, Schweizer, Österreicher und Italiener. Aber andererseits reisten schon bald auch junge Kleriker aus den missionierten Ländern zu den wegen ihrer Zucht und Gelehrsamkeit gelobten Klosterschulen in Irland, um dort zu studieren. Von Glendalough wird berichtet, daß es im 7./8. Jahrhundert die meistfrequentierte Bildungsstätte Europas war.

Theologische Grundlage der irischen Mission war der Gedanke der asketischen Heimatlosigkeit, der peregrinatio pro Christo. Da das eigene Land als vollständig christianisiert gelten konnte, wollten die Mönche ihr Bekehrungswerk in der Fremde fortsetzen. Ins benachbarte und verwandte Schottland begab sich Columba, der zur Unterscheidung vom jüngeren Columban besser mit seinem keltischen Namen Columcille genannt wird, was übrigens so viel bedeutet wie Taube der Kirche. Nachdem Columcille in Irland bereits die drei berühmten Klöster von Derry, Durrow und Kells gegründet hatte, rief er 563 auf Iona eine weitere Mönchsgemeinschaft ins Leben. Durch die Missionierung der Picten wurde zunächst Schottland für den christlichen Glauben gewonnen. Wenig später erschienen die Wandermönche von Iona in Northumbrien, wo sie 635 das nicht minder wichtige Kloster von Lindisfarne anlegten. Allerdings kam es in dem nördlichsten der angelsächsischen Königreiche zu heftigen und langwierigen Kontroversen zwischen irischen und südenglischen Geistlichen, weil man sich in Fragen der Tonsur und des Osterdatums nicht einigen konnte. Obwohl sich die prorömische Partei des Südens in diesen beiden Punkten durchsetzte, wirkte der Einfluß der Iren auf die englische Kirche noch lange nach. Das äußerte sich nicht zuletzt darin, daß die Angelsachsen den Gedanken des geistlichen Exils übernahmen und selber als Missionare auf das Festland gingen.

Während der aus diesem irisch geprägten Milieu stammende Angelsachse Bonifatius als Apostel der Deutschen verehrt wird, ist beinahe völlig in Vergessenheit geraten, daß Männer wie Columban (✝ 612), Gallus (✝ 645) und Kilian (✝ 689) – um nur die geläufigsten Namen zu erwähnen – ihm schon längst den Weg bereitet hatten. Mit der Taufe Chlodwigs waren die Merowinger zum Katholizismus übergetreten, aber nur in einem sehr oberflächlichen Sinne, wie ihre wahrhaft bluttriefende Familiengeschichte beweist. Daher stellten sich die irischen Mönche die ebenso nötige wie lohnende Aufgabe einer inneren Mission des

Frankenreichs. Nach heimatlichem Vorbild gründeten sie so viele Klöster, daß sich einem das Wort von der irofränkischen Klosterkultur geradezu aufdrängt[7]. Columban, seit etwa 590 auf dem Kontinent, unterwarf seine Schüler strengster Disziplin und verfaßte eigene Mönchs- und Bußregeln. In die dogmatischen Streitigkeiten seiner Zeit griff er ein, indem er sich mit dezidierten Vorschlägen mehrfach brieflich an den Papst wandte. Was ihn und seine Mitbrüder auszeichnete, war die konsequente Verwirklichung ihres christlichen Glaubens im täglichen Leben. Die Iren überzeugten offenbar mehr durch ihr praktisches Vorbild als durch bloßes Predigen. Doch wurde Columban wegen seiner moralischen Strenge für das merowingische Königshaus bald ein zu unbequemer Mahner, weshalb er sein Stammkloster Luxeuil in den Vogesen verlassen mußte. Über St. Gallen, das den Namen seines dort zurückgebliebenen Begleiters Gallus trägt, gelangte er ins oberitalienische Bobbio, wo er auch begraben liegt: Columban, der Apostel Europas.

In den folgenden Jahrhunderten sind die Iren aus dem kirchlichen und geistigen Leben des Kontinents nicht mehr wegzudenken, obwohl sich Persönlichkeiten vom Range Columbans kaum noch finden, abgesehen natürlich von Johannes Scottus Eriugena (810–877). Wie dieser wohl originärste und systematischste Denker des frühen Mittelalters traten auch die übrigen Männer von der grünen Insel als Gelehrte oder als Dichter und nicht mehr als Wandermönche und Klostergründer hervor. Denn durch die angelsächsische Mission wurde die typisch irische Klosterorganisation von der römisch-zentralistischen Bischofskirche abgelöst. Trotzdem gab es aber auch im hohen und späten Mittelalter noch zahlreiche Gemeinschaften irischer Mönche, allerdings unter dem leicht verwirrenden Namen der Schottenklöster, da nämlich Scoti die ursprüngliche Sammelbezeichnung für die Kelten in Irland und im westlichen Schottland war[8].

Erst mit der normannischen Invasion seit 1169 und der langen Fremdherrschaft der Engländer wurde Irland vom Festland abgeschnitten und kulturell isoliert. Welchen Ruhm es aber als Insel der Heiligen und Gelehrten in seiner großen Zeit genossen hatte, brachte um die Mitte des 9. Jahrhunderts Bischof Donatus von Fiesole bei Florenz mit folgenden, bereits zurückschauenden Versen zum Ausdruck: Der edelste Teil der Erde ist die ferne westliche Welt,/ Deren Name in alten Büchern Scottia heißt,/ Reich an Gütern, Silber, Juwelen, Tuch und Gold,/ Dem Leibe bekömmlich, von der Luft her wie von der milden Erde,/ Von Honig und

---

7 *Friedrich Prinz*, Frühes Mönchtum im Frankenreich. Kultur und Gesellschaft in Gallien, den Rheinlanden und Bayern am Beispiel der monastischen Entwicklung (4. bis 8. Jahrhundert), München/Wien 1965. Ein Nachdruck mit neuem Vorwort und aktueller Literaturübersicht ist geplant.

8 Auf Einzelbelege konnte hier verzichtet werden, da die entsprechenden Aufsätze bei *Löwe* (Hg.), Die Iren und Europa, umfangreiche Quellen- und Literaturangaben enthalten. An Neuerscheinungen ist lediglich nachzutragen *Michael Richter*, Irland im Mittelalter. Kultur und Geschichte, Stuttgart 1983. Dieses Buch behandelt das gesamte Mittelalter und reicht bis etwa 1500.

Milch fließen Irlands liebliche Ebenen über,/ An Seide und Waffen, an Kunst und Menschen, von Früchten voll,/ Wert sind die Iren, zu wohnen in diesem Land,/ Eine Menschenrasse, berühmt im Krieg, im Frieden und im Glauben.

Das Urteil des Donatus von Fiesole wirkte lange nach, und der Hinweis auf die sich durch den Glauben und die Weisheit ihrer Bewohner auszeichnende Insel ist ein Topos, der auch heute noch in der Forschung und Literatur gerne gebraucht wird[9]. So wählte selbst James Joyce für einen kulturhistorischen Essay über seine Heimat den Titel „Irland – Insel der Heiligen und Weisen"[10].

Während man sich in Tübingen vorrangig mit der Mission und Kultur der Iren auf dem Kontinent befaßt hatte, lag der Schwerpunkt des Dubliner Kolloquiums, für dessen wissenschaftliche Leitung Próinséas Ní Chatháin und Michael Richter verantwortlich zeichneten, auf der Frage nach der „Eigenentwicklung der frühen irischen Kirche im Rahmen der keltischen Zivilisation". Da Michael Richter am Schluß dieses Bandes die Ergebnisse inhaltlich zusammenfaßte, genügt hier eine kurze Übersicht über den äußeren Aufbau und Verlauf der im University College Dublin abgehaltenen internationalen Tagung.

Der Kongreß erfreute sich eines außergewöhnlich lebhaften Interesses, wovon auch noch die Vor-, Gruß- und Eröffnungsworte dieses Bandes zeugen. Als Teilnehmer konnten u. a. begrüßt werden der Kardinalprimas von Irland, Tomás Ó Fiaich, das Mitglied des Staatsrates, Frau Dr. Máirín Bean Uí Dhálaigh, der Kanzler der National University of Ireland, Dr. T. K. Whitaker, der Präsident des University College Dublin, Dr. Thomas Murphy und der Präsident der Royal Irish Academy, Professor Proinsias Mac Cana. Dazu kamen zahlreiche Vertreter politischer, diplomatischer und kultureller Einrichtungen. Besonders beachtet aber wurde die Tatsache, daß sich die Referenten nicht nur aus Europa und Übersee, sondern aus allen wissenschaftlichen Institutionen im Süden und Norden Irlands zu diesem Kolloquium über das gemeinsame historische Erbe zusammengefunden hatten. Als besondere Auszeichnung betrachteten die Veranstalter die Eröffnung des Kongresses durch den Doyen der irischen Rechts- und Kulturgeschichte, Professor D. A. Binchy.

Um das Wesen der irischen Kirche und der von ihr getragenen Kultur auf der Insel, in Britannien und auf dem Kontinent voll zu erfassen, bedarf es interdisziplinärer Fragestellungen und Methoden. Daher wurden neben allgemeinen historischen und theologischen Themen auch spezielle Probleme der Archäologie und

9 Das klingt zum Beispiel auch durch in der griffigen Formulierung von *Ingeborg Meyer-Sickendiek*, Gottes gelehrte Vaganten. Auf den Spuren der irischen Mission und Kultur in Europa, Stuttgart 1980.

10 Am leichtesten zugänglich bei *Gerd Haffmans* (Hg.), Das Diogenes Lesebuch irischer Erzähler, Zürich 1976, S. 12–34. Es handelt sich hierbei um den Vortrag „Irlanda – Isola dei Santi e dei Savi", den *Joyce* am 27. April 1907 an der Università Popolare in Triest gehalten hat.

Kunstgeschichte, der Sprach- und Literaturwissenschaft sowie der Rechtsgeschichte behandelt.

Die archäologischen Vorträge machten deutlich, daß man noch mit der Bestandsaufnahme beschäftigt ist und weitere Grabungen durchführen muß, um zu gesicherteren Ergebnissen zu gelangen, etwa bei der Rekonstruktion der Holzkirchen und der – heftig umstrittenen – Datierung der ältesten Steinkirchen. Erhebliche Fortschritte hat man indes bereits bei der Interpretation der irischen Hochkreuze gemacht, die Hilary Richardson mit den armenisch-byzantinischen Kreuzstelen in Verbindung brachte[11].

Die Neuerungen auf dem Gebiet der Sprache äußerten sich in einer umfänglichen hiberno-lateinischen Literatur, in die auch viele irische Lehnwörter eindrangen. Andererseits nahm das Irische eine große Zahl lateinischer Lehnwörter auf, so daß sich das Irische und Lateinische gegenseitig bereicherten. Selbst die Ortsnamen wurden christianisiert und latinisiert. Das Entscheidende jedoch war, daß die Mönche das System der Schriftlichkeit entwickelten und damit die nur mündlich überlieferten keltischen Mythen vor der Vergessenheit bewahrten. Durch ihre Aufzeichnungen trugen die geistlichen Schreiber zu einer Standardisierung der altirischen Orthographie und Grammatik bei und begründeten zugleich auch neben der hiberno-lateinischen Literatur die volkssprachlich-irische Literatur des frühen Mittelalters.

Besondere Aufmerksamkeit wurde noch dem weit verbreiteten Phänomen der Glossen gewidmet, wobei man linguistisch über die keltischen Sprachen und historisch über die irische Mission hinausging. Denn zusammen mit der Überlieferung irischer und bretonischer Wörter wurden auch die althochdeutschen Glossen untersucht, die aber als Ergebnis der angelsächsischen Mission zu werten sind. Überhaupt bleibt festzuhalten, daß das Irische angesichts der frühen und regen Bekehrungstätigkeit nur einen relativ geringen Einfluß auf das Althochdeutsche ausgeübt hat, was wohl am ehesten damit zu erklären ist, daß sich die Wandermönche sehr schnell der Volkssprache ihrer Gastländer bedient hätten.

Wie schon angedeutet, lebten die keltischen Traditionen sogar in Religion und Theologie fort, weshalb es naheliegt, von einer „Eigenentwicklung der frühen irischen Kirche" zu sprechen. Dabei hat man in der Forschung vor allem die irische Mönchskirche der römischen Bischofskirche gegenübergestellt. Von dieser oftmals überpointierten Differenzierung ging Patrick J. Corish aus und warnte davor, die Kategorien späterer Jahrhunderte anzulegen und einen quasi reformatorischen Gegensatz zwischen Rom und Irland zu konstruieren. Während des frühen Mittelalters gab es innerhalb des westlichen Patriarchats vielmehr eine Reihe von lokalen Kirchen. Diese „Landeskirchen" erkannten durchaus den Vorrang des apostolischen Stuhles an. Daher wandte sich auch Columban in seinen

---

11 Auf enge Beziehungen zum Festland verwies auch Peter Harbison in seinem Diskussionsbeitrag, als er die Ikonographie der Hochkreuze vom Bildprogramm der karolingischen Fresken ableitete.

Briefen an den Papst als höchste und letztentscheidende theologische Instanz. Erst die wissenschaftliche Wiederbelebung des römisch-kanonischen Rechts im 12. Jahrhundert hat aus dem theologischen principatus eine politisch-juristische plenitudo potestatis des Papsttums gemacht, wodurch in der Folgezeit die Besonderheiten der frühen irischen Kirche als nichtkanonische, fast schon „antirömische" Abweichungen erscheinen mußten.

Die Bedeutung Irlands für Europa, die von Friedrich Prinz an Columban und dem irofränkischen Mönchtum exemplifiziert worden war, betonte auch Diarmuid Ó Laoghaire in seinen Gedanken zur frühen irischen Spiritualität. Da Columcille und Columban das „weiße Martyrium" des Exils zu ertragen bereit waren, konnten sie ihr großes Missionswerk in Britannien und auf dem Festland in Angriff nehmen. Allein schon deshalb gehören sie nicht nur Irland, sondern ganz Europa.

An das ausgeprägte Europa-Bewußtsein der Iren im frühen Mittelalter erinnerte auch Francis J. Byrne in seinem Resümee zum Abschluß des Kolloquiums[12]. Auf der Insel feierte man beispielsweise ein Fest aller Heiligen Irlands, Britanniens und Europas, und Columban verdanken wir den zu seiner Zeit singulären Begriff vom gesamten Europa, „totius Europae". Im frühen Mittelalter lag Irland nicht am Rande der Welt, es pflegte vielmehr intensive Kontakte zum Festland und den mittelmeerischen Ländern, bis hin nach Ägypten, Armenien und zum Heiligen Land. Von überall her empfingen die Iren mannigfaltige Anregungen, die sie in einer eigenen, keltischen Tradition verpflichteten Weise verarbeiteten und an das werdende Abendland weitergaben. Damit begann die „irische Dimension" der europäischen Geschichte des Mittelalters.

---

12 Dieser größtenteils in der Form der freien Rede gehaltene Beitrag ist hier nicht abgedruckt.

Foreword to
"Ireland and Europe: the Early Church"

By
The European Cultural Foundation

The European Cultural Foundation, created in Geneva in 1954, is a private, international, non-governmental organisation which devotes most of its resources to the development of cultural and scientific activities in Europe, thus contributing to the development of European cooperation. As reflected in its Board of Governors, which comprises forty-seven personalities from seventeen European countries, the framework of its activities extends to Europe as a whole.

Based in Amsterdam since 1960, the Foundation first became known through organising a series of congresses in various European cities on such themes as "Cultural and Intellectual Unity in Europe", "The Past and Future in Europe", and "Youth and Europe". From 1967 to 1975 its programme was dominated by a major research project entitled "Plan Europe 2000" in which a series of future-oriented studies in the fields of education, urbanisation, agriculture and environment were carried out. More than 200 researchers were involved and by 1975, over fifty publications in nine languages had been issued. Through this programme, as well as making a major contribution to future research studies in Europe, the Foundation gained the reputation of an "international consultant". As an almost natural result of "Plan Europe 2000", the Foundation entered a new phase in 1975 with the establishment throughout Europe of a network of Institutes and Centres for research and policy studies. The purpose was to decentralise yet at the same time lend a European dimension to local, regional or national intitatives. The network now includes the following bodies:
- European Institute of Education and Social Policy (Paris, 1975),
  branch Office for Cooperation in Education (Brussels, 1976)
- Institute for European Environmental Policy (Bonn, 1976),
  Paris and London Offices opened respectively in 1978 and 1980
- European Cooperation Fund (Brussels, 1977)
- European Centre for Political Studies (London, 1978)
- European Centre for Work and Society (Maastricht, 1979)
- Central Unit of Eurydice, the Education Information Network in the European Community (Brussels, 1980)
- Centre for European Policy Studies (Brussels, 1981)
- European Institute for the Media (Manchester, 1983).

As part of its decentralisation policy, the Foundation also has National Commitees operative on its behalf in sixteen European countries.

Parallel, however, to its pursuit of scientific activities, the Foundation has, since its inception, maintained a grants programme in support of cultural undertakings. Initially, only projects which were "cultural" in the traditional sense of the word received support, whereas now projects in the following fields are eligible:
– architecture and archaeology
– fine arts, history, literature, music and cultural cooperation
– education, language and youth
– employment and social problems
– environment
– international relations, human rights and European cooperation
– the media.
Though relatively small in relation to those of the major American foundations, the Foundation's grants programme remains unique within the European framework in that it does not impose, directly or indirectly, any national conditions. On the contrary, projects will only be considered for support, if more than three European countries are involved.

Such was the case in the 1981 colloquium on "Ireland and Europe in the Early Middle Ages", organised by the Europa Zentrum Tübingen and the Board of Medieval Studies Dublin, and attended, among others, by American, British, French, German and Irish experts. Both for typifying the kind of joint initiative which the Foundation seeks to encourage, and for the success with which the project was realised, the Foundation is pleased to extend its congratulations on this occasion.

Grußwort von Máirín Bean Uí Dhálaigh

Mit großer Freude habe ich erfahren, daß das Zweite Internationale Kolloquium über Irland und Europa im früheren Mittelalter mit dem Thema „Die Eigenentwicklung der frühen irischen Kirche im Rahmen der keltischen Zivilisation" unter der Leitung des Europa Zentrums Tübingen und des Board of Medieval Studies am University College Dublin vom 25. bis 29. Mai in Dublin abgehalten wird.

Die Begegnung von Wissenschaftlern aus benachbarten Fachgebieten dient der Weitergabe der erworbenen Erkenntnisse; sie zeigt ferner auf, welche Forschungen in den verschiedenen Ländern betrieben werden; vor allem aber dient sie der gegenseitigen Anregung. Gelehrte in aller Welt bedürfen derartiger Begegnungen, aber ich bin der Ansicht, daß wir hier auf unserer kleinen Insel Irland besonders darauf angewiesen sind. Denn bei uns ist die Zahl der in der Wissenschaft Tätigen notgedrungen klein, und vielleicht neigen wir manchmal dazu, den Kontakt mit den großen Linien europäischer Forschungstätigkeit etwas zu verlieren.

Da das Thema des Kolloquiums einem Aspekt unserer eigenen frühen Geschichte gewidmet ist, können wir die Bedeutung dieser Begegnung für uns nicht hoch genug einschätzen.

Ich wünsche dem Kolloquium viel Erfolg.

Máirín Bean Uí Dhálaigh

Is breá liom a chlos go bhfuil an dara Colloquium Idirnáisiúnta faoi choimirce Bhórd Léann na Meánaoise i gColáiste Ollscoile Bhaile Atha Cliath agus Europa Zentrum Tübingen le bheith ar siúl i mBaile Atha Cliath ó Bhealtaine 25–29.

Nuair a chruinníonn na scoláirí i dteannta a chéile, go mór mhór iad siúd gur spéis leo an t-ábhar céanna nó ábhair ghaolmhara, deintear leathnú ar an léann agus faightear cur amach ar an taighde atá á dhéanamh ins na tíortha éagsúla. Agus thar aon ní eile tugann teacht le chéile dá leithéid spreagadh agus misneach dóibh.

Cé go dteastaíonn sé seo ó lucht léinn gach tíre, dar liom is fíor-riachtanas dúinn-ne é in oileán bheag na h-Eireann áit in ar beag líon na scoláirí agus in arbh fhuirist sinn a dheighliúint ó phríomhshruth an taighde san Eoraip. Rud eile de, ní féidir róthábhacht an chaidrimh seo a mheas nuair is ábhar don taighde seo cuid de luathstair ár dtíre féin.

Guím gach rath ar an gColloquium,

Máirín Bean Uí Dhálaigh

Inhalt/Contents

D. A. Binchy
Opening address 1

I. Die Entstehung der frühen irischen Kirche
The Formation of the early Irish Church

Patrick J. Corish
The early Irish Church in the Western patriarchate 9

David N. Dumville
Some British aspects of the earliest Irish Christianity 16

Deirdre Flanagan †
The Christian impact on early Ireland: place-names evidence 25

Pádraig Ó Riain
Finnian or Winniau? 52

Richard Sharpe
Armagh and Rome in the seventh century 58

Diarmuid Ó Laoghaire
Irish spirituality 73

Peter O'Dwyer
The Céli Dé reform 83

Charles Doherty
The use of relics in early Ireland 89

II. Archäologie und Kunst
Archaeology and Art

Michael Herity
The layout of Irish early Christian monasteries 105

Ann Hamlin
The study of early Irish churches 117

Hilary Richardson
The concept of the High Cross 127

Michael Ryan
The Derrynaflan and other early Irish eucharistic chalices:
some speculations 135

III. Kanonisches Recht und irisches Recht
Canon Law and Irish Law

Gearóid MacNiocaill
Christian influences in early Irish law 151

Donnchadh Ó Corráin
Irish law and canon law 157

T. M. Charles-Edwards
The Church and settlement 167

IV. Sprache und Literatur
Language and Literature

Damian MacManus
The so-called *Cothrige* and *Pátraic* strata of Latin loan words in early Irish 179

Michael Herren
Old Irish lexical and semantic influence on Hiberno-Latin 197

E. G. Quin
The Irish glosses 210

Léon Fleuriot
The Old Breton glosses and the cultural importance of Brittany in the
early Middle Ages. 218

Rolf Bergmann
Die althochdeutsche Glossenüberlieferung des 8. Jahrhunderts 226

Stefan Sonderegger
Die Bedeutung des religiösen Wortschatzes für die Entfaltung des
Althochdeutschen: von früher Vielfalt zu allmählicher Vereinheitlichung. . . . 240

Jean-Michel Picard
The metrical prose of Adomnán's *Vita Columbae*; an unusual system 258

Seán Connolly
Some palaeographical and linguistic features in early *Lives of Brigit* 272

Pádraig Ó Néill
Romani influences on seventh-century Hiberno-Latin literature. 280

Tomás Ó Cathasaigh
Pagan survivals: the evidence of early Irish narrative 291

V. Irland und Europa
Ireland and Europe

Julian Brown
The oldest Irish manuscripts and their late antique background 311

Friedrich Prinz
Papst Gregor der Große und Columban der Jüngere 328

Martin McNamara
Tradition and creativity in early Irish psalter study..................... 338

Dagmar Ó Riain-Raedel
Irish kings and bishops in the *memoria* of the German *Schottenklöster* 390

VI. Zusammenfassung
Results

Michael Richter
Irland und Europa: Die Kirche im Frühmittelalter...................... 409

Verzeichnis der Tafeln / List of Plates 433
Tafeln / Plates .... hinter Seite 434
Abkürzungen und Siglen / Abbreviations and Sigla.................... 435
Verzeichnis der zitierten Handschriften / List of Manuscripts Cited 438
Verzeichnis irischer Glossen / List of Irish Glosses 440
Verzeichnis der zitierten Rechtstexte / List of References to Legal Material ... 441
Register / Index... 442

Opening address

By
D. A. Binchy

Mr. President, Ladies and Gentlemen,

Of course it is a great privilege to open this Colloquium, but I cannot help wondering why I was chosen. The only reason I can think of is seniority. There are comparatively few octogenarians still around who have had anything to do with this subject — it seems to kill them off quite early! Or is it that on account of my age some people — perhaps some of you — would think of me as a survival from the Middle Ages, though not one of 'the last enchantments' surely? Or is it on account of my connection with this Institution, which will probably be news to most of you — *et ego in Arcadia vixi* — some years ago, as a student and even as a member of the staff? True, I left it at a time when most of the present audience, if they were around at all, were in their perambulators. But that does give me the chance at least of pointing to the difference, the enormous difference, the change in medieval studies that has taken place in this College between the years 1917 and 1981. In my student days here the 'Middle Ages' and 'Medieval' were, if anything, pejorative words. There was no chance of learning anything about the medieval world or about medieval Ireland except to some limited extent in the course of Celtic Studies. But I can't help feeling that this was a somewhat one-sided approach to medieval studies: "It is important to know something about them, but you do not have to know very much". In any event there was no question of my doing even that, for I came up to this College completely innocent of Irish.

I didn't know any Irish until I was 26 years old. I had had an excellent classical training in Clongowes and my ambition was to take the degree, the honours degree, in classics. Here it behoves me to remember the maxim *De mortuis ...*, so perhaps the best I could do would be to draw a veil over the Classics Professors of that period. Both of them were inherited from the old Royal University, what Roman lawyers would call a *damnosa hereditas*. But there was one luminous exception to the general boredom — a young assistant named Michael Tierney. He had been appointed by the President, and thus was not part of any take-over bid. I believe I would have remained in the classical faculty if he had then been a professor, as he was of course afterwards. But I have always envied the few laymen, such as my dear friend Gerard Murphy, who stuck it out. They needed heroic virtue, and I had not that virtue. Since we only had Michael Tierney in the honours class for one lecture a week — and in Greek alone, not in Latin — I decided to call it a day at the end of my second year.

1

As it happened, I had always been interested in history, and during my First Arts year I was profoundly impressed by the lectures given by the Professor of History, John Marcus O'Sullivan. So I continued to attend his classes, sometimes at the expense of the Latin Classes. John Marcus as we all called him, students and colleagues alike, had been trained as a philosopher, and he had taken a very brilliant degree in Heidelberg in philosophy, with history merely as a minor subject; but that made his lectures all the more interesting to me because he spoke more about the history of ideas than about the history of political or military events. Remember, too, that he had to deal in three years' lectures — First Arts, Second Arts and Third Arts — with the whole of European history from Clovis to Bismarck — a tall order. But he did it, as I say, from the point of view of anyone who was interested in ideas rather than in political and military developments, extremely well. And I recall him, in the course of his academic gallop through the medieval period, speaking of what he called the most remarkable philosopher of the 9th century, a man named John Scottus, adding "incidentally, an Irishman". That was my first introduction to Eriugena.

In the meantime I had switched horses, having already taken a number of the law subjects in preparation for a call to the Bar, not indeed with any intention of practising, but simply as a gesture of ancestor worship (I hoped to devote myself to scholarship rather than to making money). So, with history as a major subject, I was able to slide over (with a rather guilty conscience) from Classics to the much easier degree of Legal and Political Science. After I had graduated I got advice from one of my former teachers at Clongowes, who was by that time editor of *Studies* — advice for which I can never be grateful enough — to take up something close to Classics and close to history at the same time: medieval studies. And he suggested my going to Munich which was then, and probably is still, the Mecca of such studies. My family were financially independent; like G. K. Chesterton, "I was born of rich but honest parents". They were prepared to frank me, so I had not to look around for a Studentship. I went straight to Munich — as ignorant of German, incidentally, as I was of Irish.

The founder of the great school of Medieval Studies, Ludwig Traube, had died at a tragically early age, but his successor Paul Lehmann, who had been a prize pupil of his, was very kind to me, though he told me afterwards he had great difficulty in controlling his amusement at the appalling ignorance shown by me at our first meeting. I will not tell you some of the things I said to him because even still they bring a blush to my cheek. He asked me if I knew any of the auxiliary sciences, *historische Hilfswissenschaften,* and I said, Oh yes, I had done Latin up to B. A. honours! But he welcomed me warmly as the first Irish student he ever had. What is more, he told me that Traube, the man who did so much to establish what we would call in modern parlance "the Irish dimension" in the medieval world, had often lamented to him that though he had students, lay and clerical, from all over the world, not merely from Germany, but from France, from England, and particularly from the United States, he had never had an Irish student. Lehmann

2

gave me *Perrona Scottorum* to start with and I must say it opened a new world to me. Traube was not merely a great scholar, he was also a great artist. (He always reminds me of another scholar-artist whom I met in a very different context, F. W. Maitland). And although I am quite sure that much of what he wrote in the *Vorlesungen und Abhandlungen* has now become out of date, I would recommend any medieval student to read through these three volumes, for entertainment if nothing else.

Well, I spent three years in Munich working at a dissertation on the history of the Irish Ratisbon monasteries which was chosen for me by the Professor of Medieval History, von Grauert, and in which, to tell you the truth, I was not very interested. My main interest was to attend the lectures and seminars on literature of four great scholars: Lehmann himself; Clemens Bäumker, the leading authority on medieval philosophy; Martin Grabmann, on the Scholastic Method; and Rudolf von Heckel, who taught the *historische Hilfswissenschaften* (of whose nature I had shown myself so ignorant), palaeography, diplomatics and chronology. With three of them at least I eventually established very friendly relations, and when I was leaving they all urged me to go back to Ireland and try to teach something of what I learned from them. I must confess that I had not the slightest intention of doing this. I had no Irish, and while I had read most of the Latin works by Irish writers which had appeared in the *Monumenta Germaniae Historica,* I had an instinctive feeling that unless I knew the contemporary native language of the writer I would miss a lot (and here is something I want to rub in before I sit down: you *do* need the two languages). Besides, at that time how could one hope to make a living in the Ireland of the twenties as a medievalist? So my sights were firmly fixed on America, where there was a very wide interest in the subject, started indeed by Traube's former pupils, and I actually had letters of introduction to a few of them such as the famous palaeographer Eric Lowe (who afterwards became a close friend) and Kenneth Rand of Harvard University. But before going over there I decided to spend a year in Paris at the Sorbonne and the École des Chartes. Just about half way through that year when I was back on holidays, passing through Dublin, a chance meeting in Stephen's Green with the then all-powerful President of University College changed the whole course of my life and my studies.

This was the celebrated Dr Denis Coffey. He told me that the Chair of Roman Law and Jurisprudence would be vacant shortly, and he did not say I *ought to* go for it, he said I *was to* go for it. I demurred, pleading that I was working in Paris. He said he knew that, but all I had to do was to put in an application, return to Paris and finish my academic year and leave the rest to him. That, if I may say so Mr President, was the golden age of the Presidency! The Institution was still fairly new, and the other statutory bodies — the Academic Council, the Governing Body, even the Senate — were still eating out of his hand. It took some time for them to feel their oats. And so, by the grace of God and the favour of Dr Coffey, I joined the staff of University College to lecture on two subjects in which I had no special qualifications nor any great interest. I had told Dr Coffey at our first

3

meeting that I had only studied them for the Bar and for the B. A. degree, and thus had no special qualifications in either. His reply was typical: 'Neither has any-body else'. When I went back to Paris I met, by pure chance again, the famous expert on early English legal history, Sir Paul Vinogradoff, and he suggested to me, when he heard what I was going to teach, to take up the study of native Irish law. The result was, not exactly that I was shunted on to a siding, but that I was switched on to another line, a line running parallel to the main line of medieval studies, but joining it occasionally at some stations.

First of all, of course, I had to learn Irish, beginning with the spoken language, and I must be now one of the very few people old enough to say that I picked it up from a monoglot community in West Kerry. And then here in U.C.D. I came on to the older sources: Old and Middle Irish with Bergin, Early Irish History with MacNeill, and Welsh with John Lloyd-Jones. I think there is a lot to be said for coming to Irish from outside, from a wider background. But the essential thing is, when you do come to it, whether late or early, to get to know it thoroughly.

Now I want to stress that in working on the Irish laws I found the medieval background I had acquired extremely useful. After all, the bulk of the Irish law tracts were drafted in the seventh century and the jurists, whether they were lay or clerical, or a mixture of both, used the classical Old Irish which had been evolved in the monastic schools and based on the explanatory and expository techniques followed from late Latin grammatical and Patristic works, and above all influenced by Isidore of Seville. But besides that, there is an archaic stratum taken over from the oral tradition of the pre-Christian schools. Something less than ten per cent of the whole *Corpus Juris Hibernici* belongs to this archaic stratum, which makes a good deal of my research pre-medieval rather than medieval because a lot of it is quite clearly pre-Christian. Or take the famous *Collectio Canonum Hibernensis* — there you see the crossflow of Christianity and pre-Christian institutions, and it is sometimes quite difficult to separate them. As for the influence which Christian-ity itself had on the Irish laws, though formally it was very considerable, it always seems to me that Irish Law in this respect (and only in this) resembles the Roman Law of the *Corpus Juris Civilis,* which has a Christian façade but a pre-Christian background. The jurists did apparently strive obstinately to keep the traditional rules, say on the marriage laws, that were not merely prior to Christianity but indeed opposed to the teachings of the new religion.

Well, having offered you this over-voluminous sort of *apologia pro vita mea,* I must now confess to you that I cannot take up again the thread of general medieval studies which I snapped nearly fifty-five years ago. I despair of keeping abreast of all the work that has been done since, though I have read, as everybody must read, the remarkable works of Professor Bischoff, another successor of Traube, who has greatly extended "the Irish dimension" in the medieval world. For the rest I am just here to learn, and it is a joy to me to find so many younger scholars interested in medieval studies, and to find so many people who can speak with authority on various aspects of early medieval Ireland. How has this revolution come about between 1917 and 1981? Let me try to summarize the main reasons for it.

While I was still a member of the staff, a special Chair of Medieval History was set up, and the first occupant of it was Father Aubrey Gwynn who is happily still with us. By the time I came back from Oxford to the Dublin Institute in 1950, I found that Ludwig Bieler, with his untiring energy and enthusiasm, had introduced what one might call a Germanic thoroughness into the study of Hiberno-Latin literature. His recent death has saddened us all, though it is some consolation to remember that he has left a very generous legacy of publications, and his end was not premature like that of my friend Dr Kathleen Hughes, who was on the threshold of reaching the zenith of her career as an authority on early Irish ecclesiastical history. It was Bieler, combined with the influence of Fr Gwynn, who was the moving spirit behind something we started in the Dublin Institute for Advanced Studies: the *Scriptores Latini Hiberniae*, and it is a great consolation to know that the works of Eriugena, or at all events his masterly *Periphysion*, of which only three volumes have appeared hitherto, is to be continued by Professor O'Meara, who is certainly the ideal authority on the subject.

Now it may seem churlish to criticize a remarkable scholar like Bieler who has given us so much to be thankful for, but I never could understand why he did not learn Irish, at least enough Irish to be able to check and control the information he got from people like myself! Surely that is part of the duty of any historian? And Bieler had an ideal opportunity to learn Old and Middle Irish, situated as he was here in Dublin. His attitude contrasts very strangely with that of Kathleen Hughes, who, at great disadvantage to herself, realising how important it was to know the vernacular, had done her best to acquire a sound knowledge of Old and Middle Irish, as some members of this audience will know because they helped her to achieve her aim.

But I see I have already exceeded my quota, so it only remains for me to congratulate the promoters of this Colloquium; to wish them every success, and to stress once more, and finally, that anyone who is engaged in Irish medieval history or literature of any kind must be bilingual, must know the two languages, late Latin and Old Irish, well. This seems to me to be the main lesson that I learned from my own life. Even yet I do not know either of them well enough but I have done my best. And so, with this final appeal to Irish medievalists to become bilingual in their researches, I shall end like Patrick himself: *Haec est confessio mea antequam moriar*. I do not expect it to be remembered quite as long, but I hope a few of you will remember it in the years to come.

I.

Die Entstehung der frühen irischen Kirche
The Formation of the early Irish Church

The early Irish Church and the Western patriarchate

By
Patrick J. Corish

In the light of such things as the thoughtful essay on "The Celtic Church and the Papacy"[1] by the late Kathleen Hughes, it might well be asked if there is much more to be said on this topic. Yet while the question has escaped from the strait-jacket of religious controversy — we no longer begin by asking if St Patrick was a Protestant or a Catholic — it is nevertheless quite difficult to get rid of all the accretions of the centuries and pose our question to the early Irish Church in the way that Church would have posed it to itself; and yet anything short of this is unhistorical.

The first great name in post-Reformation Irish controversy is that of James Ussher, successively professor of divinity at Trinity College, Dublin, bishop of Meath and archbishop of Armagh. The full title of his principal book on this subject is sufficient to indicate the main line of his argument: *A discourse of the religion anciently professed by the Irish and Scottish, showing it to be for substance the same with that which at this day is by public authority established in the Church of England*. It was first published in Dublin in 1622.

The Thirty-Nine Articles contain two statements explicitly relevant to our topic: "As the Church of Jerusalem, Alexandria and Antioch have erred, so also the Church of Rome hath erred, not only in their living and manner of ceremonies, but also in matters of faith"; and "The bishop of Rome hath no jurisdiction in this realm of England"[2]. Two interconnected points are rejected: first, the unique authority of the Church of Rome in matters of faith; and second, the prerogative of the Church of Rome to exercise its authority in these and other matters by virtue of jurisdictional or legal authority.

The Reformation debates in the sixteenth century were conducted within this legal context. However, it is important to remember that the papal prerogatives had been discussed in these terms for centuries. They had been set out as a practical programme by Pope Gregory VII (1073—85) and had received theoretical elaboration in the great revival of canon law in the twelfth century. This revival had centred on the university of Bologna. Here, not long before 1140, John Gratian compiled his *Decretum*. This was to remain basic to the study of canon law for centuries. Roland Bandinelli, another professor of canon law at Bologna, and author of a commentary on Gratian's *Decretum*, became pope as Alexander III in 1159. He was the first of a distinguished line of papal canonists.

1 In C. H. *Lawrence*, ed., The English Church and the Papacy in the Middle Ages, London 1965, p. 1—28.
2 Articles 19, 37.

This is not to say that the juridical formulation of papal claims *began* in the eleventh and twelfth centuries. An elaborate formulation goes back to the fifth century, to Gelasius I (492—6) and in particular to Leo the Great (440—61). Leo formulated his position against a background of Roman law, paralleling closely the terms and concepts used by the Emperor Augustus. The pope possesses *principatus* (the term expresses a jurisdictional primacy), from which springs his *auctoritas*, his *plenitudo potestatis*. In this he differs from the other bishops: they are called *in partem sollicitudinis*, but the pope is called *in plenitudinem potestatis*[3].

To fill out the picture, two points should be noted. Leo and Gelasius elaborated a papal position: they did not originate it. Already in the second century Irenaeus of Lyons, in a much-discussed passage, was speaking of the *principalitas* of the Roman Church. The second point is that these fifth-century popes elaborated their position in the context of a sharp conflict with the emperor at Constantinople, a conflict that was in fact the seedbed of schism. It was Pope Gregory the Great (590—604) who came to recognise the full implications of the fact that outside the imperial territories there was no effective challenge to the papal *plenitudo potestatis* and who shaped the new Roman relations with the barbarian peoples, first with the Anglo-Saxons and through them with the Franks and the Germans.

Can we speak then of a continuity in the papal programme? In the English-speaking world this theme of continuity has been stressed by Walter Ullmann in particular[4]. In so far as a simple answer is given to this question, it must be "Yes". But within this continuity we can detect a genuine change of emphasis in the twelfth century. This change of emphasis may appear more clearly if set in a theological context, where it is associated with Peter the Lombard (ca. 1095—1160). Peter was born near Novara, and his earliest studies were in Italy, probably in Bologna. He then moved north to more theological climes, and settled in Paris between 1135 and 1139. Here he produced his *Four Books of the Sentences* at almost exactly the same time as Gratian was compiling his *Decretum* at Bologna. Lombard, like Gratian, was to become very influential because he had succeeded in writing a good text-book.

What concerns us here is his theology of Holy Orders. To simplify somewhat crudely, he drew a sharp distinction between what he called "power of orders" and "power of jurisdiction". He conceived a priest as having nearly all the "power of orders" and little if any "power of jurisdiction", whereas the bishop had a little additional "power of orders" and almost all the "power of jurisdiction". This remained the basis of the theology of Holy Orders in the Catholic Church until quite recent times. Some evidence that an earlier theology may be coming back into favour may be seen in the decrees of the Second Vatican Council.

---

3 Ep. 14, 1; PL 54, 671 (= JL 411).
4 See in particular Walter *Ullmann*, The Growth of Papal Government in the Middle Ages, London 1955.

This theology had been elaborated in a quite sophisticated way by Ignatius of Antioch as early as the beginning of the second century. To simplify once again: the bishop with his priests and deacons is the representative of Christ in the believing community, above all when this community is assembled for the Eucharist or for the solemn baptism which takes place within the eucharistic liturgy. The bishop sums up in himself the continuing faith of that community: to be in communion with him is the rule of faith.

As the generations passed, the Christian communities became more conscious of the continuity of their witness and stressed the witness of the holy dead, the bishops of course, but also the other witnesses, especially the martyrs — the very word means witness. Their mortal remains, their burial places, became centres of cult, especially on the anniversaries of their death. Pilgrimages from other Churches developed to the cult-centres of the more famous martyrs. Apart from the pilgrimages to the Holy Land, the first great pilgrimages to develop were to the shrines of Rome, especially to those of Peter and Paul. Excavations under St Peter's in Rome have disclosed a Petrine cult-centre going back certainly to ca. AD 160, with some indications of a cult before that date.

From an early date the Roman Church held two liturgical celebrations of St Peter. They have survived many vicissitudes and are still in its liturgy. Both are noted in a calendar from the middle of the fourth century. The better known liturgy of 29 June is in this calendar associated with a date a hundred years earlier, the middle of the third century, and the other, that of 22 February, must certainly have been in existence before the middle of the fourth. The two dates have some significance, for they go back to pre-Christian times. The foundation of Rome by Romulus had been celebrated on 29 June. The date of 22 February had been that of the pagan *parentalia* or *caristia* or *cara cognitio*, the day traditionally reserved for honouring the deceased members of a family by visiting the family tomb and holding a funeral feast there. It will be evident, even in the relatively sophisticated Christian communities of imperial Rome, that we are here at some remove from the concepts of jurisdiction and legal authority, or even of the bishop as the living rule of faith. We are moving in the world of the founding fathers, of the *patria potestas*.

This long introduction may help to set a context for assessing the relations between the early Irish Church and the see of Rome within the Western patriarchate. Two points would appear to emerge clearly. The first is that we must not take as our framework a juridico-theological system elaborated in the twelfth century. Rather, we must look to the earlier and contemporary world, and more particularly to the world as it existed after the pontificate of Gregory the Great. The second is that even within this earlier framework we must expect differences of emphasis. The popes will put things one way. Ecclesiastics of the Irish Church may put them another. What we may call "the religious mind" — which, it may or may not be necessary to say explicitly, the clergy share with the laity — may well put them another way. There will be a real tension between forms of expression that are juridical or theological, and forms of expression that are, for want of better words, "community" and "familial". It has been noted that such forms of expression had their influence among the Christian communities of the Roman empire. They may be expected to be even more influential among the kin-societies of the Celtic and Germanic peoples.

Here it is necessary to be selective. There are several papers listed for this conference that may be expected to develop in detail a number of the points I may mention here. A beginning might perhaps be made in the neighbouring island, at the synod of Whitby in 664. Bede's account[5] will be very familiar. The issue lay between the Roman and Celtic usage in calculating the date of Easter. The ecclesiastics had their learned say. Essentially, this consisted of appeals to their respective ecclesiastical traditions, to the witness of their Churches. It resolved itself into a choice between Colum Cille and Peter, the witness of Iona and the witness of "the apostolic see and indeed of the universal Church, of Peter, to whom Christ had given the keys of the kingdom of heaven". This phrase was decisive with the laity, in the person of King Oswy. He declared in favour of Peter, lest when he came to knock on the gates of the kingdom he might find the gatekeeper hostile.

The strength of this line of thought is manifested by the great numbers of Christian Anglo-Saxons who settled in the shadow of St Peter's in Rome to be buried as near as possible to the gatekeeper. Many streets in this area of Rome are still called by the Saxon name "borgo" and not by the Latin "via", and in it there still stands the church of the Saxons, S. Spirito in Sassia, built by Ine, king of Wessex, who died in Rome "on his pilgrimage" in 726.

Some thirty years before the synod of Whitby the Paschal disputes in Ireland had led to a delegation to Rome from southern Irish ecclesiastics. The well-known testimony of Cummian indicates a somewhat parallel mentality. First it shows how rare such appeals had to be at this time because of the sheer difficulty of communication. He notes that they had a good journey, in that some of them got there and some actually got back. He notes too that they were sent in accordance with a legal prescription, *ut si causae fuerint maiores, iuxta decretum synodicum, ad caput urbium sint referendae,* but the "familial" theme enters when he describes them as sent *velut natos ad matrem*[6]. He notes further a point to be noted at Whitby, that the witness of Rome was in fact the witness of the universal Church. Their report led to the acceptance of the Roman practice, if only by degrees.

There is then a juridical element, and it is important. There is a *decretum synodicum* in existence at least by the year 630, and by then of sufficient authority to be successfully invoked by at least a party in the Irish Church. This decree is repeated almost *verbatim* in the Collectio Canonum Hibernensis, where it is ascribed to "Patrick". With it there is a longer decree, of the same purport, ascribed to a

5 Bede, HE III, 25.
6 PL 87, 977.

12

sinodus Romana[7]. In the *Liber Angeli* there is an interesting development: when such a dispute arises, it is to be referred to "the see of the Irish archbishop, i.e., Patrick" and it is only if he and his wise men cannot produce a solution that the problem is to be referred to "the chair of the apostle Peter, which has authority in the city of Rome"[8].

These texts take us into dangerous waters, where I much prefer to leave the navigation to others, all the more so because there is every indication that at least some of these waters will be skilfully navigated later in this conference. Very delicate questions are involved, demanding discussion in detail — the dating of documents, or at least a relative dating that will establish an order of dependence, set against a background of debate between two reform-parties, this debate in turn set against an ecclesiastical power-contest deeply involving the church of Armagh, and involving in particular its links with the party of the *Romani*.

There was then a real juridical factor in the question, but it may very well have turned out not to have been the primary element, for such victory as the *Romani* had in the debate would seem to have been more apparent than real. The effective reform-movement in the Irish Church developed along more native lines. It appears in a completely native context with the *Céli Dé*. In consequence, one might expect the Irish Church's consciousness of itself as part of the Western patriarchate and of its relationship with the see of Rome to find expression less in juridical terms than in "community" or "familial" ones, and such, I think, proves to be the case. The authority of a Church will be linked to the quality of its witness, and this will be seen in the cumulative witness of its holy dead. Their graves afford tangible testimony to this witness. The Irish word for a cemetery is *reilig*, that is, where rest the *reliquiae*, the earthly remains of the saints. Earlier there was another word, *ruam*. This word occurs in four meanings, three of them ecclesiastical, and all three are interconnected. It means the city of Rome itself; then any great ecclesiastical centre that might fittingly be compared to Rome; and thirdly, a cemetery, especially the cemetery of such a place. All three meanings blend in the well-known quatrains in praise of the great Irish monasteries from the Prologue to the *Félire* of Oengus, a document of the *Céli Dé* of about the year 800[9]:

> The proud burgh of Aillenn has perished with its boastful throng,
> Great is triumphant Brigid, fair is her crowded *ruam*.
> The burgh of Emhain has faded away save that its stones remain,
> Thronged Glendaloch is the *ruam* of the western world ...

7 Hermann *Wasserschleben*, ed., Die irische Kanonensammlung, Leipzig ²1885, XX, 5.

8 J. *Gwynn*, ed., The Book of Armagh, Dublin 1913, fol. 21b2.

9 Whitley *Stokes*, ed., Félire Oengusso Céli Dé. The Martyrology of Oengus the Culdee, HBS 29, 1905, p. 24–26. For the translation cf. Eleanor *Knott*, Irish Classical Poetry, Dublin 1957, p. 32—33.

> The little places that were occupied by twos and threes
> They are *ruama* with multitudes, hundreds and thousands.

Rome was the chief witness to the faith for the churches of the Western patriarchate, the incomparable city of saints and martyrs, and the highest praise that could be given to another church was to compare the witness of its saints to the witness of the saints of Rome.

We may now be in a position to approach the figure of Columbanus, who has always been fairly close to the centre of this controversy. Three letters which he wrote to popes have survived. In these letters Columbanus addresses the popes with very great respect, piling one title of deference on top of another, while abasing himself. Though accepting that the Irish had received from Rome "the evangelical and apostolic teaching, the Catholic faith", at the same time he takes the pope sharply to task for his practice in regard to the date of Easter, or for what he regards as papal ambivalence, to say the least, on the theological issues of the Three Chapters' controversy. It is in his letter on this topic that his language is sharpest, and where he is very palpably out of his depth. The Three Chapters' controversy was a combination of political pressures with the ultimate refinements — it is hard not to regard them as over-refinements — of the Greek speculative intellect. It may be doubted if the Roman Church was always in full command of the complexities. It is quite certain that the Lombard bishops of northern Italy were not. Columbanus was little if anything better. He appears to have regarded the whole dispute primarily as an obstacle to his work of evangelisation.

We are dealing here with a man of single-minded saintliness, who is also proud, angry and confused. It will be apparent that we must not try to slot him into the categories of the post-Reformation controversies, nor even into those of the twelfth century, when Peter the Lombard had introduced something of the legal approach of Bologna into the theological schools of Paris, nor even into the categories of Rome before the great canonist popes. It would probably be a mistake to assume that even the categories of the Irish *Romani* were uppermost in his mind. I should be inclined to look for the core of his thinking in three short passages. The first is in his letter to Gregory the Great: "just as we read in the narrative of the learned Jerome, how some men once came to Rome from the last confines of the strand of Hyele, and, wonderful to tell, sought something other than Rome, so I too would seek, desiring now, not Rome but you, saving the reverence due to the ashes of the saints"[10]. Columbanus inserts this last saving clause because he realises that his argument is running away with him: the parallel from the learned Jerome is leading him astray. Rome is what it is, not because of the living pope, however much Columbanus may desire to meet him, but because of the ashes of the saints. The other two passages occur, perhaps significantly, in closing salutations. The first reads: "Farewell, pope most dear in Christ,

---

10 G. S. M. *Walker*, ed., Sancti Columbani Opera, SLH 2, 1957, Ep. 1, 8, p. 10.

14

mindful of us both in your holy prayers beside the ashes of the saints", while the very sharp letter to Pope Boniface concludes: "Pray for me, a most wretched sinner, and for my fellow-pilgrims, beside the holy places and the ashes of the saints, and especially beside Peter and Paul"[11].

Doctor Kathleen Hughes has given a subtle and nuanced analysis of what we may call Columbanus's theology. She notes that it was "in line with patristic opinion" and, that in at least one passage, it was "a recognition, in vague and rhetorical language, of the papal plenitude of power"[12]. She notes, however, that the juridical aspect of the question does not dominate. Picking up the idea expressed in the Prologue to the *Félire* of Oengus, she writes[13]:

> A later life of Coemgen describes Glendalough as one of the "four best Romes of burial" in Ireland. Bardsey Island, off the north-west coast of Wales, the burial ground of "twenty thousand holy confessors and martyrs", was proverbially known in the twelfth century as *Roma Britannie*. This idiomatic use of the word *ruam* clearly shows Rome's primary significance in the Celtic imagination. The living pope was respected, but it was his great predecessor Peter, with the other saints and martyrs, who drew Celtic pilgrims to Rome. The power of the dead saints was a far more potent force than that of the living pope.

There is much truth in this, but there is this danger in it, that we may be reading into the mind of a man like Columbanus distinctions that in fact were not there. Leo the Great would have seen his authority as deriving, not from his person, but from his office, the office of "vicar of Peter". This phrase is Leo's, but the idea behind it, that the pope acts by the authority of Peter, is explicit two centuries earlier. The idea occurs with the Irish Church too, and is rather central to the mind of Columbanus. What he venerated in Rome was not the saintly dead in themselves, but the saintly dead as witnesses to present faith.

In this paper I have tried to indicate the extreme complexity of the historical background that needs to be, I will not say mastered, but at least appreciated, if we are not to be in danger of reading into the early Irish Church ideas which simply could not have been there. It must always be borne in mind that the legal strand was only one in a complex weave. That it was real is clear from the history of the Paschal controversy. That it was not unique is clear from a host of considerations. What is most consistently in the foreground is the "community" or "familial" theme. Perhaps the main thread of my argument is that this must not be regarded as a distinctively Irish way of looking at things, a "Celtic particularism". It was an approach the Irish shared in particular with the Churches of the other non-Roman societies, but it also had deep roots in the Churches of imperial Rome.

11 Ibid., Ep. 3, 3, p. 24; Ep. 5, 17, p. 56.
12 As above note 1, p. 13—17.
13 Ibid., p. 23.

Some British aspects of the earliest Irish Christianity

By
David N. Dumville

Saint Patrick is, of course, the very prominent embodiment of the important British role in the establishment of Christian institutions in Ireland. It is nonetheless agreed that he does not stand at the beginning or the end of the story: in this respect too he is not the figure presented by his seventh-century and later biographers. He must rather be seen as occupying part — albeit an important part — of a much larger stage. To understand properly the context in which Patrick's mission was operative we must look backwards and ask questions about Christian antecedents in Ireland.

Pre-Patrician Irish Christianity is a subject which has been often discussed, but to relatively little profit[1]. A lack of clarity of perception about the subject of study accounts for part of the difficulty. In this paper no doubts will be entertained: here the concern is with pre-Patrician Christianity as a British phenomenon; its Britishness may be the whole of that subject, or just a part of it; but whether as the whole or as a part, the British dimension was certainly important.

Prosper Tiro, in his *Contra Collatorem* of 433 or 434, refers to the anti-Pelagian campaign of Pope Celestine I; he concludes by noting that Celestine was responsible for crushing Pelagianism in Britain and, by his ordination of a bishop for the Irish, for making Ireland Christian[2]. The way in which he links these facts has suggested irresistibly to commentators — and rightly, in my view — that Prosper, *and* Celestine, saw the two processes as linked to one another[3]. The plain implication is that there was a risk, however it be explained, that British Pelagianism would infect an Irish Christianity which had no bishop to keep it on the straight and narrow. Prosper gives us one further piece of essential information, in the famous annal for 431, when he makes it plain that Bishop Palladius was being sent to an already existing Christian Irish community (*ad Scottos in Christum credentes*)[4].

---

1 The most thorough discussion remains that of James H. *Todd*, St Patrick, Apostle of Ireland. A Memoir of his Life and Mission, Dublin 1864, p. 189—226. For the productive idea that *acta* of Palladius have been fathered on Patrick, see *Todd*, ibid., p. 265—345 (esp. 334—40), and cf. p. 393—9.

2 § 21.2: *Nec uero segniore cura ab hoc eodem morbo Britannias liberauit, quando quosdam inimicos gratiae solum suae originis occupantes etiam ab illo secreto exclusit Oceani, et ordinato Scotis episcopo dum romanam insulam studet seruare catholicam fecit etiam barbaram christianam*, PL 51, 271.

3 J. B. *Bury*, The Life of St Patrick and his Place in History, London 1905, p. 51—2, 54, gives a brief exposition of this view.

4 *Chronicon*, § 1307: *Ad Scottos in Christum credentes ordinatus a papa Caelestino Palladius primus episcopus mittitur*, ed. Theodor *Mommsen*, Chronica Minora Saec. IV. V. VI. VII., 3 vols,

16

Who these Irish Christians were must now concern us. We cannot be sure that when Prosper said *Scottos* he necessarily meant 'racially Irish'; it seems doubtful that he would be so well informed. He must be taken as meaning what seems natural in the context, especially for a distant foreigner, namely 'people who live in Ireland' without further specification.

Scholars have naturally supposed that Christianity first found its way into Ireland from Roman Britain, most likely through trading contacts; some have deduced further that the traders themselves, whether Britons or other Imperial citizens, constituted the body of 'Irish' Christians whose bishop Palladius became[5]. We have to suppose, I think, that this Christian community was Latin-speaking, whatever other languages its members may have boasted; otherwise, how would they have had access to the religion and what use would their Latin-speaking bishop have been? These remarks serve to remind us that we are here dealing with the first recognised Christian community beyond the western Imperial frontiers.

The size of such a community remains a very problematic question. The amount of trade and the number of traders must have been limited: we may doubt that, even with their dependents and those whom they may have influenced, they would have formed much of a community. Against this, however, we must set the evidence offered by a fourth-century source that a city with a community of as few as twelve Christians should have its own bishop[6]. Yet inasmuch as episcopal organisation was usually urban it was in need of specific adaptation to Irish circumstances. We do not know what Celestine expected Palladius to find on arrival in Ireland: for example, how widely dispersed could Irish Christians have been while still seeming to constitute a 'community' or 'flock' to which a single bishop might credibly minister?

St Patrick himself might be thought to answer both the main questions posed so far. Professor E. A. Thompson's astonishing paper on 'St Patrick and Coroticus'[7] now compels us to pay proper attention to the saint's remarks on these matters. In § 42 of his *Confessio*, Patrick says, in an aside, *et de genere nostro qui ibi nati sunt nescimus numerum eorum*. Very varying translations — or, rather, interpretations —

Berlin 1891—8, I. 473. *Scotti credentes* do not necessarily live in Ireland, of course; it is the passage in *Contra Collatorem* which assures us that Prosper linked Pope Celestine I and Ireland.

5 *Bury*, The Life of St Patrick, p. 10—15, places the growth of Irish Christianity in the broadest possible context; see also James F. *Kenney*, The Sources for the Early History of Ireland: Ecclesiastical. An Introduction and Guide, New York 1929; rev. imp. by L. *Bieler*, 1966, p. 159—60.

6 Gregory *Dix*, Jurisdiction in the Early Church, Episcopal and Papal, London 1938; rev. imp. by T. M. *Parker*, 1975, p. 60—1. We must remember also the rule formulated by Pope Celestine I, *Epistola IV (ad episcopos prouinciae Viennensis et Narbonensis)*, PL 50, 434: *nullus inuitis detur episcopus*.

7 Journal of Theological Studies, N. S., 31 (1980), p. 12—27.

of this passage have been offered[8]. The key-words are *genus nostrum* and *nasci*: at one semantic extreme they can mean 'Christians' and 'to be baptised', at another 'Britons' and 'to be (physically) born'. If we observe a contrast in § 42 between its main subject — *una benedicta* Scotta genetiua *nobilis pulcherrima adulta* — and those who are *genere nostro,* then the latter must be Christians. It is not, of course, clear that this is the only interpretation: for example, we might wonder whether Patrick might here consider himself Irish. I do not wish to venture further at this point into the particulars of Thompson's case, save to say that it will take very strong arguments to refute it as a whole. For it is underpinned by other evidence. It is clear from § 1 of the *Confessio* — taken together with our other evidence for Irish raiding in western Britain[9] — that, however we attempt to interpret Patrick's statement about the *tot milia* of Britons taken into captivity with him, we must allow for the existence of a substantial British servile population in fifth-century Ireland. This fact may perhaps account for the stress laid by Patrick on the servile condition of members of his flock[10]. Such captive Britons must have had Christians among their number; this British population would have formed a natural mission-field for Patrick.

If this community formed the initial body of 'Irish' Christians it is especially clear why continental ecclesiastics might have feared its contamination by Pelagianism. Palladius, we must suppose, was the first bishop of this British population in involuntary exile. One presumes that generally they were slaves, but some may perhaps with time have gained their freedom. Not later than the time of Patrick's mission, however that be dated (although I should prefer to place it in the second half of the century), a new generation of Britons was being born on Irish soil; whether this was the second generation or a subsequent one we can hardly say. With the advent of Patrick, this community had effectively acquired a

8 For some interpretations of this passage see L. *Bieler,* Libri Epistolarum Sancti Patricii Episcopi, Classica et Mediaevalia 12 (1951), p. 79—214, at p. 173; R. P. C. *Hanson,* Saint Patrick, his Origins and Career, Oxford 1968, p. 56, 137—9; *Thompson,* St Patrick and Coroticus.

9 A useful account is offered by C. *Thomas,* The Irish settlements in post-Roman western Britain: a survey of the evidence, Journal of the Royal Institution of Cornwall, N.S., 6 (1969—72), p. 251—74.

10 *Confessio,* §§ 42 und 59. But § 42, by its phrasing, makes it clear that there were members of Patrick's flock who were not slaves. One wonders whether the original Britishness of the Christian community in Ireland accounts for the possibility envisaged in the (?sixth- or seventh-century) *Sinodus Episcoporum* (§ 7) that a cleric might be a slave: see The Irish Penitentials, ed. & transl. Ludwig *Bieler,* SLH 5, 1963, p. 54, 55; for varying interpretations see also The Bishops' Synod ("The First Synod of St Patrick") A Symposium, ed. M.J. *Faris,* Liverpool 1976, p. 1, 2, and 39. For useful remarks about clerical servitude see E.A. *Thompson,* The Goths in Spain, Oxford 1969, p. 296—7, 305—6, which make the difficulties expressed by D.A. *Binchy,* St Patrick's "First Synod", Stud. Hib. 8 (1968), p. 49—59, at p. 53—4, seem rather less serious.

bishop from among its own number. Patrick's youth spent as a slave in Ireland was therefore a double qualification for his episcopal role in Ireland.

How many of the native Irish accepted Christianity at this stage (or earlier) is anything but clear. The context is strikingly analogous to that of the introduction of Christianity among the third- and fourth-century Goths in Roumania, as Thompson has pointed out[11]. Whether Palladius or any other early bishop in Ireland had attempted evangelisation we cannot say: Prosper implies this in *Contra Collatorem* where he says that Pope Celestine had made Ireland Christian, but we have already seen reasons for an alternative interpretation of the passage. In a famous sentence (*Confessio*, § 51), St Patrick tells us that he travelled *in multis periculis etiam usque ad exteras partes, ubi nemo ultra erat et ubi numquam aliquis peruenerat qui baptizauit aut clericos ordinauit aut populum consummaret*. In Patrick's day there was still plenty of missionary work ahead and we find the saint busy with it.

The identifiable existence of a British community in fifth-century Ireland perhaps makes some of the linguistic facts a little more intelligible. It provides, for example, a broader and longer-lasting channel of transmission into Ireland for the British pronunciation of Latin and for the early adoption in Irish of Latin loan-words[12]. Among these linguistic facts is the existence and extensive use in Irish personal nomenclature of hypocoristic formations of British origin. We are concerned with two such types. First, we may mention the suffix -óc, generally taken with a contracted form of the name and often with the *mo-* or *to-* possessive prefix, creating what Henry Lewis called a 'cloister-name'[13]. That the practice of giving ecclesiastics such pet-names began in Britain seems clear, for (as Thurneysen pointed out[14]) the -óc suffix is not native to Irish. Whether or not this name-type is purely monastic is less certain, although a plausible case could be made out. To this very numerous type we may add the less well evidenced, though no less certain, group in -io based on the British -ịawo- hypocoristic of which (once again) no native equivalent seems to occur in Irish[15]. The usual Irish hypocoristic terminations are the -án, -én, -ín diminutives which are certainly not restricted, in their usage, to ecclesiastics. The development of classes of foreign hypocoristics for members of the ecclesiastical establishment speaks a great deal for the early his-

11 E.A. *Thompson*, The Visigoths in the Time of Ulfila, Oxford 1966, p. XIII—XIX, 127—32; St Patrick and Coroticus, p. 18—19.

12 The standard study of loanwords remains that of Joseph *Vendryes*, De hibernicis vocabulis quae a latina lingua originem duxerunt, Paris 1902. For a broader view of Hiberno-British language-ties see Kenneth H. *Jackson*, Language and History in Early Britain, Edinburgh 1953, p. 122—93.

13 The honorific prefixes *to-* and *mo-*, ZCP 20 (1933—6), p. 138—43, at p. 143.

14 Rudolf *Thurneysen*, A Grammar of Old Irish, Dublin 1946, p. 173—4 (§ 271).

15 Ibid., p. 175 (§ 275). This form, with especial reference to the name *U(u)inniau*, is discussed at greater length in my paper, Gildas and Uinniau, in Gildas: New Approaches, ed. M. *Lapidge* & D.N. *Dumville*, Woodbridge 1984.

tory of the Church in Ireland — and, if we should regard at least the *Mernóc*-type as claustral, then for the early history of Irish monasticism too.

If we discount the possibility that wherever these name-types occur in early Irish sources they are the result of direct recourse to a written or oral source of British origin, there seem to be two available interpretations of the evidence that Irish hypocoristics of the *-óc* ((*-awc*) and *-io* ((*-iaw*) types were formed under British influence, since these suffixes are not native to Irish. The hypocoristic forms may have been given by Britons (to Irishmen, where appropriate) and subsequently have been adopted as complete forms by Irish-speakers. This explanation may suit the relatively poorly attested *-io* forms. Alternatively, we may suppose that these British hypocoristic formations were borrowed into Irish and freely used there, both at an early date and later. The latter explanation would seem to suit well the history of the *-óc* suffixes and the *Mernóc*-type formations at least. But, whichever view we accept, we seem to have here good linguistic evidence for strong British influence in the formative stages of Irish Christianity.

We can therefore gain glimpses of an extended period in which British and Irish Christianity enjoyed the closest relationship. The sense of community which this relationship engendered is still apparent, at the end of the sixth century, in Columbanus's attitude to the Insular family of Churches. In his second Epistle he refers to the opinion of *omnes ecclesiae totius occidentis*[16], and we might do well to consider that Columbanus, familiar with a number of works of British ecclesiastical literature — Gildas's *De Excidio Britanniae*[17] and letter to Uinniau[18], and the Penitential of Uinniau[19] —, saw the Celtic Churches as constituting something of a culture-province. Certainly Columbanus is found, in his continental activities, in close association with Bretons. He travelled through Brittany[20], recruited followers there (it has been suggested that he founded a monastery there[21]), and continued

16   Epistola II, § 5: G. S. M. *Walker,* ed., Sancti Columbani Opera, SLH 2, 1957, p. 16, lines 12—13.

17   M. *Winterbottom,* Columbanus and Gildas, Vigiliae Christianae 30 (1976), p. 310—17.

18   R. *Sharpe,* 'Gildas as a Father of the Church', Gildas: New Approaches, ed. *Lapidge* & *Dumville.*

19   *Walker,* Sancti Columbani Opera, p. LIII; *Bieler,* Irish Penitentials, p. 5; Jean *Laporte,* Le Pénitentiel de Saint Colomban, Tournai 1958, p. 41—4 *et passim,* stresses especially Columbanus's dependence on British sources.

20   This is denied by Louis *Gougaud,* Un point obscur de l'itinéraire de Saint Colomban venant en Gaule, Annales de Bretagne 22 (1906/7), p. 327—43, and more summarily in Les saints irlandais hors d'Irlande étudiés dans le culte et dans la dévotion traditionnelle, Louvain 1936, p. 55. Nonetheless, I still find it difficult to see how else to take the statements of Jonas, *Vita Columbani,* §§ 4—5: ed. Bruno *Krusch,* Ionae Vitae Sanctorum Columbani, Vedastis, Iohannis, MGH SS. rer. Germ. 37, 1905, p. 160—1; for translation see Edward *Peters,* Monks, Bishops and Pagans, Christian Culture in Gaul and Italy, 500—700. Sources in Translation, Philadelphia Pa. 1975, p. 79—80.

21   Jonas, §§ 13 and 20 (*Krusch,* p. 173—4 and 196; *Peters,* p. 88 and 99). For the suggestion about a foundation, see *Walker,* Sancti Columbani Opera, p. 37, n. l. A disciple, Potentinus,

to have Breton fellow-monks throughout his continental wanderings. Such ecclesiastical travel seems to have taken place within the context of trading contacts between Ireland, Brittany and the Loire valley, implying a range of contacts between the Celtic-speaking countries broader than the purely ecclesiastical[22].

What is implied by the presence of Irishmen in Brittany is far from clear. Columbanus suddenly bursts upon the scene and we have no detailed context within which to place his activities. Whether he had predecessors or whether Breton missionary clerics in Ireland had told him of comparable mission-activities on the Continent is a matter for speculation. What is surely not speculation is that the British Churches had provided manpower to develop Christianity in Ireland; to that extent they were missionary Churches, and we have no reason to suppose that their efforts would have been confined to Ireland until the Irishman Columbanus gave them a new lead. It seems possible, in fact, that one or more of those Britons with whom Jonas brings his hero into contact had preceded that saint into Francia and other parts of Germania[23].

The close Insular ecclesiastical relationships to which Columbanus bears witness seem not to have survived long in the seventh-century atmosphere of ideological conflict. But, whatever the nature of the ecclesiastical link between Ireland and Brittany at the end of the sixth century, the connexion itself seems to have been maintained. To the extent that Irish clerics wished to get to the Continent, Ireland-(Wales)-Cornwall-Brittany was an obvious route and almost certainly remained so even after that across England was opened up in the seventh century. In Breton manuscripts of the ninth and tenth centuries we find preserved a range of texts from the early Celtic Churches without which our appreciation of the period would be greatly restricted[24]. The Collectio Canonum Hibernensis is a

eventually established a monastery in Armorica, at Coutances: Jonas, § 21 (*Krusch*, p. 199; *Peters*, p. 101).

22 This seems especially plain from Jonas, § 23 (*Krusch*, p. 205—6; *Peters*, p. 104—5). On the whole subject see E. *James*, Ireland and western Gaul in the Merovingian period, in Ireland in Early Mediaeval Europe. Studies in Memory of Kathleen Hughes, ed. Dorothy *Whitelock et al.*, Cambridge 1982, p. 362—86.

23 Carantoc, in Jonas, § 7 (*Krusch*, pp. 164—6; *Peters*, pp. 82—3); Uinioc, in Jonas, §§ 15 and 17 (*Krusch*, p. 177—8 and 182—3; *Peters*, p. 89—90 and 91—2). That *Brittones* were still active in the German mission-field in the eighth century seems apparent from a letter of Pope Gregory III to the bishops of Bavaria and Alemannia (ca. 738): ed. Michael *Tangl*, Die Briefe des Heiligen Bonifatius und Lullus, MGH Epp. sel. I, 1916, p. 70—1 (no. 44); for comment see Arthur W. *Haddan* & W. *Stubbs*, ed., Councils and Ecclesiastical Documents relating to Great Britain and Ireland, 3 vols, Oxford, 1869—78, I.203, and F.E. *Warren*, The Liturgy and Ritual of the Celtic Church, Oxford 1881, p. 45. (And, according to *Haddan* & *Stubbs*, Councils, I.154n., St Gall was accompanied by a Briton.)

24 For notices and discussion of the relevant manuscripts see Hermann *Wasserschleben*, ed., Die irische Kanonensammlung, Leipzig ²1885; Henry *Bradshaw*, The Early Collection of Canons known as the Hibernensis, Cambridge 1893; *Bieler*, Irish Penitentials. On the Penitential of Uinniau (ed. *Bieler*, p. 17, 74—95, 242—5; but the text must be reconstructed) see further L. *Fleuriot*, Le "saint" breton *Winniau* et le pénitentiel dit "de Finnian"? EC 15 (1976—8), p. 607—14.

fairly extreme and relatively late example: this early eighth-century text owes its preservation very largely to Breton copies. Other and earlier canon-texts (including the *Liber ex Lege Moysi*), penitentials, and the versions of the *Hisperica Famina*, attest in their transmission this same Hiberno-Breton connexion. In particular we may suppose that Brittany remained a highway for Irishmen travelling to the Irish centres in central Europe. We see this exemplified in various ways in the text-histories of Insular works. A relatively inconspicuous case is that of the Penitential of Uinniau: it survives complete only in a ninth-century Sankt Gallen manuscript, but substantial excerpts occur in another central European manuscript of ca. 800 and others in two tenth-century Breton books. Two pieces of evidence in particular serve to reassure us that the connexion was still vital in the later ninth century. A Tegernsee codex, now in Munich, contains a ninth-century Breton manuscript of philosophical texts; it seems to have been in southern Germany at an early date after its execution[25]. Similarly, the Breton manuscript, London, BL, Royal 5.E.13 contains a copy of the allegedly Hiberno-Latin biblical commentary *Canon in Ebreica* attested already in central Europe ca. 800[26]; the Breton copy contains palaeographical features showing that it was copied from a central European exemplar. In short, we can see the Irish route between Brittany and central Europe operating in both directions.

Outside the transmission of texts the Irish seem to have left little trace of themselves in our sources for Breton history. Apart from the cult of a handful of saints with Irish names[27] we are left with that most intriguing item, the statement by Ermoldus Nigellus that the Emperor Louis the Pious caused the monks of Landevennec in 818 to replace their Irish rule with that of St Benedict of Nursia[28]. Any Celtic monastic form may have seemed Irish to Louis or Ermold, but we have insufficient grounds for denying Ermold's specific remark; that the community of

25 Bernhard *Bischoff*, Die südostdeutschen Schreibschulen und Bibliotheken in der Karolingerzeit, I, Wiesbaden ²1960, p. 161—2; C. *Ineichen-Eder*, Theologisches und philosophisches Lehrmaterial aus dem Alkuin-Kreis, DA 34 (1978), p. 192—201; *eadem*, The authenticitiy of the *Dicta Candidi*, *Dicta Albini* and some related texts, in Insular Latin Studies. Papers on Latin Texts and Manuscripts of the British Isles, ed. M.W. *Herren*, Toronto 1981, p. 179—93.

26 B. *Bischoff*, Turning-points in the history of Latin exegesis in the early middle ages, in Biblical Studies. The Medieval Irish Contribution, ed. Martin *McNamara*, Dublin 1976, p. 73—160, esp. 95 and 159 n. 126; D.N. *Dumville*, Biblical apocrypha and the early Irish: a preliminary investigation, PRIA 73 C (1973), p. 299—338, at p. 325—8.

27 *Gougaud*, Les saints irlandais hors d'Irlande, p. 9, 11—12, 23—6, 55—6, 67, 81—2, 84, 88, 117, 135—9, 147, 150, 159—66, 186, is the natural starting-point; cf. *Kenney*, Sources, p. 175—6, 180—2.

28 The relevant document is printed by *Haddan* & *Stubbs*, Councils, II. 79—80, from *Vita Wingualoei*, II. 13: ed. C. *de Smedt*, Vita S. Winwaloei primi abbatis Landevenecensis auctore Wurdestino, AB 7 (1888), p. 167—264, at p. 227. Cf. *Kenney*, Sources, p. 175—6; Robert *Latouche*, Mélanges d'histoire de Cornouaille (Ve—XIe siècle), Paris 1911, p. 37; Nora K. *Chadwick*, Early Brittany, Cardiff 1969, p. 282—3.

St Winwaloe should follow the *Regula Columbani* or any other Irish rule seems curious but is by no means to be rejected out of hand. But whatever the nature of Hiberno-Breton links from the sixth century to the ninth they were probably sundered by the Scandinavian conquest of Brittany in the 910s, and the Breton highway to central Europe supplanted by other possible routes such as that through England and the Channel-ports.

In our search for early Hiberno-British links we have wandered some way from the fifth and sixth centuries. It might be asked why we have had to pursue so many elusive fragments of evidence for the British background to Irish Christianity. Yet these items have displayed the fairly clear aspects of British relations with Ireland in its first two Christian centuries. No smooth or consistent picture of the British Church can be created as a model with which the disjointed pieces of Irish evidence can be compared. Ecclesiastical organisation, which used to offer the favourite point for discussion in this context, is a subject about which (it is now recognised) almost nothing of value can be said at present. Few will wish to follow Dr Wendy Davies in dating some of the Llandaff charters to the sixth century, or even the seventh[29]. The saints' Lives, which might be thought possible sources of information about organisation, are far too late to be of any merit, whether they speak of purely British or of Hiberno-British affairs. In fact, it is now much easier for us to write in terms of intellectual or cultural links between the Churches of the two islands in their early centuries. In particular, one notes the newly emerging evidence which sustains theories of the export from sub-Roman Britain of Insular script and a peculiar form of private charter, both of which found favour throughout the Celtic-speaking West[30]. The transmission to Ireland and the extensive seventh-century employment there of Gildas's works is no doubt an aspect of the same milieu[31]; the authority which Gildas's name acquired is evidenced in a remarkable way in the Collectio Canonum Hibernensis[32]. It has often been remarked that early Irish biblical exegetes invoke the name of Pelagius and quote from his work[33]:

29 As expounded, for example, in her *Liber Landavensis:* its construction and credibility, EHR 88 (1973), p. 335—51; for the full implications, see her books The Llandaff Charters, Aberystwyth 1979, and An Early Welsh Microcosm. Studies in the Llandaff Charters, London 1978.

30 On the subject of the origins and diffusion of Insular script we await major publications by Professor Julian Brown. On charter-forms see W. *Davies,* The Latin charter-tradition in western Britain, Brittany and Ireland in the early mediaeval period, in Ireland in Early Mediaeval Europe, ed. *Whitelock et al.,* p. 258—80.

31 *Winterbottom,* Columbanus and Gildas; *idem,* Aldhelm's prose style and its origins, Anglo-Saxon England 6 (1977), p. 39—76; *idem,* The Preface of Gildas's *De Excidio,* Transactions of the Honourable Society of Cymmrodorion (1974/5), p. 277—87; Gildas' in the Middle Ages: Studies in Textual History, ed. D.N. *Dumville* (Studies in Celtic History: Woodbridge, forthcoming).

32 *Sharpe,* Gildas as a Father of the Church.

33 See, for example, *Kenney,* p. 661—3; Heinrich *Zimmer,* Pelagius in Irland, Berlin 1901; H.J. *Frede,* Pelagius, der irische Paulustext, Sedulius Scottus, Freiburg 1961.

that their predilection is indeed an aspect of British influence on the formation of their intellectual tradition seems confirmed by the availability and copying of a major work by Pelagius in Wales in the seventh century[34]. For all this, however, it remains possible at the moment to speak only of British aspects of the earliest Irish Christianity, not of a clear British background to (and much less a British model for) the developing Irish Church.

34 Alexander *Souter*, ed., Pelagius's Expositions of Thirteen Epistles of St Paul, 3 vols, Cambridge 1922—6, I.272—81, 283—6. See further D.N. *Dumville*, Late seventh- or eigth-century evidence for the British transmission of Pelagius, Cambridge Medieval Celtic Studies, forthcoming.

The Christian impact on early Ireland: place-names evidence

By
Deirdre Flanagan

Although the incidence of place-names which, in their element-content, have specific reference to ecclesiastical settlement is small in relation to the wealth of early Irish ecclesiastical site-names[1], it is, nonetheless, sufficiently significant to afford a broad base for the study of the more frequently attested ecclesiastical generics: *domnach, cell, dísert, tech, eclais, mainistir, tempul*. The object of this paper is to observe and, where possible, clarify points of distinction in the application of these terms as place-name elements. In the interests of concentrating on these commoner terms, the less frequently attested ecclesiastical elements such as *scrín, airecal, lann, baislec*, etc. have been omitted from the discussion. The disproportionate concentration on the incidence of the term *domnach* requires little justification in view of its unique character and early context.

domnach (< Lat. dominicum)

The word *dominicum* in the specialised sense of 'church building' is attested in continental Latin manuscripts from AD 333 onwards and disappears from use in the course of the 5th century. It related to popular rather than official usage. It would seem that the only survival of *dominicum* in the sense of church building are the *domnach* names in Ireland. (For documentation and discussion cf. Doelger 1950, 175—89 and Mohrmann 1977, 223—3.)

The incidence and spread of the Anglicised element *donagh-* as initial element in the townland and parish names of Ireland (cf. maps 3 and 5) shows unequivocally that at one time the word *domnach* in the sense of church-site was part of the natural vocabulary of the people. It follows that the term *dominicum* with specific reference to church-site must have been, for at least a time, in natural use by Latin-speaking clerics in Ireland. Yet the term *dominicum*, in this sense, is not attested in the Hiberno-Latin writings that might be expected to feature it, such as the Book of Armagh Patrician documents[2]. Tírechán (late 7th century) employs *aeclessia* and *aeclessia magna* not only as an appellative with reference to churches

---

1 The generic element in most instances is topographical rather than habitative, *cluain* 'meadow' being the most commonly attested term, while *inis* and *droim* are also well represented. For the range of terms cf. Flanagan 1979, p. 6.

2 The 5th-century *domnach* usage may perhaps underlie the much debated term *dominicati rethorici* of the *Confessio* for which Mohrmann (1977, p. 340—2) suggests the translation 'learned clerics', *dominicatus* derived from *dominicum* in its specialised sense of 'church building'.

attested in subsequent documentation as *domnach*-named sites[3], but even in several instances as translation of a *domnach* generic: *Aeclessia Patricii Magna* (Tír.[4], § 10): *Domnach Pátraic* (BP[5] p. 46—7); *aeclessia magna Saeoli* (Tír., § 22): *Domnach Mór Maigi Seolae* (BP p. 59); another *aeclessia magna Patricii* (Tír., § 14): *Domnach Mór* (BP p. 82). His *aeclessia magna*[6] *Aird Licce* (Tír., § 7) is referred to later in the narrative as bearing the name Sendomnach (*fundauerunt aeclessiam in Ardd Licce, quae sic vocatur: Sendomnach*, § 27). Two further *domnach* names, Domnach Ailmaige (§ 46) and Domnach Sairigi (§ 27), he leaves in their Irish form. While *aeclessia* is the standard term employed by Tírechán for 'church', the terms *cella* and *cellola* do feature, occasionally as appellatives but more commonly as translations of the generic *cell*. *Dominicum* ('church'), on the other hand, was patently not a feature of Tírechán's literary vocabulary; its absence from this source in particular suggests that *dominicum* 'church' was not in normal use in the Latin vocabulary of the 7th-century ecclesiastics in Ireland.

The traditional association of the term *domnach* with the Patrician mission, while strongly reflected in both Latin and Irish biographical material, is most succinctly defined in the 8th-century *Liber Angeli*: ... *et omnis ubique locus qui dominicus appellatur ... in speciali societate Patricii pontificis atque heredis cathedrae eius Aird Machae esse debuerat* ... (Bieler 1979, 188). This is the nearest approach in Patrician Latin documentation to a natural use of the term; whatever the validity of Armagh's claim, the expression 'any *place* that is called *dominicus*' strongly suggests that the term *domnach* by the 8th century was regarded as no more than a place-name element, albeit an element of weighted ecclesiastical significance.

3 A number of these references can be equated with *domnach*-named sites in *Bethu Phátraic* [B P]: the *aeclessia magna* founded *in campo Itho* (§ 47) is *Domnach Mór Maigi Itha* (BP p. 92); the *aeclessia magna* founded in Maugdornai (§ 50) is seen to be *Domnach Maigen* (BP p. 111), etc. *aeclessia filio Laithphi* (§ 8), although not featured in BP, is attested in other sources as a *domnach* name — cf. Hogan's Onomasticon Goedelicum (Dublin 1910) *s. v. domnach mór mac laithbe*, ~ *mic flaithbi*. These *aeclessia* references to subsequently attested *domnach* sites are not represented on map 1, since they do not, in themselves, constitute *domnach* place-name documentation. The consequent imbalance in historical (as distinct from onomastic) representation is adjusted by the appearance of these names as *domnach* units on maps 3 (left) and 5 (left).

4 The abbreviation Tír. denotes Tírechán's *Collectanea*. The edition referred to is Bieler 1979, to which paragraph references are given with citations. This edition was also used for the *Additamenta* and the *Notulae*.

5 BP denotes *Bethu Phátraic* ed. Mulchrone (1939), the edition of the Tripartite Life used in citations throughout this paper.

6 Tírechán's use of *aeclessia magna* is seen in all instances but one to relate to subsequently attested *domnach*-named sites; the unequated instance, *aeclessia magna Sirdrommo* (§ 47), is not known to me by name from subsequent documentation. Compare Tírechán's use of *cellola/cellula magna* with reference to and as translation of Cell Mór: ... *in illo posuit celolam magnam, quae sic uocatur Cellula Magna* (§ 20), Kilmore (Rosc. OS 12, 18); *cellola magna Muaide* (§ 7), Kilmoremoy (Mayo OS 30).

In the interest of clarity, the distribution maps of the element *domnach* are presented in relation to the chronological stratification of the major sources of documentation[7]. Map 1 ('Book of Armagh') plots the *domnach* names documented in 7th-8th-century source material[8]: from Tírechán's *Collectanea*, the three named *domnach*-sites plus the three *aeclessia magna* place-names that correspond to *domnach* names; two *domnach* names from the *Additamenta*; fourteen of the sixteen *domnach* names of the *Notulae*[9]. Of the total representation only six (plus one tentative instance) survive as OS *donagh*-names; one, entered as an addition to the OS distribution map (cf. note 16 *infra*), is attested in 17th-century documentation as a *donagh*-named unit.

The traditional association of Patrick with *domnach* names is intensified in the Irish biography, *Bethu Phátraic* (compiled from earlier sources between the years 895 and 901), where a total of forty-five *domnach* sites[10] are recorded and a further six unnamed *domnach* sites[11] referred to (cf. distribution map 2). This includes twelve of the total of nineteen *domnach* names recorded (either fully in Irish or in partial translation) in the Book of Armagh.

In considering the evidence for *domnach* names in *Bethu Phátraic* (which evidence indicates beyond doubt that, in the early phase of Christianisation, *domnach* 'church' was an established and widespread appellative in the demotic Irish vocabulary), the question arises of how long *domnach* continued to remain a formative element in place-name coinage. The documentary incidence of *domnach* 'church' as a lexical item in natural expression is insignificant[12]. Were it to survive in popular usage for several centuries after its introduction, the context in which,

---

7 The main source for identification (and in map 4, documentation) of names is Hogan's invaluable Onomasticon Goedelicum; in checking the evidence for Hogan's identifications some emendations have been made. While many tentative and approximate identifications/locations have been entered on the maps, where there appeared to be a strong element of doubt, or of ambiguity, the entry has been omitted.

8 In the onomastic context here, the precise date for the final compilation of these texts is of less significance than the period in which the material was collected. Whatever the date of Tírechán's writing of the *Collectanea*, the toponymic material appears to have been collected in the course of the 7th century (Bieler 1979, p. 41—3); for dating of the *Additamenta* and the *Notulae* cf. idem., 46—52.

9 *Notulae* names which also feature in Tírechán and the *Additamenta* are distinguished by their symbols on map 1.

10 The reference to *domnach* as the name of a bush (BP p. 50) has been omitted since no associated church site is recorded. One name is not locatable.

11 *uii. ndomnaig do Pátraic lá Cianacht, im Domnach Brechmaigi* (BP p. 96). I take *Domnach Airthir Ardda*, which both Mulchrone and Stokes (1887, p. 160) have inserted in association with this statement but which in the manuscript precedes the statement, to be the actual *name* of the church founded by Patrick at Dún Cruithne, in Aird Dáilauig (Magilligan Point, Co. Derry). Dún Cruithne is in the eastern part of the Aird. *Domnach Airthir Ardda* is represented on the distribution map by a tentative symbol in the Duncrun location.

12 cf. DIL dodénta — dúus, *s. v.* domnach (b).

27

par excellence, one might expect to find it is the Irish Patrician biographical material. But in *Bethu Phátraic* the nearest approach to the use of *domnach* as a lexical item in natural expression occurs in three rather formulaic expressions: *uii. ndomnaig dó im Ochaine* (p. 94); *uii. ndomnaig do Pátraic lá Cianacht* (p. 96) *secht ndomnaig do Pátraic la Úu Turtri* (p. 100). Here the presentation seems consciously contrived. These three units of seven are represented on maps 2, 3 and 5 (left) by larger symbols[13]; they are the three areas of greatest *domnach* frequency in the text. The compiler occasionally employs a *dinnseanchas* approach to a *domnach* place-name, e. g. *Domnach Mór Maige Réta, boí Patraic and fó Domnach* (p. 117). To all appearances, he was not at his ease with the *domnach* appellative, as he was, for instance, with the term *cell*; it appears not to have been part of his natural vocabulary. *Bethu Phátraic* is seen to derive from an 8th-century Latin or Latin-Irish Vita (Bieler 1954, Mulchrone 1952, eadem 1953); if *domnach* (or *dominicum*) was a significant lexical feature of the 8th-century 'working copy', one might expect to find this echoed to some degree in *Bethu Phátraic* (other than in the three phrases cited above). Can we assume that the term *domnach*, the *dominicum* that is significantly absent from Tírechán's *Collectanea*, was outmoded as an appellative by the 7th century? The indications are that it was. Is it possible that even in the latter half of the 6th century *domnach* was no longer a productive name element? It may be noted that the term *domnach* does not occur in the context of the Columban mission (which emanated from the North, the area of strongest *domnach* distribution, as will be shown below), that, to our knowledge, it was not introduced to Scotland[14] as were *cell* and other ecclesiastical settlement terms. Or is this totally explicable in terms of the difference in character between the so-called Patrician Church and the Columban Church? The 7th century, however, is as far back as our documentary evidence for *domnach* will take us.

Two related areas of enquiry towards which the distribution maps were directed are (i) the extent to which the documentary evidence for *domnach* names finds corroboration in the OS coverage and (ii) the extent, if any, to which the element *domnach* occurred outside the parameters of the *domnach* incidence in the Patrician documentation[15]. Map 3 (left) might be termed the official Patrician *domnach* picture — a combination of the *domnach* names in the Book of Armagh and those in *Bethu Phátraic*. Bearing in mind that the larger symbols are the aforementioned groups of seven, the North and, in particular, the mid-North is

13 Although some of the *domnach* names of the first-mentioned and third-mentioned units of seven can be identified or finely located, not all can; consequently, it is less misleading to represent them on the map by a collective symbol per unit of seven.

14 I am reliably informed by Mr. Aidan MacDonald, Department of Archaeology, University College Cork, that there is no evidence for *domnach* as a place-name element in Scotland.

15 Ideally, this area of enquiry would best be served by comparing the distribution of OS *donagh*-names with the distribution of the total *churches* ascribed to, or allegedly associated with, Patrick in the Patrician documentation.

clearly the area of heaviest *domnach* incidence; a lighter, but quite significant spread is seen in the mid-East and a pocketed group (all of which are tentative or approximate locations) in the Roscommon area. In comparing this with the OS distribution[16] on the right, there is a fair correspondence in the North, although the larger symbols on the documentary map preclude a general assessment of correlation; the mid-East OS spread, while corresponding in general effect with the documentary representation, is by no means a total correlation; totally absent from the OS picture is the documented Roscommon group[17]; excepting the Limerick instance, there is nothing in the documentary picture to correspond with the spread of OS *donagh*-names (seven in all) from Cos Carlow and mid-Laois southwestwards. Map 4 shows the distribution of *domnach* names documented in Irish writing[18] — glosses on martyrologies, annalistic references, saint-lists, etc. — over and above those already noted in the Book of Armagh and *Bethu Phátraic*[19]. This, unfortunately, is but a minimal representation of the potential distribution; the greater proportion of these names, as entered in Onomasticon Goedelicum[20],

16 The distribution is, in the main, that of *donagh*- as initial element in townland (in some instances townland/parish) and parish names, as entered in the General Topographical Index, Census of Ireland, 1901. Two instances have been omitted: Donaghstown and Donaghaguy, both of which appear *not* to have been *domnach* names. (Information on the latter was kindly supplied by Rev. Bernard Treanor, citing from the papers of Dean Mooney). To the *donagh*-names have been added some additonal names, the initial element (Dona-, Dunna-, etc.) of which is seen to have been originally *domnach*. (I am indebted to Art Ó Maolfabhail, Príomhoifigeach Logainmneacha, An tSuirbhéireacht Ordanáis for much helpful direction in this sphere. On his advice I have omitted three instances of Donnybrook (Cos Clare, Cork and Tipperary), which appear to be late names modelled on Donnybrook (Dublin OS 18, 22), the original *domnach* of the name-coinage.) There is an inbuilt element of chance in the perpetuation of place-names as 'received names' in the OS townland coverage; to redress the balance, particularly towards the comparison of the documentary distribution with the OS distribution, three further names have been added to the latter: Donaghedy (Tyrone OS 12), one of the western group of seven in *Bethu Phátraic*, known to Reeves (1850, 73) as a site name; Donaghmore (Mayo OS 22), documented in Tírechán and *Bethu Phátraic*, recorded as a land-unit in the 17th century; The Donahies (Dublin OS 14, 15) currently in use but no longer a townland name. (It is quite probable that more instances, unknown to the writer, could be added.) A fourth additon is Bodoney (Tyrone OS 12), a parish name, another survivor from the western group of seven in *Bethu Phátraic*. In the writer's opinion, the place-name Toberdoney, of not infrequent occurrence, is more likely to be the well visited *ar an Domnach* than to contain, as its specific, the element *domnach* 'church'.

17 This does not necessarily imply invalidation of the tentative/approximate identifications.

18 Including later Latin Vitae.

19 While the majority of these 'extra' names, including the unidentified names, are not documented in a Patrician context, some do have alleged Patrician associations. The strongest of these is the *Domnach Mór Mac Laithbe* instance, cited in note 3 supra.

20 The total count of *domnach* names entered in the Onomasticon is misleading, if viewed superficially as an indication of the sum total of *domnach* names in Irish documentation. Some names are entered under several variant entry-forms and cross-references are not always given. Some of the entry-names are Irish postulations of Anglicised or Latinised

are unlocatable. By adding the points on map 4 to the 'official' Patrician picture (map 3, left) we have a somewhat denser picture but little further spread (map 5, left); there is a better general correspondence with the OS incidence (map 5, right), stronger in the North, stronger in the mid-East, an improvement in the aforementioned southern stretch[21], but still, that same area and, indeed, the hinterland of Dublin Bay remain the weakest spheres in the correlation of OS instances with documented instances.

The probability of sporadic missionary activity in Ireland before the Patrician mission has been voiced by a number of writers[22]; this is generally assumed to have taken place from Britain and most likely to have been in the south and east of Ireland. *Domnach* belongs to the early layer of Latin loanwords, which, according to Jackson (1953, 122 ff), were borrowed from British Latin[23]. Was the term *domnach* 'church' already in use in Ireland, as Binchy (1962, 165—66) has suggested, before the Patrician mission? If so, might this account for some of the *domnach* names that are not entered in the embracive Patrician picture? Might it also account for some of the OS *domnach* names that are not represented (in identifiable form) in Hiberno-Latin or Irish documentation? Is this what is indicated by the site-name *Sendomnach* in Tírechán[24] and the site-name *Sendomnach Maigi Aí* in *Bethu Phátraic* (both of which appear to be in Co. Roscommon)? And we have in *Bethu Phátraic* (p. 19) the ascription of a *domnach* site, *Domnach Airte*, to Palladius, if that has any validity. The onomastic consideration, as represented above, gives no definite answers to these questions; it leaves us with impressions rather than findings. The writer's impression from the overall Irish onomastic consideration (irrespective of views on the historical validity of all documented instances of Patrician association) is that the term *domnach* 'church' did have some currency in Ireland before the advent of Patrick, with the attendant corollary that some *domnach*-

entries in post-12th-century calendars, in particular the Papal Taxation ca. AD 1306; while, in the main, these postulated names appear to be acceptable (in their generic, at least) they are not part of the brief of map 4. The distribution from the calendar sources would be a valuable supplement to map 5 (left); several unidentified *domnach* names have been noted, which appear not to be represented in the established Irish documentary count. It is hoped to make this additional map available when research in this area is completed.

21 The three 'extra' names from map 4, all of which are equated with OS *donagh*-names, are *Domnach Femin* (al. *Domnach Mór Maige Feimhin*) in Co. Tipperary, *Domnach Mór Muscraige Mittine*, Co. Cork and the lightly documented *Domnach Mór Roigni* (Co. Kilkenny). The first two are positive identifications; neither appears from documentation to have alleged Patrician associations.

22 More recently Binchy 1962, p. 165—6.

23 *Dominicum* is not attested (either as appellative or generic) in the context of Latin Roman Britain. The paucity of documented terms for 'a church building' leads Thomas (1981, 149) to conclude "that, until at least the fifth century, British Latin exhibited a certain looseness in finding any one specific word to mean 'a Christian church building'. The range of terms used very probably did include *ecclesia* (though we have no early example)".

24 Equated by Bieler (1979, p. 264) with *Sendom(nach) la Au. Er(cae)* of the *Notulae*.

named sites, particularly in the South and East, may, perhaps, predate the Patrician mission, others may be roughly contemporaneous with it but independent of it. What does emerge with fair certainty from the earlier consideration is that *domnach* 'church' relates to the first phase of Christianity in Ireland and appears to have fallen into disuse by the 7th century. It follows that OS *donagh*-names[25], whether or not they have early documentation, can be dated to this period.

What, if any, was the distinctive feature of the *domnach*? Did it differ from *cell* which, in the biographies, is well represented both as generic and appellative in the Patrician context? Seán Mac Airt (1958, 79) was of the opinion that the *domnach* was the equivalent of the regional parish church, founded to serve a settled community; this certainly is the impression gained from many of the *domnach* place-name forms: *Domnach* or *Domnach Mór* qualified by a district name: *Domnach Mór Maige Críathair*, *Domnach Mór Maige Itha*, *Domnach Mór Maige Coba*, etc. The incidence of *domnach* qualified by a personal name is relatively low. The transition in Ireland from an episcopal Church to a monastic Church was, almost certainly, a factor in the decline of *domnach* as a productive element in place-names. It is quite possible also that, with the stabilisation of Christianity, the prevalence of the word *domnach* in the sense of Sunday eclipsed, in popular usage, the more specialised connotation of *domnach* 'church'. Some of the *domnach* sites are documented in the later context as monastic sites — others must certainly have survived as monastic sites that are not documented[26] – but very many of the *domnach* names fade out of documentation altogether. It is reasonable to assume that many of the documented *domnach*-named units perished at an early stage[27], which assumption might account for the numbers that can be approximately located from their documentary context but not identified.

cell (< Lat. cella)

Whatever meaning the word *cella*[28] may have had when first introduced into Ireland, by the time *cella* or *cell* makes a significant appearance in Irish sources

25 Except in a few aberrant instances, as indicated in note 16 supra.

26 *Domnach Riascad* (BP p. 100), OS Donaghrisk townland, Co. Tyrone, appears to be such an instance; it does not feature in Irish documentation outside the Patrician context, yet it is entered as a church in a range of post-Reform ecclesiastical documentation and is known from 17th-century sources to have had 'erenagh lands'. A degree of continuity can be assumed with respect to all *domnach*-named churches of the later calendar documentation.

27 This may account for only one of the unit of seven *domnach* churches among the Cianacht being referred to by name (BP p. 96).

28 As stated by Lorié (1955, p. 51), *cella* is an instance of a non-Christian Latin word affected by a semantic change under monastic influence. Commenting (ibid., p. 45—6) on the one instance in the anonymous Latin translation (ca. AD 370) of the *Vita Antonii*, (V), of *cella* used as a translation of μοναστήριον ('the dwelling place of a hermit or solitary monk') Lorié writes as follows: "… it cannot be inferred that *cella* already expresses what at a later date was to be its current meaning viz. a hermit's cell. In common Latin speech *cella* has the following meanings: 1. pantry; 2. room, apartment, cottage; 3. the central place in a temple

(i. e. by the 7th century) its reference is ecclesiastical; it meant 'church' or 'monastery' — apparently a unit rather than a room within a unit.

With the development of the Irish monastic church *cell* became the standard term for a monastic foundation (Flanagan 1969, 379—82); furthermore, the indications, both documentary and onomastic, are that *cell* referred to the monastic unit *in toto*, not specifically to an oratory or 'cell' within[29]. The Anglicised element *kil(l)*-[30] is by far the commonest ecclesiastical habitative term in the Irish OS placename coverage, but unlike *donagh*-, it cannot categorically be assigned to any one phase. While the majority of the documented *cell* names (as entered in Onomasticon Goedelicum) belong to the native period of Irish monasticism, there is evidence that *cell* continued to be used, although apparently less frequently, in placename coinage of the post-12th-century period with reference to churches and occasionally to monastic houses (Flanagan 1979, 4—6). However, as an appellative, *cell*, which was the standard ecclesiastical settlement term in the annals from the 8th century to the 12th, is replaced in the post-Reform period by the terms *mainistir* 'monastery', *tempul* 'church' and occasionally *eclais* 'church'. The indications are that the appellative *cell* in the sense of 'church' (or 'monastery') went out of use in the course of the later medieval period (Flanagan 1969, 382—3) and, it is assumed, out of use in place-name coinage, although retained in its transferred sense of 'graveyard'[31].

In using later place-name documentation (where contemporary documentation is not forthcoming) as a guide to the retrospective dating of the deployment of a habitative generic element (in this instance *cell*), the reservation that inevitably tempers the exercise is the possibility that the name by which the habitative unit is attested in documentation may, to a greater or lesser extent, postdate the establishment of the unit itself, irrespective of how reliable the attested historical associations are seen to be. With this caveat in mind, we may note two *cell* names

---

containing the image of the god; 4. cell of a bee-hive. In (V) 'cella' has the second meaning." Further to these comments, Lorié (ibid., 47—51) notes Jerome's use (AD 390) of *cella* as the equivalent of 'hermitage', Cassian's use (ca. AD 424) of *cella* and *cellula* to indicate a hermit's cottage, Benedict's use (AD 523—526) of *cella* mostly with reference to an abode of several monks (*cella novitiorum, cella infirmorum*) but in one instance standing for monastery (... *per diversorum cellas hospitantur, Reg. Ben.* 1). (I am grateful to Dr Clare Stancliffe, University of Newcastle upon Tyne, for bringing this article and other relevant reading material to my attention).

Cf. Thomas 1971, p. 88 for the suggestion that Irish *cell* (< cella) may derive from "the continental phrase *cella memoriae*, which may have been borrowed to describe specially marked graves in an undeveloped cemetery".

29 Cf. MacDonald's comment on the *cella* names in Adomnán: "... in each case it is pretty clear that the monastic settlement as a whole is referred to, not just the church itself". (MacDonald 1979, p. 18).

30 Where it is seen to represent Irish *cill* and not *coill, cúil*, etc.

31 From which some of the *cill* and *cillín* minor names may derive.

with alleged 5th-century associations: *Cell Fine,* one of the three churches ascribed to Palladius (*BP* p. 19) and *Cell Auxili* (*Notulae* 38), named from Auxilius, *puer Patricii* (Tír., § 51). There are a number of *cell* names with well-attested 6th-century associations (and, for what it is worth, with 6th-century annalistic documentation), notably *Cell Daro* and *Cell Slébe. Cell/cill* is the ecclesiastical settlement term most strongly associated with the expansion of Gaelic-speaking Christian communities in Scotland (Nicolaisen 1976, 128—34; MacDonald 1979). It is the term, associated in name, with Colum Cille himself, attested as such in *Amra Choluimb Chille*[32] and further instanced in two other poems in praise of the saint, thought to be 7th-century compositions by Bécán mac Luigdech[33]. *Cell*, as an appellative, is the only ecclesiastical settlement term significantly represented in the *Amra*[34]. While the standard terms in Adomnán's Life of Columba are *ecclesia* and *monasterium, cellula* and *cella* do feature as appellatives (Anderson and Anderson 1961, 248, 268), the former with reference to a named site in Ireland (not a *cell*-named site), the latter in connection with a named *Cella Diuini* in Scotland, represented in the Columban period context. Two further *cell*-named sites, both in Ireland, *Cell Roiss* and *cella magna Deathrib*, are also represented in a Columban context (ibid., 300, 322). The evidence from Adomnán is sufficient to indicate that *cell* had some degree of natural usage in the 7th century, both in Ireland and in Scotland. The evidence for the cited *cell*-names can, in documentary terms, be no earlier than the time of writing (late 7th century). Any case for an earlier use of *cell* as a potentially creative element in Irish place-names rests on assumption. Nevertheless, it is felt that a case can be made. (Consideration of the Scottish situation is omitted here.) If to Adomnán's two attested Irish *cell* names are added the *cell* names attested in Tírechán (as noted below), we have at least ten *cell* names with 7th-century documentation, all of them represented in earlier historical contexts. Whatever degree of credibility can be given to the expressed associations, it may at least be argued that these names denoted ecclesiastical sites which in the 7th century could safely be cited as having some element of acknowledged historicity; assuming a specific ecclesiastical term to have been used to denote the unit itself in its pre-documentary existence (and this is *but* an assumption), it seems highly improbable that the term would have been anything other than that which emerged as the generic of its name (at whatever date), viz. *cell.* (As will be shown below, it is very unlikely to have been *eclais* or *mainistir.*)

Cell is relatively well attested in the Patrician context but, in comparison with the Columban context, its credibility here is infinitely more difficult to assess.

---

32 In the LU version (*Best* and *Bergin*, Lebor na Huidre, Dublin 1929, p. 30, 1. 867). Cf. *v. l.* in *RC* 20 (1899), p. 258. The *Amra* is thought to have been composed shortly after Columba's death in AD 597.

33 Cf. Ériu 24 (1973), p. 1 ff., ZCP 8 (1912), p. 197—8.

34 *RC* 20 (1899), p. 164, 270 and possibly 160.

That the term was both natural and acceptable to Tírechán is evident from his occasional employment of *cella* and *cellola* as appellatives, admittedly generally in association with a *cell*-named site[35]; he records at least[36] eight *cell*-named units (including a *senchell, Senella Cella Dumiche*), some of which he attributes directly to Patrick. The *Additamenta* have one *cell*-named unit, which was offered to Patrick; the *Notulae* contain a sprinkling of *cell* names. *Bethu Phátraic* records twenty-seven *cell*-named units (including two *senchell* instances), some of which are represented as having been founded by Patrick. In the Patrician context the writer can see little or nothing of onomastic significance to distinguish the *cell* names from the *domnach* names[37]. The incidence of *cell* qualified by a personal name, a commonly attested pattern in *cell* names in general, is surprisingly low in the Patrician *cell* names, indeed not significantly higher than the corresponding pattern in *domnach* names[38]. *Cell* qualified by the name Patrick is not attested within this range of documentation. *Cell* qualified by either a dynastic name or a district name does occur, but the incidence is considerably lower than is the case with the *domnach* generic. *Cell Mór Maigi Glais* (Kilmore, Co. Roscommon) and *Cell Mór Óchtar Muaide* (Kilmoremoy, Co. Mayo) are the only two instances of the formula so commonly found with *domnach* names; *Cell Mór* itself is of infrequent occurrence compared with the high incidence of *Domnach Mór*. Whether or not some of these *cell* names were genuine Patrician foundations (or foundations of the Patrician period) remains an historical rather than an onomastic consideration. What does emerge with certainty is that *cell* as an ecclesiastical settlement term was not regarded by the Patrician biographers as anachronistic in the context of the 5th-century mission.

dísert (< Lat. desertum)

The third Latin borrowing to make a marked impact as an ecclesiastical habitative generic in the pre-12th-century period is *dísert*, generally translated 'hermitage'. *Desert* (and variants Disert, Dysert, etc.[39]) is more often than not unqualified in the

35 But cf. the entry *et fecit alias cellas multas in Eilniu* which follows on the reference to *Cellola Cuile Raithin* (Tír., § 48).

36 In two instances it is difficult to tell whether *cella/cellola* is employed as appellative or generic. *Cellola Cuile Raithin* has been omitted from the count; there is no evidence from subsequent documentation that this was a *cell* name.

37 The writer is not competent to comment on the significance (if any) of Tírechán's use of the diminutive *cellola*, particularly in view of the two *Cellola/Cellula Magna* names recorded. Cf. also the reference to *parua celula* in *Liber Angeli* (Bieler 1979, p. 184).

38 The difficulty in interpreting the specific element in many instances of both *domnach* names and *cell* names inevitably affects the judgement here.

39 Including some disguised instances such as Castledermot, Castlekeeran, Estersnow, etc. *Dísert* as a specific element, as in Dundesert, Co. Antrim (documented in 1306 as *ecclesia de Deserto*), is not represented here.

OS coverage; where early documentation is available the original qualification is most commonly seen to have been a personal name. Map 6 shows the distribution of the generic *desert-* (*et var.*) in OS townland (including townland/parish) and parish names; the high incidence of *desert-* as a parish name suggests some degree of ecclesiastical continuity for the named sites into the later medieval period. Kenney (1929, 468) cites the development of the *dísert* as a significant element of the ascetic reform movement from which the *Céli Dé* emerged. While some evidence points in this direction, it is difficult to quantify in onomastic terms. The *Céli Dé* movement is seen to have begun in the south of Ireland, in the district around Darinis — Lismore — Daire Eidnech (Waterford/Tipperary area), probably in the second quarter of the 8th century (O'Dwyer 1981, 193); the incidence and distribution of OS *desert*-names in the South[40] may, to some extent, be seen to relate to this movement (or to the prelude to the movement). An annalistic run of documentation on *Dísert Diarmata* (OS Castledermot, Co. Kildare), thought to have been a *Céle Dé* foundation (O'Dwyer 1981, 44), suggests to the writer that *dísert* in this name-instance may have a more specialised connotation than simply 'hermitage'; foundation recorded in the Annals of Inisfallen AD 812: *Congbáil Dísirt Diarmata ...*; Diarmait's death recorded in the Annals of Ulster AD 825: *Diarmait huae Aedha roin, anchorita et religionis doctor totius Hiberniae, obiit*; Annals of Ulster AD 843: *Cumsudh mac Derero et Moinaigh mac Sothchadaigh, duo episcopi et duo ancorite, in una nocte mortui sunt i n-disirt Diarmata*. Significantly, we have here a site name (later to become a place-name) which is sufficiently well established within some thirty years of its foundation, within eighteen years of its founder's death, to be documented without a locational gloss. There is enough to suggest that the site was consciously established as a *dísert* (i. e. that the generic was not bestowed upon it from without). Was this *dísert* a solitary hermitage which, in a very short time, became a distinguished monastic house, or did it start off life as some form of community, presumably observing a stricter rule? If the latter was the case (and the writer is inclined towards that view), then *dísert* would seem by the 9th century to have a somewhat more specialised reference, a stage removed from the general understanding of 'hermitage'.

Research on the associations of individual *dísert* names[41] (where sources are forthcoming) may add weight to the suggested association of *dísert* with the ascetic reform movement. In addition to *Dísert Diarmata*, a few other names have been noted in passing as having some element of association with the movement in general (or with the prelude to it): *Dísert Maeltuile* in Co. Westmeath (O'Dwyer 1981, 35—6), possibly *Dísert Labráin* near Limerick city (idem, 47), possibly *Daire Dísirt Dochonna*, tentatively located in Meath (idem, 48), *Dísert Aengusa*, OS Dysar-

---

40 Particularly marked is the cluster to the west of the River Barrow and, indeed, the general spread towards the Southwest.
41 As yet not undertaken to any significant extent.

tenos, Co. Louth, attributed to *Óengus Céle Dé* (Gwynn and Hadcock 1970, 383)[42] *Dísert* names are not documented in the annals before the 9th century; this would suggest that the major *dísert* sites, at least, did not relate to the earlier phase of Christianisation.

In considering the evidence for an earlier deployment of the *dísert* generic[43], we are dependent on alleged association in the absence of contemporary documentation. It has been argued that *Dísert Chaoimhghin*[44] in the Glendalough complex was the original site of Caoimhghin's 6th-century foundation (Price 1945—67, 38). The foundation of *Dísert Narbri* is ascribed in the Codex Salmanticensis (Heist 1965, 237) to Maedóc of Ferns, who died 625. There are several other *dísert*-named sites with traditionally early ascriptions, including two northern instances, *Dísert Egnich* (Desertegny, Co. Donegal) and *Dísert Hi Thuachuill* (now Desert, a minor name in Ballynameen townland, Co. Derry), both of which are reckoned by Colgan (Triadis Thaum., 494—5) among the churches founded by Colum Cille. If associations such as these are worth considering, it would suggest that the *dísert* settlement concept (and presumably the potential deployment of the generic *dísert*) began at an earlier stage with the primary meaning of 'hermitage' and had by the 8th—9th century developed a somewhat more specialised connotation, while retaining the essence of 'a place apart'.

tech

The incidence of the native word *tech* as a generic in ecclesiastical place-names of the pre-12th-century period is sufficiently impressive to warrant comment in this consideration of ecclesiastical settlement elements. *Tech* names that are documented in the period in question (or in the context of the period) are seen to have either mythological association[45] or ecclesiastical association; the names with mythological association, for the most part, have not survived, if indeed many of them were ever in use as referential place-names. *Tech* as a generic in the secular context makes little or no impression on documented place-names of this period[46], the reason presumably being that in habitative place-names the reference is generally to the unit of settlement (*dún, ráth, les,* etc.), not to a structure within the

---

42 The Desert, the name of an area in Armagh city, may, perhaps, relate to the presence of *Céli Dé* in Ard Macha (Documented in AU AD 921). Of interest are MacDonald's comments on the *dísertach*, an official at Iona and the names *Cladh an Díseirt* and *Port an Díseirt* outside the surviving *vallum* at Iona (MacDonald 1981, p. 317).

43 I have discounted the instances of *Dísert Pátraic* in *Bethu Phátraic*.

44 Earliest documentation AFM AD 1108.

45 For discussion cf. Wagner 1974.

46 *Tech/tigh* does occur with secular habitative reference in what the writer considers to be later place-name coinages (roughly 12th—15th century). Price (1945—67) has several examples from Co. Wicklow: Tinnahinch, Ir. *Tigh na hInse* (p. 468); Timullin, Ir. *Tigh an Mhuilinn* (p. 431), etc.

unit. Map 7 shows the distribution of the documented ecclesiastical *tech* names of the period under discussion; this is the minimal representation, many of the documented instances being unidentifiable[47]. Within the total count of both identified and unidentified documented instances, the formation pattern is almost invariably *tech* qualified by a personal name (or what appears to be a personal name). Most of the names represented in the distribution have survived in a relatively recognisable Anglicised form as parish or townland names. The use of the generic *tech* in the ecclesiastical context is not totally confined to the pre-12th-century period; a few later instances have been observed but they are rare examples of the usage[48].

Tech names have a respectable representation in documentation from an early stage. The earliest annalistic instance is *Tech Teille* (Tehelly, Co. Offaly), recorded in the Annals of the Four Masters AD 670 and in the Annals of Ulster AD 725. In Tírechán there is a reference to *Tech Cirpain*[49] (*gens o Thig Cirpani*, § 51), to a *Domus Martirum* founded by Patrick (§ 51) and to *Roigne Martorthige* (§ 51). The *Notulae* include one *tech* name while *Bethu Phátraic* features two further *tech* names, *Tech Laisrend* (p. 50) and *Tech Talan* (p. 110), neither of which is attributed directly to Patrick but referred to as if they were established places on the Patrician circuit; in the context of the former mention is made of the disciple Bice's tomb[50], in the latter Patrick left relics which he had with him from oversea[51]. Also recorded in *Bethu Phátraic* is the rather dubiously[52] named *Tech na Róman*, attributed to Palladius (p. 19). Other *tech* names have allegedly early associations: *Tech Baithín* (Taughboyne, Co. Donegal) and *Tech Baithín* (Tibohine, Co. Roscommon), both with 6th-century personal name attributions (Gwynn and Hadcock 1970, 406, 45); *Tech Moshacra* (Saggart, Co. Dublin), *Tech Moling* (St Mullins, Co. Carlow), *Tech Munu* (Taghmon, Co. Wexford), *Tech Mochua* (Timahoe, Co. Laois) *et al.* with 7th-century associations (idem, 403, 43, 45). While the documentary evidence for the generic *tech* can be no earlier than the 7th century, the impression gained from the diverse sources is that *tech* names in an ecclesiastical association were not traditionally regarded as a 7th-century innovation. The writer, following a tentative suggestion made by Wagner (1974, 10), is inclined to consider the deployment

47 In addition to the documented instances, quite a number of other ecclesiastical *tech* names have been established in the course of research. For additional instances in the Dublin area cf. de hÓir 1975, p. 133—4. These are not within the brief of the distribution.

48 Cf. *Tech Eoin*, Tyone Priory, Co. Tipperary and *Tech Eoin* at Rindown, Co. Roscommon, both houses of the Fratres Cruciferi (Gwynn and Hadcock 1970, p. 214—15). They are not represented on the distribution map.

49 Although perhaps not an ecclesiastical *tech* name.

50 *Fir oirthir Midi ros bathess Patraic oc Toig Laisrend indess. Itá a thiprae i ndorus inna cilli. Facaib dís dia muintir ann, i. Bice 7 Lugaid, 7 ata ferta Bice fri tiprait antuaid.* (BP p. 50).

51 *Martra sruithi tucc leis tar muir anair.* (BP p. 110).

52 The presence of the definite article in the name-composition is anachronistic in such an early context (cf. Flanagan 1980).

of the generic *tech* in the ecclesiastical context as a continuation into the Christian period of the pagan use (and, to some extent, the mythological associations) of *tech* as, for instance, in *Tech nDuind,* the traditional otherworld of the dead (cf. O'Rahilly 1946, 481—2). If viewed in this light, the Christian deployment of the generic *tech* might suggest the site of a saint's grave or relics. The tomb and relics mentioned in association with the *tech* names in *Bethu Phátraic* (and, indeed, the *Domus Martirum* and *Martorthech* in Tírechán), while in no way constituting positive evidence, may be pointers in this direction. But the situation is far form clear; other factors (in relation to possible contacts and cults of the 5th-7th-century church) may well have had a bearing on it[53]. Whatever the source of the ecclesiastical *tech* concept, it is possible that in the course of time *tech* may have become, by attraction, simply a fashion in naming.

eclais, mainistir, tempul

The terms *eclais, mainistir*[54] and *tempul* are noticeably absent from early documented place-nomenclature; this, in itself, requires some comment in view of the standard use of *ecclesia* and the not infrequent use of *monasterium* in Latin writings relevant to this study. The usage, however, is not paralleled to any significant degree in Irish writing. In the annals the incidence of the terms *eclais*[55] and *mainistir* in the earlier entries is virtually negligible. It is but from the later 12th century onwards that they feature, from which time *mainistir* begins to be used mainly of the new monastic houses, gradually replacing *cell* as the standard term for 'monastery', *eclais* begins to be used occasionally of 'church building' although *tempul* is the term that comes to be more commonly employed. (For documentation cf. Flanagan 1969, 379—84.)

Eclais. The absence of evidence for the element *eclais* in documented place-names of the pre-12th-century period strongly suggests that Eglish/Aglish names in the

---

53   There is little likelihood that the ecclesiastical *tech* generic is an Irish equivalent of the shortlived term *domus dei* (as applied to a church building), discussed by Mohrmann (1977, p. 220—22, 230). I am not competent to comment on the significance of Domus Martirum (as distinct from *martyrium*) in Tírechán (§ 51) or to speculate on whether it is a translation of Martorthech or the latter an Irish adaptation of Domus Martirum. On the other hand, Tírechán's *Domus Liacc Cennani, id est lapidum* (§ 27), with reference to *Dom-Liacc Cíanán* (as in BP p. 64) appears to be simply a hybrid translation of an existing name. Cf. O'Rahilly's discussion of the word *dam* 'house, dwelling place' and his note to the effect that he considers it to be a native word, and not a borrowing from Latin (O'Rahilly 1950, p. 332—5).

54   With one exception, discussed below.

55   Two instances in the Annals of Ulster have been noted by MacDonald (1981, p. 307), one of which appears to refer to the church of Cluain-foto (AD 890); the second instance, *ecluis Brigte,* is discussed below.

OS coverage[56] (cf. map 8) relate to churches of the post-Reform period. The fact that approximately half of the names represented in the distribution are civil parish names suggests that the generic *eclais* in all instances may have originally denoted the main church of the medieval parish. That *eclais* was not the common pan-country term for church/parish church emerges clearly from a comparison of its distribution with that of *temple-* (map 9), a corroboration of the impression gained from the later annalistic usage of the appellative *eclais* as compared with that of *tempul*. All but three of the Eglish/Aglish names are simplex forms; it may be assumed that they did originally have qualifications (if only the name of the area which they served); their survival without the requirement of a specific qualification is a further indication of their topographic singularity.

The later dating of *eclais* place-names is tempered by one reservation. *Eclais* meaning a 'church structure' was not a new linguistic concept in the Reform period, as is illustrated by several pre-12th-century annalistic references to *eclais*-named church structures (as distinct from place-names), notably *ecluis Brigte for lar Duin dalethglas* (AU AD 1007) and *eclais becc* in Clonmacnois (AFM AD 893, AD 921, passim)[57]. It is probable that other unattested *eclais*-named structures existed elsewhere. The non-emergence of such *eclais* instances as place-names may be explained by their being within a named monastic settlement unit, in like manner to the terms *dairthech* and *dam liac* (with one notable exception in the case of the latter term) which, for the same reason, are unattested as place-name generics.

Mainistir. Although the term *monasterium* appears to have been acceptable to Latin writers in the context of early Irish monastic sites, as seen in Tírechán (§ 57) and *Liber Angeli* (Bieler 1979, 185), there is no evidence, excepting one singular instance, for the use of *mainistir* in place-name composition prior to the Reform period. In this later context the generic *mainistir* is frequently attested as the equivalent of English *abbey*: Abbeylara, *Mainistir Lethrátha*; Greyabbey, *An Mhainistir Liath*; Abbeydorney, *Mainistir Ó dTorna*, etc. *Mainistir Buite* (Monasterboice, Co. Louth) is the unique instance of an early documented *mainistir* name. Buite's death is recorded in the Annals of Ulster AD 519/523. The location of Monasterboice in proximity to the east coast would support the impression gained that the generic *mainistir* here was an isolated import. Its singularity is indicated by documentary references to Mainistir as a simplex form[58], apparently without need of further qualification.

56 The distribution is that of the generic element only. Instances of *eglish/aglish* as a specific element do occur but are much more difficult to quantify.

57 Cf. also the entries *Ecclas Fuinche .i. Ross airthir dfothughadh* (AFM AD 1084) and *Ecclas Choluim Chille hi cCenannus* (ibidem, AD 807).

58 Cf. Onomasticon Goedelicum *s. v. mainistir*. While other monastic names such as *Cluain moccu Nóis* and *Cluain Ferta* are also documented without their specific, the tendency is more marked in the case of *Mainistir Buite*.

Tempul. As with *eclais*, in the absence of pre-12th-century documented *tempul* place-names it may be assumed that the OS *temple*-names are, in the main, post-Reform coinages. A sizable number of the names represented in the distribution of the generic (map 9) can be seen to be civil parish names. Price (1945—67, 505) has noted that the Co. Wicklow instances suggest that the element *temple* came into use after the Anglo-Norman invasion, denoting the principal church of a parish. Hurley (1979) has effectively demonstrated that the spread of *temple*-names in Co. Cork related to Anglo-Norman colonisation. This may also be true of other areas. Certainly the impression gained from the element-content of many of the instances (e. g. dedications to Michael, Peter, Patrick, etc.) is that of later coinage. It accords with the later annalistic usage of *tempul* as the more common term for a church.

Again as with *eclais*, the use of the term *tempul* is not an innovation of the Reform period. From the mid-11th century onwards *tempul* features sporadically in the annals with reference to a church structure within a named monastic settlement[59]; in some instances (e. g. *Cell Dara*, cf. AU AD 1050, 1067) the reference appears to be to a stone-built structure. Within the first half of the 12th century the Annals of Ulster employ *tempul* relatively frequently to denote the church or churches of monastic units such as *Cell Da Lua, Corcach, Áth Truim, Daire, Imblech Ibair,* etc. The new Romanesque *Tempal Cormaic* (CS AD 1130) is the earliest recorded instance of a *tempul* site name[60]. In the opinion of the writer, the attested use of the term *tempul* from the mid-11th century onwards (notwithstanding its initially denoting a structure within a unit) inhibits the blanket assignation of all surviving *temple*-names to the later period. Some *temple*-named churches in the West are seen structurally to predate the medieval period (e. g. *Teampall Mac-Duach* and *Teampall Bhreacáin* on Inishmore); rather than dismiss the generic in these instances as a medieval bestowal, the possibility may be entertained that such *tempul* instances may relate to the attested currency of the appellative *tempul* at an earlier period.

---

59 For discussion of the unique use of *templum* in the Annals of Ulster AD 813, with reference to the newly constructed church at Kells cf. MacDonald 1981, p. 307—8.

60 Of interest is the reference to *tempall na manach* (AU AD 1157), the church of the newly established Cistercian monastery of Mellifont.

References

Anderson A. and		
Anderson M.	1961	Adomnan's Life of Columba. Edinburgh
Bieler, L.	1954	The *Notulae* in the Book of Armagh, Scriptorium 8, 89—97
Bieler, L.	1979	The Patrician Texts in the Book of Armagh. SLH 10
Binchy, D. A.	1962	Patrick and his biographers: ancient and modern, Stud. Hib. 2
de hÓir, É.	1975	Sracfhéachaint ar logainmneacha Bhaile Átha Cliath, Stud. Hib. 15
Doelger, F. J.	1950	Antike und Christentum 6
Flanagan, D.	1969	Ecclesiastical nomenclature in Irish texts and place-names: a comparison, Proceedings of the 10th International Congress of Onomastic Sciences 2, 379—88
Flanagan, D.	1979	Common elements in Irish place-names: *ceall, cill,* Bulletin of the Ulster Place-Name Society, ser. 2, 2
Flanagan, D.	1980	Place-names in Early Irish documentations: structure and composition, Nomina 4, 41—5
Gwynn A. and		
Hadcock, R. N.	1970	Medieval Religious Houses: Ireland. London
Heist, W. W.	1965	Vitae Sanctorum Hiberniae. (Société des Bollandistes, Brussels)
Hogan, E.	1910	Onomasticon Goedelicum. Dublin, London
Hurley, V.	1979	The distribution, origins and development of Temple as a church name in the south-west of Ireland, JCHAS 84, 74—87
Jackson, K.	1953	Language and History in Early Britain. Edinburgh
Kenney, J. F.	1929	The Sources for the Early History of Ireland: Ecclesiastical. New York
Lorié, L. Th. A.	1955	Spiritual Terminology in the Latin Translations of the Vita Antonii. Nijmegen
Mac Airt, S.	1958	The churches founded by Saint Patrick, Saint Patrick, ed. *Ryan,* J. Dublin
MacDonald, A.	1979	Gaelic *cill (kil(l)-)* in Scottish place-names, Bulletin of the Ulster Place-Name Society., ser. 2, 2, 9—19
MacDonald, A.	1981	Notes on monastic archaeology and the Annals of Ulster, 650—1050, Irish Antiquity, ed. *Ó Corráin,* D. Cork
Mohrmann, C.	1977	Études sur le Latin des Chrétiens IV, Rome
Mulchrone, K.	1939	Bethu Phátraic. The Tripartite Life of Patrick. Dublin
Mulchrone, K.	1952	What are the Armagh *notulae?,* Ériu 16, 140—44
Mulchrone, K.	1953	Tírechán and the Tripartite Life, IER 79, 186—93

Nicolaisen,		
W. F. H.	1976	Scottish Place-Names. London
O'Dwyer, P.	1981	Célí Dé. Spiritual Reform in Ireland 750—900. Dublin
O'Rahilly, T. F.	1946	Early Irish History and Mythology. Dublin
O'Rahilly, T. F.	1950	Varia II: 4. *dia daim*, Celtica 1
Price, L.	1945-67	The Place-Names of Co. Wicklow 1—7. Dublin
Reeves, W.	1850	Acts of Archbishop Colton ... Visitation of the Diocese of Derry, AD 1397. Dublin
Stokes, W.	1887	The Tripartite Life of Patrick I. Dublin
Thomas, C.	1971	The Early Christian Archaeology of North Britain. Oxford
Thomas, C.	1981	Christianity in Roman Britain to AD 500. London
Wagner, H.	1974	Der königliche Palast in keltischer Tradition, ZCP 33, 6—14

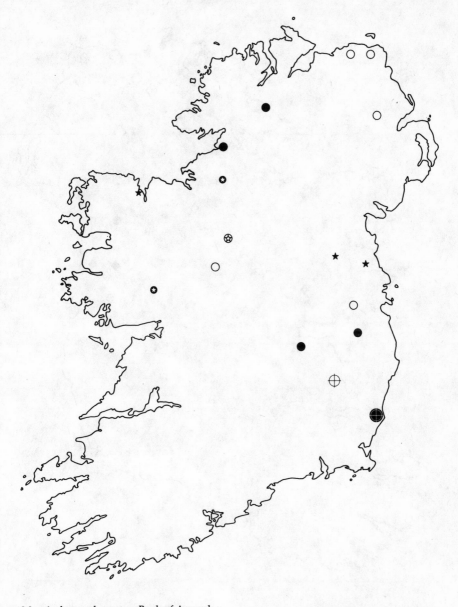

Map 1: domnach names: Book of Armagh

● Notulae, established
○ Notulae, tentative/approximate
★ Tírechán, established
✪ Tírechán + Notulae, established
✪ Tírechán + Notulae, tentative/approximate
⊕ Notulae + Additamenta, tentative/approximate
⊕ Notulae + Additamenta, established

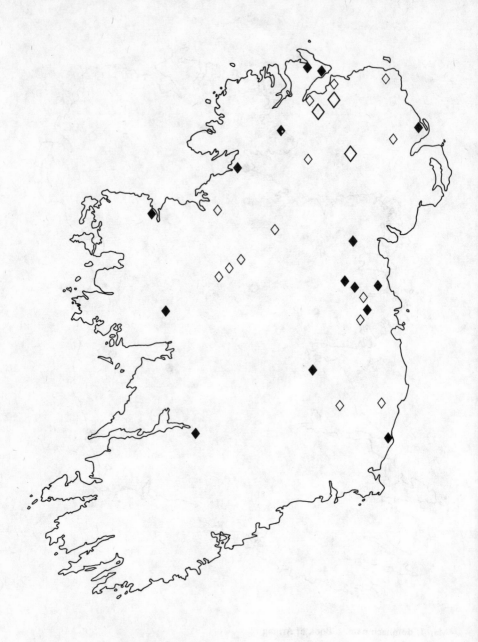

Map 2: domnach names: Bethu Phátraic

◆ established
◇ tentative/approximate
◇ unit of 7

44

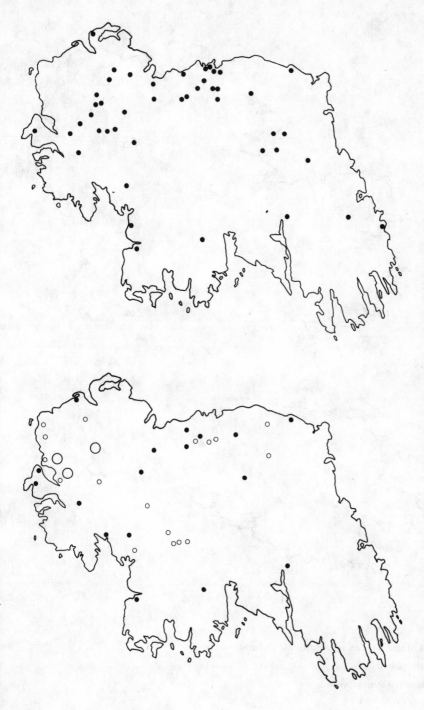

Map 3: (left) domnach names: Book of Armagh + Bethu Phátraic (right) O/S Donagh- (et var.)

• established ○ tentative/approximate ◯ unit of 7

Map 4: domnach names: Additional Documentation

▲ established

△ tentative/approximate

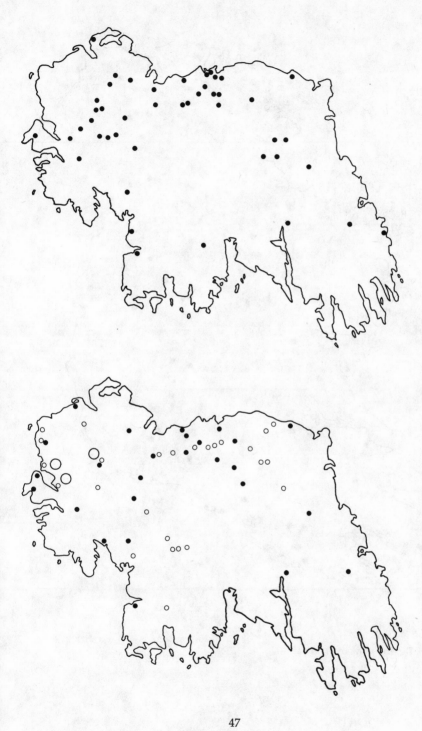

Map 5: (left) domnach names (documentary)   (right) O/S Donagh- (et var.)

● established   ○ tentative/approximate   ○ unit of 7

47

Map 6: Desert(-)/Dysart(-) (et var.)

✱ parish

● townland

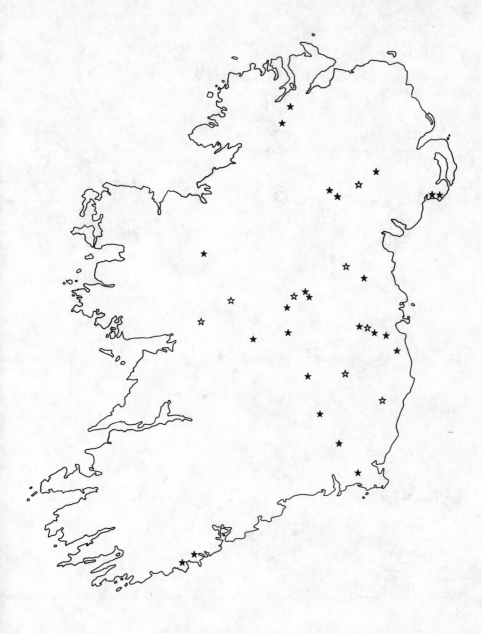

Map 7: tech names (documentary)

★ established

☆ tentative/approximate

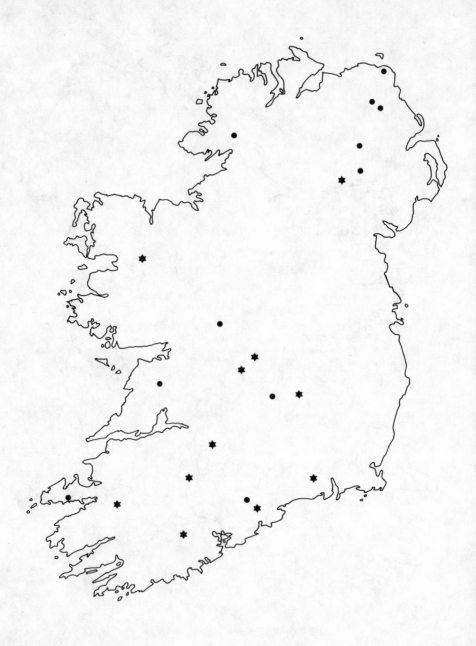

Map 8: O/S Eglish/Aglish(-)

★ parish

● townland

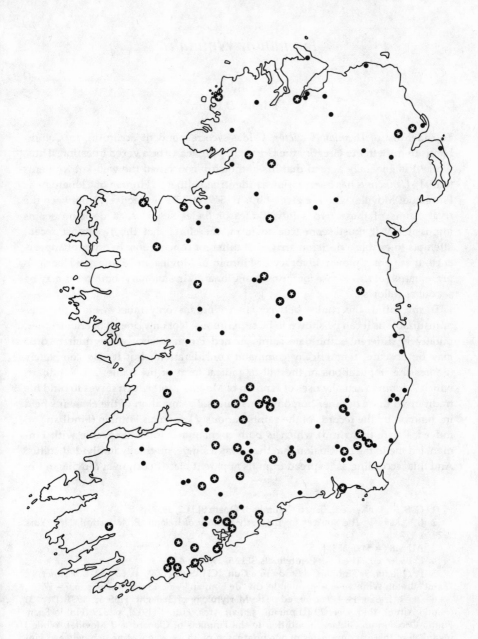

Map 9: O/S Temple

- • townland
- ✪ parish

51

Finnian or Winniau?

By
Pádraig Ó Riain

The identity of *Uennianus auctor*, Gildas's correspondent according to Columbanus in his letter to Gregory the Great[1], has proved to be a vexed question. Thus, while it is generally agreed that his authorship concerned the well-known penitential[2], *Uennianus* has been variously identified either as Finnian of Clonard or as Finnian of Moville, who are given obits of 549 and 579 respectively[3]. Between the rival claims of these two saints, Professor Bieler suggests, 'a decision seems impossible'[4]. It must seem true to form, therefore, that the two most recent attempts to enable a decision arrived at different conclusions. In order of appearance, these are my own advocacy of Finnian of Moville and Professor Fleuriot's presentation of a new case for Finnian of Clonard[5]. In summary, both cases may be set out as follows.

To my mind, the choice between two Finnians only must seem *a priori* as unjustifiable as it can be shown to be superfluous. Not only does it overlook other, putatively different, candidate saints named Finnian who, while their records may be obscure, theoretically command consideration[6], but it also completely ignores the implications of the full or radical form of the name, i. e. Findbarr, which Adomnán actually uses of Finnian of Moville[7], and which serves to bind his tradition to those of other homonymous saints. Examination of the elements held in common by the records of the saints variously known as Finnian (Findbarr) or, indeed, Bairre (Bairrfind) which is both cognate and interchangeable with Finnian, led me to the conclusion that there was a single, originally undivided cultus. And this, according as it spread from its apparent place of origin at Moville in Co.

---

1 G. S. M. *Walker*, ed., Sancti Columbani Opera SLH 2, 1957, p. 8.

2 J. F. *Kenney*, The Sources for the Early History of Ireland: Ecclesiastical, New York 1929, p. 177.

3 AU 548 (= 549), 578 (= 579).

4 L. *Bieler*, ed., The Irish Penitentials SLH 5, 1963, p. 4.

5 P. *Ó Riain*, St Finnbarr: a Study in a Cult, JCHAS 82 (1977), p. 63—82. L. *Fleuriot*, Le "Saint" Breton Winniau et le pénitentiel dit "de Finnian"?, EC 15 (1976—78), p. 607—17.

6 Cf. R. I. *Best*, H. J. *Lawlor*, ed., The Martyrology of Tallaght, HBS 68, 1931, Dec. 31 (Finnio Áirne); ibid. Dec. 29 (Uinniauii senis); Arch. Hib. 1 (1912), p. 329 (Finnio Sean, Finnio Óac, Finnio Gildae, in addition to the Finnians of Clonard and Moville). While I regard all of these as surrogates of one original saint, those who distinguish between Finnian of Clonard and his namesake of Moville clearly do not; yet, they fail to take them into account.

7 W. *Reeves*, ed., The Life of St Columba, (Ir. Arch. Celt. Soc., 1857), p. 103—4 (= II.1); A. O. and M. O. *Anderson*, ed., Adomnan's Life of Columba, Edinburgh 1961, p. 324—6 (= 53 a b).

Down, developed a number of localized forms (such as that at Clonard) for reasons which, far from being peculiar to the case of Findbarr (Finnian), were to affect, and superficially distort, the whole pattern of Irish dedications[8].

In showing preference for Finnian of Clonard, Professor Fleuriot conforms with the more common view. In justifying his choice, however, he seriously breaks with tradition by regarding the saint's connexion with the Irish monastery as the final episode of a long life which began in Brittany and which was for the most part divided between there and Britain. Two important pieces of evidence are cited in support of this view. Firstly, of the four manuscript witnesses to the penitential, two are of Breton provenance, so that the Irishman, Columbanus, who demonstrably used it[9], could easily have had access to it through his otherwise well-established Breton associations. Secondly, in early sources the saint's name is more commonly written *Uinniauus*, whence Breton Winniau, than *Uinnianus*, which may reflect the Irish form Finnian.

That scholars should hitherto have ignored these aspects of the record is attributed by Professor Fleuriot to a more general failure on their part to appreciate adequately the early British contribution to the success of Celtic Christianity. After AD 550, Anglo-Saxon encroachment had not only undermined the position of the British Church; it had also prepared the ground for the disproportionate importance thenceforth to be attached to the Irish Church; so much so, that the latter could almost forget 'qu'elle etait fille de la chrétienté brittonique'[10].

Finnian too was to succumb to this form of creeping Hibernicization. Yet, even in Irish sources, clues to his real identity remain. Thus, in Latin usage *Uinniauus* 'à la brittonique' is found together with *Uinnianus* 'à la irlandaise'. Similarly, in vernacular usage Finnio, which appears to be the earlier form[11], alternates with Finnian (Finnén). On this evidence, one can hardly speak of Finnian as a '"pur" irlandais' and, if not, should one not infer that *Uinniauus* (or Winniau), the presumptive Breton, and *Uinnianus* (or Finnian), the Irishman by convention, were one and the same? ('ne sont ils pas un seul et même personnage?'[12]) Finnian's biographer asserts that the saint spent up to thirty years in South Wales[13]. Also, the author of Samson's Vita brings his subject into contact with a very learned

8 In other articles, e. g. P. Ó Riain, Traces of Lug in Early Irish Hagiographical Tradition, ZCP 36 (1977), p. 138—56, and *idem,* Cainnech *al.* Colum Cille, Patron of Ossory, in P. *de Brún,* S. Ó Coileáin, P. Ó Riain ed., Folia Gadelica: Essays presented to Professor R. A. Breatnach, Cork 1983, I explore the traditions of saints other than Findbarr which reveal similar patterns.

9 *Bieler,* Penitentials, p. 5.

10 *Fleuriot,* p. 610.

11 Adomnán (*Reeves,* III, 4; *Anderson,* 106b) uses Finnio and provides it with a Latin accusative Finnionem. Óengus invariably uses Finnio (Findio) in his metrical calendar (*Fél.* Sept. 28, Dec. 12); only in the late commentary does Finnian, Findén etc. occur.

12 *Fleuriot,* p. 612.

13 W. W. *Heist,* Vitae Sanctorum Hiberniae, Bruxelles 1965, p. 99 (§ 11).

man named *Uinniauus* (written *Winniauus*) in North Cornwall[14]. These and certain other British traces of the saint pinpoint for Professor Fleuriot the route followed by a Breton saint Winniau while dividing his time between South Wales, Cornwall and Brittany, before finally establishing himself at Clonard[15].

The evidence then for a Breton rather than for an Irish author of the penitential breaks down into two principal components. One concerns the manner in which the text has been transmitted. The other relates to the implications of the author's name. Besides, evidence from other sources appears to confirm the presence of the saint on the British mainland, and if convention later required that this man be regarded as an Irishman, then this was due only to the disproportionate influence achieved by the Irish component of Celtic Christianity. Each of these points will now be taken in turn.

The suggestion of a link between the Breton associations of Columbanus and the provenance of at least two of the manuscript witnesses to *Uinniauus's* penitential must seem very plausible. However, it can hardly be said that it argues the case for the Breton origins of Finnian of Clonard. Thus, accepting Finnian's annalistic obit of 549[16], Columbanus, who would then have been about six years of age[17], would surely have had more than enough time to become acquainted with the penitential, regardless of its author's place of origin, before he left for the Continent in or around 590[18]. On the other hand, accepting Professor Bieler's contention that Columbanus composed his own penitential while on the Continent[19], then, since this demonstrably draws on Finnian, he must have had a copy of the earlier work in his possession. Were the question of an originally Breton Finnian never to arise, therefore, the exclusively continental manuscript tradition of the earlier penitential could be very plausibly explained along these lines. Also, the fact that the two Breton manuscript witnesses to the penitential consist of extracts only, and that these form part of a largely Irish group of texts within each manuscript[20], hardly lends support to the theory of a continental origin for the work[21].

The onomastic evidence cited by Professor Fleuriot is decidedly more impressive. Thus, the incidence of the Brittonic suffix *-iaw* in Irish (*-io*) seems limited to

---

14 F. *Plaine*, Vita Antiqua Sancti Samsonis, AB 6 (1887), p. 77—150 (107).

15 *Fleuriot*, p. 613.

16 As I point out in a further paper (P. Ó *Riain*, Towards a Methodology in Early Irish Hagiography, Peritia 1, 1982, p. 146—59), the association between Finnian and Colum Ua Crimthannáin, which appears to underlie the annal, does not say much for its authenticity.

17 *Walker*, 'the available evidence points ... to 543 as the date of Columba's birth', p. XII.

18 Ibid. (Even if the earlier possible date of Columbanus's arrival on the Continent, i. e. ca. 575, be accepted, the argument here is not affected).

19 *Bieler*, Penitentials, p. 5.

20 Ibid. p. 12 (B), p. 14 (P).

21 *Bieler* (ibid. p. 242—5) also details the slight internal evidence of insular authorship.

Finnio[22]. In Welsh, on the other hand, the suffix is extremely common e. g. *Sylio, Ceirio, Ceidio* etc. Also, as Thurneysen points out[23], *Finnio* shows Brittonic assimilation of *nd* to *nn*. Undoubtedly, therefore, while Brittonic influences were generally operative in the formation of Irish hypocorisms[24], their effect on *Finnio* was unusually marked.

It must be remembered, however, that, as far as Irish usage was concerned, the hypocoristic form accounts only for a part of the saint's onomastic record. Thus, in the same passage as Adomnán refers to *Uinniauo* (dat.) in the Brittonic fashion, he also uses the full form of the saint's name, *Findbarrum* (acc.)[25] which, with its unassimilated *nd*, seems fully Irish in character. This lack of discrimination between the full and the hypocoristic form is typical of Irish usage and, as I have shown in *Findbarr*'s case[26], the equivalence and possible exchange with the cognate form *Bairrfind (Bairrind)* must also be borne in mind. For instance, *Findbarr*, patron of Cork was formerly known as *Bairrfind*[27], whose hypocoristic form, *Bairre (Barrae)*, is still that used of the saint.

Belonging then to a series of cognate forms, of which no other representative shows traces of borrowing, *Finnio*, despite its typically Brittonic features, is firmly fixed in an Irish context, already in the earliest part of the saint's record[28]. If the theory of a British or Breton origin for the saint is to be upheld, therefore, the inference must be that the saint's arrival in Ireland was also heralded by the use of a full, i. e. non-hypocoristic, Brittonic form of his name, so close to the Irish equivalent, *Findbarr*, that this could be immediately substituted for it. In that case, however, one would expect to find in British (or Breton) sources not only a form corresponding to *Findbarr*, but also some evidence of its local use side by side with *Uinniauus*.

Here, Professor Fleuriot's case is at its weakest for while the Welsh equivalents, *Gwynfor (Findbarr)* and *Berwyn (Bairrfind)* are already used of a father and son in a sixth-century inscription from South-West Carmarthenshire in Wales, i. e. *Barrivend- filius Uendubari*[29], nowhere is there evidence to suggest that any of these forms ever interchanged with *Uinniauus*, either as such or, more importantly, in

22 However, Martyrology of Tallaght (as above note 6) (cf. Gorm.) July 25 (which, curiously, is also Findbarr's day) refers to a *Ninnio Senoir* and this form also occurs in *Gorm*. April 18.

23 R. *Thurneysen*, A Grammar of Old Irish, Dublin 1946, p. 175 (§ 275).

24 Cf. R. *Thurneysen*, Zum Namentypus abret. To-woedoc, air. Do-dimoc, ZCP 19 (1933), p. 354—67; H. *Lewis*, The Honorific Prefixes *To-* and *Mo-*, ZCP 20 (1936), p. 138—43.

25 *Reeves, Anderson* (as above note 7).

26 *Ó Riain*, St Finnbar.

27 Mart. Tall. Sept. 25, 26.

28 Adomnán (Reeves, Anderson) here represents the earliest part of the record.

29 R. A. S. *Macalister*, ed., Corpus Inscriptionum Insularum Celticarum I, Dublin 1945, p. 351—2 (§ 368). The place of the inscription, Llandawke, lay well within the area of Irish settlement in South Wales.

relation to the author of the penitential[30]. We must conclude either that the record is incomplete in this respect or, as seems more likely, that the author of the penitential first became known in Britain and beyond through Irish sources which showed the preference for the hypocoristic form exemplified by the predominance of *Finnio (Finnian)* in the records of such monasteries as Moville and, even more particularly, of Clonard[31]. The Irish context which this would suppose for the diffusion of *Finnio*'s name and, implicitly, work, draws further support from the fact that where traces of *Finnio*'s cognates do occur on the British mainland, the context is invariably Irish.

In independent articles[32], Professor Fleuriot and I have discussed in detail the implications of Finnian's connexions in South Wales, which were centred on Cadog's church at Llancarfan[33], and in Cornwall, where the learned man *Winniavus*, whom Samson encounters at St Kew, appears to have been his surrogate[34]. Professor Fleuriot views these connexions as reflexes of the saint's physical passage from Brittany to Clonard in Ireland. In doing so, however, he fails to take into account the numerous other associations of the saint with the British mainland which mostly, but not exclusively, take the form of dedications[35]. Are we to assume that the saint engaged in many a lengthy detour while on his way to Ireland, or are the dedications to Finnian in, for example, Scotland to be viewed as traces of cult rather than of person? And if the latter, then why not so in South Wales and Cornwall where the local Irish settlements would have ensured very favourable conditions for the diffusion of devotion to the Irish saints?

As I see them, Finnian's connexions in these parts of Britain reflect, indeed help to delimit, the spread of local Irish settlement[36]. And it is surely no coincidence that the saint's presence in both areas is witnessed not only by the textual evi-

30 Professor Fleuriot, for instance, while making his case for a British background to the saint, does not refer at all to the non-hypocoristic form of the name.

31 At Clonard, there is no evidence in the written record of the saint's full name. As I show elsewhere, however (*Ó Riain*, Towards a Methodology) the full form Findbarr can be inferred.

32 *Fleuriot*, Le "Saint" Breton; *Ó Riain*, The Irish Element in Welsh Hagiographical Tradition, in D. *Ó Corráin*, ed., Irish Antiquity: Essays and Studies presented to Professor M. J. O'Kelly, Cork 1981, p. 291—303.

33 *Heist*, Vitae 97 (§ 4)—99 (§ 11); W. *Stokes*, Lives of the Saints from the Book of Lismore, Oxford 1890, p. 75—6 (11. 2529—66).

34 *Plaine* (as above note 14). Cf. *Fleuriot*, p. 611, 612.

35 *Ó Riain*, St Finnbarr, p. 76—7; cf. E. G. *Bowen*, The cult of St Brigit, Stud. Celt. 8—9 (1973—4), p. 38.

36 For the Llancarfan area, see H. *Lewis* in G. H. *Doble*, Saint Illtud, Cardiff 1944, p. 33 n = G. H. *Doble* (D. S. *Evans*, ed.), Lives of the Welsh Saints, Cardiff 1971, p. 125n; G. O. *Pierce*, The Place-names of Dinas Powys Hundred, Cardiff 1968, p. 112—3. For Cornwall etc. see C. *Thomas*, The Irish Settlements in post-Roman Western Britain, a Survey of the Evidence, in Journal of the Royal Institution of Cornwall 6 (1972) pt. 4. p. 251—74.

dence of the Lives already mentioned, but also by local dedications which, of course, very often are the raw materials from which episodes in Saints' Lives are constructed[37]. In the Llancarfan district, however, despite its importance in the record of Finnian of Clonard, no local commemoration survived under that form of the saint's name, or in its Welsh guise of *Gwynn(y)aw(g)*. Instead, we find the cognate Barrock, from *Barruc*, which in turn derives from Bairre, the hypocoristic of Bairrfind *al.* Findbarr[38].

Similarly, in Cornwall, while St Kew of the Life lies near the north coast of the peninsula, the encounter between Samson and Winnavius would now seem to be best 'preserved' locally in a series of dedications further along the traditional route to Brittany, on the Fowey estuary. Here, at St Winnows and Golant, facing each other across the estuary, are dedications to Winnow (earlier Winnoc) and Samson respectively. Equally close to Samson's church, however, is another dedication, in the town of Fowey itself, to Barrianus *al.* Fymbrianus, colloquially known as Barry[39].

As in the Llancarfan tradition, then, Finnian's (or *Winniauus's*) memory appears to have been perpetuated in South Cornwall under both possible hypocoristic forms of his full name, i. e. Findbarr (Bairrfind). But, since it is only in Irish sources that this multiplicity of denomination is otherwise found in relation to the saint, it must seem likely that Irish influences were also at work on the names in these two areas which, on other grounds, are regarded as having come within the compass of Irish settlement in Britain. Once this inference is drawn, of course, the uniquely Brittonic character of the name Finnio no longer has a bearing on the career and scholarly activity of the saint (which would then have been conducted in a predominantly Irish context), but rather on the question of how those Brittonic influences on the formation of Irish hypocoristic forms in general and of Finnio in particular were exercised? The scope of this question is too wide for discussion here; yet the answer to it may well help to explain why the melting-pot of Celtic Christianity produced such a predominantly Irish tradition of the saints. As E. G. Bowen has pointed out, 'early Celtic Christianity in South-East Wales functioned in a strong Goidelic atmosphere'[40], and the same was no doubt true of other parts of Britain affected by Irish settlement. Here, in the crucial first century and a half after the conversion of the Irish to Christianity, the upperhand in the political and cultural spheres did not lie with the British, despite their part in bringing Christianity to Ireland. Does the importance traditionally attached to the Irish component of Celtic Christianity do more than reflect what must have been their cultural and political dominance at the time of its emergence? After all, St Patrick first came to Ireland as a slave.

---

37 *Ó Riain*, Towards a Methodology, *passim*.
38 For a discussion of the evidence, see *Ó Riain*, The Irish Element.
39 G. H. *Doble*, The Saints of Cornwall, Oxford 1970, p. 155.
40 E. G. *Bowen*, The Settlements of the Celtic Saints in Wales, Cardiff 1956, p. 43.

Armagh and Rome in the seventh century

By
Richard Sharpe

There is preserved in the Book of Armagh a text which lays claim to appellate jurisdiction throughout Ireland for the archbishop of Armagh, and refers any case which he cannot resolve *ad Petri apostoli cathedram auctoritatem Romae urbis habentem*. Evidence for contact between the Irish Church and Rome is very sparse indeed before the twelfth century, and the little there is has been much discussed. But the interest of this passsage goes further than the establishment of a connexion with Rome; for the decree is followed by the subscription of St Patrick[1]:

> *Item quaecumque causa ualde difficilis exorta fuerit atque ignota cunctis Scotorum gentium iudicibus, ad cathedram archiepiscopi Hibernensium .i. Patricii, atque huius antestitis examinationem recte refferenda; si uero in illa cum suis sapientibus facile sanari non poterit talis caussa praedictae negotionis, ad sedem apostolicam decreuimus esse mittendam .i. ad Petri apostoli cathedram auctoritatem Romae urbis habentem.*
>
> *Hii sunt qui de hoc decreuerunt .i.*
>
> *Auxilius   Patricius   Secundinus   Benignus*

The passage, lifted from its context and associated with the similar provision in the Collectio Canonum Hibernensis[2], was at one time treated as evidence for the position of Armagh as metropolitan and its direct relationship with the Roman see in the time of Patrick. The "Armagh Canon" was regarded as a genuine monument of Patrick's work in Ireland by many scholars as various as Whitley Stokes and Ludwig Bieler[3]; dissenting voices tended to be those of incensed Protestant

---

1 *Liber Angeli* § 28. The text is printed in J. *Gwynn* ed., The Book of Armagh, Dublin 1913, fol. 21 vb; ed. and trans. L. *Bieler*, The Patrician Texts in the Book of Armagh, SLH 10, 1979, p. 188—91.

2 F. W. H. *Wasserschleben*, Die irische Kanonensammlung (henceforth *Hib.*), Leipzig ²1885, XX.5 b; see below p. 67.

3 See for example, P. F. *Moran*, Essays on the Origins of the Irish Church, Dublin 1864, pp. 120—31; W. *Stokes*, The Tripartite Life of St Patrick, RS 89, 1887, I, CXXXV; *Idem*, The Academy 34 (1888), p. 26 [No. 845, 14 July 1888]; L. *Bieler*, The Life and Legend of St Patrick, Dublin 1949, p. 34—6 (but Bieler later rejected the canon, Patrician Texts, p. 53 n. 2). Compare J. B. *Bury*, The Life of St Patrick and his Place in History, London 1905, p. 168—70.

clergymen[4]. It is now generally recognized that the "Armagh Canon" cannot be treated in this kind of isolation[5]. Notwithstanding the singular pronoun *de hoc*, the subscription refers to the series of nine decrees which follow the heading *De speciali reuerantia Airdd Machae et honore praesulis eiusdem urbis dicamus*. These decrees, with their introductory sentences, form the second and major part of the *Liber Angeli*. Only a special desire to attach the name of Patrick to the Roman interest of the "Armagh Canon" could separate it from this context[6].

Whatever the connexion with Rome may have signified to the Irish Church, in the *Liber Angeli* it is to be associated directly with the claims of privilege made by Armagh. Particularly relevant is the paragraph naming the relics of Roman martyrs at Armagh[7]:

> *Nihilhominus uenerari debet honore summorum martyrum Petri et Pauli Stefani Laurendi et caeterorum.*

Though hagiographers tell of St Patrick's bringing these relics to Ireland from Rome, few scholars give the story credence and none has argued a date for the *Liber Angeli* within as much as a century of Patrick's lifetime. Indeed, its inflated claims have often been treated as a late development of Armagh's pretensions[8]. I aim to show that the *Liber Angeli* is not merely important evidence for any discussion of the Irish attitude to the Holy See but an absolutely key text to understanding the significance of contact with Rome in the development of Armagh's claims to greatness. The relationship which the text asserts existed between Armagh and Rome, whether real or pretended, brought Ireland closer to the hierarchy of the

---

4 Witness the discussion, 'St Patrick's doctrines', in the correspondence of The Academy 34 (1888), p. 11, 26, 41, 54—5, 73, 89, 104 [Nos. 844—50, 7 July to 18 August 1888]. This debate, in one forum, exemplifies a long-standing confrontation between sectarian apologists posing as historians; many nineteenth-century references are given by S. *Czarnowski*, Le Culte des héros et ses conditions sociales — Saint Patrick, héros nationale de l'Irlande, Paris 1919, p. 302—4.

5 D. A. *Binchy*, Patrick and his biographers, ancient and modern, Stud. Hib. 2 (1962), p. 7—173 (at p. 49—52).

6 The immediately preceding words, *Liber Angeli* § 27, relate directly to Armagh's rights of jurisdiction.

7 *Liber Angeli* § 19, but see below n. 12. On the history of the supposed relics, see M. P. *Sheehy*, The relics of the apostles and early martyrs in the mission of St Patrick, IER 5th series 95 (1961), p. 372—6.

8 So F. E. Warren thought it was more or less contemporary with the manuscript, that is, the beginning of the ninth century; see The Academy 34 (1888), p. 11 [No. 844, 7 July 1888]: "Certainly this document is as old as AD 807. Equally certainly it is a forged document of about that date to support the Primacy of Armagh. Both in language and substance it exhibits those features which such a forged document would be expected to exhibit." No reasons are advanced why the document could not have been produced with this intention and these features at an earlier date. Gwynn, in his edition of the Book of Armagh, guessed that the *Liber Angeli* dated from the late eighth century. *Gwynn*, Book of Armagh, p. LXXXVII.

Western Church than at any other time before the twelfth century. In seeking the historical context for this development, we must inquire into the date of the *Liber Angeli*.

Recently, there has been a marked divergence of opinion on this point. Kathleen Hughes, who first published a translation of the text, broadly dated its compilation to the seventh or eighth century[9]; more particularly, she saw the divergence of view as between ca. 734 and an earlier date, *ante* 670[10]. The criteria for dating are sound, so that the *Liber Angeli* can be dated quite closely. But first it is worth considering how these two different dates were arrived at.

The date ca. 734 was put forward by Heinrich Zimmer, who pointed to an entry at 734 in the Annals of Ulster, which mentions that the relics of Patrick accompanied those of St Peter and St Paul in the promulgation of a law[11]. Since these relics are referred to in the *Liber Angeli*, the text was dated to *ante* 734[12]. Such relics could not have reached Armagh until that church had adopted the Roman Easter, which Zimmer believed to have happened in conjunction with the other churches of northern Ireland in (as he thought) 701[13]. I shall return to comment on Zimmer's argument more fully, but it should be noted that his association of the *Liber Angeli*

9 The Church in Early Irish Society, London 1966, p. 69.

10 Ibid., p. 86 n.

11 H. *Zimmer*, Keltische Beiträge III, ZfdA 35 (1891), p. 1—172, in an important note, p. 76—80. He expanded this into a thesis on the development of the Irish Church as a whole, notably in his article, Keltische Kirche, Realencyklopädie für protestantische Theologie und Kirche 10 (³1901), 204—43, published in English as The Celtic Church in Britain and Ireland, London 1902.

12 *Zimmer*, Keltische Kirche, p. 242, Celtic Church, p. 126, erroneously prints the phrase in *Liber Angeli* § 19 as *Nihilominus uenerari debet honore summorum martyrum* reliquias *Petri et Pauli* etc., where in fact the word *reliquias* does not occur. MacCarthy argues that Zimmer's case therefore necessarily falls; B. *Mac Carthy*, Prof. Zimmer on the early Irish Church, IER 4th series 14 (1903), p. 385—411 (p. 392—3). Apart from other references to these relics at Armagh, the whole sense of § 19 shows that the allusion is to honour for these martyrs present as relics, and MacCarthy's attempt to give the passage a vague general sense fails. MacCarthy here ignores the evidence that, in Irish usage, Lat. *martyres* carried the meaning "relics", attested in the very annal to which Zimmer referred, AU 734: *commotatio martyrum Petir 7 Phoil 7 Phatraic;* cf. AU 742, 775 and contrast AU 783, 784, 789, 792 etc., where *reliquiae* stands as the exact equivalent. Yet compare MacCarthy's notes on the Annals of Ulster, The Academy 34 (1888), p. 209 [No. 856, 29 Sept. 1888], where he observes that *ad sargifagum martyrum*, glossed *du ferti martur* (*Liber Angeli* § 31), means "to tomb of relics". In OIr., *martyr* represents a calque on *martyr*, but the regular word for relics is *martre* (< Lat. *martyrium*); it does not seem improbable that an Irishman might use *martyr* to express Ir. *martre* in preference to *martyrium* which would be understood as "(place of) martyrdom".

13 That decision required the personal efforts of Adomnán, who must then have been one of the most respected men in the Irish Church. It did not happen until a little before 704. See Bede, HE V, 15. Zimmer himself was undecided: in Keltische Studien II: Über altirische Betonung und Verskunst, Berlin 1884, p. 198, he takes the date 701 as if from Bede. In his 1891 articles, he retains this date, but in Celtic Church, p. 82, 129, he has changed his mind to 697, confounding the agreement with the first enactment of Adomnán's Law.

with the *Lex Patricii* or *Cáin Phátraic*, mentioned in the same annals at 737 and presumed to be the same as the *lex* of 734, is incidental to his dating, though he overstates the element of identification[14]. Bury and Kenney both adopted this equation with the Law of Patrick, and through their influence a date in the early eighth century has become orthodox[15]. But there is a fundamental difficulty in the indentification: the *Liber Angeli* has no resemblance, in form or purpose, with the known *cána*, and is, indeed, inconsistent with what is reported about the *Cáin Phátraic*. A late scholiast tells us that the Law of Patrick was *cen chléirciu do marbad*, "not to kill clerics"[16]. This testimony is not of high value; but, although the scholiast somewhat misrepresents the *Cáin Adomnáin* and the *Cáin Domnaig*, one can see that his comments might relate to those texts. In no way does the *Liber Angeli* deal with the killing of clergy; it is hardly likely to be the *Cáin Phátraic*.

More recently, O'Rahilly and Professor Carney have advanced cogent arguments from within the Patrician dossier which suggest a considerably earlier date, before ca. 670. For a comparison of the *Liber Angeli* with the work of Tírechán shows that the two works are closely related in background and purpose[17]. In the *Liber Angeli* the angel tells Patrick[18]:

> donauit tibi Dominus Deus uniuersas Scotorum gentes in modum paruchiae et huic urbi tuae.

14 „Zwischen 701 und 733 (= 734 AD) ist der *Liber Angeli* entstanden und er ist höchst wahrscheinlich die *lex Patricii*, deren Einführung in Irland von 736 (= 737) an versucht wird"; ZfdA 35 (1891), p. 79 n. He later exaggerates the connexion, saying, "If the law was enforced in 743, the date of the Book of the Angel is fairly fixed. It must have been a kind of official commemorative document (eine Art offizieller Festschrift) issued by Armagh on the occasion of the tercentenary of St Patrick's arrival in Ireland (in 432), and must thus have been written about 732"; see Keltische Kirche, p. 242, Celtic Church, p. 126—7.

15 Accepted by *Bury*, Tirechan's memoir of St Patrick, EHR 17 (1902), p. 235—67, 700—704 (p. 255); St Patrick, p. 287; Zimmer's line of argument is not followed. It also seems that J. F. *Kenney*, Sources for the Early History of Ireland, New York 1929, p. 335—6, failed to see Zimmer's point: he sees the law as imposing "payment of some pecuniary or other tribute to the saint's successor", and so reasons that the Law of Patrick, "or, at least, one version of it, is preserved in the Book of the Angel"; cf. Patrician Texts, p. 239, where Bieler takes *peculiare censum (Liber Angeli* § 13) as a reference to the Law.

16 Marginalia, *saec.* XII or later, in the Liber Hymnorum, Killiney, Franciscan Library, MS A 2, ed. W. *Stokes* and J. *Strachan*, Thesaurus Palaeohibernicus, Cambridge 1903—10, II, p. 306, Cf. scholia on Félire Oengusa in Oxford, Bodleian Library, MS Laud misc. 610; W. *Stokes*, ed., Félire Oengusso, HBS 29, 1905, p. 210. It was taken up from here by Keating in his History of Ireland, ed. P. S. *Dineen*, III, p. 107.

17 T. F. *O'Rahilly*, [review of *Bieler*, The Life and Legend of St Patrick], IHS 8 (1952—3), p. 268—79 (at p. 273); J. P. *Carney*, Comments of the present state of the Patrician problem, IER 5th series 92 (1959), p. 1—28 (p. 14); *idem*, The Problem of St Patrick, Dublin 1961, p. 46. Cf. *Binchy*, Patrick and his biographers, p. 64.

18 *Liber Angeli*, § 8; *Bieler*, Patrician Texts, p. 184.

Further, the angel says, *quia donauit illi* [sc. Patricio] *Deus totam insulam ut supra diximus*. When Tírechán sets out his purpose of defending Patrick's *paruchia* from those who hate and rob and fear his church, he says[19]:

> *Si quaereret heres Patricii paruchĭam illius, potest pene totam insolam sibi reddere in paruchiam, quia Deus dedit illi totam insolam cum hominibus per anguelum Domini.*

Tírechán's words *per anguelum Domini* clinch the point: here is weighty support for the view that Tírechán, writing around 670, knew the *Liber Angeli* and saw his purpose as supplementary to it, a matter of transferring stated claims into a more detailed and circumstantial narration of how Patrick forged for his heirs that immense *paruchia*.

This opinion has been qualified by Professor Binchy, saying that the "substance" of the *Liber Angeli*, "though perhaps not its extant form, is clearly older than Tírechán's memoir, since he reproduces and expands its more extravagant claims with obvious approval"[20]. The distinction between "substance" and "form" is a problematical one. It is also drawn by Ryan and O'Rahilly, who hold that, if not the whole, at least a major part of the *Liber Angeli* was known to Tírechán[21]. Kathleen Hughes has drawn the distinction thus[22]:

> "It seems to me more likely that Tírechán used some of the same sources employed by the compilers of the *Liber Angeli* than that he had seen the text in its present form. This would mean that the sources on which the *Liber Angeli* is based were at Armagh in the late seventh century, but that the tract did not gain its present form until the eighth."

In her notes, she indicated the detailed points of correspondence between the two texts. However, she observed that in dealing with an Irish technical term Tírechán chose to express himself in different words from those used by the *Liber Angeli*[23]. On the strength of this, and of the difference between the versions of Patrick's four *petitiones*, she distinguished between the source and the present work, which she dated to the early eighth century[24]. I cannot see how this present state of the

---

19 Tírechán, § 18.2; *Bieler*, Patrician Texts, p. 138.

20 *Binchy*, Patrick and his biographers, p. 64.

21 J. *Ryan*, Irish Monasticism. Origins and Early Development, Dublin 1931, p. 75 (though contrast *idem*, Ireland and the Holy See, Studies 49 (1960), p. 1—16, where he says (p. 3 n.) that the *Liber Angeli* is ninth-century); T. F. *O'Rahilly*, IHS 8 (1952—3), p. 273.

22 *Hughes*, CEIS, p. 275.

23 In another context, Professor *Binchy* comments on minor verbal changes as a weak argument; Patrick and his biographers, p. 65 n. 169.

24 *Hughes*, CEIS, p. 275; even so, at p. 276, she regards the *Liber Angeli* as still the *textus receptus* of Armagh's claims when the Book of Armagh was written. To my mind, this implies far more stability in the eighth-century Church than other evidence can justify.

text could be dated, since the only criteria for dating treated are matters of substance rather than form. All the evidence relating to content points to the existence of the text in Tírechán's time.

Only Professor Carney has adhered firmly to an early date for the whole of the *Liber Angeli*, believing that it was known to Tírechán and was used by him[25]. Recently, he has added to this a linguistic argument: the preservation of the unsyncopated form *Brí Erigi*, he suggests, indicates a date in the period between 500 and 630[26]. This linguistic feature cannot provide a closer date, and the large timescale allows Professor Carney the theory that the *Liber Angeli* was composed about the middle of the seventh century from still older sources. This rests on verbal arguments for conflation, and on his identification of the *Liber Angeli* with the "Angel's Gospel" mentioned in the *Liber Cuanach* as having been found in Patrick's grave in the year 553[27]. The latter story must be treated as late evidence, interesting but not really worthy of credence.

Professor Bieler offers a different approach. He cites Zimmer's date, widely accepted since Bury and Kenney, but if I read him rightly, he proposes a date nearer to ca. 700[28]. About this time, he argues, an agreement was reached between the churches of Brigit and of Patrick which is recorded at the end of the text. Professor Bieler believes that the intermeshing of Patrician and Brigitine stories dates from the eighth century. Accordingly, he places the agreement, on which for him the hagiographical rapprochement depends, at the beginning of the century. More recently, however, Professor Bieler, in response to the argument that Tírechán knew the *Liber Angeli*, separated the two questions, and adopted the view that, while the paragraph at the end dealing with Brigit dates from ca. 700, the main *Liber Angeli* is earlier[29].

25   *Carney*, Comments on the present state of the Patrician problem, p. 14; Problem of St Patrick, p. 46.
26   Aspects of archaic Irish, Éigse 17 (1977—9), p. 417—35, at p. 427.
27   Comments on Patrician studies, p. 14; Problem of St Patrick, p. 119—20. The implication is that the document was specially written at the time of the invention of the relics. Cf. Richard *Sharpe*, Palaeographical considerations in the study of the Patrician documents in the Book of Armagh, Scriptorium 36 (1982), p. 3—28, at p. 24—5.
28   *Bieler*, The Celtic hagiographer, Stud. Patr. 5 (1959) [Berlin 1962] p. 243—65, at p. 252-53.
29   *Bieler*, St Patrick and the Coming of Christianity, p. 19 n. 55. This distinction between the two is no more than an expedient in response to others' arguments for an early dating of *Liber Angeli* which enables him to agree with them without having to revise his views relating to the Brigit material. His whole concatenation of arguments is unsound, and there are reasons for thinking that, though the Brigit paragraph may be later than the *Liber Angeli*, it is not later than the middle years of the seventh century. In Professor Bieler's latest statements, his views on the date of the *Liber Angeli* are unclear: Patrician Texts, p. 54, favours the qualification as to form and substance; at p. 239, on §§ 7—8, an unequivocally early opinion is expressed, adding that Muirchú as well as Tírechán adopts a phrase from the *Liber Angeli*; but ibid. on § 13, Bieler again associates the *Liber Angeli* with the *Lex Patricii*.

But if one returns to Zimmer's actual argument, instead of latching on to the conveniently dated label, *Lex Patricii*, the chronological problems disappear. It is, in fact, perfectly possible to harmonize the arguments which give the separate dates ca. 734 and *ante* 670. The core of Zimmer's argument is the presence at Armagh of the relics of Roman martyrs referred to by the *Liber Angeli*[30]. His *terminus ad quem*, therefore, was the earliest datable mention of the relics, the *lex* annal of 734. The *terminus a quo* was the date when Armagh conformed to Roman practice, which Zimmer placed around 700. Hence the limits for his date of the *Liber Angeli*. However, mention of these same relics occurs in Tírechán's *Collectanea*, which Zimmer overlooked[31]. Otherwise, he would have realised that this becomes the *terminus ad quem* and the date for Armagh's acceptance of the Roman Easter had to be considerably earlier than he had thought. So, Zimmer's argument from the Roman relics and the more recent one based on Tírechán agree in making ca. 670 the latest possible date. In order to find the *terminus a quo*, the crucial question is when did Armagh patch up its differences with the Roman Church, conforming with universal practice on the matter of Easter. Zimmer went wrong in presuming that Armagh acted at the same time as a majority of the northern churches. Kathleen Hughes's suggestion is much more likely: that Armagh conformed independently, at some point after 640, but before 688 when Aed of Sleaty, in the south, submitted to Armagh, something unlikely to have happened while Armagh still followed the uncanonical reckoning[32].

There is strong evidence suggesting that the adoption of the Roman Easter at Armagh took place in the years when we know that Tomméne, the coarb of Patrick (AU 623—61), initiated dealings with the Holy See. In this period, influences were reaching Ireland which presented opportunities for the head of a great church to achieve a more elevated status and a position of greater power than had hitherto existed anywhere among the Celtic churches. This influence is to be associated with the arrival of the Gregorian mission in Anglo-Saxon England and the outbreak of Paschal controversy; Armagh, it seems, was quick to respond to the challenge.

Not long after 600, when Columbanus was engaged in conflict in Gaul over the calculation of Easter, an Irish bishop Dagán evidently passed through Kent and met Archbishop Lawrence[33]. Whether this meeting was accidental or deliberate is not known, but the archbishop of Canterbury appears to have reacted as if he exercised over the Irish churches the same pastoral responsibility as Pope Gregory

---

30 *Kenney*, Sources, p. 336, seems to me completely to have missed this element in Zimmer's argument. It was likewise ignored by Bury, who had a low opinion of the *Liber Angeli*, St Patrick, p. 287, and of Zimmer's emphasis on the Romanizing cult of relics.

31 Tírechán § 48; cf. the misplaced passage, Book of Armagh, fol. 8 v b, Patrician Texts, p. 122 § 5.

32 *Hughes*, CEIS, p. 115—16.

33 Bede, HE II, 4.

intended his predecessor to have over the British[34]. His letter to the Irish clergy exhorted them to leave the wayward paths of the British Church and enter Roman unity. Over a decade later, Pope Honorius wrote a similar letter to the Irish churches, which may have had a gradual effect[35]. For some ten years further on, a rift occurred between those Irishmen who favoured their own customs and those who believed these should be abandoned for the sake of unity with the rest of Christendom[36]. Bede's treatment of the events in these years implies an interpretation that the English Church initially acted as intermediary between Ireland and Rome, though it was *ad admonitionem apostolicae sedis antistitis* that the Irish first learnt the canonical observance of Easter. By a fortunate chance, one central episode is well documented, the synod of Mag Léne, which is described for us by Cummian in a letter to Ségéne, abbot of Iona[37]. This synod failed to agree on conformity with Roman practice but sent envoys to Rome. The predictable answer seems to have been implemented in southern Ireland, which became catholic in practice soon afterwards.

At a date soon after Cummian and his fellows returned from Rome, where they had celebrated Easter in AD 631, we learn from Bede that in 638 Pope Severinus received a letter from Ireland, containing questions of great importance[38]. The letter is referred to as *scripta quae perlatores ad sanctae memoriae Seuerinum papam adduxerunt*, but Bede is not informative as to the questions contained, most likely because, like us, he knew only the reply from the pope-elect who became John IV. Like Pope Honorius, John IV seems to have been concerned with issues which (so far as evidence from Ireland can tell on the matter) were irrelevant to the Irish Church: persistence in the use of Pelagian teachings and a new appearance of the Quartodeciman heresy. The words of his reply, as quoted by Bede, are not explicit about where his information came from, though the natural reading is to suppose that the *scripta* from Ireland and the words of the *perlatores* were the pope's sole source of information. So, in its Irish context the letter of John IV is full of problems[39]. The key feature of the part quoted by Bede is the list of persons to whom the letter was addressed:

34 Ibid. I, 27 § 7.

35 Ibid. II, 19.

36 Ibid. III, 3.

37 The *Epistola Cummiani*, preserved only in BL MS Cotton Vitellius A XII, is a letter written by a variously identified cleric, Cummian, to Ségéne, abbot of Iona (624—52), and a hermit Beccán. Its date is established as ca. 632 or 633, on the basis of a calculation from Paschal information; see B. *MacCarthy*, Annals of Ulster IV, Dublin 1900, p. CXXXV—XLV, and *Kenney*, Sources, p. 221. The text is most accessible in PL 87, 969—78; there is a critical edition by Miss M. J. *Walsh*, Cummian's Paschal Letter, unpublished M. Phil. dissertation, University College, Dublin, 1977.

38 Bede, HE II, 19.

39 Since there is little reason to believe that Irish informants would speak of Pelagianism and Quartodecimanism, it seems possible that the English Church was another (and misleading) source of information.

Dilectissimis et sanctissimis Tomiano, Columbano, Cronano, Dimao, et
Baithano episcopis, Cronano Ernanioque, Lastriano, Scellano et Segeneo
presbyteris, Sarano ceterisque doctoribus seu abbatibus Scotis...

Most of these people can be identified, with a greater or lesser degree of confidence[40], but it is taken as axiomatic that they must belong to the northern part of Ireland because it has always been believed that the south conformed soon after Cummian's mission had reported about 632[41]. Papal protocol, conscious of distinctions in rank and seniority, would have been careful with the order in which the persons named are mentioned; but the papacy seems to have been so unsure of the prevailing circumstances in Ireland that it is probable that the order of names was taken from the order of signatures in the original *scripta*. Tomianus is undoubtedly Tomméne, bishop of Armagh (623—61 AU), but one should avoid inferring from this that the list is set out in hierarchical order, indicating that Armagh had acted as primatial see, calling a synod of the northern churches to decide where they stood in the Paschal controversy; if such authority had existed, then a unanimous decision could have been enforced. The order is something simpler. Bishops sign before priests, who precede ecclesiastics in minor orders, even where the latter hold important positions such as master of the schools or abbot. Sacerdotal standing takes precedence over the headship of important monastic foundations such as Iona, whose abbot Ségéne signs as a priest. Tomméne of Armagh may have taken the initiative in prompting the enquiry, or, as I think likely, Armagh in his time may have begun to build up a position of effective importance, which may have enabled its bishop to assign himself precedence over other bishops.

The synod which directed Cummian to Rome and the ecclesiastics apparently led by Armagh who wrote to Pope Severinus acted on the basis that Rome was the final authority in any intractable dispute. Their proximity in date may suggest a common impulse. A more direct connexion might be inferred from the fact that Cummian addressed himself to Ségéne who is then a signatory to the letter. In this attitude to Rome, we find the context which underlies the statement of appellate jurisdiction in the *Liber Angeli*.

First of all, Cummian himself quotes the relevant *decretum*, taken from a letter of Pope Innocent I to Victricius of Rouen[42]:

> *ut si causae fuerint maiores, iuxta decretum sinodicum, ad capud urbium sint*
> *referendae.*

40 C. *Plummer*, Baedae Opera Historica, Oxford 1896, II, p. 112—13; following earlier work of Colgan, Lanigan and Reeves.
41 W. *Reeves*, Adamnan's Life of St Columba, Dublin 1857, p. 27; *Plummer* II, p. 113.
42 Epistola Cummiani § 13; cf. Innoc. I decr. c. 10.

The same text occurs again in the unedited B version of the Irish canon collection[43]:

> Canones Romani dicunt: *Causa uniuscuiusque prouinciae non referenda (v. l. ferenda) ad alteram; si cause maiores fuerint exorte, ad caput urbium sunt referende.*

In the same section of the Collectio Canonum Hibernensis, *De Provincia,* there are several passages stating the nature of an ecclesiastical province and providing for its rights of jurisdiction. For example[44]:

> *Certa prouincia est quae decem ciuitates habet et unum regem et tres minores potestates sub se, et unum episcopum aliosque minores decem iudices ad quorum iudicium omnes causae ciuitatum referuntur; et si causae difficiles oriantur, ad omnium iudicium omnes decem iudicum referendae sunt.*

Contrast this definition with another from the same context[45]:

> *Quicunque causam habuerit, apud suos iudices iudicetur et ne ad alienos, causa uagandi et proterue despiciens suam patriam transeat, sed apud metropolitanum episcopum suae prouinciae iudicetur.*

Provision is also made for higher jurisdiction[46]:

> *De alienis prouinciis adeundis ad iudicandum*

> Sinodus Romana: *Si in qualibet prouincia ortae fuerint questiones, et inter clericos dissidentes non conueniat, ad maiorem sedem referantur, et si illic facile non discutiantur, ubi fuerit sinodus congregata iudicetur.*

> Patricius: *Si quae [difficiles] questiones in hac insula oriantur, ad sedem apostolicam referantur.*

These extracts were put together around 700 and draw largely on seventh-century documents. The last quotation, attributed to Patrick, brings us back to the *Liber Angeli* passage from which it probably derives. It is apparent that when the Collectio Canonum Hibernensis was assembled, there was no coherent sense of what jurisdiction was appropriate to a metropolitan bishop nor what course appeal should take. The questions which had arisen in the 620s and 630s had not been resolved over half a century later. Indeed, the desire to collocate such contradictory

---

43 At Hib. XX.3; see *Wasserschleben,* p. XXXVI, 61 n. (e).
44 Hib. XX.2 a.
45 Hib. XX.3 c.
46 Hib. XX.5. See *Binchy,* Patrick and his biographers, p. 49—51; *Hughes,* The Celtic Church and the Papacy, in The English Church and the Papacy in the Middle Ages, ed. C. H. *Lawrence,* London, 1965, p. 1—33 (at p. 19—20).

prescriptions indicates that any attempt to resolve the problems of ecclesiastical authority had been abandoned.

Here, I suggest, lies the origin of the terms *Romani* and *Hibernenses,* frequent in Irish canon material. The distinction is in part a Paschal one; hence *Romani* has come to be understood as often meaning supporters of the Roman Easter[47]. But the term is of wider significance than this. The main aspect of its use is the assertion of a belief in the oneness of Latin Christendom, with its hierarchy culminating in the papal primacy of the bishop of Rome[48]. One may perhaps contrast Cummian's account of the divisive synod of Mag Léna, where he felt that the decision to adopt catholic practice should have been adhered to, and the story of the otherwise unknown synod of Mag Ailbe reported in the Life of Munnu, in which the opposing sides agree to differ[49]. Cummian reflects the opinion of the *Romani* that the Church is one body, but the saint's Life, of the early eighth century, shows that by that date the commitment of the *Romani* to the practice of the universal Church had been overcome by the more diverse, more tolerant views of the *Hibernenses.* It was this change of attitude in the late seventh century which undermined the Paschal victory of the *Romani* and left the Irish Church to continue its independent, *laisser faire* development without the emergence of a metropolitan hierarchy.

Tírechán's use of the *Liber Angeli* shows that, as far as Armagh was concerned, this change of attitude followed the serious plagues of the 660s. For in every detail Tírechán shifts the emphasis from the Roman and metropolitan claims of the *Liber Angeli* on to the more direct relationship between Armagh and the many subordinate churches with less regard to the universal territorial claim. Let us look more closely at the claims of the *Liber Angeli.*

In the first section of the text, the narrative portion[50], the story is told how God, recognizing that Ireland owed its conversion to Patrick, whose position was small and inadequate for an apostolic church, granted through the angel a huge *terminus* around Armagh and a *paruchia* comprising all Ireland. Further, as recognition that Patrick was the *apostolicus doctor et dux principalis omnibus Hiberionacum gentibus,* it was right and proper that his church should have a *peculiare censum* over all the churches and monasteries of the island. The case is apostolic: Patrick was the apostle of Ireland, therefore his church is specially privileged. The writer of the

47 *Bury,* St Patrick, p. 237—9; *Kenney,* Sources, p. 216, 249, 325.

48 W. *Ullmann,* On the use of the term *Romani* in the sources of the earlier Middle Ages, Stud. Patr. 1 (1955) [TU 63 (Berlin, 1957)], p. 155—63.

49 *Vita S. Munnu* (S) §§ 29—30; Vitae Sanctorum Hiberniae e codice Salmanticensi, ed. W. W. *Heist,* Brussels 1965, p. 207—8. The key phrase, *Unusquisque ergo faciat quod credit et rectum sibi uideatur,* is omitted from the two later medieval versions, no doubt because twelfth-century or later redactors found such want of unified discipline intolerable or incomprehensible; see D § 27, Vitae Sanctorum Hiberniae, ed. C. *Plummer,* Oxford 1910, II, p. 237, and SO § 26, ed. *Heist,* p. 254—5.

50 §§ 1—13, 15—16.

passage knew the *Confessio* since he reflects its wording about Patrick's missionary labours, and the individual word *Hiberionacum* was surely borrowed from Patrick's writings[51]. The second, legalistic section of the text follows the argument through[52]:

> *Ista quippe ciuitas summa et libera a Deo est constituta et ab anguelo Dei et ab apostolico uiro sancto Patricio episcopo specialiter dedicata. Preest ergo quodam priuilegio omnibus aeclessiis ac monasteriis cunctorum Hibernensium uel superna auctoritate summi pontificis illius fundatoris.*

Immediately following this apostolic claim, the second and no less *(nihilhominus)* reason for Armagh's position is its possession of relics of Roman martyrs, of a cloth stained with Christ's blood and other relics[53]. The sense of logical argument continues from *quippe* and *ergo* through *idcirco* to nine statements of the peculiar privileges of Armagh[54]. The statements, some of which I have already quoted, present the claims of a metropolitan see with complete jurisdiction over its province, Ireland.

It was the exalted character of these claims which led scholars in the past to treat the *Liber Angeli* as a late document, containing Armagh's most preposterous pretensions. It was denounced as "forgery", not to be taken seriously[55]. I am in no doubt that the work is a "forgery", in the sense that it does not record a contract between God and St Patrick negotiated through an angel; but it is not for that

51 Patrick, *Conf.* 23; cf. *Ep.* 16, where Bieler brilliantly conjectures *Hiberionaci* for MSS *Hiberia nati*. An objection to this has been made by T. Ó Raifeartaigh, Leasú eagarthóra sa Litir faoi Choroticus, Stud. Hib. 2 (1962), p. 174—81; *idem*, The life of St Patrick; a new approach, IHS 16 (1968—9), p. 117—37 (p. 131), and St Patrick's twenty-eight days' journey, ibid. p. 395–416 (p. 410); *idem*, [review Hanson and Le Blant], IHS 21 (1978—9), p. 219—24 (p. 222—3). Ó Raifeartaigh holds that the only attested form, genitive plural *Hiberionacum*, implies nominative **Hiberionax, -aces*, so that *Hiberionaci* would be impossible. But this is guesswork based on Kennedy's *Latin Primer*, and overlooks the fact that such a national adjective or noun is formed with the suffix *-acos* in Primitive Irish and Brittonic (cf. *Elmetiacos*, V. E. Nash-Williams, Early Christian Monuments of Wales, Cardiff 1950, no. 87), plural *-aci*, and genitive plural *-acon* to which Patrick's inflexion is the closest available in Latin. *Hiberionacos* must be the lineal ancestor of ModIr. *Éireannach*. See R. Thurneysen, Grammar of Old Irish, Dublin 1946, § 286.

52 §§ 17—18.

53 § 19.

54 §§ 20—30. In Bieler's edition, it would seem that the initial letter of § 25 should be in bold face, and I find his splitting of §§ 28—9 unsatisfactory.

55 See above, n. 8, and compare Archbishop Healy, 'more or less open to suspicion as a record of fact', Life of St Patrick, Dublin 1905, p. 496; Bury, 'a clumsy invention, fabricated at Armagh', St Patrick, p. 287; or W. S. Kerr, 'this *Liber Angeli* is most obviously a composition constructed to maintain or extend the privileges of the See of Armagh. No one nowadays could defend its authenticity', Independence of the Celtic Church in Ireland, London 1931, p. 111; Bieler, 'the canon in question, like the remainder of the document, is an Armagh forgery', Patrician Texts, p. 53.

reason to be dismissed. It shows rather that contacts with the English and Roman hierarchy on the Paschal question had made Armagh aware that the universal Church recognized a principle whereby it was possible for an archbishop to exercise very considerable powers over the churches of his province. Armagh in the early seventh century aimed at such a position, arguably as a continuation of an ancient pre-eminence; but it lacked a real basis for it. Yet having accepted the Roman Easter, Armagh obtained (or perhaps faked) relics of Roman martyrs such as Pope Vitalian sent with Archbishop Theodore to King Oswiu[56]. The clergy of Armagh at once sought a direct association with the Holy See, and to foster the chance of elevation to metropolitan rank by promoting an apostolic connexion, via Patrick, even though they had no title to his corporeal relics[57].

The method adopted was to produce a document setting out these claims: the *Liber Angeli*. It was conjoined with the *Confessio* of St Patrick, suitably edited for the occasion. These two texts formed a book, which I have termed the *Volumen Patricii*, in accordance with its colophon, and which claimed to have been written by Patrick himself. Its heading presents it as a letter from the angel to the saint, and, if Professor Carney is right, its first person authority may have been supported by a staged discovery of the book in Patrick's grave[58].

Having the relics of Roman martyrs and claiming primatial rights, Armagh proceeded to identify itself with Rome. This shows itself in the terminology of the *Liber Angeli*, not so much where Patrick is called *summus pontifex*, a term not yet limited to the bishop of Rome, but in the repeated use of the word *urbs*. In all early medieval texts, *urbs* means pre-eminently Rome, the *caput urbium*. Yet it is applied to Armagh no fewer than five times[59]. Compare also the striking entry in the Annals of Ulster for the foundation of this city:

> [AD 444] *Ard Machae fundata est. Ab urbe condita usque ad hanc ciuitatem fundatam MCXCIIII.*

The synchronism of Armagh's foundation with Rome's by an *ab urbe condita* date was probably inspired by one of the late Roman chronicle sources used in the compilation of the Irish chronicle. But only Armagh's foundation is so linked. Thereafter, from 432 to the early years of the seventh century, the only two churches which have what appear to be full, consecutive lists of bishops are

56 Bede, HE III, 29; the exact circumstances of the gift are uncertain, involving the recognition by the pope of Oswiu's acceptance of Roman practice at the Synod of Whitby and the appointment by the pope of Theodore as archbishop of Canterbury to succeed Deusdedit. Pope Vitalian treats Wigheard as a mere messenger rather than as archbishop-designate.

57 Cf. R. *Sharpe*, St Patrick and the see of Armagh, Cambridge Medieval Celtic Studies 4 (1982), p. 33—59, at p. 40—43.

58 See n. 27 above, and R. *Sharpe*, Palaeographical considerations, p. 21—6.

59 *Liber Angeli* §§ 1 (twice), 7, 8, 15; and a sixth time in § 14, an addition.

Armagh and Rome. The papal entries cease at 607, and in 609 is entered *Finis Cronici Iusebii*. A connexion seems likely; but the papal entries were not taken from a known continuation of the chronicle of Eusebius. Eoin MacNeill and John Morris both argued that the Irish had such an expanded continuation; but, as Mrs Anderson has shown, the papal entries appear to be derived from the *Liber Pontificalis* and the chronicle of Marcellinus so that the connexion between the papal material and any text derived from the Eusebian chronicle and its continuations is obscure[60]. When these particular annal-entries were compiled is a question to which no answer can be given, but I am tempted to conjecture that there were annalists working at Armagh in the mid-seventh century, who matched the lists of popes and coarbs, and whose work was duly incorporated in the compilatory chronicles known to us.

Other Armagh entries in the annals suggest the same desire to establish an association with Rome. At 432, Patrick's arrival in Ireland is synchronized with the regnal years of the emperor and the bishop of Rome. The very year at which this is entered was determined by the desire to make Patrick's work follow on from the papal commission of Palladius, chronicled by Prosper of Aquitaine. Patrick himself is credited with some form of papal commission:

> [AD 441] *Leo ordinatus xlii Romane eclesie episcopus et probatus est in fide catholica Patricius episcopus.*

Hagiographers go so far as to say that Patrick actually visited Rome, where he was consecrated by the pope and performed sacramental duties[61]. Belief in this led Fr Gwynn to an interpretation of the curious *dictum*, supposedly an injunction of Patrick, *Aeclessia Scotorum immo Romanorum ut Christiani ita ut Romani sitis*. He suggests that this is to be taken closely with the reference to the *Kyrie* following in the manuscript, and that both stem from Patrick's having heard the *Kyrie* sung in Rome[62]. The liturgical aspect I cannot comment on. But the *dictum*, like the supposed visit to Rome, is part of the bridge-building by which Armagh aimed to buttress its claim to a special link with the Holy See. Indeed, this seems also to provide an explanation to the kernel of the Patrician problem: if there ever existed any *Acta S. Palladii*, the interweaving of its information with what was known of Patrick from the *Confessio* was surely motivated by Armagh's desire to ensure no

60 E. *MacNeill*, The authorship and structure of the "Annals of Tigernach", Ériu 7 (1913—14), p. 30—113 (at p. 62—6); J. R. *Morris*, The Chronicle of Eusebius: Irish fragments, Bulletin of the Institute of Classical Studies of the University of London 19 (1972), p. 80—93; M. O. *Anderson*, Kings and Kingship in Early Scotland, Edinburgh 1973, p. 27—9. Compare J. P. *Carney*, Studies in Irish Literature and History, Dublin 1955, p. 356—57.

61 Muirchú I 6; Tírechán, misplaced chapter, Book of Armagh fol. 9ra, Patrician Texts, p. 122; appendix to Tírechán, ibid. p. 164, c. 56; and cf. *Bieler*, Patrician Texts, p. 198.

62 A. *Gwynn*, The problem of the *Dicta Patricii*, Seanchas Ardmhacha 8 (1975—7), p. 69—80.

distinction between the apostle recognized in Ireland and the bishop recorded as having been sent from Rome[63].

The hagiographical legend took on a life of its own, and successive versions of the Life of Patrick form the backbone of Armagh's late seventh- and eighth-century propaganda. The progress in writing up the Life appears to have left the *Liber Angeli* redundant, and it survives only because the *Volumen Patricii* was copied, as an afterthought, at the end of the Patrician section of the Book of Armagh. At what point the text became redundant one can only guess. The possession of Roman relics certainly remained part of Armagh's claim to privilege, but the claim to metropolitan position was already shifting ground when Tírechán invoked the angel's grant of *paruchia* to Patrick. For Tírechán's concern was with the more direct links between Armagh and the dependent churches within its jurisdiction. Out of all the claims in the *Liber Angeli*, it was that to *specialis societas* and *peculiare censum* which continued to be developed in the later work. Appellate jurisdiction as a metropolitan was lost sight of, remaining only a theme treated in a confused way by the canonists.

It would seem, therefore, that the *Liber Angeli* provides a remarkable glimpse of a shortlived attempt to project a notion of metropolitan and hierarchical organization in the middle of the seventh century. The Irish Church had grown up and lived without the controlling hand of authority, and Armagh had not the power simply to impose, in its own interest, a hierarchical structure, in the way that Theodore was able to give order to the miscellaneous churches in England. For Armagh lacked any acknowledged right or prerogative to act in this way. Its invoking of the name Rome was evidently not sufficient to impress on the independent-minded Irish churches a structure of authority comparable to that in England or on the continent. What form opposition took can only be guessed from fragmentary references: the canonists were clearly not singleminded; Kildare for a time disputed Armagh's claim to primacy by making the same claim for its own bishop, while many churches challenged Armagh's rights of jurisdiction in particular cases[64]. These churches clearly had well-established rights which Armagh sought to take over; their resistance in the seventh century led Armagh to modify its claims, and to concentrate on strengthening its widespread particular jurisdiction, the *paruchia Patricii*. Its success in this ensured that, when Rome did finally take an active interest in the Irish Church, the coarb of Patrick emerged in the twelfth century as primate, fighting off the opposition of the entrenched monastic churches and of its archiepiscopal rival in Dublin.

63 For the view that much Patrician legend is drawn from sources dealing with Palladius, see T. F. *O'Rahilly*, The Two Patricks, Dublin 1942, p. 19, 55, and IHS 8 (1952—3), p. 275—6; *Binchy*, Patrick and his biographers, p. 83—7, 154—5, 163—4.

64 Cogitosus, *Vita S. Brigitae*, praef., c. 32 (AA SS Feb. I, 135—42, §§ 1—2, 38—9); Tírechán, §§ 18, 22, 25, 47, 48, 51.

Irish Spirituality

By
Diarmuid Ó Laoghaire, S.J.

The first, and indeed permanent, voice of our spirituality is found in the two small and touching documents left us by Saint Patrick, his Confession and his Letter to Coroticus and his soldiers. It is difficult now to trace the direct influence of the saint in our land, but it is remarkable how the special traits of our Christianity, particularly in the early days, can be traced in Patrick's account of his own life and spiritual experience. Here, by the way, I may briefly say that I speak of spirituality in the sense of the special colour that the Irish before the Normans gave to the Gospel of Christ, the expression of that Gospel in Irish terms and under Irish conditions.

Patrick speaks more than once of his being a stranger in this land for the sake of Christ, and a permanent exile, for, as he said, if he were to leave Ireland to visit Britain, his own people and the Christian community there, the Spirit would hold him responsible or guilty[1]. Whether the old Irish imitated him consciously in that matter we cannot tell. We do know that the father of all the faithful, Abraham, was regarded as the supreme example of one who would go into exile and lasting pilgrimage (as was said) for love of God[2]. Such exile was the highest point of asceticism. Saint Colum Cille, our first exile, as he has been called, left Ireland for Iona, according to his biographer Adomnán, as an exile for the sake of Christ[3]. Saint Patrick speaks in very human terms of his desire to visit his own people: "How dearly would I love to go ... God knows I yearned for it ..."[4]. That same humanity is found in the Irish exiles. In the Life of Colum Cille compiled from many ancient sources, including Adomnán, by Maghnus Ua Domhnaill in the early sixteenth century, we have several passages and poems (the latter attributed to the saint himself) expressing the loneliness and nostalgia of the exile. "It is the parting of soul and body for a man," we are told, "to leave his kindred and country and to go from them to strange, distant lands, in exile and perpetual pilgrimage"[5]. We are told too that "Colum Cille had so much human feeling and love for his own country and fatherland that his sorrow on parting from them was hardly greater

---

1 L. *Bieler*, Libri epistolarum S. Patricii episcopi 1, Dublin 1952 (= Classica et Mediaevalia 11, 1950, p. 1 ff), Confession 43; Letter 10.

2 Whitley *Stokes*, ed., Lives of Saints from the Book of Lismore, Oxford 1882, p. 20.

3 A. O. *Anderson*, M. O. *Anderson*, ed., Adomnan's Life of Columba, London 1961, in the second preface.

4 Confession 43.

5 A. *O'Kelleher*, G. *Schoepperle*, ed., Betha Colaim Chille. Life of Columcille, Urbana, Illinois 1918, § 190.

than his sorrow at leaving the seagulls and birds of Loch Feabhail"[6]. And he is recorded as saying of the place of his first monastery, remembered in exile, "The great cry of the people of Doire (Derry) has broken my heart in four"[7].

Although there were a thousand years between the time of Colum Cille and that of his later biographer, I think we may take it that this following passage represents very well the mind and heart of the saint and of his contemporaries in regard to exile:

> When Colum Cille was going into exile to Scotland, Mochonna, this holy child of whom we have spoken, said that he would go with him. "Don't go," said Colum Cille, "but remain with your father and mother in your own country." "You are my father," said Mochonna, "and the Church is my mother, and the place in which I can give most service to God is my country," said he, "and since it is you, Colum Cille, who has bound me to Christ, I will follow you till you bring me to where he is." And then he took the vow of pilgrimage[8].

That same Colum Cille, we are told, asked of God three things, virginity, wisdom and pilgrimage, all of which he received[9]. Five centuries later, so constant is the tradition, the poet and learned monk of Armagh, Maol Íosa Ua Brolcháin († 1086), asks for that same gift of pilgrimage:

> The virtue (or victory) of piety, the virtue of pilgrimage,
> the virtue of repentance for my soul,
> Christ, without fault the slightest,
> grant them all to me likewise[10].

Saint Adomnán of Iona († 704), whom we have already mentioned, biographer and successor of Colum Cille as abbot, is credited with a verse about three definite steps one can take: to go to visit the sick, to go on pilgrimage, to go to church[11]. Oengus the Céile Dé gives in his Martyrology at the end of the eighth century what is fitting for the monk:

> A strange abbot over thee,
> thy family absent from thee till the day of thy death,
> strange soil over thee at the end of thy journey[12].

6 Betha Colaim Chille § 192.
7 Betha Colaim Chille § 191.
8 Betha Colaim Chille § 250.
9 Betha Colaim Chille §§ 65, 67.
10 Whitley *Stokes*, Kuno *Meyer*, ed., Archiv für celtische Lexikographie 3, Halle 1907, p. 230.
11 Ibid., p. 215.
12 Whitley *Stokes*, ed., Félire Oengusso Céli Dé. The Martyrology of Oengus the Culdee, HBS 29, 1905, p. CLXXX 5.

In the early ninth century Walahfrid Strabo, the abbot of Reichenau and theologian, poet and man of letters, wrote about "the Irish nation, with whom the custom of travelling into foreign parts has now become almost second nature" *(de natione Scotorum, quibus consuetudo peregrinandi iam paene in naturam conversa est)*[13]. It is fitting that in this Colloquium we should recall this outstanding feature of Irish spirituality, for without it we could hardly imagine the Colloquium taking place. Those ancient pilgrims for Christ joined Ireland to the rest of Christian Europe and Europe to Ireland with the closest of bonds. And so, Colum Cille, Columbanus and Gall, Fiachra, Fursa and Fearghal belong, not just to Ireland, but to Europe.

The ancient Irish took to the concept of life itself as a pilgrimage and felt a special kinship with Moses and the Children of Israel whom he brought safely through the Red Sea on their way to the Promised Land. They spoke of the sea of baptism and red martyrdom[14]. Saint Patrick himself they regarded as the Moses of Ireland and the Irish people. We are told of Irishmen setting off into exile, even without oars, not caring where they went. So a Saxon chronicler tells in 891 of those Irish who landed in Cornwall, having set out on pilgrimage for the love of God, without a thought of where they might go[15]. Yet, as in an excursus on pilgrimage in the life of Colum Cille in the Book of Lios Mór, we are reminded that "it is not by track of feet nor by motion of body that one draws near to God, but by practising virtue and good deeds"[16]. Later, in the time of the Céilí Dé reform, there was a reaction, perhaps in particular against those who wandered abroad without the true spirit of pilgrimage as outlined in that excursus, and we find Maol Ruain, the most notable of the Céilí Dé, speaking of such pilgrims as "deniers of Patrick in heaven and of the faith in Ireland"[17].

It appears that the original motive in going into exile and pilgrimage was precisely that second element, pilgrimage, so that the two were synonymous. However, if the primary motive was that of pilgrimage, the particular organisation of the Church in Ireland itself would have made sure that the pilgrim, when the need arose, would give himself to the spiritual needs of his new neighbours. Saint Columbanus himself tells us, "My desire was to visit the heathens, and that the Gospel be preached to them by us"[18]. The saint was writing, not before going to the Continent, but after his expulsion from the first area of his exile and apostolic work. Bede, to whom we are indebted for an account of Saint Fursa, is a witness to the fact: "He (Fursa) was anxious to live the life of a pilgrim for the Lord's sake

---

13 Quoted in *Kenney*, Sources, p. 551.
14 Kuno *Meyer*, ed., Betha Colmáin maic Lúacháin, Todd Lecture Series 17, Dublin 1911, § 104.
15 Quoted in *Kenney*, Sources, p. 487.
16 Book of Lismore (as above note 2), line 712.
17 E. J. *Gwynn*, W. J. *Purton*, The Monastery of Tallaght, PRIA 29 C (1911), § 17.
18 G. S. M. *Walker*, ed., Sancti Columbani Opera, SLH 2, 1957, letter IV, § 5.

whenever opportunity offered. When he came to the kingdom of the East Angles he was honourably received by the king, and followed his usual task of preaching the Gospel"[19].

So now we return to where our talk might have begun. For any understanding of the various facets of early Irish spirituality, it is essential to realise that the Church in Ireland was on a monastic basis. Within about a hundred years of Saint Patrick's time that situation had come about whereby areas were looked after spiritually, not by diocesan bishops, as on the Continent, but by abbots of important monasteries whose *paruchiae* (whence the Irish word *fairche*, meaning now 'diocese') those areas were. We are not surprised, then, to find that the Irish monks abroad gave themselves to the work of evangelisation, since they were accustomed to such in Ireland.

Pilgrims also went to definite shrines, both at home and abroad, to Jerusalem and to Rome. In fact the word *rómh* (Rome) became a common noun, meaning a holy burying ground, a place, therefore of pilgrimage. We are told of soil from Peter's tomb and from the graves of other apostles and saints in Rome being brought home to Ireland to spread in Irish graveyards[20]. The love of pilgrimage for the sake of Christ, for the eternal fatherland or some other of the high motives mentioned is one outstanding sign of the great earnestness with which the spiritual life was practised. Another no less sure sign of that earnestness was the cultivation of the sacrament of penance. In that matter, as in the matter of prayer, the Irish influence on the Continent was seminal. If the Irish monks did not introduce private penance, auricular confession, to the Continent, at least they popularised it, so that after Columbanus's death it seems to have become common practice. In the life of Saint Molua we read, "As the floor is brushed clean every day, so the soul is cleansed by daily confession"[21]. Further evidence of that deep earnestness and intensity of spiritual life is the practice of *anamchairdeas* or soul-friendship. That friendship or spiritual guidance was given by the *anamchara* ('soul-friend'), and not merely to religious but also to lay-people. Whence we have the profound proverb, "Colainn gan cheann duine gan anamchara" ('A person without a soul-friend is a body without a head').

I suppose when people think of the old monks the first thing that comes to mind is their great corporal austerity. Yet, as in so many things concerning their spiritual practice, it is easy to exaggerate, and this practice of *anamchairdeas* shows a great care for the individual and a realisation that even under a common rule not all are lead the same way by God. The austere Columbanus stresses continually that principle. What he demands is a pure and single heart. So, for instance, he speaks of the choir office, "... although the length of standing or singing may be

19   Bede, HE, ed. C. *Plummer*, Oxford 1896, III, 19.
20   In Betha Colmáin maic Lúacháin (as above note 14), 77, 82.
21   C. *Plummer*, ed., Vitae Sanctorum Hiberniae, 2 vols., Oxford 1910, Vita Sancti Moluae, XXX.

various, yet the identity of prayer in the heart and mental concentration that is unceasing with God's help will be of a single excellence"[22]. Again he says, "... if temperance exceeds measure, it will be a vice and not a virtue"[23]. Many other examples of that wise understanding of human nature could be cited. It is interesting, in fact, to note that some of the "Rules" attributed to various monastic founders seem not to be rules in the legislative sense, but rather outlines of spiritual and mental outlook, hortative rather than juridical. Typical is the introduction we find to some of these "Rules": to quote again Saint Columbanus: "Here begins the Monks' Rule of Saint Columbanus the Abbot. First of all things we are taught to love God with the whole heart and the whole mind and all our strength, and our neighbour as ourselves; next, our works"[24]. In the Rule of Saint Ailbhe we read: "Let it not be too strict, let it not be too lax; let it not be a rule without knowledge, that each may be able to bear his yoke and not leave his enclosure"[25].

One of the great principles of the spiritual life was that popularised by the celebrated fourth and fifth century Gaul, John Cassian, *Contraria contrariis sanantur* ('contraries are healed by their contraries'). It appears in any number of texts, both in prose and poetry. So, for instance, in the Penitential of Finnian: "But, by contraries ... let us make haste to cure contraries and to cleanse away these faults from our hearts and introduce heavenly virtues in their place: patience must arise for wrathfulness; kindliness, or the love of God and of one's neighbour, for envy; for detraction, restraint of heart and tongue; for dejection, spiritual joy; for greed, liberality"[26].

Saint Patrick in his *Confessio* tells us how in his captivity he used to pray constantly, day and night — in the woods and on the mountainside, no matter how severe the weather[27]. Later tradition credited Patrick with reciting a third of the psalter by night in icy water. The old Irish were firm believers in making the body share in prayer. Genuflexions and prostrations were commonplace. Long prayers would be recited with the arms extended to form a cross, *crosfhighil (crucis vigilia)*. They knew the need to do penance, and they had no illusions about the weakness of the flesh, nor yet of its power to dominate the whole man, and so they were quite severe. In the monasteries, although usage, as we said, could vary, food was taken sparingly and seldom. There were three lents in the year, of Elias during Advent, of Jesus during the forty days before Easter, of Moses during the forty days immediately after Pentecost.

Long prayers, we said. And also at time very prolix, particularly the penitential prayers, where the penitent accused himself or herself of sins and faults innumer-

---

22 Sancti Columbani Opera, p. 132.
23 Ibid., p. 126.
24 Ibid., p. 122.
25 Ériu 3 (1907), p. 104.
26 L. *Bieler*, ed., The Irish Penitentials, SLH 5, 1963, § 29.
27 Confession 16.

able. There are a number of such latter prayers in Latin, of unmistakably Irish composition, in the ninth century Book of Cerne from Mercia in England. By way of contrast there are in the same book the brief, concise and beautiful Roman prayers. You would not be far wrong in saying that Irish prayer seems to have more in common with the East than with the West. At the same time we must not forget the telegrammatic brevity and the beauty of much of the ancient religious and so-called nature poetry, and if it comes to discipline, the extreme control as shown in such a work as the Book of Kells.

In recent times, thanks especially to the efforts of Professor Bernhard Bishoff, it has come to light that the influence of the Irish on scriptural studies in the early Middle Ages was far greater than anyone had previously realised[28]. We are told that they were the first Latin writers in the West to comment on the catholic epistles and Hebrews, and that between 650 and 850 more than half the biblical commentaries in the West were by Irishmen or their pupils. Again, without seeing a direct link with Saint Patrick, it is well-known that his short writings abound in quotations and echoes from the Scripture, especially from Saint Paul. The same holds for the early Irish spiritual writers and prayers. The whole cast of mind was scriptural. To be learned was, above all, to be learned in the Scriptures. Bede tells us that "many of the nobility and of the lower ranks of the English nation ... at that time (mid-seventh century) ... retired thither (to Ireland), either for the sake of sacred studies or of a more ascetic life"[29]. The highest powers of artistry were devoted to honouring the word of God, as in that shrine of the Gospels, the Book of Kells; as in the High Crosses and their portrayal of the history of salvation. The Irish popularised devotion to the saints of the Old Testament. We are told in a poem of the ninth or tenth century of five fastings not pleasing to the King of kings, and one of them is "fasting from wise learning and searching the Scriptures"[30]. As one typical example of that scriptural learning, perception and spirituality, let this small excerpt from an eighth-century Latin text stand for the rest. It speaks of Jesus:

> He is the first and the last.
> He is the second Adam and the brother of the first Adam.
> He is the way, the truth and the life, and the mountain upon which the city is placed.
> He is the true vine and the root of Jesse.
> He is the consuming fire and the sacrificial lamb.
> He is the bread from heaven divided among the saints.

---

28 Bernhard *Bischoff*, Wendepunkte in der Geschichte der lateinischen Exegese im Frühmittelalter, Sacris Erudiri 6 (1954), p. 189—281; in English translation in: Biblical Studies. The Medieval Irish Contribution, ed. M. *McNamara*, Dublin 1976, part II.

29 Bede, HE III, 27.

30 Ériu 19 (1962), p. 8.

He is the strong lion of the tribe of Judah.

He is the flower of the field and the lily of the glen.

He is the sun of justice and the cornerstone, the giver of the law and the great physician[31].

The psalms were the prayer par excellence and permeate all prayer. The Irish made their own, even as a common term of enumeration, *na trí caogaid*, the three fifties of the psalter. Again, the influence was seminal, for from that derived the Pater Noster Psalter, the Rhyming Psalter, and eventually, Mary's Psalter or the Rosary.

A notable feature of the ancient prayers as exemplified in the *loricae* or breastplate prayers and many other similar litanic prayers, often in poetic form, is the enumeration, firstly, it could be, of the members of the body for which God's protection is sought, or again the various classes of the heavenly and earthly Church and the different stages of our Lord's life from nativity to ascension and second coming, for the sake of which God's help is implored. Whether the *lorica* is originally a pagan charm against natural evils and dangers matters little. It became a Christian thing, not least in its stress on the inner dangers from man's own weakness and sinfulness, and on God's strengthening grace. Well-known is the ninth-century *lorica* attributed to Saint Patrick and the ever-popular and very spiritual prayer towards its end: "Críost liom, Críost romham ..."

It is helpful sometimes to show up things by way of contrast. An important study of our subject, which oddly bypassed the scholars, was published as far back as 1963 by Dom Willibrord Godel O.S.B. in *Zeitschrift für Katholische Theologie: Irisches Beten im frühen Mittelalter*. It is currently being published in English by Fr Patrick Rogers C. P. in *Milltown Studies*. The article is long, quite a book in itself, covering 130 pages in the *Zeitschrift*. There are many illuminating observations. Theological and other influences on Irish spirituality and prayer are discussed and help towards a deeper appreciation of the subject. Impossible here to assess fully the article, but if I appear to be rather negative in some of my remarks, it is, as I think, to counterbalance some of the author's judgments.

As Dom Godel well shows, early Irish Christianity certainly shared in the over-stress on Christ as God in opposition to the Arianism for so long rampant in Europe, whereby Christ was regarded as only a creature. However, I do not think I could admit this statement: "The image of the faithful as members of the Body of Christ is rarely used"[32]. On the contrary, it is quite often used. I myself have come across about fifty explicit mentions of it, mostly but not all in the biblical commentaries. In fact it could be said that in ancient Ireland there was an intense devotion to Christ, both God and Man, and to his Body, the Church. In passing, we notice

---

31 R. E. *McNally*, Christus in the Pseudo-Isidorian 'Liber de Ortu et Obitu Patriarcharum', Traditio 21 (1965), p. 177.

32 Zeitschrift für Katholische Theologie 85 (1963), p. 407.

capping a number of our High Crosses a church-shaped carving. On the crosses themselves, as we said, we have depicted the history of salvation, centred on Christ. All is summed up in the cross itself. Perhaps the Church might stand for the spiritual building of which Christ is the cornerstone. Incidentally, the word *cros* itself can also mean "church". The editor of Saint Columbanus's works speaks well of the saint's understanding of the Church as being corporate rather than hierarchical. The saint in that, as in so much else, was truly representative of his people.

We know that it is vital to any understanding of Ireland, even to this very day, but much more so the further back we go into an Ireland more truly herself, to realise that the country was untouched by the direct rule and power of Rome. What is termed "original" may at times just mean "non-Roman". Equally vital, and especially so from the point of view of Christianity here, is it necessary to realise that in ancient Ireland there were no cities and that the many small *tuatha* ('states') must have made for great intimacy within their bounds. So, when we read of Christ being addressed as *rí* ('king') we should realise that it is a term of intimacy, or at least not of remoteness. The king was one of his people. It is a point of no small importance, given the fondness of the Irish for its use in regard to God and Christ. The great importance of kinship in the *tuath* also would ensure a constant understanding of Christ's kinship with us through his Mother, in other words, his humanity.

Dom Godel speaks of "the essentially beleagured character of Irish Christianity"[33]; "the heavy emphasis on Christ's divinity went with a negative estimate of the world and a highly developed consciousness of sin"[34]. There are many other such references backed up with quotations. Stress is laid on the individualism of Irish prayer, the "I" rather than the "we"[35]. In regard to that latter remark, we might remember that some of these prayers may have been composed by anchorites, but in general, I think that with all the emphasis on sin and man's weakness we must also place the plentiful evidence of trust in God and in his mercy. The two things are obviously not incompatible. As regards individualism in prayer it is sufficient to refer to the concept of the Body of Christ. Another all-pervading feature of Irish spirituality which would, I imagine, have caused some modification of Dom Godel's views, is that of *muintearas* or intimacy. The word *muintir* from which it comes is the equivalent of the Latin *familia* or monastic family and itself is generally held to be from Latin *monasterium*, but meaning, significantly, not the place itself but the people who dwell in it.

A few instances of that intimacy must do. In the ancient poem about 800 attributed to Suibhne Geilt, God himself is addressed as *mu chridecán*, "my little

---

33 Ibid., p. 390.
34 Ibid., p. 399.
35 Ibid., p. 420ff.

heart"[36]. The humanity of our Lord is greatly stressed in the poems of Blathmhac[37], which of course are a prime witness to a mature devotion to our Lady in the mid-eighth century. The poet speaks (line 593) of consoling the heart of Mary (do airchisecht do chridi). Could anything be more human than the description of Christ's arrival in heaven after his death? The poet addresses Mary (lines 732—6): "When the household of heaven welcomed their true heart, Mary, your beautiful son broke into tears in their presence." We have that note of intimacy also in the little poem from about 900 attributed to Saint Íde, Ísucán ('little Jesus')[38], a poem remarkable for its untranslatable diminutives, such as a mother might use with her child, one of the verbs even appearing in a diminutive and completely untranslatable form! The hypocoristic or pet-names of the saints point also to familiarity and affection: M'Íde, Mocholmóg, Mo Bhí etc., (We are reminded of the modern Mo dhuine!). Incidentally, we should note the great devotion the ancient Irish had towards their holy ones, whose cult they propagated so zealously on the Continent that it still lives today. That devotion was shown by the dedication of men and women to their saints, signified by the prefix Maol, meaning "tonsured": Maol Phádraig, Maol Choluim, Maol Bhrighde. I suppose those would originally have been monastic names. Apart from the native saints we find few others so honoured. Maol Íosa and Maol Mhuire there are, but not mentioned in the annals before the tenth century. We also have Maol Mhichíl (the old Irish had a notable devotion to Michael the Archangel), Maol Pheadair, Maol Phóil, Maol Mharthain, Maol Ghiric (Cyric(i)us the child-martyr much esteemed in Ireland and Wales), Maol Domhnaigh. Only later on, if we can judge by the entries in the annals, do we find Giolla used in the same way (from the tenth century).

There is time left only to make bare mention of some other facets of the ancient spirituality. The old Irish had a feeling for their pagan ancestors and passed on the pagan literary inheritance without necessarily approving of paganism. There was a tradition that Patrick accepted everything in the old recht aicnid or natural law that did not clash with the recht litre or law of the Scripture. That understanding of natural goodness and custom may have helped Colum Cille in his successful work with the Picts and Aidan, so loved of Bede, in his evangelisation of the Angles[39].

For the old Irish the guest was always in Christian times Christ. Almsgiving was held in the highest esteem. Finally, mention must be made, however briefly, of the many attractive incidents we read of concerning the old saints and animals. For instance, the little bird weeping in the Calendar of Oengus at the death of Molua who had never killed a living thing[40].

36 Gerard Murphy, Early Irish Lyrics, eighth to twelfth century, Oxford 1956, p. 112.
37 James Carney, ed., The Poems of Blathmac, son of Cú Brettan, ITS 47, 1964.
38 Murphy, Lyrics, p. 26.
39 Charles Donahue, Beowulf and Christian Tradition: A Reconsideration from a Celtic Stance, Traditio 21 (1965), p. 55—116.
40 Félire Oengusso (as above note 12), p. 56.

We have dealt all too sketchily with some of the mechanics, as it were, of the spirituality of the ancients, but there are the higher and deeper reaches of holiness that we can hardly treat of. Power over animals, luminous and mysteriously clear treatment in verse of God's creation, all point, I think, to an inner detachment, harmony and power, achieved only by a loving, interior and exterior asceticism, centred on Christ and his Cross. A holiness such as was exemplified in later times by Saint Francis.

The Céli Dé reform

By
Peter O'Dwyer, O.Carm.

A movement of reform must have a charismatic and juridical aspect and be supported by a competent authority. These three are complementary. The charism or inspiration which God gives to individuals is marked by spontaneity, freshness and vitality but runs the risk of falling into error or illusion. It may also experience great difficulty in maintaining its 'first fervour' sufficiently long to ensure stability, continuity and diffusion. The juridical aspect runs the risk of losing the original spirit of authentic renewal and the letter may tend to prevail over the spirit. It may lack adaptability, and authority may not be prepared to suit the structures to what the times need. Yet without the juridical aspect and support from on top movements from below will fail to be effective[1]. This would seem to sum up the efforts of the culdee reform as regards lasting effects in external observance.

This reform movement which we follow from ca. 750 till 900 hoped to counterbalance a tendency towards laxity in the 'older churches'. It aimed at restoring monastic studies to their rightful place and at maintaining proper respect for the person of the cleric. It was also meant to counteract what was to be one of the chief causes of the downfall of Irish monasticism in the twelfth century: namely the introduction of the lay-abbot. Its insistence on poverty was one of the means to that end. Probably from the seventh century onwards the growth in monastic property had begun to affect religious observance. This was due primarily to the kindness of the donors who gave the monastery the land, and secondly to the profitable labour of the monks whose work, of course, was free. The temptation to hoard or to keep the surplus was strong and the reform forbade this several times. That the monasteries were rich is evident from the fact that the Vikings, who came mainly for plunder, concentrated their attention on them[2]. Probably the continuance of the lay-abbot or *airchinnech*, due to family interests, proved to be the greater obstacle. At this period the Church was experiencing similar difficulties with local rulers in Europe, and the papacy itself was being dominated by Italian family interests. In Ireland there was as yet no diocesan structure in the Church and no individual abbot or king was powerful enough and willing to combat the abuses.

The movement began in the south of Ireland, in the district round Darinis-Lismore-Daire Eidnech probably in the second quarter of the eighth century. One

---

1 G. *Martina*, La Chiesa nell' età dell' Assolutismo, del Liberalismo, del Totalitarismo, Brescia 1970, p. 136—37.
2 J. *Ryan*, Irish Monasticism, Dublin 1931, p. 245—46.

of the monks of Darinis, Ruben, collaborated with Cucuimne of Iona to compile the collection of canons known as the Collectio Canonum Hibernensis[3]. Though non-official in origin it came to be held in high favour before long. It is a compilation of aphorisms and enactments, arranged without any apparent order in sixty-seven books, each subdivided into a number of chapters, and deals with matters pertaining to Christian discipline, the religious life and direction of souls. The aphorisms and laws are drawn chiefly from Holy Scripture, the Fathers, decisions of foreign and local councils and native practices. This is the most developed and most important of the canonical collections of Celtic origin so far known[4].

The principal man of the reform was undoubtedly Maelruain. His tutor was Ferdácrích, native of Daire Eidnech[5] and abbot of Darinis. The Tallaght documents[6] look back with great respect to men like Mac Uige, Mocholmóc Ua Liatháin and Caincomhrac, all of Lismore, who were noted for their sincerity and wisdom in spiritual matters. The Collectio Canonum Hibernensis and very probably the Alphabet of Piety are also from this district and from about this time[7]. So it is a fair inference that the reform owes much of its inspiration to these monks. Two other persons are connected with the early stage of the movement, Samthann of Clonbroney and Maeltuile of Dísert Maeltuile, Co. Meath. The Unity of Maelruain indicates the spread of the reform. It continued in the place of its birth under such men as Flann son of Faircheallach and Flann son of Duibthuinne, both from Daire na bhFlann. It found its real home in Tallaght round the last quarter of the eigth century with Maelruain and the monks who came to be directed by him. Thence it spread to Tipperary, Cork, Kildare and Westmeath and seems to have lasted longest in the monastery of Terryglass, Co. Tipperary.

The period of the reform is marked by the rise of what has been called the anchorite movement, the aim of which was to give the monk the opportunity for solitude close to the monastery. His life was a poor one. Prayer, work, reading and especially growth in charity were his daily occupations. The core of the anchorite rule was charity, self-denial, useful occupation and perseverance. This useful occupation frequently took the form of intellectual labour[8]. Flower, in discussing the personal poems which evolved from this movement, says that they "are a scanty gleaning after the great harvest produced by the mysterious impulse of the eighth century which made the culdee movement possible in Ireland and was the driving force behind the Irish scholars who did so much for the culture of the

3 Peter *O'Dwyer*, Célí Dé, Dublin 1981, p. 4 (henceforth: Célí Dé).

4 L. *Gougaud*, Christianity in Celtic Lands, London 1932, p. 278—81.

5 Daire Eidnech or Daire na bhFlann as it is later called, lies about a mile or two from the village of Horse and Jockey near Cashel. The Derrynavlan Chalice was found there in 1980.

6 Cf. Célí Dé XIV, n. 4 and p. 122—23.

7 Ibid., p. 177—82.

8 Diarmait of Dísert Diarmata (825) might be taken as a good example of this aspect of the movement.

Carolingian Empire. The piety was often misguided as the scholarship was erratic and uncertain. But the passion for sincerity of faith and life was as noble in one as the eager thirst for knowledge in the other. And both of them left an ineffaceable stamp on Irish literature. The study of their own language was pushed almost to grotesque lengths in the Irish schools. But the accurate forms of verse perfected in this period held out for a long time against the exuberant tendencies developed in Irish prose. And whenever the verse of the later poets touched personal things, it is always distinguished by an extraordinary sincerity and directness of feeling. It had gone to school with religious emotion when that emotion was quick with the new hopes and the spiritual awakening of an intense and passionate race. The best of these poems are all fire and air, praise, prayer and dedication of the heart, touching little upon dogma or miracle, but content and eager with a new joy and a young revelation. These men only ask to serve and pray, and it is clear that the best reward they ask is to have their praise accepted"[9].

The monasteries of Tallaght and Finglas were known as the "two eyes of Ireland". The application is not explained by the writer of the Triads but there are two very obvious ones in the light of eighth- and ninth-century Ireland. Firstly it may be very well applied to the impetus given to learning by these monasteries and secondly it may be applied perhaps with more propriety and justice to the ascetical movement sponsored mainly by them. Flower continuing the metaphor says that these monks brought into their "environment an eye washed miraculously clear by a continual spiritual exercise" and "that they first in Europe, had that strange vision of natural things in an almost unnatural purity"[10]. The monk of the reform, typified in the *céle dé* (culdee), recognized and stressed his total dependence on God and his consequent abandonment to His divine providence[11]. The common but indispensable means for salvation and perfection were used by them. Mass, the Sacraments (especially Penance and the Eucharist) were the regular sources of grace for them. Prayer was an important duty and occupied a goodly portion of each day. Their minds and hearts must have been well stocked from the daily recitation of the Psalter. Mortification was a very important part of their observance. The first year was spent in constant purification, which was both external and internal. The monk was expected to come to the monastery with great generosity and to take the straight road to sanctity through self-denial. Yet this mortification was not an end in itself. It was aimed at overcoming the old Adam, was taken as a test of sincerity, and prepared the soul for the beautiful experiences recounted in the poems of these monks. On the other hand, excessive mortification was frowned upon, and the monk was expected to keep himself fit for the life

9 R. *Flower*, The Irish Tradition, Oxford 1947, p. 47—48. His insights may prove very valuable for the studies of the roots of Irish spirituality at present in progress.

10 *Flower*, p. 42.

11 W. *Stokes*, J. *Strachan*, Thesaurus Palaeohibernicus I, p. 65, Ml. 30 c 3.

of prayer and work[12]. At the festive seasons of the year relaxations were allowed so that the minds of the monks would be elevated to the life which awaited them after their resurrection. Thus their spiritual life consisted chiefly in renunciation, prayer and work. This penitential note has always marked and still marks genuine Irish spirituality.

The virtue most stressed by them would seem to be perseverance. The path to holiness is delineated by Fothad[13] in the law of charity, the ten commandments and more specifically in prayer, vigil, reading and work. In the poetry of the time it is often marked by the same virtues, though on occasion it is denoted by prudence, obedience and patience. The Alphabet of Piety recommends prudent holiness for clerics, avoidance of boasting and other vices etc. While it does not give an itinerarium to sanctity in the strict sense of the word the following recommendations are as near to it as can be found in this literature: Four things to be fulfilled: duty to God, kindness to man, devotedness to all, thought of death. Four duties of the sons of life: suppression of wishes, fear of pain, love of suffering, hope of reward. Four ways to heaven: perseverance, detachment, devotion, endurance[14].

The literature connected with this reform includes a number of monastic rules which date from about this time[15], thereby showing that a general revival of the monastic spirit of the founders of Irish monasticism was sought after by a number of monasteries in the country. Tallaght was well to the fore not alone in the detail of its legislation but also in other sections of the religious life, particularly in catering for its liturgical needs. The vernacular tract on the Mass in the Stowe Missal is unique for its period in Celtic lands. But these monks were much more interested in the records of the saints, and they have left clear testimony of their industry in two Martyrologies written within a period of about ten years of each other[16]. Works like these could not have come into existence without unremitting research into the traditions of the Irish Church, and the hagiographical memoranda in the Notes to the Félire and the collections of this nature in the Book of Leinster are the obvious fruits of this activity. But this interest was not merely cultural. It was primarily religious and devotional. The litanies show that the monks who busied themselves in amassing these materials hoped to reap a big reward in the next life for their labours here. Furthermore the composition of some of the Vitae Sanctorum in this period was undertaken with a view to providing spiritual reading for all, and reading such as this was expected to have appropriate results in the lives of all who read or heard them read.

12 Céli Dé, p. 111.
13 Ibid., p. 125 ff.
14 V. Hull, Celtica 8 (1968), p. 72.
15 Céli Dé, p. 122—39.
16 The Martyrology of Tallaght, ed. Best, Lawlor, London 1931 and The Félire of Oengus, ed. Stokes, London 1905.

Nor was the reform without some effect on secular literature also. Cormac mac Cuillenáin was connected with Dísert Diarmata[17]. In the Book of Leinster there is a versified form of the Unity of Maelruain attributed to him[18]. He was educated at Dísert Diarmata by Snedgus, who died AD 888[19]. Later he became king of Cashel and is described as scribe, bishop, anchorite and wisest of the Irish[20]. A Brussels MS describes him as "surpassingly learned in the Irish language"[21]. He is certainly a very important figure in the literary history of the country and has the distinction of being the author of the first etymological dictionary in the vernacular[22]. He also wrote the Psalter of Cashel which is now lost[23]. In addition to these there are numerous poems attributed to him and the rule which bears his name dates from his period[24]. Many other works were written during the eighth and ninth centuries and have since been lost. There was a set of Annals of Clonenagh and also a Book of Clonenagh[25]. As this was a monastery intimately connected with the reform these works and others of the period may be a further indication of the extent of the literary activity of the movement.

Reform is a recurring factor in the history of the Church and comes about when men ask themselves with a new urgency how they are to be sincere with God. In the middle of the eighth century a group of monks strove to live a life in full conformity with their ideal. In doing this they introduced a freshness and vigour, though somewhat austere and occasionally puritanical, into the religious life, which is always inclined to follow the easier course, an inclination which is often the more marked according as the body or institute is farther removed from the time of its founder or reformer.

The abuses which it was expected to counteract were, at this time, but in their initial stages and were trifling in comparison with those which affected the life of the contemporary Church on the Continent, or the life of the Church in Ireland in later times. Yet these abuses developed during the succeeding centuries and finally led to the downfall of Irish monasticism in the twelfth century. The coming of the Vikings certainly hindered this movement from having a lasting effect on the religious life of the country. The monasteries of Tallaght and Finglas, so closely connected with the reform, were almost on the spot where the Vikings made their first landing and in time built their great stronghold in Dublin. But it is worthy of note that the annals have no reference to Vikings attacking either monastery.

17 Célí Dé, p. 44.
18 LL fol. 370 b.
19 AFM 885.
20 CS 901, 907; AI 901.
21 Bibl. Royale MS 2324—40, fol. 10.
22 Sanas Cormaic. Best, Bibl. 1913—41, nn. 39—44 a.
23 Kenney, Sources, p. 11—12.
24 Célí Dé, p. 133.
25 R. Flower, Catalogue of Irish Manuscripts in the British Museum II, p. 284—85. Oengus mac Oengobann, author of the Félire, had strong links with Clonenagh.

In the monastery of Tallaght we may see a detailed picture of the typical monastery of the reform, which, if strict and austere, was also prudent. We must resist the temptation to judge life in the eighth century in the light of present-day conditions and ideas. From Tallaght it spread to other monasteries throughout the country, notably to Clonmacnois, Terryglass and Clonenagh and probably influenced other monastic centres.

As Mac Niocaill has said: "The ascetic reform had however no machinery for renewing itself. Each church attached to the reform during Maelruain's lifetime was dependent on the character of its abbot to maintain its level of asceticism. No authority existed to maintain a check on any individual monastery, to prevent it slipping away from its standards. The ascetic reform had indeed a future, but not an institutional one: it survived rather as an inspiration to small groups of ascetics and individuals"[26].

That it had a good effect on the religious life of the country is evident from the spiritual writings of these centuries. Most of these had the aim of inculcating a spirit of minute religious observance. The Rule of Fothad, the Alphabet of Piety and the Tallaght documents provide the most detailed picture that we can get of Irish monasticism at any period, and this serves not only for this period but also helps to fill in lacunae for earlier periods in the history of Celtic monasticism. To these must be added the Martyrologies, Missals, Gospels, Ritual, psalters, Scripture studies, sermons, Lives of saints, litanies, hymns and other compositions produced by or connected with the movement[27]. It should also be noted that two great literary collections were executed in monasteries influenced by the movement, Clonmacnois and Terryglass, the *Lebor na hUidre* and the Book of Leinster. Large sections of the latter are obviously derived from labours begun in Tallaght.

Few events in early Irish history had such a wide effect on Irish monastic life after its first fervour and on Irish literature as this ascetical movement which resulted in the foundation or reform of monasteries, bequeathed to them a large corpus of literature, made a very important contribution to devotion to the saints and inspired those delicately wrought lyrics which show us the inner depths of these monks and which are, to my mind, one of the most attractive features of the whole of Irish literature.

---

26 Gearóid *Mac Niocaill*, Ireland before the Vikings, Dublin 1972, p. 151.
27 Célí Dé, p. 122—191.

The use of relics in early Ireland

By
Charles Doherty

The cult of relics is not specifically Christian. In general humanity has had a respect for the dead, their places of burial and objects associated with them. The cult of relics in Antiquity was closely bound up with the cult of the hero, and indeed it would appear that some aspects of the pagan cult are found in the exterior forms of the cult of the saints. Recently Nicole Herrmann-Mascard has made a masterly survey and analysis of the cult of relics, especially the legal developments relating to them[1]. She has pointed out the fundamental difference that exists between the pagan cult and that of the early Christians[2]. On the same theme Peter Brown has argued, with finesse, that late antique society underwent a deep psychological reorientation as it became Christian. 'Their intimacy [that of the martyrs] with God was a *sine qua non* of their ability to intercede for and, so, to protect their fellow mortals. The martyr was the "friend of God". He was an intercessor in a way which the hero could never have been'[3].

Worship at the tombs of martyrs could lead to accusations of idolatry, and it was to defend against such accusations that St Augustine stated that the sacrifice of the Mass was not offered to Peter or Paul or Cyprian, 'but it is to God who crowns martyrs that the sacrifice is offered'[3a]. In the fourth century the doctrine of the Church wisely stressed that the sanctity of relics could save only those who imitated the saints. The cult as such was reserved for God and the saints, and an excessive devotion towards relics was regarded as heretical and superstitious. Such a distinction on the part of the theologians was not recognised by the faithful, however, for whom the relics had a power in themselves. Among the barbarian peoples it was the miraculous aspect of relics that most impressed[4].

The rapid and somewhat anarchic development of the cult of relics was influenced more by custom than by Church legislation. It was not until the beginning of the thirteenth century that the Church was able, finally, to impose upon the cult a discipline compatible with the evolution of the Christian religion[5].

---

1 N. *Herrmann-Mascard*, Les reliques des saints, formation coutumière d'un droit, Paris 1975.

2 *Herrmann-Mascard*, Reliques, p. 13—15.

3 P. *Brown*, The cult of the saints, Chicago and London 1981, p. 6.

3a The Irish canon lawyers adopt this idea quoting Isidore, cf. H. *Wasserschleben*, ed., Die irische Kanonensammlung, Leipzig ²1885 (1966), p. 207, Book XLIX, c. 11.

4 *Herrmann-Mascard*, Reliques, p. 15—17.

5 Ibid., p. 18.

The very brief outline of the development of the cult of relics above and in the few paragraphs below is based mainly on the clear exposition of Herrmann-Mascard. It is given to provide a framework within which the Irish evidence may be discussed.

The development of the cult of relics at Rome itself was much slower than elsewhere because Roman law forbade interference with a *locus religiosus* except under exceptional circumstances. The papacy followed Roman law wishing on the one hand to avoid abuses and on the other to maintain the status of Rome as the treasure house of the remains of the martyrs. Until the seventh and eighth centuries it was the exceptions to Roman law that were appealed to at Rome in order to effect translations. In the East translations with solemn processions were taking place already in the fourth century. In the writings of Gregory of Tours it is clear that they were happening in the West by the sixth century. In the East increasing demand led to the dismembering of bodies and St Basil himself partitioned the bones of martyrs and divided them among the Eastern Greek Churches. Fragmentation in the West, however, became common only from the ninth century onwards, although there were exceptions to this rule also.

Cemeteries in Roman law had to be outside towns. In Rome itself, with the exception of saints John and Paul on Mount Coelius, there are no known Christian burials within the walls until the mid-seventh century. Pope Theodore (642—648) took the initiative and transferred bodies into the Basilica of St Stephen. Although some popes tried to maintain and repair the catacombs they fell increasingly into disuse and ruin, and this caused many translations to be made in the eighth century. Pope Paul I (757—67) carried out more than 100 translations[6].

From the mid-eighth century onwards the export of relics from Rome, mainly to Gaul and Germany, increased considerably in volume. It was a means by which the papacy could maintain direct links with those areas to the north of the Alps. Indeed the great reformer bishop Chrodegang of Metz was one of the first, it would seem, to benefit from the more relaxed attitude of Pope Paul I and carry back to Gaul in 764—5 the bodies of the saints Nabor and Nazarius to which he had added, more or less fraudulently, the body of St Gorgon[7].

To the north of the Alps, particularly in Gaul, the displacement of bodies multiplied rapidly from the middle of the ninth century onwards, mainly owing to the disruption brought about by the invasions of the Norse. By this time too the trade from Rome had increased to such an extent that highly organised groups of relic prospectors existed. Deusdona, a deacon of the Roman Church who would appear to have been in charge of the catacombs in one of the Roman cemeteries, is probably the most famous of the ninth-century entrepreneurs[8]. During the winter he and his brothers collected relics from the cemetery. In the spring they fitted out

6 Ibid., p. 50f.
7 Ibid., p. 58—59.
8 Ibid., p. 342—344.

a caravan and crossed the Alps, timing their journey so that they would arrive at the monasteries of their customers on important feast days. This was big business. England in the tenth, eleventh, and twelfth centuries was a major market for relic merchants. Aethelstan had an absolute passion for relics and was possibly the greatest collector of his century[9]. By this stage, however, we are in the full flowering of the cult of relics of the Middle Ages.

What of the relics themselves? The commonest type of relic up to the eighth century had been the *palliola*. This was a fabric which had been used in the celebration of mass near a saint's tomb, or one which had been in contact with a venerated tomb. Other representative relics included objects or linen which had been in contact with the body of a saint. These were called variously, *pignora, brandea, sanctuaria, beneficia. Brandea,* little pieces of cloth or silk, were enclosed in small cases and hung around the neck. At the end of the fifth century in North Africa clothes and flowers which had been in contact with martyrs' tombs were sanctified. Oil lit before a tomb was a kind of relic kept by pilgrims in little glass phials. The everyday objects used by saints, their clothes, shoes, utensils, and beds were regarded as relics and in particular the implements of torture such as chains which had been associated with martyrs were especially treasured[10]. North of the Alps where there were very few martyrs real non-corporeal material of this kind was in very short supply and *brandea* were the normal type of relic until the eighth century.

Bede claims that Germanus had a casket hung around his neck which contained the relics of the Apostles. He also claims that Mellitus in 601 brought relics of the Apostles and martyrs to England. In 655 Pope Vitalian sent relics of the blessed Apostles Peter and Paul, and of the holy martyrs Laurence, John and Paul, Gregory and Pancras. He also sent a cross with a golden key made from the fetters of the blessed Apostles Peter and Paul[11]. This last-mentioned type of relic was given only to important personages on whom the pope wished to confer favour. It is in the seventh century in Britain and in Ireland that the cult of relics really begins to develop.

One would suspect that the early missionaries to Ireland had brought relics with them. We have allusions to these in later sources. The *Vita Tripartita* of St Patrick, dating ca. 900 but based on earlier materials, claims that Palladius left his books, the casket with the relics of Paul and Peter, and his writing board in Cell Fine in Leinster[12]. It is likely that Palladius, who was sent to Ireland directly by the papacy, would have brought the most important Roman relics with him as a sign

9 P. *Geary*, Furta sacra, Princeton 1978, p. 52.

10 *Herrmann-Mascard*, Reliques, p. 42—49.

11 Bede, Historia ecclesiastica gentis Anglorum, ed. C. *Plummer*, Oxford 1896 (1961) I, XVIII, p. 36; I, XXIX, p. 63; III, XXIX, p. 198.

12 K. *Mulchrone*, Bethu Phátraic, Dublin 1939, p. 19 = W. *Stokes*, The Tripartite Life of Patrick, RS 89, 1887, vol. I, p. 30.

of his authority[13]. His mission was to establish a Church organization among those of the Irish already Christian, and also, like Germanus mentioned above, he was sent to prevent the spread of the Pelagian heresy. It was thus all the more important to have the new Church in Ireland bound closely to the Holy See. The use of the relics of Paul and Peter would have been of the utmost importance in achieving this. Also the fact that they were found in a relatively obscure Leinster church that had been taken over by Armagh suggests that the tradition was genuine. In a similar way at a later period Pope Gregory the Great gave a relic of St Peter to Augustine when he set out for England.

In the notes on early foundations (much of it confused traditions) gathered by Tírechán shortly after 684 there are two references to *Bassilica Sanctorum*[14]. The name is now preserved in Baslick in Co. Roscommon. It was close to Cruachu, the 'capital' of the Connachta. Tradition associated the church with 'Patrick's Franks'. Its bishop was Sachellus. He and another, Caeticus, were accused of operating independently of Patrick in Connacht[15]. It is likely that here we have the residue of tradition concerning fifth-century Gaulish activity in this area. The title of this church implied that it was an early foundation and that it contained relics. It was undoubtedly the main church of the province and was an extremely important church politically right down to the eighth century[16]. We do not know what relics were kept there but it was almost certainly a rival to Armagh. The word *basilica* may have been used specifically of those churches which had major relics. Armagh herself had a basilica in the southern quarter of the site[17]. Tírechán tells us that Patrick gave Sachellus 'a portion of the relics of Peter and Paul, Stephen and Laurence which are in Armagh'[18]. Since it is unlikely that Armagh possessed these relics herself before the 630s we can suggest that this is an attempt by Armagh to outdo and overcome a powerful rival[19].

What major relics Armagh had she acquired relatively late. After all she was embarrassed by the fact that she did not possess the body of her patron saint, Patrick, who was buried at Downpatrick. As the episode in Muirchú's 'Life' of Patrick, written in the late seventh century, suggests there may have been an unsuccessful and unseemly struggle for possession of the body some time ear-

13 J. *Ryan*, The early Irish Church and the Holy See, Studies 49 (1960), p. 1—16; M. P. *Sheehy*, The relics of the Apostles and early martyrs in the mission of St Patrick, IER 95 (1961), p. 372—376.

14 L. *Bieler*, The Patrician Texts in the Book of Armagh, SLH 10, 1979, p. 146, 148.

15 Ibid., p. 122—124.

16 F. J. *Byrne*, Irish Kings and High-kings, London 1973, p. 247, 251.

17 *Bieler*, Patrician Texts, p. 186.

18 Ibid., p. 123.

19 This may have happened later since relics could have been sent with the bearer of the letter of John, Pope-Elect, and the clergy of Rome, to the clergy of northern Ireland in 640. Tomméne, bishop and abbot of Armagh headed the list of those addressed in the letter, HE II, XIX, p. 122—123.

lier[20]. She had, therefore, to rely all the more heavily on possession of the *insignia* of the saint. Already by the mid-seventh century fines were established for insulting or for the violation of the consecrated *insignia*[21]. It is almost certain that Armagh valued even more the possession of the relics of the principal martyrs. These she probably acquired as a result of the embassy which was sent to Rome in about 630 on the question of the dating of Easter. The Irish were in the Holy City for the celebration of Easter 631. They returned to Ireland in 632. As a result of this mission Cumméne wrote a letter to Ségéne, abbot of Iona, in which the power of these relics which were brought back was extolled: *Et nos in reliquiis sanctorum martyrum et scripturis quas attulerunt, probavimus inesse virtutem Dei. Vidimus oculis nostris puellam coecam omnino ad has reliquias oculos aperientem, et paralyticum ambulantem, et multa daemonia ejecta*[22].

It was not long before possession of these relics became an essential part of Armagh's claims to supremacy within Ireland and to be the highest court of appeal outside of Rome, as can be seen in the *Liber Angeli*, the earlier part of which may date to the 630s or 640s: 'Furthermore, it [Armagh] ought to be venerated in honour of the principal martyrs Peter and Paul, Stephen, Lawrence, and the others. How much more should it be venerated and diligently honoured by all because of the holy admiration for a gift to us, beyond praise above other things, (namely) that in it, by a secret dispensation, is preserved the most holy blood of Jesus Christ the redeemer of the human race in a sacred linen cloth, together with relics of saints in the southern church, where there rest the bodies of holy men from abroad who had come with Patrick from across the sea, and of other just men!' The Sunday liturgy for processing to and from the southern church (the *basilica*) was '*Domine clamavi ad te* to the end, *Ut quid Deus repulisti* to the end, and *Beati immaculati* to the end of the blessing, and the fifteen gradual psalms'[23].

By the end of the seventh century Tírechán records that Patrick is said to have given 'a portion of the relics of Peter and Paul and others and a veil to protect the relics' to bishop Olcanus at Dún Sobairche[24]. Armagh would appear to have used these relics in a manner similar to the papacy in an attempt to bring churches directly under her wing. This process continued as she built up her *paruchia* in the following centuries.

Indeed much of the activity of Tírechán as revealed in his notes in the Book of Armagh is concerned with the origins of churches and anything they might have possessed by way of authentication. He was very interested in graves — some of them pagan. In this way we get references to the remains of holy men. He refers to

20 *Bieler*, Patrician Texts, p. 120–122.

21 Ibid., p. 189.

22 J. *Ussher*, Veterum epistolarum Hibernicarum sylloge, Dublin 1632 in: C. R. *Elrington*, and J. H. *Todd*, The whole works of the Most Rev. James Ussher, DD., Dublin (1847—1864) vol. IV p. 443.

23 *Bieler*, Patrician Texts, p. 186, 190, 240 (16).

24 Ibid., p. 160.

a *Domus Martirum* in Leinster[25]. Relics were used to seal a treaty of *amicitia* between churches[26]. He refers to a pagan burial which he calls a *ferta* (OIr. *fertae*, 'a grave-mound') but which he says is a *relic*, a grave[27]. By the late seventh century then, *reliquiae*, the 'relics of the saints' had acquired its normal meaning when borrowed into Irish *(reilic)* of 'cemetery'. In the Sligo area the chasuble of Bishop Brón and the tooth of Patrick were preserved as relics[28]. Most interestingly he gives us what is probably the earliest reference to a translation: 'And he came to Mag Réin and ordained Bruscus a priest and founded a church for him; Bruscus said something extraordinary after his death to another holy man, who was in the monastery of the family of Cothirbe: "All is well with you because you have a son; I loathe my death because I am alone in a solitary church, a church deserted and empty, and no priests offer beside me." For three nights (the holy man) had this dream; on the third day he got up, took ... an iron shovel and dug up the moat of the grave and took the bones of holy Bruscus with him to the monastery where they (now) are, and (Bruscus) spoke no more'[29]. It is interesting to note that dreams were necessary to justify interference with a grave even though the church would appear to have been abandoned. It is likely that translations as such were not as yet very common.

As the work of Tírechán shows, the cult of native saints was well under way towards the second half of the seventh century. Hagiography begins in Ireland in the same century and it reflects the development of the organised 'cult' of various saints. It is the written counterpart to the interest in the physical remains.

The detailed description of the great church *(basilica)* of Kildare by Cogitosus about the middle of the seventh century shows how well orchestrated was the cult of Saint Brigit and Bishop Conlaeth there: *Nec et de miraculo in reparatione eclesiae facto tacendum est in qua gloriosa amborum hoc est archiepiscopi Conlaeth et huius virginis florentissimae Brigidae corpora a dextris et a sinistris altaris decorati in monumentis posita ornatis vario cultu auri et argenti et gemmarum et praetiosi lapidis atque coronis aureis et argenteis desuper pendentibus, ac diversis imaginibus cum celaturis variis et coloribus requiescunt et in veteri nova res adnascitur actu*[30]. The bodies of the saints had been translated and had been placed in sumptuous coffins on either side of the altar. With the rich and colourful paintings and linens on the partition wall closing off the sanctuary and in particular the crowns of gold and silver suspended from the ceiling one is reminded of the scene in Visigothic churches, as Charles Thomas has pointed out[31]. We are clearly in a royal church.

25 Ibid., p. 162.
26 Ibid., p. 142.
27 Ibid., p. 144.
28 Ibid., p. 158.
29 Ibid., p. 136.
30 I wish to thank Dr. Seán Connolly for providing me with the text of his new edition (in preparation) of the *Vita Brigitae*.
31 C. *Thomas*, The early Christian archaeology of north Britain, Glasgow 1971, p. 146.

The splendour of Kildare reflects the position of the church as chief church of the Leinstermen. By the seventh century it was controlled by the main dynasty of Leinster, the Uí Dúnlainge, and challenged the position of Armagh. Áed Dub, *ríg-epscop Cille Dara 7 Lagen uile* 'royal bishop of Kildare and of all Leinster', died in 638. Áed Dub was son of the king of Leinster, Colmán, and the praise poem written about Áed is full of references to his royal connections. His nephew Óengus also became bishop of Kildare[32]. Patrick and Brigit were the 'two pillars' of the Irish, and it would appear that an accommodation or treaty of co-existence was worked out between the two churches during the course of the seventh century[33].

These major cults stood somewhat apart from the intensely local cults that were to be found everywhere. There must have been much continuity from the pagan past. The word *érlam*, a 'patron saint', originally meant 'tutelar deity', the 'god of the tribe'[34]. The word *cretair* means a 'relic', 'halidom', 'blessed object', and is found also in Welsh. Vendryes suggested that originally in pre-Christian times it meant 'that which has magical power within it', a 'talisman', a 'fetish', 'something which assures help and protection'[35]. Kathleen Hughes has pointed to the relationship between major tribal cult centres and church sites[36]. Some smaller churches were probably Christianized local pagan cult centres. Many of the attributes of local saints as reflected in the hagiography may be the attributes of the site itself or the well associated with it and in this way there would have been unconscious continuity with the pagan past[37]. The local saint and his relics was a concept which was easy for the pagan Irish to accept and understand.

In a tribal society the identity of the saint with the local community was intense. He was thought of as part of the family. Not all cults expanded, however. The churches dedicated to Abbán moccu Cormaic did not thrive. Abbán, as his name indicates, belonged to the Dál Cormaic, a powerful group in Leinster at the opening of the historical period. When they lost power to the Uí Dúnlainge dynasty their churches faded into the background. This was a pattern which repeats itself all over the country and to some extent accounts for the churches which were without patronage or even clergy in the seventh century as we have already seen in the writings of Tírechán.

After the great plague of 664 and the diseases and famines which recurred in the closing years of the seventh century and the beginning of the eighth there would appear to have been an increase in stress and disorder in society. This is reflected

---

32 *Byrne*, Kings and High-kings, p. 152.

33 *Bieler*, Patrician Texts, p. 190.

34 D. A. *Binchy*, Patrick and his biographers: ancient and modern, Stud. Hib. 2 (1962), p. 166.

35 J. *Vendryes*, A propos du verbe 'croire' et de la 'croyance', RC 44 (1927), p. 90—96.

36 K. *Hughes*, Early Christian Ireland: Introduction to the Sources, London 1972, p. 74f.

37 C. *Plummer*, Vitae Sanctorum Hiberniae, Oxford 1910, vol. I, p. CXXIX—CLXXXVIII.

in the amount of archival activity that took place. The collecting of law tracts, canons, genealogies, and annals would seem to fall within this period. Dynasties that were to remain on the scene until the twelfth century come to the surface in these years[38]. Relics assumed an added importance against this background of unrest.

About seventeen years before Adomnán wrote his 'Life' of Columba (ca. 692—697) there had been a great drought in the spring which threatened to ruin the recently planted seeds. The elders at Iona decided upon a plan to carry the white tunic of Columba and books in his own handwriting around the fields. They raised his tunic, the one he wore on his deathbed, three times in the air and shook it and opened his books and read them. Rain duly fell. 'Thus the commemoration of the name of one blessed man, made with his tunic and books, on that occasion brought saving and timely help to many districts and peoples'[39]. This circuit of relics to ward off natural disaster was a forerunner of the many relic circuits which took place throughout the eighth century.

The relics of Adomnán († 704) were brought to Ireland in 727 (AU) and his *lex* (protection of non-combatants in war) was renewed. The relics returned to Iona three years later. In 734 (AU) the *commotatio*[40] of the relics of Peter and Paul and Patrick took place to 'fulfill the law' (protection of clerics). Throughout the eighth century and into the ninth the circuits of many different saints became common. They often followed years of bad weather, diseases in men and cattle, famine, the burning of churches (presumably during raids to acquire food) and general disorder. The provincial kings were quick to act as protectors and guarantors of the relics as they were proclaimed throughout their kingdoms. This was particularly the case with the relics of Patrick[41].

Although a great deal of income came to the churches as a result of these circuits it would be wrong to regard them as taking place simply for the collection of revenue[42]. Indeed in the canon collection the section *De Martyribus* (quoting Augustine) gives as a reason for the translation of relics an increase in the evils in society[43]. Fines were levied for infringement of these laws, and from this it was

38 F. J. *Byrne*, Tribes and tribalism in early Ireland, Ériu 22 (1971), p. 153.

39 A. O. and M. O. *Anderson*, Adomnan's Life of Columba, London 1961, p. 450—452.

40 This word is not found in Latin dictionaries with the meaning of 'translation of holy bodies'. It is found in a commentary on Vergil, Aen. IV 301—302, by Servius Honoratus where it is used of the moving of the statues of the gods in pagan temples when they are opened for festivals; cf. G. *Thilo*, and H. *Hagen*, Servii Grammatici, Hildesheim 1961, vol. I, p. 517—518; P. *Jahn*, (ed.) Vergils Gedichte, Dublin/Zürich 1912 (1973), vol. III, p. 167 and notes 301—303. It was from such a source, if not exactly this particular commentary, that the Irish derived this usage. cf. also D. A. *Bullough*, Columba, Adomnan and Iona, SHR 44 (1965), p. 24—25.

41 Cf. AU s.a. 667, 726, 729, 733, 742, 743, 771, 773, 774, 775, 776, 779, 781, 782, 783, 784, 786, 787, 788, 789, 792, 793, 797, 798 etc.

42 *pace* F. *Ó Briain*, The hagiography of Leinster, in: J. *Ryan*, (ed.), Féilsgríbhinn Eoin Mhic Néill, Dublin 1940, p. 454—464.

43 *Wasserschleben*, Kanonensammlung, p. 206, Book XLIX, c. 8.

but a short step to the idea that the law was promulgated in order to demand tribute. A commentary on the secular law tracts dating to a later period mentions the 'wages of a reliquary': *Tuillem meinistri .i. log ar comairce do'n minn .i. imtuillit na minna bitt for aister .i. do dechmaduib 7 primittib 7 almsanaib.* 'The wages of a reliquary, i.e. pay for protection to the relic i.e. which is earned by the relics that are carried about i.e. of tithes and first-fruits and alms'[44]. It is the Latin word *lex* which is used in the Annals of Ulster until 782 when *cáin* appears for the first time. The vernacular term acquired the meaning of 'rent', 'tribute' as well as 'law', and it is possible that the mercenary attitude was beginning to appear by the late eighth century. It is certainly clear by the late tenth and eleventh centuries when the word *cúairt*, 'circuit' is used of specifically tribute collecting activity at a time when relics are being used in a similar fashion on the Continent[45].

Although the enshrining of relics may have been taking place from a relatively early period the first reference I have come across in the annals is in AU 800 for the *positio* 'placing' of the relics of Conlaed (bishop of Kildare) in a shrine of gold and silver. In the following year the relics of Ronan son of Berach (from Dromiskin, Co. Louth) were placed in an arc of gold and silver. These are likely to have been portable reliquaries made for taking on circuit.

The earliest non-portable type would appear to have been tent-shaped stone tombs with a hole at the gable end allowing the bones to be touched. They may have replaced wooden structures[46]. This activity might represent the second stage in the development of a site. Professor M. J. O'Kelly's excavations at Church Island indicated the replacement of a timber church by a stone one in the late seventh or early eighth century, and a similar sequence has been discovered on a number of other sites. At Reask a low stone wall was erected to separate the graveyard, oratory, shrine, and possibly abbot's house from the rest of the enclosure[47]. This reorganizing would appear to be reflected in the canon collection compiled in the early eighth century but containing earlier legislation, much of it probably seventh century. It is clear that there was concern over the violation of cemeteries and holy places. This is also reflected in a story in Adomnán's 'Life' of Columba[48]. Book XLV of the Collectio Canonum Hibernensis, *De Locis,* has two chapters, XXX, *De numero terminorum sancti loci* and XXXI, *De decreto sinodi Hibernensis in reliquiis violandis,* which attempt to provide a solution to this problem[49]. The solution was

44 R. *Atkinson,* Ancient Laws of Ireland, vol. V (1901), p. 266; CIH I, p. 40.

45 K. *Hughes,* The Church in early Irish society, London 1966, p. 151 and note 2; *Herrmann-Mascard,* Reliques, p. 296.

46 *Thomas,* Christian archaeology, c. 5.

47 T. *Fanning,* Excavation of an early Christian cemetery and settlement at Reask, county Kerry PRIA 81 (1981), p. 150.

48 *Anderson,* Columba, p. 248—250.

49 This book, XLV in *Sheehy's* forthcoming edition, = *Wasserschleben,* Hib. p. 175—176.

to divide cemeteries internally according to the ecclesiastical status of those buried in them on the one hand and to separate the cemetery with its oratory and shrine from the more profane parts of the site by establishing different areas of sanctuary with the holy of holies lying at the core. This allowed a site to remain sacred at its centre, while at the same time it could expand and acquire many urban characteristics[50].

We may infer that relics were part of a bishop's equipment in the eighth century from the list of articles given to Bishop Fíacc of Sléibte (Co. Carlow) by Patrick in the *Additamenta* in the Book of Armagh: *idon clocc 7 menstir 7 bachall 7 poolire*, 'i.e. a bell, a reliquary (means collectively the objects necessary for the cult, in particular sacred vessels, sometimes containing relics), a crozier and *pólaire* (a word of doubtful meaning, perhaps a satchel for carrying books or a portable altar stone)'[51].

From the ninth century onwards we enter the full flowering of the cult of relics in Ireland, having all the ingredients that are to be found on the Continent. There were shrines of various shapes suggested by the relics enclosed. Some of them may have been very elaborate such as the 'Model of Solomon's Temple' stolen from Clonmacnois in 1129. There were book-shrines, bell-shrines, croziers, arms, hands, St Patrick's jaw, his thumb, tooth, St Brigit's shoe, St Domongart's shoe, and the paten of St Tighernán[52].

There were famous collectors too. The earliest, albeit in a literary medium, was Óengus whose great work, *Félire Óengusso,* or Martyrology was compiled ca. 800[53]. This work and the notes added to it in the course of the centuries provide a treasure house of information on the relic cults. It is in these later notes that we learn of Onchú of Clúain Mór Maedóc (Clonmore, Co. Carlow); a collector so avid that he would not remain in a church which refused to give him some of her relics, and indeed anyone with a reputation for sanctity was in danger of losing a limb to him while still alive[54]. Adomnán, too, was famous as a collector. The eleventh or twelfth century text 'The Reliquary of Adomnán'[55] gives an interesting list: a gospel book, a piece of Mary's clothing, a cloth with Christ's blood on it, a piece of the tree on which Paul was killed, a piece of the tree on which Christ was crucified, the girdle of Paul, the cloak of Martin, a tooth of Patrick, a tooth of Declan, some of the Virgin Mary's hair, St Brigit's hairshirt, Senach's cloak, a stone from Molua's island, a rib from Fínán Camm's body, the mantle of Énda of Aran,

50 C. *Doherty,* Exchange and trade in early medieval Ireland, JRSAI 110 (1980), p. 81f.

51 *Bieler,* Patrician Texts, p. 176.

52 H. S. *Crawford,* A descriptive list of Irish shrines and reliquaries, JRSAI 53 (1923), p. 74—93, 151—176; C. *Bourke,* Early Irish hand-bells, JRSAI 110 (1980), p. 52—66.

53 W. *Stokes,* Félire Óengusso, HBS 29, 1905.

54 Ibid., p. 70.

55 L. *Gwynn,* The reliquary of Adomnán, Arch. Hib. 4 (1915), p. 199—214. See now James *Carney's* edition in Celtica 15 (1983), p. 25—41, who dates the poem to the late seventh century.

the vestment[56] of St Donnán, the shoulder-blade of Colmán mac Crimthain, Columba's tunic, a hymn of Brendan, the skulls of Mochuda, Mochóe and Mocháemóg, Cainnech's cloak, and the cloth that Bairre's body had been wrapped in for seven years. Some of the more exotic of these relics had already arrived in Ireland by the late ninth century according to the *Vita Tripartita* of St Patrick.

According to the text Patrick was taken by an angel to Waterford harbour to await a ship from *Burdigala* (Bordeaux) to take him to Rome. Once there the typical Irish theft took place — the inhabitants of Rome fell into a sleep while Patrick gathered what he wished of relics. He returned with 365 relics together with the relics of Paul and Peter and Laurence and Stephen and many others including a sheet with Christ's blood on it and some of the Virgin Mary's hair. These Patrick left in Armagh[57].

It is clear that Armagh was taking no chances; she had an answer for each day of the year. The word *burdgal* is of interest here. This word and the word *Rúam* (Rome) were both used by Óengus writing about the year 800. One of the main meanings of *rúam* was in the sense of cemetery. Places such as Glendalough are *rúama* of the Western world. In hagiography written between the tenth and the twelfth centuries 'the soil of Rome' is a common motif. Saints bring back cartloads of soil which they sprinkle over their cemeteries. In this way a church can attract burial in the soil of Rome, which ought to be of help on the last day. Richard Warner has suggested that the finds of sherds of *terra sigillata* pottery on various sites may reflect this practice[58].

The word *burdgal* is a borrowing of *Burdigala* with a range of meaning: 'famous resort, gathering, assembly, meeting place, goal of pilgrimage'. It is a placename in a few places in Ireland and has been connected with the wine trade. It made a considerable impact on the minds of the Irish, not least because it was probably the major port for the relic trade[59].

In the hagiography of the tenth to twelfth centuries it is the economic aspect of relics that is to the fore. The great circuits of the eighth century would appear to have been institutionalized. Armagh, for example, was particularly successful in this matter. She had stewards in churches in various parts of the country who looked after the collection of tribute in each area. There was a steward in Meath, and the church of Ard Patrick in Limerick was a great collecting point for the tribute of Munster. The insignia of the saint, his bells, books, and croziers were used to demand tribute. The virtues of each relic were extolled and the power of each was described by appeal to one extravagant miracle after the other. Some of

56 I wish to thank Dr Próinséas Ní Chatháin for making this text known to me and also for translating *almu*, a word which puzzled Gwynn.

57 *Mulchrone*, BP, p. 141—142 = *Stokes*, Vita Tripartita. Vol. I, p. 238—240.

58 R. B. *Warner*, Some observations on the context and importation of exotic material in Ireland, from the first century BC to the second century AD, PRIA 76 (1976), p. 285—288.

59 *Doherty*, Exchange and trade, p. 77—78.

these miracles, such as the removal of unwanted pregnancy, seem rather unsavoury to say the least. Relics were used for the swearing of oaths. It is for this reason that the word for the insignia in Irish, *mind,* 'a crown, diadem, venerated object' came to mean oath. Kings were encouraged or rather threatened as much as anyone else for not protecting the clergy or for interfering with Church property. In return for services at the inauguration ceremonies great dues were demanded[60].

In the 'Lives' of the twelfth century we can see that federations of monasteries had agreements whereby the clergy of one mother-house could go on a great collecting circuit every so many years in the territory of the other. This arrangement probably evolved as a means of reducing friction between churches in the eighth century and later[61]. It was part of an elaborate system of exchange or reciprocity. One could list many more examples of the mercenary aspect, but perhaps something should be said on the credit side. The Church redistributed a great deal of its tribute in the form of alms — it looked after the poor, the destitute, and the lepers, it supported a literate elite and schools of craftsmen and students, and it lavished much of its wealth on buildings, monuments and shrines. If we wish to see the religious life of the Church in these later centuries we have to look at literature other than the hagiographical documents, which are to a large extent a reflection of the economic structure of the institution.

The Church's role as peacemaker is very much in evidence from the late tenth century onwards[62]. This was related to the Peace of God movement on the Continent. The relics were of major importance in establishing a truce between warring factions. Armagh was to the fore in this area. Truces were often broken and relics frequently violated, but without such restraints the situation would probably have been much worse.

Relics for both the Church and the kings were on two different levels. There were the relics of the local saints on the one hand, and the relics of the apostles, martyrs, Christ and Mary on the other. Any church that wished to rise above merely local significance, or even compete for burial rights, had to have at least the 'soil of Rome'. A major church such as Armagh needed as many important relics as possible to maintain her respect as the chief church in Ireland. This was not lost on those provincial kings who protected Armagh's interests. Brian Bóruma in 1005 showed he was aware of the significance of Armagh's position by having his legend, *Brian imperator Scotorum,* inscribed in the Book of Armagh, by then one of

---

60 This information is to be found scattered through the great collections of 'Lives' of the saints. For a bibliography cf. D. *Ó Corráin,* A hand-list of publications on early Irish history, Historical Studies 10 (1978), § 4 p. 179—183.

61 C. *Doherty,* Some aspects of hagiography as a source for Irish economic history, Peritia 1 (1982) p. 300—328.

62 D. *Ó Corráin,* Nationality and kingship in pre-Norman Ireland, in: T. W. *Moody,* ed., Nationality and the pursuit of national Independence, Historical Studies 11, Belfast 1978, p. 23 and note 91.

the church's major relics[63]. When he was killed in the battle of Clontarf he was buried in the *mausoleum regum* in the city[64]. Armagh was aware of the need to attract royal support, and the first reference to burial in the royal cemetery there, *in cimeterio regum,* is AU 935.

Major kings, therefore, had intense loyalty to local churches which they exploited economically, and acted violently towards the churches of their opponents, but at the same time they were usually very careful of the rights of Armagh. By the twelfth century those kings whose ambitions embraced the whole country are at the forefront of the reform of the Church. They support the international orders and the bishops. Kingship is also taking on a European dimension. From seventh century Spain there survives a scenario which may help to throw light on developments in twelfth century Ireland: 'This development of Toledo into the ceremonial centre of the Visigothic kingdom during the last part of the seventh century can clearly be seen from other sources too. Many of the actions of the king were coming increasingly to be put into a liturgical context. Some of the parts of what we may call this late seventh-century royal liturgy have fortunately survived. The most complete of these are the liturgical ceremonies created to mark the departure of the king on a military expedition: the *Ordo Quando Rex Cum Exercitu Ad Proelium Egreditur.* These ceremonies are specifically stated in the text to take place in the church of Ss Peter and Paul, wherein which, of course Wamba was anointed, as too will the liturgy to mark the return of the king and of his army. In the course of the service the king receives the golden cross, containing a fragment of the True Cross, that will be borne before him throughout the expedition'[65].

In ca. 1123 one of the most powerful kings in Ireland, Toirrdelbach Ua Conchobair, had a European-style processional cross made into which was placed a fragment of the True Cross. He created a new capital at Tuam and built a cathedral there. The twelfth-century Corpus Christi Missal contains a similar liturgy of kingship: *Ut regem hibernensium et exercitum eius conservare digneris: ut eis vitam et sanitatem atque victoriam dones.* There are prayers *Pro Rege.* Although this liturgy goes back to a much earlier period, its inclusion in the missal suggests that it was in current use. The missal has not been given a firm location, but it is tempting to envisage the use of such a liturgy by Ua Conchobair in his new cathedral in Tuam in the presence of the True Cross[66].

63 E. J. *Gwynn,* ed., Book of Armagh. The Patrician documents, Dublin 1937, p. 15 v.

64 *Byrne,* Kings and High-kings, p. 256.

65 P. *Sawyer,* and I. N. *Wood,* ed., Early medieval kingship, Leeds 1977, p. 46.

66 Ó *Corráin,* Nationality and kingship, p. 30; J. T. *Gilbert,* Facsimilies of National Manuscripts of Ireland, London 1878, part II, p. XXV.

Acknowledgements: I wish to thank Dr Próinséas Ní Chatháin for reading this paper and suggesting a number of improvements.

II

Archäologie und Kunst
Archaeology and Art

The layout of Irish early Christian monasteries

By
Michael Herity

In an issue of the *Irish University Review* dedicated to the poet Richard Murphy, I described the ruined remains of the early Christian site on his *Ard Oileán*, High Island, Co. Galway, and published a reconstructed plan (1977, 55—61, fig. 2), noting that three elements, a cross-slab, saint's tomb and rectangular oratory, are located at the focus of this simple hermitage. In this it followed a pattern noted by Dr Françoise Henry (1957, 154—56), who pointed out that in the Iveragh peninsula of Kerry the oratory and its 'annexes' are whenever possible sited on a raised terrace or at least separated from the rest of the enclosure by a wall or a fence of slabs. She described these annexes of the oratory as 'a slab or a shrine-shaped tomb or some other kind of slab-tomb', suggesting an analogy with the *martyria* of the first Christian centuries, 'those small funerary chapels erected over the tomb of a martyr and later of some revered dead'.

Just as these elements, cross-slab, saint's tomb and oratory, are found at the focus of western foundations, I suggested that their equivalents are often found close together, usually in a more developed form, at the centre of the larger monasteries of the midlands and east, like Clonmacnois (1977, 66). From this it appears 'that the conjunction of oratory, cross-slab and founder's tomb was once common throughout the country, east and west, developing later into something more elaborate in the richer east, retaining its primitive cast in the ascetic and conservative west' (1977, 66—68). The inquiry is continued in this paper, towards appreciating and understanding the canons influencing the layout of early Christian monasteries in Ireland.

At first sight, plans may appear confused because of the proliferation of later medieval churches and more recent burials and grave-slabs. Perhaps for this reason the question has received little attention; though Macalister published plans of Clonmacnois (1909, frontispiece) and Monasterboice (1946, 18) he gave as his opinion: 'The most conspicuous buildings ... of which any relics remain, are the churches ... Of these there were several, scattered over the area of the monastic enclosure. The monastic settlements at Clonmacnois and at Glendalough have each a number of small churches, obviously of very different dates and *not designed to carry out any uniform symbolic or other scheme'* (1946, 16, italics mine).

Dr Henry, who presented plans of Nendrum, Duvillaun, Loher, Armagh, Glendalough, Dublin, Clonmacnois and Inishcealtra (1965, 52, 78; 1967, figs. 2—5; 1970, 37, 43) gave a rather similar opinion, perhaps surprisingly, in view of the insight quoted above: 'within the enclosure of the monastery, all sorts of buildings were scattered, *probably without much order*, one or two stone churches being surrounded by wooden buildings of various shapes' (1965, 91; italics mine).

Examination of a number of sites in the west suggests that the three focal monuments and the burials are arranged in a recurring standard plan somewhat apart from the domestic buildings of the hermitage or monastery.

The remains of the early Christian hermitage of Killabuonia (fig. 1b) are sited on a series of south-facing terraces about 300 feet above sea-level at the landward end of a valley opening to the Atlantic at St Finan's Bay, opposite *Sceilg Mhichíl* at the west end of the Iveragh peninsula in Kerry (Henry 1957, 102, fig. 18). On an upper terrace at the focus is the rectangular boat-shaped oratory, its doorway facing west into an open space. On the opposite, north-west side of this open area, 11 m away, is a circular *clochán* (stone-built beehive hut), its doorway facing that of the oratory. On the next terrace down, 7.6 m south-west of the oratory, is another *clochán*, its doorway opening beside the high retaining wall of the upper terrace; 6.4 m east of it is the short stone stairway leading up to the open area in front of the oratory. In line with the west face of the oratory and south of it, to the right as one ascends the steps, are a cross-inscribed slab facing west and a slab-tomb with a circular hole in its triangular west gable. The slab-tomb, traditionally regarded as that of the founder saint, appears to be regarded as a reliquary by pilgrims, who could see or touch the bones within through the hole in the west gable (Henry 1957, 101—04).

At the main hermitage on the island of *Sceilg Mhichíl* (fig. 1d), the buildings are also on a series of terraces which run north-east and south-west, and the ancient enclosure had a focus similar to that of Killabuonia (de Paor 1955; Henry 1957, 121—27). Towards the east end of the main terrace is the principal ancient oratory, its tiny east light looking over the sea to the mainland. On the north side of the oratory is a platform with two upright cross-slabs; on its south side are two further cross-slabs. At the east side is the walled platform of the 'Monks' Grave-yard', with several simple cross-slabs standing erect on it. The north platform may also mark early graves. Set into the terrace to the north and running west from the north side of the oratory are five *clocháns*, apparently the cells of the monks, those at the west and east ends a little apart from the others and somewhat larger than them. A space 10.7 m long between the door of the most westerly *clochán* and the west door of the oratory is now largely occupied by the much later St Michael's Church but can be presumed to be originally an open space analogous to that of Killabuonia.

One of the few monastic sites to be excavated in modern times is the enclosure at Reask on the Dingle peninsula investigated by Fanning (1981). A stone oratory with associated cross-slabs was found at the east side of the enclosure (fig. 2b). Here was the burial area of the monastery, as at *Sceilg Mhichíl*, there being 42 lintel-graves on a rough north-south line through the oratory, some of them earlier than the oratory itself. A slab-shrine sited north-west of the doorway of the ora-tory, built presumably to house an important early burial, was contemporary with some of these lintel-graves. Two postholes immediately to the south of this and in line east and west may have been part of an original wooden oratory. Reask may thus document a development in which the presumed earliest wooden oratory is replaced by a stone-built one near the same site. A slab-shrine is among the earliest monuments in the immediate area and some of the cross-slabs found in this part of the enclosure may also belong to the earliest discernible phases of life in this monastery, which are dated to the seventh century at latest by the occurrence of imported Bii ware (Fanning 1981, 155). The oratory and almost all of the burials were separated from the rest of the monastic enclosure by a wall running a serpentine course roughly north-east to south-west across the enclosure. In the western sector were the living-quarters, two double *clocháns* and a third single one. The general resemblance to the apposition of oratory and burials, on the one hand, and domestic buildings on the other, at *Sceilg Mhichíl* and Killabuonia, is striking.

At Labbamolaga, near Mitchelstown Co. Cork, a similar group was recorded in 1845 by G. V. du Noyer and later published by Lord Dunraven (RIA MS 12 N 22, 1875, Vol. I, 26—36). The site gets its name from the Irish *Leaba Molaga* (Molaga's tomb, literally bed), which was in the south side of a small rectangular building with antae measuring 4 by 3 m externally, apparently a reliquary building of developed form (fig. 1a). North of this was a larger rectangular church with engaged pilasters on the façade and measuring 11.6 by 7.3 m; this had originally had a small stone finial 25 cm across. Between the two buildings and standing at the east end was a cross-slab with a cross-in-circle in relief on the west face and an incised Greek cross on the east. Both church and reliquary appear to be of late date, perhaps of the twelfth century, but they probably mark the position of an earlier group of simpler form.

Saint's tomb, church and cross-slabs are present in a similar developed form at St Molaise's foundation on Inishmurray island (fig. 2a), off the Sligo coast (Wakeman 1893). The principal church, *Teampall Molaise, Teampall Mór* or *Teampall na bhFear* stands apart towards the east end of the enclosure. Three cross-slabs stand in line with its west façade, two on the north side, one on the south. The open space surrounding the church was until the last century the burial-place of the men (Wakeman 1893, 50). Within this part of the enclosure and near the north wall is the tiny *Teach Molaise* (Molaise's House), measuring only 2.7 by 2.4 m internally, with a bench of solid masonry along the south wall, as at Labbamolaga, which is reputedly the burial-place of Molaise, the founder (1893, 42). As at Reask the area surrounding the principal church is separated from the rest of the monastic enclosure by a stone wall, beyond which is the so-called 'school house', the only circular *clochán* now visible within the enclosure. In front of the west façade of *Teampall Mór*, the principal church, is the only open space of any size in the whole complex. This arrangement of living quarters in the western sector beyond an open space and possibly an internal division in the enclosure appears also at Illaunloghan and Loher in Kerry (Henry 1957, figs. 16, 25) and at *Ard Oileán* (Herity 1977, fig. 2).

St Ciaran's foundation at Clonmacnois on the Shannon has a dispersed arrangement not unlike that of Inishmurray on the remains of a series of east-west terraces near the west end of the present assemblage of monastic buildings (fig. 2c). At the focus is the cathedral, called the *Daimhliag Mór* (Great Stone Church) which can be assumed to be on or near the original site of the principal church.

About 12 m south and 4 m east of its present façade stands the South Cross, made about 800, the only figured scene on its shaft or arms a Crucifixion on the west face. The same distance north, and similarly placed east of the façade of the church, is the so-called North Cross, a decorated pillar dating to roughly the same time, the east face of which is plain. One can envisage the west façade of the *Daimhliag* or its predecessor, about 800, as close to the line of these two decorated pillars which extended its façade by having their principal decorated faces looking on to an open space to the west; records tell of its erection and possible enlargement early in the tenth century (Henry 1980, 37, 45).

These monuments may have replaced earlier cross-slabs of the western type, like those at Inishmurray. Alternatively, new canons of siting deriving from a separate High Cross tradition may have influenced their siting. The eighth-century Ahenny High Crosses, which appear to be typologically the earliest Irish developments of the type independent in form of the stone cross-slab tradition, are sited close together north and south with their principal faces east and west; the base of a third cross to the east forms a triangle with them.

North-east of the *Daimhliag Mór* is a small stone building 3.8 by 2.45 m called *Teampall Chiaráin*, traditionally the burial-place of the founder (Macalister 1909, 141). In 1684, Bishop Dopping recorded that the saint's hand — it may have been enshrined — was kept here (O'Donovan 1857, 447) and early in the nineteenth century the twelfth-century crozier of the abbots was found here with a chalice and a wine vessel, a rosary of brass wire and a hollow brass ball (Macalister 1909, 155). This may be the *Teampall Bearnáin Chiaráin* mentioned in the Annals of Tigernach (s. a. 1077); if so, the word *Bearnán* may suggest that it housed a bell-shrine. It appears to be both saint's tomb and reliquary.

The Round Tower called O'Rourke's tower is apparently tenth century in date and stands at the edge of the terrace 30 m north-west of the west doorway of the *Daimhliag Mór*, its doorway facing that of the church. Its siting gives some idea of the extent of the open space in front of the *Daimhliag* in the tenth century.

The Cross of the Scriptures, a new and politically important development of the early tenth century (Henry 1980; Ó Murchadha 1980), with scripture panels on all four faces, was erected on a prominent position in this open space 12.5 m from the west façade. It marks a fundamental change in that it is to be viewed from all sides as a separate monument surrounded by space, rather than as part of a façade fronting an open area, as most crosses and cross-slabs up to this period appear to have been conceived. Its siting, form and figured scenes underline and confirm the existence of the area surrounding it as a public open space shortly after the year 900. (Pl. 1)

The open space at the west façade of the oratory or principal church of the early

108

Irish monastery is so widespread that it seems to have been established at an early stage, if not with the coming of Christianity. It appears to have been present at Reask (Fanning 1981, 155) about the seventh century, possibly even at the foundation some centuries earlier, and to have been an established feature of Clonmacnois by the time the North and South Crosses were erected, shortly after 800. Adomnán, writing his Life of Colum Cille a little before 700, describes a small open area called the *plateola* in the monastery in Iona within which the monks could walk (Anderson and Anderson 1961, 114). It was probably on ground that the monks had to cross to reach the church from their sleepinghouses (1961, 114, 528–9), so a layout like those of *Ard Oileán*, Inishmurray and Reask is probable.

A rather larger open space is implied by a passage in the same Life describing the visit of Colum Cille to the monastery of Conall, bishop of Cul-raithin (Coleraine), on his return from the Convention of Druimmcete near Limavady in Derry about 575. Conall had collected from the people of the plain of Eilne a large number of gifts, which were presented to Columba for benediction, laid out 'in the courtyard of the monastery' *(in platea monasterii strata)*. The story suggests a large area, possibly paved, which may be equated with the open area recognised above (Anderson and Anderson 1961, 114, f. 51a). Another passage relates how the brethren of Clonmacnois, hearing that he was near the monastery on his way from Durrow to visit, came from the fields on every side and joined those inside. They then passed outside the boundary of their monastery, accompanied by their abbot Alither, and meeting the saint led him with honour to the church on an improvised litter (Anderson and Anderson 1961, 215/6). This story suggests a space within the monastery large enough for the brethren to congregate in and possibly a processional way in front of the principal church, and thus accords with the archaeological evidence.

It seems likely that the focal monuments, oratory or principal church, cross-slab or High Cross, and saint's tomb, slab-shrine, reliquary or *martyrium* originally stood close to one another at the east side of this open space. Explanation in ritual terms is to be found in a passage in Bede's prose Life of St Cuthbert. Shortly before his death in 687, Cuthbert retired to a hermitage on the island of Farne, asking his friend Herefrid to bury him 'in this dwelling near my oratory towards the south, on the eastern side of the holy cross which I have erected there', wrapping him in a cloth and placing him in a sarcophagus provided by Abbot Cudda (Colgrave 1969, 273). Incidentally, the guesthouse of this hermitage was at the perimeter, as Cuthbert is described as coming from the inner buildings of the monastery to the guest-chamber (Cramp 1980, 11).

The hypothesis developed here can explain the layout of some Irish monasteries and the disposition of the principal buildings and monuments and the *platea* or *plateola* as well as the living-quarters within it. It may be useful in indicating the siting of buildings which are to be expected on comparative or historical grounds but which are no longer visible on the ground.

The ecclesiastical remains in the town of *Ceannanas Mór*, Kells, Co. Meath (fig.

3b), can be interpreted on the model of those of Clonmacnois. In the open space opposite the west doorway of the present church stands the Broken Cross, originally about 6 m high, a developed tenth-century Scripture Cross of the same family as the Cross of the Scriptures which is similarly sited at Clonmacnois. To the south, 25 m away, is the Round Tower, its doorway facing across the open space to the west façade of the church; beside it is the Cross of Patrick and Columba, related in style and iconography to Iona and Northumbria and dated shortly after 800 (Henry 1965, 138).

North-west of the west façade of the church, 90 m away, is St Columb's House, in its present form a stone-roofed building probably of the twelfth century (Leask 1955, Vol 1, 33—4). The name, as at Inishmurray, seems to imply the tomb and/or reliquary of the founder saint. All these sites are concentrated near the top of a low rise and the street-pattern between Carrick St. and Cannon St. to the north and south, and the Fair Green and Church St. on the west and east, suggests that they follow the original curvilinear outline of the monastic *vallum* which may have been over 300 m across (Henry 1967, 43). It was probably a considerable monastic town like Armagh. On the lower ground at the east end of Market St., immediately east of this street pattern, stands the Market Cross, possibly on the site of a market already established before the year 1000 which would have required a new open space just outside the confines of the monastery.

The remains at Armagh (fig. 3a) can be reconstructed with the aid of a plan made by Bartlett shortly after 1600 and from other sources (Henry 1967, 39—43, fig. 2). Near the flat-topped rise on which the main monastery stood was the oldest foundation of St Patrick, called *Na Ferta* ([Church of] the Relics). Within the rath, the enclosure on the rise, 240 m across, stood the *Daimhliag*, mentioned in the Annals before 800. Two other buildings, the *Sabhall* and the *Toi*, stood on the south side, the *Toi* parallel to the nave of the latest church and touching the south transept; apparently it had originally been a separate building. These two buildings were built of stone in 1020, according to the Annals. Over from the west door of the church to the northwest was the abbot's house, surrounded by thatched huts in 1600 (Henry 1967, 41). This may have been close to the original living-quarters of the monastery; in this general area, on comparative grounds, we should expect to find the Round Tower, mentioned in the same annalistic entries for 1020: Ard Macha was all burned, the great *Daimhliac* with its roof of lead, and the *Cloictech* with its bells ... (AU s. a. 1020).

Henry has fully outlined the evidence for the monastic town divided in *Trians* (thirds), estimated its population at up to 4000 in the mid-ninth century and referred to the High Cross at the gate of the rath on the west side, which was placed inside the cathedral in 1819 (1967, 42). This cross is similar to the Broken Cross at Kells. As it stood just outside the enclosure in a small open space between two of the *Trians* of the town, at the head of what is now Market St., it may have been a market cross, probably confirming the existence of a market here as at Kells (Doherty 1980, 83).

At Slane in Meath, the gable ends of what appears to be a slab-shrine stand east and west, 20 m south of the oldest part of the late medieval ecclesiastical buildings and opposite its west end. Wilde has published a sketch dating to 1849 and recorded that each corpse was laid beside this shrine for a short time on the way to its burial-place (1949, 158—9). If the open space at Slane was west of shrine and church, then in the arc west of this space would have stood the Round Tower recorded in the Annals of Ulster (s. a. 949, *recte* 950): the *cloictech* was burnt by the Vikings and the crozier of St Erc, the founder, and 'a bell that was the best of bells' were destroyed on it. (A similar monument at Kilranelagh in Wicklow, called the Gates of Heaven, may also be part of a slab-shrine; the coffins of all those buried in the graveyard were carried through it [Drury 1903, 296]).

The remains of St Kevin's monastery at Glendalough in Wicklow (fig. 2d) are in two main groups, an earlier near the Upper Lake, including the church of Reefert *(Rígferta)*, and a later on a series of terraces running east and west beside the present cathedral (Leask n. d.; Henry 1967, 45, figs. 5, 6).

South of the west façade of the cathedral *(Daimhliag)* is a plain granite High Cross. To the north-west of this façade, 15 m away, is the Round Tower, its doorway facing across the open space to the cathedral. Within a small rectangular burial enclosure on a lower terrace 27 m to the south-west is a tiny building called the Priests' House, traditionally the burial-place of some of the clergy of the district and possibly built to house some monastic relics (Leask n. d., 18); over the doorway in the south wall is a tympanum with a central, seated figure between two others who hold a crozier and a bell respectively, possibly a clue to its original contents (Petrie 1845, 264; Henry 1970, 183). An enigmatic feature is a blind Romanesque arch which dominates the outer face of its east wall framing a single tall window (Leask 1955, 160). If the building was a reliquary, perhaps even for the bones of St Kevin, the founder, can it be that this façade, oriented as it is towards the open space between it and the High Cross, was ornamented because pilgrims in the twelfth century were allowed to view or touch the monastic relics here, congregating at a gable wall decorated in the contemporary fashion, yet analogous to the simple west gable of the slab-shrine at Killabuonia?

In the twelfth century Ireland was opened to a stream of new continental influences which transformed the organisation of the Irish Church and the art and architecture of Irish monasteries (Henry 1970, *passim*). New housings for important relics were constructed under the patronage of new rulers including the O'Connors of Connacht, like the Cross of Cong and the Crozier of the abbots of Clonmacnois. Cormac MacCarthaigh's chapel on the rock of Cashel in the fashionable Romanesque style was begun in 1127 and finished in 1134; a doorway in this style was inserted into the *Daimhliag* of Clonmacnois; a completely new tower with elegant string-courses was built at Ardmore in Waterford. Stone-built reliquaries like those of Clones, Co. Monaghan, and Glendalough were refurbished or replaced by buildings in the new style. High crosses were made according to new canons and erected within the monastic enclosures at Drumcliff, Boho, Kilfenora,

Dysert O'Dea, Killaloe, Roscrea, Glendalough and Cashel; one was erected at the market-place of the O'Connor capital at Tuam, Co. Galway.

New churches, each with a diminutive round tower belfry, an adoption of a continental Romanesque feature, were added at the edges of the monastic enclosures at Temple Finghin, Clonmacnois, and St Kevin's Kitchen, Glendalough. Further churches were added at the perimeter of Glendalough: St Mary's and Trinity; St Saviour's, with its elaborate late decoration, at a new site east of the main enclosure. At Clonmacnois, stone churches began to be added, possibly under the stimulus of a growing pilgrimage traffic, in the twelfth century by local patrons, first Temple Dowling, Temple Uí Ceallaigh and possibly Temple Conor, disposed on the north, east and south sides of the *Daimhliag* but avoiding the open space at its west side.

In the early hermitages, the *plateola* or central open space appears to have had the special status of a claustral area private to the hermits themselves. This is implied in the story of Herefrid's visit to Cuthbert on Farne, who gave the customary signal to warn his close friend Cuthbert inside the hermitage that he had arrived. When the monastery grew bigger and the open space was no longer a diminutive *plateola*, the public apparently had access to it, as is implied in Adomnán's story about the gifts laid out in the courtyard of Conall's monastery near Coleraine. This is suggested also by the public nature of the Cross of the Scriptures and its inscription at Clonmacnois.

In 1142, the rectilinear cloister ultimately of Roman derivation was introduced by the Cistercians to Mellifont beside Monasterboice, implying a return to the kind of enclosed cloister arrangement documented at *Sceilg Mhichíl*, Killabuonia and *Ard Oileán*, though now on a much more organised and grander foreign scale. These Cistercians also built larger churches than the Irish had so far been in the habit of building. When large late medieval churches intruded into the old monasteries, as at Cashel and Ardmore, Waterford, the old native canons of layout were apparently abandoned.

References

Anderson, A. O.		
and M. O	1961	Adomnan's Life of Columba. London
AFM		Annals of the Kingdom of Ireland by the Four Masters
AU		Annals of Ulster
Colgrave, B., ed.	1969	Two Lives of Cuthbert. Cambridge 1939, reprinted New York
Cramp, R.	1980	The Background to St Cuthbert's Life. Durham Cathedral Lecture. Durham
de Paor, L.	1955	A Survey of Sceilg Mhichíl, JRSAI 85, p. 174—187
Doherty, C.	1980	Exchange and Trade in Early Medieval Ireland, JRSAI 110, p. 67—89

Drury, E.	1903	The Gates of Heaven, in: Preservation of the Memorials of the Dead, Ireland 5, 296
Dunraven, Lord	1875	Notes on Irish Architecture, 2 vols. London
Fanning, T.	1981	Excavation of an Early Christian Cemetery and Settlement at Reask, County Kerry, PRIA 81 C 3, p. 67—172
Henry, F.	1957	Early Monasteries, Beehive Huts, and Dry-stone Houses in the Neighbourhood of Caherciveen and Waterville (Co. Kerry), PRIA 58 C 3, p. 45—166.
Henry, F.	1965	Irish Art in the Early Christian Period (to 800 A. D.). London
Henry, F.	1967	Irish Art during the Viking Invasions (800—1020 A. D.). London
Henry, F.	1970	Irish Art in the Romanesque Period (1020—1170 A. D.). London
Henry, F.	1980	Around an Inscription: The Cross of the Scriptures at Clonmacnois, JRSAI 110, p. 36—46
Herity, M.	1977	The High Island Hermitage, Irish University Review 7 (Spring), p. 52—69
Leask, H. G.	1955	Irish Churches and Monastic Buildings, vol. 1, Dundalk
Leask, H. G.	n. d.	Glendalough, Co. Wicklow. Official Historical and Descriptive Guide. Dublin
Macalister, R.A.S.	1909	The Memorial Slabs of Clonmacnois, King's County. Dublin
Macalister, R.A.S.	1946	Monasterboice, Co. Louth. Dundalk
O'Donovan, J.	1857	The Registry of Clonmacnois; with Notes and Introductory Remarks, JRSAI 4, p. 444—60
Ó Murchadha, D.	1980	Rubbings taken of the Cross of the Scriptures at Clonmacnois, JRSAI 110, p. 47—51
Petrie, G.	1845	The Ecclesiastical Architecture of Ireland. Dublin
Royal Irish Academy MS 12N22		
Wakeman, W. F.	1875	On the Ecclesiastical Antiquities of Cluain-Eois, now Clones, County of Monaghan, JRSAI 13, p. 327—40
Wakeman, W. F.	1893	A Survey of the Antiquarian Remains on the Island of Inishmurray. Dublin, London, Edinburgh
Wilde, W.	1949	The Beauties of the Boyne and its Tributary the Blackwater. Dublin 1849, reprint Dublin

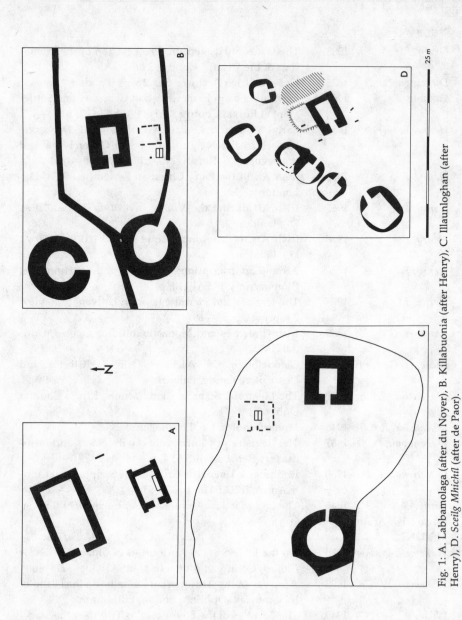

Fig. 1: A. Labbamolaga (after du Noyer). B. Killabuonia (after Henry). C. Illaunloghan (after Henry). D. *Sceilg Mhichíl* (after de Paor).

114

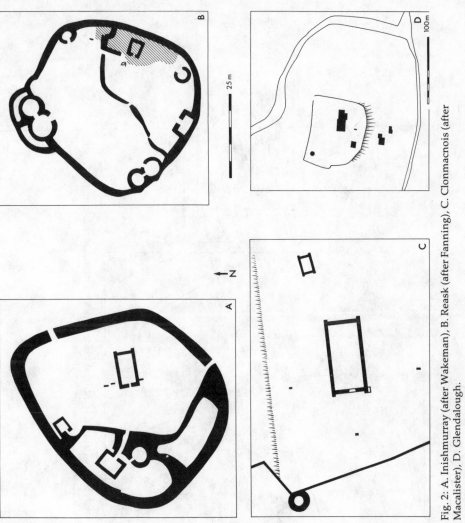

Fig. 2: A. Inishmurray (after Wakeman), B. Reask (after Fanning), C. Clonmacnois (after Macalister), D. Glendalough.

115

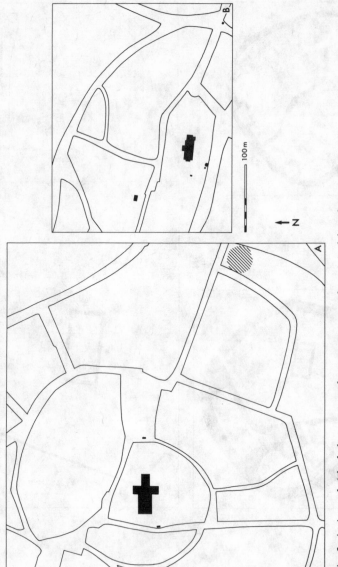

Fig. 3: A. Armagh (shaded area at south-east represents the original foundation, *Na Ferta*), B. Kells, with the Market Cross near the South-east.

100 m

N ←

116

The study of early Irish churches

By
Ann Hamlin

Our knowledge of early Irish churches is still very far from complete. The rich written sources have not been sufficiently exploited, the surviving stone churches are difficult to date, and few early churches have yet been excavated. This international colloquium, with its wide range of specialist fields, is exactly the kind of interdisciplinary forum from which future research could grow. Rather than attempting any overall coverage of the subject I shall concentrate on sources and methodology, surveying the ways in which the study of early Irish churches has been treated and suggesting some directions for future work[1].

Written Sources

Much of what we do know comes from written sources and I begin by outlining briefly the range of this knowledge. At a very simple level we learn from the earliest sources that there *were* churches. The earliest canons, for example, regulated the consecration of churches[2]. In the laws distinctions were carefully made between different kinds or grades of churches, distinguished by different words[3]. The meanings of the words are not always well understood, but they must indicate differences, and these may have been reflected in the buildings themselves. The Rule of Patrick refers to 'any church in which there is an ordained man of the small churches of the tribe apart from the great churches'[4]. There are indications that certain churches were reserved for the use of particular groups. At Armagh the *Liber Angeli* tells us that bishops, priests and anchorites worshipped in the south church, and 'virgins, penitents and those serving the church in legitimate matrimony' in the north church[5].

We hear from many different sources of the kinds of materials from which churches were built. Different rates of pay are laid down in the laws for builders of

---

1 When I gave my paper in Dublin neither I nor the colloquium organisers knew that Dr Peter Harbison had submitted a paper on the same topic for publication in the Proceedings of the previous colloquium. This has appeared as Early Irish Churches in Die Iren und Europa im früheren Mittelalter, ed. H. *Löwe*, Stuttgart 1982, p. 618—629. I have not retraced the ground covered there so the two papers are to some extent complementary.

2 L. *Bieler*, The Works of St Patrick, London 1953, p. 50—54.

3 ALI Vol. 3, especially p. 65—79.

4 J. G. *O'Keeffe*, ed., Ériu 1 (1904), p. 223.

5 K. *Hughes*, CEIS (1966), p. 277.

timber and stone churches[6]. Particularly valuable in the annals is the distinction drawn between the *dairthech* (literally 'oak-house', meaning wooden church) and the *damliac* (stone church): wooden churches were blown away in the great storm of 892, but the church burned at Ardstraw in 1099 was of stone[7]. There are references in saints' Lives to churches built of smooth planks, wattles, and occasionally mud or clay. Tírechán's account of St Patrick's work twice specifies a church built of earth. In one case Patrick *fecit ibi aeclessiam terrenam de humo quadratam quia non prope erat silua*, so clearly wood was considered the usual material[8]. Monenna's church at Killevy was built *tabulis dedolatis iuxta morem Scotticarum gentium*, and Samthann sent carpenters to a nearby wood *oratorium de lignis levigatis construere volens*[9]. Mochaoi of Nendrum began his long sleep of 150 years while collecting wattles to build a church[10], and on a visit to Scotland Malachy built an oratory of woven twigs[11].

I believe that the place-name Duleek *(damliac)* deserves more discussion than Dr Harbison allowed it[12]. The Life of Mochua with its explanation of the name may be far later than St Cianán's time, but it could be based on an early Duleek tradition: *Interea sanctissimus vir Kyennanus ... ecclesiam cepit Domino edificare lapideam; quia ante illam in Hibernia non fuit usus construendi ex lapidibus ecclesias*[13]. We should not overlook an annal reference to Duleek in 724 (AU) and still earlier the appearance of the name in Tírechán's account of St Patrick: *Domnach Sairigi iuxta Domum Liacc Cennani, id est lapidum*[14]. This reference is at least a century earlier than the first mention of a stone church in the annals, in 789 at Armagh (AU). It does seem likely that Duleek was so named because it had an early and unusual stone church at a time when churches were normally built of wood. Its easterly position, within easy reach of sea contact with Britain and the Continent, may well be significant.

Information about the detailed planning of churches, their size, shape and internal arrangements is much harder to find. Writers on the whole took their physical surroundings for granted and were not concerned to describe them. References in annals to churches in the plural suggest the multiplication of buildings still to be seen at Clonmacnois and Glendalough. In 845 the Vikings burned

6 G. *Petrie*, The Ecclesiastical Architecture of Ireland, Dublin 1845, p. 364—6 and C. A. Ralegh *Radford*, The Earliest Irish Churches, in Ulster Journal of Archaeology 40 (1977), p. 1—2.

7 AU, discussed also by *Radford* (see note 6) and P. *Harbison* in Medieval Archaeology 14 (1970).

8 L. *Bieler*, The Patrician Texts in the Book of Armagh, SLH 10, 1979, p. 158f.

9 M. *Esposito*, Conchubrani Vita Sanctae Monennae, PRIA 12C (1910), p. 237; C. Plummer, VSH 1910 vol. 2, p. 254 and more generally vol. 1, p. cxix.

10 J. H. *Todd* and W. *Reeves*, The Martyrology of Donegal, Dublin 1864, p. 177.

11 H. J. *Lawlor*, The Life of St Malachy of Armagh by St Bernard of Clairvaux, London 1920, p. 79.

12 See note 1, p. 620 and 629, also Radford's paper (note 6) p. 5.

13 C. *Plummer*, VSH 1910 vol. 2, p. 187.

14 L. *Bieler*, Patrician Texts, p. 146.

Clonmacnois 'with its oratories', and Glendalough was burned 'with its oratories' in 1020[15]. We get an impression of a range in size from small to large, from the hermit's church holding 'twice six in the church, both north and south'[16], to the church at Trevet, burned with 260 people in it in 850 according to the Annals of Ulster. There are hints of complexities of plan: in 1006 the great gospel book of Colum Cille was wickedly stolen in the night out of a western annex (erdam) of the great stone church at Kells (AU). The written sources have little occasion to mention church orientation, but there are indications of a few exceptions to the normal east-west pattern. Cell tarsna, listed in the Martyrology of Gorman at 20 January, is explained in a gloss as 'a transverse church, whose orientation is north and south, not east and west'[17], and according to late traditions the churches at Derry and Saul were built north and south[18]. One well-known surviving north-south church is Temple Benen on Inishmore, largest of the Aran Islands.

There are rare glimpses of internal arrangements. From the Rule of Tallaght, for example, we hear that 'it was not customary for them to pass between the altar and the transverse choir which is in front of the altar'[19]. Outstanding in its detail and well-known is Cogitosus's description of the 7th-century church at Kildare, with its screens, tombs and rich decoration[20]. Also of the 7th century, but until recently less widely known, is the description of the wooden church in Hisperica Famina. Professor Herren has pointed out the interest of this passage for archaeologists, suggesting as it does a square church of massive timbers with a western porticus, a central altar and four steeples[21].

If we look to written sources for help in dating churches we find that they can provide a broad chronological framework, and I agree with Dr Harbison's general conclusions, that stone churches were found on a few important sites in the 8th and 9th centuries but were not commonly built until the 10th century, still then at important sites, increasing in the 11th and 12th centuries[22]. The use of written sources for dating particular buildings is, however, full of problems. A foundation date, or the founder's obit, can be used only to provide a terminus post quem date for material on a site. 19th-century scholars, like Petrie, tended to be over-

15 Both AU.

16 K. Meyer, Selections from Early Irish Poetry, London 1959, p. 30.

17 W. Stokes, The Martyrology of Gorman, HBS 9, 1895, p. 301.

18 A. O'Kelleher and G. Schoepperle, Betha Colaim Chille, Illinois 1918, p. 84—5 and W. Reeves, Ecclesiastical Antiquities of Down, Connor and Dromore, Dublin 1847, p. 220—222.

19 E. J. Gwynn, The Teaching of Mael Ruain, Hermathena 44 (1917) supplementary volume, p. 11.

20 Recently discussed by Radford, who offers a suggested reconstruction drawing (see note 6).

21 M. Herren, Hisperica Famina, Toronto 1974, p. 109, quoted by Harbison (see note 1). H. M. Taylor has discussed centrally-placed altars in Anglo-Saxon churches in Antiquaries Journal 53 (1973), p. 52—58.

22 See note 1 and see also Radford's paper (note 6).

credulous, equating foundation dates with surviving remains. Dated events involving buildings are potentially useful, but these dates also have to be used with caution. St Columb's House at Kells has often been dated to the time following the flight from Iona in 807, but this is highly unlikely. The church is much more likely to date from the 12th century. The erenagh of Nendrum was burned in his own house in 976 (AU), and reporting on his 1922—4 excavations H. C. Lawlor assumed that monastic occupation on the site ended in 976[23]. It does, however, seem quite likely that occupation continued, perhaps right through to the Anglo-Norman invasion of 1177.

Material Remains

The second main approach is through the surviving remains, those small, simple stone structures which form the popular vision of early Irish churches. Dr Harbison has dealt with plan types and their dating in the previous colloquium volume[24] and I shall not retrace this ground, but rather look back to how earlier scholars have regarded these buildings as I think there is an important lesson to be learned from the story of their study.

The great 19th-century student of early Irish architecture was George Petrie, whose prize-winning essay on Round Towers in 1833 provided the basis for his important 1845 book, The Round Towers and Ancient Architecture of Ireland. Petrie's treatment was admirably full, based on wide study of written sources as well as prodigious fieldwork: 'The Towers have been all subjected to a careful examination ... I have examined, for the purpose of comparison with the Towers, not only all the vestiges of early Christian architecture remaining in Ireland, but all those monuments of known or probable Pagan origin'[25]. Petrie's work set the study of early Irish architecture on a new, sound basis, but he did fall into the common trap of over-reliance on written sources for dating buildings. He believed that 'the Irish erected churches and cells of stone, without cement, at the very earliest period after the introduction of Christianity into the country', and argued that many of the surviving churches dated from the time of their founders in the 6th and 7th centuries[26].

An important landmark twenty years later, now largely forgotten, was a series of papers in The Gentleman's Magazine of 1864—5 by John Henry Parker of Oxford[27]. He was the publisher of many architectural books but also a consider-

23 H. C. *Lawlor*, The Monastery of St Mochaoi of Nendrum, Belfast 1925, p. 72. M. *Craig*, The Architecture of Ireland, London 1982, p. 25 accepts 974 (correctly 976) as the end of the early monastic occupation of Nendrum.

24 Cited in note 1.

25 G. *Petrie*, The Ecclesiastical Architecture of Ireland, Dublin 1845, p. 2.

26 Ibid., p. 136

27 J. H. *Parker*, The Gentleman's Magazine 216 (1864), p. 3—20 and following issues.

able student of architectural history in his own right, in the tradition established by Thomas Rickman in his seminal 1817 An Attempt to Discriminate the Styles of Architecture in England. Rickman expounded a stylistic and chronological succession for English churches and for the first time defined a group of pre-Conquest churches[28]. Parker's background in the 1860s was in British and European architecture, and on the basis of the Irish buildings and their features he concluded that few if any stone churches in Ireland could date from before the 10th century. A similar conclusion was reached by the English architect, Arthur Champneys, in a series of articles in The Builder, later published in book form in 1910[29].

Harold Leask's Irish Churches and Monastic Buildings: Early Phases and the Romanesque, first published in 1955, is the best-known and most accessible study of early Irish churches and is valuable for its descriptive material, but from the point of view of dating it is not a reliable guide. Leask acknowledged the existence of timber churches but traced a long development for stone churches and emphasised the largely western, corbelled stone-roofed churches as early in the sequence. His attempts at dating were based mainly on typology, but with such simple material and so few dates to serve as fixed points, typological dating is a very imprecise and unreliable tool. In spreading the surviving stone churches through her three volumes of Early Irish Art, Françoise Henry also implied a long chronology for their development. When Dr Harbison published his paper 'How old is Gallarus Oratory?' in 1970[30], the suggestion that it could be as late as the 12th century came as a surprise to holders of the widely accepted Leask-influenced view of dating, but we have seen that this line of argument can be traced back at least to Parker in the 1860s.

The general point that seems to me to emerge from this history of the study is the need to view the evidence not in a purely Irish context but against the background of the material in Britain and the Continent, areas with which Irish churchmen had active contacts. This point has recently been developed by Dr Radford[31] and is one that hardly needs labouring in the context of an international colloquium, yet it is not always sufficiently acknowledged by students of the material[32].

Comparison with the British evidence is immediately instructive in one respect. The map of surviving pre-Conquest church remains in England shows a very

28 T. Rickman, An Attempt to Discriminate the Styles of Architecture in England, London 1817 and many subsequent editions.
29 A. C. Champneys, Irish Ecclesiastical Architecture, London 1910, especially chap. 3.
30 See note 7.
31 See note 6.
32 G. L. Barrow, The Round Towers of Ireland, Dublin 1979, in arguing an Irish origin and early date for Round Towers ignores the weight of comparative British and Continental evidence.

marked thinning from east to west. In Devon only two surviving fragments of Anglo-Saxon churches have been recognised with certainty, and in Wales there are no known pre-Conquest churches standing at all[33]. In these western areas of Britain, as in Ireland, the traditional building material before the 12th century was clearly wood. The Irish were certainly in contact with many areas overseas where stone churches were being built: travelling Irish churchmen would have seen stone churches in Northumbria and elsewhere in England, in France, Germany and Italy. If they continued to build in wood it was not through ignorance but by choice, keeping faith with a deeply revered inherited tradition.

No pre-Romanesque Irish church is datable by inscription. We have nothing like the Jarrow dedication slab which can be dated to 23 April 684 or 685, or the inscribed sundial built into Kirkdale Church (Yorkshire) between 1055 and 1065[34]. The date 474 on the west door of Banagher church (Londonderry) was carved in the 1730s by a mason who *knew* that the church was built in St Patrick's time[35]!

A well-quarried source of information about early Irish churches, especially the lost timber buildings, are the depictions of churches in manuscripts, metalwork and stone-carving. The 'temple' in the Book of Kells Temptation scene is not altogether easy to interpret, but it does suggest an ornate building with brightly painted decoration, and a hipped shingled roof with prominent finials[36]. The small group of shrine- or church-shaped reliquaries suggest hipped roofs, ridge poles and sturdy angle posts, perhaps later translated into stone *antae*[37]. Those High Cross caps which seem to represent churches have shingled roofs with ridge poles, finials and barge boards, for example on Muiredach's cross at Monasterboice (Louth) and at Durrow (Offaly) (Pl. 2a, b), whilst the west side of the 12th-century 'Doorty' cross at Kilfenora (Clare) shows a shingled roof with finials[38]. It is not clear whether the massive stone 'sarcophagus' at Clones (Monaghan) is based on a timber or stone church, but in spite of weathering its barge boards and finials are clear[39]. (Pl. 2c)

33 H. M. and J. *Taylor*, Anglo-Saxon Architecture, Cambridge 1965, maps in end papers; D. B. *Hague*, Scottish Archaeological Forum 5, Edinburgh 1973, p. 17—35.

34 *Taylor*, see note 33, vol. 1, p. 338, 359.

35 D. M. *Waterman*, Banagher Church, County Derry, Ulster Journal of Archaeology 39 (1976), p. 29, 40.

36 F. *Henry*, Irish Art during the Viking Invasions (800—1020 A. D.) London 1967, pl. B. Dr Radford based the elevation view of his Kildare reconstruction on this depiction (see note 6).

37 A. *Mahr*, Christian Art in Ancient Ireland, vol. 1, Dublin 1932, plates 9, 10, 16, 17.

38 H. G. *Leask*, Irish Churches and Monastic Buildings, vol. 1, Dundalk 1955, p. 46—7; F. *Henry*, Irish Art in the Romanesque Period (1020—1170), pl. 56.

39 D. M. *Waterman*, An Early Christian Mortuary House at Saul, Ulster Journal of Archaeology 23 (1960), p. 82—88, pl. 9d.

Excavation

It will, however, mainly be through excavation that we shall gradually learn more about the lost stone buildings and generations of vanished timber structures. There are hints of wooden churches in early excavation reports. H. C. Lawlor in his 1922—4 work at Nendrum found burials under the east wall of the stone church and suggested that they were associated with an earlier, smaller, wooden church, but his were certainly not the methods for finding its traces[40]! It is doubtful from the report how far the interior of Keeill Woirrey on the Isle of Man was excavated, but the published plan shows a suitably shaped space free of burials within the stone ruin, suggesting again the possibility of an earlier, smaller timber structure[41].

Dr Harbison has reviewed some of the results of more recent excavations, at Reask and Church Island in Co. Kerry, Carnsore, Co. Wexford, Ardagh, Co. Longford, and Inishcaltra, Co. Clare[42]. I will confine myself here to the northern work of recent years which contributes to the picture. D. M. Waterman demonstrated in a small excavation in White Island Church, Co. Fermanagh, that the stone church of about 1200 succeeded a timber structure of two or three phases, on a similar alignment to the stone church but separated from it by a thick layer suggesting a period of disuse[43]. (Pl. 3a) At Derry near Portaferry in the Ards peninsula of Co. Down he found a wall of mixed construction — dry-stone with timber uprights — under the south wall of the south church (Pl. 3b) which is a small simple structure with *antae*. Finds suggested use of the site from at least the 8th century onwards, but the excavated wall could not be closely dated[44]. Recently N. F. Brannon excavated at St John's Point in Co. Down another small church with *antae* (Pl. 4a), to investigate subsidence of the north wall and discovered early burials running under the wall[45]. (Pl. 4b) The possibility clearly arises here, as at Nendrum, that the burials were associated with a smaller wooden church, replaced by the stone building. We can note that the same pattern is emerging from excavation in south-west Scotland and south Wales[46].

40 See note 23, p. 133—4.

41 P. M. C. *Kermode*, The Manx Archaeological Survey, second report, reissued 1968, Manx Museum and National Trust, p. 3—5.

42 See note 1, p. 627—9.

43 D. *Lowry-Corry*, B. C. S. *Wilson* and D. M. *Waterman*, A Newly Discovered Statue at the Church on White Island, Ulster Journal of Archaeology 22 (1959), p. 59—66.

44 D. M. *Waterman*, The Early Christian Churches and Cemetery at Derry, Co. Down, Ulster Journal of Archaeology 30 (1967), p. 53—75.

45 N. F. *Brannon*, A Trial Excavation at St John's Point Church, County Down, Ulster Journal of Archaeology 43 (1980), p. 59—64.

46 Summarised by C. *Thomas*, The Early Christian Archaeology of North Britain, Oxford 1971, p. 68—74. We can note that recent excavations of old-established parish churches in England are showing that the earliest (Anglo-Saxon period) structure is often of wood. Wharram Percy (Yorks) is only one example: J. G. *Hurst* in The Archaeological Study of

In all the three areas of study I have discussed – written sources, standing remains and excavation — there is scope for progress. The rich written sources must have much more to tell us about early churches, especially if historians and archaeologists approach their study together, to a greater extent than in the past. Secondly there must be far more, and more detailed, recording and analysis of the remains above ground. It is surprising, considering the amount of interest lavished on early churches, that the state of the published record is so poor. There is no published distribution map of early Irish churches. A few buildings are well known and much illustrated, but some have never been properly recorded and published, and for many we have only old publications. To take just one example, although the fascinating group of churches on Inchcleraun in Lough Ree (Longford) was described by F. J. Bigger in 1900, it badly needs a fresh study[47].

It is also important to disentangle and record the fragments of early churches which survive, incorporated into later buildings. A good recent example is J. T. Smith's study of Ardmore Cathedral, Co. Waterford, in which the pre-Romanesque fabric is distinguished from the many later additions and alterations[48]. It is possible to point to early fabric incorporated into later, usually medieval, churches, some published but others not: these include early churches with *antae* at Lorrha (Tipperary), Tullaherin (Kilkenny) (Pl. 5a) and Temple Doolin at Clonmacnois (Offaly) (Pl. 5b), with eaves corbels at Terryglass (Tipperary), and with west doors superseded by medieval south doors at Drumacoo (Galway) and Inishmacsaint (Fermanagh) (Pl. 5c). A full corpus of such evidence would greatly extend the body of known pre-Romanesque material, less dramatically than the finding of a 'new' Gallarus, but telling us a great deal about the original distribution of these early stone churches.

Once identified, whether surviving largely intact or in only fragmentary condition, these early churches need to be recorded in great detail. Harold Leask suggested some dating criteria on the basis of typology, especially length: breadth proportions, and discussions often include quantifiable terms like 'common', 'unusual', 'sometimes', 'rarely' and so on. But the state of the existing record is not full or detailed enough to enable such statements to be tested. Further progress will surely be limited until the churches are well recorded and the record made widely available[49].

Churches, ed. P. *Addyman* and R. *Morris*, C. B. A. Research Report no. 13, London 1976, p. 36—39.

47 F. J. *Bigger*, Inis Clothran, Lough Ree, JRSAI 30 (1900), p. 69—90.

48 J. T. *Smith*, Ardmore Cathedral, JRSAI 102 (1972), p. 1—13.

49 This need for detailed recording extends to many types of archaeological material in Ireland. There are published surveys of megaliths and Round Towers, but An Archaeological Survey of County Down, Belfast, H. M. S. O. 1966 and An Archaeological Survey of County Donegal, ed. B. *Lacy*, Lifford 1983 remain the only county inventories.

The recent study of Anglo-Saxon churches in England can provide an example close at hand. After many years of recording H. M. Taylor produced both the record in volumes 1 and 2 of Anglo-Saxon Architecture (1965) and analysis and synthesis in volume 3 (1978), as well as many articles, amongst which we can note particularly his 'Structural criticism: a plea for more systematic study of Anglo-Saxon buildings' in 1972[50]. Taylor has used written sources, for example the description of the church in the 9th-century Northumbrian text De Abbatibus, and unpublished records of earlier scholars, like J. T. Irvine's at Bradford-on-Avon in Wiltshire[51]. He has subjected the surviving Anglo-Saxon churches to detailed record and analysis and has collaborated with archaeologists excavating at Deerhust, Gloucestershire, and Repton, Derbyshire[52].

There is, of course, a limit to how far the study can progress from above-ground remains alone. The ruined early stone churches are only the visible tip of a large iceberg. In Northern Ireland, for example, we have remains of only seven certainly pre-Romanesque churches, yet we know from written sources that many stone churches at important sites have completely disappeared — at Ardstraw, Armagh, Bangor, Derry and elsewhere[53]. On the island monastic site of Devenish there were six centuries of activity before the time of the earliest standing remains — the 12th-century Round Tower and the small church known as St Molaise's House. This was almost certainly a rebuilding in stone of an ancient, greatly revered timber church, associated with the founding saint, burned in a recorded fire in 1153[54]. In our reconstruction drawing of pre 12th-century Devenish (Pl. 6) we show wooden churches where the two stone ruins now stand, a timber tower on the site of the 12th-century Round Tower, and wooden buildings in the many earthwork enclosures: cells, abbot's house, scriptorium, school-room, workshops, kitchen, refectory, guesthouse, agricultural buildings — a reminder that although this paper concentrates on churches, the church was often only part of a large monastic complex, and that the buildings were commonly of wood.

It would be wrong to suggest that excavation will often provide very firm dates for individual buildings, though there is the possibility of closely datable finds, or of wood or charcoal for radiocarbon dating, as at Carnsore, Co. Wexford[55]. Excava-

---

50 Anglo-Saxon England 1 (1972), p. 259—72.

51 The Architectural Interest of Aethelwulf's De Abbatibus, Anglo-Saxon England 3 (1974), p. 163—173; J. T. Irvine's Work at Bradford-on-Avon, Archaeological Journal 129 (1972), p. 89—118.

52 P. A. Rahtz, Deerhurst 1971—73, London, C. B. A. Research Report no. 15 (1976). Photogrammetric recording has been used successfully in recent work on churches in England.

53 Chap. 6ii in my unpublished Ph. D. thesis deals with the northern churches: The Archaeology of Early Christianity in the North of Ireland, Queen's University, Belfast 1976.

54 C. A. R. Radford, Devenish, Ulster Journal of Archaeology 33 (1970), p. 55—62.

55 M. J. O'Kelly, Archaeological Survey and Excavation of St Vogue's Church, Carnsore Point, Dublin 1975, p. 62.

tion will, however, help us to see the surviving, above-ground ruins in the context of the development of the site as a whole over many centuries. This chronological perspective is lacking in Leask's book, and is badly needed. Nor will progress from excavation come rapidly or easily. Churches are often badly disturbed by burials, and recent burial can offer a formidable barrier to archaeological excavation. At long-occupied sites the material record may be very complicated and the excavator may encounter much evidence of post-medieval and medieval occupation before he reaches the earlier material. But as opportunities for work arise, whether in the context of rescue excavation or research, excavation will gradually increase our knowledge of early churches and help to create a clearer chronological perspective.

In looking at the material remains of the early Irish Church we are confronted by a marked contrast between the small, simple stone churches which survive and the carved stones, metalwork and manuscripts on which such care and expertise were lavished[56]. These arts still shine brightly to us across a millennium, but when we look for the churches we see small stone 'boxes' or a few excavated postholes or slots. Perhaps the Irish did not lay great emphasis on the physical setting for worship, or perhaps their main efforts went into the building and adorning of fine timber churches. The 150 years of study since Petrie's book was published do not allow us to explain this contrast satisfactorily, but if work can continue on the lines I have suggested our archaeological knowledge of early Irish churches should gradually become fuller and clearer. The study may no longer be in its infancy, but John Henry Parker's comment is as true today as it was in 1865: 'the study will require the labour of many heads and hands to work it out as it ought to be'[57].

56 A contrast pointed out by R. *Stalley* in The Irish World, ed. B. *de Breffny*, London 1977, p. 81.
57 The Gentleman's Magazine 218 (1865), p. 283.

The concept of the High Cross

By
Hilary Richardson

The High Crosses are virtually unique documents in the history of Western Art. Except for the carvings of the same period in Britain, they are an isolated phenomenon. The Irish crosses and their offshoots in Western Scotland form a really impressive coherent body of monuments. To quote Professor Domhnall Ó Murchadha, Ireland "established the first School of Sculpture in Western Europe"[1].

Why did this happen and how did the peculiarly characteristic shape of the ringed cross arise? In spite of much outstanding work, notably by such scholars as Henry Crawford, Kingsley Porter, Françoise Henry and Helen Roe, certain problems still remain to be resolved.

Accordingly, I should like to put forward a few tentative proposals, more in the nature of a reconnaissance than anything else. In the first place I should like to suggest the reason why the Ahenny group of crosses imitate metal prototypes. Secondly, I should like to offer an explanation for the shape of their capstones; and thirdly I should like to indicate the existence of an outlook shared in common between Irish and Caucasian carvings.

To begin it is helpful to consider the structure of two superb crosses, spaced perhaps two hundred years apart and representative of two very different groups. These are the North Cross at Ahenny in Tipperary and the Cross of Muiredach at Monasterboice.

The Cross of Muiredach, dating to the tenth century, is probably the finest of all High Crosses. (Pl. 7) Its scale places it outside the range of ordinary carving and almost within the sphere of monumental architecture.

With the end of the Roman world in Europe there was a total closing down of carving on any large scale, just as building programmes more or less came to a full stop. In Ireland there never had been a tradition of building in cut stone. However, megaliths show a continuity in the erection of monuments stretching back over centuries. Perhaps this is significant because in Transcaucasia, where early Christian stone monuments also appear, there was a megalithic culture too, with dolmens and standing stones.

There can be no doubt that the figuration of the cross itself was the fundamental reason for setting up the High Crosses. In examining the ornament or iconogra-

---

1 Domhnall Ó *Murchadha*, Stone Sculpture in Pre-Norman Ireland, The Capuchin Annual, 1969, p. 172.

phy of the scenes this fact may be obscured. In Athanasius's Life of St Anthony he tells how St Anthony directed houses to be marked with the cross 'which takes the place of the Lord'[2]. The cross replaced the figure of Christ, but was not an allusion to Christ's passion: it was an expression of Divine Power. This is where the study of the liturgy and early texts provides illumination as it is necessary to get inside the thinking of the period. Work produced in early Christian Ireland was always specific in intent.

The cross at Monasterboice consists of a base, into which is set the shaft. The shaft, in combination with the huge ring, is made from one enormous block of stone. A capstone tops the monument.

The capstone is an integral part, completing the image the sculptor had of the cross in its entirety. It is in the shape of a small oratory or church, with a shingled roof and finials, like the picture of Solomon's temple in the Book of Kells (fol. 202v).

These scripture crosses are characterised by clearly defined legible scenes of figure carving with a narrative approach. This was something new. It was the first departure of Irish artists from their native Celtic expressionism. A descriptive or didactic quality was a striking innovation. (Pl. 8b)

The word *sign* links two themes connected with the cross. A major idea uppermost in medieval thought was the Second Coming of Christ. In the Scripture Crosses the Last Judgement usually occupies one side of the crosshead and may very well have been the dominant imagery. In the Cross of Muiredach the depiction of this scene is spread over the entire sweep of the eastern face of the crosshead and cannot fail to impress the spectator. (Pl. 8a)

A key text for the Second Coming is St Matthew's Gospel, chapter 24, verse 30, where it says: 'And then shall appear the Sign of the Son of Man in Heaven'. It is the only passage on this subject where the word 'sign' occurs. This verse is actually one of the readings in the Stowe Missal in an Office for the Visitation of the Sick. It is hard to draw any conclusion from this, but it is worth noting. Perhaps it is more than coincidence. Interestingly enough, the treatise on the Mass at the end of the Stowe Missal, dated to 800, plainly refers to the ring as being part of a normal cross. In the directions given for the fraction, the bread is to be arranged in the shape of a cross, and there are to be twenty particles in the *circle-wheel* (Ir. *cuairtroth*)[3].

The second manifestation of the word 'sign', which was in widespread circulation, is associated with the vision of Constantine. This was followed by the finding of the True Cross, Constantine's building over the Holy Sepulchre, and the jewelled cross set up on Golgotha containing the relic of the True Cross.

2 *Migne*, Patrologia Graeco-Latina 26, 893.
3 G. F. *Warner*, ed., The Stowe Missal, 2 vols., HBS 31, 1906, 32, 1915; for a diagram of the possible arrangement of the fraction see Peter *O'Dwyer*, Célí Dé, Dublin 1981, p. 157.

Before his victory at the Milvian Bridge in 312 Constantine had a vision which he later recounted to Eusebius, bishop of Caesarea, who recorded the story. While Constantine prayed for help "a most marvellous sign appeared to him from heaven. He said that about noon he saw with his own eyes a cross of light in the heavens, above the sun, and bearing the inscription 'by this sign shalt thou conquer'". The victory achieved through the cross seen by Constantine was followed by the building of his triumphal arch in 315 to celebrate the victory and glorifying the Triumph of the Cross. Again, this theme has implications for the Irish High Crosses.

The North Cross at Ahenny is perhaps the finest example of the earliest ringed crosses which are grouped within a few miles of each other in Tipperary and Kilkenny. It is dated to the eighth century through parallels in manuscripts and metalwork, with its fine interlace and angular patterns. The silhouette is quite different from Monasterboice: the stepping of the base is more strongly emphasized, the ring is much larger in proportion to its height, and the capstone is beehive shaped. (Pl. 9)

It has long been recognised that these crosses are based on metalwork jewelled prototypes. Helen Roe has suggested that the stepped base follows the model set up on Golgotha, which was of worldwide renown in Christendom[4]. Some representations of jewelled crosses are well dated, for example those in mosaics in Ravenna, in the Arian Baptistry or in the apse of St Apollinare in Classe. (Pl. 10b) The most remarkable actual instance of such a cross of insular workmanship which survives is the Rupert Cross, now in Salzburg, which resembles Northumbrian crosses in shape, having no ring, and also in the treatment of the vinescroll. The narrow sides have panels of interlace and the remaining glass studs give an idea of the sort of technique the Ahenny crosses were imitating. (Pl. 11) Interestingly enough, the see of Salzburg was administered by an Irishman, St Virgil, in the third quarter of the eighth century. He was an Irish monk who had spent very many years in the area, dying in Salzburg in 784. The ingenious theory put forward by Seán P. Ó Ríordáin that the ring developed from diagonal braces to support a wooden cross is not convincing. As W. D. Lamont points out, no self-respecting carpenter would be satisfied in making such a bad joint that it would need strengthening[5].

The observation that the Ahenny crosses are skeuomorphs of metal covered wooden crosses may only be half the truth. They may in fact be the sculptor's version in stone of the jewelled cross set up on Golgotha. This was described by Arculf, for instance, among the many pilgrims who flocked to the holy sites. Adomnán writes: "Towards the east, in the place that is called in Hebrew Golgotha, another very large church has been erected. In the upper regions of this a

---

4 H. M. *Roe*, The Irish High Cross: Morphology and Iconography, JRSAI 95 (1965), p. 224.

5 W. D. *Lamont*, Sculptured Stones of Islay, Glasgow 1968, p. 10.

great round bronze chandelier with lamps is suspended by ropes and underneath it is placed a large cross of silver, erected in the selfsame place where once the wooden cross stood embedded, on which suffered the Saviour of the human race"[6].

The Anglo-Saxon poem *Elene* (St Helena finds the True Cross), composed soon after 750, gives a vivid picture of this prototype. Incidentally St Helena, the mother of the Emperor Constantine, should be the patron saint of archaeologists as hers is the first recorded excavation. In the poem, Helena in Jerusalem receives a message from her son to build a church on Calvary.The poem goes on:

> The queen bade seek men dowered with skill,
> The best who could cunningly build in stone,
> To rear God's temple on that spot of ground.
> According to the word of the Warden of heaven
> She had the Rood garnished with gold and gems,
> Skilfully set with precious stones
> And enclosed with clasps in a casket of silver.
> There from that time the Tree of life,
> Best Tree of triumph, has had its abode
> In beauty unbroken[7].

This too is the meaning intended by the sculptor of the Ahenny cross. The extraordinary elaboration in stone towards the appearance of metal techniques which we find in the Slievenamon group must be a deliberate re-creation of the revered cross at Golgotha associated with the True Cross itself. There is a later Irish *Invention of the Cross* which uses similar sources to the Anglo-Saxon poem[8].

My second proposition concerns the capstones of the Ahenny group. It is hardly likely that the crowning portion of the cross would be devoid of meaning. Kingsley Porter explained these capstones as bishop's mitres but otherwise they have remained a puzzle. The small church buildings on the top of the Scripture Crosses have been identified as simulating the Holy Sepulchre. On analogy with this, the capstones of the Ahenny group might represent a *clochán*, but more likely represent a domed building, which was in fact the actual shape of the building erected above the Holy Sepulchre.

After the restoration of Jerusalem by Constantine, the presence of pilgrims from all over Christendom is well attested. Many versions of the shrines built above Christ's tomb were depicted, sometimes on souvenirs for pilgrims visiting the Holy Places. A few examples will suffice to show the range of illustration.

6 D. *Meehan*, ed., Adomnán's *De Locis Sanctis*, SLH 3, 1958, p. 49.
7 Translated by C. W. *Kennedy*, Early English Christian Poetry, New York 1963, p. 206.
8 M. *McNamara*, M. S. C., The Apocrypha in the Irish Church, Dublin 1975, p. 78—79.

The composition in the apse of Santa Pudenziana in Rome and the Madaba map are well-known representations in mosaics. (Pl. 10 a, 12 a) The lid of the small wooden reliquary box in the Vatican shows the Rotunda very clearly in the scene of the Holy Women at the Tomb. (Pl. 12 b) The same scene occurs in this Carolingian ivory (Pl. 13 b) where the round buildings in the lower corner contrast with the building in the Pentecost scene above. In Armenian manuscripts domes are frequently represented in the architectural background. (Pl. 14 a) A church or the temple at Jerusalem is a common marginal illustration. (Pl. 14 c) Miniature domed buildings repeat the theme on church roofs, for example the west end of the cathedral at Mtskheta. (Pl. 15) It even appears on fairly recent gravestones in Georgia. (Pl. 14 b)

This building symbolises the Triumph of the Cross, the symbol of salvation for every Christian. André Grabar has extensively examined this model church evoking Sion. The symbolic sanctuary proclaims the victory of the Cross over death[9].

Although domed buildings are remote from Ireland, extraordinary as it may seem the best description of the buildings at Jerusalem in the seventh century is that of Arculf, who sketched the sepulchre and the church built over it on a waxed tablet for Adomnán and the community of Iona about 683. The account Adomnán gives of this in *De Locis Sanctis* is entitled: "Concerning a church of round shape that is built over the Lord's Sepulchre and concerning the Sepulchre itself and of its domed structure"[10]. Arculf describes the Church of the Holy Sepulchre "all of stone, and shaped to wondrous roundness on every side" and centrally placed in the interior, a round domed structure "carved out of one and the same rock, in which it is possible for thrice three men to pray standing". This, he says, is covered with marble and its summit supports a "fairly large golden cross". The entrance of this domed structure faces east. He reproduces this circular shape in his celebrated plan of the Church of the Holy Sepulchre. (Pl. 13 a)

Only a short distance from Ahenny, in the graveyard at Kilkieran, two of the crosses have the beehive cap. O'Neill's lithograph in the nineteenth century shows the Plain Cross in fragments with the capstone lying on its side. The Tall Cross near it has a lightly hatched moulding, badly worn. The cap has now been replaced on the Plain Cross and the Decorated Cross at Kilkieran has a fine beehive cap too, rather high and pointed. (Pl. 16, 18 a)

The dome itself may be extended further to imply the Dome of Heaven. For example, the versified hymn of North East Syrian origin to celebrate the building of the cathedral at Edessa in the mid-sixth century treats the dome of the church as a microcosm. This extract describes the edifice:

> For it truly is a wonder that its smallness is like the wide world,
> Not in size but in type; like the sea, waters surround it.

9 Cahiers Archéologiques 27 (1978), p. 63—83.
10 *De Locis Sanctis* (as above note 6), I, 2.

Behold! Its ceiling is stretched out like the sky and without columns
(it is) arched and simple,
And it is also decorated with golden mosaic, as the firmament (is) with
shining stars.
And its lofty dome — behold, it resembles the highest heaven,
And like a helmet it is firmly placed on its lower (part)[11].

The multiple allusions to the architecture and decoration of the building make this hymn of great interest from an archaeological standpoint, although no trace of the cathedral remains. Grabar has shown that the comparison of the dome to a helmet solidly placed on its base must refer to a view encompassing the outside of the church[12].

The same dual interpretation is witnessed in the Pentecost scene of the Armenian Gospel of 1262 (Walters MS 539), from Cilicia, where the dome of the upper chamber is considered at the same time as the dome of heaven. The vivid blue of the vault emphasises this concept. (Pl. 18 b)

A humbler version appears in a marginal illustration in an Armenian hymnal, Chester Beatty MS 593. Here the forty martyrs of Sebastia are represented only by their heads, visible in a large dish. Their forty crowns are above, and Christ in half profile looks down from Heaven, from a segment of sky coloured a brilliant blue. (Pl. 18 c)

In interpreting the Eucharist, early Christian writers too use a constant theme that the temple in which the Eucharist is celebrated is an image of the new transfigured cosmos.[13]

These are very difficult ideas to illustrate, let alone carve in three dimensions. One must remember though that Celtic artists for centuries had been dealing in the symbolic. The Ahenny group with their distinctive beehive capstones would be the closest among the High Crosses to the actual time when Arculf was dictating his experiences to Adomnán. Perhaps the craftsmen had never seen a domed church but the fame of Jerusalem and its holy buildings must have been part of everyday tradition[14]. In shaping the capstones of these crosses the sculptor created his own idea of the domed building over the Holy Sepulchre in Jerusalem in the best way he could.

11 This translation was supplied by Professor Kathleen *McVey*, Princeton Theological Seminary, for her lecture 'The Domed Church as Microcosm: Greek vs. Syriac Literary Roots of an Architectural Symbol'. Symposium on "East of Byzantium: Syria and Armenia in the Formative Period", Dumbarton Oaks, May 1980.

12 A. *Dupont-Sommer*, Une Hymne Syriaque sur la Cathédrale d'Édesse, Cahiers Archéologiques 2 (1947), p. 29—39; A. *Grabar*, Le Témoignage d'une Hymne Syriaque sur l'architecture de la Cathédrale d'Édesse au VIe siècle et sur la symbolique de l'édifice Chrétien, ibid., p. 41—67.

13 J. *Meyendorff*, Byzantine Theology, Oxford 1975, p. 208.

14 It is clear from the scene on the east side of the base of the North Cross at Ahenny that the artist was familiar with palm trees.

It is remarkable that the Holy Sepulchre building also occurs on early Caucasian carvings. These provide an important parallel development in erecting Christian monuments, of especial interest because they pre-date the Irish crosses. Considerable remains of cross-bearing monuments dating from the mid-fourth to mid-seventh century show that they were widespread[15].

The stele of Khandisi discovered in 1961 dates to the second half of the sixth century. It is a stele carved on all four sides with figured panels and ornament, such as the vinescroll. The flat graphic style is characteristic of the period. Above the figure of Christ in Majesty is the building representing the Holy Sepulchre — here with the horse-shoe shaped arches found in contemporary architecture in Georgia and seen in the arches of canon tables, like those of the Rabbula Gospels. (Pl. 19, 20b) There is a hollow on top of the shaft where a missing cross once fitted.

In the sixth-century Sion church at Edsani, a complete monument is recorded in a relief carved in the east wall. It is 60 cm high and shows a perfect model. (Pl. 17a) The base is in separate steps, the top one with a cross inscribed in a circle. The shaft has a decorative moulding and tapers slightly upwards. On top, a small cubic block is slightly wider than the shaft and supports the last element, a little Holy Sepulchre building. The cross fitted into this.

This carving is extremely important since it shows the design of monuments which lasted for several centuries. The inscription, now destroyed, but read by Brosset, said: "This cross I, (Teog)ed, built as a prayer for our souls, whoever reads this let him pray for me".

In the case of all these monuments only one or two elements remain out of the complete structure depicted in the Edsani model. The sixth-century base at Pantiani was discovered in 1966 and probably stood to the north of an ancient church. It has a seven line inscription on the back, with a similar dedication. Here the favourite motif of the *Exaltation of the Cross* is carved on the front, with archangels supporting the cross inscribed in a circle. There is a vine and birds below and the cross is mounted on a stele decorated with a typical sixth-century motif. (Pl. 22)

The stele of Brdadzor is the tallest monument surviving, being six metres high. All four sides are carved, three with motifs such as the vinescroll, but the front is divided into separate panels and it is possible to identify a number of biblical scenes, such as the sacrifice of Isaac. A cross would have surmounted the monument. (Pl. 17b, 20a)

The Kachagani cross would have been the final element surmounting a whole monument. Again, the *Exaltation of the Cross* is the main theme. (Pl. 21)

15 The references to the Georgian material may be found in N. *Chubinashvili*, Khandisi, Tbilisi 1972; see also N. *Aladashvili*, Georgian monumental sculpture. Russian text, English summary, Tbilisi 1977.

This special concentration on the cross goes back to the conversion of Georgia when in the fourth decade of the fourth century, St Nino set up a cross on the mountain crag overlooking the capital of Mtskheta. (Pl. 23 a)

In the second half of the sixth century the ruler of Kartli had a small church built beside the cross. The large church called Djvari or Holy Cross in Georgian was built in the last decade of the sixth century above the revered cross erected by St Nino, to enshrine it. (Pl. 23 b) The carved doorways here again celebrate the *Exaltation of the Cross;* the smaller lintel with Christ in a medallion supported by angels, the South doorway having a cross inscribed in a circle above a free-standing cross. (Pl. 24 b, a)

Returning once more to Ahenny (Pl. 25) and remembering that the cross stands both for the person and symbol of Christ, in an interchangeable way as seen in the Georgian carvings, surely the best explanation of the ring is as a glory or halo around Christ or the Cross. This was the simple solution put forward by Macalister and it is hard to disagree with it when faced with the arresting outline of the Ahenny crosses.

Acknowledgements

I should like to thank all those listed in the illustrations for their help. N. M. is the National Monuments Branch of the Office of Public Works, Ireland. Phot. Arch. indicates the Photographic Archives of the Department of Archaeology, U. C. D. Special thanks are due to the following for their generous assistance: Zaga Gavrilović, Elinor Wiltshire, Lt. Col. Martin Bates, Prof. V. Beridze, Helen Simpkiss, Prof. Sirarpie Der Nersessian, Prof. Kathleen McVey, Rev. Prof. Martin McNamara, Dr. P. Ní Chatháin, Anahit Arshakian Ó Cathail.

The Derrynaflan and other early Irish eucharistic chalices: some speculations

by

Michael Ryan

In 1980 a hoard of ecclesiastical objects was found in the ancient monastic site of Derrynaflan, in the townland of Lurgoe, near the villages of Horse and Jockey and Ballinure, Co. Tipperary, Ireland. The find consisted of an elaborate silver paten together with its foot or stand, a decorated bronze ladle adapted for use as a strainer, a silver chalice and a large bronze basin which had partly covered and protected the objects (Ryan 1980, Ó Ríordáin 1980, a and b). The objects had been buried in a shallow pit excavated into the side of a bank near the ruined church of Derrynaflan. The date of concealment is unknown.

While this paper is concerned with the chalice and its analogues, it is necessary first to give a brief account of the other objects in the hoard. The paten is a large, complex and unusual piece. It is decorated with sheets of gilt-silver die-stamped foil, twenty four gold filigree panels, cast imitation 'kerbschnitt'-work, glass and enamel, trichonopoly work and gilding. Twelve letters in half-uncial script are engraved on the surface of the silver. They were presumably part of a code for assembling the piece. The use of the letters and, in particular, 'k' which was not employed in spelling the Irish language but was associated with Latin learning, suggests that a literate, scholarly person played a part in the conception of the paten. The decoration of the object can be compared with that of well-known pieces of 8th century metalwork such as the 'Tara' Brooch and larger Ardagh Chalice (Ryan 1980). The foot is a hoop of silver decorated with stamped foil panels and glass and enamel studs and in appearance reflects the design of the side of the paten. There is evidence to suggest that at one stage it was fastened to the underside of the paten to form a foot or pedestal, although it is now separated from it.

The strainer-ladle is of bronze, it consists of a hemispherical bowl with a long handle terminating in a round finial. It is decorated with glass and enamel studs bearing inlaid step-and-cross-patterns and millefiori flowerets, stamped gilt-bronze sheets, blue and red glass, a polished rock crystal and gilt-bronze mouldings. The bowl is divided in two by a semi-circular perforated strainer-plate. Closely comparable in many respects with plain bronze ladles known from Ireland, western and northern Britain and from some 9th century Viking graves, an 8th century date for the Derrynaflan example seems plausible.

The basin is very badly decayed, it is large with a flat rim and a groove forming a slight shoulder just below it, a convex wall and a dimpled base. It was formed by hammering and finished by means of polishing on a lathe. In general it is similar to the series of smaller vessels known as hanging bowls (Henry 1936) although,

135

unlike them, it is not equipped with hooks for suspension. By analogy with the later hanging bowls, an 8th or 9th century date seems to be indicated.

As will be argued in detail below, the chalice appears to be of 9th century date. The hoard can thus be seen to represent a group of objects in somewhat different styles manufactured at different times — they do not therefore form a matched set of altar plate, rather they are to be viewed as a treasure accumulated over a fairly long period much in the same manner as the Ardagh hoard (Dunraven 1874, Gogan 1932). The important consequence of this, for the present discussion, is that the find illustrates a continuity of the finest vernacular metal-working traditions in Ireland over a substantial period, perhaps a couple of generations or more.

The Chalice

While the paten is the most elaborate, ambitious and accomplished object in the hoard, the chalice does not fall far short of it in interest. Except for some wear on the handles, some cracked amber studs and some slight damage to its filigree ornaments, the chalice is intact. It consists of a large, two-handled bowl with a plain, flared rim, a cast, cylindrical copper-alloy stem and a flanged sub-conical foot (Pl. 26a, b) The handles are applied to the bowl; they are small, of cast silver-gilt, each with a decorative escutcheon. The stem is composite, consisting of a cylindrical trunk presumably rebated at each end to engage with two separately cast broad rings: an upper one designed to seat the bowl and a lower one to engage the foot. The outer edge of the upper ring has a high, decorative flange which projects downwards. Radiographs recently taken in the British Museum Research Laboratory show that the stem is hollow and that the whole assembly is united by a stout, round-sectioned pin, tightened with washers and an internal system of lugs and stops not yet fully understood but clearly designed to prevent the rotation of the components. Cast, gilt copper-alloy decorative plates are riveted to the upper surface of the flange of the foot. An ornamental roundel of cast, gilt copper-alloy with seven hemispherical amber studs decorates the under-side of the foot and conceals the structure of the stem-foot junction. The bowl and foot are formed by 'raising' — that is hammering on a 'stake' or anvil specially devised for bowl-making. They are finished by means of lathe-polishing. The purity of the silver is about 70% showing that the craftsman had access to a supply of metal of good quality in contrast to the debased material noted on some roughly contemporary objects in Scotland (Small et al. 1973).

The chalice is slightly lopsided because the bowl is not quite seated true on the upper ring of the stem. It is 19.2 cm in maximum and 18.75 cm in minimum height. The rim diameter varies between 20.7 and 21 cm; the depth of the bowl is 11.5 cm. The diameter of the foot plus its flange is 16.7 cm. The rim thickness varies between 0.8 and 1 mm.

The handles, escutcheons, stem, flange of the foot and a band or girdle around the body of the bowl just below the rim are embellished with filigree panels,

136

eighty-four in all not counting the gold insets on the six principal amber studs on the escutcheons. Fifty-seven amber studs decorate the chalice: both hemispherical and rectilinear shapes with both rounded and facetted surfaces, are used.

It has been argued elsewhere that the chalice should be dated to the 9th century AD (Ryan 1980 and 1983). The arguments may be briefly stated here.

The majority of the filigree panels carry animal ornament — quadrupeds, beast and bird-heads being most frequently depicted. With the exception of two panels of crude, bird-headed interlace, the animals are never shown as interlaced or entwined as is extremely common on the metalwork of the 8th century. Whole panels are frequently devoted to the depiction of single beasts and, while these are often contorted to fit the frames provided, they are never twisted into the fanciful knotwork of those on, for example, the 'Tara' brooch or the Steeple Bumpstead boss (Henry 1965, plates 42, 43). On the contrary, in the frequent clear depiction of eyes, tongues and genitalia, there is an obvious attempt at a true naturalism — this is especially marked on some panels devoted to beasts (lions? dogs?) shown running at full stretch. The ultimate source of much of this animal style lies in the art of the late antique rather than the Germanic world — perhaps the evangelist symbols in MSS illumination (see especially those in the Book of Armagh [Mitchell 1977, no. 43]) played a part in their formation. Certainly some of the interlinear animals in the Book of Kells are also apt comparisons for the feeling of the chalice's zoomorphic style. In carvings, something of the same spirit can be seen on Pictish slabs of 8th-9th century date — e. g. the Papil cross-slab, the Aberlemno slab (panel to right of the head of the cross), Dunfallandy (front) (Allen and Anderson 1903, 10—15, 209, 286; Cruden 1964, plates 4, 9, 11 for modern photographs of these).

One animal represented both in filigree and in imitation 'kerbschnitt' is a squatting, dog-like beast with back-turned head. It is closely comparable with the well-known beasts on the reverse of the 9th century Killamery brooch (Mitchell 1977, no. 47). A long-snouted or beaked animal in a similar pose is occasionally represented on the chalice and here, too, by analogy with other 9th century tendencies such as the long-snouted animals on bossed silver penannular and other brooches (Johansen 1973, 76 figs. 15—17) a 9th century date is indicated.

There are two round panels of filigree in each escutcheon. Each bears an elaborate triscele device in beaded wire and gold ribbon built up of interlocking 'C' and trumpet scrolls in the ultimate La Tène style. This style was an important component of the art of the 8th century and is well represented on metalwork of the period such as the 'Tara' brooch, the Ardagh Chalice and the Derrynaflan paten. In MSS illumination it occurs in codices ranging in date from the Book of Durrow (7th century) to the Book of Kells (later 8th century?). By the time the chalice came to be made, the ultimate La Tène style was clearly in decline and, by the end of the 9th century as far as can be judged it was, for all practical purposes, extinct. An object as elaborate and important as the chalice could scarcely have failed to reflect in its decorative scheme what was fashionable at the time. The rarity of the ultimate La Tène ornament on it seems therefore significant.

137

Other filigree panels, especially some of those on the bowl girdle, depict animal and bird heads and are clearly, I believe, to be interpreted as fossil versions of ornamental detail of an earlier period. One panel shows two beast heads each one grasping in its jaws a human head. It appears to be an attenuated version of the motif of the snake-bodied beast grasping a human head on the St Germain finials (Henry 1965, pl. 66), or the human head clasped in the animal jaws on the Ekerö crozier (Henry 1965, pl. 69). It may be significant that the only other anthropomorphic representations in *filigree* known in early Irish art are on the Derrynaflan paten.

A further argument for a 9th rather than an 8th century date may well be the use of amber studs to the exclusion of *any* glass or enamel. Amber does not occur in Ireland and so must have been imported. Indeed Ó Corráin (1972, 71) refers to records of its importation. In Europe, in ancient times, it was most plentiful on the shores of the Baltic but was available to a lesser extent on the coasts of the North Sea. Although it was known in prehistoric Ireland, it makes its first appearance in the early historic period metalwork on objects of 8th century date where, as a rare substance, it is used sparingly as a variation for glass and enamel on, for example, the 'Tara' brooch and in minute quantities on the larger Ardagh Chalice. During the 9th century, the fashion for glass and enamel declined (Henry 1967, 131), and brooches of that period tended more and more frequently to have amber studs in their settings (Ryan, 1982, 21—22) or instead, metal bosses sometimes gilded and decorated (Graham-Campbell 1972, 116—117 and 124). Glass and enamel where it occurs tends to be poorly done as, for example, on the Killamery brooch (Mitchell 1977, no. 47). It may be argued, therefore, that the Derrynaflan chalice fits readily into that period when amber was becoming fairly abundant (perhaps as a result of Viking trade contacts) and when the fashion for brightly coloured enamels which were such a major part of the 'polychrome effect' of 8th century Irish metalwork (Graham-Campbell 1972, 124) was in decline.

As an important commission it is clear that the chalice must embody the best craftsmanship available to the patron at the time. In comparable 8th century works, the range of techniques used, and well-used, is impressive. A more restricted variety was employed in the manufacture of the chalice — apart from the absence of enamels there are, for example, no die-stamping, trichonopoly-work or other knitted wire mesh. In filigree, gold ribbon, beaded, plain and twisted round-sectioned gold wire and granules are used and all are relatively coarse. There are none of the complex wires of the filigree of the Ardagh Chalice, 'Tara' Brooch or Derrynaflan paten present — no simulated plaiting of wires, no stamping of ribbon for filigree and very little of the delicacy of finish so characteristic of the best Irish 8th century work. In standards of accomplishment it stands much closer to the goldwork on the 9th century Killamery and Roscrea brooches (Mitchell 1977, nos. 46 and 47 and Ryan 1982). While, admittedly, it can be argued that much of this might be attributable to the relative lack of skill of the craftsman, nevertheless I believe that we can can see here that impoverishment of technique which can be observed in the period after the great 8th century flowering of the art of the metalworker in Ireland (Henry 1967, 112). I would argue, therefore, that the balance of evidence favours the suggestion that the Derrynaflan Chalice was made sometime after the 8th century climax of Irish art and that it belongs most probably to the early or mid-9th century because, while displaying the later traits sketched above, it remains firmly in the mainstream of native traditions of ornament and construction. If this dating is accepted, then it follows that it was possible and apparently reasonable to commission and to execute a major, portable work of art in precious materials during the earlier part of the Viking period in Ireland (Ó Corráin 1972, 82—89, Graham-Campbell 1978—79).

Other Irish Chalices

The closest analogue of the Derrynaflan Chalice is the 8th century (Henry 1965, 106—108) silver one from the Ardagh hoard (Dunraven 1874, 435—442, Gogan 1932, 27—42, Organ 1973, Rynne forthcoming). Too well known to require further detailed description here, it is a two-handled chalice with a bowl and flanged foot of beaten, lathe-polished silver and a cast cylindrical copper alloy stem with two separately-cast rings similar to those of the Derrynaflan Chalice (Pl. 27a). The ornamental scheme is also strikingly similar — in addition to equivalents of all the decorated areas on the Derrynaflan Chalice, the Ardagh vessel has two decorated roundels on the body of the bowl, elaborate ornament on the underside of the flange of the foot, an inscribed band below the bowl girdle (recording the names of eleven original apostles and St Paul in the possessive case in Latin) and further incised decoration below the roundels and escutcheons and on the base of the bowl at its junction with the stem. The rim of the bowl of the Ardagh Chalice is covered by a round-sectioned binding strip reminiscent of some of the later hanging bowls (Henry 1936, fig. 5, d) but, apart from this, the profile of the bowl and its method of manufacture are closely similar to that of Derrynaflan.

Organ has shown in detail how the Ardagh Chalice was assembled (Organ 1973, fig. 25). The various components of the stem and foot were united by a stout pin in a manner remarkably closely paralleled on the Derrynaflan Chalice as radiography has now shown. There are other striking technical correspondences between the two chalices, for example in the choice of materials for different components viz. silver for the bowls, feet, handles and escutcheons, but gilded copper alloy for the stem, stem rings and ornament of the underside.

The Ardagh Chalice differs in proportions from that of Derrynaflan — it is less tall and somewhat broader in relation to its height. Other differences explicable as due to the tastes of different times can be seen in the range of techniques, materials and sophistication and delicacy of the ornaments which are not matched on the Derrynaflan Chalice.

The third surviving early Irish chalice is the plain bronze example from the Ardagh hoard (Gogan 1932, 56, Mitchell 1977, no. 34, 138—139). Damaged at the time of discovery, it was restored in the 19th century. Its bowl is almost intact: it is nearly hemispherical in shape with a flared rim and a pronounced horizontal groove below it. The bowl is of beaten bronze, finished on a lathe. The foot was broken off at the time of finding and only the lower portion of it survives: it was short, perhaps 3—4 cm long but perhaps longer, as far as can be judged, tubular and with a flared mouth (Pl. 27b).

Gogan (1932, 42—43) remarked of the two Ardagh chalices that each was the other's closest analogue. True at the time, it is, since the Derrynaflan discovery, no longer so. The two large silver chalices have much more in common than either has with the bronze vessel. Nevertheless all three Irish chalices share important characteristics. The form and method of manufacture of their bowls are closely similar. They quite clearly belong to native traditions of vessel-making as represented by the hanging bowls (Gogan 1932, 44, Wilson 1961, 91—92, Elbern 1965, 118). The use of bronze, the short, trumpet-shaped foot and the lack of either handles or ornament on the smaller Ardagh vessel clearly indicate that there was some variety in chalice design in early Ireland — a point which is emphasised by the goblet illustrated on the opening page of St Luke's Gospel in the Book of Kells (fol. 188r). Some of these differences may be explicable in terms of function — the smaller size and lack of handles of the bronze chalice may be due to the fact that it was a *calix minor* or *calix sanctus* used by the celebrant of Mass and not like the larger, handled, silver minsterial chalices, intended for administering the sacrament to the faithful (Gogan 1932, 68—69, Elbern 1963, 48). There is, however, also the question of chronology: while the silver Ardagh Chalice may with some confidence be ascribed to the 8th century, being plain, the date of the bronze vessel is less certain. The often assumed 10th century date for the deposition of the hoard on the basis of the inclusion in it of a thistle brooch provides only a *terminus ante quem* for the manufacture of the smaller Ardagh Chalice.

In summary, therefore, it can be seen that all three surviving Irish chalices have a common form of bowl. Of the three, the two great silver ministerial chalices are remarkably similar in design, choice of materials for specific components and means of solving technical problems of assembly which, without dismantling or radiography, are not immediately apparent. There is a remarkable correspondence also in the form of decoration and in the areas chosen for ornament. These prompt the question: is the Derrynaflan a copy of the Ardagh Chalice? If not how might these similarities be explained? The answer to the first question is, I believe, no and the reasons for it are to be found in an examination of the relationships of the Irish chalices.

Insular Chalices

In his paper, carefully entitled *Eine Gruppe insularer Kelche* — the use of the indefinite article is significant — Elbern (1965) linked all the then known surviving chalices from Britain and Ireland — that is, the two from Ardagh and the

140

Trewhiddle (Pl. 28a) and Hexham (Pl. 28b) vessels together with continental examples such as the Lebuinus (Deventer, Netherlands) and Silos (Spain) chalices which he felt showed insular influence. Traits which he saw as characterising the insular chalices — although all are not present on each one — were the large, domed, flanged foot and the cylindrial knopless stem. Insular chalices were further distinguished in Wilson and Blunt's view by the use of beaten rather than cast metal for the major components and a certain complexity of construction (Wilson and Blunt 1961, 88—92) in contrast to many larger continental Carolingian and later examples — such as the Tassilo Chalice at Kremsmünster, Austria, — where casting was regularly used (Haseloff 1951, 1977; Stollenmayer and Widder 1976, plates pp. 85, 89). In proportions, too, the insular chalices stand apart in being somewhat broad in relation to their height in contrast to continental pre-Carolingian, Carolingian and Ottonian chalices which tend to be more slender (see also below pp. 142 f.).

Three major difficulties beset the discussion of the insular chalices. Firstly, the size of the sample is very small: only four examples from Britain and Ireland were known to Elbern (1965). The second problem is chronological: the larger Ardagh Chalice was made probably during the 8th century, the date of the bronze vessel is less certain. The Trewhiddle chalice was deposited towards the end of the 9th century — its date of manufacture is unknown. The Hexham chalice probably belongs to the 11th century (Elbern 1963, 1965). The third difficulty is the problem of ornament (Elbern 1965, 122). The Lebuinus chalice — regarded as insular in form — betrays no insular influence in its carvings. The ornament has been identified as the work of the Aachen court school (Lasko 1972, 15). The Tassilo Chalice, clearly not in the tradition of design of surviving British and Irish chalices, is elaborately decorated in a style widely regarded as heavily influenced from insular art (Haseloff 1977). Nevertheless, the existence of an insular tradition of chalice form gains force when the sum of contrasts with contemporary chalices on the continent are considered.

The discovery of the Derrynaflan chalice requires a refinement of our view of insular chalices. It and the Ardagh silver vessel can be seen to have so many formal characteristics in common, and, if design is any guide, appear to have been made for the same liturgical ritual, that they are closer to each other than to any of the other insular examples. They both have, in common with Trewhiddle and Hexham, the large flanged foot and with the much later Silos chalice, the foot and cylindrical stem (Elbern 1963, 73; 1965, 115—116). The bowl form and the technique of manufacture are common to all three together with Trewhiddle. The two great silver ministerial chalices are not, therefore, to be seen in isolation but rather to be representatives of a regional tradition of making sacred vessels, albeit particularly sumptuous and liturgically specialised representatives.

Continental Chalices: Further Contrasts:

Some technical and formal contrasts between insular and continental pre-Gothic chalices have been mentioned above. The *corpus* has been surveyed by Braun (1932) and Elbern (1963). Cup shapes are rarely hemi-spherical or nearly so; half-ovoid forms and variations are most common. Engraved decoration occurs on, for example, the 8th century Tassilo Chalice (Haseloff 1951) and on the Cunpald chalice from Petöhaza, Hungary (Elbern 1963, 74). Applied decoration — in the form of filigree and semi-precious stones is known on the early 6th century Gour-don chalice (Elbern 1963, 72), semi-precious inlay (garnet?) on the destroyed Eligius chalice (Vierck 1974, 312—314) and on the bowl girdle and medallions of the 10th century Gauzelin chalice at Nancy (Elbern 1963, 72, Lasko 1972, 85). Feet are normally broad, trumpet-shaped and elaborate widely flared forms seem to be a late feature. Occasionally the rim of the foot is flanged as on the well-known Grimfridus chalice (Elbern 1963, 16 fig. 7). Feet and cups are normally united by knops: an uncommon feature is the placement of the knop a short distance below the bowl so that a near cylindrical portion intervenes e.g. on the Ursus chalice (Elbern 1963, 17 fig. 8). Handles occur occasionally on for example, the Gourdon and Gauzelin chalices and on that depicted on the gold altar of Sant' Ambrogio, Milan (Lasko 1972, 50—55 and plate 47 panel top left). These are however never like the small strap handles of the two Irish ministerial chalices — they are normally much larger in relation to the size of the cup and often take the form of 'S' scrolls and they lack escutcheons (see also Elbern 1963, 35 plates 32, 33).

It is well known that altar plate developed from the table ware of late antiquity and, as Painter (1977, 22) has pointed out, specialised liturgical vessels appear relatively late. At one stage utensils were used interchangeably for secular and religious purposes. Such a vessel may well be the cup from the late 4th century hoard of silver from Water Newton (Painter 1977). Vessels of this sort must have contributed heavily to the formation of metal chalice styles in Western Europe, and Lasko (1971, 34—35) regards the Gourdon chalice and paten as showing "clearly a synthesis of Roman forms and the orientalizing barbaric taste for rich and colourful decoration ...". Given the strong British and Gaulish element in the early missions to Ireland, one would have expected that Irish chalice types would have been broadly in line with those of Western Europe, particularly as there is a strong tradition that St Patrick was accompanied by metalworkers. Examples of the work of one of these, Assicus, were said to have survived into the 7th century. It is clear, however, that the antecedents of the larger Irish chalices must be sought elsewhere.

Silver chalices are an important component of hoards of Byzantine ecclesiastical metalwork deposited in the 6th or 7th centuries AD (Dodd 1973 esp. 54—57 for the close links between various finds). The types of chalice show limited variation in design. They normally consist of a large bowl sometimes hemi-spherical in shape, more often with an incurved rim, standing on what is usually a dispropor-tionately narrow, trumpet-shaped foot. The mouth of the foot is often flanged for greater stability. Knops are a common feature; they are not normally placed at the bowl-foot junction but some way down the foot and sometimes separated from the bowl by a short cylindrical section. The chalices vary in size but tend in the main to be large (for a summary see Dodd 1973 and Weitzmann 1979, 592—609). Inscribed bands, often a dedicatory or memorial inscription, are common; they normally encircle the bowl just below the rim and are often confined within gilded mouldings (Dodd 1973, 13—15). Occasionally, roundels bearing the sacred images are placed on the body of the bowl (Dodd 1973, 18 fig. 9, 10). A particularly interesting example is the 6th century chalice from Rusafa in Syria (Dodd 1973, 15, fig. 7). With a pair of small ring handles at the rim, an inscribed band within gilt mouldings and a chi-rho on the body of the bowl, the composition of the upper part compares closely with that of the Ardagh silver chalice.

Such chalices were not confined to the outer part of the Empire: some are undoubtedly of provincial workmanship, others are the products of the style of the capital (Dodd 1973, 53—54) such as that from Hama, Syria. Pictorial evidence exists — a mosaic at San Vitale, Ravenna, shows the Empress Theodora carrying a large jewelled chalice of this general type. Gold versions of Avar workmanship occurred in the Albanian hoard now in the Metropolitan Museum, New York.

A later group of Byzantine chalices, together with other sacred vessels, is pre-served in the cathedral treasury of St Mark in Venice (Dalton 1911, 552; Grabar 1971). Thought to have been looted by crusaders they may be dated to the 10th century. One of them bears the name of Basil, a distinguished official, general and patron of the arts at Byzantium and a bastard son of Romanus I and dates to the second half of the tenth century (Grabar 1971, 59—60; Beckwith 1979, 210—213, plate 178). Two other St Mark's chalices bear inscriptions which may refer to the Emperor Romanus II (AD 959—963). The Venice chalices are composite pieces, the bowls being made of semi-precious stone bound with jewelled metal strips and equipped with applied stems and, sometimes, large handles. In general they may be described as having large bowls and narrow stems.

The chalices in Venice are important because they constitute the best preserved group of sacred vessels in media other than metal. Glass, semi-precious stone, and even wood are attested as materials used to make chalices but surviving examples of early date are difficult to demonstrate. Fragments of early glass vessels of vari-ous forms with incised, moulded or inlaid gold Christian motifs are well known from France and western Germany (Beckwith 1979, 25, fig. 10, Böhme and Schulze

1980, 114—116, nos. 135—145). Handled glass cups of *kantharos* form are widely known in late Roman contexts — for example from a 4th century woman's grave at Strasbourg (Schulze 1980, 80 No. 77). Elbern (1965, 121, 122, fig. 7) compared the bowl of a similar glass cup from Cologne with that of the Lebuinus chalice. The use of glass for chalice-making is attested at a later date by the so-called Heinrichskelch in the Residenz treasury in Munich where an exotic glass cup was remounted in the early 11th century for liturgical use (Braun 1932, 47; Brunner 1977, 5). Chalices of stone are very rare in Western Europe. An antique sardonyx cup in the Cabinet des Medailles in Paris may at one time have been used as a companion chalice with the paten of Charles the Bald, itself a classical serpentine dish remounted in Carolingian times (Lasko 1972, 66).

The earlier metal chalices, therefore, embody only a part of the range of materials, designs and techniques liturgically permissible. Different media call for different approaches to design and construction. It is possible, however, that features, structurally necessary in one medium, were borrowed for decorative use on a vessel of different materials. Thus, for example, decorative bowl girdles on metal chalices may owe something to the binding strips necessary to carry applied handles on vessels of stone or glass. It is tempting also to compare the downward projecting flange at the base of the bowl of the Derrynaflan Chalice with the treatment of the base-stem junction in the Venice chalice (Grabar 1971, 59—60; Beckwith 1971, 210, plate 178). There are dangers in attempting to force these analogies; they are offered here merely to point to the problem that much of the evidence for chalice development is lost and many strands of influence may be represented in the surviving pieces.

It has long been accepted that the larger Ardagh Chalice owes a great deal to Byzantine influence. Indeed, Gogan went so far as to refer to Adomnán's recounting of Arculf's description of the cup of the Last Supper preserved in Jerusalem as the 'perfect exemplar' of the Ardagh vessel (Gogan 1932, 44). He noted also the long survival of the description in Irish scholarly tradition, quoting the *Leabhar Breac* that the chalice was silver, two-handled and equivalent in capacity to a sextarius. The large bowl, the roundels with their cross patterns (clearly chi-rho equivalents, see Thomas 1971, 108, 109, fig. 49), inscribed band, and pair of small handles secured at the rim, all point in the direction of the Byzantine world. The same applies with equal force to the Derrynaflan Chalice. One can only conclude that the insular craftsmen felt that the great bowl required to be balanced by a large foot. When and in which island this modification occurred is unknown.

The smaller Ardagh chalice with its narrow trumpet-shaped foot can be seen clearly as an insular version of a handleless Byzantine chalice (Gogan 1932, 56). Gogan (1932, 44) assumed it to be a type which was widespread in Ireland and which provided some at least of the elements of design for the larger vessel — this may be so but it cannot be demonstrated.

Conclusion

We have seen how the two large Irish silver chalices differ from their West European equivalents and have noted the presence of a degree of Byzantine influence in their design. Nevertheless they remain, in the present state of knowledge, peculiarly Irish products: native traditions of bowl-making formed the vessels, local traditions of decoration provided the ornaments, local inventiveness modified the borrowed design. The problems of assembling a large and complex piece were solved in what is for the period a unique and elaborate manner. Short of dismantling an existing chalice, a craftsman a generation or so later would not see enough to reproduce the methods closely. If, however, he could draw on a body of teaching, then he could be expected to solve technical problems in a similar way. Given the strong hints in the literature of clerics engaging in metalworking and given the use of the letter code on the Derrynaflan paten, it is tempting to postulate the existence in 8th and 9th century Ireland, not alone of pattern books for the design of objects but also of a technical manual embodying perhaps both the native and late classical technology. The problems of the origin and usefulness of early treatises with instructions for processes are discussed in detail by Hawthorne and Smith (1979, XXVII—XXXV).

The method of transmission of ideas is relevant to this suggestion. It is not necessary to postulate actual imports of Byzantine vessels into Ireland — the dissemination of patterns and written guidance, perhaps through the medium of monasteries such as Bobbio, could have sufficed. Earlier direct contacts with the eastern Mediterranean are, however, attested (Thomas 1971, 22—25). The problem of eastern influence on all aspects of early Irish art has been dealt with in a refreshingly sceptical way by Raftery (1965, but see Henry 1965, 64—65) but there is need now to reopen the question as has so successfully been done for another region of Europe by Vierck (1981).

To return to our questions, I would argue that the Derrynaflan Chalice is not a copy of the Ardagh Chalice. Both are to be seen as partaking of insular and exotic influences and any one of their characteristics occurs so widely as to render the hypothesis of copying unnecessary. They must be seen as representatives of the design which had come to be considered suitable for ministerial chalices in 8th and 9th century Ireland. Their sumptuousness marks them as objects of special importance and suggests that they were commissioned by wealthy patrons, whether laymen or clerics we cannot tell. Their richness may have had a great deal to do with their survival: as treasures, their concealment in times of trouble must have been of great importance and the success of the measures taken to safeguard them have provided us, out of a tiny sample of three Irish chalices, two exceptionally magnificent examples. We must assume the former existence of many more vessels about which we know nothing.

I hope that this short offering to the colloquium sheds some light on its theme. A great deal of interest has perforce to be left unsaid — the source of raw materials for the chalices, the origins of the techniques of decoration and fabrication, the liturgical context of the pieces, all would illustrate exotic influences on Irish life and on native response to these. The question of the origin of the forms of altar plate in early Christian Ireland mirrors exactly the problems posed in other areas such as ecclesiastical organisation and liturgy: an initial introduction with the early missionaries of models current in the late Roman West is hypothesised or demonstrated, but radically different patterns are to be seen a century or so later when native sources begin to be reliable. The notion that Ireland was isolated in that century is not tenable if the Church was being penetrated by such profound new influences.

References

Allen, J. R. and Anderson, J.	1903	The Early Christian Monuments of Scotland. Edinburgh
Beckwith, J.	1979	Early Christian and Byzantine Art. Second edition. London
Böhme, H.	1980	Gallien in der Spätantike (exhibition catalogue entries) Mainz
Braun, J.	1932	Das christliche Altargerät, in seinem Sein und in seiner Entwicklung. München
Brunner, H.	1977	The Treasury in the Residenz. München
Cruden, S.	1964	The Early Christian and Pictish Monuments of Scotland. Edinburgh
Dalton, O. M.	1911	Byzantine Art and Archaeology. London
Dodd, E. C.	1973	Byzantine Silver Treasures. Åbegg Stiftung. Bern
Dunraven, Earl of	1874	On the Ancient Chalice and Brooches lately found at Ardagh in the County of Limerick. Transactions of the Royal Irish Academy 24, part 3, p. 433—454
Elbern, V.	1963	Der eucharistische Kelch im frühen Mittelalter, Zeitschrift des deutschen Vereins für Kunstwissenschaft 17, p. 1—76
Elbern, V.	1965	Eine Gruppe insularer Kelche des frühen Mittelalters, Schlegel, U., Zoege, C., ed., Festschrift für Peter Metz. Berlin
Gogan, L.	1932	The Ardagh Chalice. Dublin
Grabar, A.	1971	'Calici Bizantini E Patene Bizantine Medievali' in: Volbach, W. F., Grabar, A., Erdman, K., Hahnloser, H. R., et al., Il Tesoro Di San Marco, Florence 1971, 55—90
Graham-Campbell, J.	1972	Two Groups of Ninth-Century Irish Brooches, JRSAI 102, p. 113—128
Graham-Campbell, J.	1978/79	The Initial Impact of the Vikings on Irish Art, Saga Book 20, 1—2, p. 42—48

Haseloff, G.	1951	Der Tassilokelch. Münchener Beiträge für Vor- und Frühgeschichte I
Haseloff, G.	1977	Zum Stand der Forschung über den Tassilokelch, Baiernzeit in Oberösterreich (exhibition catalogue), Linz, p. 221—236
Hawthorne, J. G. and Smith, C. S.	1979	ed. and transl., Theophilus On Diverse Arts. Second Edition. New York
Henry, Françoise	1936	Hanging Bowls, JRSAI 66, p. 209—246
Henry, Françoise	1965	Irish Art in the Early Christian Period to 800 A. D. London
Henry, Françoise	1967	Irish Art during the Viking Invasions 800—1020 A. D. London
Johansen, O. S.	1973	Bossed Penannular Brooches: A Systematization and Study of their Cultural Affinities, Acta Archaeologica 44, p. 63—124
Lasko, P.	1971	The Kingdom of the Franks. London
Lasko, P.	1972	Ars Sacra. London
Mitchell, G. F.	1977	Treasures of Early Irish Art (exhibition catalogue entries), Metropolitan Museum of Art. New York
Ó Corráin, D.	1972	Ireland before the Normans. Dublin
Ó Ríordáin, A. B.	1980	The Derrynaflan Hoard, Antiquity 54, p. 216—217, plates XXI—XXIII
Organ, R.	1973	Examination of the Ardagh Chalice — a Case History, Young, W. J., ed., Application of Science in Examination of Works of Art. Boston. p. 238—271
Painter, K.	1977	The Water Newton Early Christian Silver. British Museum. London
Raftery, J.	1965	Ex Oriente ..., JRSAI 95, p. 193—204
Ryan, M.	1980	The Derrynaflan Hoard, Ireland Today, April, p. 2—5
Ryan, M.	1982	The Roscrea Brooch, Éile 1, p. 6—24
Ryan, M.	1983	in: The Derrynaflan Hoard: A Preliminary Account, National Museum of Ireland. Dublin
Rynne, E. forthcoming		The Ardagh Chalice. National Museum of Ireland. Dublin
Schulze, M.	1980	Gallien in der Spätantike (exhibition catalogue entries) Mainz
Small, A., Thomas, C., Wilson, D. M.	1973	St Ninian's Isle and its Treasures, 2 vols. Aberdeen
Stollenmayer, P., Widder, E.	1976	Der Kelch des Herzogs Tassilo. Rosenheim
Thomas, C.	1971	The Early Christian Archaeology of North Britain. London

Vierck, H.   1974   Werke des Eligius, *Kossack, G., Ulbert, G.*, ed., Studien für Vor- und Frühgeschichtliche Archäologie, II, p. 309—80

Vierck, H.,   1981   *Imitatio imperii* und *interpretatio Germanica* vor der Wikingerzeit, *Zettler, R.*, ed., Les Pays du Nord et Byzance (Scandinavie et Byzance), Acta Universitatis Upsaliensis, NS 19. Uppsala, p. 63—113

Weitzmann, K.   1979   Age of Spirituality: Late Antique and Early Christian Art. Third to Seventh Century (exhibition catalogue, *Weitzmann*, ed., entries). New York

Wilson, D. M. and   1961   The Trewhiddle Hoard, Archaeologia 98, p. 75—122
Blunt, C. E.

III

Kanonisches Recht und irisches Recht
Canon Law and Irish Law

Christian influences in early Irish law

By
Gearóid Mac Niocaill

What I have to say here is restricted to the period of the classical Irish law texts, that is, Irish law of the seventh and eighth centuries. The period preceding this is represented by fragmentary, and largely obscure, aphorisms cited in the classical texts; the following period, from the ninth century onwards, is that of the glossators, whose aim is to expound and reconcile texts which they may not understand, and to defend as best they can the application of rules which social, and perhaps economic, change have rendered obsolete. It is as well also to be clear about what we mean by influence. This is something more than simple verbal borrowing — of Latin *testis*, for example, or *adaltrach*. And whether or not it is true that the relatively fluent expository prose of the classical texts owes something or everything to the Church, or whether indeed churchmen are responsible for setting down these texts, as has been suggested, is not itself to the point: we must distinguish between channels of transmission and what was flowing in those channels. And, furthermore, mere acceptance of Christianity by the lawyers does not necessarily of itself lead them to accept Christian influence in their law: it persuades them to concede a status *ex officio* to the members of the clerical hierarchy, certainly, in much the same way as a club may accept fresh members, without necessarily producing a change in the rules of the club.

Indeed, it would be unrealistic to expect any early change. The period from about the mid-sixth century to the early seventh, that of the early monastic foundations, of Comgall of Bangor, of Colum Cille and the various cousins of his later commemorated as saints, is that in which Christianity became acceptable, one might almost say respectable. It is that in which Christians changed from being the oddities and outsiders implied by the sixth-century canons studied by Kathleen Hughes[1] to being, in some sense, the establishment. This put the Church in a position of potential influence, but also left it more open to secular influence. For example, it is quite likely that granting a specific status to persons in ecclesiastical orders in fairly short order ensured that mainly persons of the equivalent secular status would henceforth gravitate into the Church: the field of recruitment was narrowed, so that whereas in the sixth century persons of dubious and obscure origin could make their mark in the Church, the churchmen remembered from the seventh and eighth centuries are overwhelmingly of gentle origins. This is the period when the canonical, 'classical' Irish law-texts were put together, the period also when, partly as a result of the Easter controversy, there was considerable

---

1 K. *Hughes*, The Church in Early Irish Society, London 1966, p. 44 f.

canonistic activity in the Irish Church, and the period in which, if the Church does in fact exercise Christian influence on the law, it should be detectable.

What we in fact observe is superficial and insubstantial, and insofar as influence was exercised, it seems to have been exercised in the opposite direction, by secular society, of which the law-tracts provided the theoretical and conservative articulation, on the church.

Take the field of procedure first. Early Irish law acknowledges two types of evidence, that of the eye-witness (fiadu) who was present and saw the blow struck or heard the words of the contract spoken; and that of oath-helpers, prepared to swear that they believed or supported their principal's version of events[2]. The oath obviously offers some scope for Christianisation: the pre-Christian oath 'I swear by what my people swear by', or 'I swear by the god by whom my people swear'[3], which is found, fossilized, in the saga-texts, is in law-texts replaced by 'I swear by God' or 'by the God of Heaven'[4]. But this is clearly a superficial shift: once Christianity is accepted and official, the 'god by whom my people swear' is, officially, the 'God of Heaven'. Legally, nothing substantial has changed. So with sureties: as well as purely human sureties, we find traces in the saga-texts of the elements being invoked as sureties[5], which are later replaced by the creator of the elements and his saints. Again nothing substantial is involved.

Perhaps the closest we come to a substantial Christian importation in this field is in the form of the teist, from Latin testis, which some have interpreted as meaning, or being capable of meaning, evidence as to character[6]. Of the examples I have been able to find from the classical period, only one can be used in support: athlaech ara tabair anmchara a thest 'an ex-layman for whom [his] confessor gives evidence'[7], — and even this can be interpreted as evidence of what the confessor has heard and seen of the ex-layman, although obviously this shades over, of necessity, into character evidence. This possible example apart, all the other examples I have found support Thurneysen's interpretation of it as the zeugnisfähig[8], the vir honestus whose status is unspotted by any of those disreputable acts, such as defaulting as a surety, briefly listed by the Críth Gablach[9]; and by extension, the

2 G. Mac Niocaill, Admissible and inadmissible evidence in early Irish law, Irish Jurist ns. 4 (1969), p. 332—7.

3 E. g. Tongu na-tongat mo thuath (Scéla Mucce Meic Dathó[2] § 16); Tongu-ssa a tongas mo thúath (Mesca Ulad[2] 1020); Tongu a toingend mo thúatha (Bruiden Da Derga[2] 698); Tongusa a toingthe mo thúatha (ibid. 707); etc.

4 R. Thurneysen, Die Bürgschaft im irischen Recht (Abh. Berlin, Phil.-Hist. Kl. Nr. 2, 1928), p. 22—3 § 65.

5 See examples cited in DIL, R, 17.23—37, including (significantly) one from the Law of Adomnán § 22.

6 D. A. Binchy, Linguistic and legal archaisms in the Celtic law-books, Transactions of the Philological Society 1959, p. 23.

7 ALI IV 366.9 = CIH, p. 598.

8 R. Thurneysen, Cóic conara fugill (Abh. Berlin, Phil.-Hist. Kl. Nr. 7, 1926), p. 68.

9 D. A. Binchy, ed., Críth Gablach, Dublin 1941, p. 12 § 21.

evidence given by such a man. The semantic development of the later, postclassical, sense of 'recommendation' is straightforward. And it is as well here to recall that oath-helpers in effect commit themselves publicly to the support of their principal's truthfulness and accuracy — in fact, to what amounts to a character recommendation.

In much the same way, slight though our knowledge of it is, the use of written evidence, in matters of title to land, for example, stands in a direct line of descent from the *ogam isin gallán*[10], the ogham inscription on the standing stone, used as sound evidence of a boundary line. The later *senscríbenn déoda*, the 'godly old writing', which seems to be found mostly in ecclesiastical contexts[11], merely extends this from stone to calf-skin.

In the field of family law, again, the evidence for Christian influence is thin. The suggestion has been put forward that Christian influence no doubt did something to raise the standing of women who, in the earliest law-texts, are portrayed as being in as complete a state of legal incapacity as in Roman law. The suggestion, unfortunately, has not been backed by any solid evidence, and I would incline to the view that their standing was more likely to be raised by the existence of a fair number of propertied women, of *banchomarbai*, 'female heirs', than by the Church. It is noteworthy that, by the period of the classical texts, the woman with the highest status is the woman of property[12].

It is in the field of property and the family — the two are hardly separable — that the instinct of the early jurists to limit Church influence perhaps appears at its clearest. Take the example of the soulscot, the *tertia Deo* which was studied some years ago by Eberhard Bruck[13]. The section of the *Senchas Már* entitled *Córus Béscna* 'customary law' preserves a number of rules on the disposition of property[14]. The patrimony *(fintiu)* is of course sacrosanct, and may not be alienated without the consent of the *fine*, the kin-group, the ultimate heirs, which is unlikely to be forthcoming. But as well as this, a man may also have acquisitions, either in land or movables, over which he has some power of alienation without the consent of his kin. The *Córus Béscna* lays down, firstly, that such property may be left, to the Church, for example, up to the value of seven *cumals* — the fixed penalty for homicide — and, secondly, proceeds to hedge this liberty round with restrictions. If the acquisitions are the produce of the patrimony — an increase in his livestock, for example — at least two-thirds of them must be left to the kin, the heirs; if they are additions to the patrimony — perhaps land cleared and reclaimed by the testator — then he may alienate up to half of it; and finally if the acquisi-

---

10 CIH 748.18, 1566.6, 2143.39.

11 *Mac Niocaill*, Admissible and inadmissible evidence (as above note 2), p. 333.

12 D. A. *Binchy*, ed., Studies in early Irish law, Dublin 1936, p. 226—7.

13 E. *Bruck*, Kirchenväter und soziales Erbrecht: Wanderungen religiöser Ideen durch die Rechte der östlichen und westlichen Welt, Berlin 1956, p. 172 ff.

14 ALI III, 48.

tions are neither of these, but the pure fruit of his labour, he may alienate up to two-thirds. Throughout, what the Church may get is in inverse proportion to the closeness of the link with the testator's patrimony. Note also that throughout there is no implication that a certain amount must go to the Church, that the Church has a right to it: the emphasis is on the testator's limited liberty to alienate.

The claims of the Church, not unexpectedly, went further than this. The Collectio Canonum Hibernensis[15] of the same period has one passage (XXXII, 13) laying down that a dying man should leave a third of his *hereditas*, his patrimony, to his sons, a third to *Caesar*, his lord, and a third to the Church; if he had no church, a third to the poor; and if he had neither church nor lord, his *hereditas* should be divided equally between his sons and the poor. Elsewhere, a certain synod is cited as laying down that *omnis hereditas sub censu regis et ecclesiae alligata in tres partes dividatur: prima pars heredibus sine sorte detur, secunda regibus ... tertia vero Deo* (XLVIII, 1). More extreme, though less precise, claims are made in another canon (XXXII, 14): that a dying man should commend all he has to God, should yield a part to *Caesar*, and God by men's hands will see to the sons or kin.

The jurists viewed these canonist claims with a distinct lack of sympathy: one text remarks flatly that one may not bequeathe anything without the consent of the kin-group, and notes — significantly in the context — that it is not a commandment of God that a man should pass over his kin which brought him forth, who carry responsibility for his misdeeds, who reared him to manhood, and not leave them their due[16]. In only one case were the jurists prepared to acknowledge some liberty: that of the woman who has neither kin nor liabilities, and may therefore leave to the Church whatever she has acquired by her own labour[17] — but equally, of course, to anyone else. It is not evidence that the Church was able to breach the solidarity of the kin-group and to loosen its grip on the patrimony.

The jurists' tactics in invoking the will of God in support of their view are worth noting. They were never unwilling to draw precedent from the Bible as and when appropriate — more or less: so, Adam's loss of Paradise for the sake of the fruit of the tree of good and evil was regarded as exemplification of the principle that inadequacy of consideration is not ground for avoiding a contract[18]. In another field they were able to turn this weapon back against the clergy who insisted on monogamy, while the secular nobility often practised, and the secular jurists defended, forms of polygamy, even if they accepted the Christian term *adaltrach* for the secondary wife. So, in one demure passage, a jurist notes there is a disagreement as to whether a plurality of marriages or only one is the more proper — 'for the chosen people of God were in a plurality of marriages, so that it is no

15 H. *Wasserschleben*, ed., Die irische Kanonensammlung, Leipzig ²1885.
16 R. *Thurneysen*, Irisches Recht (Abh. Berlin, Phil.-Hist. Kl. Nr. 2, 1931), p. 33 § 35.
17 Ibid., p. 32 § 34.
18 ALI, III, 52.

easier to censure it than to praise it'[19] — in short, a matter of indifference. In the same way, although early Irish canonists rejected divorce, the early jurists devote much attention to the grounds for divorce and its implications for the property of the couple, provoking August Knoch to the comment, 'Angesichts dieser Blüte christlichen Lebens ist es erstaunlich … daß trotz aller Klöster und großartig wirkender heiliger Männer und Frauen das irische Volk als Masse vom christlichen Lebensideal noch weit entfernt war'[20]. If we cast an eye over the contemporary, and officially Christian, barbarian kingdoms of the Franks and the Visigoths, it may seem to us less *erstaunlich* than it did to Knoch[21].

Instead of Christian influence on early Irish law, what seems to me most noticeable is the extent and substantiality of the influence of the secular ethos expressed in the laws on the Christian Church in Ireland — in hereditary or familial succession within monasteries, for example, and in the adaptation of the secular system of clientship to the relations of superiors and subordinates within monasteries. Perhaps the most notable example is the borrowing of the native institution of the *maigen dígona*[22] for ecclesiastical purposes, and its extension. The *maigen dígona* was the area, varying according to rank, around the residence of a freeholder. Any offence committed against even a third person within this area constituted a breach of 'house-peace', a violation of the householder's protection, and for this the freeholder was entitled to compensation. This institution the Church borrowed, as *termonn* (<Lat. *terminus*), but extended it substantially: late seventh-century sources claim for Patrick, that is, the church of Armagh, a *terminus vastissimus*, an area comprising the Airgialla with parts of the neighbouring kingdoms of Ulaid and Dál nAraide[23]. Obviously, there may well be a gap between claim and reality, but it seems clear that in this period various churches were claiming to exercise some form of protection over particular areas, or particular sections of society, claims which were usually described as *leges* or *cána*. The earliest is the *Lex Innocentium*, or *Cáin Adomnáin* of 697, which extended special protection to clerics, women and children. Anyone injuring these was liable not only to the normal penalties, but also to an extra penalty payable to Adomnán's church, presumably Raphoe. It was renewed again in 727, but was soon superseded by the Law of Patrick, at least as far as clerics were concerned, between 734 and 737; and the latter was renewed and proclaimed several times. In the eighth century there was a spate of such *leges* — the law of Colum Cille, of Ua Suanaigh, of Brendan, Ciarán, Ailbe and so on; no major monastery, without damage to its self-respect, could refrain from promulgating one.

19 D. A. *Binchy*, Bretha Crólige, Ériu 12 (1938) p. 44 § 57.
20 *Binchy*, ed., Studies in early Irish law, p. 261.
21 For the Franks, see Gregory of Tours passim; for the Visigoths, P. D. *King*, Law and society in the Visigothic kingdom, Cambridge 1972, p. 235—6.
22 Cf. *Binchy*, Críth Gablach, p. 83.
23 *Hughes*, CEIS, p. 86.

Nothing is known of the contents of most, but one thing is clear, that they could be proclaimed and applied only with the consent and support of the secular rulers, more than once mentioned in the annals. I doubt that this support was for nothing, and the *Proemium* to the Law of Adomnán proper is careful to note that Adomnán does not deprive of their dues *(fiacha)* the chieftain and church and kin to whom they are due. It is, moreover, possible that this co-operation of ecclesiastical and secular rulers stimulated the latter to expand their *de facto* powers in the same way as those of the Church: I think that I can detect hints of this in the period from the eighth century onwards[24]. But this does not constitute substantial Christian influence on early Irish law: it is, rather, acceptance of that law by both Churchman and layman, and exploitation of its potentialities, much to their material profit.

Kathleen Hughes has written that 'the general effect of Christianity upon Irish law was to modify it without dislocating it: its rigidity was reduced, and the result was a strengthening of native institutions'[25]. I would be inclined to reverse this verdict, and to suggest that on the contrary, it was Irish law that modified Christian institutions in Ireland, and reduced their rigidity.

24 *Mac Niocaill*, Jetsam, treasure trove and the lord's share in medieval Ireland, Irish Jurist ns. 6 (1971), p. 103—10 at 108—9.
25 *Hughes*, CEIS, p. 153.

Irish law and canon law

By
Donnchadh Ó Corráin

In the early part of the seventh century — and no doubt earlier — native Irish law and canon law appear to have already profoundly influenced one another. This is particularly evident in the prose law tracts which most authorities date to the seventh century, itself a period of great activity in the field of canon law. Indeed, it is likely that the secular prose law tracts — and prose indicates a written as distinct from an oral legal tradition — owe much to the example, if not the labour, of the canonists. The impression one gets is that the churchmen were much concerned with secular law and had a large part in giving it its shape. There is textual evidence for this from the seventh century and solid annalistic evidence from the ninth[1]. Conversely, influence flowed in the other direction and canon lawyers took over many of the institutions and legal concepts of their secular peers. It may yet be possible to show that the two streams had flowed together and that effectively there was only one legal profession with a broad spectrum of individual interests and special skills, but a great deal more research needs to be done before such a hypothesis can be proved or disproved. Given that and other limitations, I propose to examine briefly just three selected topics which bear on the question of the interrelationships of the two legal traditions: (I) the rules governing marriage within the kindred and especially the marriage of an heiress; (II) the rules governing the parting of an abbot from his monastery; and (III) the rules governing compensation for personal injuries in the case of a cleric of high status. In each case, there are materials or at least interesting parallels, of respectable antiquity in both legal traditions which may be useful in estimating the degree of interpenetration.

I.
Marriage within the kindred and marriage of heiresses

The general Church rules governing the marriage of close relatives raised serious problems for Irish lawyers and canonists. As is well known, the Church took over the prohibitions of Roman law and added to them. Roman law forbade all mar-

---

1 *Uraicecht Becc* provides the most explicit information ot this point: D. A. *Binchy*, ed., CIH, p. 634—55, p. 1590—1618, p. 2255—7, p. 2261—82. The text is annotated and translated by Eoin *MacNeill*, Ancient Irish law: the law of status or franchise, PRIA 36 C (1923), p. 265—281. The annalistic evidence is collected in D. *Ó Corráin*, Nationality and kingship in pre-Norman Ireland, T. W. *Moody* ed., Nationality and the pursuit of national independence, Belfast 1978, p. 1—35.

riages in the direct ascent and descent, all unions between brothers and sisters, and marriage between first cousins, though not unlawful, was contrary to what was felt to be fitting. Taking its cue from Leviticus 18: 6 (*Omnis homo ad proximam sanguinis suae non accedat ut revelet turpitudinem eius*) but going much further, the Church forbade marriage with a widening circle of kindred. Marriage with paternal first cousins was forbidden in the early fifth century or before — *patrueles fratres qui sibi quarto sociatur gradu*, as Ambrose put it in his letter to Paternus in 397 (PL 16, 1184). Augustine deals with the same matter (*De Civitate Dei* XV 16) and while he admits that such unions were allowed in the Old Testament he states that Christians avoided them even before they were forbidden by Theodosius in 384. Churchmen found a convenient delimitation in the law of inheritance: those not entitled to inherit were not accounted kindred and the Church's prohibition was extended to that conventional limit. This embraced the sixth degree and some categories from the seventh. In the sixth century, a number of Gaulish and Spanish synods forbade marriage within the six degrees and the councils of Auvergne (535), Orleans (538), Tours (567) and Auxerre (585) declared marriage with second cousins (the sixth degree) to be incestuous and thus forbidden. The same prohibition held good in Spain as we learn from Isidore (Etymologiae IX 6 — a text very probably familiar to the Irish) and the laws of Chindaswind. Gregory the Great, in his letter to St Augustine of Canterbury (601) setting out the rules for the newly converted Anglo-Saxons and no doubt making concessions, absolutely rules out marriage of first cousins but concedes that the Anglo-Saxons might marry their second and third cousins[2].

When one transfers these rules (even the most lenient of them) to the circumstances of Irish lineage society they give rise to hefty problems for the canonists, and it is scarcely surprising that the major reference to the matter in what has been taken to be a *Romani* document, ,Synodus II Patricii', rings of controversy:

> *De consanguinitate in coniugio. Intellege quod lex loquitur, non minos nec plus: quod autem observatur apud nos, ut quattuor genera diuidantur, nec vidisse dicunt nec legisse.* 'Understand what the law says, neither less nor more: but what is observed among us, that they be separated by four degrees, they say they have neither seen nor read'[3].

The method of computation here is by no means clear: at the minimum (*computatio legalis*) it forbids marriage with first cousins; at the maximum (*computatio canonica*) the prohibition extends to and includes third cousins. Whichever way one takes it, there was good reason for the dogmatic assertion of those who opposed the *Romani:* in Irish lineage terms, the rule that one could not marry

<hr />

2 J. *Gaudemet*, L'église dans l'empire romain, Paris 1958, p. 524—8; G. H. *Joyce*, Christian marriage, London 1933, p. 505—43.

3 L. *Bieler*, ed., The Irish Penitentials, SLH 5, 1963, p. 196. The translation is that of Bieler.

within the fourth degree (i. e. first cousin or closer) ruled out all members of one's *gelfhine;* prohibition of the sixth degree (i. e. second cousin) ruled out all members of one's *derbfhine;* and the further extension of the rule to the eighth degree (i. e. third cousin) excluded all members of one's *iarfine.*

The problems raised by these rules were most pressing in the matter of inheriting females in a lineage society such as that of the Irish. The normal rule was that where there was a son or sons, daughters did not inherit real estate or moveables (excepting three limited categories of this latter type of property)[4]. Where there were no sons, a daughter inherited a life-interest in her father's estate which reverted on her death to her father's surviving agnates within the *gelfhine* or, in default of these, to the agnates within the *derbfhine.* There was however a possible compromise — and it appears to be an ancient solution to the problem[5] — by which the inheriting female married one of the ultimate heirs and so preserved an interest in the estate (though not an exclusive one) for her own issue. There is evidence in two archaic poems that this was the normal solution. The first of these, *Inlongad bandtaig banchora,* has been dated by Dr Thomas Charles-Edwards to the late sixth century or to the first half of the seventh[6]. It is certainly no later and it is far from clear. According to this poem the senior of the *gelfhine* 'binds forward' the family inheritance, i. e. he causes sureties to be given that it will not be alienated permanently. There is some evidence that within the *gelfhine* property was divided *fo lín gabal (per stirpes);* the *senior* who acts would then belong to another branch of the *gelfhine* and would most probably be the *flaith gelfhine.* If the entire *gelfhine* is extinct, a member of the *derbfhine* acts instead *(manip sese[d] imbera).* A further section of the poem (which is difficult to interpret) states that the son of such an heiress does not inherit the property if, when his mother's family contests it, his father has not a better claim by kin-right[7]. That is to say, his mother must marry her father's inheriting agnate or one of them in order to insure an interest in the estate for her issue. This is none other than prescribed parallel cousin marriage amongst first cousins. The second archaic text, *Din Techtugud*[8], supports this interpretation. Seither, who makes formal entry on an estate which is the property of her 'head' *(cond)* and her kindred *(cenél),* is described as 'a woman who sprang from two forks' *(ba-ch bé degabail chinnes)* i. e. an heiress issuing from a parallel cousin marriage. The text goes on to say that her family *(fine)* accepted her taking possession 'because it was a case [entailing] reversion' *(fo bíth ba n-adba taisic).*

---

4 D. A. *Binchy,* ed., Studies in early Irish law, Dublin 1936, p. 133; R. *Thurneysen,* Irisches Recht, Abh. Berlin, Phil.-Hist. Kl. Nr. 2 (1931), p. 20.

5 SEIL p. 181—6.

6 The poem is edited by Myles *Dillon* in SEIL p. 135—76. T. M. *Charles-Edwards,* Kinship, status and the origin of the hide, Past and Present 56 (1972), p. 3—33.

7 SEIL p. 150.

8 Celtica 6 (1963), p. 234—5 (text and translation by Binchy).

The evidence of these archaic texts is amply borne out by the provisions of Irish canon law which pay particular attention to the matter of inheriting females:

> *De his qui addunt auctores ecclesiae in feminis heredibus.* Sinodus
> Hibernensis: *Auctores ecclesiae hic multa addunt, ut feminae heredes dent
> ratas et stipulationes, ne transferatur hereditas ad alienos; Dominus enim dicit*
> [Num 27: 10, 11]: *Transibit hereditas earum fratribus patris sui, inde
> propinquis. Sciendum est, utrum dabunt partem Domino; si tacuerint
> propinqui earum, Domini erit, quod dabunt, sin autem, irritum erit. Sciendum
> est, quid dabunt in testamentum, hoc est, vaccas, vestes et vasa. Sciendum est,
> quid dabunt ministris, hoc est partem de ovibus et lanam: si vero de propinquis
> fuerint ministri, dabunt eis aliquid de hereditate, et si ecclesiae habuerint
> partem* [vl: *ecclesiam habuerint paternam*], *dabunt ei de sua hereditate, et si
> genuerint filios, viris suae cognationis dabunt hereditatem* [vl: *Si peperint
> filios viris cognationis, hereditas paterna filiorum erit*][9].

The provisions of canon law are borrowed from secular law and are almost identical in all respects. And while not prescribed, parallel cousin marriage is clearly taken to be normal and the rights of the issue of such marriages are clearly asserted. Justification for this, merely hinted at here, is set out in full in the preceding paragraph of the collection where the matter is dealt with thoroughly and the grounds for the accomodation with Irish law fully explained.

The way out of the difficulty was found, of course, in the Old Testament. Jewish law forbids marriage with the following relatives: mother, sister, father's sister, mother's sister, son's daughter and daughter's daughter (Lev 17—20). This leaves the way open for parallel cousin marriage, but the Irish canon lawyers did not leave the matter at the stage of general principle. As evidence in support of the general legal principle *De eo quod feminae dividunt hereditatem non tamen principalem* ('that women take a share in the family land but not as ultimate heirs') they cite in detail the case of the daughters of Salphaad. Their father died without sons and they demanded an inheritance: *date nobis possessionem inter cognatos patris nostri* (Num 27). The leaders of the lineage raised the problem of the alienation of family land should they marry outsiders. The answer of Moses (which was the Lord's answer) was that they should marry whom they wished but only within a family of their father's tribe. A careful collation of the genealogies in Num 26: 28—34 with the text in Num 36: 10—12 shows without any doubt that they married sons of their father's brothers. This genealogical point would not be missed by an élite much given to the cultivation of genealogy. Here then was sound and explicit biblical support for the type of parallel cousin marriage common in Irish society and a citation so apt and pointed that we have to postulate an

---

9 H. *Wasserschleben*, ed., Die irische Kanonensammlung, Leipzig [2]1885, p. 116 (XXXII, 20).

exactly formulated question and a carefully researched answer. Marriage within the *gelfhine* and therefore of first cousins, contracted for reasons of property, had therefore explicit divine sanction. The terminology is that of Irish law: *ratae* and *stipulationes* are identical with *ráth* and *naidm* of Irish law and the expression *si tacuerint* is a fair rendering of the ideas behind the secular expressions *cnet* and *fogurred*[10].

II.
The parting of an abbot from his monastery

The remarkable passage in the Collectio Canonum Hibernensis which deals with the parting of a *princeps* from his church and which Dr Hughes felt belonged to the seventh century, shows how the canonists adopted not only the terminology but also the conceptual framework of secular law.

> *De eo, qui dat locum alicui, si separati fuerint, hoc modo separabuntur.*
> Sinodus Hibernensis: *Placuit, ut princeps, qui se ipsum non dedit aut sua, sed tamen servabit ecclesiae, si ejectus fuerit, aut voluerit abscedere, dimittat dimidium seminis in pecoribus ecclesiae, et quod ei datum, relinquat intactum, nisi quod necessitas loci illius exegerit ab eo, et quod secum intulit, tollat. Si ipse dominatricem aut ministros conduxit, in sua parte erunt, si vero causa loci conduxit, cum parte loci exibunt, et omnes oblationes alienorum inter principem et ecclesiam dividentur in separatione; sed si princeps sacerdos catholicus sit, omnes autem labores, quos ille fecit, et omnia loci ornamenta, loci erunt, et quidquid ipse laborans impenderit, de substantia loci non reddet, exceptis rebus maximis et propriis, id est, specialibus ecclesiae vasis. Aliis vero placuit, quod in primo anno sparsit, quando egenus fuit, in separatione non reddet*[11].

Another text, preserved in a different recension of the same collection, deals with the same matter.

> *De his qui loca pro tempore tenent, qualiter recedentes separari debent.*
> Sinodus: *Qui pro tempore locum tenent, sed voluerint recedere, quartam partem substantiae dimittere debent loco, et quantum in sua parte retinere debebunt substantiae. Item. Antiqua institutio est, ut dimidiam partem seminis et* [om. ?] *pecorum secum habeat, et alteram relinquat in loco, et quod eis* [recte *ei*] *commissum est, relinquat sanum et intactum in jure loci, nisi quod necessitate ejus loci exegerit, et quod secum portavit, secum tolle* [recte *tollat*].

---

10 SEIL p. 39. Tob 6: 10 is appositely adduced as a solution to the same problem elsewhere; on which see *Wasserschleben*, p. 177 n.
11 *Wasserschleben*, p. 173 (XLIII, 6); K. *Hughes*, The church in early Irish society, London 1966, p. 158—9.

> *Si autem ipsa* [recte *ipse*] *dominatricem aut ministros conduxit, in sua parte erunt, si vero causa loci conduxit, cum parte loci exibunt. Omnes oblationes aliorum inter propinquos*[?] *et ecclesiam dividentur in separationem. Omnes labores, quos hic fecit, loci erunt, et quicquid ipse laborans expenderit de substantia loci, non reddet. Alii tamen judices volunt, quod in primo anno expenderit, quando egenus fuit, non reddet in separationem*[12].

These texts are by no means easy to construe, and how these provisions worked out in real life remains obscure to a degee. Evidently, they deal with a *locum tenens* who acts as *princeps* of a church or monastery, possibly when the owners of the institution could not or did not provide a suitable candidate (and the secular laws envisage such a situation)[13], and the framers of the rules confine themselves to the practical problems of property and service when such a *locum tenens* resigns or is dismissed. Two matters are of particular interest: the terms used in regard to the division of the herds and, more generally, the model for the whole arrangement.

The terms *dimidium seminis in pecoribus* and *dimidiam partem seminis (et) pecorum* appear nowhere else to my knowledge and the meaning is not immediately obvious. However, the idea which lies behind it is common enough in the secular law tracts and is expressed in the technical term *indoth (indad)*. It occurs notably and in a context identical with that of the canons in the tract on marriage law, *Cáin Lánamna*[14]. The term *indoth* I take to be a compound of *in* and *doth* 'bearing, bringing forth, hatching' and it means 'young, young of cattle'. It seems to be used in particular by the secular lawyers in reference to the offspring of cattle born within a determined period, such for example as the period during which a contract was in force. The term is used in *Cáin Lánamna* with reference to the division of marital property on the occasion of a divorce in *lánamnas comthinchuir* ('marriage of equal contribution', the usual type of secular marriage in the seventh century):

> 'A third of all yield *(torad)* except handiwork [of the woman] goes to [the owner of] the land; a third of the cattle born during the duration of the marriage to [the owner of] the stock from which they sprang; a third to [whomsoever supplied] the labour'[15].

This type of division does not take place in the case of *lánamnas for ferthinchur*, where the man provided the bulk of the marriage goods. It only arose when the woman made a substantial contribution to the marriage goods and this, as Professor Binchy has shown, was a later development[16]. A text edited by Binchy points to an intermediate stage:

12 *Wasserschleben*, p. 179 n.
13 ALI III, p. 70—72 = CIH p. 1820, 1929.
14 SEIL p. 1—75.
15 SEIL p. 28; CIH p. 507.
16 SEIL p. 180—86; p. 207—34.

162

Ni beir an ben ba o fhir do indud cethra acht ag cach dhini, dairt 7 colpthach 7 samaisc 'the woman takes nothing from the man of the young of the cattle [born during the marriage] but an ox [i. e. full-grown animal of either sex] of each [year's] group, a year old heifer, a yearling and a two year old heifer'[17].

It appears to me that the Latin expressions of the canon lawyer are none other than an attempt to render the precise shade of meaning which *indoth* has in regard to the division of property on the dissolution of a contract in which property was held in common. The contract he had in mind was a secular marriage contract, and he drew his principles of division from those in use in the secular law of divorce in the case of the commonest type of marriage in the seventh century and perhaps earlier. This is borne out by an excursus of the compiler of *Cáin Lanamna* at the beginning of his text in which he discusses the different types of *lánamnas* 'bonding' recognized by Irish law. Amongst those he lists are: *flaith fria aicgillne, eclais fria manchu ... fear fria ben* 'the relationship of a lord to his base clients, of a church [to be understood church superior here] to its monastic tenantry ..., of a man to his wife'[18]. In commenting on this passage, Thurneysen pointed out that since definition was foreign to Irish lawyers the compiler simply lists all the associations which could properly be called *lánamnas*[19]. This is quite true but it is clear that the compiler of *Cáin Lánamna* was well aware of the parallels between the rules of division in divorce law and those which applied in the case of an abbot and his church. He may even have been aware of the precise rules of canon law under discussion. In fact, the principles of division are exceptionally close in both cases. What the marriage partner contributes in the first instance, he/she takes away on the dissolution of the contract, what is lawfully expended to appropriate ends entails neither penalty nor restitution, and the increase in wealth (essentially an increase in the herds) is divided according to fixed proportions between the partners[20]. Given the difference in circumstances of the two types of partnerships, the resemblances are so remarkably close that we must postulate that the one is modelled on the other. It would seem that the canon law is based on the property division in use in *lánamnas comthinchuir*, the latest type of marriage to emerge in the Irish system. Its canon law imitation is described, as we have seen, as *antiqua institutio* in a text which can scarcely be later than AD 700. Can we take it that if this order of things is called old and thought customary about AD 700 it was in existence at that time for a generation or two? If so, we must place the emergence of its model in the early seventh century or before. If one wished to turn the tables, one could argue that the provisions for the division of property in secular divorce were based on those governing the parting of an abbot from his church. I know of

17 CIH p. 2105.
18 SEIL p. 16; CIH p. 502—4.
19 SEIL p. 4.
20 SEIL p. 18—45.

no evidence to support this unlikely hypothesis but even if any can be found one must still conclude that the two legal systems were deeply intermeshed and shared personnel as well as principles.

III.
Personal injuries in the case of a cleric of high status

In the archaic portion of the medico-legal tract, *Bretha Déin Chécht*, — the follow-ing lines occur:

> *dí-rirt[h]er bronn-ór bronn-arcat*
> *huile n-ard n-úag*
> *ar- séotu -saig*
> *la cumail cech aonuig*
> *la sét cach aidbriuda*
> *ima ruide rus*[21].

I translate tentatively;

> 'With refined gold with refined silver shall every high celibate be paid. He has a claim to *séoit* together with a *cumal* for every assembly [and] a *sét* for every advertisement for which his cheek blushes'.

As Professor Binchy points out, this section of the text has to do with the archaic institution of *iarmbrethemnas* or *iartaige* 'further compensation for bodily injury if the injury proved permanent'. § 30 states that this arises only after inspection by a leech and then proceeds to list the *iarmbrethemnas* appropriate for injuries to the leg, the thigh and the hand. § 31 deals with the head and facial injuries, and these of course are very obvious ones and involve embarrassment to the person who has suffered them. I consider the last six lines of this section to have reference to injuries to clerics of high status and this is borne out by a parallel passage in the very early *Canones Hibernenses*:

> *Sanguis episcopi uel excelsi principis uel scribae qui ad terram effunditur, si colirio indiguerit, eum qui effuderit sapientes crucifigi iudicant uel .vii. ancel-las reddat. Si in specie, tertiam partem de argento et conparem uerticis de auro latitudinem nec non et similem occuli de gemma praeciosa magnitudinem reddat; et pro eius liuoris uel uulneris admiratione in conuentu uel in qualibet multitudine usque ad tertium annum aut eo amplius, si non indulgeat, praetium ancelle si qui comisit reddat*[22].

A later tract, dated by Professor Binchy to the first half of the eighth century at latest, throws some further light on this — and on the closeness of the relationship

---

21 D. A. *Binchy*, Bretha Déin Chécht, Ériu 20 (1966), p. 1—66: 40.
22 *Bieler*, Penitentials, p. 170.

of secular and canon lawyer —, but since it is so close to the text of the *Canones Hibernenses* that it can be none other than a free rendering of it or of the text on which it is based I do not propose to discuss it in detail here[23].

The *Canones Hibernenses*, in the case of this section at least, are universally agreed to be early. McNeill-Gamer, Haddan and Stubbs, and Kenney assign them to the seventh century and Bieler suggests that they are not later than the middle of the seventh century. This early date is now well supported by a number of other considerations. The passage under discussion quite clearly reflects the matter contained in the very archaic poetic section of *Bretha Déin Chécht*, the part attributed to the poet-jurist, Laidcenn mac Ercaid (of whom nothing else is known) and which Professor Binchy assigns to the Archaic Old Irish period and considers likely to be a product of the poetico-legal school where the *Nemed* tracts originated[24]. The section dealing with clerics is one of a piece with the rest of the archaic poem in language and in diction and cannot be rejected as an interpolation.

The canons accurately reflect both the matter and the linguistic terms of the archaic poem: *uulneris admiratione in conuentu uel in qualibet multitudine* is a fair rendering of *aidbriud* and *si colirio indiguerit* conveys the archaic legal term *inindraig* (which occurs in an ancient rule)[25] perfectly adequately. Besides, the canons supply additional information on the archaic institution of *iarmbrethemnas*. The payment of a *cumal* falls due for a disfigurement and may be claimed each year up to three years or more in the case of an injured bishop, leading abbot or scribe unless he chose not to enforce his claim. It should logically follow that the *sét* for every *aidbriud* should run the same term.

What of the possibility that the canons have been drawn on by the archaic poem? There are serious reasons against this, not least the probability that the poem belongs to the oral teaching of the law schools, but quite apart from the explicit reference to a celibate cleric, there is a least one tiny piece of evidence in support of this notion. That is the reference to *bronn-ór, bronn-arcat*, which looks like an attempt to render *in specie* which may be taken to be gold and silver of a fairly uniform standard of purity used for exchange. The poem lists all compensations in terms of the normal native units — *séoit, cumala* and livestock — with two exceptions: the *cumal* for the hand is paid in silver of unspecified quality and the present references to gold and silver. Have we to do here with sub-Roman ideas? It is likely, given Professor Binchy's demonstration of the archaism of *othrus*, that knowledge of *iarmbrethemnas* can only have come from the native law schools at a very early period. It seems not unlikely that the two texts are roughly coaeval. The date of the poem must be in doubt because of the complexities in the dating of

23   ALI IV p. 362 = CIH p. 588; *Binchy*, Stud. Hib. 2 (1962), p. 63 n 166.
24   *Binchy*, Ériu 20, p. 3—4.
25   *Binchy*, Ériu 12 (1934), p. 131.

Archaic Old Irish, not least the problem of different but contemporary registers, but it is probably safe to place it in the sixth century.

We can conclude that by the sixth century there is evidence for wide-ranging borrowing between the two legal systems and since, in such matters as family inheritance and marital rules, traditional societies do not usually undergo abrupt and rapid change, we can reasonably posit a lengthy period of acculturalization anterior to the putative date of these documents. And that canons which may be dated to the sixth century should retail archaic rules on personal injuries, obsolescent in the seventh century and certainly obsolete by the beginning of the eighth, points to the same conclusion.

The Church and settlement

By

T. M. Charles-Edwards

The impact of the Church on patterns of Irish settlement is difficult to gauge even if we limit ourselves to the seventh and eighth centuries. There is useful evidence in the Laws as well as in early hagiographical texts such as the Patrician material in the Book of Armagh[1]. The evidence is, however, patchy, and crucial questions, such as the status of the *manach* 'monastic tenant', remain obscure.

Many churches must have been very small-scale economic enterprises, in effect the lands of one branch of a not very wealthy family dedicated to the support of a church held by that branch. The worldly advantages of creating a church within the family may have been tangible: freedom from royal dues was at least a possibility, and there was also the ability to pay burial dues to a church within one's own kindred[2]. There is no reason to think, however, that such churches would make much impact on patterns of settlement while they remained under the control of the family or kindred. Their importance lies, perhaps, in their vulnerability to seizure by outsiders. Such a church will have been ruled by an *airchinnech*, 'erenagh', who might himself be a layman and free from the spiritual authority of an abbot (CIH 2.4)[3]. Should such a church fall below certain minimum standards of behaviour, it would lose its legal status (CIH 1.1). In such circumstances it may well have found it necessary to subject itself to a powerful monastic patron from outside the *túath* (the *déorad Dé* of CIH 3.33) or be forcibly taken over by the king and, perhaps, given to another church. Inadequacy of spiritual life, then, could make a church legally vulnerable and lead to loss of its independence. Such disputes were one source of accumulation of Church property. Accumulation would not, of itself, affect patterns of settlement, but it might be the occasion of changes in the form of agricultural exploitation.

Even the *prímchell na túaithe* 'chief church of the túath' (CIH 577.34) might lose its independence. In Adomnán's Vita S. Columbae Cúl Rathin (Coleraine) is an

---

1 References to the laws are to D. A. *Binchy*, ed., Corpus Iuris Hibernici, Dublin, 1978, and are to page and line. References to Patrician material are to L. *Bieler*, ed., The Patrician Texts in the Book of Armagh, SLH 10, 1979, and are given according to Bieler's numbering, thus T 12.2 = paragraph 12, sub-section 2 of Tírechán Collectanea; references are to Tírechán (T), the *Additamenta (Addit.)* and the *Notulae*.

2 *Addit.*, 8.1, 3; CIH 532.1—534.21.

3 There is considerable variety in scholars' statements on the *airchinnech*: J. *Ryan*, Irish Monasticism, Dublin 1931, p. 264, n. 5; K. *Hughes*, The Church in Early Irish Society, London 1966, p. 223. The difference is in part a matter of date: Ryan's "extern (generally lay) manager of the church property" is true of a period later than the seventh century. But I doubt whether the identity of *airchinnech* and *ap*, implied by Hughes, is correct for any period.

episcopal church, the *prímchell* of Mag nEilni, one of the Cruithnian *túatha*[4]. Tírechán, however, mentions it as a former episcopal church and speaks of the acquisitions of the church of Connor in Mag nEilni[5]. The *Notulae* suggest aggrandisement on the part of the Uí Chóelbad, the ruling family of Mag Line to the south, which conquered Mag nEilni during the seventh century[6]. Within the Church, therefore, large accumulations of land were possible not only through the peaceful development of *paruchiae* but also through the forcible subjection of the churches of a conquered *túath* to the favoured church of the conqueror. This may, indeed, have been the easiest way for the conqueror to acquire territorial interests in the subject kingdom.

Part of the stimulus behind the growth of *paruchiae* was the wish to defend oneself from the tentacles of a powerful ecclesiastical neighbour by seeking the patronage of more distant church. Much of Tírechán's work suggests a readiness on the part of Armagh to fulfil such a role[7]. The material on Sletty, in Tírechán and in the *Additamenta*, appears to reflect an outstanding case[8]. Sletty, within the kingdom of Uí Bairrche, had much to fear from Kildare, the ecclesiastical wing of Uí Dúnlainge power, to the north. Remote Armagh was a prestigious patron unlikely to be in a position to cause much trouble. Áed's subjection of Sletty to Armagh in the late seventh century coincides with the rise of the Uí Dúnlainge and a period of novel prominence for Kildare[9]. Moreover the terms of the testament by which the subjection was achieved may have secured Áed's candidate as the successor to Sletty itself[10]. In this case the extension of a *paruchia* will have merely defended the *status quo* and thus it will not have caused of itself any change in the economic position of the newly subject church beyond some, possibly token, tribute. When considering the growth of ecclesiastical federations, everything depends upon the circumstances in which a link was created: in some cases a genuine accumulation of economic resources will have been achieved, in others it will, on the contrary, have been averted. In some cases the patron church will aspire to nothing more than an alliance with its associates, as Tírechán plainly implies for Armagh[11]; in others there will have been direct subordination expressed in the payment of *cís*, 'tribute'[12]. Just as an individual church may be nothing more, in terms of settlement, than a tonsured kindred[13], so a federation of such

4 Adomnán, Vita S. Columbae, ed. A. O. *Anderson* and M. O. *Anderson*, London 1961, I. 50.
5 T 48.2,3.
6 *Notulae* (15).
7 E.g. T 18.2; 22.4; 25.2; 47.4.
8 T 51.4; *Addit.*, 14.3; 16.1—2.
9 Cf. F. J. *Byrne*, Irish Kings and High-Kings, London 1973, p. 152.
10 *Addit.*, 16 (in lines 8, 9, 10 read *a idacht* for *aidacht*).
11 T 25.2.
12 CIH 38.21 (*cís flatha nó ecalsa*).
13 CIH 54.32—3 (*fine ecalsa*).

churches may be only a defensive alliance in the interests of preserving economic independence.

Once such federations or *paruchiae* begin to raise the dominant church to a position in which it has a relatively large community and lands to sustain its size, then they will make an impact upon settlement patterns. A major monastery of the seventh century appears to have depended heavily on the direct exploitation of lands adjacent to the monastery: so much is implied by Adomnán for both Iona and Clonmacnois[14]. The arable lands of Iona seem to have been concentrated in the *occidentalis campus* 'western plain' of the island. *Campus*, here, like its Irish equivalent *mag*, seems to be used of an area of land consisting of arable or permanent pasture, to be distinguished from temporary pasture such as *móin* 'bog-land', *lénae* 'riverine pasture', *slíab* 'mountain pasture' (the latter apparently usually exploited in common). Thus the *Additamenta* in the Book of Armagh record the purchase of Ochter Achid *cona seilb, iter fid 7 mag 7 lénu, cona llius 7 a llubgort*[15]. The phrasing is significant: the *selb* 'estate' includes first the assets outside the settlement itself, *fid* 'woodland', *mag* 'arable and permanent pasture', *léni* 'pastures along a river', and then the assets within the settlement, the *less* or enclosure within which the buildings lay, and the *lubgort* 'vegetable garden'. On Iona the western *campus* appears to have been primarily arable for there is a separate *bocetum* 'cow-pasture'[16]. The monks of Iona used stone walls to defend their arable from trespassing animals[17], but this was almost certainly a consequence of scarcity of timber: the lawtract *Bretha Comaithchesa* shows that fences of dead wood, not live hedges, and not usually stone walls, were the norm[18]. Major churches, then, were supported in large part by accumulations of land directly cultivated, in other words by large demesnes or home farms. These did not necessarily form cohesive blocks of territory excluding any other holdings: even on Iona Adomnán records a lay peasant[19]. They did, however, provide the normal sustenance of the monks: Adomnán has the aged Columba reflecting happily that the grain in the barn will be enough to feed the monks for an entire year[20].

The importance of lands adjacent to a major monastery raises the question of what were the economic rewards of lordship over more distant churches and lands. No doubt considerable political influence was acquired through such lordship, but one wonders what economic return there may have been beyond the right to claim hospitality, to receive gifts, and, occasionally, to impose tribute. The problem is made worse by the evidence in the Book of Armagh that grants to

---

14 Adomnán, Vita S. Columbae, I. 3; I. 37; II. 28; III. 23.
15 *Addit.*, 11.2.
16 Adomnán, III. 23.
17 Adomnán, II. 28.
18 CIH 73.7—18; cf. 65.4—6 (which could hardly be a stone wall).
19 Adomnán, II. 3.
20 Adomnán, III. 23.

churches were exceedingly varied in terms of what was granted. At one extreme Fedelmid mac Loíguiri is made to grant *regionem suam cum possesione sua et cum omnibus substantiis suis et cum omni progenie sua*[21]. Another grants one son together with his inheritance[22]. The sons of Fíachrae grant a *campus, cum seruis in eo sibi famulantibus*[23]. Others grant cows or pasture rights or both[24]. The lawtract *Córus Béscna* suggests that churches might attract many small grants in the form of burial dues: the man who has merely maintained his inheritance without making any further acquisitions may only grant the value of his honour price[25]. An *aire désa*, for example, the lowest grade of nobleman, can grant the value of five cows. Gifts of cows or of silver were no doubt always acceptable; grants of land together with its free occupants or with its servile cultivators were also manageable, but grants of odd parcels of pasture or arable must often have posed a difficulty unless they were immediately rented out to a neighbouring farmer. The more distant a piece of land was the more obviously advantageous it will have been to exploit it indirectly through rent-paying tenants. Even so it will have been something of a problem for churches like Iona or Clonmacnois even to collect rent from all their scattered possessions. One must assume local *rechtairi* 'stewards', based in churches subject to the leading church of a *paruchia*, and charged with rent collection[26]. The consequence of grants of land at a distance from the church will have been the multiplication of rent-paying tenures.

The *Additamenta* in the Book of Armagh record, as we have seen, grants of land together with, on the one hand, the *progenies* of the grantor, and, on the other, the *serui* cultivating the land. These examples raise the issue of the relationship to the land of free and servile occupants and the position of *manaig* 'monastic' or 'ecclesiastical tenants'. It is probably approximately true to say that, in seventh-century Ireland, dispersed settlement was the expression of free status, nucleated settlement the expression of servile or semi-servile status. The sharing of land within free kindreds was carried out in such a way that the farmsteads of adult kinsmen tended to form dispersed clusters, each farmstead forming the centre of the kinsman's land-holding[27]. For the servile and semi-servile population, however, the critical economic relationship was to the lord rather than to the kindred. For them the dispersing effect of the division of inherited land did not operate, and hence it seems likely that their function as labourers for their lords drew them together into nucleated settlements. It will also, therefore, be approximately true

<hr>

21 *Addit.*, 1.6.
22 *Addit.*, 10.1; T 15.2.
23 *Addit.*, 5.2.
24 *Addit.*, 5.4; T 22.3.
25 CIH 532.1ff.
26 Cf. the *rechtairi* of Adomnán's *cáin*, K. Meyer, ed., Cáin Adamnáin, Oxford 1905, para. 48.
27 CIH 64.18—20; 444.12—16; 447.4—31; 457.11—18; 460.7—461.9.

to say that settlement in dispersed clusters was the expression of kinship whereas nucleated settlement was the expression of lordship. In terms of settlement, then, the grant of land together with the free kindred of the grantor will have been quite different from the grant of land together with servile labourers. This must be borne in mind when we turn to examine the nature of the class of *manaig*.

Manach is the Irish word derived from Latin *monachus* 'monk'. Though modern scholars distinguish two quite distinct senses of the word, (a) 'monk' and (b) 'monastic tenant', such a distinction may perhaps obsure the issue to some extent. One has to remember that the dividing line between the monk and other regular forms of the religious life was less easy to draw until the reforms of Benedict of Aniane made Benedictine monasticism the rule throughout the Carolingian Empire and introduced a separate rule for canons. The existence of a separate religious profession, that of the canon, made the position of the monk quite distinct. But in the seventh century this was all in the future: indeed such distinctions were not to gain a hold in Ireland until the twelfth century. Hence the term *manach* could be extended to cover all those living a regular life under the authority of an abbot even though they had not taken two of the three standard vows of poverty, chastity and obedience. The problem arose, so one may suggest, from the subjection to the authority of the abbot, or other head of a church, of men living at a distance from the church. Such subjections were sometimes, as we have seen, of a whole kindred or of a branch of a kindred. Enough clues have survived to suggest that this was due to the existence of a device — the solemn oral declaration known as an *audacht (edacht, idacht)* — by with the head of a kindred, with the consent of this fellow kinsmen, could create obligations binding upon the whole kindred[28]. Typically such a declaration was made to create obligations which became operative after the death of the person making the declaration. The *audacht*, therefore, enabled legal arrangements to persist after the death of the head of the kindred who had initiated them. This provided a way in which a kindred and its lands could be permanently subjected to external authority such as that of a church. A kindred subjected to a church became bound by a strict penitential regime; it was subject to the authority of the head of the church; its lands were granted to the church so that it occupied them as tenants; but since it was itself subjected to the church *qua* continuing kindred its members were not bound by a rule of celibacy, only by an un-Irish rule of monogamy and periodic sexual abstinence. While *manaig* of this sort might be subject to the abbot of a regular monastery, there is no reason to think that any church was unable to accept such *manaig*. The eighth-century *Ríagail Phátraic* envisages *manaig* subject to an *airchinnech* and, as we have seen, the Laws do not identify *airchinnech* and *ap*, erenagh and abbot[29]. The *airchinnech* is simply the head of a church and its

28 See T. M. *Charles-Edwards* and F. *Kelly*, Bechbretha, Dublin 1983, notes to § 49.
29 CIH 2129.32—35; 2130.18—19; 2.4.

171

familia. This *familia* includes the *manaig* and is termed in Irish *muinter* (probably from Lat. *monasterium*, but already by the eighth century used for any household: *muinter* = *'familia* including *manaig'* I take to be a principal stage in this semantic progression[30]). The creation of such a class provided an answer to the problem of administration at a distance and to the problem of kindred solidarity. However, not only free kindreds but also slaves were subjected to churches, including monasteries. The heterogeneous social origins of ecclesiastical dependants makes one wonder whether the *manaig* formed a single class, or whether *manach* was a blanket term covering quite disparate social groups.

The principal category of legal evidence for the *manach* consists of the lists of legal dependants or non-competents. In the majority of these lists, six out of the ten I have collected, the *manach* is associated with the *mug* 'slave' or *fuidir* 'half-free dependant', and also with the *macc* 'son' and *ingen* 'daughter' in a group of close legal dependants[31]. For example, among the five contracts which are to be rescinded according to the old introduction to the *Senchas Már* are the contract of a *mug* without the authorisation of his lord, the contract of a *manach* without the authorisation of his abbot and the contract of a 'son of a living father' without the authorisation of his father. The authority to which the *manach* is said to be subject is either the *ap* 'abbot', *eclais* 'church' or the *airchinnech* 'erenagh'. There are, among these lists, four in which the *manach* is associated, not with the *mug* 'slave', but with the *céile* 'client'[32]. The *céile*, unlike the *mug*, is of free status, a vassal who owes fixed food renders to his lord. The tracts in which *manach* is associated with *céile* all received their present form relatively late in the classical period of legal writing, probably in the early eighth century. The earlier association with the *mug*, however, persisted alongside the later association with the *céile*, so that one may suppose that the position of the *manach* bore some resemblance to both *mug* and *céile*. The lists of dependants are mainly concerned with legal capacity in such things as suretyship and contracts. In these, except for one list, the association is with the *mug*. Those lists in which the *céile* appears are, with the same one exception, concerned with more general relationships or with the capacity of the superior in regard to his dependant rather than the other way round. In legal capacity, then, the *manach* resembles the *mug*; his resemblance to the *céile* lay elsewhere. If this conclusion be accepted, then the larger number of associations with *mug* than with *céile* is merely a consequence of the interest of such lists in legal capacity. Similarly the relatively late date of the tracts in which *manach* is associated with *céile* may prove nothing: the extension of the coverage of lists of

---

30 For a different view see J. *Vendryes*, Lexique Étymologique de l'Irlandais Ancien (M, N, O, P) Paris 1960, s. v. *muntar*.

31 CIH 47.1; 220.2; 351.25; 536.24; 593.35. At 522.1 the *dóermanach ecalsa* is associated with the semi-free *fuidir*.

32 CIH 240.33; 503.7—10; 592.24; 592.35.

dependants to topics other than legal capacity would suffice to account for the appearance of the *céile*. No real legal or social change need be assumed.

Outside the lists the most important evidence on the *manach* comes from the lawtract *Córus Béscna*, a text probably to be assigned to the early eighth century, but containing, as so often, earlier material. It, like the *Díre* tract, emphasises the *goire* 'pietas' owed by the *manach* to the church[33]. More importantly, however, it contains evidence on the status and the obligations of the *manach*. It contains a version of the legend of the encounter of Patrick with Lóegaire, king of Tara, in which a druid is made to prophesy to Lóegaire that Patrick would "steal from him the living and the dead":

> "He will free slaves *(mugo)*, he will exalt base kindreds through the grades of the church and through the service of penitence to God." For the kingdom of heaven is open to every kindred of men after the coming of the Faith, both free kindreds and base kindreds. So, likewise, is the Church open to every man whoever should submit to the Law[34].

A slightly later reference makes it clear that the phrase "through the service of penitence to God" was intended to refer (though not necessarily exclusively) to the *manach*[35]. The implication of the passage, then, is that Christianity has changed slaves into free *manaig*: the *mug* has become the *manach*.

The *manach* is a member of the body of his church just as the kinsman is a member of the body of his kindred[36]. The authority of the head of the church over the *manach* replaces the authority of the head of the kindred over his kinsman[37]. According to *Córus Béscna* the right of a church from its members (namely, in this context, its *manaig*) consists of first-born, first-fruits and tithes[38]. The basis is obviously Old Testament law, but it has been adapted to make it more like the food-renders paid by the client *(céile)*. Thus, among the tithes we have an annual render of every tenth calf, lamb and young of other livestock alongside the first-fruits which include the first-born of each class of livestock. A *manach* with fifteen breeding cows would, therefore, expect to pay two calves each year. This is undoubtedly a lower rate of render than that of the *céile*, but one has to remember that the *céile*'s livestock is a grant from the lord which passes into the *céile*'s possession on his lord's death and is kept by his heirs should he predecease his lord[39]. A higher rate of return on grants of livestock to *céili* would be necessary to redress the situation in the lord's favour and assure that in the long term lords and

---

33 CIH 530.24—26; 440.24—26; also 433.25—27.
34 CIH 527.28—528.12 (omitting the later addition, 528.1—4).
35 CIH 530.2—3.
36 CIH 530.1—3, 24—26, 32—33; 488.25—26; cf. 220.2.
37 CIH 455.1—4.
38 CIH 530.32—531.24.
39 CIH 483.12—37; 486.24—33.

their heirs held the bulk of existing livestock so as to continue to be able to grant it out. The *manach* is in a quite different position: his lord, being an institution, will never die, and his subjection, unlike that of the *céile*, is permanent.

The personal services of a *manach* to his church appear to have resembled, in principle at least, those of the *céile* to his lord[40]. At a period, however, at which agricultural labour was performed by monks resident in the monastery, *manaig* living at a distance can hardly have performed many economic services: they were, from the economic point of view, essentially rent-payers. It may have been desirable to have *manaig* adjacent to good summer-pasture and thus able to herd the church's cattle, so that living at a distance will not have precluded all labour-dues. But if the bulk of direct cultivation was concentrated on land adjacent to the church or monastery, distant tenants can never have been a significant element in the labour force.

The growth of a class of *manaig*, therefore, will have reinforced the importance of food-rents in the economy. Since *manaig* were freemen, and a *manach* may often have been an enfranchised *mug*, the growth of the class of *manaig* may also have strengthened the tendency towards dispersed settlement, except in the area close to the church or monastery to which they were subject. Here one may well have seen larger nucleated settlements. With the *manach*, as elsewhere, the effect of the Church on settlement patterns was not in any way revolutionary. Certain existing forces were reinforced at the expense of others. One can imagine that among the free, the economically weaker kindred may have been more likely to subject itself to a church or monastery, especially perhaps a distant church or monastery. The weight of their obligations would probably be reduced. As the druid declared in his prophecy to Lóegaire, the main impact of the Church may have been to exalt the *mug* and the *dochenél* — the slave and the base kindred.

The class of *manaig* appears to have been a genuine social and economic group. They may well have varied widely in wealth — as did the *céili* — but the close dependence upon their churches, in which they resembled the *mug*, and their regular annual food-renders, in which they resembled the *céile*, gave the class a genuine unity. Notable also is the way their relationship to their churches, for all the display of Old Testament Law, was assimilated to Irish categories: a *manach* was to his church as a kinsman to his kindred, and thus a collective term *mainche* was formed parallel to *fine* 'kindred'[41]; a *manach* owed *goire* 'pietas' to his church as a son to his parents. The assimilation enabled concepts to be transferred from application simply to the *manach* to embrace the *céile* as well: *manchaine*, the services due from the *manach*, became the term for the personal services of the *céile*. Yet, however Irish the form given to this new class, it nonetheless bore a certain resemblance to the *colonus* of the Roman and ex-Roman world: *manaig*

40 CIH 525.21—28.
41 CIH 530.9, 24; 1819.1; *Addit.*, 12.8.

formed a class of men hereditarily subjected, with their land, to their lord, just as the *colonus* was tied to his land, and yet they were of free status like the *colonus*. It may even be that the *manach* owes his origin to an attempt by early missionaries to transform slaves granted to them, or bought by them, into something approximating to the *colonus*[42].

42 Cf. Patrick, Epistola ad Coroticum, 14. The account of the *manach* in K. *Hughes*, CEIS, p. 136—137, is unduly dependent on glosses and commentary; but her account of the ecclesiastical and especially the canonical evidence, p. 138—140, is very useful.

IV

Sprache und Literatur
Language and Literature

The so-called Cothrige *and* Pátraic *strata of Latin loan-words in early Irish**

by
Damian McManus

§ 1 It was the Danish scholar Christoph Sarauw (IS, p. 1ff) who first expounded the theory that the dichotomy observable in the rendering of certain Latin consonantal sounds in the loan-words in Old Irish could be best explained in terms of two chronologically distinct periods of borrowing. In a short but well thought out discussion he set out his criteria for the relative chronology of these words, and in doing so paved the way for later more detailed expositions on this subject. Despite its flaws, his work, which did not receive due recognition until 1953 (§ 21 below), deserves to be regarded as one of the most important contributions to the study of the foreign element in the vocabulary of Old Irish.

§ 2 Sarauw observes (IS, p. 5ff) that the Lat. phoneme /p/ appears in the loanwords in OIr., in initial position, as either /k/ (written *c*) or /p/ (*Cothrige*< *Patricius, paiter* <*pater*), and he explains that as IE *p had been lost in Celtic the Lat. phoneme was foreign to the phonemic inventory of PIr., and was consequently replaced by the nearest approximation, native /kw/. The somewhat later adoption of /p/ was necessitated, he argues, by the loss of the labial element in /kw/, whereby original /kw/ and /k/ fell together as /k/, OIr. *c*. Once this element had been lost the native phoneme was no longer felt to be a suitable substitute for foreign /p/ "og saa blev de nødt til at laere at sige *p*". This explanation of the dichotomy is to be preferred to that of Zimmer (KZ 33 [1895], p. 280ff and IER 3rd Ser. 5 [1884], p. 242ff) and Güterbock (LLI p. 100f.), both of whom explain OIr. /k/ for Lat. /p/ as due to conscious substitution on the analogy of the separate reflexes of the IE voiceless labiovelar *kw in Insular Celtic.

§ 3 In words with OIr. /k/ for Lat. /p/ Sarauw saw that Lat. intervocalic /t/ and /k/ appear as /θ/ and /x/ (or /ð/ and /γ/ in unstressed syllables) respectively (*cuithe* < *puteus, cruimther* <*presbyter, Cothrige* <*Patricius*). He explains, no doubt correctly, that these words were borrowed before lenition took place in PIr. As this type of lenition is not found in words which retain Lat. /p/ (*paiter* <*pater, póc* <*pācem*) these are ascribed to the post-lenition period.

§ 4 To the above chronological criteria Sarauw adds (IS p. 8—9) the treatment of the Lat. endings *-ius, -ium* etc. In words with the earlier treatment of Lat. /p/ and intervocalic /t/ and /k/ these appear as *-e* (*Cothrige, cuithe, caille* <*pallium*) whereas they have completely disappeared in the later borrowings (*Pátric* <*Patricius, proind* <*prandium, purgatóir* <*purgatōrium*). The earlier words were, he argues,

---

* For a list of abbreviations see the end of this article.

borrowed before the loss of final syllables in PIr.; the later are to be derived from British, after the loss of final syllables had taken place in that language.

§ 5   In the twofold treatment of the Lat. clusters -nt- and -nc- Sarauw sees further support for his theory (IS, p. 10—11). The earlier words, in which these clusters are replaced by native -nd- and -ng- (cland <planta, ungae <uncia), were borrowed at a time when PIr. had no native equivalents. Later these clusters were adopted into the language (cinteir <centrum, ponc <punctum, cingciges <quinguāgēsima).

§ 6   A further, less reliable, criterion is seen in the treatment of Lat. /a:/. Sarauw observes (IS, p. 12) that OIr. /o:/ for Lat. /a:/, a reflection of British influence, is found in no word with spirant for tenuis and is consequently an indication of late borrowing (oróit <orātio, altóir <altāre, póc <pācem). He suggests that the retention of Lat. /a:/ as /a:/ was the norm in the older borrowings (cáise <cāseus, Márta <Mārtius).

§ 7   Though he saw (IS, p. 14ff) that the twofold rendering of Lat. f- in the loan-words (as s-, senester <fenestra or f-, febra(e) <februārius) presented an analogous dichotomy to that of the other phonemes, Sarauw excludes this from his list of chronological criteria. He realized, undoubtedly, that his own explanation of s- for f- as being due to false delinition of the foreign phoneme on the analogy of native radical /sw/, lenited /f/ (siur/ mo fiur), implied that these words must have been borrowed after lenition had taken place; and as the retention of Lat. f- as f- was not necessarily an indication of later borrowing the contrast s-/f- was seen to be redundant as a chronological criterion.

§ 8   We may summarize Sarauw's theory as follows:

(a) There are basically two groups of Latin loan-words in Old Irish, an earlier and a later one. The characteristics of the earlier group are (1) c- <p- (2) -th-, -ch-< -t-, -c- (3) -e <-ius, -ium etc. (4) -nd-, -ng- <-nt-, -nc- (5) á <ā. Corresponding to these the later group has (1) p- (2) -t-, -c- (3) zero (4) -nt-, -nc- (5) ó.

(b) Characteristics (3) and (5) of the later group point to borrowing from British rather than from Latin.

§ 9   This analysis of the loan-words was ingenious and, no doubt, basically correct, but it was not developed by the scholars of Sarauw's day. Vendryes, for example (DHV 60ff), writing two years after the publication of Sarauw's work, prefers the latter's explanation of OIr. c- for Lat. p-, to that of Güterbock, but goes no further; while Thurneysen on the other hand sticks to the older theory of analogical substitution (Hdb. § 909, GOI § 920). Indeed, it was not until 1931 that this chronological analysis of the loan-words was carried a step further, in Mac Neill's masterly article 'Beginnings of Latin Culture in Ireland'.

§ 10   MacNeill's contribution can be summed up under the following headings:

(a) Further contrasting criteria for the two-group theory.

(b) The correction of mistakes in Sarauw's work.

(c) An historical framework.

§ 11   (a) To the criteria set up by Sarauw MacNeill adds (BLCI, p. 44f) the shortening of original long vowels in unstressed syllables (in Irish) and syncope to the characteristics of the earlier group, contrasting with the retention of the former and the absence of the latter in the later stratum (*sesra* <*sextārius*, *ortha* <**orātio* as opposed to *oróit* <**orātio*).

§ 12   (b) MacNeill corrects Sarauw's misreading of OIr. -*t*-, -*c*-, -*p*- as /t/, /c/, /p/, explaining that these represent /d/, /g/, /b/, and that the convention of representing the intervocalic mediae with the symbols for the tenues derives from the orthographical conservatism of British (and Irish) Latin. In these the intervocalic voiceless plosives had been voiced in the same way as British voiceless plosives in the same position, but they continued to be written -*t*-, -*c*-, -*p*-.

§ 13   (c) Being an historian MacNeill sought to provide an historical or absolute chronology for the two strata of loan-words. He suggests (BLCI, p. 42) that the older group belongs to the earlier part of the fifth century, as the rendering in Irish of the Latin names of historical characters of this era reflects the features of this group (*Cothriche, Sachall* <*Sacellus, Sechnall*< *Secundinus*). The later, more extensive, group belongs to the period of the great expansion of monastic institutions in Ireland and the concomitant development of Latin literary culture in this country. This expansion dates from the early part of the sixth century and was largely due to the missionary zeal of the monasteries of South Wales, especially Llancarfan and Menevia (BLCI, p. 48).

§ 14   Drawing attention to the nature of British Latin MacNeill makes the important point that many words of the later group could, and most likely did, pass "direct from the Latin language into Irish, but from a Latin which the Irish had learned to pronounce after the British manner" (BLCI, p. 40—41). In this he differed from most of his predecessors who saw British itself as playing the intermediate role in the adoption of these words into Irish.

§ 15   This objective chronological investigation of the Latin loan-words in Early Irish was to a certain extent derailed in 1942 by the publication of O'Rahilly's The Two Patricks. O'Rahilly's controversial theory of the existence of two Patricks need not be discussed here, but his employment of the loan-words to substantiate it cannot be ignored.

Not recognizing MacNeill's contribution to the study of the loan-words, O'Rahilly accepts the existence of two groups of these words, as outlined by Sarauw, but rejects that scholar's explanation of the dichotomy. He argues (TP, p. 42) that many of the words, irrespective of the group to which they belong, must have been borrowed into Irish in the fifth century, and that the "true distinction between the two types of words is not so much that they came into Irish at different periods, as that the missionaries who introduced them belonged to two groups, who differed from each other in their pronunciation of Latin". According to O'Rahilly, Sarauw's early group was introduced by the Palladian missionaries, educated Gauls and Italians of the early fifth century who had preserved in their speech the classical values of Latin consonants, while many of the words of Sarauw's later group "are not so much borrowings of Latin words direct from Latin as of British words derived from Latin" (TP, p. 43). These belong to the second half of the fifth century (i.e. to the Patrician mission) and the sixth.

§ 16   The above theory is based on the following arguments:

(a) The lenition of Lat. intervocalic -t- and -c- to /θ/ and /x/ in the earlier group suggests that these phonemes were pronounced /t/ and /k/ in the Latin from which they were borrowed. As these are the classical values of the Lat. phonemes those who introduced the words must have been educated men, most likely Gauls and Italians.

(b) The rendering of Lat. intervocalic -p-, -t-, -c- by /b/, /d/, /g/ in the later group shows that this stratum must have been borrowed from either British Latin or British itself; the complete disappearance of Lat. -ius, -ium etc. from these points to the latter as the most likely candidate.

(c) This analysis of the loan-words corroborates the twofold nature of the external influence that helped to mould the Irish Church in the early centuries of its existence.

§ 17   Notwithstanding the "striking manner" (TP, p. 44) in which this analysis substantiates O'Rahilly's major contribution to the Patrician problem there are numerous objections to it, and few scholars today would accept it *in toto*. The following is an outline of the problems, contradictions and inconsistencies associated with it:

(a) O'Rahilly's argument that many of the words, irrespective of the type to which they belong, *must* have been borrowed into Irish in the fifth century is merely an hypothesis based on his own estimation of the number and nature of religious words indispensible to a growing Christian community, and does not take into account the possibility, far from remote, that many of the earlier borrowings could have been replaced by more 'modern' equivalents in the second stratum. This possibility had been mentioned by MacNeill (BLCI, p. 46—47), whom O'Rahilly ignored, and is also suggested by Murphy (Studies 32 [1943], p. 300 n. 1).

(b) The theory that educated Gauls and Italians of the fifth century would have preserved in their speech the Classical values of Latin consonants is not supported by what is known of continental Vulgar Latin. It was precisely in Gaul and Italy that intervocalic -t- and -c- were being voiced to /d/ and /g/ already in the fourth century (LHEB 145 n. 2).

(c) O'Rahilly is extremely vague on absolute chronology. He assigns the continental group to the early fifth-century Palladian mission and the British group, the borrowing of which "continued over a considerable period of time" (TP, p. 43), to the latter part of the fifth century, presumably beginning with the episcopate of Patrick the Briton and continuing on into the sixth century. This leaves only a generation between the two strata and requires that lenition, reduction of unstressed long vowels, vowel-affection, loss of final syllables, resolution of clusters of the type spirant + resonant, and syncope could all have taken place within a relatively short period of time, an hypothesis dismissed by Jackson (LHEB p. 144) as "scarcely credible" and by Greene (SLE p. 79) as "totally impossible".

(d) O'Rahilly's readiness to accept Sarauw's theory on the /kw/ for /p/ issue, and his explanation of the acclimatization of the phoneme /p/ in the second stratum as being due to the large number of words with /p/ borrowed during this period, are hardly consistent with his own theory (The Goidels and their Predecessors, 1935) that the Goidels of the time had been hosts to a population of *p*-dialect speaking Celts for five hundred years (Shaw, Studies 32 [1943], p. 321).

(e) As we have seen O'Rahilly ignores MacNeill and brings British back into the limelight as a direct intermediary in the adoption of Latin words into Irish, arguing on the basis of the loss of Lat. *-ius, -ium* etc. in the second stratum. I hope to show elsewhere that the loss of these endings has no relevance whatsoever to the question of the identity of the lending language.

(f) As Shaw points out (ibid. p. 320), O'Rahilly's theory leaves little time for, and pays less attention to, transitional words such as *pólire, pairche* etc., but in fairness to him the same criticism might be made of Sarauw and MacNeill.

(g) Finally, the striking way in which O'Rahilly's solution to the Patrician problem is corroborated by his analysis of the loan-words might lend credibility to this analysis if the solution were acceptable. But in 1962 Binchy was prepared to go no further than Bergin in describing it as "the 'least improbable' of all the theories which at present hold the field" (Stud. Hib. 2 [1962], p. 143).

§ 18   One of the major disadvantages in O'Rahilly's theory, and in the articles by Murphy. Shaw (loc. cit.) and Ryan (IER 5th Ser. 60 [1942], p. 246ff) which it provoked, was the absence of a chronological table, relative or absolute, of the British vis-à-vis the Irish sound changes. O'Rahilly's ambiguity on dating led to counter-arguments such as that of Shaw (loc. cit. p. 316) who contends that if Lat. intervocalic *-p-, -t-, -c-* had become /b/, /d/, /g/ by the British type of lenition, these in turn should have further developed to /β/, /δ/, /γ/ respectively by Irish lenition. Had these scholars consulted MacNeill's article such arguments would not have arisen, as he had already explained the phenomena chronologically.

§ 19   The articles I have just mentioned were not written with a view to elucidating the problems inherent in the loan-words *per se*, but rather to falsify or defend O'Rahilly's The Two Patricks. As has been pointed out, the loan-words had not, as yet, been examined in the light of an absolute or relative chronology of the sound changes of both branches of Insular Celtic, nor had the exceptional or transitional forms, hitherto relegated to notes, been accommodated in the analysis of Sarauw and MacNeill. The next scholar to tackle the problem would carry out the former and attempt to classify the latter.

§ 20   1953 saw the publication of Jackson's masterly chronological survey of the British languages, Language and History in Early Britain. This work is mainly devoted to the chronological history of the *p*-variety of Insular Celtic, but includes an interesting chapter on the British Latin loan-words in Irish (p. 122ff).

Content to remain neutral on the Patrician issue, Jackson was the first scholar since MacNeill to approach the loan-words with no motive other than that of investigating their phonology with a view to establishing a sound chronology for their adoption into Irish. He had at his command a sound knowledge of British,

Primitive Irish and Vulgar Latin, and was unbiased in his use of other scholars' work.

§ 21 Dismissing O'Rahilly on the grounds of (b) and (c) above (§ 17) Jackson reviews the work of Sarauw and MacNeill, giving it for the first time its due recognition, and procedes to carry the investigation a step further. His contribution may be summed up under the following headings:

(a) A further contrasting criterion for the two-group theory and correction of mistakes.

(b) The introduction of the subsidiary group theory.

(c) An absolute chronology.

§ 22 (a) To the criteria set up by Sarauw and MacNeill Jackson adds vowel affection (LHEB, p. 132). He observes that a/o- and i/u-affection is found in the earlier borrowings *(sorn <furnus, muilenn <molīna)* but not in the later *(stoir <[hi]storia)*, and argues therefore that "stressed vowel affection occurred in Pr(imitive) I(rish) between the time of the Cothriche and Pádraig groups".

MacNeill had argued, as we have seen (§ 11), that the shortening of unstressed long vowels and syncope were characteristics of the earlier *(Cothrige)* group, but Jackson shows (LHEB, p. 135 ff) that both of these features are also found in words of the later *(Pátraic)* stratum.

Given these additions we may now tabulate the characteristic features of the earlier vis-à-vis the later stratum of Latin loan-words in Early Irish, as understood by Jackson.

early	late
1) c- <p-	p- <p-
cuithe <puteus	*paiter <pater*
2) /θ/, /x/ </t/, /c/	/d/, /g/ </d/, /g/
Cothrige <Patricius	*póc <pācem*
	not < nota
3) -e <-ius, -ium etc.	-ius, -ium etc. lost
caille <pallium	*proind < prandium*
4) nd, ng <nt, nc	nt, nc retained
cland <planta	*cinteir <centrum*
ungae <uncia	*ponc <punctum*
5) á <ā	ó <ā
cáise <cāseus	*oróit <* orātio*
6) ? s- < f-	f- < f-
senester <	*firmimint < firmāmentum*
(AIr. *senestr) < fenestra*	
7) vowel affection	no vowel affection
muide < modius	*stoir < (hi)storia*

early	late
8) long vowels in unstressed syllables shortened	long vowels in unstressed syllables retained long
srathar <	*oróit* <**orātio*
VL **stratūra* < *strātūra*	< *ōrātio*
9) syncope	no syncope
ortha <**orātio*	*epistil* < *epistula*

§ 23 (b) Having established the above mistakes in MacNeill's analysis and having explained Sarauw's reticence on the *s-/f-* issue (above § 7; LHEB p. 130), Jackson sets about accommodating the words involved in the orthodox scheme. Words with *s-* for *f-* belong to the *Cothrige* stratum, as the a/o- affection in *sorn*<PIr. **/swuRNah/*<*furnus* shows, but unlike the other words in this stratum they were borrowed after lenition, and therefore "represent a late stage" (LHEB, p. 135) of this group. *Pátraic* words in which unstressed long vowels *have* been shortened (*eclais* < VL *eclēsia*, *Laiten* <*Latīna*) were borrowed before the reduction of clusters of the type spirant + resonant, whereby new long vowels developed in Irish unstressed syllables, and therefore represent a very early stage of the later stratum (LHEB, p. 135—6). *Pátraic* words which are syncopated (*caindleóir* < *candelārius* etc. LHEB, p. 136—7) were borrowed somewhat later than these, but undoubtedly earlier than the main body of this stratum which belongs to the post-syncope period. These, then, are Jackson's three subsidiary groups.

§ 24 Before proceeding to discuss Jackson's chronological table and his accommodation of these subsidiary groups in it, it might be wise to examine the latter in more detail. With regard to the late stage of the *Cothrige* series it will suffice here to list the relevant words, all of which must have been borrowed after lenition if Sarauw's explanation, which Jackson accepts, is correct. The words are: *senester* < *fenestra*, *sorn* < *furnus*, *sléchtaid* < *flēcto*, *síbal* < *fībula*, *sroigell* < *flagellum*, *seib* < *faba*, *srían* < *frēnum*, *súst* < *fūstis*, and possibly *séire* < *fēria*, *slóch* < *floc(c)us*.

§ 25 The list of words given for Jackson's earliest subsidiary group of *Pátraic* loans, those in which (Irish) unstressed long vowels were shortened, is as follows: *eclais* <VL *eclēsia*, *Laiten* <*Latīna*, *accuis* <VL **accāsio* (<CL *occāsio*), *matan/maiten* <**ma(tu)tīna*, *saltair* <*psaltērium*, *treblait* <**tribulātio*, *cosmaid* <*consummātio*. All of these, he says, are *Pátraic* words (witness the treatment of Lat. intervocalic *-t-, -c-*, and final *-ius, -ium* etc.) but differ from the main body of this stratum in shortening the Lat. long vowels of non-initial syllables. Of those given I would exclude *treblait* and *Laiten* (see §§ 34—5) as well as *cosmaid*; the following may be added to the list:

persan <*persōna* (LHEB 136 n. 1), *airecal/aracol* <AIr. **/oragl/* <VL **orāclum* <CL *ōrāculum*, *comman(n)* < *commūnio*, *latrann* <*latrōnem*, *pardus* <AIr. **/paraðes/* < *paradīsus*, *esparta* (nom. sg. originally *espartan*) <*vespertīna (hora)*; *secal* <*secāle* and *fátal* <*fatāle* might also be included though these are more likely to be book-words. We have, then, a substantial subsidiary group of *Pátraic* loan-words in this category.

§ 26 Only two words are given in LHEB (p. 136—7) for the second subsidiary group of *Pátraic* loan-words, the syncopated *Pátraic* words: *caindleóir <candelārius*, *notlaic <nātālicia*. The sceptical scholar might justifiably object to the former of these, arguing that it is more probably a hybrid of OIr. *caindel* (*<candēla*) and *-eóir* (*<ārius*), but Jackson's derivation of *notlaic* from Primitive Welsh */Nodolig <British Latin */nodǫ:ligịa/ (LHEB, p. 136, 293) clearly shows the word to be pre-syncope. However, as the pretonic shortening of /o:/ to /o/ in Primitive Welsh "might be as early as the first half of the sixth century" (LHEB, p. 293), the word could have been borrowed at the same time as those of § 25, and even if it were not this early, Primitive Welsh */Nodo:lig/, borrowed at the same time as VL *eclēsia* etc., would have yielded OIr. *notlaic*. Thus, this particular word need not have been borrowed later than those of the first subsidiary group of the *Pátraic* stratum, and the same applies to the following, which are also ostensibly *Pátraic* and pre-syncope:

parbail <parabola, *meirtrech <meretrīcem*, *apstal <apostolus*, *epscop <episcopus*, and possibly *crapscuil* (gen.sg.) *<crepusculum*.

§ 27 (c) The following is Jackson's chronological table, given with some additions to render it more lucid.

Primitive Irish

AD

1) —400 nt, nc >/dd/, /gg/.
2) 450 Main body of *Cothrige* loan-words:
       cuithe <puteus
       cland <planta etc.
3) 450—500 a) Lenition.
       b) f->s- sub. group of *Cothrige* loan-words:
          sroigell (*<VL *fragillum*) *<flagellum*
          sorn (*<PIr. */swuRNah/*) *<furnus* etc.
       c) Reduction of unstressed long vowels:
          (*molīna* >PIr. */moli:nah/) >*/molinah/
       d) a/o-, i/u-affection of vowels in stressed syllables:
          /molinah/ >/mulinah/
          (*modius* >PIr. */moδiyah/)> */muδiyah/
          /swuRNah/ >/swoRNah/
       e) First palatalization:
          /mulinah/ >/mul'inah/
          /muδiyah/ >/muδ'iyah/
       f) a/o-affection of vowels in unstressed syllables:
          /mul'inah/ >/mul'enah/
          /muδ'iyah/ >/muδ'eyah/

4) 500   Loss of final syllables:

                     /mul'enah/ >/mul'eN/
                     /muð'eyah/ >/muð'e/
                     /swoRNah/ >/s(w)oRN/

Archaic Irish

5) 500—550   a) Earliest sub-group of *Pátraic* loan-words:
                   eclais <VL *eclēsia* etc.

                b) Reduction of clusters of type spirant + resonant and compensatory lengthening of preceding vowels in (un)stressed syllables:
                   */anaðl/ >/ana:l/
                   (*signum* >PIr. */siɣnah/> */seɣnah/> AIr. */seɣn/) >/se:n/

                c) Second sub-group of *Pátraic* loan-words:
                   notlaic <Primitive Welsh */Nodolig/ etc.

6) 550   Syncope
                     /Nodolig/ >/Nodlig/

Old Irish

7) 550—   Main body of *Pátraic* loan-words.

§ 28 The above table presents the orthodox and least controversial analysis of the Latin loan-words in Early Irish. Though the table of diacritic and shared features (§ 22) presents a degree of overlap between the two groups (features 8 and 9 found in both), this has been accounted for in the chronological table by a more detailed stratification, introducing subsidiary groups. Thus, whereas the table of features presents two *almost* distinct groups, the chronological table has two *major* distinct strata (*Cothrige* and *Pátraic*) separated by approximately one century, during which three *minor* groups are seen to have entered the language. Of the latter, the last two are characteristic of the second or *Pátraic* stratum (though they have some *Cothrige* features) and are separated from the first, which represents a late stage of the early or *Cothrige* layer, by a period of approximately fifty years. The *Cothrige* words belong clearly to the Primitive Irish period, the *Pátraic* ones to Archaic and Old Irish, the second half of the fifth century being almost devoid of loan-words. It is precisely this vacuum which justifies Jackson's ratification of the two-group theory.

§ 29 Being an upholder of the two-group theory, Jackson was obliged to account for the existence of hybrid or transitional forms such as (a) those of §§ 25—6 above and (b) words like OIr. *peccath, pridchid, pairche,* which formally contradict the table of diacritic features (§ 22). This he did with a degree of success, as we have seen, in the case of hybrids (a), by accommodating them in subsidiary groups.

With regard to hybrids (b) he argues (LHEB, p. 134—5) that it would be folly to expect rigid consistency and a clear-cut partition of linguistic changes in loan-words in a period of such rapid linguistic evolution. Thus, the accommodation of hybrids (a) in the superstructure is executed in such a way as to neutralize any threat they might pose to the two-group analysis, while hybrids (b) are bereft of their intrinsic importance and left unclassified. In the following discussion I pro-pose to show that in accommodating hybrids (b), of which there are more than is generally believed, in the chronological table, one is left with no option but to revise the two-group superstructure as set out in the foregoing paragraphs.

§ 30 The orthodox classification is a descriptive one which recognizes a vacuum in time between the two groups of loan-words in Early Irish, but does not account for it. The historical framework presented by MacNeill (§ 13) corroborates the existence of two strata, and the adoption of these into Irish is made to coincide with the two periods of influence of the British Church on the Irish one, the early fifth-century Patrician mission and the early sixth-century expansion of monastic institutions in Ireland. As is the case with O'Rahilly's theory, however, there is a tendency to impose an historical background on the classification of these words, and to seek linguistic corroboration for it on the grounds, as Christine Mohrmann puts it (The Latin of Saint Patrick 1961, p. 54), that "linguistic evidence does not tell lies". Thus, while it associates the two groups of loan-words with these two periods of Christian activity in this country, the orthodox classification does not acknowledge that it is only reasonable to assume that a more or less continuous interrelationship must have existed between the inhabitants on both sides of the Irish Sea during the period in question, and that there are apparently no historical grounds for assuming a communication breakdown between speakers of Primi-tive Irish and British Latin (or British) late in the fifth century which would account for this peculiar vacuum. In seeking to corroborate, or indeed elaborate, the historical evidence for the development of Christianity in this country, the orthodox theory, in its search for uniformity and consistency, tends to become prescriptive in nature, and to prejudge the forms of the Latin loan-words in Early Irish. This is reflected in the treatment of words which seem to transgress the boundary between the two strata, or to contradict the evidence for the dichotomy. Such erratic, non-conformist, transitional or anachronous words as hybrids (b) are explained away by the often unjustifiable and inaccurate assumptions of analogy, suffix substitution or the possibility, not yet explored, of linguistic changes in loan-words occurring at different rates in different parts of the country. Some are relegated to notes, while others are not mentioned at all. These words must now be investigated.

§ 31 We may begin for argument's sake with the OIr. word *notire* (later *notaire*) "a professional scribe" <Lat. *notārius*. Before discussing it, it might be pointed out that the evidence of this word is as equivocal as that of Jackson's *caindleóir* (see § 26 above), but it is interesting to speculate on the way in which it may have been adopted into Irish.

As it appears in OIr. the word *notire* features the later, or *Pátraic*, treatment of Lat. intervocalic *-t-*, and the earlier *(Cothrige)* rendering of Lat. *-ārius* (later *-(e)óir)*, a combination not recognized by the orthodox classification. In accordance with the strictures of that classification the word should appear in OIr. as either **nothire* or **notóir*, neither of which occurs. *Notire* is therefore to be explained as a hybrid of OIr. *not* <*nota* and *-(a)ire* <*-ārius*, a perfectly legitimate explanation. But given that lenition in British and Primitive Irish occurred, according to Jackson's chronology (LHEB 143 and 695), simultaneously, the word can also be derived direct from British Latin, if the strictures of the two-group analysis are not imposed on it. Thus, Classical Latin *notārius* would have become */noda:ri̯us/ in British Latin. Had this form been adopted into Primitive Irish after lenition, the intervocalic /d/ would regularly have been assimilated to native /d/< geminate /dd/, the opposition single/geminate having been replaced after lenition by the opposition lenited/unlenited. The development would have been as follows: CL *notārius* >BL */noda:ri̯us/ >PIr. */Noda:riyah/ > */Nodar'eyah/ >AIr. */Nodar'e/ >OIr. /Nodər'e/ = *notire*. This derivation, which shows a *Pátraic* word (OIr. -t- = /d/ for Lat. *-t-*) entering the language before vowel affection, is not possible in the orthodox classification where the earliest *Pátraic* words belong to the post-apocope period (see no. 5 in the chronological table § 27). It is valid only if the word is assumed to have been borrowed after lenition had taken place in British and Primitive Irish, and before vowel affection, at least in unstressed syllables, in the latter, i.e. at approximately the same time as the so-called "late stage" of the *Cothrige* layer, the words with OIr. *s-* for Lat. *f-* (§ 23). It is precisely at this period that the Irish word for "sword", OIr. *claideb*, seems to have entered the language.

§ 32   Vendryes's derivation of OIr. *claideb* from British */klaδiβos/ <*/klaδiδos/ < */klaδiyos/ has been discussed by Kelly in Ériu 22 (1971), p. 192 ff. Of the etymologies put forward for the OIr. word, Kelly finds that of Vendryes more convincing than those of Loth and Morris-Jones, but remains doubtful of its validity. Among his objections he argues that if it is a borrowing from British the transfer "must have taken place in or around the 6th c(entury)" after the loss of final syllables in British (ibid. 194). He rightly points out that if this were so, British */klaδiβ/ should appear in OIr. as **claidib*, with *i*-vocalism in the final syllable and a gen.sg. **claidbeo*, but adds that a "foreign origin might also explain why the OIr. word is not **cladab*, in accordance with the general rules set out by Thurneysen", referring to GOI § 166.

Now as the suffix *-eb* does not appear elsewhere in Irish, and seems to have no obvious progenitor among the IE suffixes, the theory of British origin, which carries a tentative explanation for it does, as Kelly observes, hold considerable attraction. But what of the objections above? If Kelly's "in or around the 6th c." can be given more latitude than he seems to have allowed it, one of these can be removed immediately. No reason is advanced to explain why the word *must* have been borrowed after the loss of final syllables in British, nor is any apparent to me. Why could not the post-lenition fifth-century British form */klaδiβos/ have been borrowed into Primitive Irish? Entering the language before vowel affection, this form would have developed regularly in the following way: */klaδiβos/ >PIr. */klaδiβah/ > */klaδ'eβah/ >AIr. */klaδ'eβ/ >OIr. /klaδ'əβ/ = *claideb*. The reason the word does not appear in OIr. as *claidib* is, then, that it was borrowed before vowel affection, and the palatal /δ/ of *claideb*, as distinct from Kelly's hypothetical *cladab*, is not due to its being a borrowed word, as he suggests, nor to the influence of the gen.sg. and nom.pl. *claidib* as suggested by Thurneysen (GOI § 166), but is the regular reflex of /i/ in */klaδiβah/, the phonemicization of palatalization having begun before the merger of /i/ and /e/ in unstressed syllables followed by /a/ and /o/.

Note the same reflex of /i/ in

OIr. *cainnenn*	< PIr. */kaN'ina/
OIr. *cailech*	< Lat. *calicem*
OIr. *sroigell*	< VL *fragillum*
OIr. *saiget*	< Lat. *sagitta*

§ 33   The following are examples of hybrids (b): (Note that they are characterized in form by a combination of the so-called *Cothrige* feature of vowel affection and the *Pátraic* treatment of Lat. intervocalic *-t-, -c-, -p-,* and *-ius, -ium* etc., a combination which, as we have already seen, is inconsistent with the orthodox analysis. The adoption of these words into Irish would seem to have been simultaneous with that of *claideb,* and possibly with that of *notire.*)

§ 34   (a) *treblait* "tribulation, illness", Lat. *trībulātiō:*

We have already noted (§ 25) Jackson's inclusion of the OIr. word *treblait* in his earliest sub-group of the *Pátraic* series. His derivation of it from British Latin */triβula:dịọ:/ or */triβulọ:dịọ:/ (LHEB p. 146—7) is accompanied by the alternative suggestion (LHEB, p. 136) that the *-ait* of the OIr. form may be due to suffix substitution, in which case there would be no question of shortening of Lat. *-ā-* and the word would have to be excluded from the list. But whatever about the question of substitution, which will be discussed presently, Jackson does not seem to have been troubled by the vocalism of the first syllable of *treblait,* despite the fact that neither of his hypothetical British Latin forms could have given an Irish *treb-,* but rather **trib-(*triblait),* with which the later borrowing (from Latin or English?) *triobloid* might be compared. *Treblait* cannot derive directly from */triβula:dịọ:/ or */triβulọ:dịọ:/.*

The vocalism of OIr. *treblait* (Mod. Ir. *treabhlaid*) suggests a progenitor with /i/ in the first syllable and /a/, /a:/, /o/ or /o:/ in the second — not a sequence /i/ — /u/ as in the hypothetical forms above — and the phonology of Vulgar Latin can easily provide us with the required form. We have seen that syncope of intertonic syllables and subsequent pretonic vowel shortening were regular features of Vulgar Latin. If we apply these to CL *trībulātiō* we get the following VL development: /tri:bula:tio:/ >VL */tri:bla:tịo:/ >*/tribla:tịo:/. The form */tribla:tịo:/ became */triβla:dịọ:/ in British Latin, and this was borrowed into Irish giving a PIr. form

*/triβla:diya:/ (fem. *iā*-stem, cf. acc.pl. *treblaiti* Fél. p. 44,32.). As this PIr. form should have yielded a nom.sg. *treblaite* (< */treβlad'eya/) Jackson's theory of suffix substitution may be invoked at this stage to account for the form *treblait*. Alternatively, we may have here an example of the process, noted by Mac Eoin (ZCP 33 (1974), p. 64) in later Irish, whereby an old nominative becomes the new genitive.

Compare

OIr. nom.sg.	*cáise* (masc.)		Mod. Ir.	*cáis* (fem.)
OIr. gen.sg.	*cáise*		Mod. Ir.	*cáise*
OIr. nom.sg.	*sochraite*		Mod. Ir.	*sochraid*
OIr. gen.sg.	*sochraite*		Mod. Ir.	*sochraide*

The vocalism of the first syllable of OIr. *treblait*, then, clearly shows the word to have been borrowed before vowel affection in Primitive Irish.

§ 35   (b) *Laiten* "the Latin language", Lat. *Latīna*.

Though this word does not appear in the nom.sg. in OIr. its inflection as a fem. *ā*-stem in the Glosses (dat.sg. *latin* Ml. 3a15) and its gen.sg. *Laitne* (Auraic. 3016) suggest an original nom.sg. *Laiten* (Mod. Ir. *Laidean*). The occurrence of nom.sg. *Laitin* (Auraic, 27) can easily be explained as due to the frequent replacement of nom.sg. by oblique forms (acc. or dat. sg.) in the fem. *ā*-stems. As Jackson's date for the adoption of *Latīna* into Irish (see § 25 above) would have resulted in a nom.sg. *Laitin* (gen.sg *Laitneo?* cf. Kelly's *claidib* gen.sg. *claidbeo* § 32 above), it is more probable that the word entered the language before vowel affection. It is, indeed, hardly unreasonable to suggest that the name of the Latin language might have been adopted into Irish at an early stage, and the form in which it survived into Mod. Ir. probably ousted an original (nom.sg.) *Laithen* (cf. *Dúil Laithne*).

§ 36   (c) *cucann* "kitchen, ration of food", Lat. *coquīna*.

The VL form of *coquīna* was undoubtedly */koki:na/, and this became */kogi:na/ in British Latin. That OIr. *cucann* was borrowed from the latter is clear from the British lenition reflected in the -*c*- (= /g/), a typically *Pátraic* characteristic, but the vocalism of the first syllable shows, once again, that the transfer took place before vowel affection. The development was as follows: BL */kogi:na/ >PIr. */kogi:na:/ (fem. *ā*-stem)>*/kogina/ >*/kugena/ >OIr. */kugən/ (cf. nom.sg. *cucan* Sg. 68a 7) >/kugəN/. The non-palatal guttural /g/ of *cucann* is regular, as palatalization did not take place when a labial or guttural consonant (or consonant group) was preceded by /u/ and followed by an /i/ which does not undergo syncope (cf. OIr. *ungae* <Lat. *uncia*, OIr. gen.sg. *lungae* <PIr. */LuNgiyah/ Lat. *longa*, OIr. *tugae* PIr. */tuɣiya/, (Greene, GPI p. 130). When the /i/ is syncopated palatalization regularly occurs (cf. gen.sg. *cuicne* <PIr. */koginiyah/).

§ 37   (d) *screpul(l)* "a scruple etc.", Lat. *scrīpulus*.

The Irish borrowing from Lat. *scrīpulus* occurs in two forms, *screpul(l)* and *scripul(l)*; the former undoubtedly the earlier, the latter probably due to secondary learned influence. The borrowing *scrubul* <*scrūpulus* is distinct.

Though both Old Welsh *scribl* and OIr. *screpul(l)* derive ultimately from VL forms in which the penultimate syllable has been lost, *scribl* preserves the original long quantity of the vowel of the first syllable (EL § 51) whereas *screpul(l)* points to a VL form with a short /i/ (*/skriplus/).

In British Latin */skriplus/ became */skriblus/, and this form was borrowed into Primitive Irish as */skriblah/ (masc. *o*-stem) whence AIr. */skrebl/. When this AIr. form became disyllabic, shortly before the Classical Old Irish period, it had a final lenited (i.e. single) /l/ (cf. *screpul*, Thes. ii p. 346; Corm. Y 1150) as in OIr. *cétal* < */ke:dl (GOI § 120) but a variant form with −ll (= /L/) was to develop later and eventually ousted the earlier form. Note, once again, that *screpul(l)* is a typical hybrid form with *Cothrige* vowel affection and *Pátraic* /b/ for Lat. *-p-*.

§ 38 Three contemporaneous borrowings with the *(Pátraic)* phoneme /p/ may be added to those above:

(e) MIr. *sopp* "a wisp" <BL *suppa* <VL *stuppa* "a bundle of fibres", Greene, Ériu 26 (1975), p. 178 ff, with /o/ from /u/ by vowel affection.

(f) MIr. *cepp* "a tree-stump, log, block" <Lat. *cippus*, Sarauw IS p. 9—10. One may tentatively suggest an intermediate PIr. stage */kipah/.

(g) OIr. gen.sg. *screptra/screptaire*, Lat. *scrīptūra*.

The editor of DIL cites the gen.sg. forms *screptra/screptaire* under the lemma *scriptuir* and correctly points out that these represent the original form of the borrowing. The same is true of the nom.pl. *screptra*. All these forms suggest a defective ā-stem, the nom.sg. of which, were it to occur, would probably be *screptar*. The /e/ in these can be explained by assuming that a VL *scriptūra* (cf. Welsh *ysgrythur* <VL *scrittūra*, EL § 48 c) was adopted into PIr. with substitution of the native suffix *-trā*, as in *bríathar*, for Lat. *-tūra*, giving a PIr. nom.sg. */skriptra:/ whence *screptar*. The nom.pl. *screptra* is regular from PIr. */skriptra:h/, but the PIr. gen.sg. */skriptriya:h/(with /iya:h/ of the *iā*-stems, GOI § 296) should have yielded OIr. *scriptre/scriptire*, not *screptra/screptaire*. Here, then, as in OIr. *cruth* <*kwritu, gen.sg. *crotho* (irregularly) <*kwritous, the vocalism of the nom. prevailed.

Note the unorthodox combination of vowel affection and the preservation of Lat. /p/ in these three words.

§ 39 All the hybrids discussed so far are pre-affection loans, though *Pátraic* in form. The following *Pátraic* words (witness initial *p-*) are even earlier; they were undoubtedly borrowed before lenition:

§ 40 (h) *Pólire* "writing tablet(s)", Lat.*pugillāres, pugillāria*.

According to Thurneysen (GOI § 918), the OIr. word *pólire* recalls British *poullōr* (whence Middle Welsh *peullawr*); and Jackson (LHEB p. 442) seems to accept this derivation. But whatever about the development of Lat. *pugillāres* to Welsh *peullawr*, which itself is doubtful (LHEB, p. 442), it is not clear, and nowhere clarified, how the hypothetical British form could have yielded OIr. *pólire*, with its intervocalic /l/ and final /e/. In fact, *pólire* can be derived regularly from a VL syncopated form *pugllāria*, as Pedersen (VGKS i p. 222) rather tentatively suggests. I would propose the following derivation: *pugillāria* >VL */pugLa:rịa/ >PIr. */puɣla:riyah/ (masc. *io*-stem) >*/poɣlare'yah/ >AIr. */poɣlar'e/ >*/po:lar'e/ >OIr. /po:lər'e/ = *pólire*. The lenition of /gL/ to /ɣl/, the lowering of /u/ to /o/, the vocalization of /ɣ/ before /l/ and accompaniying compensatory lengthening of the preceding /o/ to /o:/, and the final /e/ are all regular if we accept, in spite of the orthodox analysis, that initial /p/ could be retained in a word borrowed before lenition.

§ 41   (i) *Pridchid/pridchaid* "preaches, teaches", Lat. *praedicāre*.

According to Sarauw (IS p. 8), whom Jackson (LHEB p. 135) follows, the inconsistent -*ch*- (<Lat. -*c*-) in a word with initial /p/ can be explained by assuming that "Verbet *predach*- <*praedicāre* har rettet sig efter *bendach*-", and the suggested analogy with the Irish loan from Lat. *benedico* could be accepted if Sarauw's *predach*- constituted the verbal stem of the borrowing from *praedicāre* in OIr., but this is not the case.

The verb, which is frequently used in the OIr. glosses, normally appears with the stem *pridcha*- (with neutral -*dch*-) or *pridche-/pridchi*- (with palatal -*dch*-), cf. pres. indic. 3rd. sg. *pridchaid; Wb.* 13a22; 3rd. pl. *pridchit*, 12d37 etc. The vowel -*e*- seldom appears in the root (cf. *prechite*, 5a5), and when it does it probably owes its origin to the influence of the verbal noun *precept*, while the stems *praidch*- and *praitch*- are, no doubt, learned imitations of Lat. *praed*-.

Pridchaid, like most verbs borrowed from Latin, is a weak verb of Thurneysen's A 1 class (GOI § 546), and this fact may provide an explanation for the varying quality of the cluster -*dch*- alluded to above. *Praedicāre*, which in VL was pronounced /predika:re/, was, like */pugLa:ria/, borrowed into PIr. before lenition. The pre-lenition PIr. form of the 3rd. sg. pres. indic. was probably */predika:ti/, and this passed through */preðixa:θi/ >*/pr'ið'exaθ'i/ >AIr. */pr'ið'exaθ'/ >EOIr. */pr'iðx'aθ'/ (by syncope of /e/). The last form is regularly written *pridchid* in OIr., the -*i*- of the last syllable (which represents) /ə/ <EOIr.- /a/ in this position) being regular between palatal consonants (GOI § 102, 1). The neutral quality of -*dch*- reflected in OIr. *pridchaid* is secondary and owes its origin to the analogy of other verbs in the A 1 class.

Pridchid/pridchaid, then, presents no problem if we accept that the Lat. vb. endings were replaced by the corresponding native ones on adoption, and that the adoption of the word pre-dated lenition. The verb *bendachaid* can hardly be invoked, and indeed need not be, to account for the /x/ of *pridchid*.

§ 42   (j) *Pairche* "a parish etc.", Lat.(ecclesiastical) *paroecia*, (corrupt *parochia*, *paruchia*)

Seeking once again to explain away the inconsistent combination of /p/ <Lat. /p/ and /x/ <Lat -*c*- in this loan-word, Sarauw (IS p. 8) ascribes OIr. /x/ in *pairche* to the orthographical influence of the corrupt Lat. form *parochia*. Jackson (LHEB p. 135 n. 2), however, is undoubtedly correct in dismissing this suggestion and accepting O'Rahilly's unqualified observation (TP, p. 80) that *pairche* conforms to the *Cothrige* type in everything but its initial /p/. The syncope and final -*e* of

pairche suggest that it can hardly be a book-word. It is clearly an early pre-lenition borrowing, like *pólire* and *pridchid*, from VL */pare:kia/ (< *paroecia*), the development being as follows: */pare:kia/ >PIr. */pare:xiya:/ (fem *iā*-stem) >*/parex'eya/ >AIr. */parex'e/ > EOIr. /parx'e/ = *pairche*.

§ 43 (k) *Peccath* "sin", Lat. *peccātum*.

If the final /θ/ (also written -*d* = /ð/) of this word is due to the lenition of Lat. -*t*- we have here another loan-word which combines the retention of /p/ with the regular *Cothrige* treatment of the Lat. intervocalic voiceless dental stop. It is, however, not improbable that we have here a case of suffix substitution (IS p. 8) of the native verbal noun suffix, OIr. -*ad*/-*ath*. This suggestion, which O'Rahilly supports (TP, p. 80), goes back to Ebel (KZ 1 [1852], p. 174), and is probably correct in view of the declension of OIr. *peccath* as a *u*-stem.

§ 44 These hybrids, which find no place in the scheme set out by Jackson (see § 23 ff. above), must now be included in a revised version of the chronological table. Giving them their rightful place in the table, and retaining the orthodox terminology (*Cothrige*, *Pátraic*), one is presented with the following result: (§ 27)

Primitive Irish

1) As above
2) Main body of *Cothrige* loan-words PLUS some *Pátraic* words (*pólire, pridchid, pairche*).
3) a) Lenition
   b) *f- s-* sub-group of *Cothrige* loans PLUS a number of *Pátraic* words (*treblait, Laiten, cucann, screpul(l), sopp, cepp, *screptar*) PLUS British loan-words like *claideb*, and possibly the *Pātraic* word *notire*.
   c), d), e), f) as above.
4) As above.

Archaic Irish

5) a) A sub-group of *Pátraic* loan-words (see § 25).
   b) As above.
   c) Another sub-group of *Pátraic* loan-words, though all could belong to 5c (= 5[a]) (see § 26).
6) As above.

Old Irish

7) Main body of *Pátraic* loan-words.

§ 45 We have here an intricate and rather confusing tabulation, confusing, however, it will be noted, only in the loan-word terminology. The two distinct (?) groups of loan-words are seen to have been entering the language simultaneously; that is to say, our inclusion of the hybrids above in the superstructure leads us to recognize only *one* continuous series of loans, or one period of borrowing. Fur-

194

thermore, of the seven diacritic features of the *Cothrige* series given above (§ 22) numbers 2, 3, 4, 5 and 7 are all to be found in *Pátraic* loans:

2) *pairche, pridchid*

3) *pairche, pólire, notire, (treblait* see § 34)

4) *pennaind (<poenitentia)*

5) *Enáir (<Iānuarius)*

7) *treblait, pólire, pridchid, cucann* etc.

Feature 6 *(s-<f-)* is considered *Cothrige* by Jackson because, as we have seen (§ 23), *sorn <furnus* shows vowel affection, and Jackson believes this to be a *Cothrige* characteristic (§ 22). It is now clear, however, that vowel affection is no more *Cothrige* than *Pátraic* (*treblait, pólire* etc.), so feature 6 need not be strictly *Cothrige*. This leaves only one so-called (distinctively) *Cothrige* feature, the rendering of Lat. *p-* by PIr. /kw/, OIr. *c-*. The reason no loan-word with the *Pátraic* (or British) type of lenition, has OIr. *c-* for Lat. *p-* is simply that the phoneme /p/ had been naturalized in Irish, as is clear from *pólire, pridchid* etc., before the period of Insular Celtic lenition.

Where, then, do we draw the line between the two groups?

§ 46   Given, (1) the degree of overlap, both in terms of phonological features and periods of borrowing, to which the hybrids examined above testify, (2) the inadvisability of distinguishing main and subsidiary groups, (3) that the circumstances of the lending language offer no grounds for an *a priori* division into two groups, (4) the confusion arising from the retention of the *Cothrige/Pátraic* classification in the chronological table, and (5) the misleading historical overtones of these terms, I would propose that this orthodox division of the loan-words into two distinct groups should be abandoned. In its stead I would suggest that there is one series of Latin loan-words in Early Irish, the borrowing of which was nonintermittent and continued over an extensive period of time. During the earlier years of this period the transfer of these loans to Irish was characterized by phoneme substitution, and a tendency on their part to conform to the exigencies of the Irish accentual and phonemic systems. As familiarity with Latin became more widespread with the development of Christianity, this type of assimilation yielded to a degree of phoneme transfer, and even to a recognition of the foreign accentual pattern. At all times, however, assimilation to the native inflectional pattern was strictly observed.

§ 47   The major objection to the orthodox classification is that it precludes the objective investigation of the chronology of these words, and gives a distorted view of the relative dates of transfer of INDIVIDUAL loans. If one argues, for example, that there is a group of loan-words in Early Irish characterized by the Irish type of lenition (e.g. *-th-* for Lat. *-t-*) and final *-e* for Lat. *-ius* etc., one is effectively saying that between the time of lenition and the loss of final syllables, a period of approximately forty years, no Lat. loan-words were borrowed into Irish. But while it follows that a word borrowed early enough to undergo the Irish type of lenition will naturally undergo affection, given the appropriate conditions, this

195

does not mean that a word which shows affection was necessarily borrowed before the time of lenition. Each individual feature, such as lenition, vowel affection etc., has its own *terminus ante quem*, but classification on the basis of a plurality of features, as in the orthodox system, effectively renders all but that with the earliest *terminus a. q.* redundant as chronological criteria. This classification thus provides no mechanism for the analysis of what in terms of its own strictures must be labelled as anachronous or transitional words. Once a word is tagged with a diacritic feature all segments of it are expected to exhibit, consistently and continually, a uniform set of phonological peculiarities. This straitjacket of uniformity tends to disregard the continuity of the borrowing process as reflected in these words, a continuity consistent, I might add, with what is known of traffic across the Irish Sea during the fifth and sixth centuries of our era.

Abbreviations not to be found in DIL are:

BLCI   Beginnings of Latin Culture in Ireland (Eoin *MacNeill*, Studies 20 (1931), p. 39—48; 449—60

DHV   De Hibernicis Vocabulis quae a Latina lingua Originem duxerunt (J. *Vendryes*, Paris 1902)

EL   Yr Elfen Ladin yn yr Iaith Gymraeg (H. *Lewis*, Cardiff 1943)

GOI   A Grammar of Old Irish (R. *Thurneysen*, Dublin 1946)

GPI   The Growth of Palatalization in Irish (D. *Greene*, Transactions of the Philological Society 1973, p. 127—36)

Hdb.   Handbuch des Altirischen (R. *Thurneysen*, Heidelberg 1909)

IS   Irske Studier (C. *Sarauw*, Copenhagen 1900)

LHEB   Language and History in Early Britain (K. *Jackson*, Edingburgh 1953)

LLI   Bemerkungen über die lateinischen Lehnwörter im Irischen: Erster Teil: Zur Lautlehre (B. G. *Güterbock*, Leipzig 1882)

SLE   Some Linguistic Evidence Relating to the British Church (D. *Greene*, in: M. W. *Barley*, R. P. C. *Hanson*, ed., Christianity in Britain 300—700, Leicester 1968, p. 75—86)

TP   The Two Patricks (T. F. *O'Rahilly*, Dublin 1941, reprint 1971)

VGKS   Vergleichende Grammatik der Keltischen Sprachen (H. *Pedersen*, Göttingen 1909)

AIr. = Archaic Irish; BL = British Latin; CL = Classical Latin; EOIr. = Early Old Irish; IE = Indo-European; MIr. = Middle Irish; Mod. Ir. = Modern Irish; OIr. = Old Irish; PIr. = Primitive Irish; VL = Vulgar Latin.

Old Irish lexical and semantic influence on Hiberno-Latin*

By
Michael Herren

In my Tübingen paper[1], I discussed several types of orthographical peculiarities that occur in Latin texts of Irish origin. I concluded that certain of these features (Class I) could be used as sure evidence that a given text was transmitted by the Irish. Other features (Class II), if they occur frequently, could also point in the direction of Irish transmission. The Class I features owe their origin exclusively to the influence ot the Irish language, whereas the Class II spellings just possibly reflect the influence of the pre-Carolingian orthographical tradition in Gaul.

In the present paper, I should like to call attention to the lexical and semantic influence of Old Irish on Latin. This influence was exercised chiefly in three ways: (1) actual loan words, that is, Irish words with Latin endings; (2) Irish etymologies for Latin words; (3) meaning shifts in Latin words attributable to the influence of Old Irish. I regard the presence of any of these features, where firmly established, as good evidence for Irish authorship of a given text. Indeed, it is hard to think of better evidence.

Up to now very little has been said on the subject of Irish loan words in Latin, although there has been some discussion of meaning shifts attributable to Irish influence[2]. There seems to be some reluctance on the part of Celtic scholars to accept any list of Hibernisms that has not been established by professional Celtic scholars. This attitude is understandable, since most practising Celticists possess a good grounding in Latin as well as Celtic languages, while their colleagues from the classics are often hampered by an imperfect command of Irish and Welsh. Yet, I think, the Latinist can occasionally shed light on what is essentially a Celtic problem. Most scholars are now aware that a good many curious words occur in texts of Celtic Latin origin, and not only in such creations as the *Hisperica Famina*

* I should like to express my gratitude to three Irish scholars who have assisted me in matters of the Irish language and Hiberno-Latin texts: Mr. Aidan Breen of Trinity College, Dublin; Dr Próinséas Ní Chatháin of University College, Dublin; Dr Dáibhí Ó Cróinín of University College, Galway.

1 „Sprachliche Eigentümlichkeiten in den hibernolateinischen Texten des 7. und 8. Jahrhunderts" in: H. *Löwe*, ed., Die Iren und Europa im früheren Mittelalter. Vol. I, Stuttgart 1982, p. 425—433.

2 See A. O. and M. O. *Anderson*, Adomnan's Life of Columba, London 1961, p. 162 (brief remarks); the discussions by G. B. *Adams* and M. J. *McGann* in: M. J. *Faris*, The Bishops' Synod ("The First Synod of St. Patrick"): A Symposium with Text, Translation and Commentary, Liverpool 1976, p. 19—26.

or in technical works such as penitentials. In cases where the etymology of a given word is unknown, the Latinist is able to say whether the word ever at any point belonged to the Latin language (up to say, the sixth century AD) or whether the word, by reason of its root or formation, could possibly have been Latin. Of course, it is well known now that the insular Celts and the Bretons laced their Latin compositions with words of Greek, Hebrew, and other Semitic origin[3]. Still there are words in Celtic Latin texts that cannot be traced to any of these languages. In these cases one must remain open to the possibility of loan words from Celtic. Naturally, each case must be judged on its own merits, and in some instances it must simply be admitted that a definitive etymology cannot be established.

I know of only one piece of external evidence to show that the Irish engaged in the practice of using latinized Irish words in Latin compositions, and that evidence, unfortunately, is indirect. In the latter part of the ninth century Hincmar of Reims wrote a letter to his nephew Hincmar of Laon condemning him for numerous excesses, some of them stylistic:

> *Qui enim linguam, in qua natus es, non solum non loqui, verum nec intelligere nisi per interpretem potes, cum suppeterent sufficienter verba Latina, quae in his locis ponere poteras, ubi Graeca, et obstrusa, et interdum Scottica et alia barbara, ut tibi visum fuit, nothata atque corrupta posuisti, paret quia non ex humilitate, vel ad manifestationem, ea quae dicere voluisti Graeca verba, quae ipse non intelligis, inconvenientissime posuisti, sed ad ostentationem illa insipientissime inseruisti, ut omnes qui illa legerint intelligere possint, te illa velle vomere quae non glutiisti[4].*

Even though this letter is a diatribe by one non-Irishman against another, I believe it to be a fair inference that the unfortunate Scotophile of Laon would not have indulged in the linguistic antics, for which he was, perhaps, justly censured, had he lacked examples provided him by Irish scholars on the Continent.

It is not surprising that we find vernacular technical terms in Latin texts, especially when they relate to the fields of law and administration. That practice occurred in other jurisdictions[5]. What is much more curious is the use of Latinized Irish words for which there exist perfectly normal Latin equivalents. The employment of these non-technical Irishisms appears to begin with the *Hisperica Famina* around the middle of the seventh century and with Virgilius Maro Grammaticus,

---

3 See my paper, Some New Light on the Life of Virgilius Maro Grammaticus, PRIA 79 C (1979), p. 60—62.

4 Hincmarus S. Metropolis Ecclesiae Rhemorum Episcopus Hincmaro Laudunensi coepiscopo nostro, PL 126, col. 448B.

5 See E. *Lerch*, Germanische Wörter im Vulgärlatain, Romanische Forschungen 60 (1947), p. 647—684.

who was a contemporary of the faminators, or else wrote a little earlier[6]. The faminators drew their vocabulary from Latin, Greek, and Hebrew lexical sources. This appears to be a rather radical extension of a tradition at least as old as Columbanus, whereby Latin words were glossed in the other two "sacred languages"[7]. The faminators, however, following Virgilius Maro (?), seem to have begun the curious practice of using Hebrew words as a *subtitute* for Latin ones[8]. Now Irish and other Celtic[9] words also occur in the *Famina* as substitutes for normal Latin. This phenomenon may possibly have coincided with the conferral of a special status on the Irish language by the Irish mythographers. In the *Auraicept na nÉces*, a treatise written in Irish comparing the Irish language with Latin and other languages, we read:

> The Irish Language ... on account of its comprehensiveness beyond
> every speech ... was the first language brought from the Tower (sc. of
> Babel)[10].

Now according to Irish tradition, portions of the *Auraicept*, including the passage just cited regarding the origin of the Irish language, go back to Cenn Faelad, an authenticated scholar, whose death is placed in 679[11]. Did the author of the primer portion of the *Auraicept* somehow interact with the faminators and Virgilius Maro? Whatever the answer to this question, it is at least of interest that the mixing of Irish with the "three sacred languages" in Latin compositions coincides with the attempt by Irish mythographers to give their language an important place in the "mythology of speech". The reason for the creation of this macaronic language will perhaps remain obscure. But I have the impression that the motives ascribed to Hincmar of Laon by his acerbic uncle apply to the Irish *sapientes* as well[12].

The non-technical words constitute the larger group and are found in virtually every genre of Hiberno-Latin writing: hagiography, *itineraria*, grammatical works, and poems. The technical words are limited, to my knowledge, to the penitentials, and to one or two possible examples in Adomnán's Vita Columbae,

---

6 M. *Herren* (as above note 3), p. 42—47. See now D. Ó Cróinín, A Seventh-Century Irish Computus from the Circle of Cummianus, PRIA 82 C (1982), p. 413—14, 424—25. This article clearly shows that Virgilius was cited in Ireland by ca. 658.

7 R. E. *McNally*, The *Tres Linguae Sacrae* in Early Irish Bible Exegesis, Theological Studies 19 (1958), p. 395—403.

8 M. *Herren*, The Hisperica Famina: I. The A-Text: A New Critical Edition with English Translation and Philological Commentary, Toronto 1974, p. 45—46.

9 Ibid.

10 G. *Calder*, ed., Auraicept na nÉces, the Scholars' Primer, Edinburgh 1917, p. 5.

11 *Calder*, p. XXVII—XXVIII. But see now the cautionary remarks of A. *Ahlqvist* regarding this attribution in his The Early Irish Linguist: an Edition of the Canonical Part of the *Auraicept na nÉces*, Helsinki 1983, p. 18.

12 See D. A. *Binchy*, The Background of Early Irish Literature, Stud. Hib. 1 (1961), p. 13.

plus one in Muirchú. The certain and possible Old Irish loan words in the penitentials have been discussed by Bieler and Binchy[13]. The one certain case of an Old Irish loan word is *arreum*, "commutation (of penance)", which occurs several times in Hi II. *Arra* or *arrae* (the older form) is a neuter io-stem; thus the choice of Latin *-um* as an ending preserves the original Old Irish gender.

A more difficult case is that of *bardicatio* (Hi I.26) and *bardigium* (Bi IV 6.2). Bieler refers to these words as "Hibernicisms". But are they Irish? Let us look at the evidence:

> Bi IV.6.2 *Penitentia bardicationis glandellae post obitum laici uel laicae .l. dies et noctes in pane et aqua.*
> Hi I.26 *Poenitentia bardigi capalbiae post laicum uel laicam .l. dies in pane et aqua.*

It is clear that these are parallel passages and that *bardicatio* and *bardigium* are collateral forms. The editor(s) translate by "wailing" in both instances. A clue to the meaning of these collateral forms is given by the Bigotian Penitential (IV.6), where the rubric is addressed to prohibitions against *clamor*. Now since we have a regulation against keening, it seems unlikely that our word bears any connection to Irish *bard*, or that it is a compound of Irish *barae*, "anger", "hostility", and Latin *dicare*, as I early suggested[14]. The best explanation, in my view, is that the word is based on Germanic Latin *barditus* or *barritus*[15]. In Tacitus *barditus/barritus* refers to the war cry of the Germans[16], but the scholiast to Statius, *Thebaid* 4.394 glosses it with the meaning "wailing of the Amazons"[17]. A verbal form *bardit*, presumably from *bardio, -ire*, is also attested[18]. We may therefore posit the frequentive **bardicare* on which *bardicatio* is based. *Bardigium*, however, is probably a corruption of an original **barditio*, formed like *auditio*, based directly on **bardire*. **Barditio* would have gone through the stages: **barditio>*bardicio>*bardigio>bardigium*. Confirmatory evidence is provided by the adjective *bardigiosus* (compare *superstitiosus* from *superstitio*), attested in Felix, Vita Guthlaci 12: *non ruricolarum bardigiosos vagitus imitabatur.* The Dictionary of Medieval Latin from British Sources has, I think, wrongly connected the word with Latin (?) *bardus*, "stupid"[19].

Of the other possible lexical Hibernisms mentioned by Bieler, *capalbia* appears to be inscrutable, although its meaning as an equivalent of *glandella* = *clientella*,

---

13 The Irish Penitentials, SLH 5, 1963, p. 37—38, 50—51.
14 In the oral presentation of this paper in Dublin.
15 See the Thesaurus Linguae Latinae, II, fascs. VIII—IX, s. *barditus* (col. 1750) and *barritus* (col. 1759).
16 Germ. 3: *quorum (carminum) relatu, quem barditum vocant, accendunt animos.*
17 *ululatum: quod Amazones cum finitimis bellare dicuntur, quorum ululatus barritus, id est barbarus ritus.*
18 *Goetz*, Corpus Glossariorum Latinorum II, 294, 31. This verb doubtless belongs to the fourth conjugation along with numerous other verbs expressing sounds, e. g. *hinnio, grunnio.*
19 Fasc. I, A—B, p. 182.

"female dependent" or "wife" appears to be certain. At the moment a convincing etymon is not in sight.

There are three latinized Irish words in Adomnán's Vita Columbae which are not proper names: *tigernus* 43b, *curucus* 100ab, and possibly *clocca* 18 and 129b. Of these, only *curucus* = Irish *curach* is in any way a technical word, as it refers to a specific type of boat of Irish manufacture. In the passages just cited the curachs are used for the towing of timber across the water for the construction of houses and full-sized ships[20]. Elsewhere *curucus* is employed by Gildas in the De Excidio Britanniae ch. 19 to refer to the boats of the Picts and the Irish[21]. In neither Gildas nor in Adomnán is *curucus* used as a simple substitute for "boat" or "ship".

In Muirchú's Life of Patrick, (I, 25 [23]) (ed. L. *Bieler*, SLH 10, p. 106), we hear about pagans working on a Sunday, *facientium fossam rathi* (var. *castelli*). The editor translates with "moat of a rath". *Rathi* can only be a latinization of OIr. *ráth*, *-o* (m. and f. of originally doubtful gender) (see DIL, s.v. 2), with a Latin genitive singular ending in place of the Irish genitive represented variously as *-o*, *-a*, and *-e* and by the form *ráith*. This might be regarded as a technical usage, since a *rath* refers to a particular kind of fortification peculiar to the Celts and would have no precise Latin equivalent (though *uallum* would be closer than *castellum*).

Let us now turn to the non-technical words, beginning with the ones in Adomnán. In the Vita Columbae at 43b we find the heading:

> De duobus tigernis sancti vaticinatio viri,
> qui ambo motuis (i.e. mutuis) vulneribus disperierant.

The *tigerni* are later described as *duo quidam nunc regii generis viri in Scotia*. Does the use of *tigerni*, which is a latinization of Irish *tigern* or *tigerna*, imply that the men belong to the royal *derbfhine*? The examples for *tigern* and *tigerna* given by the Dictionary of the Irish Language do not appear to support a technical meaning. The Irish words mean simply "lord" or "chief", and *tigerna* is also used in ecclesiastical contexts at a later period. The use of the latinized form, therefore, appears to be stylistic. Latin *nobiles* would probably have done just as well.

Of great interest is the occurrence in two places in the Vita of the word *cloca*: 18a *Pulsa clocam*; 129b *pulsata personante cloca*. Here and virtually everywhere else in the Latin literature *cloca* refers to a church or monastery bell. The entry under Irish *cloc* in DIL gives Late Latin *cloc(c)a* as the etymon of the Irish word, qualify-

---

20 Adomnán distinguishes three types of sea vessel: the *longa navis* (cf. OIr. *long*), which was a full-sized sailing ship; the *scafa* ("skiff") and the *curucus* or „coracle". See the *Andersons'* note, p. 452.

21 *Itaque illis (sc. Romanis) ad sua remeantibus emergunt certatim de curucis, quibus sunt trans Tithicam vallem evecti, quasi in alto Titane incalescenteque caumate de artissimis foraminum caverniculis fusci vermiculorum cunei, tetri Scottorum Pictorumque greges ...*

ing that derivation thus: "otherwise Thurneysen, Grammar, p. 87"[22]. A derivation of Irish *cloc* from Latin *cloca* has a false ring to my ears, since the two *loci* in Adomnán given above are, to my knowledge, the earliest attestations of a Latin word *cloca*. The fact that this word is found in no continental source earlier than Adomnán is indeed telling. Our next examples come from English circles on the Continent, including those of Willibald, Wynnebald, and Alcuin, none earlier than the second half of the eighth century. Dr. Ingrid Strasser has made a thoroughgoing study of the problem of the relation of Hiberno-Latin *cloca* in her "Irisches im Althochdeutschen"[23] and makes a powerful case to show that this word is derived from a native Irish word *cloc* rather than the reverse. Furthermore she bolsters the earlier case made by Meyer-Lübke[24] that the Germanic reflexes of this word (*glocka*, etc.) are derived from the Irish[25].

The collective evidence shows that Latin *cloc(c)a* had its origins in an Irish milieu in the seventh century, then travelled quickly to English circles with close Irish connections[26]. However, the distribution of *cloc(c)a* was so wide that the word rivalled *campana* as a normal medieval Latin word for "church bell"[27]. We must conclude from this distribution and from the reflexes in both Romance and Germanic that we cannot regard the presence of *cloc(c)a* in a Latin text as evidence of Irish origin or even of transmission.

Another word of problematic origin employed by Adomnán in his *De Locis Sanctis* (II. 30.20) is *tollus*: *ulterius nauem procere kataractae, hoc est fluminales aquarum tolli, non sinunt. Tollus*, also spelled *tolus*, appears several times in the A and B versions of the *Hisperica Famina*[28]:

A60 *ac inmensus urbani tenoris manasset faucibus tollus*

A87 *Ceu montosus scropias tranat tollus per macides*

A109 *Haud hispericum propinabis auido gutture tollum.*

A490 *quod spumaticum rapuit tol <l> o diluuium.*

B135 *(glas) ne tellatum procellosis fluctibus operiat tolum*

B136 *et glaucum mundiano artauit limbum tolum*

---

22 It is not clear whether Thurneysen lists OE *clugge* as the etymon of OIr. *cloc*: "The *g* instead of *c* in Mod. Ir. cloigeann 'skull', earlier *clocenn*, lit. 'stone-head' from *cloch* and *cenn* (cf. W. *pen-glog*) may be due to the influence of Mod. Ir. *clog* 'bell', Mid. Ir. *cloc* (OE *clugge*)."
23 In *Löwe* (as above note 1), I, p. 399—424.
24 Romanisches Etymologisches Wörterbuch, ⁵1972, s. v. *clocca*.
25 I should prefer to say that *gloka* comes from Hiberno-Latin *cloc(c)a* rather than from Irish *cloc*.
26 For similar developments in word histories see now my Insular Latin *(C(h)araxare (Craxare)* and Its Derivatives, Peritia 1 (1982), p. 273—80, along with the earlier study by A. K. *Brown*, Bede, a Hisperic etymology and sea poetry, Mediaeval Studies 37 (1975), p. 410—32.
27 *Strasser* (as above note 23), p. 405 and note 54.
28 The passages from the A-Text are cited from my edition (as in note 8); passages from the B-Text are taken from F. *Jenkinson*, The Hisperica Famina, Cambridge 1908.

Plummer, in his edition of the Vitae Sanctorum Hiberniae, gives instances of *tollus* and an alternate spelling *tullus*, with the meanings "cataract" and "rapid"[29]. A definition of the word is given in the interpolated chapter 44 of Isidore's *De Natura Rerum: Tulli aquarum proiectus, quales sunt in Aniensi flumine quam maxime praecipiti*[30]. This word is also used to gloss the word *euripus*, which is Greek for "a strait or narrow where the flux and reflux is violent"[31]; *euripus* in turn is a gloss on the Hisperic word *ledones* in the Karlsruhe version of Bede's *De Rerum Natura*, ch. 29[32]. Finally, the word occurs in a poem of Eriugena's, where the context is a moral interpretation of the Hebrews' passage through the walls made from the Red Sea:

> *Nos virtutis iter medium dum carpimus, altae*
> *Instant phantasiae nequitaeque toli.*
> While we cling to the middle path of virtue,
> the high cataracts of phantasy and of evil draw nigh[33].

There can be little question from all this evidence that *tollus/tolus* (and *tullus*) refer to a "cataract", "flood", or "mass of water", and by extension, to "an abundance" or "great quantity" (see especially *Hisperica Famina* A60 and A 109, where the reference is to "a flood of speech" or "great quantity").

As to the question of etymology, I do not think that *tollus* can be Latin. Latin *tollo*, "lift up", "raise", "support", can of course be used of water, and it would not be unnatural to think of a flood of water as "that which raises". But *tollus* is unattested in Latin literature until its first appearance in Hiberno-Latin texts of the seventh century. Moreover, the *o*-suffix in Latin is apparently not used to extend vocabulary in the Late Latin period by combination with a verbal stem. Of the ninety commonest nominal suffixes in Vulgar Latin mentioned by Grandgent, *o* (i.e. *-us*) does not even figure[34]. Nor is it likely that *tollus* is a fanciful Hisperic coinage. I can think of no example from the Hisperic corpus where a word is coined by adding *-us* directly to a verbal stem.

It seems highly probable, therefore, that Latin *tollus/tolus* is coined from a Celtic word. Here there are two possibilities: Brythonic *tolo* and Irish *tólae*[34a]. Brythonic

---

29 See the Latin Clossary, II, 384.

30 Ed. J. *Fontaine*, Bordeaux 1960, p. 134. For the different versions of this text, see W. *Stevens*, Scientific Instruction in Early Insular Schools in: M. *Herren*, ed., Insular Latin Studies: Papers on Latin Texts and Manuscripts of the British Isles: 550—1066, Toronto 1981, p. 99—101.

31 H. G. *Liddell* and R. *Scott*, A Greek-English Lexicon, rev. H. S. *Jones*, 9th ed., 1940, s. v.

32 See W. *Stokes* and J. *Strachan*, ed., Thes., II, 24. I am grateful to Dr Dáibhí Ó Cróinín for this reference.

33 Iohannes Scottus, Carmina II.ii, 40, ed. L. *Traube*, MGH, Poetae Aevi Carolini III, Berlin 1896, p. 530. I am grateful to Professor Édouard *Jeauneau* for this reference.

34 C. H. *Grandgent*, An Introduction to Vulgar Latin, Boston 1907, p. 18—23.

34a [See also OIr. *tuile*, io-stem n., v.n. of *do-lín*, Edd.].

tolo appears in Breton only in the compound *ectoll, ectell,* for which the Greek gloss *euripus,* "strait" or "tide" is given[35]. Welsh *tolo* has a variety of meanings: "sound of waves", "noise", "flood", "scale"[36]. (The last meaning seems to connect the word to Latin *tollo* and to classical Sanskrit *tula*[37]; the relation of all these words requires more investigation.) Against the rather ambiguous evidence of Brythonic, Irish *tólae* (*-io,* n.) is clearcut. In classical Old Irish the word means "flood", "inundation", and by extension, "abundance", "large quantity"[38]. This very neatly matches the Latin evidence.

The double *l* found in the spelling *tollus* may reflect scribal habits and hence be purely arbitrary[39]. Yet the early occurrence of *tollus* in the A-Text of the *Hisperica Famina* may reflect an authorial attempt to distinguish between this word and another word *tolus,* which stood for Greek θόλος (examples at A253, A256; possibly also at D60)[40]. Still, one point about *tollus,* if derived from Irish *tólae,* is perplexing. Why is this word latinized as *tollus* rather than as *tollum* or *tollium*? Compare the treatment of *arreum* from Old Irish *arrae, io.*

There are two *possible* latinized Irish words in Hisperic compositions that are problematic: one because of its usage, the other because of its form. The first is *iaras* (acc. pl.), *iaris* (abl. pl.):

> B89—80 *Ut aquifluam cinereo propinauerit letheam leuitorio*
> *quatinus spumanti salsi licuminis fluctu*
> *crinitas elixauerit iaras.*

To pour a draft of water into a basin of ashes, so that with a frothy flood of salty liquid it can cleanse our long-haired manes.

Again, in the *Lorica* of Laidcenn at line 33:

> *gigram cephalem cum iaris et conas*[41]

---

35 L. *Fleuriot,* Dictionnaire des gloses en vieux breton, Paris 1964, p. 154. Interestingly, *ectoll* is glossed by *euripi.* Did the Breton glossators know the Karlsruhe Bede (see note 32)? According to the editors of the Thes., internal evidence and the language of the glosses combine to support a dating of ca. 850 for this MS (see II, X—XI). There is a ninth-century fragment now in Vienna (see ibid.) of the same text by Bede glossed in both Irish and Latin.

36 For Welsh *tolo,* see J. *Loth,* RC 37 (1917—19), p. 297. See the references to this word in Ifor *Williams,* ed., Canu Llywarch Hen, Cardiff 1935, p. 172, p. 244; also, the Y Geiriadur Mawr, s.v. *tolo.* I am grateful to Professor *Fleuriot* for these references.

37 See A. *Ernout* and A. *Meillet,* Dictionnaire Etymologique de la Langue Latine, 4th ed., rev. J. *André,* Paris 1959, p. 694.

38 DIL, fasc. TO—TU, Dublin 1948, col. 238.

39 On this tendency in Hiberno-Latin texts, see B. *Löfstedt,* Der hibernolateinische Grammatiker Malsachanus, Uppsala 1965, p. 102—103. Löfstedt is correct in noting that the writing of double consonants for single and vice-versa is widerspread outside the Irish area. I do not think that *ss* for *s* and vice-versa necessarily constitutes an exception; this phenomenon is "pan-insular".

40 See *my* commentary (as above note 8), p. 134, p. 167.

41 Ed. *Jenkinson* (as above note 28), p. 52.

And *Rubisca* 37:

> *Iaris sauris tam pectinatis*[42]

The glossarial evidence of these last two works leaves no doubt that *iara, -ae* means "hair"[43]. There is, however, no Latin, Greek, or Hebrew word *iara* with that meaning[44]. Whether the word is of Celtic origin is not certain, but it is of some interest that the *Cóir Anmann* (twelfth century) contains the glosses: *íarghlás .i. folt ghlas bái fair* and *íar .i. folt*[45]. It is at least a possibility that we have a metaphorical extension of the nominal use of Old Irish *iar* to mean "extremity"[46].

The second case is the word *tona*, glossed *mortalem* in the Echternach Glossary, a set of glosses believed to be based on a lost version of *Hisperica Famina* (C-Text)[47]. There is also the curious word *tonaliter*, glossed *mortaliter*, in line 3 of the *Adelphus Adelpha Meter*. However, it must be noted that in the other extant manuscript of this poem we find the reading *tanaliter*, a word repeated in a number of Anglo-Latin texts[48]. I suspect that *tona* itself is a noun, and hence should be glossed by *mors*. The DIL lists a word *tona .i. bás*, which is labelled as *Bérla na Filed* (language of the poets). We may speculate that *tona* is not real Irish, but rather an Hisperic Latin word based on OIr. *tonnad* (-o, m.). *Tona* could be formed on the Irish plural form *tonna;* cf. the phrase *tri tonna* cited in DIL s.v. *tonnad.* The Irish glossator labelled *tona* as *Bérla na Filed* possibly because he recognized it as a Latin formation based on an Irish word.

Another possible instance where an Irish neuter plural ending in *-a* became a Latin feminine singular is that of *scamnae* (line 54 of the *Rubisca*): *gnunctae (= iunctae) tam scamnae/plumaria tergora quam costae. Scamna*, in my view, is a syncopated form of OIr. *scamána*, "little lungs", of which *scamán* is the singular. "Lungs", or better, "little lungs", makes good sense in the context of the verse. Moreover, according to Stokes, Irish Glosses[49], *cusin scaman* stood as a gloss to *cum pulmone* at *Lorica* 73. The *Rubisca* poet knew the *Lorica*, probably in an Irish manuscript[50].

---

42 Ed. *Jenkinson* (as above note 28), p. 56.

43 This evidence receives a full treatment in *my* Hisperica Famina II.

44 There is a Greek word ἴαρ for αἷμα = "blood"; cf. *Liddell* and *Scott* (as above note 31), s.v. ἴαρ and ἔαρ. Hebrew *jar* or *iar* has a variety of meanings, but none corresponds to "hair"; see *jar* and also *jare* in M. *Thiel*, Grundlagen und Gestalt der Hebräischkenntnisse des frühen Mittelalters, Spoleto 1973, p. 323.

45 DIL, fasc. I, col. 18, s. *íar* (3).

46 See ibid., s.v. *íar* (2).

47 No. 136, ed. *Jenkinson*, p. 39. This word, along with *tonaliter*, are discussed in detail in my Hisperica Famina II.

48 In a donation by Cenfrith to Malmesbury, *Ehwald*, Aldhelmi Opera, MGH AA 15, p. 510; also in a charter of Athelstan's, ed. W. *de Gray Birch*, Cartularium II, p. 402.

49 P. 141, note 221.

50 M. *Herren*, Some Conjectures on the Origins and Tradition of the Hisperic Poem *Rubisca*, Ériu 25 (1974), p. 76—77.

A few other words that occur in the *Hisperica Famina* should be noted here on account of their formation. *Ligo, -onis* (A207 and 499) derives, according to Grosjean[51], from OIr. *lí, líg* (f.), "colour, brilliance, beauty". This is doubtless right. The faminators skilfully adapted this guttural stem to the Latin third declension feminine type *origo, vertigo*. A very interesting case is that of *besu* (D6—7)[52]:

> Gemello titicus circonicat besu drimus
> litoreum uelicat adsisa planetum etc.

The field of the sea moves about in two-fold fashion: sometimes the tide covers the plain of the shore; at other times it takes back its waters to its bosom.

Besu here, which I translated as "fashion", cannot be Latin *bes*, which means "two thirds of a unit"! The obvious etymon is Old Irish *bés*, "habit", "custom", "manner", "way", etc., which is a masculine *u*-stem. *Bés* here and in Virgilius Maro has been transferred to the Latin fourth declension, i.e. the masculine *u*-stems. The cases of *ligo* and *besus*, like that of *arreum*, indicate considerable care in the transfer of an Irish word to Latin. Similarly, *curucus* and *tigernus* retain the gender of *curach* and *tigern*, as does *broccus* from *brocc*, "badger", in the Vitae Sanctorum Hiberniae[53]. *Scamna* and *tona* appear to be derived from the plural forms *scamana* and *tonna*. In the case of *barthanus*, "little bard", from *bardán* in the Vitae[54], the masculine Latin ending has been added directly to the Irish diminutive. Perhaps the most glaring exception to the usual practice of analogous formation is that of the feminine *cloc(c)a* from the masculine *cloc*. This discrepancy must have been felt by some Hiberno-Latin writers, for we do find an instance of *cloccos* (accusative plural) in an early Patrick life[55].

To my knowledge, there is only one instance of a latinized Irish verbal form in Hiberno-Latin texts. That is *orgo* from Old Irish *orgid*, which occurs in the *Ars Malsachani* (Löfstedt, p. 226) and in the Corpus Glossary 0—238, *orge: occide*[56].

A few words show evidence of "recycling", that is to say, words coming from Latin into Irish are re-latinized. Thus Irish *abgitir*, "alphabet", for example, comes from Latin *abecedarium*. *Abgitir* reappears in Latin guise as *abicitorium* in *Auraicept na nÉces* and in the curious *Ars Sergilii*, a product of Virgil the Grammarian's circle[57]. Even more striking is the case of Greco-Latin *parochia*, "diocese", which

51 Confusa Caligo, Remarques sur les Hisperica Famina, Celtica 3 (1956), p. 62.
52 Ed. *Jenkinson*, p. 43, with my translation.
53 Vita S. Ciarani de Saigir, V. and VI. = Vol. I, 219. *Capgrave* reads *taxus* for *broccus*.
54 Ibid., IV.
55 Tírechán II, 1, ed. L. *Bieler*, The Patrician Texts in the Book of Armagh, SLH 10, 1979, p. 122. *Strasser* (as above note 23) cites the variant *cloccum*, p. 403.
56 See J. D. *Pheifer*, Old English Glosses in the Epinal-Erfurt Glossary, Oxford 1974, p. vii.
57 For Sergilius, see V. *Law*, The Insular Latin Grammarians, Woodbridge 1982, p. 51—52.

went into Irish as *pairche*, then was "recycled" as *parcium* (gen. pl.) in the Vitae[58], though to be sure *parochia* remained the usual Latin word (usually spelled *paruchia*). Other possible examples may be adduced[59].

We turn now to the second item: the etymologizing of Latin words from Irish. Not surprisingly, the majority of cases are found in grammatical treatises. One exception concerns the connection made between Latin *beo, -are*, "to bless", and Old Irish *béo*, "living", "immortal", as in the phrase *tír na mbéo*. The two words are joined through the obvious association of the *beati*, "blessed ones", with the notion of eternal life. Thus in a Matthew commentary noted by Bischoff: *Apud veteres vivatus pro beato lectitabatur*[60]. This etymology has been attributed to Sergius the Grammarian[61]. There is even one instance of *béo* used as a substitute for *beatus;* this occurs in the *De Abbatibus* of Aethelwulf, who was thought to be active in a daughter house of Lindisfarne: (v. 577): *alitibus testatus erat, pia castra beorum*[62].

As far as I can tell, this kind of etymologyzing began with Virgil the Grammarian and his school around the middle of the seventh century. I pointed out three examples of this phenomenon in my paper on Virgilius[63]:

> *Bestia dicitur de bessu, hoc est more ferocitatis*[64]

> "Beast" is derived from *bessus*, to wit, the *habit* of ferocity.

The word play here is between *bestia*, "beast", and *bessus*, "custom", "habit", a word derived from Irish *bés* that we met above (p. 206) in the D-Text of the *Hisperica Famina*[65].

> *Belua marina, bel enim a philosophis mare uocatur*[66]

> The word for whale means "marine", because the sea is called *bel* by the philosophers.

---

58 *In confinio duarum parcium*, Vita S. Ciarani de Saigir, IV., II, 219.

59 See the examples in my paper (as above note 3), p. 55.

60 No. 21 in his catalogue: Wendepunkte in der Geschichte der lateinischen Exegese im Frühmittelalter, Mittelalterliche Studien I, p. 252—254 (quotation on p. 254). Also, R. L. Ramsay, ZCP 8 (1912), p. 472.

61 See P. Ó Néill, The Old-Irish Treatise on the Psalter and Its Hiberno-Latin Background, Ériu 30 (1979), p. 152—154. Ó Néill cites a passage from the Old Irish Treatise that specifically derives Latin *béo* from a word *bes* "of the fourth kind of Roman rhetoric", which means *vita*. Ó Néill argues for a parallel or source in Virgilius Maro.

62 See the edition and study by A. Campbell, Oxford 1967, p. 577. See *Campbell's* discussion, p. XXI—XXXV.

63 As above note 3, p. 53.

64 See now the text by G. Polara and L. Caruso, Virgilio Marone Grammatico, Epitomi ed Epistole, Naples 1979, p. 150.

65 The etymology *bestia* from *bés* occurs in three other Hiberno-Latin texts: the *De XII Abusivis Saeculi*, the Collectio Canonum Hibernensis, and the Glossary of Cormac. See V. Law, The Insular Latin Grammarians, Woodbridge 1982, p. 48, n. 39; K. Meyer, Learning in Ireland in the Fifth Century, Dublin 1913, p. 22, note 6.

66 See *Polara's* text, ibid.

Bél is Old Irish for "mouth", or "aperture". Its close association with the sea, in the sense of "gulf" is attested by O'Clery and Cormac (see examples in the DIL s.v. *bél* IIb). But the etymology may be more complex. *Bél*, which is the normal Irish word for "mouth", is used in a number of instances to gloss *mén*, its poetic equivalent. The phrase *mén mara* and also *mén* alone are glossed by Irish words meaning "sea monster" or "whale"[67]. As there are no cases in Latin, Greek, or Hebrew of a word with the element *bel* with the meaning "sea"[68], it would seem that Irish *bél* = "abyss", "cavern" best explains the fanciful etymology of *belua* given here.

> *Gloria ex eo dicitur quia alti quique ut sunt dii apud filosophos glores di-cuntur*[69].

> "Glory" is so called, because those beings on high are called *glores* as though gods by the philosophers.

Now Latin *glores*, "sisters-in-law", cannot possibly be associated with *gloria*. *Glores* and *gloria* were doubtless associated by the etymologizer with Old Irish *glór*, "pure", "clear", "bright".

The third category is that of sense borrowings. Here each case must be examined closely to ascertain that only *Irish* semantic influence — and no other — is the cause of a particular meaning shift in a Latin word. The case of *alius* used as an equivalent of *quidam* because of the influence of Old Irish *alaile* has been mentioned by a number of writers and may now be considered a certain instance of "Hibernism". On the other hand, the interchange of the prepositions *cum* and *apud* through the alleged influence of Irish *la*, which has both meanings, is a more doubtful case. Bengt Löfstedt has adduced a number of instances of this confusion that occur entirely outside areas of Celtic influence[70].

A fairly clear case of a sense borrowing from Irish would be the use of *calvus*, "bald", in a monk's name in imitation of the Irish *Mael*, e. g. *Calvus Brigidae* = Maelbrighde[71]. Irish *Mael*, used in the formation of masculine names, means primarily a cropped headed person who is a slave or servant; in a Christian context the element means "devoted to", to wit, a particular saint[72]. Latin *calvus* could never mean "servant of" or "devoted to" without help from Irish. Another good case, adduced by Plummer, is the use of *letitia* in the sense of "welcome" rather than merely "joy", under the influence of Irish *fáilte*. A clear instance occurs

---

67 DIL, s.v. *mén* (c) [where it is taken by the ed. as a 'mistaken inference', Edd.].

68 See the references under *Baal, bal, bel* in *Thiel* (as above note 44); the only possibility in Greek is βέλλαι, glossed in Hesychius by ῥαφίδες θαλάσσιαι. But the first element is related to βελονη, which means "needle", and the phrase means "the garfish". I think that a Greek etymology can be safely excluded.

69 See *Polara's* text (as above note 64), p. 156.

70 As above note 39, p. 118—120.

71 J. *Armitage Robinson*, The Times of St Dunstan, Oxford 1923, p. 57.

72 DIL, s.v. *mael* (3). The entry lists other examples of the equation with *calvus*.

in the Life of Ciaran of Clonmacnois, I. 204: *Numquid ibi pro Christo congruam leticiam invenistis?* The use of *congruam* "fitting", with *leticiam* shows that the word is heavily coloured by Irish *fáilte*. The meaning must be: "Did you find a fitting welcome there for Christ?" Other good examples from the Vitae are: (1) *amicus animae*, meaning "confessor", calqued on *anmchara*[73]; (2) *manum tenere*, meaning to "expel", based on *gabáil lámae*[74]; (3) *quinta pars*, meaning "province", obviously calqued on *cóiced*[75].

These few examples can doubtless be expanded by Irish specialists[76]. Certainly it would be worthwhile to examine the claims made by Fr. William Most regarding the influence of Old Irish syntax on the Latin of the Vitae[77]. Many of Most's examples involve semantic as well as syntactical influence. A philological study of Irish saints lives in Latin with special attention to the Irish semantic substrate would be of enormous benefit to the entire field of Hiberno-Latin studies, since the results from works of certain origin could be applied to saints' Lives, biblical commentaries and perhaps even grammars of unknown provenance. Ideally such a study would be conducted by a team with equal strengths in Latin and Irish. The study of the influence of Latin upon Irish has received a great deal of attention; the study of the reverse, but little. A history of Irish semantic influence on Latin remains to be written. If and when this is accomplished, we shall probably know a good deal more about the Irish contribution to the mainstream of medieval Latin literature.

73 See *Plummer's* Index, II, p. 381.

74 Ibid., p. 383.

75 Ibid., p. 384. This index is a valuable repository of calques on Irish.

76 See, for instance, the discussion of Irish lexical influence on Latin *sentis* by C. *Plummer*, Glossary of Du Cange: Addenda et Corrigenda, Archivum Latinitatis Medii Aevi 2 (1925), p. 26; P. *Grosjean*, Sentis: un prétendu mot gaulois à restituer en latin, ibid. 17 (1942), p. 73—77.

77 The Syntax of the Vitae Sanctorum Hiberniae, Diss., Washington, D. C., 1946.

The Irish glosses

By

E. G. Quin

Irish glosses fall into two main categories, those on native (i. e. Irish) texts and those on foreign (i. e. Latin) texts. In this paper some account will be given of the former, but the main emphasis will be on the latter, as having the greater theological interest.

The Irish texts in question are of an archaic, arcane nature and for one reason or another were held in some reverence. Not only is the language archaic but it is frequently and no doubt intentionally obscure. As a first example we may consider the text called *Imacallam in da Thúaraid* 'The colloquy of the two sages'[1]. Here we have a conversation between two poets on various matters where one can only guess at the meaning most of the time. This, however, was no obstacle to the glossators. Most of the obscurities are 'explained' in fluent, apparently convincing Middle Irish, and the would-be modern editor is left with the problem of how far, if at all, he can trust the native interpretation. The same applies to the even more obscure *Amra Con Roí* 'The eulogy of Cú Roí'[2]. In *Coire Goriath* (usually translated 'The cauldron of poesy', though the meaning of the word *goriath* is unclear) we have, again with plenty of glosses, a text which is almost intelligible and has been plausibly dealt with by Breatnach[3] and Henry[4].

In the Brehon Laws we have a large corpus of legal material in Old Irish at various stages of archaism, with glosses and commentary in later (and therefore intelligible) Irish. To this the early scholars Eugene O'Curry and John O'Donovan[5] applied their not inconsiderable knowledge and talents with seeming success, relying largely, as was natural at the time, on the native glosses and commentaries, themselves, as we have seen, belonging to different stages of Middle and Modern Irish. But these two scholars, learned as they were, belonged to a tradition where everything was translated whether understood or not, and it was not long before other thoughts prevailed. Scholars like MacNeill[6], Thurneysen[7] and Binchy[8] have

---

1　Whitley *Stokes*, The colloquy of the two sages, RC 26 (1905), p. 4—64.

2　R. I. *Best*, The tragic death of Cúroí mac Dári, Ériu 2 (1905), p. 18—35.

3　Liam *Breatnach*, The cauldron of poesy, Ériu 32 (1981), p. 45—93.

4　P. L. *Henry*, id., Stud. Celt. 14—15 (1979—80), p. 114—28.

5　John *O'Donovan*, Eugene *O'Curry*, Robert *Atkinson* and others, ed., ALI, 6 vols., Dublin 1865—91; D. A. *Binchy*, ed., CIH, 6 vols., Dublin 1978.

6　Eoin *MacNeill*, Early Irish laws and institutions, London 1935 and numerous other publications.

7　Rudolf *Thurneysen*, Aus dem irischen Recht, ZCP 14 (1923), p. 335—94, and numerous other publications.

made us realise that to understand the Laws and therefore the early Irish legal system it was necessary to work from the text itself without relying on the glosses and commentary. With this considerable progress has been made, and it is safe to say that modern scholars understand the law-texts a good deal better than did the old glossators.

The glosses in the Laws are sometimes quite near the mark, but most of the time they are of the *Volksetymologie* type. This has been luminously explained by Binchy[9], who gives as an example a fanciful one composed by Osborn Bergin. In this Shakespeare's 'darraign (arrange, draw up) your battle' is given a number of alternative analyses and hence meanings — 'do ruin', 'die ere you run', 'dare in', 'tear around', 'dear rain'. Binchy writes: 'That this parody is in no way exaggerated could be proved by several examples of legal glossing in which the alternative explanations are more numerous still and just as far-fetched.'

It should further be noted that although the commentary always sounds quite plausible most of it relates to a much later period than that described by the texts. The commentators are describing the usage of their own day, or so it would seem, and are apparently unaware that the text they claim to be elucidating deals with things quite remote from them.

This is all very much to be regretted, the more so as the whole operation was very meticulously mounted in the law-schools. This is clear from the care with which some of the legal MSS were compiled. In a typical case[10] we find considerably less than half the area of available vellum occupied by the text proper. This is written in beautifully formed letters a good quarter of an inch high, and is evidently the work of a highly-skilled scribe. A good deal of the remaining space, though not all, is occupied by glosses and commentary. The whole is an artistic and beautiful production showing none of the crowding and squeezing characteristic of so many Irish manuscripts. But as far as the text and its elucidation are concerned it is somewhat of a whited sepulchre.

The foregoing are all secular texts. We turn now to the ecclesiastical. Yet the transition is not violent, for in the *Amra Coluim Chille* 'The eulogy of Colum Cille'[11] we find a text with glosses and commentary quite strongly reminiscent of those already mentioned. It consists of a long series of *dicta* about the saint in archaic Irish with the type of interlined commentary we have come to expect. In language and style and general treatment it is so like the texts already mentioned that it

8 D. A. *Binchy*, as above note 5, and numerous other publications. For modern work on the Laws see R. I. *Best*, Bibliography of Irish philology and manuscript literature, Dublin 1942, p. 170 ff.

9 D. A. *Binchy*, Linguistic and historical value of the Irish law tracts (Sir Johns Rhys Memorial Lecture) PBA 20 (1943), p. 20.

10 R. I. *Best* and Rudolf *Thurneysen*, Facsimiles in collotype of Irish manuscripts. I. Senchas Már. Facsimile of the oldest fragments, Dublin 1931.

11 Whitley *Stokes*, The Bodleian Amra Choluimb Chille, RC 20 (1899), p. 30—55, 132—83, 248—89, 400—37.

forms an interesting link between the so-called pagan texts and the overtly Christian ones dealt with below. The *Amra Senáin* 'The eulogy of Senán'[12], ascribed, like the *Amra Coluim Chille*, to Dallán Forgaill (an alleged sixth-century poet) is shorter but of the same type.

We now turn to a work in what has come to be called classical Old Irish, *i. e.* ninth-century Irish as distinct from 'archaic' (and often obscure) Irish. This is the *Félire Óengusso* 'The calendar of Oengus'[13], which lists saints (inclusive of Irish ones) arranged under their feast-days for all 365 days of the year and provided with a prologue and epilogue. Apart from sporadic difficulties it is completely intelligible, and the fact that it is in verse with well-established metrical rules means that forms can be checked and where necessary emended with confidence. It is heavily loaded with glosses and commentary, and in at least one MS (the 14th century *Lebor Brecc*[14]) the set-out of the page is as described for the legal MSS. The glosses too are of the type described above. One example will suffice. The word *bordgala* (pl.) is from the Latin form *Burdigala* (Bordeaux), and is used of places of resort and intercourse. It is explained in the gloss as: *it lana conice a* mbord *domilib* congail *chrabuid accu* 'they are full to their *edge* with warriors imbued with spiritual *valour*'[15]. The commentary is copious and touches on a variety of subjects, anecdotes, history, explanations of place-names, poems (including the very popular *Ísucán*[16]), even one highly unsuitable description of the birth of a saint[17].

The glosses on Latin (and mainly ecclesiastical) texts are naturally of a very different type from those so far described, and it is an interesting fact that Latin was known a good deal better in the monastic schools than archaic Irish in the secular ones. For the modern scholar the roles are of course reversed. Where the old ecclesiastics explained the Latin in Irish modern scholarship frequently finds the Latin helpful in explaining the Irish.

In these glosses three main types can be distinguished — glosses giving the meaning of individual Latin words; fairly close translations of Latin sentences, exegetic glosses (of special interest for the light they throw on teaching methods in the monastic schools). In this paper it will be impossible to deal with more than three of the collections. These are, however, large in extent and on the whole typical of the whole corpus.

---

12 Whitley *Stokes*, Amra Senáin, ZCP 3 (1901), p. 220—25.

13 Whitley *Stokes*, On the Calendar of Oengus, Transactions of the Royal Irish Academy, Irish MSS Series I, 1880; *idem,* The martyrology of Oengus the Culdee, HBS 29, 1905.

14 Leabhar Breac ... now for the first time published from the original manuscript in the library of the Royal Irish Academy, Dublin 1872—76.

15 Whitley *Stokes*, On the calendar of Oengus (as above note 13) p. XXIV.

16 E. G. *Quin*, The early Irish poem *Ísucán*, Cambridge Medieval Celtic Studies 1 (1981), p. 39—52.

17 Whitley *Stokes*, On the Calendar of Oengus (as above note 13), p. LXXXIX.

The first is not religious in content, though no doubt written in a religious environment. It is the Codex Sangallensis (St Gall) No. 904, which contains the Latin text of the first sixteen books of the Latin grammar of Priscian (*fl.* AD 450) with numerous Irish glosses and some Latin ones. The Irish glosses belong roughly to the ninth century, but the exact dating has not been settled. Unfortunately no facsimile of this important codex is available, the more so as the official edition in Thesaurus Palaeohibernicus[18] gives neither the full Latin text of Priscian nor the Latin glosses. From the point of view of vocabulary two points may be mentioned for these glosses. In the first place Priscian often gives lists of Latin words to illustrate his rules. For these Irish equivalents are given, some of which are *hápax legómena* and others not otherwise attested in ninth-century texts. Thus *forcrach*[19] glosses *faux* and *muirmóru*[20] glosses *siren*, while *cletecháin*[21] glosses *aclydes* and appears again only in an eighteenth-century poem[22] and in a different meaning, 'quill pen', doubtless a new formation. But more importantly we here find an illustration of the great ingenuity of the glossators in coping with Latin grammatical terms. Several methods are used. Firstly there is straightforward borrowing (and subjecting to the Irish sound-system) — *adiecht (adjectivus)*, *comparit (comparativus)*, *genitiu (genitivus)*, etc. Then there is loan-translation or calque — *dobríathar (do* 'to' *bríathar* 'verb') *adverbium*, *comsuidigud (com* 'together' *suidigud* 'placing') *compositio*, *rangabál (rann* 'part' *gabál* 'taking') *participium*. Finally there is the use of a native word in a grammatical sense — *áram* (lit. 'counting') 'number', *bríathar* (lit. 'word') 'verb', *césad* v. *gním* (lit. 'suffering' v. 'action') 'passive' v. 'active', *tinfeth* (lit. 'breathing') 'aspiration'[23].

Approximate translation of Latin sentences may be exemplified by — *In Latinis tamen dictionibus nos quoque pro* ph *coepimus* f *scribere* glossed (I translate the Irish) 'We have, however, formed one character — *f* instead of *p* with aspiration, in Latin words'[24]; *Itaque omnis modus finitus potest per hunc modum interpretari* 'through it is expressed the meaning of every mood'[25].

As examples of exegetic glosses we may cite — *'Euripides' non Euripi filius sed ab Eurupo sic nominatus est* ''tis therefore that name was given to him (Euripides), because that is the day on which he was born, not because he was born in that

18 Whitley *Stokes* and John *Strachan*, ed., Thesaurus Palaeohibernicus II, Cambridge 1903, p. 49—224. Vol I, 1901, gives the Milan (Ml.) and Würzburg (Wb.) glosses dealt with below. For details of glosses published subsequently see *Best*, Bibliography (as above note 5), p. 53—55.
19 Sg. 24b5.
20 Sg. 96b5.
21 Sg. 66a23.
22 Patrick S. *Dineen* and Tadhg *O'Donoghue*, ed., Dánta Aodhagáin Uí Rathaille, ITS 1911, p. 260.31.
23 For these words see DIL.
24 Sg. 9a22.
25 Sg. 148b7.

place'[26]. Further — *Inueniuntur tamen etiam propria differentiae causa in fine circumflexa, ut 'Leenâs, Leenatis'* 'for not for the sake of distinction is that which we have said hitherto'[27].

The most extensive of the three collections is contained in the Codex Ambrosianus C. 301 in the Ambrosian Library in Milan, and for this we have an excellent facsimile edited by R. I. Best[28]. The Latin here is a commentary of doubtful authorship on the Psalter, and the Irish glosses (ninth century) are on this commentary (unfortunately not on the Psalms themselves. One thinks enviously of the biblical translations available for Gothic, Armenian and Old Church Slavonic). Here again we may use the classification of glosses given above. For individual words we have — *emulari* glossed (with choice of four meanings) 'to admire *i.e.* to emulate, *i.e.* to strive after or to love'[29], *adloquitur* glossed *adgládathar* 'addresses'[30], *offensam* glossed *frithorcuin*[31]. For fairly close translation we quote — *noli in tua patientia sustinere* with the gloss 'shew not patience'[32] and *docens ut non magno stupore capiantur earum rerum quae in hac uita gloriosa creduntur* 'though it be that one sees the glorious things of this world, that it may not put him in stupor and admiration to love them and to desire them'[33].

For exegesis a single long example will suffice (there are others of comparable length). Psalm 35 is introduced in the commentary with the words — *Cum Sauelis insidiis urgeretur, hunc psalmum cecinit, eo praecipue tempore cum in suam potestatem insidiator [Saul] uenisset, ab eiusque internecione temperasset, sublato tamen scipho et [sublata] hasta pro manifestatione negotii*. The Irish gloss tells the well-known story in a fine piece of continuous Old-Irish prose — 'When David went into exile before Saul, Saul went afterwards to pursue him with a host, and a camp was pitched by Saul against him for protection. David then went the following night to them into their camp, and he went to the place in which the king was and removed the king's cup, and removed the spear, and fixed it beside one of Saul's cheeks in the ground. And afterwards David went to the hill that was next the army, and called to them thence that they did not guard the king well — Behold ye his cup and his arms, how they are'[34].

We come finally to the Codex Paulinus Wirzburgensis, containing the thirteen epistles of St Paul with copious glosses in Latin and Irish, arguably the most precious Irish text we have. The codex was published in facsimile by Stern in

26 Sg. 31a6.
27 Sg. 55b5.
28 R. I. *Best,* The commentary on the Psalms preserved in the Ambrosian Library, collotype facsimile, Dublin 1936.
29 Ml. 56b39.
30 Ml. 74a8.
31 Ml. 22d21.
32 Ml. 55a1.
33 Ml. 68b9.
34 Ml. 55c1. Cf. 1 Reg 26.

1910[35]. There are three hands, the oldest going back to about AD 700, with the bulk of the glosses belonging to the eighth century. The main source of the glosses is apparently Pelagius (fifth century). Curiously, even where a gloss is in Irish, a Latin word is often retained though an Irish word is available — *gloria* (OIr. *inducbál*[36]), *mortuorum* (OIr. *inna mmarb*[37]), *spiritus* (OIr. *spirut*, itself a borrowing[38]). Though the Irish words are themselves also used in some of the glosses, it may have been felt that in particular cases a religious overtone would have been lost by using one.

Glossing by single words is frequent — *turpitudinem* is glossed by *mebuil*[39], *(cimbalem) tinniens* by *astóidi*[40] and *fogrigedar* and *tibia* by *buinne*[41]. Straightforward translation too is frequent, and one may note here the simplification process used for St Paul's sometimes rather elusive sayings. For instance at 1 Cor 15:45 *Factus est primus homo Adam in animam viventem; novissimus Adam in spiritum vivificantem* the Irish simply has 'the spirit vivifies the body this time'[42]. There is a more direct translation in the case of Gal 4:15 *Si fieri posset, oculos uestros eruissetis et dedissetis mihi* 'though I had asked for your eyes, ye would have given them to me'[43]; Rom 11:11 *Numquid sic offenderunt ut caderent?* 'have they offended so greatly that all should fall *a fide Christi?'* (where note the use of a Latin phrase[44]); 2 Cor 9:2 *De uobis glorior apud Macedonas* 'I am wont to boast about you to the Macedonians'[45].

But undoubtedly the most interesting Würzburg glosses (as is indeed the case with the other two codices) are those offering exegesis. And here the down-to-earth method of the glossator is particularly evident. Thus at Rom 8:26 *Similiter autem et spiritus adjuvat infirmitatem nostram* we find the long explanation — 'so it is then that *Spiritus* helps our weakness when we have the same desire in body and soul and spirit (ir. *spirut*. Note the distinction here). This then is the right way of prayer, but we cannot do that unless the Spirit inspire it: thus then our prayer is feeble if they be present things which we ask, and the Spirit helps us not therein: then doth the Spirit help when we beseech glory for our body and for our soul after resurrection'[46]. Again at 2 Cor 2:5 *Si quis autem contristauit, non me contristauit sed ex parte, ut non onerem omnes uos* 'so that I may not count sin with you all, or so that I may give aid to you lest it be heavy on you by yourselves'[47].

35 L. C. *Stern*, ed., Epistolae Beati Pauli glosatae glosa lineali, Halle 1910.
36 Wb. 21d3.
37 Wb. 13b19.
38 Wb. 4a27.
39 Wb. 1c2.
40 Wb. 12b28.
41 Wb. 12c41.
42 Wb. 13d7.
43 Wb. 19d24.
44 Wb. 5b11.
45 Wb. 16d8.
46 Wb. 4a27.
47 Wb. 14d17.

215

One further point is of interest. It is impossible to read St Paul without being struck by his fondness for the metaphor of the race. I have counted eight cases where he has used it, of which four have been glossed in the Würzburg codex. One example will suffice. At Phil 3:14 we read *Ad destinatum persequor, ad bradium supernae uocationis Dei in Christo Iesu.* This is glossed 'this is a similitude which he has to a soldier who runs unto the crown of victory, that is, this is his custom, he counteth not what (part) of the way lies behind him, but (only) what is before him, until he comes past it, and reaches the crown. In that wise hath Paul been, and thus ought every one to be, that is, in constant penance till he attains to the crown, that is, to the heavenly reward'[48].

In this very broadly-based analysis of the Latin to Irish glosses these have been considered purely as glosses, explanations of Latin. Linguistic considerations have as far as possible been avoided, and would be best dealt with in a separate study. Indeed, by far the greater part of the work done on the glosses has been on the language side, for it is on them that our knowledge of the grammar of classical Old Irish is based. And though Zeuss[49], Zimmer[50] and Thurneysen[51] in their various publications have given lengthy and continuous passages of the Latin of the codices, thus facilitating the kind of approach used in this paper, even here the emphasis is on the language. On the other hand, in the widely used selection given by Strachan[52] the approach is quite brutally linguistic. Here individual glosses from all three codices and a few others are arranged so as to exemplify the various parts of the verb. This is of course very valuable, the verb being the most difficult part of Old Irish grammar. But glosses on Priscian, the Psalter and St Paul rubbing shoulders with each other and each without any really convincing context (the more so as only the barest minimum of Latin is given) do not make for rewarding reading. The grammar of classical Old Irish is now fairly well established[53]. The way thus lies open for an approach different from the traditional one. The methods exemplified in these teaching-books are of considerable interest, and in this area much remains to be done[54].

48 Wb. 24a17.

49 I. C. *Zeuss*, Grammatica Celtica, editio altera curavit H. *Ebel*, Berlin 1871.

50 Heinrich *Zimmer*, Glossae Hibernicae e codicibus Wirziburgensi Carolisruhensibus aliis ..., Berlin 1881.

51 Rudolf *Thurneysen*, Old Irish Reader, Dublin 1949.

52 John *Strachan*, Old-Irish paradigms and selections from the old-Irish glosses, fourth edition revised by Osborn *Bergin*, Dublin 1949.

53 Rudolf *Thurneysen*, Grammar of Old Irish, Dublin 1946.

54 The following are exceptions to the traditional and strictly linguistic approach: Maartje *Draak*, Construe-marks in Hiberno-Latin manuscripts, Mededelingen der Koninklijke Nederlandse Akademie van Wetenschappen, afd. Letterkunde, Nieuwe Reeks, Deel 20, No. 10, Amsterdam 1957; *ead.*, The higher teaching of Latin grammar in Ireland during the ninth century, ibid. Deel 30 No. 4, 1967. In these the writer, with helpful photographs, demonstrates from the St Gall glosses the use of syntax marks and *signes de renvoi*. Brian *Ó Cuív* in his Medieval Irish scholars and classical Latin literature, PRIA 81 C No. 9

(1981) points out, with examples, that in the glosses on Priscian the glossators 'show familiarity with the traditions of Greece and Rome and with the work of the Classical authors' (i. e. over and above the requirements of particular glosses).

The Old Breton glosses and the cultural importance of Brittany in the early Middle Ages

By
Léon Fleuriot

The only purpose of this brief study is to give a general view of the problem of the Old Breton glosses, to sum up and appreciate the weight of the information they give us on the older stages of the language, and to underline the role of Brittany in former times as a land of contact between the Celtic, Germanic and Romance speaking worlds throughout several centuries. The glosses themselves are witness to the relationships between the different cultures.

I.

The corpus of Old Breton glosses is not very large, but we know it better than we did, and thanks to the work of such prominent researchers as Professor Bischoff, we have a more precise view of what remains of the output of old Breton scriptoria. This is a more general problem, as two thirds of the known Breton MSS have no glosses, but when we speak of Breton MSS here, we refer only to those dating from the eleventh century and before, with the greater part of them belonging to the ninth century.

Professor Bischoff's work has been used and continued successfully by Dr Dumville who presented a remarkable review of our present knowledge of old Breton MSS at the Oxford Colloquium in January 1981. Possibly some one hundred and twenty-five to one hundred and fifty MSS remain from the aforesaid period. This is a small number, but it should be remembered that this region suffered so many wars and such destruction that the few remaining MSS are found now in places outside Brittany.

The Normans were the chief culprits, but a large part of the destruction must be attributed to the Frankish armies and then to Plantagenet forces. Civil and internal feudal wars must also have taken a heavy toll of the monasteries. In comparing the number of ninth-century MSS from England, Dr Dumville underlined the fact that about eighty-six Breton MSS from this period have been identified. The corresponding number of MSS from England would be under thirty.

This comparison is of better value than another comparison less favourable to Brittany, that is the comparison of this hundred or so MSS with the total number of six thousand five hundred MSS from the ninth century. It must be borne in mind that many regions in Italy, Germany and France have been better preserved from the calamities of those times than Brittany or England. The dispersal of what was spared is further testimony of the tribulations suffered by Breton monasteries and churches.

New light has been cast on the travels of the few remaining MSS by the recent thesis, undertaken at the University of Paris under the direction of Professor Riché, and as yet unpublished. Its title is 'L'exode des reliques des saints de l'ouest de la France aux IXe et Xe siècles' (Université de Paris X, Nanterre, 1979); the monks who saved these relics also managed to save some of their MSS.

Their path of escape up the Loire valley explains the dispersal of MSS in later times from monasteries such as Saint Gildas-en-Berry or Fleury-sur-Loire. Other monks followed another way eastwards along the Channel, and found shelter in some of the abbeys of the Île-de-France, or at Montreuil-sur-Mer. This explains the later diffusion of some of the surviving Breton MSS in Belgium, the Netherlands, Germany and Switzerland.

About fifteen of these MSS went northwards to Britain. The main explanation of this fact must be sought in the policy of alliance with the Bretons promoted by Aethelstan against their common enemies the Vikings. Moreover Aethelstan was fond of relics and books. The cult of Breton saints was thus brought back to the country of their origin.

Towards the end of the eleventh century, the large participation of Breton troops in William the Conqueror's expedition, and the vast tracts of land they received in England, brought a new wave of Breton saints to Britain. Here it must be said that the work in progress in this field of research of Mr Michael Jones has thrown new light on the importance of the Breton element among "Normans" in the eleventh and twelfth centuries. This is another instance of the role of go-between played by Brittany in the Middle Ages.

To return to Old Breton MSS, we must mention another group slightly later than those dealt with above, and of which our knowledge has been much improved in recent times. This group contains "neumatic notation" of Breton origin. The main researcher in this field is M. Huglo whose fundamental article has been republished with illustrations[1]. About a hundred MSS are quoted in Huglo's work, many of them different from those numbered in Professor Bischoff's lists. The maps illustrate the wide expansion of this notation which was also used in Italy at Pavia.

All these facts are related. If this Breton neumatic notation was known far away from Brittany, it is in large part due to the scattering of Breton monks, relics and MSS in the tenth century. But it is also due to the ancestral habit, already quoted by Gildas, arising from the delight of Britons or Bretons, just as that of Irishmen, in travelling far and wide.

Before turning to glossed MSS we must say something of another and very ancient group of Breton MSS now beginning to be better known. These are the Gospel Books. The main source of information in this field is the book by Francis

---

1 M. *Huglo*, Le domaine de la notation bretonne, Britannia Christiana, Daoulas, Finistère 1981, I, p. 12—52.

Wormald and Jonathan Alexander, An Early Breton Gospel Book[2]. This magnificent work, with a wealth of plates and illustrations, is mainly devoted to a study of the art, but in the chapter entitled "A note on the Breton Gospel Books" one finds many valuable indications serving as a guide to further research.

So far about twelve Gospel Books from the ninth century have been traced back to Brittany, but some fifteen others may also be of Breton origin, a fact which stresses the need for further investigations. Only the patient work of comparison, the labours of many researchers to come, can give us a more exact view of an area which has been so neglected, a region whose role has been underestimated.

The amount of work to be done may be appreciated when we consider that we do not know how to distinguish the Breton scriptoria; we are not able to ascribe a group of MSS to Dol or to Landevennec, to Saint-Mathieu or to Saint-Gildas-de-Rhuys. But this will probably be possible in the future.

The Gospel Books we have just cited are unglossed, but this review of our present knowledge of old Breton MSS helps to remind us that the glossed MSS are not in isolation. They number forty or so out of a total of some hundred and fifty, perhaps close on two hundred when the research work is completed. The glosses were not written indiscriminately on every kind of MS; the Gospel Books which were in the churches and not in the class rooms were not intended to bear glosses or explanations of the text.

On the other hand the grammar books, the books relating to religious celebrations, the computations of Easter, were heavily glossed. Such was also the case for the books used in the monastic schools in teaching good Latin, the works of some poets, notably and pre-eminently Virgil. The canonical treatises containing religious legislation and not uncommonly Celtic laws bear numerous glosses owing to their general use in Brittany. They are commomly and somewhat improperly called Irish canons.

The repute and fame of the Irish was so great between the seventh and the tenth centuries that the more ancient Brittonic element, essential in the previous period from the fourth to the seventh centuries, has quite often been forgotten even in Brittonic countries. However in recent times some scholars have underlined the importance of this ancient British Church whose most famous member is Patrick. Indeed, many of the so-called *canones Hibernenses* contain matter which is ultimately of Brittonic origin, and it is not merely by chance that the MSS which have preserved it are essentially Breton.

We need not repeat here in detail the list of the thirty-six old Breton MSS which contain Old Breton glosses. They are found in our 'Dictionnaire des gloses en vieux-breton'[3]. Some others were since discovered. BN MS lat. 4389, identified

2 F. *Wormald*, J. *Alexander*, An Early Breton Gospel Book, Cambridge 1977.
3 L. *Fleuriot*, Dictionnaire des gloses en vieux-breton (Collection linguistique 62), Paris 1964, p. 4—7.

when the Dictionnaire was nearing completion, was included in it[4], bringing the number to thirty-seven.

A more important MS discovered long ago by Father Hanssens was inadvertedly omitted. This MS, to which the number thirty-eight may be given, is BN MS nouv. acq. lat. 1983. The glosses from this MS have been published[5].

The *membra disiecta* of yet another, bringing the total to thirty-nine, were found by Ludwig Bieler in various German libraries. This is a MS of Isidore of which the most important folio is from Herdringen. The glosses, some of which are difficult to explain, have been published[6].

Another MS of Isidore with Old Breton glosses has not been published. It is BL Harleian MS 3941[7]. It is to be published by Dr Dumville along with some newly-discovered Irish glosses from Laon.

We must also draw attention to the excellent edition by Daniel Huws of a fragment of a MS glossed in Old Welsh[8] containing five glosses which are very similar to the Old Breton glosses, a very frequent occurrence. Professor Hamp published his very important Notes on Old Breton[9]. A study by Mr. P. Y. Lambert on the glosses of BN MS lat. 10290 is to appear soon[10].

This summary of the present knowledge of the corpus of Old Breton glosses may be completed with the statement of the intention to publish all the glosses, in Paris, under the title *Thesaurus Palaeobritannicus*. This will contain lengthy extracts from the Latin texts on the model of the far greater *Thesaurus Palaeohibernicus*. I had done this work for the two main manuscripts, Angers MS 477 and BN MS lat. 10290 before the formulation of the Dictionnaire but financial problems delayed this publication. It should be done with the co-operation of a little team interested in this project.

II.

We may now turn to the importance of Old Breton glosses and Old Welsh glosses for the knowledge of previous stages of these languages when they were both rather different from their present state, and far closer to each other. Thus we may speak as late as the tenth century of differences between dialects rather than of differences between clear-cut languages. It is important to underline the fact that contemporaries speak as late as the eleventh century, of *lingua britannica* and *britonnicum* and not of Cornish, Welsh and Breton.

4 Ibid., p. 339 f.

5 L. *Fleuriot*, Nouvelles gloses vieilles-bretonnes à Amalarius, EC 11 (1964—67), p. 415—64.

6 L. *Fleuriot*, Gloses inédites en vieux-breton, EC 16 (1979), p. 197—208.

7 CLA XII, no. 1704.

8 D. *Huws*, A Welsh Manuscript of Bede's *De Natura Rerum*, BBCS 27 (1976—78), p. 491—504.

9 E. *Hamp*, Notes on Old Breton, EC 15 (1976—78), p. 191—93, 569—72.

10 EC 19 (forthcoming).

The disappearance of forms very different in ancient times from the present form of these Brittonic languages has widened the gap between them. It appears from the testimony of the Old Welsh glosses that ancient Welsh also had the preposition *guar* 'on', surviving only in Cornish and Breton. Old Welsh proper names tell us that Welsh formerly knew the word *bresel* 'war', still common in Breton. On the other hand, Old Breton glosses and to a greater extent the wealth of Old Breton names in the cartularies, show us that Middle and Modern Breton have lost hundreds or thousands of words which have been better preserved in Middle and even Modern Welsh, thanks to a vigorous and unbroken literary tradition. Even minor finds are meaningful in this respect. For instance, newly discovered Old Welsh glosses show that formerly Welsh had a by-form *riberthi* 'spring-tide' closer to Old Breton *rebirthi*, modern *reverzi*, than the later Welsh form *rhyferthwy*.

More telling and more important is the information supplied by the ancient glosses on morphology and syntax. They give us evidence which no reconstruction based on the present state of the languages could provide, concerning facts long obsolete everywhere. For instance, all the early texts show us that the Brittonic languages knew a type of sentence very similar to the well-known Irish type: *is cóir duit an feur do bhaint*. The Old Welsh Computus sentence: *is aries isid in arcimeir O* 'it is the "ram" that is in front of O', is paralleled in Old Breton, with an inflected verbal form as the second verb of the sentence: *ir is guolou bid nos in ocos da di ...* 'for it is bright that the night is, close to the daylight ...', *is petguar blidan iu em* 'it is of four years that this (period) is (made)'.

The second verb of the sentence may be a verbal noun, which can be preceded by a possessive: *is ret i degurmehim* 'its adding is necessary', *is ret dudo em gudbut* 'its knowledge (knowing) is necessary for him'. Middle Welsh still retains this type of sentence in decreasing use: *ys mi ae eirch* 'it is I who ask for it'. Afterwards, *is* was dropped apart from compounds or petrified expressions. The idiom *is em* was reduced to *sef* 'here is' in Welsh. In Breton the origin of the idiom *setu, sede* 'voici' may have to be reconsidered in the light of the early language. It may preserve a trace of *is*, just as *so* and *si-* in *sioaz, si-ken*, reflect the earlier *isi* and *isio* (corresponding to Welsh *ysydd*), attested in Old Breton.

Another good instance of the necessity for studying these documents in order to have a better understanding of the development of all the Celtic languages is the existence in early Brittonic of the system of absolute and conjunct forms of the verb, exactly parallel to what is well attested in Irish. In this case the testimony of the Old Welsh and Old Breton glosses is completed by examples which are still found in early Middle Welsh.

Absolute forms of the verb are mainly found when the verb is at the head of the sentence or isolated in glosses. For instance in Old Welsh: *rodesit Elcu guetig equs* 'Elcu afterwards gave a horse'; in the *Canu Aneirin* v. 325: *seinnyessit e gledyf ym penn mameu* 'his sword resounded in the head of mothers'; further examples are given in Études Celtiques[11]. Let us cite here only the opposition between Old

222

Breton *acupot* 'he holds' and Old Welsh *ni-s-acup* 'does not hold it'; the absolute ending *-ot* is dropped in the second instance, the verb being preceded by the negative *ni*.

Here we can give only a glimpse of what may be gathered from the study of the language of the early documents, and more especially of the glosses. This material is and will be treated at length in other studies by many scholars.

III.

The glosses and especially the Old Breton glosses are witnesses to many contacts between different languages and cultures. First of all, they show in detail how Latin culture was taught and understood in Celtic monasteries. An amazing fact is that the glosses are often bilingual, either beginning or ending in Latin, the rest being Celtic. Sometimes only one word is Latin or Celtic, while the remainder of the sentence is in the vernacular or in Latin. The very faults which we find in the understanding of Latin by our glossators are of great interest. A study that could and should be made of Brittonic Latin would show that many Latin sentences merely overlie a Celtic syntax.

It is difficult to account for such a sentence as *miraculum erat cum eis* 'they witnessed a miracle' without thinking about a Brittonic sentence such as **gwerthut oi cantdo* ... In the Life of Iudicael by Ingomar, the expression *materia comitis* is an obvious calque on a Brittonic **damhnidh cont*, of a type common in Old Irish *rígdamnae*, in early Welsh *defnydd fy naw* and still in use in Breton: *danvez beleg* 'stuff of a priest' i. e. a seminarist. This latter instance is not taken from the glosses but from a saint's life, another field of investigation.

The glossed MSS are also good witnesses for contacts between Celtic countries. It is rather common to find glosses in various Celtic languages in the same work. This is not only so because of the travels of the MSS themselves but also because of the mixed population of Celtic monasteries. The movements of the migrations lasted for a long time, particularly in the case of Brittany. Intercourse between Brittany and Wales was very common down to the eleventh century. The saints' Lives constantly refer to the seaways in the Celtic seas, and Bowen's work has brought many facts to light.

Archaeology has obliged us to reconsider the critical use made of these early texts. The discovery of pottery from Aquitaine or from Mediterranean countries and the numerous studies published by Professor Thomas have shown us how far and wide the Celtic sailors voyaged in the early Middle Ages. We cannot give a detailed account here of the progress made during the last twenty years in this respect.

It will suffice for us to point here to the numerous glosses which have Old Welsh characteristics in the main manuscripts, BN MS lat. 10290 and Angers MS 477. It is perhaps wrong to call them Old Welsh when contemporaries termed

11   EC 18 (1981), p. 98—101.

these languages as simply *lingua Britannica* using only a single term. In fact, *these forms are Old Breton, too,* but a dialectal variant of it, spoken by immigrants coming from what is now Wales. We cannot know whether they were newcomers to Brittany themselves, or descendants who retained some ancestral speech-habits of earlier migrants, but we have pointed to the fact that the so-called Welsh forms are also found in early Breton cartularies[12].

These remarks seem to have remained unnoticed so that we must draw attention particularly to this again. We have some examples of the form *haiarn* beside the 'regular' Old Breton *hoiarn*, some forms in *-auc* in contrast to the more common *-oc*. It also seems quite natural to find dialectal forms belonging to different stages of the speech of the ancient *Cornovii* in the area where they were so numerous that it still bears their name in our own time, and similarly in the case of the *Dumnonii.*

The predominance, in later Breton, of forms pertaining to South-western Brittonic stems from a number of facts. First the importance of the migration from Devon, underlined in the masterly work of Kenneth Jackson. Secondly the prolonged intercourse between Brittany and Cornwall, far more intimate and longer lasting than the corresponding relations between Brittany and Wales.

Miss Ditmas has recently studied the role of Breton noblemen in Cornwall after Hastings, and all the drama texts in Middle Cornish and Middle Breton betray affinities in every respect: language, literary themes and even the location of events. It is known that a large part of the play *Beunans Meriasek* is located near Pontivy and Rohan.

The glosses show us that in the early period, the dialectal forms akin to Old Welsh words were more numerous than in later times for the reasons we have just given. Since the relaxation of the links between Wales and Brittany was earlier than that of the links between Cornwall and Brittany, it is not surprising that Cornish and Breton remained so close until the sixteenth century.

What is less to be expected is the fact that numerous *Irish* glosses are also found in old Breton MSS. The main body of these is to be found in the oft-cited BN MS lat. 10290. These Irish glosses have been studied by Professor Bachellery[13], and P.-Y. Lambert will publish some additional remarks about them soon[14]. Three short sentences in Old Irish are written in the Breton BN MS lat. 12021[15]; two glosses in Irish are found in BN MS lat. 13029, fol. 12r; another MS, Munich Staatsbibliothek 14846, has a number of Old Irish and Old Breton glosses, in both cases recopied from an older MS. The Cambridge Corpus Christi College MS 279 has an Old Breton gloss *anre* among Irish glosses.

---

12 See the preface to *Fleuriot,* Dictionnaire (as above note 3), p. 15f.
13 E. *Bachellery,* Les gloses irlandaises du manuscrit Paris Latin 10290, EC 11 (1964—67), p. 100—130.
14 As above note 10.
15 See RC 4 (1879—80), p. 325, note 3.

The case of these Irish glosses may be different in some respects from that of the so-called "Welsh" glosses written by immigrants. In many instances it seems that glosses in Old Irish were already written in MSS which were used later among Brittonic monks who merely kept them. Sometimes they tried to understand and translate them. Perhaps in some cases there was an Irish monk among the Brittonic brethren.

This comes as no surprise when we have dedications to Irish saints in Brittonic countries, and when we see Columbanus passing through Brittany on his way to Eastern Gaul. The Life of Saint Winwaloe (Gwenole) shows us Breton sailors at Brehat island about to set sail for Ireland. This brings us back to the works on the sea-routes discussed above.

When we turn to other matters such as the spread of the "Matière de Bretagne" we must not forget the part played by Brittany in sea-trade until the end of the Middle Ages, from the Lower Rhine to Spain and the Mediterranean. The complex nature of the Breton glosses is only a minor fact, the meaning of which is confirmed and clarified by much information from various other fields.

It is worth noting that the study of these glosses has never been purely a Breton undertaking. The first great scholars to draw attention to them were Bradshaw and Whitley Stokes, followed by Joseph Loth and Rudolf Thurneysen. Ifor Williams made use of them for purposes of comparison with early Welsh. When Kenneth Jackson published his great work 'Language and History in Early Britain', it gave me the idea of exploring this field over again. Professor Bischoff's findings and his kind help have always been given to many a researcher. More recently Thomas Charles-Edwards, Wendy Davies and David Dumville have begun very promising work in the early Breton field and not restricted it to the study of glosses. It is fortunate that these studies take no heed of national boundaries just as in ancient times Celtic countries were in constant communication.

Die althochdeutsche Glossenüberlieferung des 8. Jahrhunderts[1]

Von

Rolf Bergmann

I.

Die Frage nach den frühesten deutschen Glossen führt unmittelbar in zentrale Probleme des Anfangs der deutschen Sprach- und Literaturgeschichte: die Entstehung der deutschen Sprache aus verschiedenen kontinentalgermanischen Stammesdialekten[2] und die Entstehung einer deutschsprachigen Schriftlichkeit[3] neben der beherrschenden lateinischen Überlieferung. Die Frage führt zeitlich in das 8. Jahrhundert und damit in den Zeitraum intensiver insularer Einflüsse auf dem Kontinent. Es wird zu zeigen sein, daß gerade in diesem Zusammenhang die im Kontext des Dubliner Kolloquiums vorgegebene Fragestellung geeignet ist, noch neue Einsichten aus einem scheinbar altbekannten Quellenmaterial gewinnen zu lassen.

Im folgenden sollen zunächst und in erster Linie gesicherte Daten über den Gegenstand geliefert werden. Die Zahl der Handschriften und die Zahl der in ihnen enthaltenen Glossen sind möglichst genau zu bestimmen, ihre zeitliche Verteilung innerhalb des 8. Jahrhunderts und ihre geographische Verteilung innerhalb des althochdeutschen Sprachgebietes ist zu beschreiben. Ferner ist nach den glossierten Texten und nach den paläographischen Aufschlüssen zu fragen. Schließlich führt die Berücksichtigung der geschichtlichen, insbesondere kirchen- und bildungsgeschichtlichen Zusammenhänge der Glossenüberlieferung zu einer Interpretation ihrer sprach- und literaturgeschichtlichen Aussagen. Bei der Ermittlung der betreffenden Glossenhandschriften ist das der Themenstellung entsprechende Alterskriterium entscheidend. Die bekannte Überlieferung

---

1 Mit Rücksicht auf den breiteren Leserkreis dieses Bandes wurde dem Vortrag der Charakter eines knappen Überblicks belassen; die Anmerkungen bleiben auf die notwendigsten Angaben beschränkt; eine ausführlichere Darstellung mit eingehender Diskussion der Einzelprobleme wird an anderer Stelle gegeben werden: Nachrichten der Akademie der Wissenschaften in Göttingen, I. Philologisch-Historische Klasse. Jahrgang 1983, Nr. 1.

2 Vgl. Adolf *Bach*, Geschichte der deutschen Sprache, Bibliographischer Nachtrag von Rudolf *Schützeichel*, Heidelberg ⁹1970, §§ 56ff.; Rudolf *Schützeichel*, Die Grundlagen des westlichen Mitteldeutschen. Studien zur historischen Sprachgeographie, Hermaea. Germanistische Forschungen N. F. 10, Tübingen ²1976, mit umfangreichen Literaturhinweisen.

3 Helmut *de Boor*, Die deutsche Literatur von Karl dem Großen bis zum Beginn der höfischen Dichtung, bearbeitet von Herbert *Kolb*, Geschichte der deutschen Literatur von den Anfängen bis zur Gegenwart 1, München ⁹1979; Gustav *Ehrismann*, Geschichte der deutschen Literatur bis zum Ausgang des Mittelalters, I. Die althochdeutsche Literatur, München ²1932, Nachdruck München 1959.

althochdeutscher Glossen[4] ist daher auf Handschriften des 8. Jahrhunderts durchzusehen, wobei die Datierungen in den Editionen, also vor allem bei E. Steinmeyer, den Ausgangspunkt liefern. Eine besondere Hilfe hierfür bieten E. A. Lowes Codices Latini Antiquiores sowie die Arbeiten Bernhard Bischoffs[5]. Nun können Glossen selbstverständlich jünger als die Handschrift selbst sein; in einigen Fällen sind daher Handschriften des 8. Jahrhunderts auszuschließen, weil die althochdeutschen Glossen in ihnen erst im 9. Jahrhundert oder später eingetragen wurden[6]. Freilich liegen nicht zu allen Glossierungen begründete Aussagen über ihr Alter vor, was auf die insgesamt nicht geringen Datierungs- und Ermittlungsprobleme führt. Nicht nur die Glossen, auch die Handschriften selbst sind nicht immer sicher datiert, so daß im Einzelfall noch mit Korrekturen an der hier gegebenen Darstellung zu rechnen ist. Darüber hinaus ergeben sich Schwierigkeiten aus der Art der Überlieferung selbst. Ein beträchtlicher Teil der Glossen des 8. Jahrhunderts ist nämlich mit dem Griffel eingeritzt. Diese Griffelglossen sind oft und lange übersehen worden. In manchen Handschriften haben sich auch nicht alle Griffelglossen entziffern lassen, und es muß daher in Anbetracht der Entdeckungsgeschichte der Griffelglossen damit gerechnet werden, daß weitere Handschriften mit bisher übersehenen Griffelglossen existieren. Schließlich wird die Aufgabe auch dadurch erschwert, daß für eine Reihe von Handschriften keine Zuweisung zu einem Scriptorium möglich ist. Die Verschiedenartigkeit der vor-

4 Elias *Steinmeyer* und Eduard *Sievers*, Die althochdeutschen Glossen, I—V, Berlin 1879—1922, Nachdruck Dublin/Zürich 1968—1969; Herbert *Thoma*, Althochdeutsche Glossen, Reallexikon der deutschen Literaturgeschichte. Neu bearbeitet und unter redaktioneller Mitarbeit von Klaus *Kanzog* herausgegeben von Werner *Kohlschmidt* und Wolfgang *Mohr*, I, Berlin ²1958, S. 579—589; Rolf *Bergmann*, Verzeichnis der althochdeutschen und altsächsischen Glossenhandschriften. Mit Bibliographie der Glosseneditionen, der Handschriftenbeschreibungen und der Dialektbestimmungen, Arbeiten zur Frühmittelalterforschung 6, Berlin, New York 1973; Rolf *Bergmann*, Liste der in dem Verzeichnis der althochdeutschen und altsächsischen Glossenhandschriften nachzutragenden Handschriften, in: Rudolf *Schützeichel*, Addenda und Corrigenda zu Steinmeyers Glossensammlung, Nachrichten der Akademie der Wissenschaften in Göttingen, I. Philologisch-historische Klasse, Jahrgang 1982, Nr. 6, Göttingen 1982, S. 12—17.
5 Codices Latini Antiquiores. A palaeographical guide to Latin manuscripts prior to the ninth century, ed. by Elias A. *Lowe*, I—XI, Oxford 1934—1966; Bernhard *Bischoff*, Die südostdeutschen Schreibschulen und Bibliotheken in der Karolingerzeit, I, Wiesbaden ²1960, II, Wiesbaden 1980.
6 Die Glossenhandschriften werden hier und im folgenden nur mit ihrer Nummer in dem in Anmerkung 4 genannten Verzeichnis von Rolf *Bergmann* angeführt, dem alle weiteren Angaben zur Überlieferung und Edition entnommen werden können; ergänzende Hinweise betreffen vor allem seit dem Erscheinen des Verzeichnisses neu hinzugekommene Editionen und Handschriften. — Handschriften des 8. Jahrhunderts mit jüngeren Glossen sind Nr. 30, 33, 34, 103, 184, 297, 330, 338, 494, 515, 517, 733, 735, 768, 839a, 842, 865, 914, 931, 934, 983, 989, 992, 994. Ausgeschieden wurden natürlich auch Handschriften, die aus verschieden alten Teilen bestehen und in den Teilen aus dem 8. Jahrhundert keine althochdeutschen Glossen enthalten, wie Nr. 47, 208, 317. Nicht berücksichtigt wurden ferner Nr. 56, 58, 61, 159, 372, 477, 576, 607, 725, 747, 915, 978, die wohl erst aus dem 9. Jahrhundert stammen.

gefundenen Handschriftendatierungen nötigt ferner zu näherer Erläuterung des Zeitraums des 8. Jahrhunderts. Unproblematisch sind dabei alle Datierungen in das 8. Jahrhundert, beispielsweise seine erste oder zweite Hälfte. Die Gesamtbedingungen der frühmittelalterlichen Überlieferung im deutschen Sprachgebiet bringen es aber mit sich, daß diese Datierungen die Ausnahme bilden. Einbezogen werden daher auch die Handschriften, die ins ausgehende 8. Jahrhundert datiert werden, sowie die mit der Angabe „8./9. Jahrhundert" eingeordneten Handschriften. Bei diesen um die Jahrhundertwende datierten Codices wird ja immerhin die Möglichkeit gesehen, daß sie noch aus dem 8. Jahrhundert stammen. Ausgeschlossen bleiben aber natürlich alle Handschriften, die ins 9. Jahrhundert, und sei es auch ins früheste 9. Jahrhundert, datiert werden. Mit der ausschließlichen Orientierung an der paläographischen Datierung von Handschrift und Glossen wird gegenüber der germanistischen Forschungstradition eine methodisch kritische Haltung eingenommen. Insbesondere Georg Baesecke und seine Schüler haben nämlich aus späterer Überlieferung, vor allem des 9. Jahrhunderts, zu miteinander verwandten Glossierungen Vorstufen und Originale rekonstruiert, die ins 8. Jahrhundert datiert werden[7]. Derartige Rekonstruktionen müssen aber vorerst außer Betracht bleiben. Sie können erst dann auf ihre Plausibilität überprüft werden, wenn die Originalüberlieferung des 8. Jahrhunderts sichere zeitliche und geographische Kriterien liefert. Daß damit die Ergebnisse dieser Forschungsrichtung nicht pauschal abgewertet werden sollen, sei ausdrücklich betont.

II.

Von den eintausend Handschriften mit althochdeutschen Glossen vom 8. bis 12./13. Jahrhundert sind 49 Handschriften mit rund 10670 Wortformen als Originalüberlieferung des 8. Jahrhunderts anzusehen[8]. Dieser Befund ist zunächst unter

7 Georg *Baesecke*, Der deutsche Abrogans und die Herkunft des deutschen Schrifttums, Halle 1930; vgl. Herbert *Thoma*, Reallexikon der deutschen Literaturgeschichte, I, S. 587 f., mit Hinweisen auf die Einzeluntersuchungen.

8 R. *Bergmann*, Verzeichnis, Nr. 29, 31, 110 (ediert von Hartwig *Mayer*, Althochdeutsche Glossen. Nachträge, Toronto o. J. [1973], S. 27), 168, 169, 179, 199, 204, 205, 247, 252, 253, 254, 255, 275, 277a, 296, 334, 355, 370 (ediert in: MGH SS rer. Merov. II, Hannover 1888, S. 76, Anm. h; vgl. H. *Mayer*, Althochdeutsche Glossen. Nachträge, S. XVIII), 467, 478, 479, 488, 496, 506 (vgl. H. *Mayer*, Althochdeutsche Glossen. Nachträge, S. XIX), 523 (ediert von H. *Mayer*, Althochdeutsche Glossen. Nachträge, S. 74—79), 524 (ediert von H. *Mayer*, Althochdeutsche Glossen. Nachträge, S. 80—81), 525, 526 (ediert von H. *Mayer*, Althochdeutsche Glossen. Nachträge, S. 82), 544 (ediert von H. *Mayer*, Althochdeutsche Glossen. Nachträge, S. 83), 567, 584 (ediert von H. *Mayer*, Althochdeutsche Glossen. Nachträge, S. 89—90), 598, 635, 652 (dazu Nachträge bei H. *Mayer*, Althochdeutsche Glossen. Nachträge, S. 97—98), 745, 777, 783, 816, 839 (ediert von H. *Mayer*, Althochdeutsche Glossen. Nachträge, S. 128), 921, 924, 960a (ediert von H. *Mayer*, Vier althochdeutsche Glossen aus Köln und Wolfenbüttel, Amsterdamer Beiträge zur älteren Germanistik 13 [1978] S. 32—34), 980, 981, 987, 990 (ediert von H. *Mayer*, Althochdeutsche Glossen. Nachträge, S. 148; vgl. dazu Werner *Wegstein*, Anzeiger für deutsches Altertum und deutsche Literatur 90 [1979] S. 131), 997.

quantitativem Aspekt zu erläutern. Wenn man diese Zahl von 49 Handschriften der Gesamtüberlieferung althochdeutscher Glossen in etwas über 1000 Handschriften gegenüberstellt, so ist dabei zu berücksichtigen, daß zu dieser Gesamtüberlieferung nicht wenige Handschriften des 11., 12., ja sogar des 13. Jahrhunderts gerechnet werden, die in der Tradition bestimmter weitverbreiteter Glossare stehen. Die Zahl von 49 Handschriften mit althochdeutschen Glossen des 8. Jahrhunderts darf im Hinblick auf die Gesamtlage der Überlieferung des 8. Jahrhunderts im althochdeutschen Sprachraum als überraschend groß angesehen werden. Der Umfang der Glossierungen ist in den einzelnen Handschriften verschieden. In drei Fünfteln der Handschriften (nämlich 29) stehen jeweils weniger als zehn althochdeutsche Glossen; in zehn Handschriften handelt es sich sogar um nur ein einziges althochdeutsches Wort. Diese 29 Handschriften enthalten insgesamt nur 72 Wörter, sind aber dennoch als Zeugnisse der Glossierungstätigkeit überhaupt wichtig. Dreizehn weitere Handschriften mit Glossierungen zwischen 10 und 50 althochdeutschen Wörtern überliefern etwa 390 Wörter. Die restlichen sieben Handschriften sind als Einzelfälle zu nennen: Es sind St. Galler Glossen zu Paulus-Briefen (Nr. 179) mit 155 Wörtern, Freisinger Gregor-Glossen (Nr. 523) mit 184 Wörtern, neben denen noch etwa 50 nicht entzifferbare Glossen stehen, Tegernseer Gregorglossen (Nr. 652) mit 132 Wörtern, die St. Pauler Glossen zum Lukas-Evangelium (Nr. 777) mit 350 Wörtern, der Vocabularius Sti. Galli (Nr. 254) mit etwa 450 Wörtern, das Reichenauer Glossar Rb (Nr. 296) mit etwa 2090 Wörtern und die St. Galler Handschrift 911 mit dem deutschen Abrogansglossar (Nr. 253) mit etwa 6650 Wörtern.

Die beiden zuletzt genannten Handschriften sind nicht nur quantitativ Sonderfälle. Die Reichenauer Handschrift in Karlsruhe enthält verschiedene Glossare aus verschiedenen Zeiten, von denen das Bibelglossar Rb um die Wende vom 8. zum 9. Jahrhundert, „wenn nicht ins ausgehende 8. Jahrhundert" datiert wird[9]. Die St. Galler Handschrift 911 ist die Handschrift K des Abrogans-Glossars, die noch dem Ende des 8. Jahrhunderts angehört, während die beiden anderen Überlieferungen der Abrogans-Verdeutschung dem frühen 9. Jahrhundert zugewiesen werden[10]. Auf das Problem der Datierung und Lokalisierung des Originals ist noch einzugehen. Rechnet man diese beiden am Ende des Jahrhunderts stehenden Glossare ab, so bleiben immerhin noch etwa 1930 althochdeutsche Wortformen in 47 Handschriften des 8. Jahrhunderts übrig.

Die quantitative Bedeutung dieser Überlieferung erhellt aus einem Vergleich mit der Textüberlieferung[11].

---

9 Bernhard *Bischoff*, Paläographische Fragen deutscher Denkmäler der Karolingerzeit, FMSt. 5 (1971), S. 107.

10 B. *Bischoff*, FMSt. 5 (1971), S. 119.

11 Eine vollständige Übersicht über die althochdeutsche Textüberlieferung mit Angaben zu den Editionen und weiterer Literatur bietet Rudolf *Schützeichel*, Althochdeutsches Wörterbuch, Tübingen ³1981, S. XIII—XXV.

Nur ein verschwindend geringer Teil der althochdeutschen Texte ist in Handschriften des 8. Jahrhunderts überliefert, ohne Einschränkung nur die Basler Rezepte mit etwa 220 Wortformen in der auch Glossen enthaltenden Handschrift Basel F III 15a (Nr. 29). Das St. Galler Paternoster und Credo mit etwa 250 Wortformen steht in der genannten Abrogans-Handschrift vom Ende des 8. Jahrhunderts (Nr. 253). In der paläographischen Zugehörigkeit zum 8. Jahrhundert unsicher sind die Altbairische Beichte und das Wessobrunner Schöpfungsgedicht und Gebet mit je etwa 100 Wortformen. Der älteste größere Text, die althochdeutsche Isidor-Übersetzung mit etwa 5800 Wortformen ist in einer um a. 800 datierten Handschrift überliefert. Den insgesamt 10 670 in Glossen enthaltenen Wortformen stehen also nur etwa 6500 Wortformen in Textüberlieferung gegenüber. Klammert man die beiden umfangreichen späten Glossare auf der einen Seite und die unsicher datierten Texte sowie die Isidor-Übersetzung auf der anderen Seite aus, so stehen neben 1930 Wortformen in 47 Glossenhandschriften ganze 220 Wortformen in dem einen Text der Basler Rezepte, was die quantitative Bedeutung der Glossenüberlieferung für das 8. Jahrhundert verdeutlicht.

III.

Die zeitliche und räumliche Verteilung der Handschriften ergibt ein differenziertes Bild der althochdeutschen Schriftlichkeit des 8. Jahrhunderts, wie es bisher nicht gesehen wurde. Die zeitliche Verteilung allein bietet zunächst kein überraschendes Bild. Sie entspricht vielmehr dem Gesamtbild der Überlieferung im 8. Jahrhundert. Handschriften der ersten Hälfte des 8. Jahrhunderts sind im deutschen Sprachgebiet insgesamt selten, die Schriftlichkeit nimmt erst in der zweiten Hälfte größeren Umfang an. So ist auch nur eine Glossenhandschrift bekannt, deren Glossen in der ersten Hälfte, zum Teil sogar im ersten Drittel des 8. Jahrhunderts, eingetragen sind (Nr. 275), und nur eine Handschrift, deren Glossen in die Mitte des 8. Jahrhunderts datiert werden (Nr. 355). Zwei Handschriften sind ohne nähere Eingrenzung dem 8. Jahrhundert zugewiesen (Nr. 168 und Nr. 255), sieben der zweiten Jahrhunderthälfte (Nr. 31, 179, 254, 523, 980, 981, 997) und zwei dem letzten Drittel (Nr. 506, 987). Diesen insgesamt dreizehn stehen dreiundzwanzig aus dem ausgehenden 8. Jahrhundert gegenüber (Nr. 29, 110, 169, 247, 253, 296 (Rb), 467, 479, 488, 496, 525, 526, 544, 567, 584, 635, 652, 745, 783, 839, 921, 924, 990) sowie weitere sechzehn, die mit der Angabe ‚8./9. Jahrhundert‘ um die Jahrhundertwende datiert sind (Nr. 31, 168, 199, 204, 205, 252, 277a, 296 (Rz), 334, 370, 478, 524, 598, 777, 816, 960a). Insgesamt sind demnach 36 Handschriften ohne jede Einschränkung dem 8. Jahrhundert zugewiesen.

Bei der Darstellung der geographischen Verteilung sind einige Unsicherheitsfaktoren und methodische Probleme zu bedenken. Zu den Handschriften liegen in der Regel paläographisch und bibliotheksgeschichtlich begründete Zuweisungen zu bestimmten Scriptorien vor, die sich auf die lateinischen Texte beziehen. Es bedarf der eigenen Prüfung, ob diese Zuweisungen auch für die Glossen übernommen werden dürfen. In Einzelfällen ergibt sich dabei ein differenziertes Bild von der Entstehung und Wanderung einer Handschrift mit späterer Glossierung an anderem Ort. Schließlich bleiben sieben Handschriften, die nicht einem bestimmten Scriptorium, sondern nur einer Schreibprovinz zugeordnet werden können, sowie drei, die überhaupt nicht lokalisierbar sind. Dies sind eine in Norditalien entstandene, heute in Einsiedeln befindliche Handschrift (Nr. 110), deren zwei Griffelglossen nicht erst in dem a. 934 gegründeten Einsiedeln eingetragen worden sein können, eine früher in der Dombibliothek Augsburg aufbewahrte Handschrift unbekannter Herkunft (Nr. 467) sowie die St. Galler Handschrift 913 (Nr. 254) mit dem 450 Wörter umfassenden Vocabularius Sti. Galli. Dieser, wie B. Bischoff[12] sagt, „persönlich zusammengestellte Taschencodex" ist aufgrund seiner besonderen Entstehungsbedingungen keinem Scriptorium zuzuordnen. Die lokalisierbaren Handschriften verteilen sich folgendermaßen: Köln, Echternach, Mainz und Lorsch sind mit je einer Glossenhandschrift des 8. Jahrhunderts vertreten (Nr. 355, 275, 277a, 816). Ihnen läßt sich eine heute Wolfenbüttler Handschrift (Nr. 960a) zuordnen, die nur allgemein einem fränkischen Zentrum zugewiesen wird.

Einen ausgesprochenen Schwerpunkt bilden Fulda und Würzburg. Fünf heute in der Würzburger Universitätsbibliothek aufbewahrte Glossenhandschriften (Nr. 980, 981, 987, 990, 997) stammen aus der Dombibliothek und wurden dort oder in unbekannten Scriptorien des Würzburger Raumes glossiert. Auf Fulda lassen sich wenigstens vier Handschriften zurückführen, die entsprechend dem Schicksal der Fuldaer Klosterbibliothek heute in Basel, Kassel und Fulda selbst aufbewahrt werden (Nr. 29, 31, 168, 334). Nach einer fuldischen Vorlage, aus der eine althochdeutsche Glosse mitübernommen wurde, entstand zwischen a. 779 und 797 in Monte Cassino eine jetzt in Paris befindliche Handschrift (Nr. 754). Achtzehn Handschriften stammen aus Scriptorien im bairischen Raum, fünf aus Freising (Nr. 523, 524, 525, 526, 544), eine aus Freising oder Tegernsee (Nr. 506), zwei aus Tegernsee (Nr. 635, 652), drei aus Benediktbeuern oder Kochel (Nr. 478, 479, 488), vier aus Regensburg (Nr. 567, 584, 598, 783), und drei aus Salzburg (Nr. 496, 839, 924). Bis auf die noch in Salzburg befindliche Handschrift liegen heute alle in der Staatsbibliothek in München. Den vier Regensburger Handschriften ist noch eine bereits bei den Würzburger Handschriften mitberücksichtigte zuzurechnen (Nr. 987), die in Regensburg entstanden ist, und dort sowie anschließend in Würzburg glossiert wurde. Der Südwesten des deutschen Sprachgebiets tritt mit zwölf Handschriften gegenüber dem Südosten und gegenüber dem Raum Fulda-Würzburg etwas zurück. Sieben dieser Handschriften lassen sich mehr oder weniger sicher St. Gallen zuordnen (Nr. 169, 179, 204, 205, 247, 252, 255), nur eine der Reichenau (Nr. 296). Die St. Pauler Lukasglossen (Nr. 777) und eine Leidener Handschrift (Nr. 370) lassen sich dem Bodenseeraum insgesamt zuordnen, die in St. Gallen befindliche Abrogans-Handschrift (Nr. 253) nur Süd-

---

12 B. *Bischoff*, FMSt. 5 (1971), S. 118.

deutschland im allgemeinen, eine andere St. Galler Handschrift (Nr. 199) nur einem alemannischen Zentrum im allgemeinen. Auch eine heute in Wien befindliche Handschrift (Nr. 921) läßt sich nur ganz allgemein dem Südwesten oder Westen des deutschen Sprachgebietes zuordnen.

Diese geographischen Einordnungen sind paläographisch begründet; sie beruhen nicht auf dem Dialekt der Glossen. Soweit die Glossen bisher untersucht sind, stimmt aber die sprachgeographische Einordnung mit der paläographischen Lokalisierung zusammen. Freilich sind noch nicht alle Glossierungen genauer untersucht worden, insbesondere nicht die erst neuerdings publizierten. Manche nur wenige Wörter umfassende Glossierungen enthalten für eine sprachgeographische Bestimmung ohnehin keine aussagekräftigen Erscheinungen.

Die Lokalisierung der Handschriften auf dreizehn namentlich bekannte und weitere wenigstens landschaftlich bestimmbare Scriptorien ergibt im ganzen eine aussagekräftige Streuung über das althochdeutsche Sprachgebiet des 8. Jahrhunderts. Diese Verteilung gewinnt noch eine zusätzliche Profilierung, wenn auch nach den Lücken gefragt wird, also nach Klöstern und Bischofssitzen, aus denen keine Glossenhandschriften des 8. Jahrhunderts bekannt sind. In diesem Sinne fehlen im bairischen Raum etwa Passau, Niederaltaich, Metten und andere, im bairisch-fränkischen Übergangsgebiet vor allem Eichstätt, Heidenheim, Solnhofen und so weiter. Im Südwesten sind nur St. Gallen und die Reichenau faßbar, sonst weder weitere Klöster wie Murbach und Weißenburg, noch Bischofssitze wie Konstanz, Basel, Straßburg, Speyer, Worms. Die thüringisch-hessische Mitte ist nur durch Würzburg und Fulda vertreten, das Rheinland und der Moselraum nur durch Echternach, Köln, Mainz und Lorsch.

Dieser negative Befund ist — wenigstens teilweise — wichtig für die Einschätzung des positiven Befundes. Aus methodischen Gründen ist zunächst die Möglichkeit zu prüfen, ob der negative Befund in der Forschungslage bedingt ist. In der Tat existieren noch nicht zu allen frühen Scriptorien vergleichbare Spezialuntersuchungen wie etwa zu Würzburg, Lorsch, Salzburg und den bairischen Scriptorien insgesamt[13]. Andererseits ist aber doch die Gesamtüberlieferung bis zum Jahre 800 in den Codices Latini Antiquiores erfaßt, so daß Forschungslücken erst in zweiter oder dritter Linie Ursachen für den Negativbefund sein können. In beträchtlichem Umfang ist vielmehr mit Überlieferungslücken zu rechnen. Zahlreiche Scriptorien, mit deren Existenz aus guten historischen Gründen gerechnet werden kann, lassen sich in den erhaltenen Handschriften überhaupt nicht oder

---

13 B. *Bischoff*, Die südostdeutschen Schreibschulen und Bibliotheken in der Karolingerzeit, I, II; B. *Bischoff*, Lorsch im Spiegel seiner Handschriften, Münchener Beiträge zur Mediävistik und Renaissance-Forschung. Beiheft, München 1974; B. *Bischoff* und J. *Hofmann*, Libri Sancti Kyliani. Die Würzburger Schreibschule und die Dombibliothek im VIII. und IX. Jahrhundert, Quellen und Forschungen zur Geschichte des Bistums und Hochstifts Würzburg 6, Würzburg 1952; Karl *Forstner*, Die karolingischen Handschriften und Fragmente in den Salzburger Bibliotheken (Ende des 8. Jh. bis Ende des 9. Jh.), Mitteilungen der Gesellschaft für Salzburger Landeskunde, Ergänzungsband 3, Salzburg 1962.

nur ganz unsicher nachweisen. Es ist beispielsweise keine Forschungslücke, sondern eine Überlieferungslücke, was B. Bischoff hinsichtlich der Schreibschulen der Diözese Eichstätt beschreibt: „Es bleibt dabei, daß keine einzige karolingische Handschrift mit Gewißheit für irgendeine der im folgenden aufgezählten geistlichen Gemeinschaften — und Schreibschulen — der Diözese in Anspruch genommen werden kann: das Domstift Eichstätt und St. Walburg, Heidenheim, Solnhofen, Herrieden, Spalt, Gunzenhausen, Monheim und Auhausen"[14], von denen ein Teil jedenfalls schon im 8. Jahrhundert bestand. In manchen Fällen lassen sich plausible Gründe für das Fehlen karolingischer Handschriften anführen, beispielsweise die Zerstörung des Klosters Tegernsee durch die Ungarn, die Plünderung Triers durch die Normannen. Auch an die bekannten bibliotheksgeschichtlichen Auswirkungen des Dreißigjährigen Krieges und der Säkularisation ist zu erinnern. Doch reichen wohl die sicher umfangreichen Zerstörungen und Verluste zu den verschiedenen Zeiten nicht aus, um die geographische Verteilung der erhaltenen Glossen-Handschriften des 8. Jahrhunderts ausschließlich aus zufälliger Bewahrung zu erklären. Vielmehr muß doch auch mit der Möglichkeit gerechnet werden, daß diese Verteilung wenigstens in gewissen Zügen auch der tatsächlichen geschichtlichen Lage entspricht, womit dann auch die Frage nach den für diese Verteilung bestimmenden Faktoren gestellt ist. Eine Beantwortung dieser Frage setzt aber die Verbindung des chronologischen und des geographischen Aspekts voraus. Die ältesten Glossierungen aus der ersten Hälfte und der Mitte des 8. Jahrhunderts sind in Echternach und Köln beheimatet. In der zweiten Hälfte des Jahrhunderts sind Fulda, Würzburg, Freising und St. Gallen als Glossenschreiborte bezeugt. Die Reichenau, Benediktbeuern, Tegernsee, Salzburg und Regensburg treten erstmals mit Glossen-Handschriften des ausgehenden 8. Jahrhunderts in Erscheinung, Lorsch und Mainz erst mit Handschriften von der Jahrhundertwende. Auf die ältesten Handschriften und ihre Herkunft ist unter dem Aspekt der Entstehung der althochdeutschen Glossographie zurückzukommen.

IV.

Die Frage nach den glossierten Texten führt in den Zusammenhang der lateinischen Textüberlieferung vor dem Jahre 800 überhaupt[15]. Die Feststellung der glossierten Texte sagt keineswegs etwas über diese Überlieferung insgesamt aus. Sie erlaubt auch keine besonderen Aussagen darüber, welche Texte gelesen wurden. Solange nicht im Einzelfall die genaue Funktion der Glossen bestimmt ist, kann lediglich gesagt werden, welche lateinischen Texte Gegenstand übersetzender Bemühung althochdeutscher Sprecher waren.

14 B. *Bischoff*, Schreibschulen, I, S. 57.
15 Geschichte der Textüberlieferung der antiken und mittelalterlichen Literatur, I. Antikes und mittelalterliches Buch- und Schriftwesen. Überlieferungsgeschichte der antiken Literatur von Herbert *Hunger*, Otto *Stegmüller*, Hartmut *Erbse*, Max *Imhof*, Karl *Brückner*, Hans-Georg *Beck*, Horst *Rüdiger*, Zürich 1961.

Die Bibel und Bibelkommentare bilden nach der Zahl der Handschriften und der Glossen einen Schwerpunkt der Glossierung. In vier Handschriften sind Teile des Neuen Testaments mit etwa 735 Wörtern glossiert (Nr. 169, 179, 275, 777), in elf Handschriften Kommentare zu biblischen Büchern, unter anderem von Augustinus, Hieronymus, Gregor und Isidor, mit insgesamt etwa 360 Wörtern (Nr. 110, 506, 523, 524, 526, 567, 584, 839, 921, 981, 997). Diesen etwa 1095 Glossenwörtern sind noch etwa 1600 Wörter der Glossare Rb und Rz zuzurechnen, die sich auf das ganze Alte Testament beziehen (Nr. 296). Die restlichen 530 Wörter des Glossars Rb gehören zu Gregors des Großen Homilien. Mit neun Handschriften (Nr. 204, 205, 467, 488, 523, 652, 783, 990, 997) und 435 Wörtern ragt Gregor ohnehin unter den Handschriften theologischen Inhalts heraus: 31 von 49 Handschriften enthalten Bibelkommentare oder andere theologische Texte mit insgesamt etwa 790 Glossenwörtern. Rechnet man die vier Handschriften mit Teilen des Neuen Testaments mit ihren etwa 735 Glossen und die auf die Bibel und Gregor den Großen bezüglichen Glossare Rb und Rz mit ihren 2130 Wörtern hinzu, so sind 36 von 49 Handschriften mit 3655 Wörtern mit der allgemeinen Kennzeichnung biblisch-theologisch erfaßt.

Die mit dieser inhaltlichen Kennzeichnung nicht erfaßten Handschriften bilden in gewisser Hinsicht alle Sonderfälle: Eine Fuldaer Handschrift enthält ein althochdeutsches Wort in dem ältesten Fuldaer Bücherverzeichnis (Nr. 29); in einer in Leiden aufbewahrten Handschrift aus dem Raum St. Gallen-Reichenau steht in der Chronik Fredegars eine Glosse ohne Beziehung zum Text (Nr. 370); auch die drei althochdeutschen Wörter auf dem St. Galler Fragment des Markus-Evangeliums haben keinen Textbezug (Nr. 255). In einer in Wolfenbüttel befindlichen Handschrift aus einem fränkischen Zentrum finden sich zwei Glossen zu der *Cosmographia* des Aethicus Ister, die Virgil von Salzburg zugeschrieben wird (Nr. 960a); ihr lassen sich vereinzelte Glossen zu Iordanes (Nr. 277a), Hegesippus (Nr. 334), zum Cento der Proba (Nr. 816) sowie zu Donat (Nr. 247), Priscian (Nr. 252) und zu Bedas *De orthographia* (Nr. 745) anreihen.

Schließlich bleiben noch die beiden Glossare, die nicht mit Texten verbunden werden können, der Abrogans (Nr. 253) und der Vocabularius Sti. Galli (Nr. 254). Das Abrogans-Glossar[16] geht zurück auf ein spätantikes, lateinisch-lateinisches Synonymwörterbuch, das durchgehend althochdeutsch glossiert wurde. Es steht in der Tradition lateinischer Glossare wie *Abba*-Glossar, *Abavus minor*, *Affatim*-Glossar; sein Wortbestand ist literarischen Ursprungs, läßt sich aber nur mittelbar über die Glossare auf Texte von Terenz bis zu Aldhelm zurückführen.

Der sogenannte Vocabularius Sti. Galli[17] bildet neben all dem die singuläre Ausnahmeerscheinung. Die in St. Gallen aufbewahrte Handschrift ist schon

16 G. *Baesecke*, Der deutsche Abrogans und die Herkunft des deutschen Schrifttums, Halle 1930; Jochen *Splett*, Abrogans-Studien. Kommentar zum ältesten deutschen Wörterbuch, Wiesbaden 1976; J. *Splett*, Die deutsche Literatur des Mittelalters. Verfasserlexikon, I, Berlin, New York ²1978, Sp. 12—15.

17 G. *Baesecke*, Der Vocabularius Sti. Galli in der angelsächsischen Mission, Halle 1933.

paläographisch ein Unikum, ein als Taschenbuch von 10 × 8—9 cm angelegter privater Gebrauchscodex, der neben den verschiedenartigsten lateinischen Auszügen ein etwa 450 Wörter umfassendes, sachlich geordnetes Wörterbuch mit ausgesprochenem Alltagswortschatz enthält, beispielsweise Bezeichnungen von Körperteilen, von Gebäuden mit ihren Teilen, von Geräten, Materialien, sozialen und rechtlichen Verhältnissen, einfachen Eigenschaften und Tätigkeiten und so weiter. Selbst wenn für Auswahl und Anordnung der Wörter literarische Quellen wie etwa Isidors Etymologien benützt wurden, so darf der Zweck des Glossars im praktischen Leben gesucht werden[18]. Es diente ganz offensichtlich der Verdeutschung und setzt einen anderssprachigen Benutzer voraus. Alle anderen Glossenhandschriften des 8. Jahrhunderts dienten dem Verständnis lateinischer Texte und setzen deutschsprachige Glossatoren und Benutzer voraus.

V.

Zahlreiche Einzelbeobachtungen stellen die althochdeutschen Glossenhandschriften des 8. Jahrhunderts in den Zusammenhang insularer, und zwar insbesondere angelsächsischer Einflüsse. Diesen Erscheinungen soll nun im Hinblick auf die historische Auswertung des Materials nachgegangen werden. Für eine Reihe von Handschriften ist Entstehung oder frühe Aufbewahrung in England sicher oder wahrscheinlich. Eine heute nach Kassel gehörige Fuldaer Handschrift, eine Unzialhandschrift des 6. Jahrhunderts, entstand in Italien und gelangte über England nach Fulda (Nr. 334). Einträge in angelsächsischer Minuskel und Einritzungen altenglischer Runen verdeutlichen diesen Weg. Die einzige Kölner Glossenhandschrift des 8. Jahrhunderts ist in Northumbrien entstanden (Nr. 355). In einem Fall ist nicht sicher erkennbar, ob die später mit althochdeutschen Glossen versehene Handschrift in England entstand oder in einem angelsächsisch geprägten Scriptorium auf dem Kontinent geschrieben wurde (Nr. 990). Angelsächsische Minuskel als Textschrift oder angelsächsische Einflüsse in der Schrift zeigt in der einen oder anderen Form fast die Hälfte der althochdeutschen Glossenhandschriften des 8. Jahrhunderts (Nr. 29, 31, 168, 179, 254, 275, 277a, 296 (Rz), 334, 355, 467, 479, 506, 523, 524, 544, 567, 584, 839, 980, 981, 987, 990, 997). Bei den Handschriften aus Echternach, Fulda und Würzburg ist diese Beobachtung nicht überraschend, da diese Scriptorien im 8. Jahrhundert ganz angelsächsisch geprägt sind. Besondere Beachtung verdient aber im Hinblick auf die germanistische Forschungsgeschichte der insulare Anteil an den bairischen Scriptorien des 8. Jahrhunderts. In dem ansonsten nach B. Bischoff[19] rein „festländisch geprägten" Benediktbeurer Scriptorium taucht wenigstens eine insuleske Hand auf (Nr. 479). Die Anfänge des Regensburger Scriptoriums stehen unter der Vorherrschaft der angelsächsischen Schrift. Eine der Glossenhandschriften zeigt insularen Schrifteinfluß

---

18 H. *Thoma*, Reallexikon der deutschen Literaturgeschichte, 2. A., I, S. 584 f.
19 B. *Bischoff*, Schreibschulen, I, S. 23.

(Nr. 584), eine andere Spuren einer insularen Vorlage (Nr. 567). In Freising wirkte im 8. Jahrhundert ein insularer, wohl aus Northumbrien stammender Schreiber Peregrinus[20], von dem auch eine der Freisinger Glossenhandschriften stammt (Nr. 544). Der Gesamtbefund ist natürlich kein spezifisches Kennzeichen der glossierten Handschriften allein. Es ist vielmehr hinreichend bekannt, daß im Zusammenhang mit der angelsächsischen Mission Handschriften aus England auf den Kontinent kamen und daß das Schriftwesen im 8. Jahrhundert unter insularem Einfluß stand[21]. Für die geschichtliche Beurteilung der althochdeutschen Glossenüberlieferung des 8. Jahrhunderts ist es aber von besonderer Bedeutung, die starke angelsächsische Prägung gerade auch dieser Handschriften bewußt zu machen.

Eine weitere wichtige Beobachtung ist in dieser Hinsicht die Feststellung des Nebeneinanders von althochdeutschen und altenglischen Glossen in denselben Handschriften, das unter den Handschriften mit Glossen des 8. Jahrhunderts in wenigstens vier Fällen anzutreffen ist (Nr. 168, 275, 334, 355; vgl. ferner Nr. 29, 254, 296 Rz). In der schon erwähnten Kölner Handschrift (Nr. 355) ergibt sich so insgesamt eine paläographische und sprachliche Schichtung. Der lateinische Canonestext wurde in Northumbrien in angelsächsischer Majuskel und Minuskel in der ersten Hälfte des 8. Jahrhunderts geschrieben. In angelsächsischer Minuskel des 8. Jahrhunderts wurde eine altenglische Glosse eingeritzt, in fränkischer Minuskel wohl der Mitte des 8. Jahrhunderts eine althochdeutsche Glosse. Die ebenfalls schon genannte ehemalige Fuldaer Unzialhandschrift (Nr. 334) des 6. Jahrhunderts zeigt ebenfalls altenglische und althochdeutsche Glossen.

Zwei weitere Handschriften mit altenglischen und althochdeutschen Glossen führen unmittelbar in den Umkreis der beiden bedeutendsten angelsächsischen Missionare Willibrord und Bonifatius und lassen so den Hintergrund der althochdeutschen Anfänge ganz deutlich werden. Der in der ersten Hälfte des 8. Jahrhunderts in Luxeuil entstandene Ragyndrudis-Codex im Fuldaer Domschatz (Nr. 168) stammt aus dem persönlichen Umkreis des Bonifatius und ist bekanntlich nach alter Tradition bei der Ermordung des Bonifatius am Einband beschädigt worden. Die zahlreichen Griffeleinritzungen konnten nur zu einem kleinen Teil von Josef Hofmann entziffert werden[22]. Immerhin sind vier altenglische, eine althochdeutsche und eine altenglische oder althochdeutsche Glosse gesichert, die alle in insularer Schrift eingeritzt wurden. Das nach der früheren Aufbewahrung der Oettingen-Wallersteinschen Bibliothek benannte Maihinger Evangeliar (Nr. 275) stammt

20 B. *Bischoff*, Schreibschulen, I, S. 61 ff.

21 Vgl. beispielsweise Wilhelm *Levison*, England and the Continent in the Eighth Century, Oxford 1946; Theodor *Schieffer*, Winfrid-Bonifatius und die christliche Grundlegung Europas. Mit einem Nachwort zum Neudruck, Darmstadt 1972.

22 Josef *Hofmann*, Altenglische und althochdeutsche Glossen aus Würzburg und dem weiteren angelsächsischen Missionsgebiet, Beiträge zur Geschichte der deutschen Sprache und Literatur 85 (Halle 1963), S. 27—131, 456; S. 52—57.

unmittelbar aus Willibrords Echternacher Mitarbeiterkreis. Es wurde in angelsächsischer Majuskel von derselben Hand geschrieben, die zwischen a. 702 und 731, wahrscheinlich schon vor a. 709 das Calendarium Willibrordi schrieb. Der in einem Akrostichon auftretende Name Laurentius wird auf einen von a. 704 bis 721 nachweisbaren Schreiber bezogen. Die vierzehn altenglischen und sechzehn althochdeutschen Griffelglossen stammen von verschiedenen insularen und insulesken Händen des frühen und späten 8. Jahrhunderts. Die älteren althochdeutschen Glossen des Maihinger Evangeliars sind nach B. Bischoff gleich alt wie die altenglischen Glossen. Seine nur anmerkungsweise hierzu geäußerte Schlußfolgerung verdient größere Beachtung: „Einige der ältesten [althochdeutschen Glosseneintragungen] können durch das Vorbild glossierender Angelsachsen in den von Willibrord, Bonifatius und anderen ihrer Landsleute gegründeten Stätten zustandegekommen sein"[23]. Noch vor der Veröffentlichung der Griffelglossen aus dem Maihinger Evangeliar und dem Ragyndrudis-Codex hatte Herbert Thoma entsprechende Gedanken formuliert: „Die Anregung zu systematischer Glossierung in dt. Sprache darf im insularen Vorbild gesehen werden. Iren und Angelsachsen hatten aus antiker Tradition gelernt, und aus ihrem Bereich kam der Gebrauch mit der Mission nach Deutschland"[24]. Die maßgebliche Literaturgeschichte der althochdeutschen Zeit von Helmut de Boor[25] stellt aber auch noch in der 9. Auflage vom Jahre 1979 „an die Spitze des deutschen Schrifttums" „den Abrogans". Die Forschungsergebnisse G. Baeseckes[26] aus den dreißiger Jahren zum Abrogans und zu dem als Hermeneumata bezeichneten Vocabularius Sti. Galli bestimmen das Bild der Entstehung der althochdeutschen Schriftlichkeit bei H. de Boor: „Abrogans und Hermeneumata, Freising und Fulda, langobardische und angelsächsische Vermittlung spätantiker Bildungswerte — das ist das Gepräge des ältesten deutschen Schrifttums"[27]. Wenn bei H. de Boor unter den Orten der ältesten Glossierungen neben Fulda und Freising die Reichenau genannt wird, während Echternach und Würzburg fehlen, wird vollends deutlich, daß der durch die Glossenveröffentlichungen der letzten zwanzig Jahre erbrachte Erkenntnisgewinn noch nicht in die Darstellung der Anfänge des deutschen Schrifttums eingegangen ist. Deshalb muß hier wenigstens kurz auf die Konsequenzen eingegangen werden, die aus dem Befund der Originalüberlieferung des 8. Jahrhunderts zu ziehen sind. Soweit anhand des Vocabularius Sti. Galli bisher schon der angelsächsische Einfluß gesehen wurde, ist dem nur zuzustimmen. Dieses in angelsächsischer Schrift geschriebene Sachglossar mit seinem ausgesprochenen Alltagswortschatz kann man sich durchaus als „ersten Sprachführer

23 B. *Bischoff*, FMSt. 5 (1971), S. 102f.
24 H. *Thoma*, Reallexikon der deutschen Literaturgeschichte, 2. A., I, S. 583.
25 H. *de Boor*, Die deutsche Literatur von Karl dem Großen bis zum Beginn der höfischen Dichtung, S. 15.
26 Vgl. oben Anm. 16 und 17.
27 H. *de Boor*, Die deutsche Literatur von Karl dem Großen bis zum Beginn der höfischen Dichtung, S. 16.

für Angelsachsen und andere des Lateins, aber nicht des Ahd. kundige Missionare"[28] vorstellen. Kritischer Diskussion bedarf aber die von G. Baesecke mit dem Abrogansglossar verbundene langobardisch-italienische Komponente der Anfänge des deutschen Schrifttums.

G. Baesecke hat aus den drei Abrogans-Handschriften, von denen nur eine noch dem Ende des 8. Jahrhunderts angehört, ein Original der althochdeutschen Glossierung rekonstruiert und mit den Eigennamenschreibungen in Freisinger Urkunden des 8. Jahrhunderts verglichen, die er ebenfalls aus kopialer Überlieferung des 9. Jahrhunderts rekonstruieren mußte. Aus dem Vergleich der Rekonstruktionen gewann er die Lokalisierung des Originals des althochdeutschen Abrogans in Freising. Bischof Arbeo von Freising habe das lateinische Glossar aus Oberitalien mitgebracht und um a. 765 seine althochdeutsche Glossierung veranlaßt. In unserem Zusammenhang muß zunächst gesehen werden, daß selbst bei einer Annahme von G. Baeseckes Hypothesen auch eine um a. 765 in Freising erfolgte althochdeutsche Glossierung des Abrogans nicht die weitreichenden Schlußfolgerungen über eine langobardische Vermittlung antiken Bildungsgutes zwingend stützen könnte. Zum einen wären neben Arbeos oberitalienischen Beziehungen seine Verbindung zu dem Iren Virgil von Salzburg und seine Ausbildung durch den von Bonifatius eingesetzten Bischof Erembert von Freising zu berücksichtigen. Friedrich Prinz[29] hat Arbeo, vor allem gestützt auf eine Untersuchung von Heinz Löwe[30], „geradezu eine Testfigur für die mannigfach sich mengenden Kulturströme" genannt, „denen Bayern im 8. Jahrhundert offenstand." Zum anderen wäre an die zu Arbeos Zeit in Freising in der Person des Schreibers Peregrinus greifbaren angelsächsischen Einflüsse im Schriftwesen[31] zu erinnern, die freilich auch G. Baesecke schon bekannt waren. Vor allem aber wäre auf die G. Baesecke noch unbekannten Glossen hinzuweisen, die in der Echternacher Handschrift des Maihinger Evangeliars (Nr. 275) und in anderen Fuldaer und Würzburger Handschriften (Nr. 168, 334, 980, 981, 987, 997) bereits vor a. 765 oder gleichzeitig anzutreffen sind.

Aber G. Baeseckes These kann ja trotz ihrer Übernahme in die Literaturgeschichten keineswegs als gesichert gelten. Eine seinerzeit von Dietrich von Kralik[32] aufgestellte Gegenthese, die zwar ebenfalls ungesichert, aber im vorliegenden Zusammenhang und vor dem Hintergrund des vollständigeren Bildes der Glossenüberlieferung des 8. Jahrhunderts neuer Beachtung wert ist, stellte den

---

28 Georg *Baesecke* — Werner *Betz*, Althochdeutsche Literatur, Reallexikon der deutschen Literaturgeschichte, 2. A., I, S. 24—39, S. 29.

29 Friedrich *Prinz*, Frühes Mönchtum im Frankenreich. Kultur und Gesellschaft in Gallien, den Rheinlanden und Bayern am Beispiel der monastischen Entwicklung, München 1965, S. 340.

30 Heinz *Löwe*, Arbeo von Freising. Eine Studie zu Religiosität und Bildung im 8. Jahrhundert, Rheinische Vierteljahrsblätter 15/16 (1950/51), S. 87—120.

31 Vgl. oben Anm. 20.

32 Dietrich von *Kralik*, Deutsche Literaturzeitung 52 (1931), Sp. 1461—1468.

Abrogans in den Zusammenhang mit Virgil von Salzburg und der angelsächsischen Mission. Auch Werner Wissmann[33] hat später darauf hingewiesen, daß im Abrogans an angelsächsischen Einfluß zu denken sei. Diesen Hinweisen ist noch nicht systematisch nachgegangen worden. Sie erlauben es aber, G. Baeseckes Abrogans-These mit Skepsis zu betrachten und damit den behaupteten langobardisch-oberitalienischen Anteil im Gepräge des ältesten deutschen Schrifttums, für den auch sonst keine Anhaltspunkte gegeben sind, zu bezweifeln[34].

Die althochdeutsche Glossenüberlieferung des 8. Jahrhunderts, neben der wie gesagt die Textüberlieferung noch fast ganz zurücktritt, erlaubt es vielmehr, ein etwas anderes Bild von den Anfängen der deutschen Schriftlichkeit zu zeichnen. Dabei ist noch einmal auf den methodischen Neuansatz zurückzukommen, der in der Sammlung aller aus dem 8. Jahrhundert stammenden Zeugnisse, auch der scheinbar geringfügigsten, bestand und von der Rekonstruktion aus späteren Glossensammlungen absah. Die nach Zahl und geographischer Streuung insgesamt unerwartet eindrucksvollen Zeugnisse gehören vor allem in den frühen und frühesten Handschriften voll und ganz in den Zusammenhang der angelsächsischen Mission. Das Auftreten althochdeutscher Glossen folgt geradezu und unmittelbar dem Auftreten der angelsächsischen Missionare und ihrem Einfluß auf die kontinentale Schriftkultur. Die Schwerpunkte ihrer Tätigkeit sind auch die Schwerpunkte der althochdeutschen Glossierung im 8. Jahrhundert[35].

33 Werner *Wissmann*, Zum Abrogans, Fragen und Forschungen im Bereich und Umkreis der germanischen Philologie. Festgabe für Theodor *Frings* zum 70. Geburtstag. 23. Juli 1956, Deutsche Akademie der Wissenschaften zu Berlin. Veröffentlichungen des Instituts für Deutsche Sprache und Literatur 8, Berlin 1956, S. 80—113; Werner *Wissmann*, Die Bildungen auf -lih von Partizipien und der Abrogans, Festgabe für Ulrich Pretzel zum 65. Geburtstag, Berlin 1963, S. 308—315.

34 Vgl. Rolf *Bergmann*, Mittelfränkische Glossen. Studien zu ihrer Ermittlung und sprachgeographischen Einordnung, Rheinisches Archiv 61, Bonn ²1977, S. 325, 327.

35 Zu den Glossen des 8. Jahrhunderts ist jetzt auch auf die große Arbeit von Lothar *Voetz* hinzuweisen: Studien zu den Anfängen althochdeutscher Textglossierung, Habilitationsschrift Münster 1982 (in Druckvorbereitung).

Die Bedeutung des religiösen Wortschatzes für die Entfaltung des Althochdeutschen: von früher Vielfalt zu allmählicher Vereinheitlichung

Von

Stefan Sonderegger

Als Althochdeutsch bezeichnen wir bekanntlich die älteste schriftlich bezeugte Sprachstufe des Deutschen vom späten 8. Jahrhundert bis über die Mitte des 11. Jahrhunderts[1]. Doch schon mit dieser scheinbar einfachen sprachhistorischen Definition sind eine Reihe weiterer Fragen verbunden, mit denen wir uns nur gerade andeutungsweise beschäftigen können. Althochdeutsch als älteste schriftlich bezeugte Sprachstufe des Deutschen — diese Formulierung impliziert auch schon den eben erst in althochdeutscher Zeit einsetzenden Verschriftungsprozeß deutscher Volkssprache für Kirche, Schule und literarische Bildung. Demnach gilt es zu fragen: welches sind denn eigentlich die Stufen eines volkssprachlichen Verschriftungsprozesses seit der ersten, im wesentlichen seit der zweiten Hälfte des 8. Jahrhunderts, wo seine Vorbilder und Voraussetzungen? Die Stufen des althochdeutschen Verschriftungsprozesses lassen sich, ausgehend von den beiden durch die gesamte althochdeutsche Zeit reichenden Grundströmen der Namen- und Glossenüberlieferung, mehr oder weniger nach Aufbau- und Ausbauschritten bestimmen, wenn auch daneben frühe Vorbrüche wie die Übersetzungen der Isidor-Sippe um und nach 800 zu beachten bleiben: diese Stufen beginnen mit der Glossierung (Einzelwortglossierung, Einfach- bis Mehrfachglossierung; Glossierung einzelner Wendungen, Phraseologismen), führen weiter zu den Interlinearversionen, wobei auch hier Untergruppen festzustellen sind, sowie zu mehr oder weniger interlinearartigen Übersetzungstexten, welche sich noch starr und stark, vielleicht von einzelnen Ausnahmen abgesehen, an die lateinischen Vorlagen halten, um dann zu freieren Übersetzungen auszugreifen und mit der spätalthochdeutschen Übersetzungskunst Notkers des Deutschen von St. Gallen im Übergang vom 10. zum 11. Jahrhundert, seines Schülers Ekkeharts IV., des sprachkünstlerischen Glossators von Notkers Psalter, in der ersten Hälfte des 11. Jahrhunderts, sowie Willirams von Ebersberg nach der Mitte des 11. Jahrhunderts zu enden[2]. Demgegenüber erscheint die Überlieferung der wenigen

---

1 Vgl. Stefan *Sonderegger*, Althochdeutsche Sprache und Literatur, Eine Einführung in das älteste Deutsch (Sammlung Göschen 8005), Berlin — New York 1974, ²1984 (mit Lit.). Zur Begriffsbestimmung Stefan *Sonderegger*, Althochdeutsch, in Lexikon der Germanistischen Linguistik, Tübingen ²1980, S. 569—570 (Definition nach verschiedenen Gesichtspunkten).

2 Diese Stufung bei Stefan *Sonderegger*, Althochdeutsche Sprache und Literatur (Anm. 1), S. 83—129 (mit Lit.). Vgl. auch Stefan *Sonderegger*, Frühe Übersetzungsschichten im Althochdeutschen, in Philologia Deutsch, Festschrift Walter Henzen, Bern 1965, S. 101—114.

autochthonen althochdeutschen Texte — mit Ausnahme von Otfrids von Weissenburg Evangelienharmonie, bei welcher der Verfasser eine planvolle und mehrfache kunstvolle Verschriftung im Scriptorium seines Klosters im dritten Viertel des 9. Jahrhunderts persönlich überwachte — meist zufällig und oft am Rande lateinisch geschriebener Bücher oder Pergamentblätter[3]. Vorbild volkssprachlicher Verschriftung bleibt die frühmittelalterliche lateinische Buch- und Schrifttradition Westeuropas, besonders Italiens, des westfränkischen und angelsächsischen, aber auch altirischen Bereichs[4]. Voraussetzung dafür ist allein die merowingisch-karolingische und ottonische Klosterkultur, welche die für das Althochdeutsche entscheidenden Scriptorien entstehen und auswachsen ließ.

Was den christlich-religiösen Wortschatz betrifft, ist darauf hinzuweisen, daß am Anfang der althochdeutschen Überlieferung im 8. und frühen 9. Jahrhundert die zwei hauptsächlichen Überlieferungsströme Glossen bzw. Glossare — darunter das älteste deutsche Buch, der lateinisch-althochdeutsche Abrogans, ferner Bibelglossen — und die volkssprachliche Katechetik stehen. Im Gefolge der karlischen *Admonitio generalis* von 789 und weiterer Reichsgesetze und Weisungen aus der Zeit vor und nach 800 entsteht an ganz verschiedenen Orten der althochdeutschen Überlieferung größtenteils unabhängig voneinander eine reiche volkssprachliche Katechetik, die sich bis ins 11. und 12. Jahrhundert weiterzieht. Diese althochdeutsche Katechetik umfaßt die folgenden für den Aufbau eines kirchlichen Wortschatzes wichtigen Gruppen[5]:

Anders gewichtet freilich Jörg *Lippert*, Beiträge zu Technik und Syntax althochdeutscher Übersetzungen unter besonderer Berücksichtigung der Isidorgruppe und des althochdeutschen Tatian (Medium Aevum, Philologische Studien Bd. 25), München 1974. Zur Isidor-Sippe Klaus *Matzel*, Untersuchungen zur Verfasserschaft, Sprache und Herkunft der althochdeutschen Übersetzungen der Isidor-Sippe, Rheinisches Archiv 75, Bonn 1970. Zu Notker zu St. Gallen Anton *Näf*, Die Wortstellung in Notkers Consolatio, Untersuchungen zur Syntax und Übersetzungstechnik (Das Althochdeutsche von St. Gallen Bd. 5), Berlin — New York 1979. Zu Ekkehart IV. als Glossator der lateinischen Reservate in Notkers des Deutschen kommentierter Psalmenübersetzung Stefan *Sonderegger*, Althochdeutsch in St. Gallen, Ergebnisse und Probleme der althochdeutschen Sprachüberlieferung in St. Gallen vom 8. bis ins 12. Jahrhundert, St. Gallen — Sigmaringen 1970, S. 113—123.

3 Friedrich *Neumann*, Überlieferungsgeschichte der altdeutschen Literatur, in Geschichte der Textüberlieferung der antiken und mittelalterlichen Literatur, Bd. II Überlieferungsgeschichte der mittelalterlichen Literatur, Zürich 1964, S. 641 ff. Hanns *Fischer*, Schrifttafeln zum althochdeutschen Lesebuch, Tübingen 1966. Zu Otfrid Wolfgang *Kleiber*, Otfrid von Weissenburg, Untersuchungen zur handschriftlichen Überlieferung und Studien zum Aufbau des Evangelienbuches (Bibliotheca Germanica 14), Bern und München 1971.

4 Vgl. Bernhard *Bischoff*, Paläographie des römischen Altertums und des abendländischen Mittelalters (Grundlagen der Germanistik 24), Berlin 1979, in Kapitel „Die Handschrift in der Kulturgeschichte, 2. Frühmittelalter und 3. Karolingische Zeit" S. 237—265.

5 Vgl. die Aufstellungen bei Stefan *Sonderegger*, Althochdeutsche Sprache und Literatur (Anm. 1), S. 76 ff., 85 ff., 115. Die weiteren Zusammenhänge in den einschlägigen Literaturgeschichtsdarstellungen, zuletzt Helmut *de Boor*, Die deutsche Literatur von Karl dem Großen bis zum Beginn der höfischen Dichtung 770—1170, neunte Aufl. von Herbert *Kolb*, München 1979 (mit Literaturnachweis).

(1) die althochdeutschen Parternoster-Übersetzungen und -Interpretationen vom späten 8. bis zum 11. Jh.

(2) die althochdeutschen Glaubensbekenntnisse vom Ende des 8. bis ins 12. Jh.

(3) die althochdeutschen Beichten des 9. bis 11. Jh., sodann Glauben und Beichten kombiniert im späten 11. und 12. Jh.

(4) der althochdeutsche Katechismus aus Weissenburg um 810—820

(5) das fränkische Taufgelöbnis um 800

(6) die Freisinger *Exhortatio ad plebem christianam* nach 800

(7) die verschiedenen mehr persönlichen althochdeutschen Gebete vom 9. bis 11. Jh., darunter auch Reimgebete.

Neben diesem katechetischen Überlieferungsstrom in der Volkssprache, welcher durch die ganze althochdeutsche Zeit reicht, aber einen deutlichen missionarisch-verfestigenden Schwerpunkt im Frühalthochdeutschen um das Jahr 800 aufweist, entfaltet sich ebenfalls seit dem Übergang vom 8. zum 9. Jahrhundert wiederum an ganz verschiedenen Orten eine althochdeutsche Bibelübersetzung in Psalter (verschiedene Psalmenfragmente 9. bis 11. Jh., dichterische Bearbeitung von Psalm 138 10. Jh., Notkers des Deutschen Psalter und Cantica mit Kommentar nach 1000) und Evangelien (St. Pauler Lukasglossen um 800, Monseer Matthäusfragmente um 800, fuldische Tatian-Übersetzung um 830, viele weitere Zitate) sowie in der spätalthochdeutschen Hohelied-Paraphrase des Williram von Ebersberg um 1060. Zur christlichen Übersetzungsliteratur gehören sodann die althochdeutsche Übersetzung von Isidors von Sevilla Traktat *De fide catholica contra Judaeos* um 800, die Monseer Bruchstücke zu Isidor und Augustinus um 800 sowie die sanktgallische Interlinearversion der *Regula Sancti Benedicti* aus dem zweiten Jahrzehnt des 9. Jahrhunderts, während man die Übersetzungen christlicher Hymnendichtung (Reichenau-Murbacher Hymnen im frühen 9. Jh., *Carmen ad Deum* Mitte 9. Jh.) als Sonderfall dichterischer Interlinearversionen bezeichnen darf. Von hier geht der religiöse Überlieferungsstrom weiter bis zur althochdeutschen Bibeldichtung, vor allem der Evangelienharmonie Otfrids von Weissenburg (863—871 entstanden) und zur christlichen Legenden-, Preis- und Heiligendichtung in Reimversen seit der zweiten Hälfte des 9. Jahrhunderts.

Die vorrangige Bedeutung des religiösen Wortschatzes für die sprachgeschichtliche Entfaltung des Althochdeutschen ist seit langem bekannt und wird in der wissenschaftlichen Forschung intensiv diskutiert[6]. Bei einer für die übergreifende Sprachgeschichte des Deutschen sich aufdrängenden Gesamtbeurteilung wird man von einer Komponentenlehre ausgehen müssen, welche zunächst die frühe Vielfalt des kirchlichen Wortschatzes aus ganz verschiedenen Wurzeln begreifen muß:

6 Literatur in Deutsche Wortgeschichte, hg. von Friedrich *Maurer* und Heinz *Rupp*, Bd. I (Grundriß der germanischen Philologie 17/I), Berlin — New York ³1974: Deutsche Frühzeit von Josef *Weisweiler* und Werner *Betz*, S. 55—133, besonders S. 86—106.

(1) als Nachleben und christliche Umfunktionierung altgermanischer Sakralausdrücke, soweit sie in den althochdeutschen Dialekten noch greifbar sind, so wie z. B. das im Altgermanischen verankerte Wort aus dem Opferbereich ahdt. *zebar* n. ‚Opfertier, Blutopfer, Opfer' (got. *tibr*, ags. *tīber, tīfer*, n., an. *tafn* n., *tívurr* m.) mit dreizehn althochdeutschen Belegen aus verschiedenen Dialekten vom ältesten deutschen Buch Abrogans (Ende 8. Jh. mit Textzeugen bis 1. Viertel 9. Jh.) bis zur Tatianübersetzung um 830, u. a. für das Blutopfer Christi (z. B. Murbacher Hymnen 12,2,3 *saliges lambes zebar* für *beati agni hostia*) verwendet[7].

(2) als Nutzbarmachung altgermanischer Rechtswörter für den christlichen Glaubensbereich, wie ahdt. *truhtĭn* m. ‚Gefolgsherr, Herrscher, Herrgott, Herr Christus' (as. *druhtin, drohtin*, ags. *dryhten* ‚Herr', an. *drótinn* ‚Fürst, Herr', alle zu germ. **dreugan* ‚wirken, leisten, Kriegsdienst leisten', **druhtiz* f. ‚Gefolge'), im Althochdeutschen vom Abrogans bis zu Notker außerordentlich reich bezeugt[8].

(3) durch frühe Missionseinflüsse aus dem gotisch-arianischen (-griechischen), aus dem lateinisch-westeuropäischen, aus dem angelsächsischen und selbst aus dem altirischen Bereich[9].

(4) unabhängig von den Missionseinflüssen durch die reich bezeugten Lehnprägungen (Lehnbildungen, Lehnbedeutungen) aus der mächtigen lateinischen Tradition, aber mit volkssprachlichem Wortgut in semantischer oder semantisch-formaler Anlehnung an die lateinischen Wörter im Rahmen der klösterlichen Übersetzungstätigkeit und Bildungserneuerung geschaffen[10].

(5) durch die jahrhundertelange kontinuierliche Übernahme von Wortgut aus der lateinischen und frühromanischen Kirchensprache, auch nach der eigentlichen

7 Belege bei Heinrich *Wesche*, Beiträge zu einer Geschichte des deutschen Heidentums, *Paul* und *Braunes* Beiträge zur Geschichte der deutschen Sprache und Literatur (PBB) 61, 1937, S. 44—47. Zur Etymologie Julius *Pokorny*, Indogermanisches etymologisches Wörterbuch, Bern—München 1959, S. 222; Jan *de Vries*, Altnordisches etymologisches Wörterbuch, Leiden 1962, S. 579—580 und 590 *(tafn, tívurr)*; Jacob und Wilhelm *Grimm*, Deutsches Wörterbuch Bd. XI, 3. Abt., Leipzig 1936, Sp. 943—944 *(Ungeziefer)*.

8 Vgl. etwa Gerhard Lebrecht *Wiens*, Die frühchristlichen Gottesbezeichnungen im Germanisch-Altdeutschen (Neue Forschung 25), Berlin 1935, S. 54—60; ausführlich D. H. *Green*, The Carolingian Lord, Semantic Studies on four Old High German Words balder, frô, truhtin, hêrro, Cambridge 1965, S. 57—401. Zur Etymologie Julius *Pokorny*, Indogermanisches etymologisches Wörterbuch, Bern—München 1959, Sp. 255; Jan *de Vries*, Altnordisches etymologisches Wörterbuch, Leiden 1962, Sp. 84—85.

9 Vgl. die wertvolle Zusammenfassung von Hans *Eggers*, Die Annahme des Christentums im Spiegel der deutschen Sprachgeschichte, in Kirchengeschichte als Missionsgeschichte, Bd. II Die Kirche des früheren Mittelalters, 1. Halbband, hg. von Knut *Schäferdiek*, München 1978, S. 466—504 (mit Lit.).

10 Zusammenfassung bei Werner *Betz*, Lehnwörter und Lehnprägungen im Vor- und Frühdeutschen, in Deutsche Wortgeschichte, hg. von Friedrich *Maurer* und Heinz *Rupp*, Bd. I, Berlin—New York ³1974, S. 135—163.

Missionierung der althochdeutschen Stämme, insbesondere in den klösterlichen Scriptorien[11].

Jedenfalls bietet eine Komponentenlehre die Möglichkeit, den wortgeschichtlich-sprachhistorischen Entwicklungsgang im Aufbau der altdeutschen Kirchensprache zu erklären und in den verschiedenen Auf- und Ausbaustufen zu begreifen — denn das uns durch die Sprachquellen ersichtliche diachronische Bild des Althochdeutschen ist keine Folge von Zufällen, sondern es lassen sich aufeinander bezügliche sprachgeschichtliche Entfaltungstendenzen vom 8. bis ins 11./12. Jahrhundert erkennen, die in einzelne Phasen zerlegt werden können[12]. Wie in anderen Wortschatzbereichen von Recht und Bildung lassen sich im christlich-religiösen Wortschatz des Althochdeutschen neben den oben genannten verschiedenen Aufbaukomponenten die folgenden drei sprachgeschichtlichen Stufen aufzeigen:

Stufe 1 Frühalthochdeutsche Vielfalt des kirchlich-religiösen Lexikons aus ganz verschiedenen Wurzeln seit dem späten 8. Jahrhundert, in der Regel bis zur althochdeutschen Tatianübersetzung um 830, z. T. sogar bis zu Otfrid von Weissenburg um 870 reichend.

Stufe 2 Zunehmende, in einzelnen Bereichen durchgehende Vereinheitlichung des religiösen Wortschatzes vom 9. bis zum 11. Jahrhundert, nicht zuletzt unter dem Einfluß festgewordener Lehnwörter von allgemeiner, überregionaler Bedeutung.

Stufe 3 Übersetzungstechnische Differenzierung und Varietät in spätalthochdeutscher Zeit auf dem Hintergrund eines allgemein gefestigten christlichen Wortschatzes bei einzelnen Sprachmeistern wie Notker dem Deutschen und dem St. Galler Glossator von Notkers Psalter, die sich zusätzlich eine neue stilistische Fülle interpretatorisch-variierender Textausgestaltung erlauben können und dies auch bewußt wollen, ohne daß dabei der einmal erreichte kirchliche Grundwortschatz in seiner relativen Einheitlichkeit grundsätzlich wieder aufgelöst würde.

Zunächst geht es beim Aufbau des christlich-religiösen Wortschatzes in frühalthochdeutscher Zeit um die Bewältigungsphase der vielen neuen Begriffe in der erstmals schriftlich fixierten Volkssprache. Da eine althochdeutsche Katechetik, wie wir oben betont haben, in karolingischer Zeit polygenetisch und fast gleichzeitig an ganz verschiedenen Orten in verschiedenen Scriptorien entsteht und auch die Einflußbereiche von außen in verschiedener Intensität sowie regional

11 Übersicht bei Theodor *Frings*, Germania Romana I, hg. von Gertraud *Müller*, Halle (Saale) ²1966 sowie Gertraud *Müller* und Theodor *Frings*, Germania Romana II, Dreißig Jahre Forschung, Romanische Wörter, Halle (Saale) 1968.

12 Vgl. dazu auch Stefan *Sonderegger*, Tendenzen zu einem überregional geschriebenen Althochdeutsch, in Aspekte der Nationenbildung im Mittelalter, Ergebnisse der Marburger Rundgespräche 1972—1975, hg. von Helmut *Beumann* und Werner *Schröder* (Nationes Bd. 1), Sigmaringen 1978, S. 229—273.

ganz unterschiedlich auf das Althochdeutsche einwirken — wie z. B. Gotisches auf das Oberdeutsche, insbesondere auf das Altbairische, Angelsächsisches vor allem auf das Altfränkische —, so ergibt sich eine sowohl sprachgeographisch als auch übersetzungstechnisch und lehnwortkundlich ausscheidbare Vielfalt innerhalb der Stufe 1. So erscheinen für lateinisch *ecclesia* ,Kirche' (im Sinn von Gemeinschaft der Gläubigen) im Frühalthochdeutschen und bis zur Tatianübersetzung die folgenden volkssprachlichen Entsprechungen:

(a) *kirihha, chirihha* f. (Abrogans Pa/Kb, St. Galler Credo, Isidorübersetzung, Monseer Fragmente, Murbacher Hymnen, Tatian), Lehnwort aus dem griechischen κυριακόν ,Haus der Herrn', vielleicht über gotische oder langobardische Vermittlung, wenn nicht Lehnwort der Rheinlinie (*kyriaka*, Isidor *chiriihha*)[13]. Außerdem nennt das Fränkische Taufgelöbnis (ohne lat. Vorlage) die (Akk.) *heilaga gotes chirichun.*

(b) *gimeinida* f. (Dat. Sg. *kimeinithu*: Abrogans Kb neben *khirihhun*)

(c) *ladunga* f. (Weissenburger Katechismus Akk. Sg. *ladhunga*), das als etymologisierende Übersetzung von *ecclesia* (griech. ἐκκλησία, zu ἐκ-καλέω ,rufen', also ,Zusammenrufung, Ladung, Versammlung') gedeutet werden muß

(d) *samanunga* f. (Glosse zum Weissenburger Katechismus, Murbacher Hymnen, Benediktinerregel, Tatian)

(e) *christanheit* f. (Monseer Fragmente, *Exhortatio ad plebem christianam* A)

Zum Teil wird noch geschieden zwischen *chirihha* f. ,Ort des Gebetes, *oratorium*' und *samanunga* f. ,Gemeinschaft der Gläubigen (oder Mönche), *ecclesia, coenobium, congregatio*': so in der Interlinearversion der Benediktinerregel.

In der Folge geht es um die vereinheitlichende Konsolidierungsphase im althochdeutschen Wortschatz, um den Prozeß von Ausscheidung und Beschränkung der frühalthochdeutschen Vielfalt auf wenige sich in den Texten des 9. bis 11. Jahrhunderts allgemein durchsetzende Begriffe (Stufe 2), wobei zu unterscheiden ist zwischen einer zwar überregionalen, aber nicht gesamtalthochdeutschen Vereinheitlichung und einer gesamtalthochdeutschen, somit räumlich das gesamte Sprachgebiet erfassenden Konsolidierung. So erweist sich *kirihha, chirihha* (bei Notker von St. Gallen *chîlicha*) mehr und mehr als das gesamtalthochdeutsche Leitwort, während *samanunga* (Trierer Kapitulare, Notker) und *christenheit* (Notker, St. Galler Glauben und Beichte II, Wessobrunner Glauben und Beichte II, ahdt. Physiologus) noch einigermaßen überregional verwendet werden.

Schließlich geht es in spätalthochdeutscher Zeit um die neuen Möglichkeiten stilistischer Differenzierung und Variation im Rahmen der persönlichen Stilbildung, so daß man von Notkers Fülle und seines Psalmenglossators Variationsreichtum sprechen darf. So übersetzt Notker *ecclesia* mit *samenunga, gesamenunga, gesemine* und *christenheit*, während *chîlicha* mehr für das Gotteshaus — allerdings auch in der allgemeinen Bedeutung Kirche in Psalm 143:12 — sowie für Heilig-

---

13 *Müller-Frings*, Germania Romana II (Anm. 11), S. 116—118.

tum und Tempel steht[14]. Dabei bleibt zu bedenken, daß *ecclesia* in Notkers Psalter häufig zu den nicht übersetzten lateinischen Reservaten zählt. Außerordentlich reich ist, neben dem verfestigten *chilcha, chilecha,* die Variationsbreite beim St. Galler Glossator von Notkers Psalter, in welchem Ekkehart IV. zu sehen ist und wo Notkers lateinische Reservate sprachspielerisch immer wieder aufs neue ins Althochdeutsche übertragen werden. So stehen für *ecclesia* beispielsweise neben *samenunga* die Komposita *wîhsamenunga* und *brûtsamenunga,* sogar *gotes prût* oder *brûtsamina,* ferner häufig auch *cristenheit,* neben weiteren Bildungen, und selbst *chil(e)cha* wird einmal zu *liutchilcha* erweitert[15]: Psalm 34:18 *Confitebor tibi in ęcclesia magna. in populo graui laudabo te. In dero uuîtun ęcclesia* [Glossator: *liûtchîlchun] iîho ih dir. in suâremo liûte lóbon ih dih —* um unmittelbar anschließend im folgenden Satz das Notkersche *ęcclesia* wiederum variierend mit *christanheit* zu übersetzen *(In dero ęcclesia* [Glossator *christanhêite] sint kenuôge die an Got iêhent. unde siê în dóh nelóbont.)*

Aus der Fülle weiterer möglicher Beispiele zur Erläuterung dieses sprachgeschichtlichen Entwicklungsprozesses von vier Jahrhunderten wollen wir einen weiteren Fall herausgreifen, nämlich die althochdeutschen Übersetzungen von lateinisch *evangelium.* Die älteste Verdeutschung begegnet im ersten deutschen Buch, dem lateinisch-althochdeutschen Abrogans bairisch-alemannischer Herkunft aus der zweiten Hälfte des 8. Jahrhunderts (Textzeugen etwas jünger)[16]:

lateinisch	Pariser Hs.	St. Galler Hs.
(Ahdt. Gl. I, 136,34—35)	(9. Jh. 1. Viertel, bair.)	(Ende 8. Jh., alem.)
Euangelium	*euangeliũ*	*koad aruntporo*
bona adnuntiatio	*cot aruntporo*	*endi koat poto*
	anti cot poto	*endi*
		khouuntheo
		[= ahdt. *kuntheo,* wenn
		nicht *kot kuntheo*]

---

14 Emil *Luginbühl,* Studien zu Notkers Übersetzungskunst, Diss. Zürich, Weida 1933 (Nachdruck in der Reihe Das Althochdeutsche von St. Gallen Bd. 1, Berlin 1970), S. 45—46, 51—52 sowie die Wörterbücher zu Notker.

15 Vgl. die Aufstellung bei Gustav *Ehrismann,* Geschichte der deutschen Literatur bis zum Ausgang des Mittelalters, Erster Teil: Die althochdeutsche Literatur, München [2]1932, S. 442. Die folgende Textstelle aus Paul *Piper,* Die Schriften Notkers und seiner Schule, Bd. II, Freiburg i. Br. und Tübingen 1883, S. 120, 22—26.

16 Text bei Elias von *Steinmeyer* und Eduard *Sievers,* Die althochdeutschen Glossen, Bd. I, Berlin 1879 (Nachdruck Dublin—Zürich 1968), S. 1—270 (zitiert Ahdt. Gl.). Die älteste Handschrift in Das älteste deutsche Buch, die ‹Abrogans›—Handschrift der Stiftsbibliothek St. Gallen, Im Facsimile hg. und beschrieben von Bernhard *Bischoff,* Johannes *Duft,* Stefan *Sonderegger,* Mit Transkription des Glossars und des althochdeutschen Anhangs von Stefan *Sonderegger,* St. Gallen 1977 (Facsimile- und Kommentarband). Zu Text und sprachlicher Deutung Jochen *Splett,* Abrogans-Studien, Kommentar zum ältesten deutschen Wörterbuch, Wiesbaden 1976.

Nach Jochen Splett sind als lateinische Quellen das Abba-Glossar mit der Glosse *Evangelium: bonum nuntium* und eine Eucheriusstelle *euangelium bona adnuntiatio siue bonum nuntium* zu nennen[17]. Ähnlich begegnet für lateinisch *evangelizare* althochdeutsch *cuatspellon* in den reichenauischen St. Pauler Lukasglossen vom Ende des 8. Jahrhunderts[18]. Zusammensetzungen mit althochdeutsch *guot*, altalemannisch *guat, cuat* kennt auch die in St. Gallen geschriebene Interlinearversion der Benediktinerregel aus dem 2. Jahrzehnt des 9. Jahrhunderts[19]:

Prolog	*in praeparatione evangeli[c]i pacis*
	in garauuidu des cuatchundin fridoo (adjektivische Wendung)
Kap. VII	*publicanus ille evangelicus*
	achiuuizfirinari der cuatchundento (Part. Praes. in adjektivischer Funktion)
Kap. IX	*lectionem de evangelia*
	[lec]zun f[ona] cuatchundidu
Kap. XVII	*canticum de evangelio*
	sanc f[ona] cuatchundidu

Demnach liegen genügend Belege für die frühalemannische Bildung *cuat-chundida* f. ‚evangelium', *cuat-chunden* ‚evangelizare' (dazu *cuatchundento* Part. Praes. swm. Sg.), *cuatchund* ‚evangelicus' vor, und die Belege aus der sanktgallischen Benediktinerregel stellen sich zu dem Abrogansbeleg *koat poto endi khouuntheo* (= *khuntheo*, sonst auch *chundeo*, zu *kundo* m. ‚Zeuge, Verkündiger') aus der St. Galler Handschrift (Kb), die nach Bernhard Bischoff in einem „von der karolingischen Erneuerung wohl noch kaum gestreiften Kloster im Südwesten des deutschen Sprachgebiets in den letzten Jahren des 8. Jahrhunderts geschrieben wurde"[20]. Das Lehnwort althochdeutsch *euangēlisc* für lateinisch *evangelica* verwenden dagegen die reichenauischen Murbacher Hymnen an einer Stelle[21]:

I,7,2	*quo uoce euangelica*
	demu stimmi euangelisceru

Dem altalemannischen Typus *kuat-chund-* steht der westliche, fränkische wie altsächsische Typus *gotspel/godspell* n. gegenüber. Aus der westfränkisch (südrheinfränkisch-lothringisch) mitbestimmten Isidor-Übersetzungsgruppe verwenden

---

17 Jochen *Splett*, Abrogans-Studien (Anm. 16), S. 207—208 mit Hinweis auf Gl. Lat. V,EV,1 und Eucherius, Instructiones S. 161,4.

18 Drei Reichenauer Denkmäler der altalemannischen Frühzeit, hg. von Ursula *Daab* (Altdeutsche Textbibliothek Nr. 57), Tübingen 1963, S. 9 (Ahdt. Gl. I,731,29) und S. 132.

19 Ausgaben: Elias von *Steinmeyer*, Die kleineren althochdeutschen Sprachdenkmäler, Berlin 1916 (Nachdruck Berlin—Zürich 1963), Nr. XXXVI, S. 190—289; Die Althochdeutsche Benediktinerregel des Cod. Sang. 916, hg. von Ursula *Daab* (Altdeutsche Textbibliothek Nr. 50), Tübingen 1959. Die folgenden Stellen *Daab* S. 11, 35, 39, 43.

20 Das älteste deutsche Buch, Die ‹Abrogans›-Handschrift der Stiftsbibliothek St. Gallen (wie Anm. 16), Kommentarband S. 82.

21 Drei Reichenauer Denkmäler der altalemannischen Frühzeit (wie Anm. 18), S. 31.

die um 800 in bairischer Sprachumformung geschriebenen Monseer Fragmente *gotspel* an drei Stellen[22]:

XXXVII,14   *Hear saget fona gotspelle* [usw.]

    17   *Euangelium quod ... Diz gotspel daz ...*

XXX,18   *in euangelio ... in gotspelle*

Auch die althochdeutsche Tatianübersetzung unter Hrabanus Maurus in Fulda setzt für *evangelium* um das Jahr 830 zweimal *gotspel,* während die lateinische Form *evangelium* an weiteren vier Stellen unübersetzt in den althochdeutschen Text Eingang findet[23]:

(a) übersetzt

22,1   *et praedicans evangelium regni* (Matth. 4:23)
    inti predigonti gótspel ríhhes

145,10   *Et predicabitur hoc evangelium regni in universo orbe* (Matth. 24:14)
    Inti uuirdit gipredigot thiz gotspel riches in alleru uueralti

(b) nicht übersetzt, sondern als lat. Wort integriert

18,5   *et credite in evangelio* (Matth. 4:17)
    inti giloubet themo euangelio

106,6   *et propter evangelium* (Mark. 10:29)
    inti thuruh euangelium

138,6   *ubicumque predicatum fuerit evangelium* (Matth. 26:12)
    so uuar gipredigot uuirdit thiz euangelium

242,2   *praedicate evangelium* (Mark. 16:15)
    praedigot euangelium

Für *evangelizare* steht außerdem an drei Stellen das von *gotspel* n. abgeleitete Verb *gotspellōn* (18,2; 22,4; 13,25). Auch im altsächsischen Heliand steht *godspell* (Fitte 1, V. 25 *godspell that guoda*) neben *éuangelium* (Fitte 1, V. 13a, im Stab mit *enan* ‚als einzige'), während in einer freieren Fügung Hrabans *evangelicam margaritam* (Kommentar zu Matth. 7:6) in Vers 1732 als *spraka godes endi spell managa* C (bzw. *spraca godes endi spel managu*) wiedergegeben ist[24]. *Evangelizare* ist volkssprachlich durch *cūthian* repräsentiert (Verse 123,399). Synonym zu *godspell* ist offenbar *ārundi godes* in Vers 2456[25].

---

22 The Monsee Fragments, newly collated text ... edited by George Allison *Hench,* Straßburg 1890. Die Stellen S. 60—61, 46—47.

23 Tatian, Lateinisch und altdeutsch mit ausführlichem Glossar hg. von Eduard *Sievers,* 2. Ausgabe Paderborn 1892, Nachdruck Darmstadt 1961. Friedrich *Köhler,* Lateinisch-althochdeutsches Glossar zur Tatianübersetzung, Paderborn 1914, Nachdruck Darmstadt 1962. Karl *Toth,* Der Lehnwortschatz der althochdeutschen Tatianübersetzung, Würzburg 1980.

24 Heliand, hg. von Eduard *Sievers* (Germanistische Handbibliothek IV), Halle 1878, Berlin ²1935. Edward H. *Sehrt,* Vollständiges Wörterbuch zum Heliand und zur altsächsischen Genesis. 2. durchgesehene Aufl. Göttingen 1966.

25 Peter *Ilkow,* Die Nominalkomposita der altsächsischen Bibeldichtung, Ein semantisch-kulturgeschichtliches Glossar, hg. von W. *Wissmann* und H.-Fr. *Rosenfeld,* Göttingen 1968, S. 151.

Vollständig auf der Lehnwortstufe steht dagegen Otfrid von Weissenburg im dritten Viertel des 9. Jahrhunderts, welcher das aus lateinisch *evangelium* eingedeutschte und durchflektierte schwache Maskulinum *êuangélio* m. an achtzehn Stellen seiner dichterischen Evangelienharmonie verwendet, davon neunmal sogar im allerdings immer gleich oder fast gleich strukturierten Reim[26]. Die Reimstellen lauten.

Lud. 89	*Er híar in thesen rédion*	*mag hóren evangélion*
II,9,71	*Lis sélbo, theih thir rédion*	*in sínen evangélion*
III,14,4	*thie scríbent evangélion;*	*lis sélbo theih thir redion*
III,20,143	*Bigónd er in tho rédion*	*sélb these evangélion*
IV,34,13	*Thaz zéllent evangélion*	*al so ih thir rédion*
V,6,6	*gidóugno, so ih thir rédion,*	*in thésen evangélion*
V,13,20	*ouh thrí, so ih thir rédinon*	*(thaz zéllent evangélion)*
V,25,33	*Thaz íh in thesen rédion*	*ni lúgi in thevangélion*
Hart. 2	*gikrúmpti thero rédino*	*thero quít ther evangélio*

Dergestalt steht das eingedeutschte Wort *êvangélio* m. ausschließlich im Reim mit den Verben *redinōn* ,darlegen, erzählen', *rediōn* ,erörtern, erzählen' und dem Substantiv *redina* f. ,Erzählung, Geschichte, Deutung'. Für *evangelizare* verwendet Otfrid *kunden* (I,4,63) und *wuntar sagēn* (*evangelizo* I,12,7 *ih scal iu sagen wúntar*), während für *evangelista gotes drutman* (II, 11, 42) steht[27].

Im spätalthochdeutschen Übersetzungswerk Notkers des Deutschen findet sich keine Übersetzung von *evangelium*, da dieses wichtige Wort in den Kommentarstellen Notkers zum deutschen Psalter als lateinisches Reservat verbleibt. Dagegen eröffnet sich die spätalthochdeutsche Variationsfülle wiederum bei Ekkehart IV. als Glossator von Notkers Psalter, und hier sind für *evangelium* drei verschiedene Übersetzungen anzutreffen:

(a) *gûot ârende* n. ,gute Botschaft':

Psalm 32:5 (Piper II,107,21) *Vuanda euangelium* [Glossator: *kuôt ârende*] *chómen ist unde fides [kelôuba] unde baptismum [tôuffi] in alla diê erda.*

(b) *betinbrôt* n. ,erbetenes Brot (eigentlich *betan brôt*), geistliche Nahrung'[28]:

Psalm 29:10 (Piper II,95,2) *Vuirdo ih redactus in puluerem* [Glossator: *praht ze stuppe*]. *uuâr sint danne diê ih uzfrúmme. predicare euangelium omni creaturę?* [Glossator: *prédigon pétinbrot állero geschéphido*].

---

26 Otfrids Evangelienbuch ... hg. von Paul *Piper*, I. Theil Einleitung und Text, Freiburg i. Br. und Tübingen ²1882, II. Theil Glossar und Abriss der Grammatik Freiburg i. Br. 1887. Handausgabe von Oskar *Erdmann*, Edward *Schröder*, Ludwig *Wolff* (Altdeutsche Textbibliothek Nr. 49), Tübingen ³1957.

27 Vgl. Gerhard *Köbler*, Verzeichnis der Übersetzungsgleichungen Otfrids von Weissenburg (Göttinger Studien zur Rechtsgeschichte Sonderband 11), Göttingen 1971, S. 38.

28 Vgl. Edward H. *Sehrt*, Notker-Glossar, Ein Althochdeutsch-Lateinisch-Neuhochdeutsches Wörterbuch zu Notkers des Deutschen Schriften, Tübingen 1962, mit Hinweis auf *Grimm*, Deutsches Wörterbuch Bd. II, Leipzig 1860, Sp. 274. Sodann Althochdeutsches Wörterbuch, begründet von Elisabeth *Karg-Gasterstädt* und Theodor *Frings*, Bd. 1 (Lieferung 13), Berlin 1961, Sp. 926—927 (mit weiteren Hinweisen).

(c) *brediga* f. ‚das Predigen des Evangeliums, Predigt'
Zwei Stellen des häufiger belegten Wortes, das u. a. für *verbum dei* steht,
übersetzen *evangelium:*
Psalm 69:10 (Piper II,228,17—19) *Ih sendo dára calciatos pedes in preparatione
euangelii pacis* [Glossator: *kescuôhto fuôzze ze fúreuuárno déro prédigo fridis]*
Psalm 107:10 (Piper II,467,19) *Ioh ze írdisken ménniscon ferrécho ih mîn eu-
vangelium* [Glossator: *prediga].*
Zu diesen Stellen ist auch die neue gemäßigt diplomatische Ausgabe von Notkers
Psalter durch Petrus W. Tax seit 1979 zu vergleichen: *kûotârende* erscheint dabei
als Kompositum[28a].
Der spätalthochdeutsche Physiologus aus dem 11. Jahrhundert beläßt *evangelium* dagegen lateinisch, wenn der Verfasser die Stelle *Item in evangelio dicit* ... mit
Oûh gibûdét uns gót in einemo euangelio ... übersetzt[29].
Alles in allem lassen sich demnach auch beim Übersetzungsvorgang von althochdeutsch *evangelium* die oben genannten drei sprachgeschichtlichen Stufen
vom 8. bis ins 11. Jahrhundert nachzeichnen:
(1) die frühalthochdeutsche Bewältigungsphase mit ihrer Vielfalt sprachgeographisch wie philologisch auseinanderstrebender Übersetzungen wie (normalisiert) *guot aruntporo, guot boto enti kundeo* (Abrogans), *guatchundida* u. ä. (Benediktinerregel), *gotspel* (Monseer Fragmente, Tatian) neben lateinisch unverän-
dertem *euangelium* (Tatian) und dem Lehnwort *euangēlisc* ‚evangelisch' (Murbacher Hymnen)
(2) die mit Otfrid von Weissenburg gegebene Konsolidierungsphase, welche sich
trotz häufiger Verwendung auf das eine Lehnwort *êuangélio* m. beschränkt,
dieses völlig althochdeutsch als schwaches Maskulinum dekliniert, aber mit
lateinisch-romanischer Betonung in die Volkssprache einverleibt
(3) die durch den stilistischen Willen einzelner Persönlichkeiten geprägte spätalthochdeutsche Differenzierungsphase auf im übrigen konsolidiertem Hintergrund, wo das Notkersche *euangelium* — lateinisches Reservat, nicht übersetzt,
insofern Otfrids *êvangélio* vergleichbar — beim Glossator von Notkers Psalter
sprachkünstlerisch aufs neue variiert wird, wobei allerdings *gûot ârende* an die
älteren Bildungen mit *guot* anschließt, was bei Ekkehart IV. Ausdruck eines
etymologischen Bewußtseins wie der Kenntnis üblicher christlicher Erklärung
— u. a. bei Isidor von Sevilla[30] — sein kann.

28a Notker der Deutsche, Der Psalter, hg. von Petrus W. *Tax,* Tübingen 1979—83 (in Die
Werke Notkers des Deutschen, Neue Ausgabe, Begonnen von Edward H. *Sehrt* und Taylor
Starck, Fortgesetzt von James C. *King* und Petrus W. *Tax,* Bd. 8—10).
29 Elias von *Steinmeyer,* Die kleineren althochdeutschen Sprachdenkmäler (wie Anm.
19) Nr. XXVII, S. 131, 121 und 146.
30 Etymologiae sive Origines ed. W. M. *Lindsay,* Oxonii 1911 (reprinted 1957, 1962, 1966
usw.), VI,2,43 (tom. I): *Evangelium autem interpretatur bona adnuntiatio. Graece enim* εὖ *bonum,*
ἀγγελία *adnuntiatio dicitur.*

Mit dieser übersetzungsgeschichtlichen Stufung ist der schon oben erwähnte sprachgeographische Befund zu vergleichen, der außerdem die Einflüsse von außen, aus den dem Althochdeutschen benachbarten oder dieses bildungsmäßig überlagernden Sprachkreisen widerspiegelt. Dabei ist auf den sich fächerartig verbreiternden Nord-Süd-Gegensatz zwischen fränkisch *gotspel* (Tatian, wie altsächs. *godspell*) gegenüber der oberdeutschen, vor allem alemannischen Vielfalt von (normalisiert) *guot ārunti, guot āruntboro* u. ä., *guotkundida* hinzuweisen, während das südöstliche *gotspel* der Monseer Fragmente aus den Nordwestzusammenhängen der Isidor-Sippe zu erklären ist. Immerhin wird dieser Gegensatz durch *cuatspellon* für *evangelizare* der St. Pauler Lukasglossen für die frühalthochdeutsche Bewältigungsphase etwas gemildert, wenn auch die Bildung mit *cuat*-typisch oberdeutsch bleibt. Althochdeutsch *gotspel* beruht auf dem angelsächsischen Einfluß von altenglisch *gōdspell*, d. h. auf der durch frühe Kürzung entstandenen Nebenform *gŏdspell* — auch altnordisch *gudspjall* geht darauf zurück —, welche einen Anschluß an altenglisch *god*, ahdt. *got* (auch an. *gud*) ‚Gott' möglich machte[31]. Doch zeigt auch die altenglische Glossierung der älteren Zeit die Verankerung in der etymologischen Erklärungstradition: *Euuangelium* (sic!), *id est, bonum nuntium, godspel*[32]. Für altenglisch *gōdspell* gibt Alfred Bammesberger zu erwägen, „daß der unmittelbare Ausgangspunkt für die altenglische Lehnbildung auch altirisch *soscéle* ‚Evangelium', eine völlig transparente Lehnbildung von *euaggélion* ‚gute Botschaft', sein könnte"[33]. Die gleiche Vermutung eines irischen Einflusses hat Josef Weisweiler seit 1943 für die süddeutschen Typen der Übersetzung von *evangelium* mit *guot* geäußert: „Wenn ‚*evangelium*' in Reichenau (Ben.-R.) mit *cuat-chundida*, in St. Gallen (Gl. zu Notkers Ps 32:5) mit *kuôt ârende* übersetzt wird, so erinnert das an altirisch *so-scélae*, ebenso wie *arm-herzî* und *arm-herzida* für ‚misericordia' an altirisch *trócaire* (vgl. ir. *is tróg limm ‚me miseret'*, zu *tróg, trúag ‚miser'), fora-scouuunga* und *fore-siht* für ‚providentia' an altirisch *remdéicsiu* usw"[34]. Diese Gesichtspunkte hat Hans Eggers wieder aufgenommen und vertieft, wobei er besonderes Gewicht auf die althochdeutschen Übersetzun-

31 Walter W. *Skeat*, An Etymological Dictionary of the English Language, New Edition Oxford 1909, reprinted 1961, S. 246; Alfred *Bammesberger*, Beiträge zu einem etymologischen Wörterbuch des Altenglischen, Berichtigungen und Nachträge zum Altenglischen etymologischen Wörterbuch von Ferdinand *Holthausen*, (Anglistische Forschungen 139), Heidelberg 1979, S. 67. Zum ahdt. Wort Wilhelm *Braune*, Althochdeutsch und Angelsächsisch, in PBB 43, 1918, S. 393 ff. Weitere Literatur bei Josef *Weisweiler* — Werner *Betz* (Anm. 6), S. 92 mit Anm. 183.

32 Thomas *Wright*, Anglo-Saxon and Old English Vocabularies, Second Edition, Edited and Collated bei Richard Paul *Wülcker*, vol. I, London 1884 (Nachdruck Darmstadt 1968), S. 314, 8—9.

33 *Bammesberger* (wie Anm. 31), S. 67.

34 Josef *Weisweiler*, Deutsche Frühzeit, in Deutsche Wortgeschichte, hg. von Friedrich *Maurer* und Friedrich *Stroh*, Bd. I (Grundriß der germanischen Philologie 17/I), Berlin ²1959, S. 85 bzw. Josef *Weisweiler* und Werner *Betz* (Anm. 6), S. 94 (gleicher Wortlaut wie in 2. Aufl.); die erste Auflage war 1943 erschienen.

gen von lateinisch *tristitia* mit Negativ-Präfixbildungen vom Typus *tristitia unfre-wida, tristis unfrō, (con)tristare (ga)unfrewen* legt, die auffälligerweise den altiri-schen Bildungen *anfáilid* ,tristis', *anfáilte* ,tristitia' entsprechen, während sie sich gleichzeitig innerhalb des Althochdeutschen auf einen leicht erweiterten südli-chen Raum (Oberdeutsch, auch Otfrid von Weissenburg im Übergangsgebiet Ale-mannisch-Rheinfränkisch, weitere vereinzelte Belege außerhalb des Alemann-isch-Bairischen) beschränken und im übrigen innerhalb der *tristitia/tristis*-Über-setzungen des Altgermanischen isoliert stehen[35].

Mit weiteren Kriterien im größeren missions- und kirchengeschichtlichen Zusammenhang hat Ingo Reiffenstein mögliche irische Einflüsse auf das Althoch-deutsche im oberdeutschen Raum dargestellt[36]. Damit konnte selbst das umsich-tige, die ältere Forschung zusammenfassende und bahnbrechend neue Erkennt-nisse vermittelnde Bild über „die Spuren der irischen Mission in der Entwicklung der deutschen Sprache" von Leo Weisgerber aus dem Jahre 1952 erweitert wer-den[37]. Noch weiter geht neuerdings Gustav Must, der einerseits in bisher als verderbt oder als mit Schreibfehlern behaftet angesehenen Formen des St. Galler Paternoster, andererseits von der Diktion sowie von der Aufarbeitung liturgischer Textvorlagen des St. Galler Paternoster und Credo her einen direkten altirischen Einfluß glaubt nachweisen zu können, in welchen Denkmälern er charakteristi-sche Züge des wandernden Mönchtums auf irischer Grundlage erkennen will[38]. Die Folgerungen Musts erscheinen in manchem, vor allem was die Texthinter-gründe betrifft, sehr erwägenswert, doch ist die paläographisch-schreibgeschicht-liche Seite keineswegs sicher abgestützt, ja zum Teil ganz einfach unrichtig[39].

35 Hans *Eggers*, Deutsche Sprachgeschichte I, Das Althochdeutsche, Reinbek bei Ham-burg 1963, S. 154—163, besonders S. 161 f.; neuerdings Hans *Eggers*, Die Annahme des Chri-stentums im Spiegel der deutschen Sprachgeschichte (Anm. 9), S. 493—494. Das ahdt. Wort-material ist aufgearbeitet bei Dietrich *Ruprecht*, Tristitia, Wortschatz und Vorstellung in den althochdeutschen Sprachdenkmälern (Palaestra Bd. 227), Göttingen 1959, S. 25—31.

36 Ingo *Reiffenstein*, Das Althochdeutsche und die irische Mission im oberdeutschen Raum (Innsbrucker Beiträge zur Kulturwissenschaft, Sonderheft 6), Innsbruck 1958; Ingo *Reiffenstein*, Die althochdeutsche Kirchensprache, in Germanistische Abhandlungen, hg. von Karl Kurt *Klein* und Eugen *Thurnher* (Innsbrucker Beiträge zur Kulturwissenschaft Bd. 6), Innsbruck 1959, S. 41—58.

37 Leo *Weisgerber*, Die Spuren der irischen Mission in der Entwicklung der deutschen Sprache, in Rheinische Vierteljahrsblätter 17 (1952), S. 8—41, bzw. Leo *Weisberger*, Rhenania Germano-Celtica, Gesammelte Abhandlungen, hg. von Johann *Knobloch* und Rudolf *Schütz-eichel*, Bonn 1969, S. 184—212.

38 Gustav *Must*, Das St. Galler Paternoster, in Akten des V. Internationalen Germani-sten-Kongresses Cambridge 1975, Jahrbuch für Internationale Germanistik, Reihe A, Kongreßberichte, Bd. 2, Bern—Frankfurt a. M. 1976, S. 396—403; Gustav *Must*, Das altale-mannische Wort ,kiscat', in Akten des VI. Internationalen Germanisten-Kongresses Basel 1980, Jahrbuch für Internationale Germanistik, Reihe A, Kongreßberichte, Bd. 8, Teil 2, Bern—Frankfurt a. M. — Las Vegas 1980, S. 399—403; Gustav *Must*, Das St. Galler Credo, in FMSt. (1981), S. 371—386. Zur weiteren Literatur vgl. Stefan *Sonderegger*, St. Galler Paternoster und Credo, in Die deutsche Literatur des Mittelalters, Verfasserlexikon, Bd. 2, Berlin—New York 1980, Sp. 1044—1047.

Kehren wir noch einmal zur Verdeutschung des Wortes *evangelium* in der althochdeutschen Kirchensprache zurück, um daraus mehr grundsätzliche Schlußfolgerungen zu ziehen. *Evangelium* zeigt in althochdeutscher Zeit die folgenden vier Möglichkeiten einer Einverleibung in die Volkssprache:

1. Übernahme des griechisch-lateinischen Wortes als Fremdwort.
So wird lateinisch *evangelium*, spätlat. *evangelio*, als ahdt. *ēvangélio* m. bei Otfrid von Weissenburg übernommen (vgl. auch das Adjektiv *euangelisc* in den Murbacher Hymnen)[40]. Gradmesser für diese während der gesamten althochdeutschen Zeit mögliche Direktübernahme des Wortes bleiben die vielen oben genannten Fälle der Aufnahme einer rein lateinischen Wortform in verschiedenen althochdeutschen Texten (Tatian, Notker, Physiologus). In mittelhochdeutscher Zeit erscheint dann die neutrale Form *êw/vangêli*, *êw/vangelje*, die auch neuhochdeutsch noch nachlebt *(das Evangeli)*[41]. Auf der gleichen Lehnwortstufe verblieb das Gotische des Missionsbischofs Wulfila in der Mitte des 4. Jahrhunderts mit den Formen *aiwaggēljō* f. (überwiegende Form in den Evangelien und Briefen, ferner in der Skeireins), *aiwaggēli* n. (sechsmal in den Briefen), wozu noch *aiwaggēljan* (für griech. εὐαγγελίζεσθαι) und *aiwaggēlista* m. (für griech. εὐαγγελιστής, lat. *evangelista*) kommen.

---

39 So behauptet *Must* FMSt. 15 (1981), S. 385, „daß die Übersetzung des St. Galler Paternoster und Credo entweder Anfang des achten oder Ende des siebenten Jahrhunderts an einem nicht bestimmbaren Schreibort entstanden ist, aber die Kopie derselben, die wir noch besitzen, höchstwahrscheinlich etwa um das Jahr 760 in St. Gallen angefertigt wurde." Nun hat aber Bernhard *Bischoff* schon 1977 klar dargetan, daß der althochdeutsche Anhang zur sanktgallischen Abrogans-Handschrift 911 mit dem sog. St. Galler Paternoster und Credo „mit einem kaum ins Gewicht fallenden zeitlichen Abstand" hinzugefügt wurde, also wie der gesamte Codex „in den letzten Jahren des 8. Jahrhunderts", während gerade der Sprachstand von St. Galler Paternoster und Credo auch schon jüngere Merkmale aufweist, die nicht älter als vom Ende des 8. Jahrhunderts sein können (Bernhard *Bischoff*, Anlage, Schrift und Ausstattung der St. Galler ‚Abrogans'-Handschrift, in Das älteste deutsche Buch, Die ‚Abrogans'-Handschrift der Stiftsbibliothek St. Gallen, Im Facsimile hg. und beschrieben von Bernhard *Bischoff*, Johannes *Duft*, Stefan *Sonderegger*, Mit Transkription des Glossars und des althochdeutschen Anhangs von Stefan *Sonderegger*, St. Gallen 1977, S. 61—82, die zitierten Stellen S. 66 und S. 82; zum Sprachstand des Anhangs Stefan *Sonderegger*, Die germanistische Bedeutung des ‹Abrogans› und der St. Galler ‹Abrogans›-Handschrift, ebenda S. 113 ff.). Außerdem lehnt *Bischoff* eine Entstehung des Codex (mit Anhang) in St. Gallen ab, ohne eine nähere Eingliederung über den deutschen Südwesten hinaus zu vollziehen (a.a.O., S. 79—82), wobei auch offen bleibt, ob die Handschrift „irisch oder angelsächsisch bestimmt war" (a.a.O., S. 82).

40 Vgl. Karl *Helm*, Althochdeutsch evangeljo sw. M., in PBB 40, 1915, S. 162—165, der freilich an ein gotisches Lehnwort dachte, was Wilhelm *Streitberg*, Germanisch (Wortforschung), in Wilhelm *Streitberg* — Victor *Michels* — Max Hermann *Jellinek*, Die Erforschung der indogermanischen Sprachen II, Germanisch, 1. Allgemeiner Teil mit Lautlehre, Berlin und Leipzig 1936, S. 106, ablehnte.

41 Matthias *Lexer*, Mittelhochdeutsches Handwörterbuch Bd. I, Leipzig 1872, Sp. 715, Jacob und Wilhelm *Grimm*, Deutsches Wörterbuch Bd. III, Leipzig 1862, Sp. 1199.

2. Frühe Lehnübersetzungen auf der Basis eines etymologischen Verständnisses. Hier kommen zwei Möglichkeiten in Betracht. Zunächst die griechisch-lateinische Basis, d. h. griech. εὐαγγέλιον, lat. *evangelium* mit der etymologisierenden Erklärung *bona adnuntiatio sive bonum nuntium* u. ä., wie wir sie oben bereits genannt haben, was zu den althochdeutschen Bildungen altalemannisch /*kuat-*/ und /*-Lexem* für Verkündigung, Botschaft/ führen konnte. Sodann muß hier aber auch selbständig oder verstärkend dazu die altirische Basis *soscéle* (Genitiv *soscéli*) m. bedacht werden, wie sie z. B. in den altirischen Würzburger Glossen zu den Paulinischen Briefen begegnet[42]. Das altirische Wort beruht auf dem griechischen Verständnis des Wortes, da die frühchristlichen Iren einen bemerkenswerten Zugang zum Griechischen hatten[43]. Jedenfalls kann die breite süddeutsche Vertretung des etymologischen Typus /*kuat-*/+/*Lexem* für Verkündigung, Botschaft/ im altalemannischen Frühalthochdeutschen durch die altirische Tradition mitbeeinflußt sein. Schwergewichtig erscheint dieser althochdeutsche Typus im Abrogans, in St. Gallen und auf der Reichenau: beide Klöster des Bodenseeraums haben auch Anteil an der altirischen Glossierung[44].

3. Übernahme des angelsächsischen Wortes unter Angleichung an die althochdeutsche Lautung.

Dies ist der Fall bei ahdt. *gotspel* (Monseer Fragmente, Tatian), Umdeutung aus altenglisch *gōdspell* über *gŏdspell*, mit Anlehnung an *got* ‚Gott'. Das Beispiel gehört in die größeren Zusammenhänge des angelsächsischen Einflusses auf das Althochdeutsche[45].

---

42 Thesaurus Palaeohibernicus, A Collection of Old-Irish Glosses, Scholia, Prose and Verse, Edited by Whitley *Stokes* and John *Strachan*, vol. I, reprinted Dublin 1975, S. 500, 619, 643. Zur Etymologie vgl. J[oseph] *Vendryes*, Lexique étymologique de l'irlandais ancien, Dublin 1959 ff. (Stichwort *soscéle*).

43 Vgl. Leo *Weisgerber*, Spuren (wie Anm. 37), S. 40—41 bzw. 211 (mit Lit.), wo immerhin steht „Natürlich wird man Beispiele wie evangelium, propheta u. a., wo die lateinischen Erklärungen der griechischen Wörter aus Isidor und anderen Quellen allgemein geläufig waren, nicht als beweiskräftig einbeziehen."

44 St. Gallen, vor allem Priscian-Glossen Codex 904 der Stiftsbibliothek; Reichenau, vor allem Karlsruher Codices Augienses No. CXCV (Glossen zu Augustins Soliloquia), No. CLXVII (Glossen zu Beda, versch. Werke), No. CXXXII (Priscian-Glossen), vgl. Thesaurus Palaeohibernicus (wie Anm. 42), vol. II, reprinted Dublin 1975. Zu den irischen Manuskripten im St. Galler Bestand vgl. Johannes *Duft*, Die Beziehungen zwischen Irland und St. Gallen im Rahmen der sanktgallischen Stiftsbibliothek und Die irischen Handschriften der Stiftsbibliothek St. Gallen, in Die irischen Miniaturen der Stiftsbibliothek St. Gallen, hg. von Johannes *Duft* und Peter *Meyer*, Olten—Bern—Lausanne 1953, S. 10—61 und 63—83.

45 Vgl. Theodor *Frings*, Germania Romana, 2. Aufl. besorgt von Gertraud *Müller* (Mitteldeutsche Studien 19/I), Bd. I, Halle (Saale) 1966, Kap. 1 Einleitung: Angelsächsisch, Althochdeutsch, Gotisch, S. 9—44; Hans *Eggers*, Deutsche Sprachgeschichte I, Das Althochdeutsche, Reinbek bei Hamburg 1963, S. 163—168, bzw. Die Annahme des Christentums im Spiegel der deutschen Sprachgeschichte (wie Anm. 9), S. 491—499.

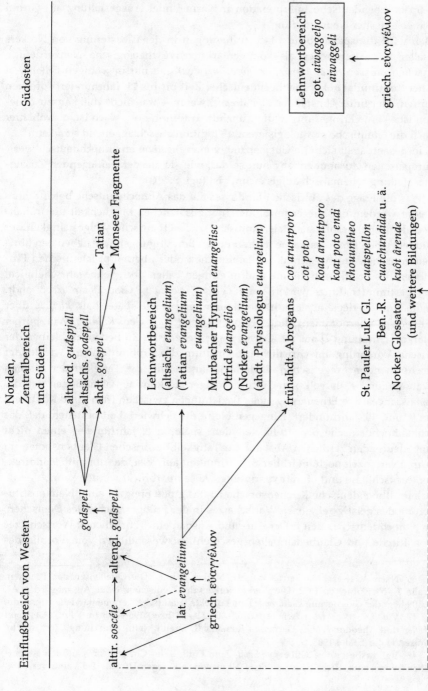

4. Spätalthochdeutsche Interpretation in variierender Ausgestaltung auf Grund theologischer Neuvertiefung.

Man wird die spätalthochdeutschen Fügungen in der Glossierung von Notkers Psalter im wesentlichen als kommentarintensive theologische Neuvertiefung ansehen müssen *(kuôt ârende, pétinbrot, prédiga)* und nur in wenigen Fällen von einer Kontinuität aus frühalthochdeutscher Zeit bis ins 11. Jahrhundert sprechen dürfen: hier unter Umständen *kuôt ârende,* wenn — was nicht völlig auszuschließen ist — eine Erinnerung an die frühahdt. Tradition noch wach ist, obwohl hier auch die lateinische etymologisierende Tradition ausschlaggebend sein kann[46].

Insgesamt stellt sich die Übersetzung von *evangelium* im althochdeutsch-westeuropäischen Zusammenhang nun so dar, wie sie auf der beiliegenden Zusammenstellung schematisch aufgezeichnet ist (vgl. S. 255).

Was die Frage des altirischen Einflusses auf das Althochdeutsche betrifft, muß betont werden, daß dieser im Sinne einer zusätzlichen Möglichkeit die frühalthochdeutsche, besonders altalemannische, z. T. altbairische Vielgestaltigkeit der süddeutschen Kirchensprache in ihrer ersten Bewältigungsphase neben den übrigen gotischen und westfränkisch-lateinischen oder überhaupt lateinischen Einflüssen besser erklären könnte und in einigen Fällen doch sehr wahrscheinlich, bei bestimmten Einzelwörtern (ahdt. *glocca, clocca* f. ‚Glocke' air. *clocc;* ahdt. *chlǐrich* m. ‚clericus' altalem. [Benediktinerregel] sowie später bair. *klerich,* über air. *clérech* übernommen; ahdt. Personenname *Kilian,* Gen. *Kilianes* [Würzburger Markbeschreibung 2] aus air. *Céléne)* sogar sicher ist[47]. Zu bedenken bleiben der irische Vorsprung im christlichen Schrifttum des Frühmittelalters wie in der hochstehenden exegetischen altirischen Glossierung, die Tätigkeit der irischen Wandermönche als volkssprachliche Prediger auf kontinentalem Boden wie die renaissanceartige Erneuerung vieler Beziehungen zwischen Irland und Kontinent im 9. und 10. Jahrhundert. Hingegen bleibt die Schwierigkeit bestehen, daß das frühalthochdeutsche Schrifttum seit dem späteren 8. Jahrhundert einen nicht unbedeutenden zeitlichen Abstand zur Tätigkeit der irischen Glaubensboten im 7. und vereinzelt noch im frühen 8. Jahrhundert aufweist, der nur mittels indirekter Rückschlüsse und oft nur vermutungsweise überbrückt werden kann.

Die althochdeutsche Kirchensprache ist das große Ereignis einer Neukonstituierung des geistig-religiösen Wortschatzes in der Frühgeschichte des Deutschen, in althochdeutscher Zeit[48]. Der Auf- und Ausbau eines christlichen Wortschatzes von Kirche und Glaubensinhalten geschieht im wesentlichen vom Vorbild des

---

46 Nach Ausweis von Petrus W. *Tax,* Notker latinus, Die Quellen zu den Psalmen, Psalm 1—50, Tübingen 1972 (Die Werke Notkers des Deutschen, Neue Ausgabe Bd. 8 A), S. 109 liegt der Glossierung *kûotârende* keine direkte lateinische Kommentarstelle zugrunde.

47 Vgl. Leo *Weisgerber* (wie Anm. 37), S. 22—25 bzw. 196—198 (mit Lit.); Gertraud *Müller* und Theodor *Frings,* Germania Romana II, Dreißig Jahre Forschung, Romanische Wörter, Halle (Saale) 1968, S. 189—192.

48 Vgl. insbesondere Gilbert *de Smet,* Zum Einfluß des Christentums auf den altdeutschen Wortschatz, Rede Universiteit te Nijmegen, Nijmegen-Utrecht 1957, und verschie-

Lateinischen her, zunächst mit Schwergewicht auf den Lehnprägungen mit altheimischem Sprachmaterial und unter Beizug altgermanischer Sakralwörter, zunächst so vielfältig wie uneinheitlich, im Verlauf der Jahrhunderte aber mehr und mehr — nicht zuletzt unter der Klammer wichtiger Fremd- oder Lehnwörter aus dem Lateinischen — zusammenwachsend. Unter den nachweisbaren Einflüssen von außen darf auch die altirische Einwirkung auf die süddeutsche Kirchensprache in althochdeutscher Zeit als eine der Aufbaukomponenten begriffen werden.

---

dene weitere Aufsätze desselben Verfassers (vgl. das Literaturverzeichnis bei *Moser-Wellmann-Wolf,* Geschichte der deutschen Sprache, Bd. 1: Althochdeutsch-Mittelhochdeutsch, von Norbert Richard *Wolf,* [UTB 1139] Heidelberg 1981, S. 255); Emil *Luginbühl,* Die altdeutsche Kirchensprache, Wissenschaftliche Beilage zum 80. Programm der St. Gallischen Kantonsschule für das Schuljahr 1936/37, St. Gallen 1936 (Nachdruck bei Emil *Luginbühl,* Studien zu Notkers Übersetzungskunst, Reihe Das Althochdeutsche von St. Gallen, hg. von Stefan *Sonderegger,* Bd. 1, Berlin 1970, S. 137—171); Hans *Eggers,* Die Annahme des Christentums im Spiegel der deutschen Sprachgeschichte (wie Anm. 9), mit weiterer Lit.

The metrical prose of Adomnán's Vita Columbae: an unsual system

By

Jean-Michel Picard

It is now generally agreed among scholars, especially since the studies of Gertrud Lindholm and Tore Janson[1], that the teaching of *cursus*, far from being extinct between the 6th and 11th centuries, was kept alive in several areas of Western Europe. It is also accepted that Ireland was not one of these areas, as Hiberno-Latin authors do not show any acquaintance with the rules of prose rhythm. This is what Michael Winterbottom has demonstrated for several 6th and 7th century writers : Columbanus, the authors of the *De mirabilibus Sacrae Scripturae, De duodecim abusiuis saeculi, De ordine creaturarum,* and Adomnán[2]. However, he warned his readers about drawing final conclusions from his survey, as it was based on samples of only one hundred sentences from each author, and it was not checked. In the case of Adomnán, my study of the whole of Book I of the Vita Columbae fully confirms his indications.

I have in the first place analysed the 599 sentence endings of Book I according to the method of internal comparison developed by Janson[3]. From this total it was necessary to exclude 58 sentence endings containing a word the accentuation of which was uncertain[4], and 107 (i. e. 17.86 %) in which the collision of a final vowel or an *m* with an initial vowel occurred. From this last figure it appears that

---

1 G. *Lindholm,* Studien zum mittellateinischen Prosarhythmus: Seine Entwicklung und sein Abklingen in der Briefliteratur Italiens, Stockholm 1963; T. *Janson,* Prose Rhythm in Medieval Latin from the 9th to the 13th Century, Stockholm 1975, p. 35—59.

2 M. *Winterbottom,* Aldhelm's prose style and its origins, Anglo-Saxon England 6 (1977), p. 71—73.

3 *Janson,* Prose Rhythm, p. 10—34. Briefly summarised, the method used is as follows: the notation *p* (for paroxyton), *pp* (proparoxyton), 2 (used instead of *p* for final dissyllables) and 1 (monosyllable) is used to indicate the possible combinations of the two last words of the sentence. This gives us a list of 25 possible sentence endings, the frequency of whose occurrence we can then observe. Next, on the principle that 'the frequency for each type of ending can be fully explained as a function of the general frequency of the first component and the last component', we can deduce an expected frequency for each cadence. We then use an accepted method of statistical comparison: the X^2 test or Pearson's test, which is intended to show the extent to which a given table of observed frequencies deviates from the table that would be expected given a random choice. Application of this test indicates whether the figures as a whole show any more than random variation between expected and observed frequency. One considers that the X^2 test is positive when the probability of the rhythmical system being due to random variation is less than 5 %.

4 *Clausulae* are considered doubtful when they contain one of the following:
— short vowel followed by *muta cum liquida* or *qu;*

Adomnán does not pay much attention to rhythm, as we know that rhythmical authors tend to keep their texts free of such collisions[5]. The analysis of the remaining 434 *clausulae* confirms that Adomnán is not a rhythmical author (see table 1). Firstly the difference between observed and expected frequencies is negligible and secondly, to corroborate this, the X^2 test is negative with a total of 6.769. This means that there is more than a 90 % chance for the system to be due to random variation[6]. We may recollect that, according to Janson, this percentage would be less than 5 % for a rhythmical author[7]. Thus, not only does Adomnán seem not to have been acquainted with the rules of *cursus*, but he appears not to care at all about rhythm.

This lack of interest in accentual rhythm is not peculiar to Adomnán and is also found in British authors. In his study of the Latin of Gildas, François Kerlouégan has shown that the British masters of the 6th century, who knew the rules of prosody and metric, were not concerned about the accent. He also suggested that this was due to the fact that they pronounced their Latin *à la bretonne*, that is to say with the accent on the penultimate syllable[8]. If so, the problem must have been all the greater for the Irish for whom Latin was an even more recently imported second language and whose mother tongue had a stress put on the first syllable. From the evidence found in the small number of Irish authors already mentioned, it seems that this aspect of the teaching of Latin was neglected in the 6th and 7th century insular schools and that Iona was not an exception to this.

However, while the results of my study of rhythm in the Vita Columbae are negative, the metrical aspect shows definite positive elements. For the analysis of Adomnán's metrical *clausulae*, I have followed the method developed by Harald Hagendahl, after the system of De Groot, which is commonly used for the study of the prose of Late Latin authors[9]. The metrical patterns of the eight last syllables of the sentences are classified in 128 combinations, which are then grouped into 19 metrical types. When this grouping is complete, the percentage use of each type is calculated and compared to the figures given on the one hand for unmetrical

— combination of two *i*'s in substantives and adjectives of the second declension (e.g. *dii, diis*);
— genitives *illius, unius, ipsius*;
— final *o* in the nominatives of the third declension, in adverbs and in the first person singular of verbs;
— desinences *erimus* and *eritis* in the future perfect indicative and perfect subjunctive.
— words known for their doubtful prosody such as *nihil* and *prehendere*.

5 See T. *Janson*, Word, syllable and letter in Latin, Eranos 65 (1967), p. 49—64.

6 Cf. Table de distribution du X^2 in Ch. *Muller*, Initiation aux méthodes de la statistique linguistique, Paris 1973.

7 *Janson*, Prose Rhythm, p. 21—22.

8 *Kerlouégan*, Les destinées de la culture latine dans la Bretagne du VIe siècle: recherches sur le De excidio Britanniae de Gildas, Thèse de Doctorat d'État, Université de Paris IV, 1977, p. 425—427.

9 A. W. *de Groot*, La prose métrique des anciens, Paris 1926; H. *Hagendahl*, La prose métrique d'Arnobe, contribution à la connaissance littéraire de l'Empire, Göteborg 1937.

prose, and on the other hand for acknowledged metrical authors. Table 2 shows the figures for Book I of the Vita Columbae; has in table 1, our analysis is based only on the 434 reliable sentence endings. The remaining 107 *clausulae*, which contain a *hiatus*, will be dealt with towards the end of my paper.

Table 3 gives figures for other Late Latin, especially Christian, writers of the preceding centuries. One can see from a comparison between these two tables that Adomnán does not follow the practice of the good writers of the Early Christian Church who, like the majority of Late Latin authors, used a metrical system based on the combination of the two feet favoured by Cicero: the cretic and the trochee. Out of all the possible combinations, three basic forms were commonly used: cretic-trochee (no. 18 in Hagendahl's classification), dicretic (no. 9) and ditrochee (no. 15). Adomnán's total percentage for these three forms is 32.95. This is lower than the figures for Jerome and Augustine (50.8 % and 53 %), and significantly lower than the frequencies found in virtuosi like Arnobius and Symmachus (80.8 % and 76 %). On the other hand, the difference between this percentage and that of unmetrical prose, which is called relative frequency in my tables, is only 1.13. The calculation of relative frequency is important as it shows the point at which a metrical *clausula* or system is the result of a conscious process and is not merely random. With a relative frequeny of 1.13, Adomnán's use of the three basic *clausulae* is only sligthly higher than that of unmetrical authors and could hardly represent a deliberate system. This modest result does not mean, however, that Adomnán's prose is unmetrical: he could have used a system different from that of the rhetors of Late Antiquity. For instance, we have in these islands the case of Gildas whose percentage for the three basic *clausulae* is only 32.15, but who nevertheless follows an acknowledged metrical system based on the use of the cretic[10]. One should not therefore expect Adomnán's to have followed the canons of composition of the 'good' Late Latin authors. The proper procedure of analysis is then to examine whether he favours any particular *clausulae* and, if so, whether these *clausulae* form a system.

Like Kerlouégan in his study of Gildas's Latin, I have postulated, in my preliminary examination, that *clausulae* with a relative frequency equal to or greater than 1.2 could be considered as favoured, and those with less than 0.8 could be seen as rejected by the author. Between 0.8 and 1.2, *clausulae* would be considered provisionally as neutral. Looking back to the figures on our Table 2, we can suppose that Adomnán favoured the following *clausulae*:

Type 9	- ∪ - - ∪ -,	relative frequency : 2.4
Type 17	- ∪ ∪ - - -,	relative frequency : 2.14
Type 4	- - ∪ ∪ -,	relative frequency : 1.55
Type 8	∪ ∪ - - ∪ -,	relative frequency : 1.28
Type 10	- - - ∪ -,	relative frequency : 1.27
Type 6	- ∪ ∪ - ∪ -,	relative frequency : 1.22

---

10 See *Kerlouégan*, Destinées, p. 421—423.

These *clausulae* have been favoured to the detriment of other sequences, that is to say:

Type 12   ◡ ◡ ◡ - -, relative frequency : 0.42

Type 5   ◡ ◡ ◡ - ◡ -, relative frequency : 0.63

Type 13   - ◡ ◡ ◡ - -, relative frequency : 0.66

Type 14   - ◡ ◡ - -, relative frequency : 0.75

What conclusions can be drawn from these figures?

Firstly we notice that the *clausulae* Adomnán rejects belong to two categories: those consisting of three or more consecutive short syllables (types 12, 5 and 13) and the *clausula heroa* (no. 14). Now, because the *clausula heroa* was the ending of the dactylic hexameter, its avoidance at the end of sentences was one of the golden rules of the Latin grammarians, and this rule was striclty observed by metrical authors. Its frequency is 8.6 % in unmetrical prose, but only 1.9 % in Cicero, 0.4 % in Arnobius, nil in Symmachus, 0.6 % in Jerome, 1.1 % in Augustine and 0.4 % in Cassiodorus. In contrast, Adomnán has a figure of 6.45 % for this *clausula* so it appears that he was not as scrupulous about its use as these authors, but it must be pointed out that he does manage to avoid obvious hexameter endings such as *condere gentem* and *conde sepulchro* which were expressly forbidden by the purists. I have found only four examples of this kind in Book I, that is 0.92 % compared to 3.3 % in unmetrical prose. Although Adomnán is not as strict as Arnobius, Jerome or Cassiodorus, he seems nevertheless to conform to the teaching of the grammarians.

With regard to the *clausulae* which contain a series of three short syllables, types 5 and 12 were neglected by most metrical authors (see Table 3), but type 13 is a special case: it is the well-known Ciceronian *clausula esse uideatur*. As a metrical equivalent of the cretic-trochee (type 18), it was also employed by Lactantius (7.2 %) and Symmachus (5.6 %), who used it more often than Cicero (4.7 %). On the other hand, authors who also cared about accentuation, such as Ammianus Marcellinus and Quodvultdeus, tended to avoid it, because this *clausula* produces three unaccented syllables between the two accents instead of the two or four syllables required[11]. But we have seen that Adomnán is not interested in rhythm. It seems then that, by his modest use of type 13, he wanted, as in the case of types 5 and 12, to avoid using a *clausula* with a sequence of three short syllables.

A similar moderation can be seen in the sequences of four long syllables (types 11 and 19). Without being explicitly rejected, they are found in a smaller proportion than in unmetrical prose (relative frequency 0.81 and 0.83).

One can then perceive in Adomnán's prose a deliberate moderation which corresponds to the precepts of the grammarians: he avoids, on the one hand, the lightness and frivolity of successions of short syllables and, on the other hand, the heaviness of successions of long syllables.

11 See R. *Braun*, Quodvultdeus: Livre des promesses et des prédictions de Dieu, Paris 1964, p. 681 & note 5.

Adomnán's liking for moderation is also illustrated in his choice of metres. These are the cretic which, despite the uneven number of syllables, is perfectly symmetrical, and the three isorrhythmic feet (that is where *arsis* and *thesis* are of equal duration): the anapaest, the dactyl and the spondee. The qualities of equal duration and symmetry are fully highlighted in the dicretic. This happens to be precisely the favourite *clausula* of Adomnán who uses it nearly two and a half times more often than unmetrical authors. The percentage for this *clausula* (5.53) may seem small compared to the 16.8 % of Arnobius or the 18.1 % of Jerome, but it is very near the 5.9 % of Quodvultdeus who, like his model Augustine, follows the pattern of traditional metric, or the 5.02 % of Gildas who also uses it prominently in his system. One must point out that the dicretic was not only sought after by the adherents of the Ciceronian school but also, as Jacques Perret has shown, by the Latin Atticists[12]. This is an interesting point as we will see that, in his other preferred *clausulae*, Adomnán clearly departs from the more widespread Ciceronian practice and appears to follow the tradition of the Attic school of *Kunstprosa* which, despising trochee and ditrochee, favoured isorrhythmic feet. This is obvious in the case of type 17 (anapaest-spondee) and type 4 (spondee-anapaest). For type 17, we have only 1.4 % in Cicero (which is the same percentage as unmetrical prose), no example in Symmachus, 0.6 % in Lactantius, as in Jerome, and 0.8 % in Cassiodorus. Compared to these low figures, Adomnán's 3 % is significant and shows a tendency comparable to the 4.3 % of Sallust for this same *clausula*. A similar trend can be seen in the case of the spondee-anapaest: we have 1.8 % in Cicero, 0.2 % in Arnobius, 0.4 % in Symmachus, 1.3 % in Cassiodorus as against the 7.09 % of Adomnán. This last percentage is smaller than that of Atticists (10.1 % in Sallust, 11.3 % in Livy and 12 % in Brutus), but it is more closely related to their practice than to that of the more common tradition. One will notice that the anapaest-spondee is also found in type 16 but Adomnán tends not to use this sequence because it contains three consecutive short syllables. The dislike of series of short syllables, already discussed for types 5, 12 and 13, is another feature of the Atticists[13]. Jacques Perret has shown that Sallust prefers to use the anapaest-spondee preceded by a long vowel which isolates the two short syllables of the *arsis* of the feet[14]. If Adomnán prefers type 17 to type 16, it is probably for the same reasons.

The remaining three sequences on my list make the following *clausulae*: dactyl-cretic (type 6), anapaest-cretic (type 8) and spondee-cretic (type 10). This last *clausula* is also found in type 11, but Adomnán does not use this sequence because it begins with four long syllables. One can see that the six favoured *clausulae* are all based on the combination of the cretic and isorrhytmic feet and form a logical

12 See J. *Perret*, Salluste et la prose métrique, problèmes de méthode et de perspectives historiques, Revue des Études Anciennes 65 (1963), p. 344 & 347.

13 *Perret*, Salluste et la prose métrique, p. 343—344.

14 *Perret*, Salluste et la prose métrique, p. 336; this effect is not unique to Sallust and it is also found in Cicero.

system. To complete this system, one has to add the cretic-spondee (type 18) to the list. It was provisionally set aside in my preliminary study, but, with a relative frequency of 1.18, it is significant enough to merit inclusion.

The percentage occurrence of the seven *clausulae* of Adomnán's system in the Vita Columbae is 35,02 as against 24.1 % in unmetrical prose, which gives us a relative frequency of 1.45 (see table 4). It is obvious that Adomnán gives less place to his system in his prose than Arnobius or Symmachus in theirs (80.8 % and 76 % respectively), but it is well known that it was not necessary for an author to use a favourite rhythm to excess in order for his readers to appreciate it. We have the example of the famous *clausula esse uideatur* which, according to Tacitus and Quintilian[15], was overused by Cicero, but the percentage for this sequence is only 4.7. In the same way, the discrepancy between a favoured *clausula* and the common practice of unmetrical prose, that is to say relative frequency, did not have to be wide. For instance, Cicero's detractors accused him of making excessive use of the ditrochee[16], but the relative frequency for this *clausula* is 1.33 and again we can see that this is not extreme. Furthermore, if we consider the system as a whole, Adomnán's figures compare quite well with an author like Sallust. The total for the latter's favoured *clausulae* reaches 53 % but the relative frequency is 1.3. With a relative frequency of 1.45, Adomnán's system could easily have been perceived by readers capable of appreciating it. We may add that the *clausulae* of Adomnán's system are rare and difficult to compose. While it is easy to produce dispondee or ditrochee at the end of a Latin sentence, it requires a much more conscious process to make dicretic of anapaest-spondee.

Before reaching a final conclusion, it is necessary to come back to the 107 sentence-endings containing a collision of vowels to see which possibility, *hiatus* or elision, would be more compatible with the system. This was the procedure used by Hagendahl at the end of his analysis of Arnobius's prose. This method is useful on the one hand because it may throw some light on the author's pronunciation, and on the other hand because knowledge of the distribution of these endings may strengthen or weaken our theory. Elision goes against the trend of the Vita Columbae, but *hiatus* confirms our theory: putting the occurrences of *hiatus* together with the other examples, the total percentage for our seven *clausulae* is still roughly the same, that is 34.9, with the same relative frequency of 1.45 (see table 5).

I think therefore that there is evidence to indicate a specific metrical system in Adomnán's prose. The existence of such a system requires the following remarks. At the end of the seventh century, the quantitative system of metrical *clausulae* is giving way to the accentual system of prose rhythm, but it seems that among the Irish, or at least in Iona, the rules of prosody and metric were still taught and put

15 *Tacitus*, Dialogus de oratoribus 23; *Quintilianus*, De institutione oratoria 9, 4, 73.
16 *Cicero*, Orator ad M. Brutum 212—214.

to good use. We know from the *De locis sanctis* that Adomnán knew the terminology of prosody and that he could tell the difference between long and short vowels[17]. Moreover, the care with which he avoids the heroic *clausula* and the rarity with which he uses the successions of long and short syllables show that he must have known the traditional rules of the *compositio uerborum*. However, while most Late Latin and Early Christian writers employed the traditional Ciceronian system based on the combination of the cretic and the trochee, Adomnán gives his preference to a system based on the cretic and the isorrhythmic feet. The choice of such a system can only be explained in the context of the theories of the Atticists about *Kunstprosa*. It is true that Cicero speaks of the use of the dactyl or the spondee at the end of the period, but with reservation. However those feet are praised for their greatness, dignity, gravity and nobleness by the theoreticians of the Attic tradition like Dionysius of Halicarnassus, Hermogenes, or Pseudo-Longinus[18]. Dionysius also praised the cretic for its nobility. One can then understand why Adomnán should have favoured the combination of the cretic with the three isorrhythmic feet: his *Vita Columbae* had to be written in a tone dignified and grave enough to suit not only the greatness and the nobility of Columba, but also the seriousness and the gravity of its author. Moreover, let us remember that these feet were recommended for the writing of great historical works: we find them in Sallust and Livy as well as in Thucydides. But, contrary to the Latin historians, we do not find in Adomnán the combination of dactyls and spondees which was expressly forbidden by the grammarians. This seems to confirm the character of conservatism and obedience to the rules which can be observed in the syntax of the *Vita Columbae*[19].

Now our interpretation of Adomnán's system leads to further questions. How did the Irish come to know at least part of the tradition of the Attic *Kunstprosa*? Was the knowledge limited to Iona or did it reach other monasteries in Ireland? Research into the rhythms of the prose of insular authors has only recently begun and an examination of more texts would be required. However, I have analysed all the sentence endings of the works of two other seventh century Irish hagiographers: Cogitosus's *Vita Brigitae* and Muirchú's *Vita Patricii*. Neither of these writers follows the rules of *cursus*, but they show preference for certain metrical *clausulae*. Cogitosus seems to favour a different system based on the use of the cretic, anapaest and trochee, but Muirchú follows a system similar to that of Adomnán. Although he is not as strict as Adomnán in avoiding the use of the sequence of three short syllables and four long syllables, his favourite *clausulae* are also spondee-anapaest, dactyl-cretic, anapaest-cretic, dicretic, spondee-cretic, anapaest-spondee and cretic-spondee. His total for these *clausulae* is 41.17 %, with

17 De locis sanctis 2, 27, 6.
18 See *Perret*, Salluste et la prose métrique, p. 343—344 & 348.
19 See J.-M. *Picard*, Une préfiguration du latin carolingien: la syntaxe de la *Vita Columbae* d'Adomnán, auteur irlandais du VIIᵉ siècle, Romanobarbarica 6 (1981—82), p. 235—89.

a relative frequency of 1.46, figures which are somewhat higher than Adomnán's (see table 6).

As regards the problem of the transmission of the Attic system, it would hardly be possible to see Adomnán as a successor of Dionysius of Halicarnassus or Hermogenes and, on the Latin side, a knowledge of Sallust or Livy is not very likely. It is true, though, that Adomnán, who undoubtedly wants to present himself as *historicus*, uses some Sallustian devices, most of which he could have known through the works of Sulpicius Severus and which could also have been the remnants of the teaching of the Gaulish masters of the fifth century[20]. But these masters did not teach the use of the Attic system of metrical prose, as the metric of the fifth century Gaulish rhetors belongs to the Ciceronian tradition. On the other hand, even if Adomnán had known parts of Sallust, that in itself would not have been sufficient to revive the old Attic system. The adornment of *clausulae* was an artificial technique and would have had to be formally taught.

Research in the texts of the Latin grammarians might then give us some clues. It is true that none of them mentions the Attic system of *clausulae*, but they do not specify the three basic *clausulae* of the more common system either. No-one can deny, however, that the latter was taught and that its use was widespread among Late Latin authors. Elements of an oral tradition in the teaching of *Kunstprosa* must also be taken into account. Moreover, the Late Latin grammarians did not recommend the exclusive use of a system based on Ciceronian feet: for instance Terentianus Maurus advocates a system where prominence is given to the cretic and Pompeius Messalinus gives a list of feet used by Sallust[21]. Among the various systems given by Rufinus of Antioch, a fifth-century grammarian, we even find mention of a school of rhetors, who, like the late theoreticians of Attic prose Hermogenes and Pseudo-Longinus, recommend the use of the spondee and the dactylic feet for writing history or the lives of remarkable men and for apologetic purposes[22]. Is this to say that the precepts of the Atticist school of *Kunstprosa* were still taught in Antioch in the fifth century? Research in metrical prose is still a marginal area of post-classical studies and one would need to examine Byzantine authors in order to give a definite answer. However, it is possible that texts such as that of Rufinus of Antioch may have reached Ireland. We know from the studies of Father Martin McNamara the importance of the school of Antioch in Irish

20 About the importance of Sallust in the teaching of Latin in the Early Medieval period, see G. *Glauche*, Schullektüre im Mittelalter. Entstehung und Wandlungen des Lektürekanons bis 1200 nach den Quellen dargestellt, München 1970, passim.

21 Terentianus Maurus, De metris, 1428—1444 (ed. H. *Keil*, Grammatici latini, reprint Hildesheim 1961, vol. 6, p. 368; Pompeius Messalinus is cited by Rufinus, Commentarius de numeris oratorum (ed. *Keil*, Grammatici latini, vol. 6, p. 575).

22 Rufinus, Commentarius de numeris oratorum (ed. *Keil*, Grammatici latini, vol. 6, p. 566—567): *Spondeo narrare solent rhetores acta, quod grauis et tardus res gestas mentibus adfert; dactylicis certant pedibus, quia currere possunt; dicimus egregios Theopompi more labores, et uitam insignem laudamus Isocratis arte: hic stilus historiis, hic laudibus aptior haeret.*

biblical exegesis[23]. We also know that exposition of the Scriptures and the teaching of grammar often went hand in hand[24]. If a tradition of Atticism was still alive in the East, there is no reason why it could not have travelled to Ireland in the same way as the works of Theodore of Mopsuestia did. As I have said, there remains a good deal of research to be done on the Irish side as well as on possible foreign influences, and I am sure that further studies in this field can only yield interesting results as to the nature and origin of Latin learning in Early Christian Ireland[25].

23 *McNamara*, Psalter text and Psalter study in the Early Irish Church (AD 600—1200), PRIA 73 C (1973), p. 255—257.

24 See *McNamara*, Psalter text and Psalter study, p. 259.

25 I wish to thank Jacques Perret and François Kerlouégan for their comments on this article while in preparation. The ideas expressed and the errors are entirely my own responsibility.

Table 1: The rhythmical *clausulae* of Adomnán's *Vita Columbae*

Type of cadence	Example	Observed frequency	Expected frequency	X^2 $\dfrac{(of - ef)^2}{ef}$
6p	uaticinatiónem	6	—	—
6pp	confabulámini	4	—	—
1 5p	húc sepeliétur	2	2	0
p 5p	decapitáti disperiérunt	18	16	0.250
pp 5p	perspíciens speculabátur	5	7	0.571
1 5pp		0	1	1
p 5pp	sóli disperíerant	5	5	0
pp 5pp	mirábilem praesciéntiam	3	2	0.5
p 1 4p	fuísse sunt conprobáta	3 ⎫ 6	5	0.2
pp 1 4p	bréuiter sunt demonstránda	3 ⎭		
p 4p	osculátus benedíxit	39	39	0
pp 4p	tángere uidebátur	15	16	0.062
p 1 4pp	prolocútus est tempóribus	1 ⎫ 4	3	0.333
pp 1 4pp	penitúdinem mox aduéniet	3 ⎭		
p 4pp	acéruo sepéliunt	25	26	0.038
pp 4pp	humíliter expóstulat	11	10	0.1
p 1 3p	sánctus sic profátus	6 ⎫ 8	7	0.142
pp 1 3 p	tempóribus sunt expléta	2 ⎭		
p 3p	perpéssos sanáuit	52	57	0.438
pp 3p	ouículas minábat	27	23	0.695
p 1 3pp	sánctum non látuit	5 ⎫ 5	6	0.166
pp 1 3pp	—	0 ⎭		
p 3pp	habére méruit	42	44	0.09
pp 3pp	fíeri mónacus	20	18	0.222
p 1 2	potítus es párte	6 ⎫ 9	10	0.1
pp 1 2	mónacus non érit	3 ⎭		
p 2 2	humánus áptus érit	18 ⎫		
pp 2 2	ínerant náutae uídent	3 ⎬ 81	74	0.662
p 2	potestáte súmus	60 ⎭		
pp 2	práecipit díe	24	30	1.2
1	confiteri uúlt	23	—	—
Sum total		434		6.769

267

Table 2: Adomnán's *Vita Columbae*, Book 1
Repartition of metrical *clausulae* according to Hagendahl's classification

Type of *clausula*	Observed frequency	Percent	Percent unmetrical prose	Relative frequency
1. ⏑⏑⏑⏒	14	3.23	3.2	1.01
2. ⏑⏑-⏑⏑⏒	6	1.38	1.2	1.15
3. -⏑-⏑⏑⏒	8	1.84	2.1	0.88
4. --⏑⏑⏒	33	7.6	4.9	1.55
5. ⏑⏑⏑-⏑⏒	3	0.69	1.1	0.63
6. -⏑⏑-⏑⏒	9	2.07	1.7	1.22
7. -⏑-⏑⏒	22	5.07	4.6	1.1
8. ⏑⏑--⏑⏒	10	2.3	1.8	1.28
9. -⏑--⏑⏒	24	5.53	2.3	2.4
10. ⏑---⏑⏒	21	4.84	3.8	1.27
11. ----⏑⏒	21	4.84	5.8	0.83
12. ⏑⏑⏑⏑-⏒	2	0.46	1.1	0.42
13. -⏑⏑⏑-⏒	8	1.84	2.8	0.66
14. -⏑⏑-⏒	28	6.45	8.6	0.75
15. -⏑-⏒	77	17.74	18.9	0.94
16. ⏑⏑⏑--⏒	10	2.3	2	1.15
17. -⏑⏑--⏒	13	3	1.4	2.14
18. -⏑--⏒	42	9.68	8.2	1.18
19. ---⏒	83	19.12	23.7	0.81
Total	434	99.98	99.2	1

Table 3: Percentages of metrical *clausulae* for Cicero and Late Latin authors of the Ciceronian tradition (2nd-6th cent.) compared to unmetrical prose

No.	Type of clausula	Unmetrical prose	Cicero	Arnobius	Lactantius	Symmachus	Ammianus Marcellinus	Jerome	Augustine	Quodvultdeus	Cassiodorus
1.	◡◡◡⏓	3.2	2.3	0.1	0.9	0.5	0.4	0.7		2.2	1.5
2.	◡◡-◡◡⏓	1.2	0.5	0.5	0.8	0	0.4	0.8		0.5	0
3.	-◡-◡◡⏓	2.1	2.8	2.5	5.2	7.4	1.4	18.1	3.7	4.1	7.1
4.	--◡◡⏓	4.9	1.8	0.2	1.7	0.4	0.9	2.8		1.8	1.3
5.	◡◡◡-◡⏓	1.1	0.5	0.2	0.8	0.7	0.4	0.8		0.5	0.4
6.	-◡◡-◡⏓	1.7	1.2	0.4	0.3	0.2	1.8	2.2		2.1	0.4
7.	-◡-◡⏓	4.6	4.9	0.7	5	3.5	4.6	3.4		4.1	0.4
8.	◡◡-◡⏓	1.8	4.1	2.4	1.2	0.9	0.4	1.7		2.5	0.6
9.	-◡-◡⏓	2.3	8.3	16.8	10.8	19.5	4.6	18.1	10.6	5.9	11.2
10.	◡---◡⏓	3.8	4.2	0.8	2	0	0.9	2.5		4.1	0.2
11.	---◡⏓	5.8	9.7	0.9	3.3	1.3	2.7	4		4.5	1.3
12.	◡◡◡-⏓	1.1	1	0.2	0.1	0.7	0.9	0.3		0.7	2.9
13.	-◡◡◡-⏓	2.8	4.7	1.9	7.2	5.6	0.4	3.1	3.5	0.9	4.8
14.	-◡◡-⏓	8.6	1.9	0.4	1.4	0	1.8	0.6	1.1	3.4	0.4
15.	-◡-⏓	18.9	25.3	26	24.4	33.8	20.5 *	15.3	15.5	14.8	30.6
16.	◡◡◡--⏓	2	2.8	1.5	6.4	1.3	2.3	2.3	0.4	1.9	0
17.	-◡◡--⏓	1.4	1.4	2.7	0.6	0	2.3	0.6		3.7	0.8
18.	-◡--⏓	8.2	16.2	37.9	24.7	22.8	22.8	17.3	27	20.3	29
19.	---⏓	23.7	6.4	3.6	3	1.3	30.6	4.2	12.5	18.6	7

These percentages are based on the figures given by H. *Hagendahl* (La prose métrique d'Arnobe, Göteborg 1937) and R. *Braun* (Quodvultdeus, Livre des promesses et des prédictions de Dieu, t. 2, Paris 1964, pp. 675—692).

Table 4: Adomnán's metrical system

Type of *clausula*	Observed frequency	Percent	Relative frequency
1. Dicretic (no 9: - ∪ - - ∪ -)	24	5.53	2.4
2. Anapaest-spondee (no 17: ∪ ∪ - - -)	13	3	2.14
3. Spondee-anapaest (no 4: - - ∪ ∪ -)	33	7.6	1.55
4. Anapaest-cretic (no 8: ∪ ∪ - - ∪ -)	10	2.3	1.28
5. Spondee-cretic (no 10: - - - ∪ -)	21	4.84	1.27
6. Dactyl-cretic (no 6: - ∪ ∪ - ∪ -)	9	2.07	1.22
7. Cretic-spondee (no 18: - ∪ - - -)	42	9.68	1.18
Total	152	35.02	1.45

Table 5: The metrical *clausulae* of Adomnán's *Vita Columbae* including hiatus

Type of *clausula*	observed frequency	percent	percent unmetrical prose	relative frequency
1. ∪ ∪ ∪ ͝	19	3.51	3.2	1.09
2. ∪ ∪ - ∪ ∪ ͝	8	1.47	1.2	1.22
3. - ∪ - ∪ ∪ ͝	10	1.84	2.1	0.88
*4. - - ∪ ∪ ͝	41	7.57	4.9	1.54
5. ∪ ∪ ∪ - ∪ ͝	4	0.73	1.1	0.66
*6. - ∪ ∪ - ∪ ͝	13	2.40	1.7	1.41
7. - ∪ - ∪ ͝	28	5.17	4.6	1.12
*8. ∪ ∪ - - ∪ ͝	12	2.21	1.8	1.22
*9. - ∪ - - ∪ ͝	30	5.54	2.3	2.4
*10. ∪ - - - ∪ ͝	31	5.73	3.8	1.5
11. - - - - ∪ ͝	29	5.36	5.8	0.92
12. ∪ ∪ ∪ ∪ ͝	2	0.36	1.1	0.32
13. - ∪ ∪ ∪ - ͝	9	1.66	2.8	0.59
14. - ∪ ∪ - ͝	36	6.65	8.6	0.77
15. - ∪ - ͝	82	15.15	18.9	0.80
16. ∪ ∪ ∪ - - ͝	11	2.03	2.0	1.01

270

Type of clausula	observed frequency	percent	percent unmetrical prose	relative frequency
*17. – ◡◡ – – ×	14	2.58	1.4	1.84
*18. – ◡ – – ×	48	8.87	8.2	1.08
19. – – – ×	114	21.07	23.7	0.88
Total	541	99.90	99.2	1.00

Total percentage for the clausulae of Adomnán system: 34.9; relative frequency: 1.45.

Table 6: Muirchú's *Vita Patricii*
Metrical *clausulae*

Type of clausula	observed frequency	Percent	Percent unmetrical prose	Relative frequency
1. ◡ ◡ ◡ ×	11	5.09	3.2	1.59
2. ◡ ◡ – ◡ ◡ ×	1	0.46	1.2	0.38
3. – ◡ – ◡ ◡ ×	2	0.92	2.1	0.43
*4. – – ◡ ◡ ×	17	7.87	4.9	1.60
5. ◡ ◡ ◡ – ◡ ×	2	0.92	1.1	0.83
*6. – ◡ ◡ – ◡ ×	8	3.70	1.7	2.17
7. – ◡ – ◡ ×	6	2.77	4.6	0.60
*8. ◡ ◡ – – ◡ ×	6	2.77	1.8	1.53
*9. – ◡ – – ◡ ×	7	3.24	2.3	1.40
*10. ◡ – – – ◡ ×	6	2.77	3.8	0.72
11. – – – – ◡ ×	18	8.33	5.8	1.43
12. ◡ ◡ ◡ ◡ – ×	1	0.46	1.1	0.41
13. – ◡ ◡ ◡ – ×	2	0.92	2.8	0.32
14. – ◡ ◡ – ×	13	6.01	8.6	0.69
15. – ◡ – ×	29	13.42	18.9	0.71
*16. ◡ ◡ ◡ – – ×	6	2.77	2.0	1.38
*17. – ◡ ◡ – – ×	6	2.77	1.4	1.97
*18. – ◡ – – ×	21	9.72	8.2	1.18
19. – – – ×	54	25.00	23.7	1.05
Total	216	99.91	99.2	1.00

Some palaeographical and linguistic features in early Lives of Birgit

By
Seán Connolly

The single most noteworthy graphic feature of the Rawlinson MS B 512, which alone has preserved the *Bethu Brigte (BB)* or Old Irish Life of Brigit, is the very frequent addition, omission or misgrouping of minims. This is compounded by the confusion of the letters *u* and 'open *a*'. Even a cursory reading of the recent critical edition of the *Bethu Brigte*[1] reveals how frequent are emendations adding or deleting letters like *i, n, m, h* or *l,* or having to do with the regrouping of minims as in the letters *m* or the words *in, ni* or *hi*. Some of the more obvious examples[2] are *am chaince* for *ain chaince* 5; *am* for *ar ni* 450; *immum* for *immimm* 103; *mara* for *mira* 46; *manan-thi* for *manim-thi* 243; *arnachim-erla* for (suggested) *arnachin-erla* 439; *namique* for *namque* 446; *asan* for *asin* 477; *aluiriga* for *al* (i.e. *ol*) *auriga.* 99; *imundus* for *mundus* 228. Perhaps the most illustrative example is the reading *indius* 354 which Dr Ó hAodha has emended to *in dus*, following Eleanor Knott[3]. Her conjecture is that *indius* is a misreading of *in dús = in dtuus* 'at first'. In other words, the scribe added one minim. The emendation to *in dús* is substantially correct and is supported by the word *prius* of the Latin pendant in *Vita I*[4]. However, it is at least equally probable that in his exemplar the scribe had before him the form *induus* and dropped one of the minims of the first *u*.

To anyone accustomed to deciphering codices, especially in insular script, such scribal errors are run of the mill but in Rawlinson B 512 they are so numerous as

---

1 Ed. by Dr Donncha Ó hAodha, Dublin Institute for Advanced Studies 1978, and referred to in this article as *BB*.

2 References are to line numbers of text in *BB*.

3 Ériu 14 (1943), p. 146.

4 *Vita Prima Sanctae Brigitae* (here abbreviated to *VP*) so-called because it comes first in the series of Latin Lives of St Brigit published by the Bollandists in *Acta Sanctorum, Februarius* I. For both *VP* and the *Vita Sanctae Brigitae* by Cogitosus references in this article are to page, section and paragraph of the 1658 edition of AA SS. The *VP* was critically edited with introduction, linguistic commentary and indexes by the writer of the present article under the supervision of the late Prof. L. Bieler and submitted in 1970 as a dissertation for the degree of Ph. D. of the National University of Ireland. It is shortly to be published in CCSL. In many passages the text of my edition differs appreciably from that of the Bollandists which is based on fewer and less reliable manuscripts. In this article I quote from my own edition, giving the reference to the corresponding passage in the AA SS. The same applies to the *Vita Sanctae Brigitae* by Cogitosus of which I am currently preparing a critical edition. Portion of the *VP* corresponds closely, sometimes almost verbatim, to *BB*, hence the frequent mention of pendants in one or the other.

to have posed awkward editorial problems, some unresolved, others, in my view, resolved unsatisfactorily. One such occurs on line 186 of *BB* where the codex reads: *Post haec obtuilit pleps locum ubi nomine Ached hI in Saltu Avis.* Here Dr Ó hAodha follows the Irish Texts edition[5] and says to read *cui nomen* for *ubi nomine.* To me the *lenior medela* would be to read *ibi* for *ubi*, i.e. reduce the *u* of *ubi* by one minim: *Post haec obtuilit pleps locum ibi, nomine Ached hI, in Saltu Avis.* 'Afterwards the people offered her a place there in Saltus Avis called Ached hÍ.' This emendation not only makes good sense but does less violence to the text and is in line with the scribe's habit of misreading minims. Another garbled reading which has so far defied all editors occurs on line 134. Dr Ó hAodha leaves it unresolved and prints the sentence as follows: *Maceram tunc virgini rex donat, eaque pretiosam inn-.* The crux is the word after *pretiosam* which in *BB* is printed *inn-.* The Irish Texts edition has *hinqto.* In the apparatus criticus Dr Ó hAodha says: '*inn* is followed by a character like a *c* with the lower stroke continued downwards perpendicularly. Over this is *vel* o.' He has reservations about Grosjean's suggestion[6] that the text was a corruption of *eaque patri donavit.* Personally, I do not believe any such elaborate emendation as Grosjean's is called for and suggest reading: *Maceram tunc virgini rex donat eamque pretiosam nimis.* Emending *eaque* to *eamque* poses little difficulty because our scribe often omits nasal suspensions. For the rest, the explanation, as I see it, is this: in the exemplar the ending of the last word was unclear, the final letter possibly being an ill-formed, blurred or partly obliterated *s* which the scribe first copied as a *c* and later doctored into an *s* by adding a descender. Admittedly this would still be two minims short of the number required for *nimis* but that is no cause for surprise considering our scribe's wholesale neglect of minims and his poor knowledge of Latin. Afterwards a corrector wrote *vel o* above the last letter to suggest emending the word to *nimio.* The meaning of the sentence then would be: 'Then the king gives a sword, and that an exceedingly precious one, to the maiden.'

In *BB* line 356 we meet the curious word *manach* for the devil. This may be a variant of the word *monach* which, among other things, can mean 'trickster'[7], a meaning which would fit quite well here. But Irish scholars seem to be in some doubt about the word in this context. Hogan[8] thought it might be a mistake for *námait.* The pendant in *Vita Prima (VP)* has *inimicum* which would lend plausibility to this view. Dr Ó hAodha says 'this would take us far from the MS reading'[9]. I am not so sure that it does, considering the nature and frequency of scribal blunders in the codex. The number of minims in the phrase *in manach* is fifteen, allowing one minim for *c* which could be the second element of an ill-formed *a.*

5 Irish Texts i, 1931, p. 2—16.
6 AB 59 (1941), p. 319—22.
7 DIL, s.v. *monach.*
8 Edmund *Hogan*, S. J., The Latin Lives of the Saints, Todd Lecture series, RIA, 5, p. 74.
9 *BB* p. 56.

The phrase *in námait* by the same token would have fourteen minims. One might even with some plausibility suggest that *in manach* is a garbling of the word *inimicum* which on the same reckoning amounts to fourteen minims. However, this is no more than a conjecture. The last instance of an editorial problem in *BB* which may be resolved in this way is the word which appears in Dr Ó hAodha's edition on line 235 as *mim*. The Irish Texts editors read *inim*. The Latin conjunction *enim* would fit the meaning but since it cannot come first in a sentence it must be ruled out. I submit that the correct reading is *nam*. Like *mim* and *inim* it consists of seven minims, the third and fourth being accounted for by 'open *a*'. The text then would run: '*Ni rag-sa tra*', *ar in clam*, '*on c[h]u[u]ch rom-icc: nam minister ero 7 lignarius vester*'. 'I shall not go', said the leper, 'from the cup which has healed me, for I shall be your servant and woodman'.

Another graphic feature of Rawlinson B 512 is the transposition of letters. Examples are *fraxeinum* for *fraxineum* 176, *sainruith* for *sainriuth* 12 and *eustutis* for *aestatis* 430, the last two being instances of vowel metathesis. Now, on line 78 the MS reading is *senior caillige craibdigi*, 'an old pious nun' (thus Ó hAodha, who adds 'but *senior* really means a nun who was a religious superior'[10]). Personally I am of the view that the word *senior* is not a Latin word in this instance but a vowel metathesis for the Irish word *senoir*. In the Contributions to a Dictionary of the Irish Language under the headword *caillech* which literally means 'a veiled one', hence 'a nun', we find the lemma *senoir caildidi* 'senior nun' and then in brackets' (opposed to *mac-caillige* 'a young nun'). Since *senóir caillige* is an attested Irish form I feel that this is what was intended here but misspelt by the scribe or in his exemplar. The reading *eustutis* for *aestatis* 430 already referred to exemplifies not only vowel metathesis but the confusion of *u* and 'open *a*' which is common in this codex, e.g. *alterum* for *alteram* 68, *manam* for *manum* 222, *paruliticas* for *paraliticas* (recte *paralyticas*) 272, *campam* for *campum* 296, *circamfunde* for *circumfunde* 307 and *recusabunt* for *recusabant* 546. Our scribe also often omits nasal suspensions and other letters, especially finals, e.g. *iteri* for *interim* 176, *commess* for *commessa (comesa)* 68 and so on. A typically Irish or insular scribal error occurs on line 371 where the codex has *favefactae* for *pavefactae*. The same kind of error occurs in two of the earliest and best MSS of *VP* viz. BL, MS Add. 34124 and Zürich, Zentralbibliothek, MS Rheinau 81 which have *proferemus* for *properemus*[11]. This shows that their exemplar was written in insular script in which, on account of the shape of the letter *f*, an imperfectly formed *p* could be mistaken for it or vice versa.

Returning to a feature just mentioned, namely, the omission of letters, Dr Ó hAodha is in most cases quite right to restore. However, in a few instances I would question his decision to do so. Take the phrase *post tergum* 131/132. Here the Rawlinson codex has *postergum* (one *t*). In all the older codices of *VP* we find

10 *BB* p. 41.
11 AA SS 130E 84.

postergum. The same form occurs frequently in the *Vita Metrica*[12] and indeed seems to be the one generally used in Hiberno-Latin writings. The final *-t* of *post* was dropped in certain environments even in classical Latin. Cicero in his *Orator* 4 157, beside *postmeridianas*, has *pomeridianas* from *posmeridianas*. Likewise Quintilian, *Institutiones* IX 4. 39, has *pomeridiem* from *posmeridiem* (cf. Italian 'pomeriggio'). *Pos* for *post* was common in inscriptions and vulgar Latin texts, e.g. Pompei[13] 6820 *pos fata*, 4966 *posquam* and even 2058 *pos Idus*. Grandgent says: 'According to Velius Longus, Cicero favored *posmeridianus;* Marius Victorinus preferred *posquam*'[14]. In the Romance languages it is only the reduced form of *post* that has survived: cf. French 'puis', Spanish 'pues', Provençal and Portuguese 'pos' and Italian 'poi'. To return to the expression *post tergum*, it is worth pointing out that in six out of seven instances in Gregory of Tours it appears as *postergum*. Examples of the same kind too numerous to list from several other authors of this period show that the form was well established in Late Latin and should have been left unchanged in *Bethu Brigte*. In this connection it is interesting to note that in the Appendix to *Bethu Brigte* in Rawlinson B 512 the form *poste* (abbreviated to p°e) occurs. Dr Ó hAodha emends to poste[a] without comment in his notes or apparatus. Admittedly, *poste* would be unlikely in a Latin document of this date but it should at least have been adverted to as a form well attested in Latin as far back as Ennius, *Annales* 230 *poste recumbite* and Plautus, *Asinaria* 915, *Menaechmi* 838 and passim.

The words *parvulus* and *pluvia* appear in the forms *parulo* and *pluiam* on lines 273 and 559 respectively of *BB*. Both are interesting and in my opinion ought to have been allowed to stand in the text with perhaps an explanatory note in the apparatus. Forms like *parulo* have a long history in Latin and are accounted for by the fact that before the homorganic vowels *o* and *u*, the semivowel *u* in medial position tended to disappear from the very earliest times. Thus archaic Latin *deiuos* and *Gnaiuos* become *deus* (through **deuos, *deos*) and *Gnaeus; *deuorsum* and **seuorsum* become *deorsum* and *seorsum*. As late as the Appendix Probi spellings of the same kind as *parulo* are proscribed: cf. App. Pr. 29 *auus non aus*, 174 *riuus non rius* (cf. Italian, Spanish and Portuguese 'rio') and 176 *pauor non paor* (cf. Fr. 'peur', It. 'paura'). In the Zürich MS of *Vita Prima s. Brigitae* the words *seruus* and *longeuus* appear as *serus* and *longeus*. In explanation of the form *pluiam* it should be pointed out that when *i* or *u* preceded a vowel of a different quality thus forming two syllables, there developed between the two syllables a transitional semivowel, *j*

12   Vita Metrica Sanctae Brigidae, ed. D. N. *Kissane*, PRIA 77 C 3, verses 809 and 1448; the form *posterga* occurs in verse 1122.

13   C. *Zangemeister*, ed., Inscriptiones parietariae Pompeianae ..., Corpus Inscriptionum Latinarum 4 and Suppl. 1, Berlin 1871, 1898.

14   An Introduction to Vulgar Latin, New York 1962, p. 121; cf. E. *Seelmann*, Die Aussprache des Latein nach physiologisch-historischen Grundsätzen, Heilbronn 1885, p. 368.

after *i* and *v* after *u*. Here it should be recalled that the use of the characters *j* and minuscule *v* in Latin to represent the semivocalic values of *i* and *u* is quite recent. They were introduced by the humanists, especially the French philosopher and grammarian, Pierre La Ramée (1515—1572), from whom they get their name 'lettres ramistes'. These parasitic phonemes were not normally represented in the written word but only in speech. So whereas *diu* was the written form, it was pronounced *diju;* likewise *pluit* was pronounced *pluvit, duo* pronounced *duvo* (*v* sounding like *w*), *uia* pronounced *uija* and so on[15]. The letter *v* was sometimes dropped even where it was original as in *struo* for *struvo* from **strug^{v}o, fluo* for *fluvo* from **flug^{v}o, frui* for *fruvi* from **frug^{v}i.* Cf. the form *fluvius* beside *fluo.* However, as the Latin alphabet made no distinction between *i* and *j* or *u* and *v,* spellings like *iventa* 'youth' and *plvia* 'rain' eventually came to be written *ivventa* and *plvvia* to avoid ambiguity[16]. It is doubtless from a form such as *pluia* which developed into **ploja* that French 'pluie' and Italian 'pioggia' have descended. But apart from the fact that it is linguistically interesting, an added reason for not emending *pluiam* is that it is a spelling particularly widespread in Hiberno-Latin texts. An instance of a related feature is the word *boellium* which occurs in Cogitosus's *Vita s. Brigitae*[17]. This word, of which I have so far discovered some eight or nine variants, one spelt *bubīle* and all the rest beginning with either *bov-* or, exceptionally, *bob-,* has been borrowed into Irish as *buaile* (Anglo-Irish 'booley' and 'booleying'). It means 'a cow-byre' and most probably is a by-form of *bovilium,* itself a by-form of *būbīle.* The *-ī-,* as frequently happens, changes to *e* and the *-v-* disappears as in *pluia.* Hence *boellium.*

In the Zürich MS of *VP* already referred to we meet the form *equs* for *equus.* Similar spellings occur nine or ten times in the *Vita Metrica s. Brigitae,* e. g. line 596 *locuntur* (one MS *loquntur*), line 1134 *lincunt* for *linquunt;* also *langor,* line 744 and elsewhere. These forms trace back to early Latin when *qu-* and *gu-*were reduced to *q-* and *g-* before the vowels *u* and *o.* Hence the form *secundus* 'the one following' which is an old participle of *sequor* with the exceptional form ending in *-undus* like *oriundus* from *orior.* In Virgil's Aeneid VII 651 the expression *equum domitor* 'tamer of horses' appears in some MSS as *ecum domitor* (*equum* being the old genitive plural). Later on, from the 2nd to the 4th century, *qu* was reduced to *q* before the

---

15 In the *Vita Metrica s. B.* verse 1101 one codex has a variant, *sepius* for *sepibus,* which is rather interesting in the present context. In the *Vita Metrica u* for *b* is especially frequent, e.g. *(h)aven(ae)* six times for *habenae, cavallus* twice for *caballus* and *libida* for *livida* (the reverse phenomenon). *Sepius* for *sepibus* may, of course, be a mere scribal blunder. On the other hand it could indicate that *sepius* represents a pronunciation *sepiuus.*

16 Cf. M. *Niedermann,* Phonétique historique du latin, Paris 1953, p. 104—107.

17 Cf. AA SS 137D 19 where the corrupt reading *boekium* is received. The best MSS read *boellium. Ernout* and *Meillet,* Dictionnaire étymologique de la langue française, Paris 1959, s.v. *bos* cite the form *bubīle* and add: 'irl(andais) *buaile*'. But *boellium* is more likely to have been the direct ancestor of *buaile,* since the borrowing would comply with the rule for borrowings into Irish: the loss of the final syllable plus one *mora.*

other vowels *a, e* and *i* and so we have in the *Vita Prima* and *Bethu Brigte coccīna* for *coquīna* 'kitchen', from which the Irish loan-word *cucann* derives. Similarly through a reduction of *quaestio* to *qestio* we get Irish *ceist* 'question'; *quadragesima* reduced to *qaragesma* (French 'Carême') gives Irish *corgus* (Mod. Ir. 'carghas'). In the Milan Glosses we have the form *aequinocht* beside *ecenocht* from Latin *aequinoctium* obviously reduced to *equinoctium* or *ecinoctium*[18]. The word *inquisita* in *VP*[19] appears as *incessita* in the manuscrit de base, L (BL MS Add. 34124, 9th cent.) and as *incesta* in the second oldest MS, Z (= Zürich, Zentralbibliothek, MS Rheinau 81, 10th cent.). In Secundinus's Hymn on St Patrick in the Antiphonary of Bangor, verse 54, *quisquilia* is spelt *cescilia*. The same process took place with *gu-* + vowel as is evident from doublets like *unguo* and *ungo* 'I smear' and *unguella, ungella* 'a little claw'. Thus in *BB* 307 *sanguine* is spelt *sangine*.

These and other spellings to be discussed presently shed light on the pronunciation of Latin in Ireland at different periods. In *BB* we find the spellings *usci (cuad n-usci)* 232 beside *usque* 284, to cite but two examples. Inversely *vertice* is spelt *vertique* 304, which shows that *c* before a front vowel was still sounded as *k* at least when the archetype of *Bethu Brigte* was written. The form *sangine* for *sanguine* shows the same thing in reverse, i.e. *g-* + front vowel was still velar not affricate as in later Latin (Church) pronunciation. On the other hand, beside these spellings the Rawlinson B 512 has several which are late, indicating palatalization of *c* before a front vowel, e.g. *ansilla* 9, *sussepit* 299, *nesio* 304, *seperunt* 399. It is worth noting that in Irish itself the same fluctuation in the pronunciation of Latin loanwords is found, e.g. *caingeal* and *cainseal* for *cancellus*, *cearcal* and *siorcal* for *circulus*, *ciombal* and *siombail* for *cymbalum*, *selam* and *celam* for *caelum*.

Idiomatic and Syntactic Features.

The use of *cum* for *ab* to express agency has often been pointed out as a Hibernicism in Latin texts of Irish provenance. For example in *VP* we are told that 'a certain leper came to St Brigit that his clothes might be washed by her', *quidam leprosus venit ad sanctam Brigitam ut cum ea sua vestimenta lavarentur*[20]. And again the saint was once asked to go to a certain king *ad liberandum virum qui erat in vinculis cum rege*[21] 'to free a man who was imprisoned by the king' (Modern Irish would say *fear a bhí i slabhraí (i ngéibheann) ag an rí*. Old Irish would say ... *lasind ríg* for *cum rege*). In his monograph on the Hiberno-Latin grammarian Malsachanus, Bengt Löfstedt insists that this use of *cum* for *ab* is not confined to

18 Thes. I, Ml. 111a9.
19 AA SS 133C 101.
20 AA SS 125D 54.
21 AA SS 129C 75.

277

Hiberno-Latin and cannot be claimed as a pure Hibernicism[22]. A scholar named Graur maintained that the substitution of *cum* for *ab* was confined to Gaulish Latin and was due to the influence of a Celtic substratum. Löfstedt thinks this thesis insufficiently supported, pointing to similar semantic shifts in other languages where a Celtic influence is out of the question. However, he does make two concessions: (1) ‚Wichtig ist Graurs Hinweis auf entsprechende Bedeutungserweiterung der Präpositionen im Angloirischen und in den frz. Mundarten der Bretagne. (Vgl. die von P. L. *Henry*, An Anglo-Irish Dialect of North Roscommon, [Zürich 1957] 142 angeführten Belege, z. B. *He was killed with a motorcar*.); and (2) ‚es ist möglich, in bezug auf die Verwendung von *cum* für *ab* nicht unwahrscheinlich, daß sie in Gallien und Irland durch keltische Sprachgewohnheiten gefördert wurde.‘

The use of *cum* to denote ownership or possession in exactly the same way as its counterpart *la* in Old Irish is attested more than once in *VP*. For example, *Brigita dixit (mago): 'Tuae vaccae tecum sint'*[23], 'have your cows!' What is particularly striking is that the pendant in *BB* here, line 109, is *Bit lat do bae*, 'the cows shall be yours.' Again where *VP* has *duodecim vaccae quas mulsisti tuae sint*[24], it is worth noting that one of the Irish MSS of *VP* (Rawlinson MS B 485, 13th century) has *tecum* for *tuae*. A similar instance, this time with *cum* denoting possession rather than ownership, occurs in *VP*: *nulla vacca cum eis erat* 'they had no cow'[25]. Compare *BB* 409: *ni fil em carpat lind* 'we have no chariot'.

The use of *ex* for *ab* is attested at least three times in *VP*: *Illum medicum semper quaere qui potest morbum ex te repellere*[26]. *Venient enim latrones in via et auferent ea ex me*[27]. *'Si me obsolveris* (i.e. *absolveris*) *ex iugo regis istius, servus tuus ero in perpetuum'*[28]. The same substitution of *ex* for *ab* has been noted by the late Prof. Ludwig Bieler in Four Latin Lives: *quae ex ipsius Paladii nomine Pallere ... uocantur; altera uero ecclesia ex (a* V₄) *discipulis Palladii*, etc[29]. Prof. Binchy commenting on this in a footnote in the same volume says: 'The preposition *ex* possibly represents Ir. *ó* or perhaps even the philologically identical (Irish) *a* (from ess <*eks).' Another expression which has an Irish flavour to it is *in capite anni*[30]. It would be rash to claim this as a Hibernicism but it is strongly reminiscent of the Irish *i gceann bliana* or *cinn bhliana, cinn* or *cionn* meaning 'at the end'[31].

22 Der hibernolateinische Grammatiker Malsachanus (Studia Latina Upsaliensia 3), Uppsala 1965, p. 118—120.
23 AA SS 120B 13.
24 ibid.
25 AA SS 121A 20 has *nulla vacca apud eos erat*. The best MSS have *cum eis* for *apud eos*.
26 AA SS 121D 25.
27 AA SS 123D 42.
28 AA SS 131B 88. One codex, Rawlinson B. 485, early 13th cent., here reads *a iugo*.
29 Four Latin Lives of St Patrick, SLH 8, 1971, p. 221.
30 AA SS 127C 64.
31 R. *Thurneysen*, A Grammar of Old Irish, Dublin 1966, p. 161.

On reading the *VP* one is struck by the rather frequent use of the passive voice in preference to the active. There are at least ten instances, in a few of which even some of the scribes felt the active seemed more natural and normal and recast the sentence accordingly. Examples of the same occur in *BB*. One of the more striking of these is on line 86: '*Haec est Maria quae a me in somnis vissia* (i.e. *visa*) *est.*' It so happens that in the pendant in *VP* the active is used: '*Haec est Maria quam vidi*'[32].

This preference of the passive over the active is a feature of at least some Old Irish texts, notably *Aislinge Oengusa*[33] where it is particularly common, e.g. *timchelltar húait Ériu uile dús in n-étar huait ingen* 48,3; *tíagar úaib co Bodb* 50,2; *congairther rí in tsíde cuccuib* 58,1; *ad-cichsiter sain-éuin lee and* 60,5. Compare *BB* 321: *A medico tacta est tui, virgo, vena capitis qui me est melior satis* with its pendant in *VP*: *O virgo, medicus tetigit caput tuum qui multo melior me est*[34]. It is interesting that in Modern Irish, for example, to express 'What are you doing?' while one may say *Céard tá tú a dhéanamh?* as speakers of Connacht Irish do, purists prefer to put it in the passive as is done in the Munster dialect and say *Cad tá dhá dhéanamh agat?* literally 'What is being done by you?' This is considered by Irish scholars more idiomatic even if to some it sounds a little cumbersome. It has been pointed out by Wackernagel that the tendency to use the passive develops as a language becomes more literary and wants to express abstract ideas. Plautus rarely uses it and the passive was a relatively late development in Sanskrit and Greek[35].

---

32 AA SS 120A 12.
33 Ed. Rev. Prof. Francis *Shaw*, Dublin 1934.
34 AA SS 121D 25.
35 Jakob *Wackernagel*, Vorlesungen über Syntax mit besonderer Berücksichtigung von Griechisch, Lateinisch und Deutsch, Basel ²1926—28, I, p. 144.

Romani *influences on seventh-century Hiberno-Latin literature*

By
Pádraig Ó Néill

Already in the second half of the sixth century the presence of reformers within the Irish Church who sought to model their administration on Roman and continental usage is signalled in a series of legislative enactments. The so-called 'First' and 'Second Synod of St Patrick' attest to this reform movement in their advocacy of an episcopal, as against a monastic, Church, and in their exhortation to observe customs of marriage, dress and notarization *more Romano*[1].

The first decade of the seventh century witnessed in Ireland a movement towards liturgical reform on the continental model. Mo-Chuaróc moccu Neth Semon, "whom the *Romani* styled doctor of the whole world", abolished at his monastery (perhaps Bangor) the venerable Celtic tradition of celebrating Mass in the evening at Nones in favour of morning, the time current in the Western Church[2]. He also championed reform of the traditional 84-year cycle used by the Irish Church for determining the date of Easter, transmitting instead the computations of his teacher Sinlán, abbot of Bangor († ca. 610), who advocated the more recent cycle of Dionysius Exiguus[3].

In the third decade of this century — perhaps as a result of Pope Honorius's letter in 628/629 exhorting the Irish Church to abandon their 84-year cycle[4] — differences between reformers and conservatives intensified into a controversy about the dating of Easter. Among the reformers was Cummean whose letter to Ségéne, abbot of Iona, in 632, bears further witness to the close ties already established with Rome by a group of monasteries located in the midlands and North-West Munster. When the decision of these ecclesiastics at the Synod of Mag-Léna (631) to observe the Roman Easter fell through, they decided to refer the matter to Rome, acting — as Cummean relates — *Iuxta mandatum, ut si diversitas orbata fuerit*

---

1 On the date of the First Synod, cf. Kathleen *Hughes*, The Church in Early Irish Society, London 1966, p. 44ff., and D. A. *Binchy*, St Patrick's ‚First Synod', Stud. Hib. 8 (1968), p. 49—59; on the Second Synod, cf. Kathleen *Hughes*, Synodus II Sancti Patricii, in John J. *O'Meara* and Bernd *Naumann*, ed., Latin Script and Letters, A. D. 400—900, Leiden 1976, p. 141—47.

2 Cf. P. *Grosjean*, Recherches sur les Débuts de la Controverse Paschale chez les Celtes, AB 64 (1946), p. 200—44, at p. 220ff.

3 Ibid., p. 215—19.

4 The chronology of this letter and other events of the Paschal controversy in Ireland follows James F. *Kenney*, The Sources for the Early History of Ireland: Ecclesiastical, New York 1929; repr. with additions, 1966, p. 220—21.

inter causam ... ut si causae fuerint maiores, iuxta decretum synodicum, ad caput urbium sint referendae[5]. Cummean's words not only demonstrate that these churchmen acted according to a long-standing Roman principle, they also verbally recall the enunciation of that principle by Innocent I (404), subsequently repeated in the *Decreta* of Dionysius Exiguus, *Si maiores causae in medium fuerint devolutae* ad sedem apostolicam, sicut synodus statuit, *et beata consuetudo exigit, post iudicium episcopale* referantur[6].

Thus from the late sixth century a group of Irish ecclesiastics can be identified who cultivated closer contacts with Rome than had previously obtained. To them was given the name *Romani*. The term, in contemporary continental usage, described those Christians who supported the papal claim to primacy among the patriarchates and who were loyal to Rome in doctrinal disputes[7]. In the seventh-century Irish context the name *Romani* applied to those who followed Rome's exhortation to abandon the 84-year cycle, regarding the Paschal controversy as primarily an issue of loyalty to Rome[8]. These Irish *Romani*, although undoubtedly most concerned at first about the Easter controversy, could hardly have confined their contacts with the continental Churches to purely administrative and computistical questions. Closer relations in such matters would inevitably lead to a readier receptivity to foreign learning and to a greater flow of other kinds of ecclesiastical literature. Besides, by calling forth other issues such as Church unity and Rome's doctrinal primacy, the Paschal controversy required the *Romani* to study patristic writings more critically and more comprehensively, a fact apparent from the range of authorities cited by Cummean in his letter to Ségéne.

Indeed, evidence for *Romani* access to continental literature comes from their Irish opponents. Writing to his student Feradad (*leg.* Feradach?), a certain Calmanus (*leg.* Colmanus?) confesses that the *Romani* possess better and more complete editions of important ecclesiastical texts; he singles out Isidore's *De Ecclesiasticis Officiis*, Jerome's translation of the Eusebian Chronicle and Sedulius's *Carmen Paschale*[9]. Calmanus's letter not only indicates the fruit of closer contacts with the Continent, it also implies that the *Romani* were regarded as a distinct cultural group.

5 PL 87, 977B.

6 Cf. P. Jaffé, ed., Reg. Pont. I Leipzig [2]1885, nos. 286, 1018, 1942; and for the text of Dionysius, PL 67, 242D.

7 Cf. W. *Ullmann*, On the use of the term ‚Romani' in the Sources of the Earlier Middle Ages, Stud. Patr. II, Berlin 1957, p. 155—63, ed. by Kurt *Aland* and F. L. *Cross*.

8 Cf. *Grosjean*, op. cit., p. 215: Le terme *Romani*, en Irlande, à cette époque et en cette matière de comput, ne saurait signifier que les partisans des méthodes romaines pour la date de Pâques.

9 Cf. B. *Bischoff*, Il Monachesimo Irlandese nei suoi rapporti col continente, in Mittelalterliche Studien I, Stuttgart 1966, p. 195—205, at p. 199.

Specific evidence for a distinct tradition of biblical scholarship among the *Romani* comes from a Latin commentary on the Psalms composed ca. 700[10]. This work mentions the *Romani* by name in three instances, attributing to them Psalter interpretations different from those followed in the commentary. Thus, after supplying its usual interpretations for Ps 49, the commentary adds, *Hic salmus* secundum Romanos *de iudicio futuro canitur.* Again for Ps 52, *Hic salmus* secundum Romanos *pro insidis Saul et occisione sacerdotum in Nouae cantatur,* and for Ps 54, *Hic salmus* secundum Romanos *pro erumnis Saul cantatur.* In all three cases the *Romani* interpretations differ from those regularly supplied by the commentary, notably in their lack of any reference to the so-called second historical interpretation which found great favour among Irish Psalter exegetes[11].

Granted that the *Romani* constituted a distinct group within the Irish Church of the seventh century, a distinction initially and primarily based on their pro-Roman stand in the paschal controversy but subsequently enlarged to include differences in scholarship and exegesis, is it possible to identify products of their scholarship, or at least to isolate characteristics of it?

The bulk of surviving seventh-century Hiberno-Latin literature — exegetical, hagiographical, computistical, grammatical and didactic — has obscure origins, sometimes as regards authorship, sometimes as regards provenance. One exception is a collection of four exegetical and didactic works which, as demonstrated by Père Grosjean, emanated from a closely-knit group of ecclesiastics associated with central and southern Irish monasteries, notably Lismore, Rahan and Clonfertmulloe[12]. This part of Ireland had accepted the Roman Easter early in the Paschal controversy, as indicated by Cummean's account of their synods, and their embassy to Rome; and more generally, by Bede[13]. Furthermore, the nuclear text of the corpus, *De Mirabilibus Sacrae Scripturae*, attests to the adoption of the Victorine paschal cycle[14], one which, as Columbanus' letter to Pope Gregory (in 600) testifies[15], had been rejected by the conservatives in Ireland. Besides *De Mirabilius*, a treatise providing rationalistic explanations of the outstanding mira-

10 MS Vatican, Pal. Lat. 68; cf. Martin *McNamara*, Psalter Text and Psalter Study in the Early Irish Church (A. D. 600—1200), PRIA 73 C (1973), p. 201—98, at pp. 218—19; and *McNamara*, Ireland and Northumbria as Illustrated by a Vatican Manuscript, Thought 54 (1979), p. 274—90. The citations from this manuscript which follow, I owe to Fr. McNamara, who is preparing an edition for publication.

11 On this type of interpretation, which applied the Psalms to events in the Old Testament after David's time, cf. R. L. *Ramsay*, Theodore of Mopsuestia in England and Ireland, ZCP 8 (1912), p. 452—97, at p. 468.

12 P. *Grosjean*, Sur quelques exégètes irlandais du VIIe siècle, Sacris Erudiri 7 (1955), p. 67—98.

13 Cf. Bede's Ecclesiastical History of the English People, ed. by Bertram *Colgrave* and R. A. B. *Mynors*, Oxford 1969 (henceforth HE) III, iii.

14 Cf. edn. in PL 35, 2149—2200, at col. 2176 (Bk. II, ch. IV) where the author outlines the 532-year cycle of Victorius in his discussion of how the moon and sun stood still (Jos 10:12—14).

cles of Scripture (written in 655[16]), the corpus includes the pseudo-Isidorean *Liber De Ordine Creaturarum* (ca. 680), a cosmographical work on the hierarchy of Creation, closely dependent on *De Mirabilibus*[17]; Laidcend's abridgement of Gregory the Great's *Moralia in Iob* (before 661[18]); and the anonymous Commentary on the Catholic Epistles (ca. 650—690) which reflects the comments of Irish exegetes responsible for or mentioned in the three previous works[19]. What characteristics in these texts could plausibly be attributed to closer contacts with Rome and the continental Churches?

Among those seventh-century Irish texts which advocate or use the 'new' Easter cycles of Victorius and Dionysius, Cummean's letter best expresses the *Romani* concern in the Easter controversy: orthodoxy in the sense of the observance of practices held by the universal Church comprised of four apostolic Sees (Jerusalem, Antioch, Alexandria and Rome) and headed by Rome, the *caput urbium*. Herein lies the burden of Cummean's argument to Ségéne: the 'Celtic' side, by refusing to abandon their 84-year cycle, challenge the unity of the universal Church and impugn its orthodoxy. Bede, in his account of the Paschal controversy in Northumbria, uses the same argument — though much more frankly expressed — frequently referring to the Roman Easter as the *pascha catholicum*[20] (the orthodox Easter) and (in the mouth of Wilfrid) warning those who scorn to follow it that they sin[21]. Likewise, Aldhelm, in his letter to Geraint (705), compares those who refuse to give up the old cycle "to the Jews and to heretics"[22].

It does not follow, of course, that the *Romani* could lay sole claim to orthodoxy, but they do seem to have given greater emphasis and more concrete application to the concept than their predecessors and opponents in the Irish Church. This trend probably reflected the influence of Rome's emphasis on catholicity in the wake of fourth- and fifth-century heresies and schisms, particularly Arianism, Pelagianism and the Three Chapters' controversy. Thus the 'Second Synod of St Patrick', one of the earliest *Romani* documents, contains a canon directed against the excessive asceticism of Novatianism[23]. Pope-elect John's exhortation to the clergy of

15 *Scias namque nostris magistris et Hibernicis antiquis philosophis et sapientissimis componendi calculi computariis Victorium non fuisse receptum* ..., ed. by G. S. M. *Walker*, Sancti Columbani Opera, SLH 2, 1957, p. 6.

16 Cf. J. F. *Kenney*, Sources, p. 275—77.

17 Ed. by Manuel C. *Diaz y Diaz*, Liber De Ordine Creaturarum, Santiago de Compostela 1972.

18 Ed. by M. *Adriaen*, Egloga ... De Moralibus Iob ... CCSL 145, Turnholt 1969.

19 Ed. by Robert E. *McNally*, Scriptores Hiberniae Minores I, CCSL 108 B, Turnholt 1973, p. 3—50.

20 HE III, xxvi.

21 HE III, xxv.

22 Ed. by Rudolf *Ehwald*, MGH AA 15, p. 480—86, at p. 482—83.

23 *Quid autem inter Nouatianum et Christianum interest nisi quod Nouatianus indesinenter, Christianus uero per tempus absteneat.* Ed. by Ludwig *Bieler*, The Irish Penitentials, SLH 5, p. 188—90 (canon XIV).

northern Ireland (ca. 640) to stamp out the Pelagian heresy in their midst[24] may have originated with overzealous *Romani* — already prejudiced against the Northern clergy for their stand on the Paschal issue — who disapproved of the use of Pelagius's writings in Ireland. *De Mirabilibus* takes a strong anti-Pelagian stand; its opening chapter contains an implied attack on Pelagianism: *Clementia ergo Conditoris homo ad illam beatitudinem,* ad quam peccans adhuc non pervenit, *per passionem Domini revocatur*[25]. It recognizes the reality of original sin in its description of Christ as one *qui proprii aut* originalis peccati *nullam culpam haberet*[26]. The same work takes a strictly orthodox approach to the problem of resolving controversial theological issues. In discussing the origin of the star that guided the Magi, it concedes that various theories are permissible, *etsi* catholico sensui *nihil repugnat*[27]. Likewise, *De Ordine Creaturarum,* on the same controversial topic of the origin of light from the sun and moon declares the principles which should guide an orthodox writer in doubtful matters:

> *Haec uero lucis organa nonnulli insensibiles creaturas opinantur, sed quae diximus usitatius a catholicis auctoribus frequentantur; in his ambiguis sententiarum aestimationibus intendendum est cui plus sanctarum scripturarum auctoritas suffragatur, et si haec desit, hoc etiam amandum est quod multitudo catholicorum in fidem traxit; deuersae autem aestimationes, quae tantundem a catholicis adsertae sunt et quibus utriusque canonis sacri dicta non contrafaciunt uel ad quas aequanimiter currunt, haec arbitris lectoribus in ambiguo relinquendae sunt*[28].

In other words, Scripture should be the first authority on orthodoxy; failing that, the traditional teaching of the majority of orthodox writers, or even other catholic opinions which do not contradict Scripture. And the Commentary on the Catholic Epistles establishes at the beginning that these letters are orthodox because *fidem certam adnuntiant*[29].

Although Celtic churchmen recognized the primacy of Rome and its popes, based on the claim that Peter was the *princeps apostolorum,* nevertheless their recognition, when not merely abstract, was modified by a certain degree of inde-

---

24 *Et hoc quoque cognovimus quod virus Pelagianae hereseos apud vos denuo revivescit, quod omnino hortamur ut a vestris mentibus huiusmodi venenatum superstitionis facinus auferatur.* Ed. by Maurice P. *Sheehy,* Pontificia Hibernica, Dublin 1962, p. 4.

25 Bk. I, ch. II (PL 35, 2154); this passage is repeated *verbatim* in *De Ordine Creaturarum* Bk. VIII, 6.

26 Bk. III, ch. V (2196).

27 Bk. III, ch. IV (2195). For other references to orthodoxy cf. Bk. III, ch. XIV (2200): *Sed hoc absit a* catholica *fide;* Bk. I, ch. VI (2157): *Sed haec investigatio qualiter accipienda sit pro certo, eruditi et* catholici *viri videant.*

28 Bk. V, 11.

29 CCSL 108 B, p. 3.

pendence. Thus Gildas stressed the divine authority of the *whole* episcopate, while Columbanus recognized a power vested in the whole Church superior to that of any individual pope[30]. The *Romani*, in contrast, were ardent believers in the unique position of Peter and the doctrine of Petrine supremacy. The author of *De Mirabilibus*, for his discussion of the miracles of the New Testament other than the Four Gospels, selects only those which illustrate Peter's *apostolica virtus* and *auctoritas*[31]; he also emphasizes Peter's power to loosen and to bind[32]. It is interesting to note similar statements of Petrine primacy and papal authority in the Hymn of Secundinus from the seventh-century Antiphonary of Bangor[33], and in two Hiberno-Latin hymns in honour of Peter, *Audite fratres famina* (probably seventh century[34]) and *Sanctus Petrus apostolus*[35]. The same devotion, even more intense, is found among English *Romani* whose final argument in favour of the Roman Easter during the Paschal controversy in Northumbria was that as the heir of Peter, the bearer of the keys of Heaven, the pope could not be challenged[36].

The *Romani* had another reason for venerating Peter and promoting his cult: their support for the Roman style of tonsure, the advocates of which claimed that it had originated with Peter; the 'Celtic' tonsure of their opponents they imputed to Peter's opponent Simon the Magician (Acts 8:9). This argument occurs in the Collectio Canonum Hibernensis, an early eighth-century compilation of *Romani* legislation[37]; likewise in Aldhelm[38] and in Bede[39]. A late eight-century Hiberno-Latin biblical commentary, 'the Reference-Bible', which contains much earlier material, has a section the title of which — *De Tonsura Apostolorum* — demonstrates concern about the tonsure issue. Its opening statement, *Romanorum pictura apostolorum imagines sic depingit*, is interpreted by Professor Bischoff as referring to

30 Cf. Kathleen *Hughes*, The Celtic Church and the Papacy, in C. H. *Lawrence*, ed., The English Church and the Papacy in the Middle Ages, London 1965, p. 3—28, at p. 13—21.

31 Bk. III, ch. XVI—XVII (2200—2202).

32 Bk. III, ch. XVII (2202).

33 *Super quem aedificatur ut Petrus aecclesia*, (line 10); *Xp(istu)s illum sibi elegit in terris uicarium*, (line 81); ed. by Ludwig *Bieler*, The Hymn of St Secundinus, PRIA 55 C (1953), p. 117—27.

34 *Dudum elegit Dominus/Petrum ... ut ... essetque pastor ovium*, (st. 4); *Fundamentum dominicae/Ecclesiae catholicae*, (st. 5); ed. by Clemens *Blume*, Analecta hymnica medii aevi, LI, Leipzig 1908, p. 347—49. Cf. *Kenney*, Sources, p. 267.

35 *Animarum pontificem/Apostolorum principem/Petrum rogamus, omnium/Christi pastorem ovium*, (st. 5); ed. *Blume*, Analecta, p. 349.

36 HE III, xxv. The cult of St Peter in England also found expression in numerous dedications of churches and monuments to him; cf. the Kilnasaggart Stone, Co. Armagh (ca. 700) with its dedication to St Peter; R. A. S. *Macalister*, Corpus Inscriptionum Insularum Celticarum II, Dublin 1949, no. 946.

37 *Romani dicunt: quod quinque causis Petrus tonsuram accepit*, etc. (Bk. LII, ch. 3—4); ed. by Hermann *Wasserschleben*, Die Irische Kanonensammlung, Leipzig ²1885.

38 *Ehwald*, MGH AA 15, p. 482, lines 21—22.

39 HE V, xxi, in reporting Abbot Ceolfrith's letter to Nechtan.

a painting of Roman origin[40]. But in view of the tonsure debate in seventh-century Ireland, the Irish *Romani* — rather than the inhabitants of Rome — may have been meant. Their *pictura* of the Apostles would have served to illustrate the Petrine tonsure which they advocated[41].

By the fifth century the Canon of Scripture — the body of works recognized by the Church as divinely inspired — was well established; in the sixth century the Canon was widely propagated in Western Europe through the Decretum Gelasianum which put Christians on their guard against apocryphal and heretical writings. The same concern with canonicity is apparent in the exegetical works of the *Romani*. The author of *De Mirabilibus*, in refusing to discuss the books of Maccabees, makes it clear that he intends to treat only of canonical Scripture, *quia tantum agere proposuimus, ut de divini canonis mirabilibus exiguam*[42]. Elsewhere, in the same critical way, he rejects chapter 14 of the book of Daniel dealing with the god Bel, and Daniel in the lions' den: *De lacu vero iterum et Habacuc translato in Belis et draconis fabulis, idcirco in hoc ordine non ponitur, quod in auctoritate divinae Scripturae non habentur*[43]. In both instances he was probably influenced by Jerome's doubts — expressed in prefaces to his Vulgate text and his commentary on Daniel — but reveals himself as more uncompromising on canonicity than Jerome. The Commentary on the Catholic Epistles always refers to the Bible as *canonica scriptura*[44]. It directs one of its opening questions to the subject of these Epistles' canonicity, in response to a long-standing doubt[45]. The Catholic Epistles were not always accepted *in toto* as canonical, nor had any of the Church Fathers lent the authority of their opinion by writing commentaries on them. Presumably, the Irish commentator felt the need to establish their canonicity — specifically, James, II Peter, John (all three), and Jude — with evidence culled from Jerome's biographical sketches of the Apostles in *De Viris Illustribus*. His material comes from Jerome, but the concern with canonicity is his own.

Another aspect of the concern with canonical Scripture is the displacement of the Vetus Latina text of the Bible by Jerome's Vulgate. Although the Vulgate probably reached Ireland towards the end of the sixth century, widespread acceptance of it came only in the seventh century, a process described by Samuel Berger as

40 Bernhard *Bischoff*, Wendepunkte in der Geschichte der lateinischen Exegese im Frühmittelalter, Mittelalterliche Studien I, rev. edn., Stuttgart, 1966, p. 234—35; and, in English translation, in Martin *McNamara*, ed., Biblical Studies: The Medieval Irish Contribution, Dublin 1976, p. 73—160, at p. 101.

41 Grosjean interprets *Romanorum* here as the Irish *Romani*; cf. Édition et commentaire du *Catalogus Sanctorum Hiberniae* ..., AB 73 (1955), p. 289—322, at p. 292, note 4.

42 BK. II, ch. XXXIV (2194).

43 BK. II, ch. XXXII (2192).

44 For example, even in borrowing a passage from Gregory's Homilies on Ezechiel (PL 76, 829, 840) where Scripture is referred to as *Scriptura sacra (divina)*, the Comm. on the Catholic Epistles changes it to *Scriptura canonica* (CCSL 108B, p. 3, lines 5—8).

45 ‹*Queritur*›, *si canonice sunt* ...; *Quot sunt epistolae de quibus extitit dubitatio?*, CCSL 108B, p.3.

one of Romanization[46]. The stages of this acceptance remain unclear, both as regards the different books of the Bible and as regards the different churches in Ireland, but all four *Romani* texts used Jerome's Vulgate as their biblical text.

The Church of Rome, although the most important influence on the *Romani*, was not the only one. Close cultural relations between Ireland and Visigothic Spain have been well documented[47]. Significantly, the south of Ireland — the part most Romanized — has been suggested as the main point of contact between the two cultures[48]. The clearest manifestation of Spanish influence is the rapid diffusion of the works of Isidore of Seville, especially his *Etymologiae*. The *Romani* authors provide ample, and the earliest, evidence for the use of Isidore in Ireland. At the beginning of his abridgement of Gregory's *Moralia in Iob*, Laidcend inserts a passage from Isidore's *De Ortu et Obitu Patrum* to provide further information on Job's genealogy[49]. The Commentary on the Catholic Epistles uses most of Isidore's major works — the *Etymologiae, Differentiae, Allegoriae, Quaestiones in Vetere Testamento* — and cites him more often than any other authority except Jerome. *De Ordine Creaturarum* draws on *Differentiae* and *De Ecclesiasticis Officiis*. The same work's use of the Acts of the eleventh Council of Toledo (675) for a definition of the Trinity[50] suggests that *Romani* interest in Spanish ecclesiastical texts stemmed in part from a desire to obtain orthodox texts. Conversely, neither Adomnán in *De Locis Sanctis* nor the Vatican Psalter Commentary — two works of non-*Romani* authors — show any familiarity with Isidore, a fact all the more remarkable since both works draw heavily on onomastic and etymological lore of the kind best presented in Isidore's *Etymologiae*.

But of all their patristic authorities the *Romani* reserved the greatest reverence for Gregory the Great. In marshalling his authorities in support of catholic unity on the question of Easter observance Cummean successively cites Cyprian, Augustine and Jerome; he leaves Gregory until last because, as he explains, *etsi post omnes scripsit, tamen est merito omnibus praeferendus*[51]. Cummean's enthusiasm for Gregory is in marked contrast to the attitude of Columbanus who does not hesitate to warn Gregory that anyone impugning the authority of Jerome — including Gregory himself — must be a heretic[52]. Laidcend's abridgement of

---

46 Samuel *Berger*, L'Histoire de la Vulgate pendant les premiers siècles du Moyen Age, Paris 1893, p. 29: «L'histoire de la Vulgate suit pas à pas les progrès de l'Église romaine en Irlande ... L'histoire de la Bible dans les pays celtiques n'est pas autre chose que l'histoire des relations de ces pays avec le continent, et particulièrement avec l'Église de Rome.»

47 Cf. J. N. *Hillgarth*, Visigothic Spain and Early Christian Ireland, PRIA 62 C (1962), p. 167—94.

48 Ibid., p. 192—93.

49 Laidcend gives his source as ‹Dicta Isdori in libro de uita et exitu prophetarum.›

50 Cf. *Diaz y Diaz*, p. 36.

51 PL 87, 975A.

52 *Tua itaque consideret vigilantia, ut ... nulla sit inter te et Hieronymum in sententia promenda dissonantia ... Simpliciter enim ego tibi confiteor, quod contra sancti Hieronymi auctoritatem veniens apud occidentis ecclesias hereticus seu respuendus erit, quicumque ille fuerit,* Walker, Sancti Columbani Opera, p. 8.

Gregory's *Moralia* can be viewed as a *Romani* effort to propagate in a more accessible form the great work of their favourite author. Not only do the *Romani* use Gregory's writings in the obvious way, incorporating his widely scattered comments on particular passages of Scripture in their own commentaries where appropriate[53], but they also apply his ideas to quite unrelated contexts in their own works[54], thereby demonstrating how well they had absorbed the matter of his writings. After Jerome and Isidore, Gregory is the most frequently cited author in the Commentary on the Catholic Epistles, with excerpts from all his major works, the Homilies on Ezechiel and on the Gospels, the *Regula Pastoralis* and the *Moralia*. *De Ordine Creaturarum* uses Gregory's Homilies on the Gospels, the Dialogues, and probably the *Moralia*[55]. This enthusiastic use of Gregory stands in marked contrast with non-*Romani* works: Adomnán's works provide little or no evidence of dependence on Gregory, at most a few passages in his Vita Columbae which may echo ideas from Gregory's account of Benedictine monasticism in Dialogues, Book II[56]. The Psalter Commentary cites Gregory's name once, attributing to him a spurious etymology of *Alleluia*[57]; obviously its author was not familiar with Gregory's works.

Certain characteristics and concerns have been discussed in these four *Romani* texts which can plausibly be explained as reflecting the influence of the Roman and continental Churches on Ireland during the seventh century: more vigorous expressions of orthodoxy; greater devotion to Rome and the cult of St Peter; diligence about scriptural canonicity; early and frequent use of certain patristic writers, notably Isidore and Gregory. The occurrence of these characteristics in other contemporary Hiberno-Latin works would point to *Romani* influence or possibly even *Romani* origins for these texts. A likely example of this influence is *De duodecim abusivis saeculi*, a treatise from the mid seventh-century on twelve aspects of public morality. Its most recent editor, Hellmann, claimed *Romani* origins for it on the basis of its strong emphasis on the *unitas ecclesiae* symbolized by Christ's tunic (a symbol also occurring in the Collectio Canonum Hibernensis), its

---

53 For example, *De Ordine Creaturarum*, for its exposition on the angels (Bk. II) uses Gregory's account of the nine angelic orders in his Homilies on the Gospels (PL 76, 1249—55); the Comm. on the Catholic Epistles, discussing James 4:4, takes verbatim an incidental comment on the same verse from Gregory's Homilies on the Gospels (PL 76, 1079C).

54 Cummean, for example, in his letter (975A/B), uses Gregory's interpretation of Job 28:1, that suffering and martyrdom can be effective only for those within the Church (PL 76, 58C—59B), as an argument in support of Church unity in the Paschal controversy. The Comm. on the Catholic Epistles on James 2:8, *Diliges proximum tuum*, uses Gregory's allegorical interpretation of *coccus bis tinctus* from his Homilies on Ezechiel (PL 76, 974B) to describe dual charity.

55 Cf. *Diaz y Diaz*, p. 34—5.

56 Cf. G. *Brüning*, Adamnans *Vita Columbae* und ihre Ableitungen, ZCP 11 (1917), p. 213—304, at p. 249.

57 Cf. *McNamara*, Ireland and Northumbria, p. 285.

discussion of episcopal powers of excommunication, and its close textual and stylistic relationship to the Collectio Canonum Hibernensis[58]. Significantly, *De duodecim* exemplifies the *Romani* characteristics discussed above: use of a good Vulgate text, quotations from Isidore (*Etymologiae, De Ecclesiasticis Officiis,* and perhaps *De Ortu et Obitu Patrum*) and remarkably, the *Regula* of St Benedict, a work popularized by Gregory the Great (in his Dialogues, Bk. II), associated with the spread of Roman influence on Western monasticism[59], and unlikely to have gained acceptance from conservative Irish monasteries.

Another text to be considered is the Pseudo-Jerome Commentary on St Mark's Gospel, recently attributed to Cummean, the author of the paschal letter to Ségéne. In support of this attribution Bischoff notes, among other things, the author's warm regard for Rome, and his attack on the Quartodecimans, who are also attacked in Cummean's letter to Ségéne[60]. Significantly, both the Commentary on Mark and Cummean use the same argument of *reductio ad absurdum*:

Comm. on Mark[61]	Cummean[62]
ut nos numquam coenam Domini, ante quartam decimam lunam faciamus.	*... quinta feria, luna xiv primi mensis ... vespera procedente, accepto pane ...*
Qui facit in quarta decima resurrectionem:	*Quia si xiv luna resurrectioni deputetur (ut vos facitis), XIII in sepultura et XII*
in undecima luna coenam Domini facit: quod numquam inventum est ...	*in passione praepostero ordine fiet.*

Although a full investigation of the sources used in this Commentary on Mark remains to be done, one source seems to be Gregory the Great's Homilies on the Gospels. On the words, *Si quis vult post me sequi, deneget semetipsum,* (Mark 8:34), the commentary adds, *id est, alter ex altero efficiatur* "Let each one be perfected by the other"[63]. This comment, which might seem unrelated to the pericope's appeal for self-abnegation, becomes clear by reference to Gregory's comments on the same scriptural passage which he interprets as an exhortation to compassion and fellow-suffering: *per compassionem proximi necessitatem illius nostram putamus*[64]. Interestingly, the Cambrai Homily[65], after citing the same passage from Gregory,

58 Siegmund *Hellmann*, Pseudo-Cyprianus De XII Abusivis Saeculi, Leipzig 1909, p. 12—13.

59 Wilhelm *Levison*, England and the Continent in the Eighth Century, Oxford 1946, p. 22.

60 *Bischoff*, Wendepunkte *(McNamara)*, p. 80—82.

61 PL 30, 589—644, at col. 632C.

62 PL 87, 971D—972B.

63 Col. 614C.

64 Gregory, Homilies on the Gospels Bk. II, 32 (PL 76, 1277B)

65 A seventh-century Irish homily; ed. by Whitley *Stokes* and John *Strachan*, Thesaurus Palaeohibernicus II, Cambridge 1903, p. 244—47. For this homily's dependence on Gregory, cf. Pádraig Ó *Néill*, The Background to the Cambrai Homily, *Ériu* 32 (1981), p. 137—47.

supports it with another scriptural quotation, *portate honera uestra inuicem*, a variant of the Vetus Latina, for which the Vulgate reads, *Alter alterius onera portate*, a reading similar to the *alter ex altero* of the Commentary on Mark. Dependence on Gregory, in conjunction with the statements of loyalty to Rome, and the similar type of attack on the Quartodecimans suggests *Romani* provenance — if not origins — for the Commentary on Mark[66].

Cogitosus's Life of St Brigit betrays *Romani* symptoms. As demonstrated by his use of the prologue to the *Cursus Paschalis* of Victorius of Aquitaine, Cogitosus supported the *Romani* reform of the Easter cycle[67]. He draws freely on Gregory's Dialogues, not only for direct quotations but even as a stylistic model. His liturgical descriptions of the church at Kildare probably depend on the *Ordines Romani*, the liturgical rules proposed by Gregory the Great for the Roman churches[68]. Stylistically, his work resembles very closely *De Mirabilibus*[69], and probably comes from a *Romani* centre.

It would appear then that *Romani* centres other than the ones identified by Grosjean were producing exegetical and hagiographical works in the second half of the seventh century. Only with critical editions of all the seventh-century Hiberno-Latin works will it be possible to identify other *Romani* texts and to assess their role in establishing the tradition of Hiberno-Latin scholarship.

---

66 According to *Hillgarth*, Visigothic Spain, p. 174, note 33, the Comm. on Mark may also have used Isidore's *Allegoriae*. I have not been able to check the reference he gives there.

67 Cogitosus's *Life* was written ca. 650; ed. in PL 72, 775—90. For his sources cf. F. Ó Briain, Brigitana, ed. by F. MacDonncha, ZCP 36 (1977), p. 112—37.

68 Cf. D. A. Bullough, Columba, Adomnan and the Achievement of Iona, SHR 44 (1965), p. 17—33, at p. 18, note 4.

69 So much so that Ó Briain thought both works were by the same man.

Pagan survivals: the evidence of early Irish narrative

By
Tomás Ó Cathasaigh

In 1902, W. G. Wood-Martin said: 'Christianity is generally supposed to have annihilated heathenism in Ireland. In reality it merely smoothed over and swallowed its victim, and the contour of its prey, as in the case of the boa-constrictor, can be distinctly traced under the glistening colours of its beautiful skin. Paganism still exists, it is merely inside instead of outside'[1]. The image of the boa-constrictor is striking, not to say startling, but the claim which it supports cannot be fully sustained: it is too much to say that the contour of pre-Christian Irish heathenism can be distinctly traced. On the other hand, Christianity is not now generally supposed to have annihilated heathenism in Ireland. So far as the early literature is concerned, opinions differ as to the balance between survival and innovation, but there can be no doubt that it is heavily indebted to the pagan tradition of pre-Christian Ireland. Early medieval Ireland is, of course, by definition pre-modern, and so it is not at all surprising that such evidence as we have for the period should show that the manners and customs of the country were of a kind which we tend to find in pre-modern societies generally. What is remarkable about the Irish situation is the extent and richness of the vernacular literature which has come down to us from the early medieval period. Much of this literature is firmly rooted in ancient myth and remains robustly pagan in character; it has been used, along with other evidence, to build up at least a partial picture, not only of the pagan religion of the Irish, but also of that of the Celts, and it has even been laid under contribution in the comparative study of Indo-European mythology.

It has to be said that an immense amount of work remains to be done on early Irish literature: most of the texts stand in need of competent edition and translation, not to speak of interpretation and evaluation. The narrative material is only a part of this literature, but it is a considerable part; in treating such a subject in a short paper one must obviously be selective. I shall not attempt either to give an overview of early Irish narrative[2], or to describe the considerable body of evidence on paganism which can be gleaned from it[3]. What I propose to do is to give some

---

1 W. G. *Wood-Martin*, Traces of the Elder Faiths of Ireland, London 1902, Vol. I, p. VIII.

2 For this purpose mention may be made of Myles *Dillon*, Early Irish Literature, Chicago 1948, and of Eleanor *Knott* and Gerard *Murphy*, Early Irish Literature, London 1966. The latter volume contains an introduction by James *Carney*.

3 Myles *Dillon*, The Archaism of Irish Tradition, PBA 33 (1947) and separatim, remains an excellent introduction to survivals in Irish literature. See also Jan *de Vries*, Keltische Religion, Stuttgart 1961; Alwyn *Rees* and Brinley *Rees*, Celtic Heritage, London 1961; and Proinsias *Mac Cana*, Celtic Mythology, London 1970.

account of the ways in which the study of early Irish narrative has proceeded, to touch upon some of the problems which have arisen in the course of that study, and to exemplify these with reference to a short excerpt from what is perhaps our most important mythological text.

A framework of some kind is required so that we may order the critical theories and perspectives which have been brought to bear on early Irish narrative, and the one which I have chosen is that which was used by Mark Abrams in his study of Romantic criticism[4], and which comprises four co-ordinates: these he terms the *work*, the *artist*, the *universe*, and the *audience*[5]. One should perhaps explain what is meant by *universe* in this context. As Abrams puts it, 'the work is taken to have a subject which, directly or deviously, is derived from existing things — to be about, or signify, or reflect something which either is, or bears some relation to, an objective state of affairs'[6]. It is for this element, 'whether held to consist of people and actions, ideas and feelings, material things and events, or super-sensible essences'[7], that he uses the term *universe*. The other terms are self-explanatory, but it should be noted that for early Irish narrative *artist* is to be taken as a generic term which denotes all those who have had an active role in the composition and transmission of the work.

Among the four co-ordinates which have been mentioned, the work, being our primary datum, enjoys a privileged status: it is our point of departure, and to it we must always return. There are, of course, literary critics who would in any case argue the primacy of work-based criticism on theoretical grounds, but in regard to early Irish literature we need only appeal to the purely practical consideration that the work is virtually all that we have at our disposal in the way of evidence. Yet the tendency has been to conduct the discussion of Irish texts principally in terms either of the artists who have produced them or of the universe which is reflected in them, so that there is a pressing need to analyse the extant texts as literary works in their own right. For present purposes, however, it must be acknowledged that the co-ordinates which have been attended to are central to the question of pagan survival, since the artists are the agents of survival and the universe contains its elements. I begin, then, with authorship and transmission, and pass on in turn to the universe, the audience, and the work.

Authorship and transmission

We are dealing with a literature whose authors are not known to us by name, and which is in that sense anonymous. Two points of fact must be made at the outset. In the first place, none of our early narrative texts survives in a manuscript written

4 M. H. *Abrams*, The Mirror and the Lamp, London 1960.
5 Ibid., p. 6.
6 Ibid.
7 Ibid.

before the latter part of the eleventh century[8]. In the Irish manuscript tradition, the processes of composition and transmission cannot always be absolutely distinguished from one another, for the composition in writing of early Irish narrative can be seen as a continuous process, comprising the expansion and contraction, reshaping and redaction of matter, much of which must have been received into the literature from indigenous oral tradition, but some of which is of learned ecclesiastical provenance. It is often possible, on linguistic grounds, to assign the composition of a relatively unitary text to an approximate date, and the same can sometimes be done for a stratum or for strata of a compilatory text. But we can never hope to recover the pristine condition of any of our early texts.

Secondly, it should be noted that even to the extent that we can strip away accretions and arrive at a text approximating to the form in which a given work was first written out, we still have not got so much as a single pre-ecclesiastical text. We know that it was under the aegis of the Church that the art of writing and the skills involved in the production of manuscripts were brought to Ireland, and that it was the churchmen who adapted Latin orthography to the Irish language. For these and other reasons we have to consider the extent to which ecclesiastics may have contributed to the formation and development of early Irish narrative literature.

Kenney observed that 'the great majority of the written sources for the history of Ireland in the early middle ages are due to two sets of institutions, the monastic churches and the secular orders of learning'[9], and there can be no dispute about that. On the other hand, the evidence would not seem to support the rigid division of labour implied by Kenney's listing, first of 'the chief classes of texts which were produced or preserved in the monasteries'[10], and secondly of 'the chief classes of texts composed or transmitted by the *filid*'[11]. Kenney credits the monastic churches only with matter of ecclesiastical interest, and of the imaginative literature he allows them only 'imaginative religious literature, including voyage and vision tales and semi-apocryphal matter, to which may be added prophecies'[12]. All the rest is attributed to the secular orders of learning. But the ecclesiastical contribution to the secular literature cannot be dismissed out of hand. Binchy says: 'As we have them, (the native lore, the old sagas, the poems) are all of monastic provenance; they were usually written in monasteries, where

---

8 The earliest extant manuscript to contain Irish narrative texts is *Lebor na hUidre*. It is the work of three hands, and it has recently been suggested that all three scribes had completed their work by 1106: see Tomás Ó Concheanainn, The Reviser of Leabhar na hUidhre, Éigse 15 (1973—74), p. 277—88. For a contrary view, see Hans P. A. *Oskamp*, Mael Muire: Compiler or Reviser?, Éigse 16 (1975—76), p. 177—82.

9 James F. *Kenney*, The Sources for the Early History of Ireland, Vol. I: Ecclesiastical, New York 1929, p. 1.

10 Ibid.

11 Ibid., p. 4.

12 Ibid., p. 2.

they received a certain dressing-up from the scribes and redactors'[13]. Where opinions would now diverge is on the character and extent of what Binchy somewhat dismissively calls 'dressing-up'. James Carney has treated the Irish sagas as literary compositions by men working in a Christian literate community[14], and while Carney may overstate the specifically ecclesiastical character of some of the compositions which he has studied[15], it seems to me that the evidence supports his general contention that the early texts as we have them were indeed composed in a Christian literate community.

This brings us to the related question of the relationship between the texts which were being written out in the manuscripts and the oral tradition. If Irish literature contains survivals from Celtic and Indo-European culture — and the comparative evidence shows that it does — then clearly these elements must have been transmitted orally until such time as they were transferred into the written record. Calvert Watkins went so far as to say: 'Ireland has the oldest vernacular literature in Europe; our earliest monuments go back to the sixth century. And it is not the beginnings of a literature that we see then, but the full flowering of a long tradition, pre-Christian, pre-literate and uninfluenced by the Graeco-Roman world'[16]. The oral tradition was indeed for a long time pre-Christian, pre-literate and uninfluenced by the Graeco-Roman world, but we have no direct access to that tradition. It is true that Watkins was writing in the particular context of a discussion of early Irish poetics and that he pointed to an impressive number of inherited features in its vocabulary and cultural context[17]. Moreover, while prose is the main vehicle of narrative in the early texts, the old poetical tradition is

---

13 D. A. *Binchy*, The Background of Early Irish Literature, Stud. Hib. 1 (1961), p. 7—18, at. 7.

14 James *Carney*, Studies in Irish Literature and History, Dublin 1955, p. 77 ff. 191 ff, and 276 ff. Cf. Gearóid *Mac Eoin*, review of *Scéla Cano Meic Gartnáin*, Stud. Hib. 4 (1964), p. 244—49, at 245 f.

15 One may instance Carney's observations on *Táin Bó Cuailnge*, SILH, p. 276 ff, 321 f. His conclusions are that *Táin Bó Cúailnge* 'consists in part of traditional material, in part of imaginative reconstruction of the remote pagan Irish past in form and terms that belong to the mixed culture of early Christian Ireland. Those features which are part of the epic scale of presentation must be due to imitation of the classics or of Christian developments of them. As imitation I would include the careful drawing of character, the dramatic opening with the muster of the hosts, the technique of dramatic description, particularly as illustrated in the device of "the ignorant and knowledgeable watchers", the retrospective technique by which Cú Chulainn's early deeds are narrated by characters in the drama, the purpose of rhetorical dialogues in the *Táin* as a whole.' (SILH, p. 321 f.) The assertion that these features of *Táin Bó Cúailnge must* be due to imitation of the classics or of Christian developments of them is unproven and (I suspect) unprovable. See also Gerard *Murphy*'s review of Carney's book, Éigse 8 (1955—57), p. 152—64, especially at 157 f.

16 Calvert *Watkins*, Indo-European Metrics and Archaic Irish Verse, Celtica 6 (1963), p. 194—249, at 217.

17 Ibid., p. 212 ff.

represented in them by the species of metrical composition known as *roscada*[18], and these latter are presumably the 'archaic passages' to which Binchy refers when he remarks that 'the compilers (doubtless monastic) of saga texts in the eighth and ninth centuries, though in general they adopted the linguistic and expository techniques established by the glossators of late Latin texts, also transcribed, with varying degrees of accuracy, archaic passages derived from oral tradition'[19]. When all that has been said, however, what has been preserved in the manuscripts is by definition a written literature; the introduction of writing was an innovation on the part of people who were Christian, literate and influenced (in some degree) by the Graeco-Roman world; and what we see, already in the seventh century[20], but especially in the eight and ninth centuries, is 'the beginnings of a literature', however much it may owe to the vigorous oral tradition which not only preceded it, but continued to flourish alongside.

It has been said that 'the oral-literary question has been to Irish literary scholarship what the Patrician problem has been to historians of early Ireland. It has probably received more attention than any other question relating to the early literature without the achievement of anything approaching a consensus, except perhaps for the negative one of justified ignorance and bewilderment in the face of conflicting attitudes and theories, of inadequate evidence, and of inadequate examination of the evidence'[21]. In the absence of a consensus one must give one's own view, and it seems safe to make the following general observations. First, the comparative evidence shows that much of the matter in early Irish narrative derives from oral tradition, this being true in particular of survivals from Celtic and Indo-European culture. Secondly, the indications are that the written literature had its beginnings in the monasteries and continued to flourish in them throughout the early medieval period[22]. The ecclesiastics' contribution to that literature was therefore crucial and continuing: its nature and extent remain to be

---

18 On these see Proinsias *Mac Cana*, On the Use of the Term *Retoiric*, Celtica 7 (1966), p. 65—90.

19 D. A. *Binchy*, "Bergin's Law", Stud. Celt. 14—15 (1979—80), p. 34—53, at 39.

20 See F. J. *Byrne*, Seventh-century Documents, IER 108 (1967), p. 164—82.

21 Seán Ó *Coileáin*, Oral or Literary: Some Strands of the Argument, Stud. Hib. 17—18 (1977—78), p. 7—35, at 7.

22 The eleventh and twelfth centuries may together be regarded as a watershed in the history of Irish literature, as indeed in that of Irish culture in general. In literature this was a great age of compilation, and it saw the production of the three monastic codices which contain so much of our early narrative literature, these codices being *Lebor na hUidre* (on which see note 8 above), Rawlinson B 502, and the Book of Leinster. Following upon the reform of the Church in this period, custody of the manuscript tradition passed from the monasteries to the newly established lay schools which were to be conducted by hereditary learned families, and it was the members of these families who continued the manuscript transmission of the literature up to the seventeenth century. Fortunately, the hereditary lay scribes evinced a lively interest in the early material, for their manuscripts add much to what we have of it in the three great monastic codices.

precisely established, though a start has been made in that direction by Carney and others. In sum, then, we may say that early Irish narrative literature owes much to the vigorous oral tradition which not only preceded it but continued unabated alongside, and that the creation and survival of that literature show that the early Irish churchmen were not only open to, but deeply involved in, the extra-ecclesiastical lore of their country.

The universe

With regard to the universe of early Irish narrative, in the sense already defined, there are I think three main orientations to be discerned in the criticism, and these may be described in turn as mimetic, mythological and textualist.

The mimetic stance is that of the critics who see in the literature a reflection of events which really happened or of a state of affairs which actually existed — the universe of the work is the society in which it was produced. The most extensive and influential body of mimetic criticism devoted to early Irish literature is that of H. M. and N. K. Chadwick and their disciples, who have treated the Ulster Cycle as a celebration of a lost Heroic Age[23]. There is ample justification for regarding the Ulster Cycle in this light, but the theory of the Heroic Age has its pitfalls. One of these is a tendency to apply the theory in a reductionist way. Thus, in introducing his valuable reading of the Ulster Cycle as 'a window on the Iron Age', Kenneth Jackson says of the material that it 'contains very little that can reasonably or safely be taken for myth, or ought to be interpreted as such'[24]. There is, on the contrary, a good deal in the Ulster Cycle that can reasonably and safely be taken for myth: one need only mention, among much else, the life-crises of its great hero, Cú Chulainn[25], or the winter sleep which afflicts the Ulidians[26], or the two great bulls which confront one another in Táin Bó Cúailnge[27].

Another pitfall of the theory of the Heroic Age lies in over-estimating the historicity of the literature. It could be argued that the theory is founded on such an over-estimation: the claim that 'in matter and in the structure of its narrative (Heroic literature) is almost everywhere the same'[28], could well give rise to suspicion that we may be dealing in some measure with the diffusion of literary con-

23 H. M. *Chadwick* and Nora K. *Chadwick*, The Growth of Literature, Vol. I, Cambridge 1932, passim; Eleanor *Knott* and Gerard *Murphy*, Early Irish Literature, p. 114ff; and Kenneth Hurlstone *Jackson*, The Oldest Irish Tradition: A Window on the Iron Age, Cambridge 1964, passim.

24 Ibid., p. 2.

25 On these see *Rees* and *Rees*, Celtic Heritage, p. 217ff, 246ff, 259f, 305ff, 326f, 331ff.

26 See Tomás Ó *Broin*, What is the "Debility" of the Ulstermen?, Éigse 10 (1961—63), p. 286—299, and Cecile *O'Rahilly*, ed., Táin Bó Cúailnge: Recension I, Dublin 1976, p. 241f.

27 See Anne *Ross*, Pagan Celtic Britain, London 1967, p. 305f; David *Greene* in Myles *Dillon*, ed., Irish Sagas, Dublin 1959, p. 96.

28 *Knott* and *Murphy*, Early Irish Literature, p. 114.

ventions rather than with an independently uniform set of literary responses to more or less identical societies. (The identity of these societies might in turn be attributed, in varying degrees, to cultural diffusion or independent development.) But even if we take leave to lay aside such suspicion and accept the proposition that 'where there is heroic literature, it may ... reasonably be inferred that a Heroic Age preceded it, and that the general traits of that Age, perhaps even some of its persons, are presented to us in that literature'[29], this inference relates merely to the mimetic origin of Heroic literature. It is quite another matter to use the Heroic literature as evidence for the duration of a given Heroic Age. The battle of Allen, fought between the Uí Néill and the Laigin in 722, is described in Heroic terms in Cath Almaine[30], and it has therefore been suggested that in Ireland the Heroic Age lasted until the eighth century[31]. It seems to me, however, that Cath Almaine has more to tell us about the durability of literary conventions than about the conditions in Ireland at the time when the battle was fought.

Here we must leave the question of the Heroic Age, and turn briefly to a consideration of the historical information which may be extracted from early Irish narrative[32]. F. J. Byrne has said that 'early Irish literature cannot be properly understood except as historical documentation'[33], and he has drawn extensively on the literature for historical purposes, notably in Irish Kings and High-Kings. There is a mass of literature dealing with the origins of Irish population groups and dynasties, their territorial distribution and their status; there are also numerous tales dealing with the careers of kings, some of whom are pre-historic (and may or may not be figments of the imagination), while others are known from reliable sources to have lived in the historical period. Literary works of this kind purport to be historical and they make political claims; it is right that their historicity should be assessed and their claims measured. If, however, we cannot control this material with reliable contemporary documentation — and this, more often than not, is the position in which we find ourselves — then our verdict on

29 Ibid., p. 115.

30 Pádraig Ó Riain, Cath Almaine, Dublin 1978.

31 *Chadwick* and *Chadwick*, The Growth of Literature, Vol. I, p. 16: 'In truth, any date which may be fixed for the end of the Irish Heroic Age must be more or less arbitrary; but for practical purposes we prefer to date it early in the eighth century. We may perhaps include the story of the Battle of Allen ...' Acceptance of such a date for the end of the Heroic Age in Ireland is implicit in Francis John *Byrne's* discussion of the Battle of Allen in *idem*, Irish Kings and High-Kings, London 1973, p. 146. It has also been suggested that the Heroic Age lasted only until the end of the sixth century: see J. E. *Caerwyn Williams* and Máirín Ní *Mhuiríosa*, Traidisiún Litheartha na nGael, Dublin 1979, p. 8 (but cf. ibid., p. 12).

32 On this matter see Brian Ó *Cuív*, Literary Creation and Irish Historical Tradition, PBA 49 (1963) and separatim; Kathleen *Hughes*, The Early Celtic Ideal of History and the Modern Historian, Cambridge 1977; *eadem*, Early Christian Ireland: Introduction to the Sources, London 1972.

33 Francis John *Byrne*, Senchas: The Nature of Gaelic Historical Tradition, Historical Studies 9, Belfast 1974.

the historicity of the texts must be speculative, and it cannot go much beyond considerations of consistency and plausibility. As for the political claims of the texts, these may not always reflect the state of affairs as it really existed, but they can at least be interpreted as expressing the political aspirations of the population group or dynasty in question.

It can also be claimed that early Irish tales embody and express the ideology and value-system of the community, and here we find many elements which have been inherited from pre-Christian culture. This line of approach has not often been taken in the study of early Irish narrative, except insofar as it pertains to the mythological criticism which will be discussed presently. A recent example, however, is the analysis by Thomas Charles-Edwards of the well-known early Irish tale *Fingal Rónáin*[34] in relation to the role of honour and status in early Irish society[35], and it is an example which shows very clearly how valuable this kind of analysis can be. In general we can say that an appreciation of the conceptual framework which underlies early Irish narrative is an essential element in the criticism of individual works. But whereas, in this respect as in others, the historian can cast light on the early texts by virtue of his knowledge and interpretation of other (non-literary) sources, there are strict limits to the amount of historical information which may be extracted from what are, after all, literary texts.

The mythological interpretation of early Irish narrative had its chief exponent among modern scholars in T. F. O'Rahilly[36]. Gerard Murphy must also be mentioned here, since he attempted to uncover a mythological basis for the Fenian Cycle[37]. The mythological criticism of early Irish narrative has received a new lease of life from the work of Georges Dumézil on Indo-European comparative mythology. Dumézil has himself considered some Irish material, and his theory has been more extensively applied to it by others, notably by Alwyn and Brinley Rees[38]. Dumézil is not without his critics, and there are those who would question the very basis of his theory[39]. The validity of the theory must ultimately be judged by comparatists. Within the more limited perspective of Irish studies, it may be said in Dumézil's favour that, given the comparative theoretical framework within which he operates, it is his practice to address himself to the extant material as we have it. One of the major weaknesses of O'Rahilly's procedure is that he had a

34 David *Greene*, ed. Fingal Rónáin and Other Stories, Dublin 1955.

35 T. M. *Charles-Edwards*, Honour and Status in Some Irish and Welsh Prose Tales, Ériu 29 (1978), p. 123—141, at 130 ff.

36 His major work in this field is Early Irish History and Mythology, Dublin 1946.

37 Gerard *Murphy*, Duanaire Finn, Vol. III, Dublin 1953, passim, and (briefly) in *Knott* and *Murphy*, Early Irish Literature, p. 147 f.

38 Celtic Heritage. (It may be noted in passing that in this work the Rees brothers also use the work of Mircea Eliade whose comparisons are of the typological rather than of the genetic kind.)

39 The arguments of some of Dumézil's critics are considered in C. Scott *Littleton*, The New Comparative Mythology, Berkeley 1966, p. 176 ff.

high-handed attitude to the transmitted texts: time and again he found it necessary to contest the testimony of the manuscript texts as being at variance with his
theory, and in effect to rewrite the tales in order to make them fit that theory[40]. It is
axiomatic that any theory is valid only insofar as it accounts for the facts, and
O'Rahilly's theory falls short on this score[41]. Dumézil's work, on the other hand,
has illuminated a number of Irish texts which were hitherto shrouded in obscur-
ity. His treatment, for example, of *Cath Maige Tuired*[42] 'has the not inconsiderable
merit of recovering order and purpose from apparent chaos'[43]. It may be necessary
in the future to refine Dumézil's theory, or even wholly to replace it: in the
meantime its practical value in the elucidation of Irish narrative literature has by
no means been exhausted. Quite apart from its pragmatic value, however, there
remains the consideration that, in any account of pagan survivals in Irish narrative, the reflexes of Indo-European myth must be attended to.

Beside the mimetic and the mythological approaches to the universe of early
Irish narrative, I have mentioned another, for which I used the term *textualist*. It
might seem that textualist criticism should come up for consideration under the
rubric of the work rather than that of the universe, but we must distinguish here
between intra-textual and inter-textual criticism. Intra-textual criticism, concerned as it is with analysis of a given text, is properly to be assigned to the rubric
of the work. Moreover, the same could be argued of that variety of inter-textual
criticism which confines itself to analysis of the versions and recensions represented by the extant manuscript texts of a given tale[44]. There is also, however, a

40   See for example his treatment of *Esnada Tige Buchet* in Buchet the Herdsman, Ériu 16
(1952), p. 7—20, and of *Baile In Scáil* in EIHM, p. 283 f.
41   Since O'Rahilly never presented a definitive formulation of his theory of Irish myth,
it must be inferred by piecing together the relevant observations which are scattered
throughout his work, and by extrapolation from his treatment of the texts. Some aspects of
O'Rahilly's position are discussed in T. Ó Cathasaigh, The Heroic Biography of Cormac
Mac Airt, Dublin 1977, p. 11 ff.
42   Ed. and tr. W. *Stokes*, RC 12 (1891), p. 56 ff. Passages omitted by Stokes were published by *Thurneysen*, ZCP 12 (1918), p. 401 ff. G. *Lehmacher*'s German translation, Anthropos
26 (1931), p. 435 ff, includes some of the material omitted by Stokes.
43   P. *Mac Cana*, Celtic Mythology, p. 61.
44   The stemmatic theory of recension still holds the field in Irish studies, but there have
been rumblings of discontent: see, for example, Seán Ó Coileáin, The Structure of a Literary
Cycle, Ériu 25 (1974), p. 88—125, at 89, and Daniel F. *Melia*'s review of *Táin Bó Cúailnge:
Recension I*, Speculum 53 (1978), p. 607—09, at 608. The Lachmannian position is stoutly
defended by David N. *Dumville*, The Textual History of "Lebor Bretnach", Éigse 16
(1975—76), p. 255—273, at 273. Having noted that 'over the years, it has often been said that
the time has not yet come for the critical edition of an Irish text', Dumville says that '*Lebor
Bretnach* is the ideal text to disprove this unfortunate maxim' (ibid.). But *Lebor Bretnach* is a
Middle Irish translation of a Latin work (the *Historia Brittonum*): it can scarcely be regarded
as the ideal text upon which to base conclusions as to the relative status of the extant
manuscript texts of early Irish narrative in general. The matter requires further discussion: a
recent contribution to the debate is Edgar M. *Slotkin*, Medieval Irish Scribes and Fixed Texts,
Éigse 17 (1977—79), p. 437—450.

good deal of inter-textual criticism where the primary concern is with the relationship between and among works of literature, rather than their relationship to the world or to myth. Literature is thus deemed to be autonomous: its universe comprises other works of literature, or the constituents of those works, such as motifs or tale-types. Thurneysen's great study of the Ulster Cycle treats the manuscript tradition of Irish narrative as a closed system, and the extant texts of the cycle are described in terms of their relationship to one another[45]. The Finnish 'historical-geographical' method has not been widely used in the study of early Irish narrative: no scholar has done for Irish tradition what Kenneth Jackson did for the Welsh in The International Popular Tale and Early Welsh Tradition[46]. The great monument of the 'historical-geographical' school in our field is Tom Peete Cross's Motif-Index of Early Irish Literature[47], a work which can be useful even to those who do not subscribe to the theory on which it is based[48].

While the international popular tale may have had a relatively poor showing in the criticism of early Irish narrative, certain other tale-types have been pursued with some vigour and in a manner which is akin to that of the Finnish school. One may instance the numerous analogues which have been adduced of the Tristan-story[49]. D. A. Binchy has taken a dim view of this kind of work, remarking in his introduction to Scéla Cano Meic Gartnáin: 'It was, I think, unfortunate that Thurneysen should have entitled his translation (of Scéla Cano Meic Gartnáin) "An Irish Parallel to the Story of Tristan", for ever since there has been a tendency to judge our text according to whether this parallel stands or falls. The hunt for the "Ur-Tristan" goes merrily on, and as there does not seem to be the remotest likelihood of his ever being caught, we may expect that the relationship between Cano and Créd will continue to be scrutinised for arguments on one side or the other'[50]. This seems too harsh a view: research of this kind would seem to find ample justification in the very nature of the early literature, for there is no doubt that its authors felt free to borrow from such works as were available to them[51].

45 Rudolf *Thurneysen*, Die irische Helden- und Königssage, Halle 1921.
46 Cardiff 1961.
47 Bloomington, Indiana 1952.
48 For a critique of the Finnish school, see Alwyn D. *Rees*, Modern Evaluations of Celtic Narrative Tradition, Proceedings of the Second International Congress of Celtic Studies, Cardiff, 1966, p. 31—61, at 34 ff.
49 See Sigmund *Eisner*, The Tristan Legend: A Study in Sources, Evanston, Illinois 1969, and the works there cited.
50 D. A. *Binchy*, ed., Scéla Cano Meic Gartnáin, Dublin 1963, p. XVII.
51 One could at least go along with Rachel *Bromwich* when she says: 'The significance of the parallel which *Cano* affords with the *Tristan* ... consists merely in the fact that it is one among several Irish treatments of the "eternal triangle". But for this very reason its importance ought not to be neglected. It is a version of the theme which preserves several interesting primitive features, illustrative of the type of story-material out of which we can see that the Celtic prototype of the *Tristan* must have emerged.' (Review of Scéla Cano Meic Gartnain, Stud. Celt. 1 (1966), p. 152—155, at 155.)

So far as our theme is concerned, it may be said in general that the textualist critic qua textualist is not greatly concerned with the survival of paganism, for he is operating within a closed system. (Even when critics see reflexes of Celtic myth in medieval romance, they are, I think, positing vestiges rather than survivals.) On the other hand, the mythological critics are dedicated to the pursuit of survivals. The mimeticists are more difficult to characterise in this respect, and space does not allow a detailed discussion here. It may be said, however, that the crux of the matter is whether they are talking of the survival of literary conventions whose origins were anterior to the composition of the extant texts, on the one hand, or of a mirroring of a contemporary state of affairs or set of events, on the other.

The audience

We may pass on to the question of the audience, which Abrams defines as 'the listeners, spectators, or readers to whom the work is addressed, or to whose attention, at any rate, it becomes available'[52]. It would seem that the *fili* was expected to relate — or perhaps rather, as Seán Mac Airt has suggested[53], to expound — traditional tales to his patron, but what audience, what 'listeners, spectators, or readers' were the monastic traditors catering for? This is a question which can be addressed in two ways, the one historical and the other literary. The literary approach will rely upon the intention of the work, as discerned from analysis of its contents. A. G. van Hamel[54] has sought to establish the existence in Irish (and Celtic) tradition of what he called 'exemplary myth', explaining that 'the adjective "exemplary" ... as applied to heroes or traditions, means a hero or tradition that had to be regarded in the early Celtic society as an example which must be imitated by them ...'[55]. Van Hamel's treatment of the Irish evidence is unsatisfactory[56], but his inadequate advocacy of his case does not compel us to reject the proposition that early Irish narrative may have been exemplary in intention. I have argued elsewhere that *Cath Maige Tuired* is exemplary myth in van Hamel's sense[57]: as such it would be deemed to have had 'palpable designs' upon its audience. It has been indicated above that certain extant works are political in their purpose and content, and it is reasonable to hold that manifestly propagandist literature implies an audience which will be swayed by it.

52 The Mirror and the Lamp, p. 6.
53 *Filidecht* and *Coimge*, Ériu 18 (1958), p. 139—52, at 150.
54 Aspects of Celtic Mythology, PBA 20 (1934) and separatim, passim.
55 Ibid., p. 5. The remainder of his definition, 'or of whose example the deeds of other men must be regarded as a reflexion', need not detain us here; its relevance to *Cath Maige Tuired* is examined in the article mentioned in note 57.
56 See G. *Murphy*, Duanaire Finn, Vol. III, p. 213ff.
57 T. Ó *Cathasaigh*, Cath Maige Tuired as Exemplary Myth, in P. *de Brún*, S. Ó *Coileáin* and P. Ó *Riain*, ed., Folia Gadelica, Cork 1983.

So much for the intention which is implict in the content of the works. The historian would also wish to have evidence on the actual reception of these works which would show that we are dealing with communication rather than mere expression, or even the use of literary conventions which may have been taken over from the work of the *filid*. Francis John Byrne is in no doubt as to the social significance of Irish mythology: 'The importance of mythology for the historical understanding of an early society cannot be overstressed. The Irish concept of kingship, for instance, is rooted in mythology. Myth in turn counteracts upon history. If life may be said to imitate art, it is even more true that if in early Ireland we can isolate a characteristic myth of kingship we shall find historical kings attempting to live up to the demands of that myth'[58]. It can certainly be said that the modern scholar who seeks to understand the mythology and ideology of kingship in early Ireland must do this by examining the extant narrative texts, together with the Laws and the Wisdom Literature. What remains in question is the degree to which the mythology and the ideology were propagated and perpetuated outside the monasteries by means of texts which were written out within the monastic scriptoria.

The Work

Some years age, James Carney wrote: 'Much close work remains to be done on Irish literature, and meanwhile generalisations are very dangerous'[59], and, further, 'every saga requires careful analytic study, and every other saga, anecdote or tradition used to elucidate it must itself be subjected to scrutiny and analysis'[60]. It is true, of course, that the studies which have already been done on early Irish literature have all been intended to elucidate the material in one way or another. Thus, much of the theorising on the relationship between orality and literacy in Irish tradition has arisen from a desire to account for what have been taken to be inadequacies (or at best peculiarities) in the extant texts. The mimetic, mythological and textualist approaches to the universe of Irish narrative have to do with the content of the texts, and consideration of the audience of the tales throws light on their function in society. For all that, however, the kinds of criticism which we have been considering all share the tendency to divert attention from the need to interpret early tales as literary works.

A distinction was made above between inter-textual and intra-textual criticism. Even the latter variety tends, as it is practised in our field, to shy away from the rigorous analysis of the literary properties of the work. The usual procedure is the 'geological' one of isolating strata in the manuscript text or texts of a given work, and of striving thereby to describe its genesis. Whatever contention there may be

---

58 F. J. *Byrne, Senchas:* (as above note 32), p. 146.
59 Introduction to *Knott* and *Murphy,* Early Irish Literature, p. 2.
60 Ibid., p. 17.

about the manner in which criticism of this kind has hitherto been conducted[61], it must be conceded that, issuing as they have done from a continuous process of composition and transmission, our manuscript materials conduce by their very nature to 'geological' criticism.

All that need be said is that the attempt to rediscover the process whereby a given work of literature came into being is a valid exercise, but that it does not exhaust the critic's task: there must also be elucidation and interpretation of the product itself. What is now most urgently required in the study of early Irish narrative literature — apart from the edition and translation of texts — is the careful analysis of individual works, and, in particular, the kind of study which, as Abrams puts it, would analyse each work 'as a self-sufficient entity constituted by its parts in their internal relation'[62]. An approach of this kind would not be intended to replace existing criticism, but rather to complement and balance it.

A specimen of early Irish narrative

It has not been possible in the space at my disposal to illustrate the discussion with excerpts from the Irish texts. By way of compensation for this, a short excerpt is given here in translation from *Cath Maige Tuired*[63], the story of the war between the Túatha Dé Danann and the Fomoiri which culminated in a great battle said to have been fought at Mag Tuired (now Moytirra in Co. Sligo). The background to the passage given here is that Núadu, king of the Túatha Dé Danann, had lost an arm in battle, and had therefore to relinquish the kingship, since a king must be without physical blemish. This excerpt will serve as a minor specimen of the imaginative literature which was being written out in the monastic scriptoria, and it is followed by a brief commentary showing the relevance of the passage to the matters which have been discussed in the course of this paper.

> Now Núadu was being treated (for his disability), and a silver hand was put on him by Dían Cécht with the motion which every hand has.
> But Dían Cécht's son Míach disapproved of that. He went to fetch the hand (which had been struck off Núadu) and he said: 'Joint to joint of it, sinew to sinew!' And he healed Núadu in the course of three periods of three days. For the first three days he put it up against his side and it became covered with skin. For the second three days he put it on his breast. During the third three days he would cast white bundles (?) of black bullrushes when they had been blackened in a fire.

61 See note 44.
62 The Mirror and the Lamp, p. 26.
63 See note 42. The passage comprises §§ 33—35 of Stokes's edition. The translation is my own, but draws where possible on Stokes.

Dían Cécht disapproved of that remedy. He hurled a sword into the crown of his son's head so that it cut the skin down to the flesh on his head. The lad healed that by exercising his skill. Dían Cécht struck him again and cut his flesh as far as the bone. The lad healed this by the same means. Dían Cécht struck a third blow and reached the membrane of his brain. This too the lad healed by the same means. Dían Cécht then struck a fourth blow and cut out the brain, so that Míach died, and Dían Cécht said that no physician could heal himself of that stroke.

Then Míach was buried by Dían Cécht, and three hundred and sixty-five herbs, in accordance with the number of his joints and sinews, grew through the grave. Airmed[64] then spread out her cloak and she piled up those herbs in their proper order. But Dían Cécht came to her, and he mixed up the herbs so that their proper curative uses were not known, unless the Holy Spirit should teach them afterwards.

And Dían Cécht said: 'If Míach be not alive, Airmed shall survive.'

Commentary

Cath Maige Tuired survives in only one late manuscript[65], but it nevertheless provides a good example of the continuous process of composition and transmission in Irish manuscript tradition. The extant text is in a sixteenth-century vellum manuscript, BL Harley 5280, and it was written out by one Giolla Riabhach Ó Cléirigh[66]. We have no external evidence on the genesis of Giolla Riabhach's text; the internal evidence suggests that we have to do with a 'composite work put together by an eleventh- or twelfth-century redactor mainly from ninth-century material'[67]. While we have no information on those who preceded Giolla Riabhach in the composition and transmission of this tale, the presumption on present evidence must be that its manuscript life began in a monastic scriptorium in the Old Irish period (600—900), and continued in the monasteries until the twelfth century, when the custody of the manuscript literature passed into lay hands[68]. The language of our excerpt would indicate that it was first written down within the Old Irish period.

Cath Maige Tuired abounds in pagan survivals, and one of them occurs in our excerpt in the person of Núadu who is the Irish reflex of the Celtic god known in British as Nodons (or Nodens), and in Welsh as Nudd (and Lludd, owing to

---

64 Dían Cécht's daughter.

65 Two other tales connected with the battle are discussed in *Knott* and *Murphy*, Early Irish Literature, p. 109 f.

66 See Robin *Flower*, Catalogue of Irish Manuscripts in the British Museum, London 1926, p. 298 ff, and Paul *Walsh*, Irish Men of Learning, Dublin 1947, p. 48.

67 *Knott* and *Murphy*, Early Irish Literature, p. 109.

68 See note 22.

assimilation of the initial to that of the epithet *Llaw Ereint* 'of the Silver Hand')[69]. Núadu's name, his epithet *Airgetlám* ('of the Silver Hand'), and perhaps something of his role in *Cath Maige Tuired*[70], are traceable to Common Celtic, and must therefore have come into the written record from oral tradition. The same route was doubtless followed by the magical charm which Míach uses in healing Núadu[71]. In our text this charm is thoroughly pagan, but it is to be found in a Christianised form in the later oral tradition[72]. We are reminded, however, of the ecclesiastical dimension by the reference in our excerpt to the Holy Spirit.

Gerard Murphy said of *Cath Maige Tuired* that 'its juxtaposition of Old Irish and Middle Irish matter and its tendency to record stray scraps of lore about the characters mentioned, rather than to concentrate on episodes essential to the theme, remind one forcibly of the museum type of arrangement ... which is so common in manuscript texts of our older saga-tradition'[73]. Here Murphy is referring to his theory that 'medieval Irish manuscripts would seem indeed to be related to living storytelling much as the museum to-day is related to living material culture'[74]. In positing significant difference between oral and written storytelling, Murphy is at one with James Carney: 'I find it impossible for many reasons to believe that the form of any of the fictions or entertainments preserved in our medieval manuscripts is in any way close to the form in which they would be told when they existed (in so far as they actually did) on a purely oral level'[75]. They diverge radically, however, in that for Murphy 'any artistry in the sagas redounds to the credit of the oral storytellers; any defects are ascribable to the written tradition'[76], whereas Carney is inclined to attribute the literary qualities of the Irish texts to what he calls 'the external element'. The evidence upon which Carney bases his contention that 'those features (of *Táin Bó Cúailnge*) which are part of the epic scale of presentation must be due to imitation of the classics or of Christian developments of them'[77] includes a small number of items in the *Táin* which are comparable to the mention of the Holy Spirit in our text. *Cath Maige Tuired* also displays an epic scale of presentation, but a stray reference to the Holy Spirit is not sufficient reason for attributing this to external influence.

69 See Anne *Ross*, Pagan Celtic Britain, p. 176 ff, and P. *Mac Cana*, Celtic Mythology, p. 67 ff.

70 On this latter, see *Mac Cana*, p. 69, and Brynley F. *Roberts*, Cyfranc Lludd a Llefelys, Dublin 1975, p. XIX.

71 On this charm and others of a very similar kind, see Rolf *Ködderitzsch*, Der Zweite Merseburger Zauberspruch und seine Parallelen, ZCP 30 (1974), p. 45—57.

72 Ibid., p. 50

73 *Knott* and *Murphy*, Early Irish Literature, p. 110.

74 Ibid., p. 101.

75 James *Carney*, SILH p. 277.

76 Gearóid *Mac Eoin*, review of *Knott* and *Murphy*, Early Irish Literature, Stud. Hib. 7 (1967), p. 246—47, at 246.

77 See note 15.

This excerpt might not appear fertile ground for the mimetic critic, but Wolfgang Meid has suggested that the Celts could fit artificial limbs, his evidence being the name of a third-century Caledonian chief, one Argentocoxos ('Silver Foot')[78]. As this suggestion is, to say the least, extremely improbable, we may pass on to the mythological and textualist critics. The dispute between Dían Cécht and his son is a version of the Generation Conflict, and there has been a deal of discussion, first as to the origin and history of the Generation Conflict in general[79], and secondly as to the origin of the Irish versions in particular[80]. Schultz adduced the Ulster version of the Generation Conflict in support of his contention that Thurneysen underestimated the mythological component of the Ulster Cycle[81], and there are good grounds for seeing the Conflict as an Indo-European myth[82]. On the other hand, Tom Peete Cross argued that the Irish *literati* borrowed the Conflict from the Anglo-Saxons[83], and while his case is less than compelling, it cannot be disproved.

Whatever one may think about the origin of the Generation Conflict as it occurs in Irish literature — my own inclination is to see it as a survival rather than a borrowing — one must also attend to the manner in which it is used in this text. It is found in the anecdote about Dían Cécht and Míach, and this anecdote is told in the course of a story about Bres, king of the Fomoiri, a story which is a version of the Generation Conflict[84]. The authors of our manuscript tales were not hidebound by considerations of linear exposition: thematic iteration is a common feature of their work, and in the present excerpt we have an example of the sandwich structure in which one realisation of the Generation Conflict is slotted

78 Wolfgang *Meid*, Dichtkunst, Rechtspflege und Medizin im alten Irland, in Manfred *Mayrhofer* et al., ed., Antiquitates Indogermaniae, Innsbruck 1974, p. 21—34, at 26f. I am indebted to Liam Breatnach for this reference.

79 Of the vast secondary literature on this subject, one may mention M. A. *Potter*, Sohrab and Rustem, London 1902; Jan *de Vries*, Das Motiv des Vater-Sohn-Kampfes im Hildebrandslied, Germanisch-romanische Monatsschrift 34 (1954), p. 257—274; and A. *van der Lee*, Zum literarischen Motiv von der Vatersuche (Verhandelingen der Koninklijke Nederlandse Akademie van Wetenschappen, NR, Deel LXIII, Nr. 3, Amsterdam, 1957).

80 See Tom Peete *Cross*, 'A Note on "Sohrab and Rustum" in Ireland', The Journal of Celtic Studies 1 (1950), p. 176—182; *Knott* and *Murphy*, Early Irish Literature, p. 128, and the works there cited.

81 Wolfgang *Schultz*, review of Die irische Helden- und Königssage ZCP 14 (1923), p. 299—305, at 302.

82 See Jan *de Vries*, (as above note 79). This passage has also been interpreted in Dumézilian terms: see Jean *Puhvel*, Mythological Reflections of Indo-European Medicine, in: George *Cardona* et al. (ed.), Indo-European and Indo-Europeans, Philadelphia 1970, p. 369—82, at 378ff.

83 *Cross*, p. 180ff. See also K. H. *Jackson*, The International Popular Tale and Early Welsh Tradition, p. 70f.

84 See *Cross*, p. 179.

into another[85]. The story of how Dían Cécht killed his son may be what Murphy called 'a scrap of lore', but in our text it is integrated into a work of literature, and not treated as a mere museum-piece.

In conclusion it may be said that early Irish narrative literature is not the detritus of a lost mythology, nor yet a new phenomenon, born, like Athena, fully grown. It is the creation of a society which had two sets of cultural institutions, one indigenous, and oral in its medium, the other ecclesiastical and literate. These were sometimes hostile, sometimes amicable, but between them they contributed to the formation of a literature which combined matter drawn from the oral tradition with other elements and transmuted them into something new. It is a remarkable literature, and it must be accounted a significant achievement, not only of Ireland, but of Western Christendom.

85 One may compare the structure of the well-known tale *Scéla Mucce Meic Dathó* (ed. R. *Thurneysen*, Dublin 1935). In this tale, as in *Táin Bó Cúailnge*, the Ulaid and the Connachta are in contention for possession of a sacred animal: in the *Táin* it is the Bull of Cooley, in *Scéla Mucce* Mac Dathó's hound Ailbe. In the latter story, however, an account of how the Ulaid and the Connachta contend for possession of a sacred pig is given within the framing story of the contention for the hound.

V

Irland und Europa
Ireland and Europe

The oldest Irish manuscripts and their late antique background

By
Julian Brown

I

Surviving Insular manuscripts of the seventh century, most of which were written either in Ireland or else in Northumbria while it was still under predominantly Irish influence, differ markedly from their continental contemporaries, in construction, handwriting and decoration. By the end of the century, Northumbrian books such as the great Gospel books from Lindisfarne and the Biblical manuscripts of Wearmouth-Jarrow were already under strong Italian influence, some derived from older and some from contemporary books imported as a result of close ecclesiastical relationships with Rome itself; but the distinctive character of the Insular book persisted in England, as in Ireland, throughout the eighth century and beyond. Irish and Anglo-Saxon books, in spite of great local variation, continue to have basic characteristics in common which differentiate them very clearly from non-Insular books, and which enable us to identify books written on the Continent by Irish or Anglo-Saxon scribes, or by the pupils of such scribes — Irish at Bobbio, Anglo-Saxon at centres like Fulda or Würzburg. The purpose of this paper is to propose an historical hypothesis which could account not only for the existence of a marked contrast between Insular and non-Insular books but for the overall nature of the contrast.

Briefly stated, the hypothesis is that the character of the oldest surviving Insular books was determined by the cultural dependence of the Irish Church in the fifth and sixth centuries on a British Church which was 'provincial' even before the withdrawal of the Roman civil and military administration after AD 410, and which apparently lost touch with Rome between 454, when Pope Leo I announced a new method for calculating the date of Easter, and 457, when Victorius's system was adopted on the Continent, but not in Britain or Ireland. Virgilian mosaics in the villas of Roman Britain argue for a degree of literary culture among their no doubt wealthy and influential inhabitants; and there are grounds for thinking that the Latinity of the native magnates was of the pedantic sort to be expected in a bilingual society in which British, not Latin, was the basic language. Copies of the great Latin classics – Virgil and Cicero, perhaps even Terence and Livy – were no doubt to be found here and there in the Romano-British provinces; but books of the high, professional quality of the Bembine Terence (1, 12)[1] or the Medicean

---

1 References to E.A. *Lowe*, Codices Latini Antiquiores, parts 1—11 and Supplement, Oxford 1934—71 (2nd edn of part 2, 1972) are given in the text in round brackets, e.g. (1,12).

Virgil (3,296), in rustic capitals, or of the palimpsest *De republica* (1,35) or the Vienna Livy (10,472), in uncials, seem unlikely to have been produced even in London, for want of a big enough market. The nearest centres of professional book production to the frontier provinces of Roman Britain were no doubt Lyons and probably Trier. If 'professional' books were produced in Roman Britain, they have left no trace on the character of the oldest Irish manuscripts, which appears to derive from the semi-professional end of scale of Late Antique book production. Furthermore, there are archaic elements in the Insular systems of script and of book production which argue for a long period of isolation from developments in the main stream.

II

Which, then, are the oldest Irish manuscripts? Most primitive in script, and so perhaps earliest in date, are the set of waxed tablets from Springmount Bog (Suppl., 1684), containing Psalms 30—32, and the Gospel book generally known — mistakenly — as Codex Usserianus Primus (2,271). The handwriting of the tablets is mature and expert (to write well on wax was not easy); and the three psalms were probably written out by a senior monk for one who was not *psalteratus* to study during a longish journey, as prescribed in the *Regula Magistri*[2]. The Gospel book is also a mature performance, by two scribes of similar training. Since the techniques of stylus on wax and of a broad pen (quill or reed) on membrane are so different, and since a devotional exercise only written to be erased after a day or two is so much less consequential than a Gospel book written to do long service at the Mass, I prefer not to try to arrange these two items in chronological order. The calligraphy of both is plain and unpretentious; and both of them exhibit open loops at the tops of ascending strokes. That both are actually as well as typologically older than the next three books to be mentioned seems probable. I can think of no means to establish that the tablets were written after about AD 600 rather than before. The most hopeful-seeming clue to the date of the Gospel book is the Chi-Rho monogram with alpha and omega used as colophon decoration between Luke and Mark (fol. 149v). But is it a survival from the remote British past — the oldest known example of a similar device is in the fifth-century Lactantius from Africa now in Bologna (3,280); or is it the result of fresh contacts with Italian book-production in the period inaugurated by Columbanus's departure for the Continent in 590?

The handwriting of the next three books is all formal, or at least semi-formal, and two of them cannot be older than the first half of the seventh century. The Orosius in Milan (3,328) is partly on Insular and partly on continental membrane, and has initials which are not all typically Insular. It was at Bobbio in the fifteenth

2 Cap. *LVII*, §§ 4—9. See La Règle du Maître, ed Adalbert *de Vogüé*, vol. II, Paris 1964, p. 268.

century and was probably written there, after 613, when the house was founded. The fragment of Isidore, *Etymologiae* at St. Gallen (7,995) was either written after the posthumous 'publication' of the work in 636, or else represents the state of the text as Isidore left it at his death in 633. The Psalter called the *Cathach* of St Columba (2,266) has initials with motifs — notably a cross with expanded arms on a little stand — which evidently derive from a manuscript very similar to a Gregorius Magnus, *Cura pastoralis* (6,838), containing authorial but not autograph corrections, which was written at Rome before Gregory's death in 604[3]. This fact appears to rule out a date in the sixth century for the *Cathach;* but did the model reach Ireland soon after it was made, or — as I suspect — in about 630, brought back as a papal gift of a very usual kind to the group of clergy from South Eastern Ireland who had visited Rome to prepare themselves for the adoption of the Roman Easter reckoning?[4] The *Cathach* and the Isidore fragment are both remarkable for a very pronounced 'diminuendo' of display letters between an initial and the first text letters of standard size. The formal scripts of both the Orosius and the *Cathach* are more solemn and evolved than the script of the 'Ussher' Gospel book: instead of a loop, ascenders have a solid wedge formed by means of a separate preliminary stroke, as in most later examples of Insular half-uncial. Though lighter, the script of the Isidore fragment is also set, although cursively written punctuation and abbreviation marks show that the writer was thoroughly familiar with a rapid cursive ductus.

The fragments of Gospel text in Durham A.II.10 etc. (2,147), from a large volume which may have been a New Testament, or even perhaps a complete Bible, rather than a liturgical Gospel book, are in a half-uncial which has rather more style than those of the Orosius and the *Cathach;* but the diminuendo at the beginning of Mark (fol. 2r) is strongly reminiscent of the *Cathach* and of the Isidore fragment. Its Durham provenance suggests that A.II.10 was written in Northumbria, while Northumbria was still almost entirely dependent on Ireland for its conception of writing. The script and initials of a palimpsest Gallican Sacramentary of Irish origin (9,1298) seem to associate it closely with A.II.10.

The condition of the 'Ussher' Gospels shows that like the *Cathach* it was once enshrined in a *cumdach* — a practice that was apparently not followed at Bobbio, or elsewhere on the Continent; hence the fact that neither it, nor the Isidore fragment, appears to have been made from typically Insular membrane need not mean, as has sometimes been suggested, that either book was written at Bobbio; and even if they were, the absence of continental symptoms in the handwriting

3 Carl *Nordenfalk*, Before the Book of Durrow, Acta Archaeologica 18 (1947), p. 151—9.

4 I am not convinced by recent attempts to date the *Cathach* in the sixth century. See Bella *Schauman*, The Irish script of the MS Milan, Biblioteca Ambrosiana, S. 45 Sup. (ante ca. 625), Scriptorium 32 (1978), p. 3—18; *ead.*, Early Irish manuscripts, Expedition 21 (1979), p. 33—47; Uta *Roth*, Studien zur Ornamentik frühchristlicher Handschriften des insularen Bereichs, Sonderdruck aus Bericht der Römisch-Germanischen Kommission 60 (1979).

would still suggest that their scribes were of purely Irish formation, like the scribe of Durham A.II.10.

The cursive elements in the script of the Isidore fragment, and in the last few lines of Mark in Durham A.II.10, show that the formal script found in all the books so far discussed — though not in the tablets — was written against a background of the ability to write cursively; and the mostly set but partly cursive minuscule of the Antiphonary (3,311) written at Bangor between 680 and 691 points clearly in the same direction. The closeness of the tall, narrow minuscule found — written small — in the Book of Armagh (2,270), ca. 807, and in the Book of Mulling (2,276), which cannot be much earlier, in spite of its colophon, to early examples of minuscule from Northumbria and from South West England, suggests that our picture of Irish handwriting in the seventh century ought to be filled out by the inclusion of certain early Anglo-Saxon books written while Irish influence was still predominant. Examples of early Northumbrian minuscule are the work of three scribes in the Palatine manuscript of Paulinus of Nola (1,87), and the work of one scribe in a Jerome and an Augustine manuscript from Echternach (5,584 and 588). The handwriting of St Boniface, as seen in marginalia in the Douce manuscript of Primasius (2,257) and in the Codex Fuldensis of the New Testament (8,1196), and in part of the main text of a Corbie manuscript at Leningrad (11,1618), is probably the earliest surviving example of minuscule from South West England. The three Northumbrian books appear to have been written soon after 700; and Boniface must certainly have learned to write before 700. So we may regard early Northumbrian and early South Western minuscule (Types IA and IB, in my terminology) as seventh-century phenomena. The small Insular minuscule of parts of two grammatical manuscripts from Bobbio, now in Naples (3,391, 394 and 397b; 3,400) is very like the scripts of *Armagh* and *Mulling;* and it is all apparently contemporary with a part of one of them (3,403) which is in North Italian minuscule that is very probably to be dated between 687 and 701. If well-developed minuscule existed at the end of the seventh century in England and at Bobbio, then the common point of origin must have been Ireland — and Ireland no later than the period in the middle of the century which produced the St. Gallen fragments of Isidore and Durham A.II.10, with their minuscule symptoms.

I shall now consider how the basic palaeographical and codicological features of these books relate to Late Antique practice as known from surviving manuscripts produced in Italy, Africa and Gaul in the fifth and sixth centuries.

III

An obvious palaeographical point of departure is the absence from Irish manuscripts of any period of the two most formal scripts of Late Antiquity: rustic capitals and uncials. These entered England at the end of the seventh century; and the latter, based on seventh-century Roman models, was widespread there in the first half, at least, of the eighth century. Since the script of most of the oldest known

Insular books, Anglo-Saxon and Irish alike, is the Insular version of half-uncial, it has been said that the script from which the whole Insular system, minuscule as well as half-uncial, developed must have been continental half-uncial of the fifth and sixth centuries. But we have just seen that the predominance of half-uncial in seventh-century Irish books was less complete than appears at first sight: not only was minuscule a well established part of the Insular system of scripts by the middle of the century at the latest, but an important technical consideration suggests that Insular half-uncial is much more likely to have derived from minuscule than *vice versa*. From the fourth century onwards Roman cursive script, whether in documentary or in literary contexts, is notable for the loops at the top of ascending strokes, on the left, which enabled such strokes to be ligatured with certain preceding letters such as *a, r* and *t*. These loops were often open, but could be closed; and in either case they were functional. In the later half-uncial of manuscripts like the Basilican Hilary (1, 1a), which is based on later cursive, the loops have evolved into decorative clubbing, which can no longer serve the original purpose of the loops. But open, if triangular, loops are present in the Springmount Bog tablets and in the 'Ussher' Gospels, not yet evolved into the purely decorative wedges — made with an auxiliary fore-stroke — of the Orosius, the *Cathach* and Durham A.II.10. The two early examples seem to represent a half-way stage between non-functional wedges and the functional loops — used in straight *d* and in ligatures such as *ab* and *al* — which are much in evidence in the early Northumbrian specimens of minuscule noticed above, in one of the early specimens from Bobbio (3,391), and in the Books of Armagh and of Mulling. The fundamental place of the loop in the morphology of Insular script seems, incidentally, to rule out the possibility that the Insular script system derives from 'early half-uncial', whether in its primitive form, as in the Epitome of Livy (2,208), saec. II—III, or in the later form found in the Florentine manuscript of Justinian's *Digesta* (3,295), after 533: loops are wanting at both stages.

The archive of Flavius Abinnaeus, a Roman cavalry officer in Egypt, 340—350, shows that by then Roman cursive with functional loops was already firmly established in government circles; and since regional differences in Roman official handwriting are unknown, it is safe to conclude that similar script was in use in Roman Britain at least two generations before the withdrawal that followed the sack of Rome in 410. The script of the sixth-century Paris manuscript of Avitus on papyrus (5,573) evidently depends on tall, extravagant official cursive of the type found in the Abinnaeus archive and in contemporary, sixth-century papyrus documents from Ravenna. And a similar relationship exists between the documentary cursive of the Merovingian chancery and the literary minuscule of Luxeuil, at the end of the seventh century. If the earliest known Insular minuscule fails to conform to the pattern of new Roman cursive in provincial chanceries, it is presumably because there was no such pattern to follow, once the imperial chanceries of the Romano-British provinces had been closed. Literacy and Christianity, however, survived the political crisis. Books were as necessary as ever, for the liturgy and for basic ecclesiastical teaching; correspondence had to be carried on between churchmen; literary works, such as Patrick's and Gildas's, were drafted. Wendy Davies has recently shown good reason to believe that in the fifth century South West England knew a method of drafting and registering documents — mostly transfers of property rights and manumissions of slaves — under ecclesiastical auspices, which spread to Brittany with the migrations and to Ireland with the British missions[5]. Though creditable enough in the difficult political circumstances of the times, the prevailing level of intellectual and administrative activity in the sub-Roman Church of Britain, and so in the Irish Church which largely depended on it, was not high by continental standards.

The system of scripts needed to support such activity could have been — and surely was — a simple one. At the bottom, learners of all ages must have started with a 'script of instruction' comparable to the *scrittura di base* that has been identified among the subscriptions to Italian documents of the eighth century as the work of literate men who had not been able or willing to acquire the expert handwriting of either the literary scribe or the notary: for the learner, it is enough to have to master the basic shapes of the letters, without having to worry about style. A few examples of 'script of instruction' survive from Anglo-Saxon England; and one feature of some of them — the reduction of the Insular loop or wedge to a mere hook — makes an occasional appearance in the Springmount Bog tablets, which were expertly written — they are an aid to devotion, not an exercise in writing —, but in a difficult medium. After the indispensible *scrittura de base*, it will have been natural for the sub-Roman writing system, as for its parent and for its descendants, to bifurcate into some sort of formal script suitable for books used in the liturgy and some sort of more rapid, less formal script used for correspondence and administration, and perhaps for books in the educational rather than the liturgical field. Lack of need, lack of wealth, and lack of training will have excluded both professional book hands — rustic capitals, uncials, high-grade half-uncials — and elegant chancery hands. The lower-grade handwriting appropriate to what we think we know of ecclesiastical activity in the British Isles during the fifth and sixth centuries certainly sprang from roots in a fourth-century system of scripts that was common to the Empire as a whole; and although few examples of lower-grade handwriting have survived from other parts of the Empire during the same period, there can be no doubt that such handwriting was very widely used in a society in which literacy was still quite common and which was still being administered with a good deal of system. With books and documents, as with other artifacts, we must not underestimate the value of mere elegance as a passport to survival.

5 Wendy *Davies*, The Latin Charter-tradition in Western Britain, Brittany and Ireland in the early medieval period, in: Ireland in Early Mediaeval Europe, Studies in memory of Kathleen Hughes, ed. Dorothy *Whitelock*, Rosamond *McKitterick* and David *Dumville*, Cambridge 1982, p. 258—80.

A small papyrus codex from Egypt, now in Barcelona (Suppl., 1782) contains Cicero's first Catalinarian oration followed by a *Psalmus responsorius* in honour of the Blessed Virgin. It is probably as early as the fourth century; the contents show that the owner was a Christian with an interest in rhetoric; and the handwriting suggests that owner and scribe were one and the same. The handwriting is large, plain and careful; and the semi-cursive script, though evidently incorporating some features of contemporary cursive (notably some loops and many loops reduced to hooks), is neither literary nor administrative in style, but seems to be the work of an amateur writer — perhaps a youth who was not unaccustomed to writing but whose training had scarcely progressed beyond the level of *scrittura di base*. Compare a papyrus sheet (Suppl., 1705) with a Latin alphabet in later (*not* early) half-uncials written out as a model for school use, by Greek pupils. More numerous are the examples of the expert cursive script — called 'quarter-uncial' in CLA and 'cursive half-uncial' elsewhere, but better called 'literary cursive' — which was apparently the day-to-day handwriting of the professional scholar (*grammaticus* or *rhetoricus*); presumably of the learned cleric (a Jerome or an Augustine); and presumably of the educated layman (a Symmachus, a Boethius, a Cassiodorus). Though fully cursive in ductus and making free use of ligatures, including ligatures with looped ascenders, this kind of script is modest in size and eschews the long ascenders of chancery minuscule. Most of the known examples are in the form of marginal scholia; and the two richest sources of these are probably the late fourth-century Bembine Terence (1,12), where the scholia are either contemporary or not much later than the main text, and the Bologna Lactantius (3,280), in which main text and scholia alike appear to be of the later fifth century. The writers of such a script no doubt used it for their correspondence; but none of their innumerable letters has survived in its original form. And if they were, as they surely must have been, anything like Italian humanists of the fifteenth-century, they will often have used it to copy the main text of books for their own use. In antiquity, many such books will have been written on papyrus, like the sixth-century Josephus in Milan (3,304); and the combination of perishable material with cursive script will have greatly reduced their chances of survival. The script of the Josephus has a certain documentary flavour, but the script of the remains of two manuscripts of grammatical texts once at Bobbio, where — as we have seen — additions in Irish minuscule were made at the end of the seventh century, is characterized by a thoroughly literary restraint, which associates them with the scholia of the Bembine Terence and the Bologna Lactantius. One of them (3,397a) contains texts by Probus and Charisius, etc.; the other (3,398 and 4,462) texts by Probus and Claudius Sacerdos: matter that obviously appealed to the Bobbio Irish in the seventh century and which would have been no less welcome to British and Irish scholars in earlier centuries, since Latin was never the mother tongue of either people. Archaic features in both books argue for a date in the fifth century; and E.A. Lowe has observed that in the Claudius Sacerdos volume the shafts of *b* and *l* are apt to be sway-backed, as they are in most Insular script. In the

Probus-Charisius volume in particular, as at fol. 131v, paragraphs often begin with an enlarged letter followed by a gradual diminuendo of letters coming down to standard text size. This is evidently ancestral to the highly mannered initial-*plus*-diminuendo of the St. Gallen Isidore fragment and the *Cathach*. It is the natural outcome of starting a paragraph with a ligature such as *ter*, which would look absurd if an enlarged *t* lead straight into an *e* and an *r* of standard text size. In the Milan Josephus there is something comparable at the beginning of Book VI: the opening word — *tenentes* — begins with a ligature of *ten* in which a much-enlarged *t*, written with a very broad pen, leads into an *e* and an *n*, written with a pen of the width used for the text, which are taller than standard text size, as indeed are the remaining letters in the word[6]. Only a little more regular than the handwriting of the two grammar books is the handwriting of the Ambrose on Luke (5,654), also apparently of the fifth century, which occurs as the lower script in a palimpsest section of the Bobbio 'Missal'. Here too *b* and *l* have sway-backs; and at fol. 296v the *gn* ligature in the last line and the *eg* ligature in the fourth line up are equally close to standard Insular practice in the seventh century. The form of the *et* ligature (e.g. fol. 297v), in which the cross bar of *t* is represented by a final horizontal stroke well above the base-line, and not by an upwards continuation of the first stroke of all, as in the more usual 'ampersand' ligature, is the standard Insular form in all periods and places; and Luigi Schiaparelli pointed out long ago that in Roman documentary script this form, used in the fourth century, was superseded by another in the fifth[7]. The two grammar books and the scholia in the Terence and the Lactantius, all apparently of the fifth century, use the same form. An archaic *et* ligature is not the only ligature to distinguish Insular minuscule of the seventh century from contemporary minuscule on the Continent: several differences, and the use of subscript letters (notably *a, i, o* and *t* after *h, m* and *n*, often added cursively, without a penlift) argue for a long period of isolation during which distinct traditions could be established. The fragments of Arator (Suppl., 1740), ascribed by Lowe to North Italy, or perhaps Gaul, saec. VI—VII, which survive as offsets from pastedowns in the fifteenth-century binding of a twelfth-century manuscript from St Augustine's Canterbury, are in a small script on the borderline between literary cursive and half-uncial. The Bodleian Summary Catalogue originally described it as Insular, ninth century, but there are no specifically Insular symptoms.

A notoriously 'Insular' feature of all Insular script is the large stock of abbreviations of the type known in the early Middle Ages as *notae juris*, some of which are

---

6 The same origin for the diminuendo has been suggested independently by *McGurk*, The Irish Pocket Gospel Book, p. 256, n.3 (n.14 below), in relation to the Paris Avitus, and by Bella *Schauman* in relation to the Naples manuscript. For the Josephus, see Franz *Steffens*, Lateinische Paläographie, Trier ²1909, pl. 23a.

7 Luigi *Schiaparelli*, Intorno all'origine e ad alcuni charatteri della scrittura e del sistema abbreviativo irlandese, in his: Note paleografiche (1910—1932), ed. Giorgio *Cencetti*, Turin 1969, esp. p. 222, 230.

late versions of signs used in Tironian shorthand (*autem, con-, eius, enim, est, et*) while others (*nec, uel, uero*, etc.) are apparently translations of shorthand signs into ordinary letters accompanied by a superscript letter or by one of the standard marks of abbreviation (line or point). Many such abbreviations occur in two manuscripts of the Institutions of Gaius, in *BR* uncial and probably from Constantinople, one of which survives as the lower script of a palimpsest at Verona (4,488), while the other consists of a few fragments from Egypt, now in Florence (3,292). Their dates are probably saec. V and saec. V—VI respectively. Another source of similar abbreviations is the marginalia, but *not* the main text, of the sixth-century Reginensis of the Codex Theodosianus (1,110). These cases amply justify the term *notae juris;* but W.M. Lindsay preferred his own *notae communes*, on the ground that they are not confined to legal texts. That their use in manuscripts of the Theodosian and Justinianian codes was prohibited by the codes themselves suggested to Ludwig Traube that their occurrence in Insular script was a legacy from a South West Britain which the prohibitions — promulgated in 438 and 529 respectively — never reached, owing to the withdrawal of the imperial administration soon after 410. The manuscripts of Gaius and of the Codex Theodosianus confirm that the prohibitions were neither intended to be, nor interpreted as, general prohibitions, which would in any case have been unenforcable. Traube's hypothesis can perhaps be saved by basing it on the occurrence of *notae juris* in non-legal texts. Two of the manuscripts in literary cursive mentioned above contain such abbreviations: the Probus fragment in Turin (4,462) has one-letter abbreviations for *est* and *sunt*; the scholia in the Bembinus (1,12) have letter abbreviations for *est, esse, non, quam* and *quod*. And the late fifth-century half-uncial scholia in the Medicean Virgil (3,296) have the shorthand sign for *con-* and one-letter abbreviations for *-men, post, pro, qui, -tur* and *uel*.

Another literary context for *notae juris* is a fragmentary papyrus codex of some of Cicero's speeches (2,210), in early half-uncial of the fourth or fifth century (*est, esse, quod, tamen, tibi*). *Notae juris* are also to be found in specifically ecclesiastical contexts. Over a dozen occur in the contemporary marginalia in literary cursive in a sixth-century Augustine manuscript in half-uncials, apparently written at Verona and now divided between Paris and Leningrad (5,635 and 11, p.10). Three later manuscripts of patristic texts, all copied within the Anglo-Saxon sphere of influence, contain numerous *notae juris* in the main text which are outside the standard Insular range and so apparently derive from exemplars which were Late Antique, since no contemporary continental books contain anything similar on the same scale. These are Augustine's letters, Southern England, saec. VIII (6,737); Marius Victorinus, Lorsch, saec. VII ex. (Suppl., 1776); Augustine on music, Tours, ca. 800, Tours MS 268. The *notae* in these manuscripts seem likely to have been fed into the traditions of the three texts by learned ecclesiastics copying books for their own use in the period which produced the legal and literary manuscripts mentioned above. The script they wrote is likely to have been literary cursive: the only professionally written books in which *notae juris* occur freely in the main text are the two Gaius manuscripts in *BR* uncial mentioned above. Abbreviation in professionally written literary and patristic books of the fifth and sixth centuries is usually confined to *-bus, -que* and final *m* or *n*. If books in sub-Roman Britain were normally written by semi-professional writers, including well-educated writers, it is easy to see how a basic stock of *notae juris* could have been part of the Insular script system from its origins. The size of the stock in the seventh century, and its differences in detail from the smaller stock known at the same date on the Continent, can be explained partly in terms of Bernhard Bischoff's assumption that by the seventh century the Irish had developed their inherited system of abbreviation[8], and partly in terms of the long period of cultural isolation of the British Isles between the middle of the fifth century and the end of the sixth. The seven Insular abbreviations in the mere sixty lines of text surviving in the St. Gallen Isidore fragment, and the profusion of them in the manuscript of Adomnán (7,998) written by Dorbbéne, who died as abbot of Iona in 713, show that the abbreviations must have been firmly established in Ireland by the middle of the seventh century. If they are found rarely or not at all in the majority of seventh-century Insular books, it is only because most of those books were written for liturgical use.

And so evidence from several directions converges to support E.A. Lowe's conclusion that the ancestor of the Insular system of scripts was literary cursive — what he himself called 'quarter-uncial'[9]. If you take literary cursive, as found in the Springmount Bog tablets, remove most of the ligatures, change the ductus from cursive to set and and transform loops into wedges, the result is bound to be a kind of half-uncial, such as we find in the 'Ussher' Gospels. That the oldest Insular minuscule, as seen in the handwriting of St Boniface, in Northumbrian books like the Palatine Paulinus and the Jerome and Augustine from Echternach, and in the grammatical texts copied at Bobbio, all of the late seventh or early eighth century, developed out of literary cursive in the same sort of way but in the opposite direction is conceivable; but I am not inclined to accept Bernhard Bischoff's opinion that the Irish developed minuscule script only during the intellectual renaissance of the mid-seventh century. Half a century strikes me as a short time for a wholly new script to have spread from Ireland to Northumbria and South West England; and the early specimens from England and from Bobbio are no less sure of themselves than the very similar script in *Armagh* and *Mulling*, written about a century later. A passage in the fifth-century Bologna Lactantius (fol. 221v) shows how easily the literary cursive of a scholiast could assume a documentary aspect: longer ascenders and descenders, a few more ligatures, a somewhat accelerated ductus. As Bischoff says, the literary activity of the seventh-century Irish renaissance called for more writing. Was Insular minuscule, like humanistic cursive in the early fifteenth century, *invented* to serve a literary pur-

---

8 Bernhard *Bischoff*, Paläographie des römischen Altertums und des abendländischen Mittelalters, Berlin 1979, p. 107—15 (script), p. 192—200 (abbreviations).
   9 CLA 4, p. XXIII; cf. 2, p. XI.

pose? Or was it *appropriated* for the same purpose from the sphere of business-personal correspondence and administration, like Gothic cursive in the early fourteenth century? Or did the sub-Roman system of scripts which the Irish inherited from the British have two sides to it: a literary side capable of leading on to a local version of half-uncial; and a documentary side whose character shows through in the loops and ascenders of the oldest minuscule specimens, whether Irish or Anglo-Saxon? Fifth- and sixth-century clergy in the British Isles corresponded with each other; and they apparently kept written records of grants of land and of manumissions that involved religious establishments, and perhaps also of transactions between private individuals, although evidence for that is wanting. During the same period, ca. AD 500 to be precise, transfers of landed property between individuals in the Vandal-occupied area of Roman North Africa were being recorded in ink on wooden tablets in a cursive script which is smaller and less pretentious than the official version of New Roman Cursive, and at the same time less restrained and deliberate than literary cursive as we find it in the two fifth-century grammatical manuscripts in Naples. The type of document which the *Tablettes Albertini* respresent must once have been at least as widespread as the type of book represented by the Naples volumes; and we may reasonably suppose that the kind of unofficial documentary script in which they are written was used in Roman and sub-Roman Britain.

I conclude that the system of scripts used in the British and Irish Churches in the fifth and sixth centuries descended from the personal, unofficial end of the Later Roman script system as a whole, namely from the parts of it which were used by native writers in the period of transition — ca. 400 to ca. 450 — between Roman and sub-Roman Britain. Rustic capitals, uncials and formal half-uncials were excluded. Included were three main elements: *scrittura di base*; a literary cursive, comparable to the script of the Springmount Bog tablets, which could be formalized to produce a kind of half-uncial suitable for liturgical use, as in the 'Ussher' Gospels; and a documentary cursive, some traces of which can be detected in the fragment of Isidore from St. Gallen and in the last ten lines of Mark in Durham A.II.10, but which has left a clearer impression of itself in the oldest known Anglo-Saxon minuscule, some from Northumbria and some from the South West, and in the small Irish minuscule of the grammar texts written at Bobbio, of 'pocket Gospel-books' such as *Mulling*, and of the Book of Armagh[10].

IV

The typical quire in continental books of the fifth and sixth centuries differs in several ways from the typical quire of the oldest Insular books. In Late Antique

10 Ludwig *Bieler*, Insular palaeography: present state and problems, Scriptorium 3 (1949), p. 272—3 argues for the existence of 'quarter-uncial', half-uncial and cursive in sixth-century Ireland.

books, the thinnish membrane exhibits a strong contrast between a rougher, darker hair-side and a smoother, whiter flesh-side; quires are normally formed from four sheets folded to make eight leaves and arranged so that the first recto is a flesh-side and hair-sides and flesh-sides face each other in pairs in the rest of the quire; and sheets were ruled on the flesh-sides before folding, one or more at a time, from prickings in the outer margins or in the outer half of the written space, so that the furrows and ridges left by the hard point faced each other in pairs within the quire. From ca. 600 onwards regularly formed quires on the Continent began to be ruled on the hair-sides and to make the first recto a hair-side. Although irregularly formed quires in continental books of the seventh and eighth centuries tended to break some of these rules, membrane continued to be prepared so that hair- and flesh-sides differed considerably in appearance; and sheets continued to be pricked in outer margins only and ruled before folding. The standard quire of the period before 600, in which alternate openings within the quire consisted of pairs of ridged hair-sides followed by pairs of furrowed flesh-sides, is a well thought-out solution to the problem presented by the contrasts in appearance between hair-side and flesh-side and between ridge and furrow.

The typical Insular quire of the seventh century is made of thickish membrane, both sides of which tend to have a slight, suede-like knap, making the hair-side difficult to distinguish from the flesh-side; quires are normally formed from five sheets folded to make ten leaves and arranged with all hair-sides outwards, so that flesh-sides face hair-sides all through the quire. Having been folded, the quire was pricked in both margins and ruled vigorously with a hard point on the first recto, and then on one or more later rectos, sometimes also on the last verso, until every leaf was adequately ruled. In the ordinary way, all rectos were furrowed and all versos were ridged. In the first half of the quire, ridged flesh-sides on the left faced furrowed hair-sides on the right; in the second half, ridged hair-sides on the left faced furrowed flesh-sides on the right; between quires and the middle of quires, hair-sides faced hair-sides and flesh-sides faced flesh-sides respectively, but even here a ridged left-hand page faced a furrowed right-hand page. The thickness and the lack of contrast between hair-side and flesh-side in Insular membrane made this arrangement of the sheets less unsatisfactory than it would have been if the membrane had been prepared in the continental way, with one side smooth, white and obviously furrowed, and the other side rougher, grayish or yellowish in colour, and obviously ridged. But the confrontation between ridges and furrows in each Insular opening could be conspicuous; and ruling on a recto in the middle of a formed quire of ten leaves of thickish membrane cannot have been easy. All in all, the Insular quire of the seventh century strikes me as technologically primitive when compared to the continental quire of the fifth and sixth centuries.

Not all Insular books followed this standard method of quiring. In Irish books, the quires were often irregular — of six, eight, ten or twelve leaves — and ruling could be omitted or ignored; and the membrane was sometimes of extremely poor quality. From ca. 700 onwards Anglo-Saxon books, beginning with the Wearmouth-Jarrow Biblical volumes in uncials and the Lindisfarne Gospels (2,187), in all of which Italian influence was very strong, usually have quires of eight and not ten leaves, although arrangement, pricking and ruling remain the same as before. All the leaves in the Echternach Gospels (5,578) and some of the leaves in the Durham Gospels (2,149), both written at Lindisfarne ca. 698 by the same scribe, were apparently made from a stock of membrane prepared more or less in the continental way; and the membrane of the Stonyhurst Gospel of St John (2,260), a Wearmouth-Jarrow book also very likely of ca. 698, is also more continental than Insular in appearance. Neither the 'Ussher' Gospels nor the St. Gallen fragment of Isidore is in very good condition; but as far as one can tell, the membrane in each case has a rather continental appearance: a fact which has raised the question of of unusual membrane at Lindisfarne and Wearmouth-Jarrow look like isolated experiments with the continental method of preparation, in a period when Anglo-experiments with the continental method of preparation, in a period when Anglo-Saxon book-production was being heavily influenced by Italy; and it seems possible that the equally isolated cases of the two Irish specimens were similar experiments, inspired by the fresh contacts with Italy and/or Spain that brought on the Irish renaissance of the mid-seventh century. Normal Insular membrane occurs in the *Cathach*, the Bangor Antiphonary and the Schaffhausen Adomnán, from Ireland and Iona; in the Orosius and in other seventh-century books from Bobbio; and in all but the three mentioned above of the oldest Anglo-Saxon books, including Durham A.II.10: a pan-Insular diffusion which seems to prove that it was an early, basic feature of Irish book-production.

The Latin manuscripts of Late Antiquity whose quires diverge, according to CLA, from the Late Antique standard pattern in the direction of the Insular standard pattern are the following:

1. The Bembine Terence (1,12), Italy, saec.IV^2, in rustic capitals. Quires of ten leaves, apparently ruled after folding, several leaves at a time, on flesh-sides.
2. Seneca, *De Amicitia*, etc. (1. 69), saec. III—IV, in early half-unicals, probably from the Eastern Mediterranean. Probably ruled after folding.
3. Aulus Gellius (1,174), saec. IV, in rustic capitals, primary script in a palimpsest. Quires of ten leaves, ruled apparently after folding, on hair-sides.
4. Cicero, *In Verrem* (1,115), Italy, saec. V, in rustic capitals, primary script in a palimpsest. Quires mostly of ten leaves.
5. Lactantius (3,280), Africa, saec. V^2, in uncials. Quires normally of eight leaves, but ruled after folding on the first recto and on succeeding rectos as required.
6. Josephus, *De Antiquitatibus Judaicis* (3,304), North Italy, saec. VI, on papyrus, in cursive minuscule. Quires mostly of ten leaves.
7. Probus, etc. (3,397a), Italy, saec. V, in literary cursive. Quires mostly of eight leaves, but ruled after folding, on flesh-side or hair-side, with only a four-sided frame for the written space.

8. Gospels, Vetus Latina, Codex Bobiensis (k) (4,465), Africa, saec. IV—V, in uncials. Quires mostly of eight leaves, but ruled after folding on hair-sides, several leaves at a time. Late tradition says that the book was owned by Columbanus himself, but there are no solid grounds for thinking that he took it to Bobbio from Ireland.

The dates of these eight books suggest that in the fifth century quires of ten leaves and ruling after folding were going out of fashion, not coming in. And it is reasonable to suppose that if both practices are basic to the standard Insular quire, it is because they were known in Roman Britain early in the fifth century, in the period when local methods of book production lost touch with codicological developments on the Continent. In Ethiopia, a 'peripheral zone' which the codex form of book reached in the fifth century, quires of ten leaves are still standard[11].

Some further pointers in the same direction are obtainable from Sir Eric Turner's codicological examination[12] of the mostly fragmentary remains of Greek and Latin codices on papyrus and membrane as a whole, including much material outside the scope of CLA:

1. No codex consisting of eight-leaf quires only can be dated before the fourth century (p.62).
2. Between the third and the sixth century, the quire of ten leaves continues to be a stong rival to the quire of eight (p.63).
3. The quiring of the oldest known codices is often irregular (pp.60—64). Such irregularity is not uncommon in Irish manuscripts, although it is practically unknown in Anglo-Saxon manuscripts, on which the influence of the eight-leaf quire was strong from the end of the seventh century onwards.
4. Even in the oldest codices made of membrane hair-sides and flesh-sides usually faced each other within the quire: the natural result of folding a single skin to make four or eight leaves. But in codices made of papyrus horizontal fibres (rectos) usually faced vertical fibres (versos) (p.65); and papyrus codices in which matching pairs of vertical and horizontal fibres faced each other are less common before the fifth century than the other sort, in which vertical fibres faced horizontal fibres in unmatched pairs. Of Turner's listed examples of the former sort only about a quarter are earlier than the fifth century, while about half his examples of the latter sort are earlier (pp.66—7).

Papyrus must unquestionably have been imported into Roman Britain in large quantities down to the departure of the imperial troops and administrators after 410: the military and bureaucratic machines would soon have seized up without it. Further, the eventual triumph of membrane over papyrus as the standard material for a codex was hardly complete by the end of the fourth century; and we may reasonably suspect that at the lower end of the codicological scale, from which books produced in Roman Britain itself are likely to have come, papyrus

11 S.H. *Selassie*, Bookmaking in Ethiopia, Leiden 1981, p. 8,23.
12 E. G. *Turner*, The Typology of the early Codex, University of Pennsylvania 1977.

was still as common as, if not commoner than, membrane as the material for the manufacture of codices. With the Roman army and administration gone, regular supplies of papyrus, some of which will no doubt have been available for sale to the public, will have been cut off. When books had to be made of membrane, scribes who were not yet accustomed to folding single skins so as to bring hair-sides and flesh-sides together in matching pairs, may well have continued to form quires of membrane as if they were quires of papyrus, by making a pile of five sheets with all their hair-sides facing downward and then folding it, as if it were a pile of papyrus sheets cut from a roll (Turner, p. 43—50), with all their vertical fibres facing downwards. Papyrus codices were not normally pricked or ruled; but Insular pricking and ruling could well have been learned from imported fourth-century codices of membrane which resembled nos 1, 2 and 7 in the list on pp. 323—24 above. The result will have been a less advanced form of quire than the standard type found in the great majority of fifth-century codices on membrane.

The 'continental' type of membrane was apparently perfected long before the fifth century AD, since the quality of the Greek document from Dura Europos, third to second century BC, is reputedly excellent. Membrane of which the two sides were made to look as similar as possible was used for the earliest Hebrew books in the East and, in Yemen, down to the end of the Middle Ages; but hair-side and flesh-side alike are 'glossy', not suede-like[13]. Since Insular membrane has so little in common either with continental or with Oriental membrane, it seems reasonable to think of it as a local variant, devised in some Romano-British centre to make good the sudden disappearance of papyrus from a province in which the usual method of manufacture was not yet established. We meet it for the first time in seventh-century manuscripts of Irish and Anglo-Saxon origin; and if the Anglo-Saxons failed to give it up after their late-seventh-century love affair with Italian book production, it was probably because they found that it held ink and pigments equally well on both sides.

In most professionally produced Latin books of the fifth and sixth centuries the text is arranged in two columns; and Turner has suggested that papyrus codices with text in a single column were thought of as 'second-class' (p.37). The cache of fourth-century codices in Coptic from Nag Hamadi, made of papyrus and unpretentiously bound into leather jackets, is perhaps our best guide to the general appearance of 'second class' Christian books in late Antiquity; and all thirteen of them have text arranged in a single column. The two fifth-century grammar books at Naples, all in literary cursive, also have text in a single column. So do the 'Ussher' Gospels, the Bobbio Orosius, and the Isidore fragment at St. Gallen. The (early) eighth-century volume of glosses, partly in Anglo-Saxon and partly in Old Irish, on the Psalms (1,78), from Northumbria, in quires of ten, is strongly

13 Malachi *Beit-Arié*, Hebrew Codicology, Paris 1976, p. 22—6. Typically 'Ashkenazic' membrane, with the two sides made to look as alike as possible, began to be produced only in the twelfth century.

reminiscent of the two grammar books in Naples: modest size, minuscule script, text in a single column. Liturgical Gospel books in two columns are as old as the early fifth century (7,978a and 984), and the Anglo-Saxons used that arrangement from the late seventh century onwards; but in Ireland and England alike the tradition of the one-column Gospel book persisted until the ninth century. Early examples are the seventh-century Gospels from Bobbio (3,350), the Book of Durrow (2,273), and the Durham Gospels; later examples include the Lichfield Gospels (2,159), the Book of Kells (2,274), the Hereford Gospels (2,157), and the Gospels of MacRegol (2,231). The Irish 'pocket Gospel books' studied by Patrick McGurk are miniature volumes in some of which each Gospel occupies a quire of its own, which may contain considerably more than ten leaves[14]. Such are the Book of Mulling, with quires of 12 + 1,26 + 2,22 and 14 + 3; the Cadmug Gospels (8,1198), with quires of 14, 16, 18 and 18; the Dimma Gospels (2,275), with Matthew and Mark on separate quires and Luke and John on separate pairs of quires; the Stowe St John (2,267), with one quire of 12. This practice evokes the early period when the codex was still in its infancy, as in the Chester Beatty papyrus codices of the second and third centuries, during which the four Gospels circulated as separate volumes; and it seems right to regard it too as a survival from the Romano-British period. *Cadmug* and *Stowe* are in one column, like the fragment (2,277) associated with Mulling; the others are in two columns. The script of the Irish pocket Gospel books is almost entirely cursive in every case, and in some cases negligent; which suggests an origin as books copied by individuals for their own use.

The one basic, and pan-Insular, feature of the oldest Irish books which it seems difficult to envisage as a legacy from Roman Britain is a decorative one: the red points placed round and sometimes on top of initials. They are found in the famous Greek manuscript of the Herbal of Dioscorides, Vienna, Nationalbibliothek Med.Gr. 1, produced at Constantinople ca. 512; and the fact has been used to support the hypothesis of East Mediterranean influence in sixth-century Ireland. Another possible source of the red points is nearer home. In a Breviarium Alarici now in Munich (9,1324) red points are 'attached to the circumference' of an initial *O* (fol. 118v), not set out round it at an interval in the usual Insular way; and large, not typically small, red points are placed on an initial *S* (fol. 71v). This volume apparently originated in the south of Gaul too early in the sixth century to reflect Irish influence from the arrival of Columbanus at Luxeuil soon after 590[15].

---

14 Patrick *McGurk*, The Irish Pocket Gospel Book, Sacris Erudiri 8 (1956), p. 251—70; *id.*, Latin Gospel Books from A.D. 400 to A.D. 800, Les Publications de Scriptorium 5, Paris, etc. 1961.

15 Carl *Nordenfalk*, Die spätantiken Zierbuchstaben, Stockholm 1970, pl. VIII, 27—31, 57—9.

V

The systems of scripts and of book-production to which the oldest Irish, and indeed Anglo-Saxon, books bear witness differ in many ways from the contemporary system, or lack of system, on the Continent. Although changes at the more formal end of the script system certainly took place in the middle and second half of the seventh century, the combined idiosyncracy and consistency of most aspects of the two systems suggests that they already had a long history behind them at the moment at which we first catch sight of them. Is it an accident that most of the palaeographical and codicological aspects of them which can be matched in the continental systems point to the personal, unprofessional end of the scale of book production — and probably also to the sub-imperial end of the scale of documentation — in the years before AD 500? If these matchings are not all mere coincidences, the most likely explanation for them seems to be that the Insular systems are in most respects the direct heirs of informal systems current in the Roman and sub-Roman Church of Britain. The use of red points is an apparent exception; and the way the points are used in Insular books is closer to the way they are used in the Constantinopolitan Dioscorides than to the ways they are used in the Gaulish Breviarium Alarici. This is not the place for a discussion of East Mediterranean and/or Merovingian influences on the British Isles in the sixth century; and I will only say that the apparent evidence of red points for some sort of foreign influence exercised in the sixth century fails, in my opinion, to invalidate the palaeographical and codicological evidence of isolation in general, and archaism in particular, on which I have constructed this attempt to explain most of the basic characteristics of the Insular systems[16].

16 See also T. Julian *Brown*, The Irish Element in the Insular System of Scripts to circa A.D. 850, in: Die Iren und Europa im früheren Mittelalter, ed. Heinz *Löwe*, Stuttgart 1982, p. 101—19. The present paper differs only in detail from the concluding passage of my unpublished lectures: The Insular System of Scripts, circa 600 — circa 850 (The James P.R. Lyell Lectures in Bibliography, University of Oxford), 1977.

Papst Gregor der Große und Columban der Jüngere

Von
Friedrich Prinz

Das Thema meines Kurzreferates gilt nicht dem Gesamtbereich dieser Beziehungen, wie sie in Columbans Brief an diesen Papst (um 600) thematisiert werden, sondern ich möchte mich auf eine einzelne, wenn auch m. E. zentrale Frage beschränken, die Frage nämlich, ob die große abendländische Mönchsregel, die Regula Benedicti, durch diesen Papst an den Mönchsvater Columban (und damit ins Frankenreich) vermittelt worden ist oder nicht. Das Problem ist komplexer, als es auf den ersten Blick scheint, und es wird sich nicht vermeiden lassen, einen Strukturvergleich zwischen der Kirchen- und Klosterorganisation Italiens und des Merowingerreiches anzustellen, um gegenteilige, sich bislang ausschließende Standpunkte der Forschung nicht leichtfertig zu teilen oder zu verwerfen[1].

Papst Gregor d. Gr. spielt bekanntlich für die Geschichte des abendländischen Mönchtums eine bedeutende, aber bis heute noch nicht völlig geklärte Rolle. Nach neueren Untersuchungen war er es, der eine universale, eine wirkliche Weltmission in die Wege leitete und der damit dem Mönchtum in der Mission über den alten Orbis Romanus hinaus eine neue, zentrale Rolle zuwies[2]. Dies gilt nicht nur für die Angelsachsen-Mission[3], sondern auch für die monastische Missionstätigkeit auf dem Kontinent, im Frankenreich und im angrenzenden westslawischen Bereich[4].

Umstritten ist freilich — und damit komme ich zum Kern meines Themas — Gregors Rolle bei der Ausbreitung des benediktinischen Mönchtums über Rom und Italien hinaus. Welche Faktoren waren es hier, die der Regula Benedicti den Weg ebneten oder nicht ebneten? Die neue Edition der Benediktregel durch Adalbert de Vogüé[5] hat neuerlich die Frage nach Art und Weise des Vordringens der Regula Benedicti, ihrer Rezeption im Abendland aufgeworfen. Das Faktum selbst,

---

1 Für den Strukturvergleich zwischen Italien und dem Frankenreich vgl. F. *Prinz*, Italien, Gallien und das frühe Merowingerreich. Ein Strukturvergleich zweier monastischer Landschaften, Atti del 7° Congresso internazionale di studi sull'alto medioevo. Norcia — Subiaco — Cassino — Montecassino, 29 Settembre — 5 Ottobre 1980, Spoleto 1982, S. 117—136.

2 W. H. *Fritze*, Universalis gentium confessio. Formen, Träger und Wege universalmissionarischen Denkens im 7. Jahrhundert, FMSt. 3 (1969), S. 78—130.

3 Vgl. zuletzt K. *Schäferdiek*, Die Grundlegung der angelsächsischen Kirche im Spannungsfeld insular-keltischen und kontinental-römischen Christentums, in H. *Frohnes*, H. W. *Gensichen*, G. *Kretschmar*, hg., Kirchengeschichte als Missionsgeschichte II, München 1978, S. 149—191.

4 *Fritze*, Universalis gentium confessio.

5 A. *de Vogüé*, La Règle de S. Benoît. Introduction, traduction et notes (SC 181/I, 1972), S. 150 ff.

der Siegeszug einer einzigen Klosterordnung im frühmittelalterlichen Europa, ist dabei weniger problemgeladen als die Frage nach den historischen Faktoren und strukturellen Voraussetzungen, die ihn letztlich ermöglichten.

Welche Kräfte und welche politisch-kirchliche Konstellationen waren es also, die der cassinensischen Klosterordnung den Weg nach Gallien und ins Frankenreich ebneten, wo begegnen wir ihr zuerst, und wer förderte ihre Verbreitung? Fest steht, und dies ist m. E. im Anschluß an die Forschungen Kassius Hallingers[6] und seiner Schüler mit Nachdruck festzuhalten, daß die Ausbreitung des benediktinischen Mönchtums kein gradliniger, allein von Rom aus gelenkter Entwicklungsprozeß war. Eine gleichsam „autogene", innere Ursache des Siegeszuges der Regula Benedicti war sicher die Variabilität und Praktikabilität dieser Klosterordnung, die es dem Abt — als der gleichsam verkörperten Lebensordnung einer Mönchsgemeinschaft — erlaubte, den vorgegebenen Rahmen des Regeltextes nach eigenen Vorstellungen und Überzeugungen auszufüllen[7].

Ebenso ist mit Recht darauf hingewiesen worden, daß mit dem wachsenden Einfluß Roms in der abendländischen Kirche die Regula Benedicti, die als „römische Regel" galt, immer mehr Gewicht bekam, da seit dem 7. Jahrhundert die fränkischen Mönche und seit dem 8. Jahrhundert die fränkische Reichskirche insgesamt sich immer stärker nach dem römischen Vorbild orientierten[8]. Aber genügt das zur Erklärung dieses Erfolges einer italienischen Klosterregel im Abendland?

Man hat seit Mabillon immer wieder gemeint, Papst Gregor d. Gr. sei der wichtigste Vermittler und Propagator der Regula Benedicti im lateinischen Westen gewesen, und man berief sich dabei unter anderem auf Gregors „Dialoge", worin bekanntlich dem Leben Benedikts breiter Raum gewidmet ist. Seit Kassius Hallingers bahnbrechender Studie über Papst Gregor d. Gr. und den hl. Benedikt ist man aber hinsichtlich der Vermittlerrolle des großen Papstes bei der Ausbreitung der Regula Benedicti wesentlich skeptischer geworden. Gregor war weder selbst Benediktiner, noch organisierte er seine eigene römische Klostergründung St. Andreas nach der cassinensischen Ordnung, und im Regelbuch des Isidor von Sevilla, des Freundes Gregors, ist die Regula Benedicti ebenfalls nicht vertreten[9]. Nimmt man die frühe Wirkungsgeschichte der Regula Benedicti insge-

---

6 K. *Hallinger*, Papst Gregor der Große und der heilige Benedikt, Studia Anselmiana 42 (1957), S. 231—319; *ders.*, Corpus Consuetudinum Monasticarum I (Initia consuetudinis Benedictinae), Siegburg 1963.

7 J. *Semmler*, Zur Überlieferung der monastischen Gesetzgebung Ludwigs des Frommen, DA 16 (1960), S. 309—388; zum vieldiskutierten Problem, welche Qualitäten der Regula Benedicti deren nachweislichen Siegeszug durch das mittelalterliche Europa ermöglichten vgl. zuletzt J. *Angerer*, Das Mönchtum im karolingischen Reich, in: S. *Haider*, hg., Die Anfänge des Klosters Kremsmünster, Linz 1978, S. 11ff.

8 Vgl. zuletzt K. S. *Frank*, Grundzüge der Geschichte des christlichen Mönchtums, Darmstadt 1975, S. 53f.

9 G. *Ferrari*, Early Roman Monasteries, Rom 1957, S. 411ff; zur Bibel- und Liturgiereform vgl. B. *Fischer*, Bibeltext und Bibelreform unter Karl dem Großen, in: B. *Bischoff*, Hg.

samt, dann bleiben die frühen Entwicklungsphasen des Benediktinertums vor und nach der Zerstörung Monte Cassinos durch die Langobarden (581) in ein merkwürdiges Halbdunkel gehüllt; es war erst der Sprung nach Gallien, ins Frankenreich und zu den Angelsachsen, der den Siegeszug dieser Klosterordnung begründete. So stellt sich um so dringlicher die Frage, auf welchem Wege und durch welche Persönlichkeiten die Regula Benedicti in den Westen kam.

In Adalbert de Vogüés erwähnter Edition der Regula Benedicti wird wiederum Papst Gregor d. Gr. als die entscheidende Vermittlerfigur bezeichnet, durch dessen Eintreten für die cassinensische Klosterordnung der hl. Columban die Regula Benedicti unmittelbar kennengelernt und mit seiner eigenen rigorosen Klosterordnung kombiniert habe[10]. Nun ist es zweifellos richtig, daß Columban d. J. mit diesem Papst in brieflicher Verbindung stand[11], für den Nachweis einer direkten Vermittlung der Regel Benedikts durch diesen Papst reicht dieses Faktum allerdings noch nicht, vor allem wenn man sich Kassius Hallingers Argumentation anschließt, daß für Papst Gregor d. Gr. kein zeitgenössisches Zeugnis beizubringen ist, daß er der Propagator der Regula Benedicti gewesen sei. Dennoch bleibt die Tatsache, daß die Regula Benedicti bereits in den frühen Filialklöstern von Columbans Hauptgründung Luxeuil auftaucht, und zwar als benediktinisch-columbanische Mischregel[12]. Ebenso ist anzunehmen, daß bereits in Columbans eigener Regel — ihre Authentizität vorausgesetzt! — Elemente der Regula Benedicti Eingang gefunden haben. Jonas von Bobbio, Angehöriger und Biograph der columbanischen Klosterbewegung, weiß zu berichten, daß einer der ersten Schüler Columbans in Luxeuil, Bischof Donatus von Besançon, in seiner Bischofsstadt ein Männerkloster *in amore beati Columbani ex ipsius regula* gegründet habe, ebenso aber auch ein Frauenkloster, dessen Regel uns erhalten ist, und die auf den Klosterordnungen des Caesarius von Arles, Benedikts und Columbans beruht[13]. Bemer-

Karl der Große II, Düsseldorf 1965, S. 156—216; C. *Vogel*, La réforme liturgique sous Charlemagne, ebenda, S. 217—232.

10 *de Vogüé*, La Règle de S. Benoît, S. 149 ff.

11 G. S. M. *Walker*, Hg., Sancti Columbani Opera, SLH 2, 1957, S. 5 f. (Brief an Papst Gregor d. Gr.), worin Columban Gregors Regula pastoralis erwähnt und sich dessen Hesekiel-Traktat wünscht; von der Regula Benedicti ist nirgends die Rede, doch ist dies natürlich kein Beweis gegen die Auffassung, Columban habe die Regula Benedicti durch Gregor vermittelt bekommen. Die ältere Literatur zu Columban bei J. F. *Kenney*, The Sources for the Early History of Ireland. An Introduction and Guide. I: Ecclesiastical, New York 1929, ND 1969, S. 186 ff.

12 A. *Hauck*, Kirchengeschichte Deutschlands I, Leipzig — Berlin — ⁸1954, S. 288 Anm. 2 und S. 289 hat die m. E. unhaltbare Auffassung vertreten, daß die reine Columban-Regel sich von Luxeuil aus verbreitet habe, und daß die Erwähnung der Regula Benedicti in den Klosterprivilegien des 7. Jahrhunderts spätere Interpolation sei; vgl. dagegen F. *Prinz*, Frühes Mönchtum im Frankenreich. Kultur und Gesellschaft in Gallien, den Rheinlanden und Bayern am Beispiel der monastischen Entwicklung (4. bis 8. Jahrhundert), München — Wien 1965, S. 284 ff.

13 Text der Donatus-Regel bei *Holstenius-Brockie*, Codex Regularum III, S. 47 ff und PL 87, 274—298; dazu *Prinz*, Frühes Mönchtum, S. 285 f.

kenswert an dieser uns erhaltenen Regelkombination ist, daß die Regula Benedicti mit dreiundvierzig Kapiteln den Hauptteil der Donatusregel stellt, dann folgt Caesarius und erst an letzter Stelle Columban, der monastische Lehrer des Regelautors Donatus. Wenn aber ein früher Schüler Columbans bereits die Regula Benedicti kannte und hauptsächlich in seiner eigenen Regelschöpfung verwendete, dann liegt es nahe, daß die cassinensische Klosterordnung bereits zu Columbans Lebzeiten in Luxeuil und dessen Filiationen bekannt war und praktiziert wurde. Schon Mabillon hat dies, wie erwähnt, vermutet und Adalbert de Vogüé nahm diesen Gedanken unter Hinweis auf die briefliche Verbindung zwischen Columban und Papst Gregor d. Gr. wieder auf[14]. Mit dieser Annahme sind m. E. allerdings immer noch nicht die schwerwiegenden Argumente Kassius Hallingers gegen das „Benediktinertum" Gregors d. Gr. ausgeräumt, so daß m. E. auch noch eine andere Möglichkeit der Rezeption der Regula Benedicti in Gallien erwogen werden muß[15]. Es ist die von mir 1965 aufgestellte Hypothese, daß Südgallien als Relaisstation bei der Ausbreitung der Regula Benedicti eine gewisse Rolle gespielt haben dürfte, da die früheste Erwähnung dieser Regel diesem Raum zugeordnet ist. Die Nachricht darüber stammt aus dem Brief eines Abtes Venerandus[16]. Ihm ist zu entnehmen, daß Venerandus vor einigen Jahren das Kloster Altaripa gegründet und unter die Aufsicht des zuständigen Bischofs Fibicius von Albi gestellt habe. Fibicius ist der Onkel und Amtsvorgänger des Briefempfängers Constantius, der zwischen 620 und 630 als Bischof von Albi in den Unterschriften mehrerer Konzile bezeugt ist und der außerdem, was in unserem Zusammenhang wichtig ist, im Briefwechsel des Bischofs Desiderius von Cahors begegnet. Der Brief des Abtes Venerandus — dieser war wohl Abkömmling einer senatorischen Familie Südgalliens[17] — bildet zugleich das Vorwort eines Buches, dessen Inhalt die Lebensordnung des Klosters Altaripa war, nämlich die Regel des römischen Abtes Benedikt: *Regulam sancti Benedicti abbatis Romensis, quam praesens continet liber.* Die Bezeichnung Benedikts als römischer Abt ist selten und altertümlich und spricht für die Echtheit des Briefes, dem sonst zu entnehmen ist, daß unter dem Amtsvorgänger des Bischofs Constantius, also im ersten Viertel des 7. Jahrhunderts, in Altaripa die erste rein benediktinisch organisierte Klostergemeinschaft des Frankenreiches entstand. Da dieses Kloster, dessen genaue Lokalisierung fraglich ist, jedoch keinerlei Bedeutung erlangte, wird man sich fragen müssen, ob die Flut benediktinischer Klostergründungen im 7. und 8. Jahrhundert von dieser südgallischen Zelle in der Diözese Albi ausgegangen sein kann. Ausgeschlossen ist dies nicht, doch müssen noch andere Faktoren in Rechnung gestellt werden.

14 *de Vogüé*, La Règle de S. Benoît, S. 149 ff.

15 *Prinz*, Frühes Mönchtum, S. 288 f.

16 L. *Traube*, Textgeschichte der Regula S. Benedicti, Abh. München 1898, S. 600—731, hier S. 633 ff.

17 K. F. *Stroheker*, Der senatorische Adel im spätantiken Gallien, Tübingen 1948, Darmstadt ²1970, S. 226 Nr. 405. Ein Bischof Venerandus aus senatorischem Geschlecht ist Mitte des 5. Jahrhunderts in Clermont bezeugt.

Es war eben von Bischof Constantius von Albi die Rede, dem Empfänger jenes Briefes des Abtes Venerandus von Altaripa, in dem erstmalig im Frankenreich die Regula Benedicti erwähnt ist[18]. Constantius war aber auch Mitglied eines einflußreichen merowingischen Hofkreises, dem wir in der Briefsammlung des Bischofs Desiderius von Cahors begegnen und dem unter anderen Audoenus von Rouen, Eligius von Noyon, Paulus von Verdun, Chlodulf von Metz, Sulpitius von Bourges, der Hausmeier Grimoald, König Dagobert I. und König Sigibert III. von Metz angehörten, Männer also, die maßgeblich als Klostergründer an der Ausbreitung und Förderung des irofränkischen Mönchtums von Luxeuil beteiligt waren[19]. In den Klostergründungen dieser merowingischen Großen tauchte erstmalig die kombinierte Benedikt-Columbanregel auf, so daß man vermuten kann, die benediktinische Komponente der von diesem Kreis propagierten Mischregel gehe auf Bischof Constantius von Albi zurück, der ja durch Abt Venerandus von Altaripa die Regula Benedicti kannte[20]. Mit dieser Konjektur wäre nicht nur ein „missing link" in der Ausbreitungskette der Regula Benedicti gefunden, sondern gleichzeitig die wirkungsvolle und rapide Verbreitung des cassinensischen Klosterordnung, zusammen mit der Columbanregel, erklärbar, denn die Regula Benedicti fand durch Bischof Constantius ja gerade in jenem hochpolitischen adeligen Gesellschaftskreis Einlaß, der nicht nur die nötigen materiellen Mittel zur Gründung großer Klöster besaß, sondern auch die religiöse Begeisterung für die monastische Sache, die Columban in diesem fränkischen Hofadel geweckt hatte. Fest steht dabei auf jeden Fall, ganz gleich, ob man Columban selbst oder Abt Venerandus bzw. Constantius von Albi als „Relais" für das Eindringen der Regula Benedicti ins Frankenreich annimmt, daß die cassinensische Klosterordnung ihren Siegeszug der Propagierung durch das „irofränkische" Mönchtum des Luxeuil-Kreises und des Pariser Hofadels verdankt. Die Rezeption der Regula Benedicti im Frankenreich ist somit, soziologisch gesehen, ein Eindringen derselben in eine neue politische und gesellschaftliche Schicht, die Columban und seine Nachfolger, die Äbte Eustasius und Waldebert von Luxeuil gerade erst dem Mönchtum als Lebensform erschlossen hatten[21]. Mit anderen Worten: Erst im politisch-monastischen Verbundsystem zwischen fränkischem Adel und König-

18 *Prinz*, Frühes Mönchtum, S. 288ff; anders *de Vogüé*, La Règle de S. Benoît, S. 166ff.

19 MGH Epp. 3, S. 191—214. Die Briefe des Bischofs Constantius von Albi II, 4, II, 14, II, 15. Den ersten schrieben Constantius und Audoenus von Rouen gemeinsam; vgl. dazu *Prinz*, Frühes Mönchtum, S. 135 und S. 504f.

20 Die Hypothese, daß Venerandus die Regula Benedicti um 625 als Kurzredaktion der Regula Magistri verfaßte, wird man wohl als widerlegt betrachten müssen, an der Authentizität der Regula Benedicti ist heute wohl kein Zweifel mehr möglich. Zur Venerandus-These vgl. J. *Froger*, La Règle du Maître et les sources du monachisme bénédiction, RThAM 30 (1954), S. 285—288; *ders.*, Les anticipations du jeûne quadragésimal, Mélanges de Science Religieuse 3 (1946), S. 221—228 suchte Benedikt als Verfasser der Regula Magistri zu erweisen; vgl. dagegen A. *Mundó*, L'authenticité de la «Regula S. Benedicti», Studia Anselmiana 42 (1957), S. 105—158.

21 *Prinz*, Frühes Mönchtum, S. 288f.

tum einerseits und der von Luxeuil und etwa gleichzeitig von den angelsächsischen Benediktinern ausgehenden Klosterkultur andererseits gelangte die Regula Benedicti zu ihrer vollen Wirksamkeit und weltgeschichtlichen Entfaltungsmöglichkeit. Neben dem hohen asketisch-religiösen Rang, der Praktikabilität und der humanen Ausgewogenheit der Regula Benedicti war es also auch eine günstige politisch-gesellschaftliche Konstellation im Frankenreich, die dem benediktinischen Mönchtum hier zum Durchbruch verhalf. Der päpstliche Missionsauftrag kam als vitale Komponente hinzu. Anders als in Italien, wo das Mönchtum keine großangelegte Missionsarbeit entwickelte — selbst die antiarianische Mission in Oberitalien ging bekanntlich von der Columban-Gründung Bobbio aus — wurden Missionsarbeit, Rodung und grundherrschaftliche Organisation wichtige Elemente benediktinischer Praxis und Kulturarbeit[22] im Frankenreich ebenso wie bei den Angelsachsen.

Damit kehren wir aber zwangsläufig wieder zu der Frage zurück, ob Papst Gregor d. Gr. doch etwas mit der Ausbreitung der Regula Benedicti zu tun hatte oder nicht. Hier möchte ich eine Hypothese wagen, die zwischen den divergierenden Standpunkten Hallingers und de Vogüés vermitteln könnte, ohne das Problem selbst zu verwischen. Es ist seit Kassius Hallinger m. E. unbestreitbar, daß Gregor d. Gr. die Regula Benedicti in Rom und Italien *nicht* förderte. Dafür spricht schon, daß ein geregeltes Benediktinertum in Italien erst im 8. Jahrhundert als fränkisch-karolingischer Import oder im Falle Monte Cassinos als fränkisch-karolingische Restauration auftaucht und daß die Regula Benedicti in Rom offenbar erst im 10. Jahrhundert wieder Fuß gefaßt hat. Andererseits spricht die Bezeichnung der Regula Benedicti im frühen 7. Jahrhundert als römische Regel dafür, daß Gregor d. Gr. und Rom doch etwas mit ihr zu tun hatten. Werfen wir daher für die Zeit Papst Gregors d. Gr. einen Blick auf die episkopale Struktur Italiens und ebenso Südfrankreichs, das sozialstrukturell ja bis zum 8. Jahrhundert ebenfalls der Spätantike zuzurechnen ist, und bedenken wir deren Wirkungen auf das Klosterwesen dieser von der Stadtkultur geprägten Regionen. Die große Bedeutung bischöflicher Stadtherrschaft gilt für Rom ebenso wie für Neapel, Mailand, Ravenna, Arles, Lyon, Autun, Auxerre und Tours; sie konnte nicht ohne Folgen für die Stellung der Klöster im Bereich der spätantiken und frühmittelalterlichen Civitates sein[23] wie auch speziell für die Beziehungen zwischen Kloster und Bischof. Seit Leo Ueding[24] den Nachweis geführt hat, daß die Kanones von Chalkedon, die die Beziehungen zwischen Mönchtum und Klerus regeln,

---

22 *Prinz*, Askese und Kultur. Vor- und frühbenediktinisches Mönchtum an der Wiege Europas, München 1980, S. 68 ff; über die wachsende Bedeutung der Abtwürde, auch gegenüber dem Bischofsamt, vgl. F. *Felten*, Äbte und Laienäbte im Frankenreich. Studie zum Verhältnis von Staat und Kirche im früheren Mittelalter, Stuttgart 1980, S. 99 ff.

23 Für Rom vgl. G. *Ferrari*, Early Roman Monasteries, S. 411 ff.

24 L. *Ueding*, Die Kanones von Chalkedon in ihrer Bedeutung für Mönchtum und Klerus, in: A. *Grillmeier*, H. *Bacht*, Hg., Das Konzil von Chalkedon II, Würzburg 1953, S. 569—676.

wie die Ergebnisse dieses Konzils überhaupt nicht einfach als für die Gesamtkirche verbindlich angesehen werden können, sondern sich in verschiedenen Regionen auch unterschiedlich stark (oder auch gar nicht) auswirkten, kann das Verhältnis zwischen Mönchtum und Bistum für die Spätantike und das Frühmittelalter nur regional und deskriptiv aber kaum normativ und generell erfaßt werden.

Dies hat Konsequenzen für unsere Frage nach den Unterschieden zwischen Italien und dem Merowingerreich wie auch für die weitere Frage nach der Wirkungsgeschichte der Regula Benedicti einerseits in Italien und andererseits in Frankreich und auf den Britischen Inseln. Geht man nämlich davon aus, daß die Beschlüsse von Chalkedon im Westen relativ wenig und dann erst viel später wirksam wurden, dann liegt es auf der Hand, daß für Italien, soweit es nicht byzantinisch war, die päpstliche Stellungnahme wesentlich das Verhältnis zwischen Bistum und Kloster bestimmen mußte. Dabei geht es aber m. E. weniger um rein juristische Fragen und auch nicht in erster Linie um die Frage der Vereinbarkeit von Mönchsstand und Klerikerstand. Dieses Problem ist von den Päpsten zu verschiedenen Zeiten verschieden gesehen worden, und erst Gregor d. Gr. hat lange nach Benedikt die grundsätzliche Unvereinbarkeit beider Stände hervorgehoben[25]. Seine strenge Unterscheidung hat ihn aber für die weltkirchliche Praxis des Westens nicht daran gehindert, bei Priestermangel dennoch Mönche als Kleriker weihen zu lassen. Schließlich kam es ja schon seit dem 5. Jahrhundert nicht selten vor, daß Mönche auf Bischofsstühle gelangten und in ihrer Person die enge Verbindung von Mönchtum und Episkopat repräsentierten, wie eine prosopographische Analyse des südgallischen Großklosters Lérins bei Cannes zeigt[26]. Wichtiger ist m. E. für die tatsächliche Entwicklung, daß sich das Mönchtum Italiens und Südgalliens bis zum Ende des 6. Jahrhunderts durchaus im Bannkreis der Bischofsstädte entfaltete und damit auch unter weitgehender bischöflicher Beaufsichtigung. Mit anderen Worten: es wurde organisatorisch sehr stark in die Bistumsorganisation integriert. Man hat diesen Prozeß kürzlich treffend als eine „monastisch-klerikale Symbiose" bezeichnet, „die nicht selten bis zur Ununterscheidbarkeit ging"[27]. Semantisch läßt sich dies etwa an der Tatsache ablesen, daß bis Gregor von Tours Begriffe wie *monasterium, coenobium, abbatia* ebenso für Gemeinschaften von Mönchen wie von Klerikern verwendet wurden[28]. Gerade Papst Gregors d. Gr. Protest gegen die Vermischung beider Lebensordnungen unterstreicht das Vorhandensein und die Wirksamkeit dieser monastisch-klerikalen Symbiose und teilweisen Identität von Mönchsgemeinschaft und Basilikalgeistlichkeit[29]. Gregors dezidierte Stellungnahme kam ja gerade aus einer intimen

25 T. *McLaughlin*, Le très ancien droit monastique de l'Occident, Paris 1935, S. 115ff., S. 119ff.

26 *Prinz*, Frühes Mönchtum, S. 47ff.

27 R. *Schieffer*, Die Entstehung von Domkapiteln in Deutschland, Bonn 1976, S. 129.

28 *McLaughlin*, Droit monastique, S. 122.

29 Brief Gregors d. Gr. an Bischof Johannes von Ravenna von Sept. 594, Reg. 5,1; JE

Kenntnis dieses Zustandes auch und gerade in Rom selbst. Es war daher nicht zufällig, sondern entsprach der schon damals beispielgebenden Vorrangstellung dieser Stadt, daß sich in Rom seit Papst Leo d. Gr., d. h. seit der Mitte des 5. Jahrhunderts, der Typus der Basilikalklöster ausbildete, Klöster also, die in engstem Zusammenhang mit dem Gottesdienst an den großen stadtrömischen Basiliken entstanden und die schon aus diesem Grunde sehr fest in die allgemeine Kirchenorganisation eingegliedert waren[30]. Basilikalklöster solcher Art gibt es auch im stadtbezogenen gallischen Mönchtum des 5. und 6. Jahrhunderts und darüberhinaus im gesamten südgallischen Bereich, in dem die spätantike episkopale Organisation so gut wie völlig intakt geblieben war[31]. Was bedeuten nun solche Feststellungen für unsere Frage nach den Unterschieden zwischen italienischem und gallisch-fränkischem Mönchtum und des weiteren für das Problem der Ausbreitung der Regula Benedicti?

Erstens dies, daß im italienischen wie im südgallischen Bereich, soweit dort die Stadt und der Stadtbischof weiterexistierten und in die neue Ordnung des Merowingerreiches in toto aufgenommen worden sind[32], Bischof und Bistum ihr Übergewicht über den monastischen „Seitenstrang" der Gesamtkirche behielten, und daß die Klöster daher nur in sehr begrenztem Maße eine über die Klostermauern hinausreichende Eigeninitiative entfalten konnten.

Zweitens ist festzuhalten — und hier greife ich einen interessanten Gedanken auf, den Gregorio Penco[33] in seiner Klostergeschichte Italiens geäußert hat — daß sich die italienische monastische Entwicklung von der Frühzeit bis in die langobardisch-fränkische Epoche auch räumlich differenziert hat. Im Süden mit seinem dichten Netz von Bistümern, die oft nicht mehr als städtische Großpfarreien waren, blieben die Klöster im wesentlichen der bischöflichen Gewalt und Herrschaft untergeordnet. Im Norden Italiens hingegen mit seiner weiträumigen Bistumsorganisation und deren Störungen durch die Langobardenzeit, vermochte sich erst seit dem Frühmittelalter das Mönchtum stärker von Bischof und Bistum zu emanzipieren und sich neue Aufgabengebiete zu sichern. Dies gilt in wesentlich stärkerem Maße auch für das merowingische Mittel- und Nordgallien, wo dem Mönchtum aufgrund einer besonders günstigen Konstellation ein wirklicher und grundlegender Neuansatz seit dem ausgehenden 6. Jahrhundert gelang. Es gilt erst recht für die überragende Rolle des Mönchtums in der irischen Kirche und in der Kirche in den Reichen der Angelsachsen.

1317, CC 140, S. 266: *Nemo etenim potest et ecclesiasticis obsequiis deservire et in monachica regula ordinate persistere, ut ipse districtionem monasterii teneat, qui cotidie in obsequio ecclesiastico cogitur permanere.* Vgl. R. *Rudmann*, Mönchtum und kirchlicher Dienst in den Schriften Gregors des Großen, St. Ottilien 1956, S. 124ff und passim.

30 *Ferrari*, Roman Monasteries, S. 365ff.

31 *McLaughlin*, Droit monastique, S. 30ff.

32 F. *Prinz*, Die bischöfliche Stadtherrschaft im Frankenreich vom 5. bis zum 7. Jahrhundert, HZ 217 (1973), S. 1—35.

33 G. *Penco*, Storia del monachesimo in Italia, Rom 1961, S. 27ff.

Rom selbst wäre wegen der starken Stellung des Papstes und Stadtbischofs eher der Entwicklung im Süden Italiens zuzuordnen, doch trug es durch seinen universalen Anspruch wesentlich zu einer aufgabenmäßigen Neuorientierung des Mönchtums bei, die von schicksalhafter Bedeutung werden sollte. Allerdings galt dies nicht, wie man gleich hinzufügen muß, für den stadtrömischen Bereich, wo nach wie vor und weit ins Mittelalter hinein die Klöster eng in die stadtrömische Kirchenorganisation integriert blieben. Die päpstliche Initiative seit Gregor d. Gr. zugunsten weitgesteckter klösterlicher Aufgaben in der Mission entfaltete sich hauptsächlich außerhalb Italiens. Die Präponderanz des Bistums über das Klosterwesen in Süd- und Mittelitalien drückt sich auch in einem zahlenmäßig zu erhärtenden Phänomen aus, in der Tatsache nämlich, daß wir bis zum 8. Jahrhundert in Italien kaum eine Klosterhagiographie im engeren Sinne haben, in Gallien und im frühen Frankenreich diese Literaturgattung hingegen, dank der hauptsächlich von Columban von Luxeuil ausgelösten irofränkischen Klostergründungswelle, die hervorstechendste ist. Das Klosterwesen hatte dort aufgrund irischer Traditionen und aufgrund eigener neuer Aufgaben und ebenso durch die neuen Förderer aus den Reihen des fränkischen Königs und Adels auch ein neues, von der Bistumsorganisation unabhängiges Selbstverständnis entwickelt, das sich in einer spezifisch monastischen Hagiographie des Merowingerreiches manifestierte[34].

Es wäre daher zu überlegen, ob dieser bedeutende Papst mit seinem weltmissionarischen Anliegen die Regula Benedicti zwar als nicht geeignet für das stadtrömische Mönchtum und für das dem Stadtbischof unterworfene italienische Mönchtum insgesamt betrachtete, daß er aber andererseits die Regula Benedicti für die kirchlichen Ausbau- und Missionsgebiete des Frankenreiches und Englands sehr brauchbar hielt und daß er sie deshalb für diese Bereiche auch empfahl. Gekannt hat Papst Gregor d. Gr. die Regula Benedicti zweifellos, sonst hätte er in seinen *Dialogi* nicht Benedikt als Verfasser einer Mönchsregel bezeichnen können[35]. Der briefliterarisch belegte Kontakt zwischen Gregor d. Gr. und dem hl. Columban könnte also durchaus dazu geführt haben, daß die Regula Benedicti auf diesem direkten Wege ins Frankenreich gelangt ist und dann im weitgespannten Kommunikationssystem der irofränkischen adeligen Klostergründungen des 7. und 8. Jahrhunderts in zunehmendem Maße die abendländische Mönchsregel schlechthin werden konnte. Die angelsächsische Parallele spricht ebenfalls für Gregors Vermittlerrolle bei der Ausbreitung der Regula Benedicti im außeritalischen Bereich. Mehr als eine Hypothese kann dies vorläufig nicht sein, aber ist es wirklich so unwahrscheinlich, daß Gregor d. Gr. sich bei der Propagierung monastischer Lebensordnungen nicht auch gefragt haben sollte, für welche Regionen der christlichen Welt eine Klosterregel jeweils geeignet war? Warum dieser Papst die Regula Benedicti nicht in Rom und Italien förderte, darüber kann man nach

34 Siehe oben Anm. 1
35 Dialogi II, 36, ed. A. *de Vogüé*, Grégoire le Grand, Dialogues, 2 Bde. (Sources Chrétiennes 251), Paris 1978/79, II, S. 242.

dem oben Gesagten einige begründete Vermutungen anstellen. Vielleicht hatte
für ihn die Regula Benedicti zu viele Elemente der inneren Autonomie und der
wohldurchdachten inneren Organisation, als daß sie in das klösterliche Leben der
italienischen Bischofsstädte und Roms paßte, wo das Mönchtum im allgemeinen
doch sehr eng in die wesentlich ältere episkopale Organisation ein- und untergeordnet war. Vielleicht blieb die Regula Benedicti eben deshalb im italischen und
altgallischen Ambiente wirkungslos oder gar unerwünscht, während sie sich im
Freiraum weitmaschiger neuer Bistümer und großer Missionslandschaften als
eigene Organisationsform oft gleichberechtigt neben den Bistumssitzen entfalten
konnte, ja viele Bistümer sogar aus der Keimzelle von Klöstern sich erst entwickelten. Das königliche wie das adelige Eigenkloster des Frankenreiches und der
angelsächsischen Welt war dabei wohl die geeignete Grundlage, auf der sich die
benediktinische Lebensregel am besten entfalten und auf der materiellen Basis
der agrarischen Klostergrundherrschaft zu einer typisch mittelalterlichen Da-
seinsform werden konnte. Vielleicht hat der Strukturvergleich zwischen Italien —
Südfrankreich einerseits und den weiten Missionsgebieten des Merowingerreiches und des langobardischen Oberitalien andererseits gezeigt, daß eine historisch nicht exakt nachweisbare Entscheidung Papst Gregors d. Gr. für die Regula
Benedicti als brauchbare „mittel- und nordeuropäische Missionsregel" durchaus
im Bereich des Möglichen und Wahrscheinlichen liegt, und daß die römisch-
italienische „Klosterpolitik" dieses Papstes, die sich nach Kassius Hallingers
unumstößlichen Nachweisen in so ganz anderen Bahnen bewegte, kein stringen-
ter Gegenbeweis dafür sein kann, daß Gregor d. Gr. sich nicht unter anderen
Bedingungen auch für andere monastische Muster zu entscheiden vermochte, als
er sie in Rom und Italien förderte. Mit einer solchen Annahme wäre auch der Weg
frei für die Erkenntnis, daß Columban von Luxeuil in der Tat der wichtigste
Vermittler der Regula Benedicti im Merowingerreich gewesen ist.

Tradition and creativity in early Irish psalter study

By

Martin McNamara, M.S.C.

A. The Christian Use of the Psalms

The subject matter of this paper is tradition and creativity in early Irish Psalm exegesis. The tradition in question will in the first instance be the tradition of the Western Church which the Irish Church can be presumed to have inherited. The Western Church, however, was in good part heir to the Christian tradition of the East, in particular to that of Alexandria, though not exclusively so. I shall begin this essay, then, with a brief survey of the use and study of the Psalms in the Church during the patristic period[1].

1. The Jewish Heritage and the Early Church[2]

An inherent problem with the Psalter in the Church at any period is that it is the prayer book of the synagogue that has become the prayer book of the Church. While in some instances the Psalms are timeless prayer, in others they can be used meaningfully as Christian prayer only by reinterpretation in a Christian sense, and this at times cannot easily be done without violence to their original meaning. The most recent attempt in the Church to present the Psalter as a Christian prayer book is the Roman Catholic Breviary (Liturgia Horarum, Rome 1972), a work in which certain psalms or verses of psalms found offensive to pious ears have been omitted and in which each psalm is preceded by a brief heading giving it a Christian reference, superscriptions generally taken from the New Testament.

---

1 Summaries of this subject in Liam G. *Walsh*, O. P., The Christian Use of the Psalms according to the 'Tituli Psalmorum' of the Latin Manuscripts, unpublished thesis, University of St Thomas, Rome 1963; *idem*, The Christian Prayer of the Psalms, Placid *Murray*, ed., Studies in Pastoral Liturgy 3, Dublin 1967, p. 29—73 and separately as a booklet under the same title, Dublin 1967; Dom Pierre *Salmon*, Les 'Tituli Psalmorum' des manuscrits latins, Collectanea Biblica Latina 12, Città del Vaticano 1959, p. 9—39; *idem*, The Interpretation of the Psalms during the Formative Period of the Office, in: The Breviary through the Centuries, Collegeville 1962, p. 42—61 (French original in: L'office divin, LO no. 27); L'Antico Testamento nella Chiesa prenicena, various essays in Aug. 22, fasc. 1 et 2 (1982), esp. M. *Simonetti*, L'interpretazione patristica del Vecchio Testamento fra II e III secolo, p. 7—33; K. J. *Torjesen*, Interpretation of the Psalms: Study of the Exegesis of Ps. 37, p. 349—55.

2 Some examples of the relationship of Christian to Jewish tradition in N.R.M. *de Lange*, Origen and the Jews. Studies in Jewish-Christian Relations in Third-Century Palestine (University of Cambridge Oriental Publications), Cambridge 1976; *idem*, Origen and the Rabbis on the Hebrew Bible, Stud. Patr. 14, ed. E. A. *Livingstone*, part 3, Berlin 1976, p. 117—121. See also A. *Marmorstein*, Judaism and Christianity in the Middle of the Third Century, Hebrew Union College Annual 10 (1935), p. 223—263.

The Psalms is the Old Testament book most cited in the New Testament[3]. Jesus himself used the Psalms during his own lifetime, some of them in such a manner as if he took them as prophecies of himself (e.g. the use of Ps 109 in Mat 22:44; 26:24 and parallels; Ps 8 in Mat 21:16). He used Ps 21 as he hung on the cross (Mat 27:46; Mark 15:34). St Luke tells us (Luke 22:44) that after his resurrection he told his disciples that everything written about him in the Law of Moses, the Prophets and the Psalms had to be fulfilled. The Psalms chiefly used of Christ in the New Testament writings are psalms 109, 8, 21, 2 (Vulgate numbering throughout). In these cases the entire psalms are taken as messianic. Apart from these there are verses of other psalms understood as prophecies of Christ or of his mission.

By the year 200, if not earlier, the Christian Church was using the Psalter as its own prayer and song book[4]. This intensified the desire to see in the Psalms prophecies of Christ. The Christological interpretation of the Psalms, however, had already become commonplace in the Church before then.

By New Testament times a corpus of tradition about the Psalms, their origin, their transmission history and their interpretation can be presumed to have existed among the Jews. This continued to be developed during the early Christian centuries and influenced such Christian scholars as Origen and Jerome. The third and fourth centuries, in fact, were a period in which Jewish exegetical activity flourished, some of it now directed against the Christian interpretation of the Scriptures. Since there was direct contact between Jewish and Christian scholars in Palestine and Antioch, it is not surprising that Jewish interpretations should be mentioned, and at times adopted, by some Christian scholars. In fact, some of the material concerning the Psalms found in Origen and in the Psalm Prefaces is basically Jewish tradition[5].

2. Christological Interpretation: the School of Alexandria

Origen (died 253), the first great Christian scholar, was also the first to give a continuous interpretation of the Psalms. His approach to the Psalms was in keeping with his ideas on the sense of the Scriptures in general, and of the Old Testament in particular, i. e. the Spirit of God dictated the text of the Scriptures[6]. However, for Origen, what is written, the *littera*, is the sign of certain mysteries, the image of divine realities. Thus, the New Testament mystery is hidden, prefi-

3 The New Testament texts in question are noted in Novum Testamentum Graece et Latine, ed. E. *Nestle*, Stuttgart 1954, p. 662—65; K. *Aland et al.*, ed., The Greek New Testament, Stuttgart ²1966, p. 906—909.

4 See *Walsh*, Christian Prayer (as above note 1, booklet), p. 7, note 5, with references; B. *Fischer*, Le Christ dans les psaumes, Maison-Dieu 27 (1951), p. 86—113, revised form of Die Psalmenfrömmigkeit der Märtyrerkirche, Freiburg 1949, 1, p. 422.

5 See, for instance, *de Lange* (as above note 2), p. 119—120.

6 On Origen's exegesis see M. F. *Wiles*, Origen as Biblical Scholar, The Cambridge History of the Bible 1. From the Beginnings to Jerome, ed. P. R. *Acroyd* and C. F. *Evans*, Cambridge 1970, p. 454—89; see also *Simonetti* (as above note 1), p. 25—31.

gured, in the Old Testament. To remain in the letter is to end in, or fall into heresy. "Anyone wishing to understand the Scripture according to the letter would be better to class himself among the Jews than among Christians. Whoever wishes to be a Christian and a disciple of Paul must listen to Paul who says that the Law is spiritual" (Origen, Hom. in Gen., VI, 1; PG 12, 195 AB). For Origen, and the Alexandrian school, all Scripture did have a literal sense. The important matter for the followers of this school, however, was to penetrate beneath the letter to the spirit, to the spiritual sense.

It is necessary to make special mention of Origen because of the deep influence exercised by his writings on later Psalm exegesis, both in the East and West. Another writer worthy of mention is Eusebius of Caesarea (ca. 263—340), the Church historian who wrote an extensive commentary on the Psalms which was translated into Latin by Eusebius of Vercelli (died ca. 371). Although dependent on Origen, Eusebius is interested in the larger questions of content, literary genre, original historical setting and literal meaning of the Psalms[7].

3. The School of Antioch: Diodorus, Theodore, Chrysostom, Theodoretus

The real founder of the exegetical school of Antioch seems to have been Diodorus[8], later to become bishop of Tarsus in 378 (died 393). Two of his most famous students (about 370—375) were John Chrysostom and Theodore of Mopsuestia. His school is called by the Church historian Sozomen an *asceterium*, probably a monastery in which young people were given an intellectual and moral training before they moved elsewhere, whether to adopt a more severe monastic or ascetical life or become priests for the pastoral ministry[9].

The Church historians Socrates and Sozomen note that the avoidance of allegory and the literal explanation of the scriptures were features of Diodorus's exegesis[10]. We have no clear evidence from history that Diodorus wrote a commentary on the Psalms. However, in a series of studies from 1914 onwards[11] L.

---

7 Cf. *Salmon* (as above note 1), p. 17.

8 We know absolutely nothing of the nature of the exegesis of Lucian, for long believed to have been the founder of the School of Antioch; see M. *Simonetti*, in: La crisi ariana nel IV secolo (Studia Ephemeridis »Augustinianum«), Roma 1975, 19—20; *idem*, Le origini dell'Arianismo, Rivista di Storia e Letteratura Religiosa 7 (1971), p. 317—330.

9 Cf. R. *Leconte*, L'Asceterium de Diodore, Mélanges Bibliques rédigées en l'honneur de André Robert, Paris 1957, p. 531—36.

10 Socrates, Historia Ecclesiastica 6, 3, PG 67, 668; Sozomen, Historia Ecclesiastica 8, 2, PG 67, 1516A.

11 L. *Mariès*, Aurions-nous le commentaire sur les psaumes de Diodore de Tarse?, Revue de Philologie, de Littérature et d'Histoire anciennes 35 (1911), p. 56—70; *idem*, Les commentaires de Diodore de Tarse et de Théodore de Mopsueste sur les psaumes, RSR 5 (1914), p. 246—51; *idem*, Extraits du commentaire de Diodore de Tarse sur les psaumes. Préface du commentaire — Prologue de psaume CXVIII, RSR 9 (1919), p. 79—101; *idem*, Études préliminaires à l'édition de Diodore de Tarse sur les psaumes, Paris 1933. English translation of both preface and prologue by E. *FitzGerald*, Milltown Studies 10 (Autumn

Mariès and others have claimed to have identified a commentary on the Psalms by Diodorus in a number of Greek manuscripts. The first section (Pss 1—50) of this commentary, together with the introduction, has recently been published[12], a commentary that is remarkably like that of Theodore in all essentials. The Preface to the entire work, and the special preface to Ps 118, give a clear statement of the principles governing Antiochene exegesis, and the persons and events to which the major groups of psalms are to be referred.

Theodore's commentary is known partly through the original Greek text and partly through the Latin and Syriac translations and adaptations. Both Theodore and the commentary recently presented as that of Diodorus maintained all the Psalms were composed by David and that only four of them (Psalms 2, 8, 44, 109, LXX and Vulgate numbering) are direct prophecies of Christ. The others are to be understood as moral, didactic psalms or as referring to some event of Jewish history, such as David's time, the Assyrian (Hezekiah), Babylonian (exilic) or Maccabean periods[13].

Both John Chrysostom and Theodoretus of Cyr are representatives of the Antiochene School but declined to go along with what they must have considered the excesses of Theodore (and Diodorus) regarding the messianic psalms. In the introduction to his commentary (PG 80,859CD) Theodoretus tells us that his aim is to avoid the excesses of both allegorism and literalism. Among the Christian communities, he tells us, he found some who indulged inordinately in allegory while others so adapted prophecy to historical exposition that their interpretation agreed more with the Jews than with children of the faith — a fairly obvious reference to Theodore's exegesis. These see prophecy in more psalms than in the four accepted as messianic by Theodore. Yet neither Chrysostom nor Theodoretus has any difficulty in seeing Ps 8 as containing both teaching on the salvation of the world and on the providence of God as well as a prophecy on the Incarnation[14].

4. The Latin Fathers

The majority of the Latin Fathers were influenced directly by the Greek and Eastern tradition. Hilary (died ca. 367), a contemporary of the great Athanasius, lived for a time in the East. His exegesis is in the tradition of Origen, Eusebius and

1982), p. 76—86. On Diodorus and the commentary see also M. *McNamara*, Antiochene Commentary on the Psalms: By Diodore of Tarsus?, Milltown Studies 10 (Autumn 1982), p. 66—75.

12 Diodori Tarsensis Commentarii in Psalmos. I. Commentarii in Psalmos I — L quorum editionem principem curavit Jean-Marie *Olivier*, CCSG 6, 1980, with full bibliography on earlier research.

13 For the distribution of the psalms in Theodore's commentary see F. *Baethgen*, Zeitschrift für alttestamentliche Wissenschaft 6 (1886), p. 270f.; R. L. *Ramsay*, ZCP 8 (1912), p. 436—37; R. *Devreesse*, Essai sur Théodore de Mopsueste (Studi e Testi 141), Città del Vaticano 1948, p. 70. For the practically identical distribution in the Antiochene commentary attributed to Diodorus see *Olivier* (as above note 12), p. XXX—XXXV.

14 Comment on Psalm 8, PG 55. Thus also Theodoretus, In Psalmum VIII, 1, PG 80, 913C.

Athanasius[15]. Eusebius of Vercelli (died ca. 371), already mentioned, was exiled for a while to Palestine. He visited Antioch and Asia Minor before returning to rule his diocese. Ambrose (ca. 339—397), made bishop of Milan in 374, came from a noble Roman family and received a good education in rhetoric and law. On becoming bishop, he devoted himself to theological studies, especially to reading the Greek Fathers[16]. Jerome belongs to many traditions and to both East and West. He got his secular education in Rome, and first set out for the East and reached Antioch in 373, and was back there again for a protracted stay in 382 when he probably attended the exegetical lectures of Apollinaris of Laodicea. He came under the influence of Jewish masters, of Origen, and was in communication with the Cappadocian Fathers — Basil and the two Gregories[17]. Augustine of Hippo (354—430) follows a spiritual interpretation almost exclusively in his voluminous *Enarrationes in Psalmos*. For Augustine the Psalms are spoken by Christ (*in persona Christi*) or speak of Christ, the whole Christ, head and members[18]. Cassiodorus (ca. 490—583) is one of the most recent of the major western writers on the Psalms. Although he presents his work *Expositio Psalmorum* (completed about 548) as an abbreviation of Augustine's *Enarrationes*, he has used other writers besides.

5. Antiochene Influence in the West[19]

Antiochene influence made itself felt in Western Europe in different ways, chiefly however through the Latin translation of Theodore's commentary on the Psalms, through an Epitome of this work, and through an introduction to the Scriptures by Junilius Africanus. There were, probably, also other ways in which the influence of Antioch made its presence felt in Western exegesis.

15 On Hilary's Psalm exegesis cf. C. *Kannengiesser*, in: Hilaire et son temps (Actes du Colloque de Poitiers, 29 septembre — 3 octobre 1968), Paris 1969, p. 133—34; on Hilary's influence on Western exegesis: L'héritage d'Hilaire de Poitiers. I. Dans l'ancienne Eglise d'Occident et dans les bibliothèques médiévales, RSR 56 (1968), p. 435—50; for influence of Origen: E. *Goffinet*, L'utilisation d'Origène dans le commentaire des psaumes de saint Hilaire de Poitiers (St Hell 14), Louvain 1965.

16 See *Salmon*, 'Tituli' (as above note 1), p. 22—23; Breviary, p. 45—46.

17 For Jerome's career and work see J. N. D. *Kelly*, Jerome. His Life, Writings, Controversies, London 1975; F. *Cavallera*, Saint Jérôme. Sa vie et son œuvre (Spicilegium Sacrum Lovaniense Et. et Doc., Fasc 1), Louvain, Paris 1922; A. *Penna*, Principi e carattere dell'esegesi di S. Gerolamo (Scripta Pontificii Instituti Biblici 102), Roma 1950; H. F. D. *Sparks*, Jerome as a Biblical Scholar, CHB 1, 514—41, p. 596—97.

18 On this point see *Walsh*, Christian Prayer (as above note 1, booklet), p. 33—45; *Salmon*, 'Tituli' (as above note 1), 24—25; *Salmon*, Breviary, p. 46—47. See also G. *Bonner*, Augustine as Biblical Scholar, CHB 1, p. 541—63, 597.

19 M. L. *Laistner*, Antiochene Exegesis in Western Europe, HThR 40 (1947), p. 19—32; *idem*, Thought and Letters in Western Europe A. D. 500—900, London ²1957, index s.v.Antiochene; B. *Smalley*, The Study of the Bible in the Middle Ages, Oxford ²1952 (reprint Notre Dame 1970, Oxford ³1983), p. 14—20.

a) Latin translation of Theodore's Psalm Commentary
All that is preserved of this Latin translation of Theodore is to be found in two manuscripts of Irish provenance: Codex Amb. C 301 inf. of the Ambrosian Library, Milan, and MS F.IV.1, fasc. 5—6 of the Turin University Library[20] and in a fragment inserted into the Oxford MS, Bodl. 826 (S.C. 2715)[21]. The two Italian manuscripts are of the ninth century and came from the Library of Bobbio. In these we have the full translation of the commentary on Pss 1:1—16:11 (Cod. Amb. C 301 inf., fol. 14a—39d; Turin, F.IV, 1) and portion of the commentary on Pss 17—40:13a. The Oxford fragment, with part of the commentary on Ps 13:6—7, was copied in Normandy in the 11th century. The Latin translation is believed to have been made by the Pelagian Bishop, Julian of Eclanum (died ca. 460). Although only the translation for the commentary on Pss 1—40 is now known to exist, a translation of the entire commentary can be presumed to have once circulated. Even though what we now have has been preserved almost exclusively in Irish circles, the Commentary probably once had a broader circulation. The Oxford fragment would seem to indicate this.

b) The Epitome of Julian's Translation of Theodore's Commentary[22]
This is an abbreviation and in part adaptation of the Latin translation of Theodore's commentary. It is extant only for Ps 16:11b onwards. The opening section of the Epitome apparently got lost and was supplied in one branch of the translation (that represented in Cod. Amb. C 301 inf.) by the full Latin translation of Theodore and in another (that represented in the glosses in the Double Psalter of Rouen) by a completely different commentary with a literal or historical exposition[23]. Apart from two exceptions (glosses in the Monpellier and Vercelli Psalters, and section in the manuscript of a commentary on Pss 78 and 82 by Remigius of Auxerre), the Epitome has been transmitted directly and indirectly (through excerpts, and such like) in sources of Irish provenance. These sources, in probable order of composition, are as follows: the catena in Vatican MS Pal. lat. 68 from about AD 700 (excerpts)[24]; the historical sections of the *argumenta* in *De titulis Psalmorum* falsely attributed to Bede (8th cent.)[25] and in the related headings in the

---

20 Critically edited by R. *Devreesse* in: Le commentaire de Théodore de Mopsueste sur les psaumes (I—LXXX) (Studi e Testi 93), Città del Vaticano 1939; also in: Theodori Mopsuesteni Expositionis in Psalmos Iuliano Aeclanensi interprete in latinum versae quae supersunt, auxiliante Maria Josepha *d'Hont* edidit Lucas *de Coninck*, CCSL 88A, 1977.

21 Cf. M. *Gibson*, Theodore of Mopsuestia: A Fragment in the Bodleian Library, Journal of Theological Studies 21 (1970), p. 104—105.

22 Critical edition by *de Coninck*, as above note 20.

23 The different sources for the glosses of psalms 1,1—16, 11a in the Double Psalter of Rouen noted by the present writer in PRIA 73 C (1973), p. 240 and clearly demonstrated by *de Coninck* (as above note 20), p. XLIII—XLIV.

24 Critical edition, with introduction, by the present writer in the press (Studi e Testi).

25 These headings reprinted in PL 93, 477—1098, from *Heerwagen's* 1563 Basel edition

so-called Psalter of Charlemagne (Paris BN MS lat. 13159) of the late eighth century; the *Eclogae tractatorum in Psalterium*[26]; and in the introduction to the Psalter in the one-volume commentary (from Genesis to the Apocalypse) designated "Das Bibelwerk" by Dr. Bernhard Bischoff[27] (both late eighth century); Cod. Amb. C 301 inf. (ca. 800—850); in the glosses in the *Hebraicum* section of the Double Psalter of Rouen (Rouen, Bibl. Publ. MS 24 [A.41]) from Ps 16:11b onwards and in Dublin fragments of its sister codex (Dublin, Trinity College, MS H 3 18)[28] of the tenth century, and in some glosses in the so-called Psalter of Caimín (Franciscan Fathers Library, Killiney, Co. Dublin, MS A l), from ca. AD 1100[29].

c) The Instituta regularia divinae legis *of Junilius Africanus*[30]

Junilius, a native of Africa, held the office of Quaestor of the Sacred Palace in Constantinople. About 551, at the request of Primasius, bishop of Hadrumetum, he compiled his work, *Instituta regularia divinae legis* which was a Latin version of a short introduction to the Bible, composed by Paul the Persian (i.e. Syrian), whose acquaintance Junilius had made at Constantinople. The little work represents the basically Antiochene scriptural views of the Syriac school of Nisibis and Theodore's exegesis of the messianic psalms. The work must have been reasonably widely read in the Middle Ages. In 1880 Heinrich Kihn edited the Latin text from 13 manuscripts, one of which (St Gall 908) he dated to the 8th century. In 1947 M.L.W. Laistner[31] listed 23 manuscripts of the work, ranging from the early eighth (BL Cotton Tib. A. XV, fol. 175—180, South England) to the fifteenth century, the majority, however, from the 8th — 10th centuries. (Kihn's 8th-cent. date for Sangallensis 908 he regards as far too early.) Aldhelm used a copy of the work. It appears that copies of it were also available in Irish libraries: there are citations from it in eighth- and ninth-century Irish texts[32].

d) Glosses in the Montpellier and Vercelli Psalters

Glosses in the Psalter of Montpellier (Montpellier, Faculté de Médicine MS 409; written at Mondsee before 788) and of Vercelli (Codex LXII of Chapter Library,

---

of Bede; study by B. *Fischer*, Bedae de titulis psalmorum liber, Festschrift Bernhard Bischoff, Stuttgart 1971, p. 90—110.

26 On this see M. *McNamara*, Psalter Text and Psalter Study in the Early Irish Church (A. D. 600—1200), PRIA 73 C (1973), p. 201—72, at p. 225—27.

27 See B. *Bischoff*, Wendepunkte in der Geschichte der lateinischen Exegese im Frühmittelalter, Sacris Erudiri 6 (1954), p. 211, 223—30 (= Mittelalterliche Studien 1, Stuttgart 1966, p. 222, 231—36); English translation in: Biblical Studies. The Medieval Irish Contribution, ed. M. *McNamara*, Dublin 1976, p. 88, 97—102.

28 Published by L. *Bieler* and G. *Mac Niocaill*, Fragment of an Irish Double Psalter with Glosses in the Library of Trinity College Dublin, Celtica 5 (1960), p. 28—39.

29 See *McNamara* (as above note 26), p. 245—49, esp. p. 248.

30 In PL 68, 15—42; critical edition from 13 MSS by H. *Kihn*, Theodor von Mopsuestia und Junilius Africanus als Exegeten, Freiburg i. Br. 1880, p. 465—528.

31 As above note 19, HThR 40, p. 24—26.

32 In the *Eclogae tractatorum in Psalterium*, in „Das Bibelwerk" and in the Old Irish Treatise on the Psalter; cf. *McNamara* (as above note 26), p. 226, 229 note 42, p. 255.

mid-ninth century) have been edited by Franz Unterkircher[33]. Both sets of glosses are basically the same. The commentary they represent has Antiochene connections, although its exegesis in general is strongly christological. A few of the glosses have been identified as depending on the Epitome of Julian[34]. Occasionally, although there is no verbal connection with the Epitome, the historical reference is Antiochene and of the type found in Theodore, e. g. to Hezekiah (Ps 19), Babylonian Captivity (Pss 41, 72, 83, 136), the return from captivity (Pss 101, 125, 146), Maccabean times (Pss 43, 73, 78). (The Diodoran commentary, we may note, understands most of these psalms in like manner.) Together with this, there are instances in the glosses of the Montpellier and Vercelli Psalters where the Psalms are interpreted of later Jewish history but in a manner different from that of Theodore (or, we may now add, Diodorus) e. g. Pss 36 (of Babylon), 40, 41, 42, 65, 72 (of Maccabean times; in Theodore and Diodorus Ps 40 of Assyria; the others of Babylon). Occasionally the glosses give more than one historical reference, e. g. to Babylon and Maccabean times (Ps 41, in glosses only, not in heading), to Saul and Maccabees (Ps 42; Babylonian in Theodore and Diodorus).

There appears to be a direct reference to the Antiochenes (called *Syri*) and their exegesis in the heading to Ps 50, the *Miserere*. Despite the biblical heading, which takes this psalm as Davidic and concerning David's sin with Bathsheba, Antiochene tradition regarded it as a prayer of the captive people in Babylon (thus Theodore and Diodorus). The heading in the commentary of the Psalters of Montpellier and Vercelli disagrees with this: *Manifeste de Dauid dicitur, sicut titulus eius docet. Syri autem hunc psalmum ex persona eorum qui erant in Babylonia dicunt, quia tulerunt titulos de psalmis*[35]. The heading of this psalm and the accompanying commentary have been transmitted independently in Codex Monte Cassino 57, and were published in 1897 by G. Morin[36]. The authorship of this comment on Ps 50 has been, and still is, a matter of dispute. Some (e. g. A. Vaccari) have ascribed it to Jerome and taken it as evidence of his acquaintance with Antiochene exegesis[37]. Its original setting seems to have been where it stands in the larger commentary we are considering, and provides further evidence that this was composed in circles in the Latin Church consciously conversant with Antiochene exegesis. What these circles were has yet to be identified. For reasons other than its Antiochene connections, Franz Unterkircher believed it was composed in Ireland[38]. Certain characteristics of the exegesis found in these glosses are also found

---

33 F. *Unterkircher*, Die Glossen des Psalters von Mondsee (vor 788). (Montpellier) Faculté de Médicine MS 409 (Spicilegium Friburgense 20), Freiburg/Schweiz 1974.

34 Cf. *de Coninck* (as above note 20), p. XLIV—XLV.

35 Ed. *de Coninck*, p. 216.

36 G. *Morin*, in Anecdota Maredsolana 3 (2, 1897), p. 421—23; reproduced in Patrologiae Latinae Supplementum 2, vol. 2, p. 324—26.

37 Cf. A. *Vaccari*, in: Biblica 9 (1928), p. 83—85. See also *McNamara*, in: Irish Theological Quarterly 48 (1981), p. 278—79.

38 As above note 33, p. 23—26.

in Irish sources. Thus, for instance, the emphasis on interpreting the psalms of David: his persecution by Saul — (Pss 62, 85, 140, etc.); his flight from Saul, his return to reign after Saul's persecution and Absalom's revolt (Pss 80, 114). This however scarcely amounts to proof of Irish origin: Irish tradition may have been influenced by the tradition enshrined in this commentary even if the work itself originated outside Ireland.

e) Unidentified Antiochene-type commentary on Psalms 1—16

It has been noted earlier in this study that although the glosses on the Hebraicum of the Double Rouen Psalter from Ps 16:11b onwards are drawn from the Epitome of Julian as found in the Milan Codex Amb. C 301 inf., those on the opening section (Pss 1:1—16:11a) are not from the corresponding section of the Milan Theodorean commentary. These glosses, it would appear, represent portion of a hitherto unidentified commentary in the literal tradition of Antioch, although not that of Theodore or Diodorus. For these same psalms, and it would appear corresponding in content to these glosses, we have a series of historical Psalm headings. This series for Pss 1—16 has been transmitted to us in the Psalter of Rouen itself, in the work entitled *De titulis Psalmorum* erroneously attributed to Bede, and in the headings of the so-called Psalter of Charlemagne. Many of these headings also refer the Psalms to later Jewish history, but not in the same manner as in the commentary of Theodore. The glosses of some of the psalms, in so far as they are decipherable, correspond to the headings. Some of the expository excerpts on Pss 1—16 in „Das Bibelwerk", given under the rubric *Iosepus,* are identical with the glosses on the Rouen Psalter[39]. Since excerpts from the Epitome of Julian for Psalm 16:12 onwards in „Das Bibelwerk" are also under this same rubric *Iosepus,* it is clear that the Epitome text it drew on was completed for Ps 1:1—16:11a in the same manner as that used for the Rouen Psalter. Only after much more work has been done on these Rouen glosses will we be able to determine its place in the history of Antiochene exegesis in the West.

Antiochene exegesis did not suit the temper of medieval Europe, and for this reason was neglected. As Beryl Smalley notes[40], enough material existed in the early Middle Ages to enable a Latin reader to learn at least the principles of Antiochene exegesis and to experiment with them for himself, if he wished. Some of the early Irish scholars availed themselves of this opportunity. But they were alone in doing so. The Antiochenes in fact were generally neglected. The fate of the text of the Julian Epitome that got included in the exposition of Ps 82 in Remigius's commentary, as well as another non-verbal quotation from the same commentary, is symptomatic of this neglect: neither passage was taken up in the

39 All the texts of „Das Bibelwerk" under the heading *Iosepus* are noted, and those on texts of psalms 1—16 edited, in the critical edition of MS Pal. Lat. 68 (in Introduction note 231), mentioned in note 24 above.

40 *Smalley,* (as above note 19), p. 19, 17.

Glossa Ordinaria although his commentary was extremely popular and used by the compilers of the *Glossa*.

6. Psalm Prefaces, East and West

The great commentators of both East and West prefaced introductions to their commentaries on the Psalms, treating of the principles governing their exegesis among other things. Together with this, we have some early "introductions" to the Psalter which were never intended as prefaces to commentaries. Some of the great writers such as Jerome also wrote letters on individual points of Psalm interpretation. The commentary ascribed to Diodorus has a general introduction with detailed information on the Antiochene principles of Psalm exegesis[41]. Much of this is repeated in the introduction to Ps 118 in the same commentary[42]. No Greek text of a preface to Theodore's commentary is known. In the Latin translation of the comment on Ps 15:4 Theodore speaks of collections of peculiarities of Hebrew speech which he had made in the preface: *quod quidem inter proprietatum collectiones in praefatione signauimus*[43]. An Old Irish gloss (Ml. 37a15) on *praefatione* says: "that has not come down to us, for this is an epitome"[44].

During the Middle Ages older Psalm prefaces were being copied and new ones composed. Dom D. De Bruyne has published 84 such Psalm Prefaces from medieval Latin manuscripts[45], a few of which are, however, really Psalm Headings. An analysis of these works shows the older influences that were still operative. These prefaces may also give an idea of certain, less usual, methods of exegesis, e. g. that which asks whether *omnes psalmi proprie ad David pertinent aut omnes ad Christum, an sunt aliqui, qui ad utrumque pertinent?*[46]

7. Psalm Headings

Already in the Hebrew Bible headings were inserted before the Psalms, in part containing directions for the choir but also attempting to identify the historical situation that first occasioned the particular psalm's composition. In the Greek Septuagint translation and in the Latin ones these biblical headings tended to be multiplied.

In an effort to aid the use of the Psalter as Christian prayer new headings were composed for each psalm. These headings are especially frequent in Latin Psalter

---

41 As above note 12, p. 3—8. The preface was already published, with French translation, by L. *Mariès*, RSR 9 (1919), p. 82—89.

42 The introduction to psalm 118, with French translation, also published by *Mariès*, RSR 9 (1919), p. 90—101.

43 Ed. *Devreesse* (as above note 20), p. 94, lines 1—4; ed. *de Coninck* (as above note 20), p. 77, lines 90—94.

44 W. *Stokes*, J. *Strachan*, ed., Thesaurus Palaeohibernicus 1, Cambridge 1901 (reprint Dublin 1975), p. 95.

45 D. *de Bruyne*, Préfaces de la Bible latine, Namur 1920, part VIII, p. 42—117.

46 *de Bruyne*, Préfaces, no. 28, p. 81, lines 12—17; S. *Berger*, Les préfaces jointes aux livres de la Bible dans les manuscrits de la Vulgate, Paris 1902, no. 115.

manuscripts, from which Dom Pierre Salmon has published six full series of them[47].

The tradition of interpretation behind these headings is sometimes very old. Some of them take their inspiration from one individual commentator (Origen, Eusebius of Caesarea, Jerome, Cassiodorus). Others have names of noted churchmen attached (e. g. Augustine of Canterbury), or go back to various isolated traditions.

The Syriac Church rejected the biblical Psalm headings altogether and inserted in their stead headings dependent on the Syriac translation of Theodore's commentary[48]. There is also a series of Latin Theodorean headings, transmitted in Irish sources, which depends on the Epitome of Julian. Together with this, as noted already, we have for Pss 1—16 psalm-headings of an historical nature, of the Antiochene kind but not in the Theodorean tradition of exegesis. We shall consider these in greater detail later[49].

8. Latin Psalm Translations

Basic to all study of the Psalter is the text, in the original or in translation. By the second century at least there was a Latin translation of the Psalter. These old Latin versions are collectively known as the Vetus Latina. One of these was the *Psalterium Romanum*, once widely used in England and traditionally used in St Peter's Basilica, Rome, whence the name[50].

Jerome himself tells us that while in Rome (ca. 384) he corrected an Old Latin text of the Psalter. What became of this amended text, we cannot say. Later, having settled at Bethlehem (ca. 386—389), Jerome made another emendation of the Psalter, using for the purpose the critical work done by Origen on the Greek translation, and like Origen using the critical signs of asterisk and obelus. This emendation was destined to become the official text of the medieval Church. Because of its early acceptance as such in Gaul it came to be called the *Gallicanum*[51].

Between 389 and 392 Jerome translated the Psalms directly from the Hebrew (for him the *Hebraica Veritas*) into Latin. This version is known as *Psalterium iuxta Hebraeos*, or the *Hebraicum*[52].

47   *Salmon*, as above note 1.

48   Edited by W. *Bloemendaal*, The Headings of the Psalms in the East Syrian Church, Leiden 1960.

49   See below p. 358—60.

50   Edited by R. *Weber*, Le Psautier Romain et les autres anciens psautiers latins. Edition critique, Collectanea Biblica Latina 10, Città del Vaticano 1953.

51   Critical edition: Liber Psalmorum ex recensione Sancti Hieronymi cum praefationibus et epistula ad Sunniam et Fretelam (Biblia Sacra iuxta Latinam Vulgatam Versionem ad Codicum Fidem. 10), Roma 1953.

52   Edited by H. *de Sainte-Marie*, Sancti Hieronymi Psalterium iuxta Hebraeos, Édition critique, Collectanea Biblica Latina 11, Città del Vaticano 1954.

B. Tradition and Creativity in Early Irish Psalm Exegesis

I. Irish Psalter Texts[53]

a) The Old Latin Texts in Ireland

Dr Ludwig Bieler has shown that the Psalter text used by St Patrick was the Old Latin, of the type used in Gaul[54]. There is no trace in his writings of Hieronymian Psalter readings. We cannot say which Psalter text was used by St Columba of Iona (died 597). Adomnán says that the saint died while copying the following words of Ps 33:11: *inquirentes autem Dominum non deficient omni bono*[55]. This is the Old Latin text; the *Gallicanum* has *minuentur* for *non deficient*. One would scarcely be permitted, however, to draw any conclusion as to Columba's Psalter from this evidence, which may say more about some later Psalter than about Columba's. Apart from an occasional reading in the catena on the Psalms in Codex Vaticanus Pal. Lat. 68, Old Latin Psalter texts and readings in Ireland are noticable by their absence. All the evidence indicates that the new rendering now known as the *Gallicanum* had replaced the Old Latin by 600 or so.

b) The Gallican Psalter Text in Early Ireland

The Gallican Psalter text must have been brought to Ireland during the sixth century at the latest. There is a tradition (first recorded it would seem in Manus O'Donnell's *Life of Columcille*) that the text now known as the *Cathach* was copied by Colum Cille and that the copying of it was the cause of the battle of Cúil Dremne[56] in 561. The story is an unlikely one. Earlier forms of this story say that the book in question was a Gospel Book, not a Psalter. Besides this, there is evidence that the *Cathach* was written in the seventh, rather than in the sixth century[57]. The critical signs of the asterisk and obelus as used in the *Cathach* indicate that it has been edited against the specifically Irish family of *Hebraicum* texts[58]. Its text, then, represents textual criticism carried out in Irish schools, and

---

53 For this section see *McNamara* (as above note 26), p. 201—272.

54 L. *Bieler*, Der Bibeltext des heiligen Patrick, Biblica 28 (1947), p. 31—58; 236—63, at 244—45, 257 for Psalter text.

55 Adomnan's Life of Columba, 111, 23, ed. A. O. *Anderson* and M. O. *Anderson*, Edinburgh 1961, p. 524.

56 Cf. A. *O'Kelleher*, G. *Schoepperle*, ed., Betha Colaim Chille. Life of Columcille compiled by Manus O'Donnell in 1532, Urbana, Illinois 1918. The tradition of the copying of a book borrowed from Finnén of Druim Finn is given in § 168; the identification of the book as the *Cathach* in § 178. For a fuller discussion of 'St Finnian's Book' see H. J. *Lawlor*, PRIA 33 C (1916), p. 307, 329. W. M. *Lindsay* (PRIA 33 C, 1916, p. 397—403) and E. A. *Lowe*, CLA 11, no. 226, find a sixth-century date palaeographically acceptable; so also, more recently, B. *Schaumann*, in: Early Irish Manuscripts. The Art of the Scribes, Expedition 21 (1979), p. 33—47, at 37f. for the date of *Cathach*.

57 D. H. *Wright* assigns a date of ca. 630, cf. American Journal of Archaeology 67 (1963), p. 219. See also the paper of T. J. *Brown* in this volume.

58 See below p. 351—52.

not a direct copy of a continental model, as the tradition by Manus O'Donnell would have it.

We can presume, however, that the Gallican text was taken to Ireland during the life of Columba (521—597), if not earlier. The earliest evidence of its presence in Ireland is probably in the Springmount Bog wax tablets, which may be dated at about AD 600[59]. The tablets contain the Gallican text of Pss 30, 31 and part of 32, and were probably used to introduce students to the arts of reading and writing. The next oldest Gallican text we possess is the *Cathach*, coming probably from ca. 630—650.

Once introduced, the Gallican text soon displaced the Old Latin completely. In the *Old Irish Treatise on the Psalter* (ca. 800), it is spoken of as if it were the accepted translation[60]. In the Old Irish glosses in the Milan Commentary (Cod. Amb. C 301 inf.), from about AD 800, the Gallican text is taken as the criterion for determining deviant Psalter readings[61]. We have the Gallican text in the following Irish Psalters (apart from the *Cathach*, already mentioned)[62]: BL MS Vitellius F XI (ca. 920); the Gallican section of the Double Psalter of Rouen (Rouen, Bibl. Publique, MS 24, A. 41), from the 10th century, and in the fragments of the sister codex of this in Dublin, Trinity College, MS H 3 18, fols. 2*—3*; in MS Vat. Lat. 12910 of the 11th century; in the Southampton Psalter (St John's College, Cambridge, MS C. 9), of the early 11th century, in the abbreviated psalter of the Irish *Liber Hymnorum* of the late 11th century; in the so-called Psalter of Caimín from ca. 1100; also probably in the BL MS Cotton Galba AV of the 12th century. To these we may add two later and Cistercian manuscripts: the Coupar Angus Psalter, Vatican MS Pal. Lat. 65 (ca. 1170) and the Psalter of Cormac, BL MS Add. 36929 (ca. 1150—1200).

In reconstructing the original text of the *Gallicanum* the Benedictine editors place the *Cathach* (with the siglum C) and the text of the Rouen Psalter (with the siglum I) as the third and fourth respectively of their five basic manuscripts. These two texts which are very closely related constitute a family apart among Gallican texts. Apart from these peculiarities, this family contains a text very near to Jerome's original emendation[63].

---

59 See *Wright* (as above note 57) and *McNamara* (as above note 26), p. 213. *Schaumann* (as above note 56), p. 37, however, says that the archaic script used in the tablets argues against a date as late as the seventh century. A sixth-century date would not be unreasonable.

60 See, e.g., lines 329—342: "... What is the translation that is on the psalms? ... The translation of the Septuagint (= *Gallicanum*), truly, that is the one which is on the psalms ... Jerome corrected it under dagger and asterisk ...", ed. K. *Meyer*, Hibernica Minora, being a Fragment of an Old-Irish Treatise on the Psalter (Anecdota Oxoniensia), Oxford 1894, p. 32—33.

61 See some of the evidence in *McNamara* (as above note 26), p. 265—66. Occasionally in these glosses the *Gallicanum* is called "the Septuagint".

62 On these texts see *McNamara* (as above note 26), with summary, p. 263.

63 See the Benedictine critical edition of the *Gallicanum*; Liber Psalmorum, Roma 1953,

A feature of the *Cathach* is that it contains the critical signs of asterisk and obelus which Jerome used in his original correction of the Latin in accord with the Hebrew — following the lead given by Origen. In the introduction to this rendering (*Psalterium Romae dudum positus emendaram*) Jerome appealed to scribes not to copy his corrected Psalter text without these critical signs. Despite this, the signs were very often omitted: only one of the five basic manuscripts used by the Benedictine editors of the *Gallicanum* (i.e. Codex Reginensis Latinus 11) uses most of them. Medieval Gallican manuscripts, notably those of the Alcuin recension, do have obeli and asterisks. In many instances, however, these do not represent Jerome's original, but rather a later collation of the *Gallicanum* against Jerome's rendering from the Hebrew — the *Hebraicum*[64].

In the *Cathach* there are about 19 occurrences of the obelus and 21 of the asterisk — the former we may recall indicating passages in the Septuagint (and Jerome's Latin corrected text) but not in the Hebrew, the asterisk indicating a word or words not in the Septuagint but added from the Hebrew. Only in 2 instances (Pss 33:10; 84:11) does the obelus in the *Cathach* correspond to an obelus in Jerome's original. As Dom Henri de Sainte-Marie has noted in his excellent critical edition of Jerome's rendering from the Hebrew, 10 of these critical signs in the *Cathach* reveal their true origin, which is a revision of the *Gallicanum* against the Latin text of the *Hebraicum*. More precisely still, this revision is against the specifically Irish family of *Hebraicum* texts — of which we shall speak presently. The Irish family is characterised by certain omissions — sometimes omission of a single word, other times of an entire phrase. For instance in the *Cathach* the entire phrase *et opera manuum tuarum dirige super nos* of Ps 89:17 is *sub obelo*, indicating that it is regarded as having been absent from the Hebrew text. In fact, it is in the original Hebrew text and in the original *Hebraicum*, Jerome's Latin rendering of this. The phrase, however, is absent from the Irish family of *Hebraicum* texts, represented by the three basic manuscripts AKI, to which we can also add the (Irish) Edinburgh Psalter, Edinburgh, University Library MS 56. The presence of the obelus in the *Cathach* at Ps 97:5 and 91:11, 95:9 is to be explained in the same manner.

The purpose of the 21 asterisks in the *Cathach* is less easy to explain. Nine of them correspond to asterisks in Jerome's original, as reconstructed by the Benedictine editors. Five of the other instances would qualify for an asterisk, being on material which is in the Hebrew but not in the Septuagint. In these instances, however, no asterisk is given in the Benedictine edition of the *Gallicanum*. Comparison with the *Hebraicum* may have guided the person who inserted the asterisks in these cases. The remaining 7 texts in the *Cathach* set off by an asterisk present a greater problem, in that the asterisk comes before words that

---

XII—XIV, and D. *de Bruyne*, La réconstruction du psautier hexaplaire latin, RBén. 41 (1929), p. 297—324.

64 See further H. *de Sainte-Marie* (as above note 52), XXIII—XXIV; *McNamara* (as above note 26), p. 266—68.

are in the Septuagint. In five of these, in fact, the words under asterisk are found in all texts: the original Hebrew, the Septuagint, the Old Latin and *Gallicanum* (thus at Pss 34:15; 58:6; 65:7; 85:4; 103:7). In one of these (Ps 65:7) the words in question *(in aeternum)* is also *sub asterisco* in Codex Reginensis (R), the chief manuscript of the *Gallicanum*, although erroneously, it would appear, in the opinion of the Benedictine editors. It may have been in the exemplar of the *Cathach*, or the *Cathach* may have inserted it from comparison with a manuscript of the R type. In another instance of the 7 (Ps 49:7) the word in question *(et)* is absent from an Old Latin and one *Gallicanum* text and is *sub asterisco* also in Codex Abbatiae Sangallensis 20, of the *Gallicanum*. Unless the insertion of the asterisks in this latter group of texts was capricious, their presence in the *Cathach* may be explained through "correction" of the underlying Gallican text against some faulty Gallican or Old Latin manuscripts.

The evidence provided by this use of the obelus and asterisk, particularly the former, in the *Cathach* indicates the existence of a critical textual approach to the Psalter text in Irish schools, and this already in the sixth century or the early seventh at the latest. From the Old Irish glosses in the Milan Commentary we know that a critical interest in textual matters was also evident in the late eighth or early ninth centuries[65]. From these glosses we see that the Irish glossator was interested in the quality of the Latin text of the commentary, in the nature of the biblical text it employed and the instances in which it deviated from the text which for him was authoritative, i.e. the *Gallicanum* which he occasionally calls the Septuagint.

c) *Jerome's rendering from the Hebrew (the Hebraicum) in Early Ireland.*

We have copies, or fragments, of the *Hebraicum* rendering as used in Ireland in the following texts[66]: the Codex Amiatinus (with siglum A), from about 700 (but before 716); Karlsruhe, Cod. Augiensis XXXVIII (with siglum K), from the 9th century; Paris BN MS Fr. 2452, from the late 9th century; the Double Psalter of Rouen (Rouen, Bibl. Publique MS 14, A. 4), of the 10th century (given the siglum I and already mentioned in relation to the Gallican texts) and its Dublin sister codex in Trinity College MS H 3 18, fol. 2*—3*; the Edinburgh Psalter (about AD 1025) and the Psalter of Ricemarch, Dublin, Trinity College MS 50 (A. 4 20) (soon after 1055).

In the history of the transmission of the *Hebraicum* we have an Irish family of texts, represented by the manuscripts AKI, in the order of antiquity of the manuscripts[67]. In the order of the purity of the texts as representatives of the Irish *Hebraicum* tradition this order should be reversed, the Rouen Psalter being the most faithful representative of the original Irish *Hebraicum* text.

---

65 *McNamara* (as above note 26), p. 265f.
66 On these MSS see *McNamara* (as above note 26), with summary in p. 263f.
67 H. *de Sainte-Marie* (as above note 52), p. XXII—XXVI.

As already noted, this Irish family is characterised by certain omissions, sometimes of single words, other times of entire phrases. The fact that the insertion of
the obeli and asterisks into the *Cathach* is in dependence on this Irish family
indicates that the *Hebraicum* itself must have come to Ireland during the sixth
century at the latest. It still remains to be determined whether it was taken to
Ireland in what is now its peculiar Irish form or whether this developed in Ireland
itself. The use of an Irish text in the Codex Amiatinus indicates that it was being
used in Northumbria in the early eighth century. The same family had a wider
influence in Europe later through the form of text found in K[68].

II. Psalm Prefaces and Prologues used in Ireland

a) Jerome's Scio quosdam, Psalterium Romae dudum positus *and Pseudo-Bede's*
Dauid filius Jesse.
We know that the early Irish schools used at least these three Psalm Prefaces. All
three are found as Prefaces to the Milan Commentary, Cod. Amb. C 301 inf., and
are heavily glossed in Old Irish[69]. This latter fact indicates that they were used in
the Irish schools.

Jerome's preface *Scio quosdam* (Cod. Amb. C 301 inf., fol. 2c—3a) is introduced
as the work of Jerome: *Incipit prologus Hirunimi ad Suffronium* ... The same work
introduces his second preface (cols. 2a—b) as: *Incipt praefatio psalmorum in Christo
Iesu Domini nostro*, with *Hieronimi* interlineated in another hand after *praefatio*.
The preface *Scio quosdam* is also cited at length in the Prologue to the Psalter in the
Hiberno-Latin *Eclogae tractatorum in Psalterium*[70].

The Pseudo-Bede Preface has as title, *incipit* and *explicit*: (fol. 2b—c): *incipit
prologus psalmorum. David filius Iessae* ... *deabsalma lxxu, alleluia xxi. canticum
graduum xu*. D. De Bruyne[71] has published two variant recensions of this preface
from the MSS, both with a longer ending.

These three prefaces were widely used in the Western Church.

---

68 Ibid., p. XLI—XLIV.
69 Text in Thes. 1, p. 7—10.
70 Ed. by M. *Sheehy*, PRIA 73 C (1973), p. 285. It is without ascription in the Munich MS
of the *Eclogae*, but attributed to *Hiero(nimus)* in the St Gall MS.
71 The longer recensions published by *de Bruyne* end: ... *cantica graduum numero XV.
Psalmus primus nulli adsignatus est, quoniam omnium est; deinde quis alius intellegitur in primo
nisi primogenitus ut merito inscriptio non fuerit necessaria; deinde quia ipse psalmus christi men-
tionem facit et aduersus christum eius exponendo personam, inscribendi causum omnino non habet.
Ordines historiae inmutatos legimus et in titulis psalmorum; sed psalmi non secundum historiam,
sed secundum prophetias leguntur. Ita ordinem psalmorum turbare non potest ordo titulorum.
Psalmi omnes qui inscribuntur ipsi dauid, ad christi pertinent sacramentum, quia dauid dictus est
christus.*

b) St Basil's Psalm Preface in Rufinus's Latin Translation

In the Milan text (Cod. Amb. C 301 inf., fol. 3a—4a) we have the Psalm Preface of St Basil in Rufinus's Latin translation, but here attributed to Jerome: *Incipit praefatio psalmorum uel laus psalterii. Hirunimus dicit: Omnis scriptura diuinitus inspirata* ... It ends: ... *uideamus tandem quid etiam ipsa psalmi indicentur initia.* This Preface of Basil (PG 29, 210; 31, 1723—26) was commonly attributed to St Augustine (PL 36, 63—66). Although there appears to be an echo of it in the Introduction to the Psalter in the Hiberno-Latin Commentary on the entire Bible from the late eighth century, called by Dr. Bernhard Bischoff „Das Bibelwerk"[72] the fact that the Milan text has no Irish glosses, seems to indicate that this particular Preface was not much used in the Irish schools.

c) Psalm Introduction in Irish Commentaries

Together with these Psalm Prefaces received from the outside, we also have some introductions to the Psalter composed in the Irish schools themselves. The Preface to the *Eclogae tractatorum in Psalterium*[73], as the very title of the work suggests, is in the nature of a series of excerpts from other authors, mainly Cassiodorus but also Hilary, Isidore and Junilius as well as some pseudonymous writings and occasional items, it would appear, from Irish ecclesiastical tradition. The Introduction to the Psalter in "Das Bibelwerk"[74] also cites from some accepted patristic sources on the Psalms but is much more under the influence of what may be called the Irish approach to the Psalms and is very closely related to the Introduction to the Psalms in the *Old Irish Treatise on the Psalter* which was composed a little later (ca. 800).

d) An Antiochene Introduction to the Psalter

The chief source for Irish commentary material was the full Latin translation of the Commentary of Theodore of Mopsuestia and the Latin Epitome of this. It is possible, as we have seen[75], that Theodore's commentary was accompanied by a preface or introduction, as the Greek commentary attributed to Diodorus was. However, no Latin translation of any such work is known. One can only speculate whether any Latin Psalm Preface along the principles of Antiochene exegesis was used in the West or in Irish schools. Future research may throw light on the subject. The fact, however, that in Cod. Amb. C 301 inf. the Antiochene Commentary material is preceded by prefaces of another nature would seem to indicate that no appropriate Antiochene one was known to exist. The denial of any knowledge of such a preface in the Milan glosses (Ml. 37a15) serves to reinforce this.

---

72 Cf. *Sheehy* (as above note 70), p. 292. The preface has been edited from two manuscripts (BL Vesp. A 1 and Angers 14) by *de Bruyne* (as above note 45), p. 72 f.; *Berger* as above note 46), no. 91.

73 Partial edition from imperfect Munich MS by *Sheehy* (as above note 70), p. 265—67.

74 Ed. by *Sheehy* (as above note 70), p. 291—98, from Munich MS.

75 See above, p. 347.

III. Psalm Headings in the Early Irish Church

a) The Mystical Series of St Columba

The Series of Mystical Psalm Headings most widely used in Medieval Latin Psalter texts is Series I of Dom Pierre Salmon's edition. He calls it "Série de Saint Columba", because the oldest text in which it is found is the *Cathach* of St Columba[76]. In Dom Salmon's opinion all of the numerous witnesses to this series derive, through England, from a text being used in Ireland in the sixth century. What the history of this series before this time was is another matter. The four chief texts used by Dom Salmon for his edition are the *Cathach* (C), the Codex Amiatinus (A), which for the Psalter has the "Irish" text of the *Hebraicum*, the "mystical" section of the Argumenta of the work *De titulis Psalmorum* wrongly ascribed to Bede, and Codex Augiensis CVII (10th century) from Karlsruhe (with siglum R). Like Codex Amiatinus, R also has the "Irish" *Hebraicum* text and is very closely related to A. Despite the fact that its Psalter text is the *Hebraicum*, it has the Gallican biblical psalm headings of the Irish *Cathach* Gallican family, and both A and R have Series I of the mystical headings which are generally associated with Gallican Psalters. Another manuscript which we may associate with the above is the so-called Psalter of Charlemagne (Paris, BN MS lat. 13159) of the late eighth century in which all the introductory material, including the mystical psalm headings, is in the central Irish tradition[77]. The earliest witness to this tradition as found in the Psalter of Charlemagne is the introductory material in the incomplete catena on the Psalms (beginning imperfectly with Ps 39:11b) from about AD 700 found in the Vatican MS Pal. Lat. 68[78].

The Columba Series of Psalm headings is noted for its Christological orientation[79]. The greater portion of the Psalms are taken as spoken by Christ, the Church or the Apostles: *Vox Christi, Vox Ecclesiae, Vox apostolorum*. Only 24 are placed on the lips of the psalmist prophet himself, and then generally as direct prophecies of Christ.

It has been noted that this series has roots in very early Christian tradition. On a number of instances Tertullian's treatment of individual psalms is related to this series. Comparisons have also been made between this series and the exegesis of Origen (e.g. in Pss 7,8), Justin (Ps 13), the baptismal liturgy (Ps 22), the *Enarrationes* of St Augustine (Pss 48, 50, 56, 60, 86, 90, 115).

While some of the sources for this series can be traced back to the third century, there is no evidence of the existence of the series as such earlier than the *Cathach*.

---

76 Ed. *Salmon*, 'Tituli' (as above note 1), p. 45—74.

77 For this MS see *Lowe*, CLA 5, Oxford 1950, no. 652; K. *Gamber*, Codices liturgici latini antiquiores (Spicilegii Friburgensis Subsidia I, pars secunda), Freiburg/Schweiz 1968, no. 1619, p. 584f.; *Masai*, Observations sur le Psautier dit de Charlemagne (Paris lat. 13159), Scriptorium 6 (1952), p. 299—303; B. *Fischer* in: Festschrift Bernhard Bischoff, Stuttgart 1971, p. 96f.

78 A critical edition by the present writer is in the press (Studi e Testi).

79 See *Salmon*, 'Tituli' (as above note 1), p. 51f.

It is clear that the series was being used in Ireland in the sixth century. Whether it was actually composed in Ireland in the sixth century or earlier, or was introduced already made from outside, remains uncertain. The possibility of its being compiled in some Irish monastery or school cannot be ruled out. If it was composed there, the richness of Irish tradition and the degree of creativity in the Irish schools during these early centuries of Christianity in the island were far greater than we have been accustomed to accept.

b) Theodorean, Antiochene and Historical Psalm Headings

We are on surer grounds with regard to the creativity of the early Irish schools in the matter of the historical Psalm headings we find in such works as the catena on the Psalms of Codex Pal. Lat. 68, the *De titulis Psalmorum* of Pseudo-Bede, in the so-called Psalter of Charlemagne and in the Double Psalter of Rouen.

In the question of these historical headings we must distinguish between Theodorean headings (depending on the Epitome of Julian) and other historical headings not depending on the Commentary of Theodore or the Julian Epitome. There is a series of headings on Pss 17—150 which depends on the Epitome of Julian. Together with this, for Pss 1—16 there exists a historical series of Psalm headings which is not drawn from, nor dependent on, the Theodorean commentary. Then again, and together with these two series, we have, especially in the catena of Pal. Lat. 68 and in the so-called Psalter of Charlemagne, a series of historical headings, but not Theodorean. These headings for the greater part understand the psalms of David and his times. These different series of historical Psalm headings are intimately connected with the actual exegesis of the Psalms which we find in the expository glosses of the Vatican catena and the Double Psalter of Rouen.

α) Theodorean and Historical Psalm Headings in the Pseudo-Bedan De titulis psalmorum[80]

These were first printed in Heerwagen's *editio princeps* of Bede's works (1563), as part of the composition *In Psalmorum librum exegesis*[81]. In this work the exposition of each psalm is divided into three sections: (a) a brief *argumentum*, (b) an *explanatio* dealing with the psalm in general, followed by (c) the *Commentarius* proper. The *Commentarius* goes only as far as Ps 121, while the *argumenta* and *explanationes* cover the entire Psalter.

It has been shown that this composition in three sections is entirely arbitrary and in part due to the editor of the *editio princeps*. The *Commentarius* has nothing to do with Bede. It has been shown to be the work of the twelfth-century writer Manegold von Lautenbach[82]. The *argumenta* and *explanationes* once circulated

---

80 For a study of these see B. *Fischer* (as above note 25), p. 90—110; also R. L. *Ramsay*, ZCP 8 (1912), p. 453—56.

81 Reproduced in PL 93, 477—1098.

82 Cf. H. *Weisweiler*, Biblica 18 (1937), p. 197—204.

independently of the *Commentarius* and are found in the two manuscripts, Munich Clm 14387 (9th century) and Paris, BN MS lat. 12273 (10th century). In both these texts the *argumenta* for all the Psalms come first, after this comes further material on the Psalms (explanation of *sela, interpretatio psalterii artis* i.e. explanation of difficult words in the Psalter, and *Interpretatio nominum Hebraeorum*). After this come the *Explanationes*.

The *Explanationes* are really a summary of the introductions which Cassiodorus prefixed to his commentary on the Psalms. This summary was apparently made by Bede.

The *Argumenta* are composite, comprising two, and sometimes three parts. Section (a), a historical heading, is present for every psalm except Ps 87, and almost invariably stands first. It is the section that interests us here, and we shall return to it presently. Section (b) gives the mystical explanation, and is none other than the Irish St Columba Series which we have just considered. Section (c) when present, gives a brief moral application drawn from the works of Arnobius or Jerome.

Section (a), the historical heading, interprets the given psalm of some event in Old Testament history: of David's time, of Hezekiah or the Maccabees. From Ps 17 onwards, with few exceptions, all these historical headings of Pseudo-Bede are dependent on the Epitome of Julian, at times reproducing even its wording. The headings for Pss 1—16, although giving the literal, non-messianic, non-Christological meaning of the text, are not Theodorean. These historical headings in *De titulis psalmorum* are all connected with a particular form of exposition of the Psalms, the historical approach which we shall consider in greater detail later.

β) Theodorean and other historical headings in the catena on the Psalms of Cod. Pal. Lat. 68[83]

This catena on the Psalms contains introductory material of a historical nature regarding the understanding of the Psalms. The chief source of inspiration for the historical headings in the catena is the Epitome of Julian or more precisely the *argumenta* prefixed to the exposition proper in the Epitome. The Epitome has influenced the headings of the catena in two ways. In many cases the headings of the catena reproduce verbatim the text of the Epitome, while in others the substance of the heading in Pal. Lat. 68 is that of the *argumentum* of the Epitome, although the wording is different. In some instances the heading of the catena contains only a mere reflection of the Epitome.

Together with the heading reproducing or reflecting the text of the Epitome and Theodorean exegesis there is in the catena of Pal. Lat. 68 another series of headings interpreting the Psalms as speaking of David and his times. Sometimes both kinds of headings are found for the same psalm. On some occasions the Davidic interpretation of the psalm has influenced the very biblical Psalm heading, e.g. Ps 46: *Vox Dauid accepto regno* (= Davidic reference). *Vox plebis post reuersionem; siue*

---

83 This question is considered in greater detail in the introduction to the forthcoming ciritical edition of MS Pal. Lat. 68 in Studi e Testi.

(in tempore) Machabeorum carmen istud tamquam triumphale praecinnitur diu(i)ctis quippe gentibus uel Iudeis praeuaricatoribus (= Julian Epitome). Or again Ps 47: *Vox Dauid accepto regno pro gratiarum actione* (= Davidic reference). *Vox Ezechiae. Estimationem hominum ignorantium Deum arguit* (Julian Epitome).

These examples, taken somewhat at random, could be multiplied. As headings they reflect a particular kind of exegesis interpreting the psalms both of David and later Jewish history, exegesis found in the expository glosses of the catena. The headings themselves are as creative as the particular form of interpretation itself, which we shall consider later.

γ) *Theodorean and other historical headings in the Psalter of Charlemagne*

We have already spoken of the so-called Psalter of Charlemagne (Paris, BN MS lat. 13159) in relation to Series I (the St Columba Series) of mystical Psalm headings. All the introductory material to the Psalms in this Psalter, written hastily and with many errors of transcription ca. 795—800, is very closely related to that found in the corresponding introductory material in the Vatican catena just now considered. This holds true in a particular manner for the historical headings, both Theodorean and non-Theodorean. The heading of Ps 42 which I give here is typical of this relationship.

Psalter of Charlemagne	Catena in Cod. Pal. Lat. 68
In finem psalmus Dauid. Gratulatio reuertentis in regnum; uel queralla Dauid pro Saul. Vox plebis in Babilonia. Vox Christi ad passionem et Ecclesiae ad Christum.	*In finem salmus Dauid. De gratulatione reuersionis in regnum; uel querela Dauid pro Saul. Vox plebis in Babilonia. Vox Christi ad Patrem. Vox aeclesiae.*

With regard to this historical material there are differences as well as resemblances to be taken note of. Both texts have peculiar biblical headings with reference to David proper to themselves. With regard to the Theodorean material, both draw what they have of it from the Julian Epitome. In a number of instances the material from the Epitome in both the catena and the Psalter is identical, both in the wording and in the amount borrowed. In other cases, however, the text of the Psalter of Charlemagne draws more extensively on the Epitome than does the catena. With regard to the other historical headings not drawn from the Epitome found in the catena, some but not all of these are found in the Psalter of Charlemagne.

It is evident that the tradition preserved in the introductory material of the so-called Psalter of Charlemagne is intimately related to that found in the catena of Pal. Lat. 68. Both represent the same tradition which appears to be unique in the Western Church and to be that of the schools of Ireland and of the Celtic Church in Northumbria.

δ) *Historical Psalm Headings on Pss 1—16 in Psalters of Rouen, Charlemagne and in Pseudo-Bede's* De titulis Psalmorum

In the Double Psalter of Rouen, written in Ireland in the tenth century, the texts of both the *Gallicanum* and the *Hebraicum* are glossed, this latter much more so than the *Gallicanum*. It has been recognised for some time that the marginal gloss on the *Hebraicum* derives from the Theodorean commentary of the kind found in Cod. Amb. C 301 inf. We now know that this Milan Commentary of Cod. Amb. C 301 inf. fol. 14a—146, is actually composite, the first part (on Pss 1:1—16:11a) being a full Latin translation of the commentary of Theodore of Mopsuestia whereas the remainder (on Pss 16:11b to the end) is but an Epitome of the Latin translation, a translation now generally believed to have been made by Julian of Eclanum[84]. This Epitome, it would appear, once existed for the entire Psalter, but became imperfect through the loss of the entire opening section. In the tradition represented by the Milan Codex, this loss was made good by inserting in its stead the text of the full translation of Theodore's work.

A check of the Rouen glosses on Pss 1—16 has shown that the glosses on the portion before Ps 16:11b are not from the Theodorean commentary, whereas those on verses from 16:12 onwards are drawn from the Julian Epitome. These glosses on Pss 1:1—16:11 reveal portions of an otherwise unknown commentary, giving a sober, literal interpretation of the biblical text. Unfortunately, only parts of the glosses in question can be read with any degree of certainty, due to the fact that the handwriting is extremely small and that the close binding has made part of the glosses on the left-hand margins illegible. These difficulties are somewhat compensated for by the occurrence of the text of a few of these glosses in the section on the Psalter in the late eighth-century work known as "Das Bibelwerk".

I have studied the historical headings in the Rouen Psalter and find that for the greater part they agree almost verbatim with those in the pseudo-Bedan *De titulis psalmorum*. The identity is all the clearer in the rare heading on Ps 13, although it should also be noted that in one instance (Ps 12), the heading in the Rouen Psalter agrees with that of the Psalter of Charlemagne, rather than with Pseudo-Bede. Most of the historical headings for Pss 1—16 in the Rouen psalter are in the pages with the *Hebraicum*, although one or other is in the facing page with the *Gallicanum* text[85].

In so far as can be ascertained, these historical Psalm headings of Pseudo-Bede and the Rouen Psalter are designed to go with the kind of commentary revealed by the glosses on these same psalms found in the *Hebraicum* of the Rouen Psalter. Basically the same tradition of Psalm headings is found in the so-called Psalter of Charlemagne for Pss 1—16. Because of the importance of this series I publish here

---

84 On this point see *Devreesse* (as above note 20), p. XXVI; A. *Vaccari*, Civiltà Cattolica 67 (1916), vol 1, p. 578—93; *idem*, Biblica 4 (1923), p. 337—51; and more recently *de Coninck* (as above note 20), p. XV—XXXVII.

85 It has yet to be determined whether some of these *argumenta* were added later, from MSS such as Clm 14387 or Paris, BN MS lat. 12273; cf. *de Coninck* (as above note 20), p. XLIV, note 248.

(as an Appendix) all three series of historical Psalm headings. With the exception of those from the Psalter of Charlemagne for Pss 2[86], 3[87] and 4[88], and Ps 8[89] of the Rouen Psalter, only those from Pseudo-Bede's *De titulis psalmorum* have been published before.

IV. Psalm Commentaries of the Early Irish Church

1. Non-Antiochene Commentaries in Ireland[90]

While the material at our disposal has not as yet been sufficiently analysed to permit us draw a complete picture of the commentary material available to early Irish scholars, we have good reason to believe that for the interpretation of the Psalms they had copies of the following works: the *Commentarioli*, and probably also the *Tractatus sive Homeliae in Psalmos*, of Jerome; the *Enarrationes in Psalmos* of Augustine, or an abbreviation of them; the *Formulae spiritalis intellegentiae* and *Instructionum libri duo* of Eucherius of Lyons; Paterius's collection of expositions from the works of Gregory the Great known as *Liber testimoniorum Veteris Testamenti*[91]; the introductions to the Psalm commentaries of Hilary and Cassiodorus[92] and very probably their commentaries as well; works of Isidore relating to the various subjects encountered in the Psalter.

For our purpose here this general list, based on the evidence of extant Irish commentaries, will suffice. A more detailed study of the subject would need to specify how widespread the use of any particular commentary was, when its use was first attested, and if possible in what part of Ireland. In general we can say that by the year 800 the works noted above were available in Irish monastic libraries.

2. Theodore and Junilius

We may justly presume that at one time the Latin translation of the complete commentary on the Psalms by Theodore of Mopsuestia was available in the Western Church, at least in certain centres of learning. All that is now extant of this full

---

86 Published already by *Salmon*, 'Tituli' (as above note 1), p. 32.

87 Published ibid.

88 Published ibid.

89 Published, together with accompanying commentary, by *de Coninck* and *d'Hont* (as above note 20), p. XLIII, note 245.

90 On this subject see *McNamara* (as above note 26), p. 255–57. See also C. *Stancliffe*, Early 'Irish' Biblical Exegesis, Stud. Patr. 12, 1, ed. E. A. *Livingstone*, Berlin 1975, p. 361—70.

91 Paterius's work is cited extensively under the rubric *Gregor(ius)* in the section on the Psalter in „Das Bibelwerk".

92 The earliest series of excerpts from Cassiodorus's *Expositio Psalmorum* seems to be that in the Hiberno-Latin *Eclogae* (cf. PRIA 73 C, 1973, p. 231). The ninth-century Cassiodorus MS Laon, Bibliothèque de la Ville 26 (with Irish glosses) appears to contain only prefatory material from Cassiodorus, not the complete commentary or even part of it, see J. W. *Halporn*, Traditio 37 (1981), p. 390f.

translation are sections of the commentary on Pss 1—40. As already noted[93], almost all of this is written in Irish hands and comes from Irish monasteries. In Turin, Bibl. Univ. MS F. IV,1, fasc. 5—6 of the eighth-ninth century we have the continuous exegesis of Pss 13:7—16:15 (fasc. 6, fol. 1—6a), the *Argumentum* for Ps 37 (fol. 6c—d), a series of interpretations of different verses of Pss 17:1—4, 13a (fasc. 5, fol. 7—14a). In the Milan Cod. Amb. C 301 inf. (ca. 800) we also have sections of the full translation of Theodore's commentary in fols. 4a22—13d20 (fragments of the commentary on Pss 17:17—40:13a).

In the same codex, in fol. 14a—39d we have the full translation of Theodore's commentary on Pss 1:1—16:11, preserved for us in its entirety because it was used to make good the lost portion of the Epitome of Julian's translation of Theodore's commentary.

In the present state of research we cannot see how widely the full text of Theodore's commentary was known in the Irish schools — apart from the section on Pss 1:1—16:11 of the Milan Commentary that is. Neither the Turin nor the other Milan fragments with the full translation are glossed in Old Irish, a fact that would tend to indicate that they were not used in the Irish schools.

The full commentary on the Psalms (Cod. Amb. C 301 inf. fol. 14a—146) including the Epitome from Ps 16:11b onwards is, on the contrary, heavily glossed. It has been shown[94] that for the commentary on the Psalter from Ps 16:11b onwards, Theodore was known not through the full translation but through the Epitome. All Antiochene (Theodorean) comments on these Psalms found in the catena of Codex Pal. Lat. 68, in the *Eclogae Tractatorum in Psalterium*, in "Das Bibelwerk", in the glosses in the Montpellier and Vercelli Psalters and in the Rouen Psalter, and in the historical Psalm headings already studied, are from the Epitome, not from the full translation, even in sections where this is still extant. The fact that so many Hiberno-Latin texts from the early eighth century (Pal. Lat. 68) to about 1100 (the so-called Psalter of Caimín) excerpt from the Epitome or are dependent on it, proves beyond reasonable doubt that this Theodorean commentary must have been the basis for Psalm instruction in practically every monastery in Ireland and in Celtic Northumbria.

Although none of the extant manuscripts of Junilius comes from Ireland, the citations from his work, under his name in the *Eclogae*[95], in "Das Bibelwerk[96]" and anonymously in the *Old Irish Treatise*[97], would seem to indicate that at least some Irish libraries had copies of his work.

---

93 Above, p. 343. See in ed. *Devreesse* and *de Coninck* and *d'Hont* (as above note 20).

94 Cf. *de Coninck* and *d'Hont* (as above note 20), p. XXIX—XLV.

95 See above p. 344 and *McNamara* (as above note 26), p. 287. In the St Gall MS of the *Eclogae* (Stiftsbibliothek MS 261), 154 *Iunili* (*us*) is mentioned by name.

96 Above p. 344 and PRIA 73 C (1973), p. 293.

97 Ibid., p. 229, note 42.

3. The Historical Psalm Commentary on Ps 1:1—16:11 in the Rouen Psalter

A judgment on the real nature of the commentary contained in the glosses on Pss 1:1—16:11a in the *Hebraicum* of the Double Psalter of Rouen will be possible only after these have been published in full. The historical headings from this commentary (published below as an Appendix) are almost always practically identical with those of the pseudo-Bedan *De titulis psalmorum*. The glosses on Ps 8 published by Lucas De Coninck and Maria Josepha D'Hont[98] agree with the non-messianic heading to this psalm. The glosses of the other psalms in this section are probably in keeping with the historical headings as given in the Rouen Psalter.

This is the case in Ps 9. This according to the historical heading can be interpreted as David's prayer giving thanks that his son's evil designs were not put into effect, but that it might also be taken as Hezekiah's words on the destruction of the Assyrian army. The glosses follow this dual reference, e.g. on the opening word *"Confitebor"*: *Praesentibus beneficis praeterita tua munera mihi recordor, hoc est confesio Dauid pro gratiarum actione dum non perpetrauit Abisolon quae cogitauit contra Dauid.* A feature of this exegesis is the close manner in which it follows the biblical Psalm heading: *"In finem pro occultis filii psalmus Dauid"*. Likewise on *"in aequitate"* of v. 9: *id est in morte inimicorum, id est Abisolon cum sociis et in uiuificatione amicorum Dauid et sociorum.* The other reference of the title is also present in the glosses, e.g. on *"increpasti gentes"* of v. 6: *(Per angelum Domini?) qui uno impetu clxxxu milia occidit et regem superbum per suos filios occidit* (cf. 2 Kgs 19:35—37=Isa 37:36—38) *uel ad Abisolon cum hoste suo conuenit.* There is a similar reference to Senacherib in the gloss on *"iudicabit"* of v. 9. Likewise with regard to Ps 3. Whereas the biblical Psalm heading is here quite precise *(Psalmus David cum fugeret a facie Abessalon filii sui)*, a heading followed by Theodore in his exposition, both the heading and glosses of the Rouen Psalter interpret the psalm as appropriate to Hezekiah when surrounded by the Assyrian army. An interlinear gloss on *"multo dicunt animae meae"* of v. 2 refers us to the context of 4 Kgs 18 and Isa 37, with the account of precisely this matter.

Only when a sufficient amount of the glosses on this section of the Psalter of Rouen have been published will we be able to set about situating the commentary revealed in the context of early Irish and non-Irish exposition of the Psalter.

4. Irish Commentary Material on the Psalter

The early Irish Church inherited both the general Alexandrian and Western tradition as well as the Antiochene. At an early date Irish scholars were compiling commentary and expository material of their own on the Psalms, material that reflects the exegetical approach of their schools.

The earliest of these commentaries is the catena on the Psalms in Codex Vaticanus Palatino-Latinus 68, composed about AD 700 but in part reflecting the

---

98   *de Coninck* and *d'Hont* (as above note 20), p. XLIII, note 245.

earlier exegesis of Irish schools. About a third of its glosses are derived from the Julian Epitome. It stresses the historical approach and combines references to David's times with those to later Jewish history. From the later eighth century we have the *Eclogae tractatorum in Psalterium* which in its expository section draws mainly from the Epitome of Julian as supplemented for Ps 1:1—16:11 in the Milan Commentary. From about the same period we have the section on the Psalter in "Das Bibelwerk". This section draws on the Epitome, supplemented for Pss 1:1—16:11 as in the Rouen Psalter glosses, but also depends very much on Cassiodorus. It is a very good witness to the rather specific Irish approach to the Psalms which we shall consider in the next section. In this it is closely related to the *Old Irish Treatise on the Psalter* from about 800—850. From roughly the same period come the numerous Old Irish glosses on the Latin text of the Milan Commentary (Cod. Amb. C 301 inf.) and on the Psalm prefaces of Jerome and Pseudo-Bede. The Old Irish glosses on the Theodorean commentary adhere closely to what the Latin text itself has to say — an indication of how seriously these Irish scholars set about understanding it. From later periods we have the glosses on the Rouen Psalter and the so-called Psalter of Caimín.

Commentaries are only as creative as the exegesis they carry. By reason of the underlying expository approach, we can say that the earlier Irish commentaries are creative, while those of later times (the glosses in the Psalter of Rouen and Caimín) are carriers of this exegesis.

V. Early Irish Exegesis: Tradition and Creativity

1. The General Christian Christological Interpretation in Ireland

The early Irish Church inherited the general Christian Christological interpretation of the Psalms. That this tradition was cherished in Ireland is evident from the Psalm Headings of the *Cathach* which are Christological in orientation. We find this same series in other Psalters and commentaries used in Ireland or connected with Irish tradition, e.g. the catena of Codex Pal. Lat. 68, the Codex Amiatinus, the Double Psalter of Rouen. In the *Old Irish Treatise on the Psalter* (lines 320—328) 12 items prophesied in the Psalms are listed:

> Of what did the prophecy of the Psalms foretell? Not difficult. Of the birth of Christ and of his baptism, and of his passion, and of his resurrection, and of his ascension, and of his sitting at the right hand of God the Father in heaven, of the invitation of the heathen to the faith, of the thrusting of Judah into unbelief, of the increase of every virtue, of the spurning of every injustice, of the malediction of sinners, of the coming of Christ to judge the quick and the dead[99].

99 Ed. K. *Meyer* (as above note 60), p. 30—33. Twelve mysteries are itemised in this list. An Old Irish gloss on *ut impleam uerbum Dei* of Col I, 1:25 (Wb. 26d9; Thes. 1, 670) speaks of

The commentaries of Augustine, Hilary, Cassiodorus, and Jerome would have kept the early Irish schools conversant with this general Christian exegesis.

2. The Fourfold Sense of Scripture

About the year 800 the *Old Irish Treatise on the Psalter* thus expressed a theory about the senses of Scripture:

> There are four things that are necessary in the Psalms, to wit, the first story *(cétna stoir)*, and the second story *(stoir tánaise)*, the sense *(síens)* and the morality *(moralus)*. The *first story* refers to David and to Solomon and the above mentioned persons, to Saul, to Absalom, to the persecutors besides. The *second story* to Hezekiah, to the people, to the Maccabees. The *sense* (refers) to Christ, to the earthly and heavenly Church *(síens, síans or séns)*. The *morality* (refers) to every saint[100].

The three Irish terms *stoir* (*historia*, literal or historical meaning), *síans* or *séns* (*sensus*, mystical meaning) and *moralus* (*morale*, moral interpretation) must have established themselves by AD 800 as they are also found in the Old Irish glosses on the Milan Commentary. Two points should be noted about these terms and this fourfold scheme. First: the Latin term *sensus* (from which the Irish *síans, síens*, and *séns* are derived) with the meaning: "the mystical sense of Scripture", seems to be restricted to Hiberno-Latin texts — at least as a general usage. Outside of such texts I have found it only twice (in Jerome)[101]. It is found regularly with this meaning in Hiberno-Latin texts[102].

The second matter meriting attention is the assertion that the Psalms have a two-fold historical sense. This is something I have not found outside of Irish texts.

---

the seven things that have been prophesied of Christ. These are itemised as follows in the *Scuab Chrábuid*, ed. K. *Meyer* in Otia Merseiana 2, 1900—1901, p. 97; C. *Plummer*, Irish Litanies, London 1925, p. 42—43; "his birth, baptism, crucifixion, burial, resurrection, ascension, coming of the last judgment". Plummer's edition lists eight mysteries, the first being probably a later addition. Thus also the introduction to the Psalter in „Das Bibelwerk" (BN MS lat. 11561, fol. 56ra-b): *Modo, vii. quae leguntur de Christo, id est: natiuitas, baptismum, passio, sepulchrum, resurrectio, ascensio, aduentus ad iudicium et reliqua*, a passage all the more noteworthy in that the surrounding texts, but not this, depend on Cassiodorus, In Psalterium Praefatio 1, CCSL 97, 1958, 3—5; PL 70, 9—10. Hilary, in Instructio Psalmorum no. 6 (CSEL 27, 1893, 7) also lists seven things prophesied in the Psalms: *Haec septem quaedam signacula, quae de corporalitate eius, et passione et morte et resurrectione et gloria et regno et iudicio Dauid de eo in psalmis prophetat.*

100 Cf. ed. K. *Meyer* (as above note 60), p. 30f., lines 312—319.

101 In *Commentarioli in Psal. LXVII, 14* (CCSL 72, 1959, p. 124); cf. also on the same text his Commentary in Eccles. II, 8 (CCSL 72, p. 266).

102 Hiberno-Latin texts seem at times to have replaced such terms as *prophetia, allegoria, anagogia* of their sources with *sensus*, e.g. the text of the *Eclogae* and „Das Bibelwerk" to be cited later; *Utrum secundum historiam an secundum sensum legendi sunt psalmi*, which would appear to depend on a text such as that cited in note 71 above; *psalmi non secundum historiam sed secundum prophetias leguntur.*

Yet it seems to have been strongly embedded in the Irish tradition by the year 800. We find it asserted again in the same *Old Irish Teatise* in its incomplete exposition of Psalm 1: "The first story *(cétna stoir)* of the Psalms (evidently this particular psalm is intended) refers to the time of David; the second *(in tánaise)* to Chusai Arachitis *(iesu irechitis; varia lectio: hissu ireichidis)*. He it was that did not abandon him at the time of persecution, though everyone else abandoned him ...". The same two-fold historical sense for this psalm is found in the section on the Psalter in "Das Bibelwerk", a work, as already noted, very closely related to the *Old Irish Treatise*[103]:

> Hilar. *"Beatus uir qui non abiit". Prima historia ad Dauid pertinet, qui non abiit in consilio sociorum, qui uoluerant occidere Saul in spelunca, quando Dauid dixit: "Non contingat mihi ut mittam manum meam in Christum Domini"* (cf. 1 Sam 26:11,23). *"Beatus" reliqua. Secunda historia ad Chusai Arachitam pertinet, qui non exiit in consilium Abisolon et Achitophel, qui uoluerunt exire post Dauid quando fugit et occidere eum, usque Chusai dissipauit consilium eorum* (cf. 2 Sam 15:34; 17:14).

We seem to have a further reference to a two-fold historical sense in Psalm interpretation in unidentified sayings attributed to Ambrose, Jerome and Hilary preserved in the two later eighth-century Hiberno-Latin texts — the *Eclogae tractatorum in Psalterium* and in the section on the Psalms in "Das Bibelwerk". In the latter text we read as follows[104].

> AMB(ROSIUS). *Utrum secundum historiam an secundum sensum legendi sunt psalmi? Secundum sensum legendi sunt psalmi ut Ambrosius dicit: "Si toto affectu inuestigaueris psalmos multum laborem arripies. Nam etiam intellectu historico duplici sensu latent (Eclogae: duplices sensus latent uel habent)". Hieronimus: "Historico intellectu inuestigaui psalmos et certas personas in his consideraui". Item dicit: "Me ideo diuino labori reddidi et inserui psalmo(s) historico ordine". Hilar(ius). "Psalmos lege historico intellectu ubi diuersos modos inuenies".*

The point made in the obervation attributed to Ambrose seems to be that from the point of view of the historical interpretation *(historico intellectu)*, the Psalms have a two-fold sense — presumably the *prima historia (cétna síans)* and the *secunda historia (síans tánaiste)* of the other texts. The entire passage, with its erroneous ascriptions, is very probably a composition of the Irish schools[105].

---

103 Cited from BN MS lat. 11561, fol. 56va; same text cited from the other MS of this work, Munich, Staatsbibliothek Clm 14276, fol. 100r, by P. Ó Néill, Ériu 30 (1979), p. 161.

104 Ed. *Sheehy* (as above note 70), p. 292.

105 Compare the opening words, however, with the text of the full Psalm Preface *Dauid filius Iesse* given above in note 71; see also note 102.

This view on the two-fold historical sense of the Psalms, a two-fold historical reference, appears to have developed in Ireland itself, as I hope to show later. The theory which we find formulated in the later eighth century probably arose out of a practice of so regarding the Psalms which was a feature of Irish exegesis from at least 700.

3. Emphasis on the Historical Sense of the Psalms

All Christian tradition would assert that the Psalms, as the entire Old Testament and indeed the entire Bible, had a historical sense, a literal meaning — the *littera* as it was called. Where differences would arise was on the emphasis to be placed on this as against the "inner" or spiritual meaning. One patristic and classical attitude came to be expressed in the comment on Ps 67:14: *Pinnae columbae deargentatae et posteriora dorsi eius in pallore auri*. The *argentum* was *littera*, the historical sense; the *aurum* the inner meaning, the *sensus*, mystical or spiritual sense. Thus Jerome:

> *Et licet sit pulchritudo etiam iuxta litteram scire quae legas, tamen uis decoris omnis in sensu est. Exterior itaque uerborum ornatus in argenti nomine demonstratur: occultiora uero mysteria in reconditis auri muneribus continentur*[106].

In this presentation, both the *littera* and *sensus* or *occultiora mysteria* (mystical sense) were both to be respected. The latter, however, was the gold.

This view is also found in a Hiberno-Latin commentary on Luke 2:24. Quite the opposite approach was taken in the exposition on the Psalms. This, in part at least, was due to the influence of Theodore's commentary. In an Old Irish gloss in the Milan commentary (Ml. 14d7)[107] we read: "It is the history (*instoir* i.e. the literal or historical sense) that is most desirable for us to understand". The glossator says that he and those of like mind were prepared to leave to others "the exposition of the sense and the morality (*séns 7 moralus*), if it not be at variance with the history that we relate" (Ml. 14d10)[108].

This is but a theoretical assertion of an approach found already in our earliest Psalm commentary from the Irish Church, i.e. the catena in Codex Pal. Lat. 68. In this the exposition is predominantly historical. Deviations from this, especially in the form of Christological exegesis, are often explicitly introduced with the rubric:

---

106 *Commentarioli in psalm* LXVII, 14 (CCSL 72, p. 214). In the Hiberno-Latin commentary on Luke (II, 24) of MS Vindobon. lat. 997 we have a similar text: *Plerumque columba diuinarum scripturarum figuram tenet, quando dicitur: ‚pennae columbae deargentatae* usque *auri'. Quid argenti color nisi eloquentiam diuinae historiae significat. Per auri autem formam sensum triplicem spiritalem indicat, id est, tropologiam, anagogen, allegoriam*, ed. J. F. Kelly, CCSL 108C, 1974, p. 18, lines 219—223.

107 Thes. 1, 13.

108 Ibid.

Spiritaliter, i.e. a mystical interpretation, not the literal meaning intended by the author. The predominance of material of a historical nature in our extant Irish commentaries on the Psalms is evidence of the same interest in the literal exposition rather than the mystical, allegorical or spiritual one.

4. Interest in Jewish Traditions on Exegesis of Messianic Psalms

The Jewish interpretation, or even varying Jewish interpretations, of the Psalms accepted by Christians as Messianic are occasionally mentioned by the Church Fathers. In this way, and possibly also in other ways, Jewish exegesis could have become known to medieval scholars. It appears that certain sections of the early Irish Church were sufficiently interested in these traditions to include them in their own writings. Thus in the Psalm Headings of Pseudo-Bede for Ps 21 we find inserted, after that of Theodore, the following text from Jerome's *Commentarioli*[109]:

> *Aliter: Judaei de Esther hunc psalmum putant esse cantatum, quod videlicet ipsius periculo et interessione apud regem sit populus Israel a morte laxatus.*

From the Commentary of Theodore and the Julian Epitome it could be learned that the Jews interpreted Ps 2 of Zerubbabel or of David[110]; that they apparently understood Ps 44 of Solomon's wife[111] and believed that the speaker in Ps 109:1 is either Abraham's servant or David himself[112]. The Irish glossator in the Milan Commentary faithfully represents the meaning of the Latin text, yet notes the reference of Ps 2 to Zerubbabel or David (Ml. 16a17, 18, 16b5) and the mention of Abraham's servant in the commentary on Ps 109 and the manner in which the biblical text should be understood if the Jewish position were adopted (Ml. 127d3, 4, 5, 6)[113].

From Jerome's commentary on Ecclesiastes 1:1 Western scholars could learn that Jerome himself once believed that both Pss 44 and 71 *secundum historiam* were written concerning Solomon (thus accepting the Jewish understanding of them), even though they belonged to prophecy about Christ and the Church *(ad prophetiam Christi et Ecclesiae pertinentes)*[114]. We shall see that this tradition, too, was known to early Irish scholars. How much more of Jewish interpretation was known in the West, or at least in certain streams of Western tradition, it is difficult

---

109 In PL 93, 589D; Jerome, Commentarioli in Psal. XXI, CCSL 72, 198.

110 Cf. ed. *Devreesse*, p. 7—8 and in index *s.v. Iudaei;* ed. *de Coninck* and *d'Hont*, p. 10ff. (as above note 20).

111 *Devreesse*, p. 277f. and in index *s.v. Iudaei; de Coninck, d'Hont*, p. 198ff.

112 *de Coninck, d'Hont*, p. 351f.

113 Thes. 1, 16—17 for psalm 2; 434—35 for psalm 109.

114 Jerome, In Eccles. I, 1, CCSL 72, 250. This work composed about AD 389 comes from a period when Jerome was under the influence of Jewish rabbinic exegesis, see *Kelly*, Jerome, p. 150f.

to say. In view of the animated debates between Christians and Jews, particularly during the fourth and fifth centuries[115], it would not be surprising if more of Jewish tradition than is commonly believed was known in the medieval West.

5. The Messianic Psalms 15 and 21 in Irish Tradition

According to Theodore Ps 15 was composed by David in thanksgiving after he had defeated the surrounding nations. The whole psalm, he says, is sung in the person of the people, for whose benefit the power of the enemy was broken[116]. At the end of his exposition Theodore confronts the problem of the Apostle Peter's use of v. 10 as a direct prophecy of Christ in Acts 2:25—31 (to which one might add Paul's use in Acts 13:35—37). Although his language is somewhat obscure, Theodore's position seems to be that in this passage the blessed Apostle shows that the text of the Psalm in question was fulfilled in the person of Christ — how exactly he does not say, but apparently typically:

> Non ergo ab apostolo testimonium hoc usurpatum est, sed causae suae redditum: nam fuerat uidelicet a propheta praedictum, et ideo conuentienter est personae Domini uindicatum; nam prius in similitudine dictum fuerat et figura. Proprie ergo et secundum uerum intellectum, qui ipsis rebus impletus est, Domino conuenit, ad quem eum pertinere impletae sine dubio res loquuntur[117].

Theodore's non-messianic interpretation of this psalm was censured in the second

---

115 Jewish traditions in the works of the Fathers have been the subject of many studies. Thus, for Jerome, M. *Rahmer*, Die hebräischen Traditionen in den Werken des Hieronymus. Quaestiones in Genesim, Breslau 1871; *idem*, Die hebräischen Traditionen in den Werken des Hieronymus. Die Commentarii zu den 12 kleinen Propheten, I—II, Berlin 1902; J. M. *Lagrange*, RB 7 (1898), p. 563—66 (on Genesis); V. *Aptowitzer*, Zeitschrift für alttestamentliche Wissenschaft 29 (1909), p. 241—52; A. *Vaccari*, I fattori dell'esegesi Geronimiana, Biblica 1 (1920), p. 458—80; p. 470—77 for ›la tradizione ebraica‹ (= Scritti di erudizione e di filologia II, Roma 1958, p. 147—170, 159—66). Jews were numerous in Antioch in Diodorus's and Chrysostom's time and actively proselytized. It is to be presumed that the messianic prophecies would have formed part of the Jewish-Christian debate. For the background to John Chrysostom's anti-Jewish sermons see P. W. *Haskins*, in the introduction to St John Chrysostom. Discourses against Judaizing Christians (= Fathers of the Church 68, Washington 1979), p. XXI—LXXII. For the Jews at Antioch cf. C. H. *Kraeling*, The Jewish Community at Antioch, Journal of Biblical Literature 51 (1932), p. 130—60 (154—60 for Christian period); also M. *Simon*, La polémique antijuive de saint Jean Chrysostome et le mouvement judaisant d'Antioche, Annuaire de l'Institut de Philologie et d'Histoire orientales et slaves 4 (1930), p. 140—53; S. *Kraus*, Antioche, Revue des Études Juives 45 (1902), p. 27—49.

116 Ed. *Devreesse*, p. 90—100; ed. *de Coninck* and *d'Hont*, p. 75—81 (as above note 20). On Theodore's exegesis of psalm 15, see L. *Pirot* L'œuvre exégetique de Théodore de Mopsueste 350—428 après J. C., Scripta Pontificii Instituti Biblici, Roma 1913, p. 247—49; R. *Devreesse*, Essai sur Théodore de Mopsueste (Studi e Testi 141), Città del Vaticano 1938, p. 72.

117 Ed. *Devreesse*, p. 100; ed. *de Coninck* and *d'Hont*, p. 81 (as above note 20).

Council of Constantinople (553) and by the *Constitutum* of Pope Vigilius. The passage picked out for special condemnation was the ending of his exposition in which he treats of Peter's use of v. 10[118].

The Old Irish glosses on the Milan commentary repeat Theodore's exposition, as this was understood by the glossator at any rate, e.g. Ml. 38a3 (on *ab apostolo*): "*Aliter* the apostle did not apply it (i.e. the biblical text) according to the sense in which the prophet uttered it"[119]. Likewise, Ml. 38b4 (on *redditum*): "i.e. he applies it to support the saying that was uttered through congruence to the cause on which he was engaged"[120]. Or Ml. 38c5 (on a *profeta praedictum*): "i.e. that of which he (= the prophet Psalmist) applied it is different to that of which Peter uttered it"[121].

The tradition represented in the Psalm headings of Pseudo-Bede[122], and in the Psalters of Charlemagne and of Rouen differs from that of Theodore in understanding the Psalm as a prayer of Hezekiah in relation to his illness. To this the Psalter of Charlemagne adds a further historical heading, taking the psalm as sung by David on the restoration of his inheritance. Here, then, we have two further distinct historical and non-messianic interpretations of Ps 15.

The glosses of the Rouen Psalter also have a non-messianic interpretation, understanding the Psalm to speak of Hezekiah or of both Hezekiah and David or Saul. Thus, the interlinear gloss to *"tu es qui restitues hereditatem meam"* (v. 5): *uel restitues post mortem Saul uel Ezechiae post infirmitatem suam*. To *"laetatum est cor meum ..."* (v. 9): *quod corde conceptum est foris in labia eructat*. On *"in inferno"* (v. 10): *in humiliatione uel in sepulchro*. The important verse 10 is glossed as follows: *"non dabis ..."*: ... *tuis muneribus et re (...) unctione ornasti ... (res)tituti(one) uitae reparabis*. *"Sanctum tuum"* is glossed interlineary as *Dauid uel Ezechias*. The gloss for *"notas mihi fecisti uias uitae"* is *manifestabis quomodo (?) disperata uita per tuam potentiam restituitur uel reuelasti mihi quod Saul non occidisset me*. The gloss for *"cum uultu tuo"* is: ... *conspectum tuum in templo laetitia plenus ero semper quae et animo cogitatione et corporis habitu ostenditur uel auerso uultu tuo inimicis hoc est Sauli et amicis* (corr. from *inm* —) *eius*. The origins of this sustained non-messianic interpretation of Ps 15, which is quite distinct from that of Theodore, remain to be determined. In the dual reference to David and later Jewish history (in this case Hezekiah) it is reminiscent of the kind of exegesis we find in the catena of MS Pal. Lat. 68, which unfortunately begins only at Ps 39.

118 See *Pirot* (as above note 116), p. 248f.; *Devreesse*, Essai (as above note 116), p. 248. Devreesse notes that the Council's citation of Theodore's comment on psalm 15:10 is unfaithful and tendentious. Council and *Constitutum* texts in *Devreesse* (as above note 20), p. 99f.

119 Thes. 1, p. 99.

120 Ibid., p. 100.

121 Ibid.

122 See texts below, p. 389.

Theodore understood Ps 21 to speak of David persecuted by his son Absalom[123]. It was not composed of Christ, nor in the literal sense is it a prophecy of Christ or his passion. How could the sinless Christ say: "Far from my salvation are the words of my sins" (v. 2)? If different verses of the psalm are applied to Christ by the Evangelists, says Theodore, this is by accommodation, because of the similarity of circumstances. *Quod enim psalmus nullatenus conuenit Domino certum est. Neque enim erat Domini Christi, qui peccatum non fecit ... dicere: "Longe a salute mea uerba delictorum meorum"*[124].

Comparing the account of Christ's Passion with this psalm led St Augustine to say: *Passio Christi tam evidenter quasi euangelium recitatur*[125]. The psalm was universally accepted as a prophecy of Christ's passion in Christian tradition, apart from Theodore and the author of the commentary recently published under the name of Diodorus[126]. Theodoret of Cyr and John Chrysostom, of the Antiochene school, reverted to the traditional interpretation. Even Junilius lists the division of the clothes (Ps 21:19) among the 26 Old Testament prophecies concerning Christ[127]. Theodore's non-messianic interpretation of psalms was condemned in the Second Council of Constantinople and in the *Constitutum* of Vigilius.

The interpretation of Theodore is mollified somewhat in the Epitome of Julian by the introduction of the biblical heading, followed by a statement that Jesus's words on the cross tell us to whom this psalm should be referred[128]. This, however, is immediately and somewhat awkwardly connected with Theodore's position on the literal meaning of the psalm:

> *Domini ultima in cruce oratio docuit ad quem debeat hic psalmus referri, qui tamen suis temporibus habuit figuram illius historiae quae narrat Dauid coniuratione Abessalon in aerumnas coactum, in quibus positus hoc carmen uice orationis cecinit.*

As is his wont, the Old Irish glossator tries to bring out the meaning of the Latin text[129]. A gloss on the biblical text says that David sang this psalm concerning

---

123 Ed. *Devreesse*, p. 120—22; ed. *de Coninck* and *d'Hont*, p. 107—112 (as above note 20). On Theodore's exegesis of psalm 21 see also *Pirot*, L'œuvre, p. 251—54; *Devreesse*, Essai, p. 72f. (as above note 116).

124 Theodore's position as expressed by the *Constitutum* of Vigilius and Council II of Constantinople; text in *Devreesse* (as above note 20), p. 120f., footnote. Theodore's own text has: *Qui uolunt hunc psalmum in Domini persona, ex hoc loco praecipue conuincuntur non paruum temeritatis incurrere. Quomodo enim potest accipi quia hoc de se Dominus dixerit: longe a salute mea et reliqua* (ed. *de Coninck* and *d'Hont*, p. 108; ed. *Devreesse*, p. 120, [as above note 20]).

125 Enarratio II in Psalmum XXI, no. 2 (CCSL 38, 1956, p. 123).

126 Ed. *Olivier* (as above note 12), p. 126—37.

127 In Instituta regularia divinae legis 1, 22, PL 68, 38A; ed. *Kihn* (as above note 30), p. 518.

128 Ed. *de Coninck* and *d'Hont* (as above note 20), p. 108.

129 Cf. *McNamara* (as above note 26), p. 265f.

events that occurred the morning before Christ's passion and of his passion after that (Ml. 44b1). The same idea is repeated in a gloss on *docuit* of the new heading. A gloss on *suis temporibus*, however, says: "i.e. when this psalm was first sung it is appropriate to David when he complained with regard to Absalom, according to the literal sense (Ml. 44b4)[130]. It refers to Christ according to the mystic sense (*madurúin*)" (44b6)[131].

Both Pseudo-Bede (PL 93,589 D) and the Psalter of Charlemagne have the Theodorean interpretation, understanding it of Absalom's revolt. However, as already noted[132], the pseudo-Bedan *De titulis Psalmorum* adds as an alternative the Jewish interpretation and understanding of the psalm of Esther.

6. The Messianic Psalms 2, 8, 44, and 109 in Irish Tradition

These are the only four psalms taken by Theodore of Mopsuestia as direct prophecies of Christ[133]. Theodore's interpretation is reproduced faithfully in the full Latin translation and in the Epitome of Julian and in texts dependent on these, e.g. the *Eclogae tractatorum in Psalterium*[134]. There is, however, another Irish tradition in which none of these psalms is interpreted as a direct prophecy of Christ. This tradition is found especially in the so-called Psalter of Charlemagne for all four psalms; in the catena of Codex Pal. Lat. 68 for Pss 44 and 109 (the only two in the extant section of the catena); the Pseudo-Bedan *In titulis Psalmorum* and in the Psalter of Rouen for Pss 2 and 8. The evidence is as follows:

Psalm 2. Theodore, citing the words of Peter (Acts 4:24—25) and Paul (in Hebrews, 1:3, taken as Paul's), takes this psalm as a direct prophecy of Christ. Going on the same words of Peter, Jerome reckons any interpretation other than the Christological temerarious[135].

Theodore notes current Jewish interpretations, which understood the psalm either of Zerubbabel or of David.

Curiously enough, the glosses of the Psalters of Montpellier and Vercelli, generally given to Christological interpretation, both in the heading and the glosses interpret the psalms both of Christ and of David[136]. *In hoc psalmo continetur manifeste de xpo et de dauid secundum hystoriam* (on v. 1). In the Pseudo-Bedan *In titulis Psalmorum*, in the headings of the Psalter of Rouen and the Psalter of Charlemagne the psalm is understood of David — in the first two as a plaint of David that the gentiles and foreign nations have invaded Israel, in the last as the voice of

130 Thes. 1, p. 125.

131 Ibid.

132 Cf. above p. 367.

133 On this point see *Kihn* (as above note 30), p. 143, 454—64; *Pirot*, p. 238—47, *Devreesse*, p. 76—78 (as above note 116).

134 See the opening words on psalm 21 edited by M. *Sheehy* (as above note 70), p. 288.

135 Jerome, Commentarioli in Psalmum II, 1, CCSL 72, p. 181.

136 Ed. *Unterkircher* (as above note 33), p. 75—77.

David's comrades to the effect that the nations and Absalom have persecuted David[137].

The left-hand marginal glosses in the Rouen Psalter are difficult to read. However, a number of the interlinear ones are in keeping with the Davidic interpretation, especially as given in the heading of the Psalter of Charlemagne. Thus (p. 2) on *"gentes"* (v. 1): *Philistini;* *"tribus"* (Gallicanum: *populi*): *Abisolon cum socis; "aduersum Christum eius": omnis rex christus Domini uocatur,* (p. 4). *"Sion montem"* (v. 6): *Hierusalem quia Abisolon quaerit; "Dominus dixit ad me"* (v. 7): *regnare faciam in omnes qui te resistere uolunt; "ego hodie genui te": in die electionis in regnum; "beati omnes"* (v. 13): *Dauid cum sociis.*

Psalm 8[138]. The Old Irish glosses in the Milan Commentary reflect the Theodorean Christological interpretation on this psalm faithfully. I reproduce below the heading to this psalm as found in Pseudo-Bede, the Psalter of Rouen and the Psalter of Charlemagne[139]. In all three it is regarded as non-messianic, and as a prophetic admiration of the divine power, and providence and a thanksgiving for God's concern for man. We are fortunate in that the glosses on this particular psalm in the Rouen Psalter are very clear and legible. They agree fully with the heading and are in no way messianic or Christological.

Psalm 44[140]. From Ps 17 onwards almost all the historical headings of the *argumenta* of Pseudo-Bede are drawn from the Epitome of Julian. They are of little help, then, for ascertaining the non-Theodorean interpretation of Pss 44 and 109. The loss is here made good, however, by the presence of both headings and expository glosses of the catena of MS Pal. Lat 68, with which exegetical approach the headings of the Psalter of Charlemagne agree.

The heading of the Psalter of Charlemagne reads:

> *"In finem psalmus Dauid"* de se ipse et Salomon. Et *"de his qui commutabunt"* de exilio in requiem. „*Ad intellectum filiis Chore"*. Ex Patris persona profeta de Christo hunc psalmum (pre -?; text faded) dicit. Qui uerbum suum ante secula de utero profunde diuinitatis in sui manifestationem scientiam paternam omnibus monstrans eructauit.

In this heading we have combined a historical interpretation understanding the psalm of David and Solomon and another form of exegesis seeing in it a prophecy of Christ. The first part of the text just quoted coincides practically verbatim with the heading in Pal. lat. 68, while the second part is similar in tone. MS Pal. Lat. 68 reads:

---

137 Below, p. 384f.
138 For Theodore's interpretation see *Pirot* (as above note 116), p. 242—47.
139 Below, p. 386. The heading and glosses of the Psalter of Rouen on this psalm have been published by de Coninck and d'Hont (as above note 20), p. XLIII, note 245.
140 For Theodore's interpretation see *Pirot* (as above note 116), p. 244—45.

"In finem salmus Dauid". id est de ipso et Salomone. "Pro his qui com-
motabuntur." id est de exilio in requiem. "Ad intellectum filis Chore canticum
pro dilecto". id est de regno iusti. De Christo et aeclesia ... Totus hic salmus
refertur ad Christum de quo Pater in euangelio loquitur: "Hic est Filius meus
dilectus", licet ad Salomonem inertialis historia refertur. Vox Dauid de
Salomone. Vox Patris de Filio qui est Verbum.

In these headings we find juxtaposed two contrasting interpretations of the
psalm: one taking it as spoken by David of himself and Solomon, or of Solomon
alone; the other, citing Jerome's *Commentarioli*[141] on this psalm, saying it refers to
Christ alone and describing the "historical" reference *(historia)* to Solomon as
inertialis, "inept". This judgement on the historical interpretation is evidently
from the pen of the compiler.

The expository glosses contain the „historical" interpretation deprecated in the
introduction. In these the psalm is referred in the literal, historical sense to Solomon and only *spiritaliter* to Christ, as explicitly stated in v. 3: *Haec quae sequntur*
conueniunt Salomon historialiter et Christo spiritaliter. Again on v. 8: *"prae consor-*
tibus suis". id est Salomon secus filios Dauid; spiritaliter: Christus secus apostolos.
Likewise on v. 10: *"Adstetit regina". id est filia Faraonis* (cf. 1 Kgs 3:1), *siue regina*
austri quae uenit ... audire sapientiam Salomonis ...; spiritaliter: "Adstetit regina". id
est Christo aeclesia gentium.

The compiler had access to the Epitome of Julian from which he drew a number
of his glosses on this psalm. Likewise, the introduction to the psalm shows the
compiler personally agreed with the messianic interpretation, found in Theodore.
It seems fairly obvious that in the body of the exposition he is transmitting a form
of non-messianic exegesis with which he personally disagrees. This non-messianic interpretation may have originated in the same understanding of the psalm
which we find in Jerome's commentary on Ecclesiastes (Eccl 1:1)[142]. Much more
likely, however, it is but part of a larger pattern of approach to the understanding
of the messianic psalms, specifically those considered as prophecies of Christ by
the tradition inherited ultimately from Antioch and Theodore.

Psalm 109[143]. In view of the New Testament evidence, it is difficult to see how
this psalm could in Christian tradition have received anything but a messianic
interpretation. It is, however, given a non-messianic interpretation in the heading
of the Psalter of Charlemagne and in the catena of Pal. Lat. 68. The heading in the
Palter of Charlemagne reads:

---

141 Cf. Jerome, Commentarioli in Psalmum XLIV, 1, CCSL 72, p. 209.

142 Jerome, In Eccles. I, 1, CCSL 72, p. 250.

143 See D. M. *May*, Glory at the Right Hand: Psalm CX in Early Christianity (Society of
Biblical Literature Monograph Series) 1973. For psalm CIX (CX) in Judaism see P. *Billerbeck*,
Exkursus 18: der 110. Psalm in der Altrabbinischen Literatur, in: Kommentar zum Neuen
Testament aus Talmud und Midrasch, ed. H. *Strack*, P. *Billerbeck*, IV, 1, München 1928,
reprint 1961, p. 452—65.

In finem psalmus ad Dominum. Hic psalmus de Dauid loquitur. De inimicis suis canitur. Vel Dauid loquens ad Samuel. Vel uox Damasci Eleazari serui Abraham. Spiritaliter: Caro Christi de persona Christi. Hic psalmus pharisei profetatum. Vox Ecclesiae de Patre et Filio.

Sections of this heading seem to depend on the Epitome of Julian, e.g. the reference to Abraham's servant, to the Pharisees, *Caro Christi de persona Christi*[144]. The designation of the messianic interpretation as *spiritaliter*, however, indicates that the exposition represented by this heading must have interpreted the psalms "historically": of David, Samuel or Abraham's servant.

The catena of Pal. Lat. 68 has no heading for this psalm. Right throughout the expository glosses, however, the psalm is interpreted "historically": of David, Saul and Samuel. An appropriate heading would be *Dauid loquens ad Samuel* — found in the Psalter of Charlemagne. The person who speaks in v. 1 is Saul; the Lord addressed *(domino meo)* is Samuel. *"Ante luciferum"* is interpreted as *ante Saul*. The text then goes on to say that in the *spiritual sense* the psalm refers to Christ: *Spiritaliter haec Christo conueniunt ut Hirunimus ait ...*, after which a series of Christological interpretations are given. And as if to emphasise the fact that this understanding of the text is allegorical, in the margin it is marked by *M*, i. e. *Moraliter*, which for the greater part in the catena means *allegorice*. Immediately after these allegorical interpretations, the text is again interpreted of Samuel and of the land of Canaan. This exegesis is introduced in the text as *secundum historiam* and in the margin as *hist. Tu es sacerdos in aeternum* is interpreted *aliter* as referring to Christ, after which (at v. 5) the glosses revert to the non-messianic interpretation, designated in the margin as *hist*. And then, at the very end of the exposition, comes a statement similar to that found in the heading of Ps 44: *Totus hic salmus de Christo canitur, licet alii historialem inhertiam* (MS: *in hertiam*) *in eo contexunt, ut ostendimus* — which I render: "although some, as we have shown, give it an inept historical interpretation".

Evidently here once more we are in the presence of a form of exegesis which the compiler (or possibly a later scribe) considered it his duty to transmit but with which he personally disagreed. The origin of this non-messianic interpretation remains to be determined. It may have arisen from a reflection on the remark found in the Epitome of Julian that the person of David is intended in v. 1. It could possibly have also arisen from a tradition influenced by a Jewish interpretation which understood the psalm as God's words to David that he would reign after Saul[145]. But even if these influences were present it seems likely that this non-

---

144 Ed. *de Coninck* and *d'Hont* (as above note 20), p. 351f.

145 This interpretation is also found in Jewish sources, e. g. the Targum (Aramaic translation) of the psalm, which reads: 'The Lord promised (lit., said) in his Word to set me as Lord over all Israel but said to me: "Turn and wait for Saul ... until he dies ...; after this I will set your enemies as your footstool".' In the Midrash on the Psalms (English transl. W. G. *Braude*, New Haven 1959) this interpretation is ascribed to Rabbi Jehuda ben Shallum the Levite (ca. AD 370).

messianic exegesis of Ps 109 is but part of an overall pattern of interpretation of the traditional messianic psalms, an approach which may well have been the work of the Irish schools themselves.

7. Davidic Interpretations and Double Historical Reference in Irish Exegesis
In the Theodorean interpretation which the Irish schools inherited through the Epitome of Julian only 19 psalms were interpreted as referring to David and his times[146]. In contrast to this, a marked feature of the early Irish tradition is the frequency of the Davidic references, especially in the tradition represented in the so-called Psalter of Charlemagne and the catena of Codex Pal. Lat. 68. There is also strong emphasis in the Davidic interpretation on the Psalms in the commentary represented by the glosses of the Montpellier and Vercelli Psalters, edited by Franz Unterkircher[147]. A further feature of both the catena and the headings of the Psalter of Charlemagne is the combination of a reference to both David's times and to later Jewish history[148]. We find this both in the headings and glosses of the catena of Codex Pal. Lat. 68. It is also present in the interlinear glosses of some of the psalms in the first section (Pss 1—16) of the Psalter of Rouen. This Davidic interpretation is so strong in the Psalter of Charlemagne and the catena of Pal. Lat. 68 that it has occasioned the introduction of special headings referring to David, or of special references to David into the biblical Psalm headings themselves.

As examples of readaptation of biblical Psalm headings in favour of a Davidic reference we may instance a few of many: Ps 43 — Biblical heading: *In finem filiis Core ad intellectum;* Pal. Lat. 68 and Psalter of Charlemagne: *In finem salmus Dauid.* Ps 75 — Biblical heading: *In finem in laudibus psalmus Asaph canticum ad Assyrios;* Pal. Lat. 68 and Psalter of Charlemagne: *In finem de laudibus salmus Asaph pro uictoria Dauid et pro uictoria Ezechiae;* Ps 120 — Biblical heading: *Canticum graduum;* Pal. Lat. 68 and Psalter of Charlemagne: *Canticum gradum. Vox Dauid pro erumnis Saul.*

In keeping with this interest in David, very frequently in the headings of the psalms in both works we meet such words and phrases as *Vox Dauid, Vox (Oratio) Dauid pro (de) socis (suis), Vox Dauid in exilio, pro erumnis (a) Saul, de Saul, Querela Dauid pro Saul* etc. In line with this, the bulk of the historical interpretations in the expository glosses of the catena are of David and his contemporaries: Samuel (Pss 40:17; 109:1,3,4; 118:105, 114), Saul (several references), *Saul cum semini suo* (39:15), *Saul et domus (domum) eius* (42:1, 2; 52:6; 58:6), *Saul et Abisolon* (96:10), *Saul cum socis (suis)* (several texts; also in glosses of Psalter of Rouen, Pss 1—16), *montes Giluae* (on death of Saul), 39:15; 53:7; 55:8; 62:10; 63:9, 10), *Dauid cum*

---

146 Thus e.g. *Pirot,* p. 279; *Devreesse,* p. 70 (as above note 116) who lists 16 referring to the life of David (not reckoning psalm 71 as Pirot does), to which he adds 8 of a moral and religious nature.

147 *Unterkircher,* as above note 33.

148 This point is considered in greater detail in the introduction to the forthcoming critical edition of MS Pal. Lat. 68 in Studi e Testi.

sociis suis (several references), Agag (109:1, Achitophel and Abisolon (many references for each), Ioab (59:8, 108:6,8,11), *sacerdotes in Nob* (41:11, 52:5), *Golia* (143:16), *Philistini* (53:5), *Sephei* (53:5).

The conclusion to be drawn from this evidence is that there must have been at least one stream of tradition in the early Irish schools in which strong emphasis was placed on interpreting the Psalms of David and his times. Such an interpretative tradition would have taken the biblical Psalm headings very seriously as guides towards the meaning intended by the sacred writer.

A matter worthy of study in this regard is the possible relation between this Davidic interpretation and interest shown in the biblical Psalm titles in the *Old Irish Treatise on the Psalter,* and in the closely related introduction to the Psalter in "Das Bibelwerk". Equally worthy of study is the interest shown in the number of psalms composed by David or connected with David, Solomon and their contemporaries according to the biblical Psalm titles. The evidence of the Psalm Preface *David filius Jesse* and the Old Irish glosses on it is also relevant here. All this probably reflects exegetical activity of the early Irish schools. The composition of the biblical Psalm headings tended to be attributed to Ezra after the return from Babylon, rather than to David or his contemporaries[149]. The number of Davidic psalms *(psalmi David)* given in the sources varies: 74 according to "Das Bibelwerk"[150], 113 according to the *Old Irish Treatise*[151]. According to the preface *David filius Jesse, VIIII fecit ipse Dauid, XXXII non sunt suprascripta, LXXII in Dauid*[152]. An Old Irish gloss on this last number LXXII says: "i.e. which suit and are ascribed to the person of David[153].

With regard to the importance ascribed to the biblical headings, "Das Bibelwerk", deriving the word *titulus* from a Greek word supposed to mean *incendium* (the *Old Irish Treatise* has *titio,* "a firebrand", and *titan,* "sun"), says it lights up the meaning (of) the psalm that follows on it *(quia incendit intellectum psalmum sequentem)*[154].

A further point to be noted with regard to the number of Davidic psalms is the principle that the psalms without superscription in the Psalter (given as 14 in number in "Das Bibelwerk", 32 in the Preface *David filius Jesse*) are regarded as being governed by the heading of the preceding Psalm. Psalms recognised as

---

149 See the *Old Irish Treatise,* lines 207—217; Ezra gathered the Psalms in one book and 'wrote and arranged its title before every psalm' (ed. K. *Meyer,* p. 28f.); cf. „Das Bibelwerk", ed. M. *Sheehy,* p. 292. The tradition concerning the role of Ezra in establishing the order of the Psalms is found in Origen and in Jewish sources; see *de Lange,* Origen (as above note 2), p. 119.

150 Ed. *Sheehy,* p. 295.

151 Ed. K. *Meyer,* p. 24f.

152 Thes. 1, 8.

153 Ibid.

154 Text of „Das Bibelwerk" in ed. *Sheehy,* p. 295; The Old Irish Treatise, lines 269—71, ed. K. *Meyer,* p. 30f.

having Davidic headings, or anonymous psalms preceded by Davidic psalms, may have been a factor in the early Irish interpretation of psalms as referring to David.

A second feature of early Irish Psalm exegesis is the double historical reference given to a number of psalms. We find this in the Psalm headings of the Psalter of Charlemagne and of the catena on the Psalms in Codex Pal. Lat. 68, and also occasionally in the glosses in the Psalter of Rouen for Ps 1—16. That the double historical reference was taken seriously in the interpretation is clear from the fact that it is found both in the headings and expository glosses of the catena just mentioned. To illustrate by just two of the many examples:

Ps 40 — heading: *"Salmus Dauid". Pro erumnis a Saul. Vox Ezechiae* ... Expository gloss — *"qui intellegit".* (v. 1). *id est Dauid uel Ezechiae* ... *"inimicorum eius"* (v. 3). *id est Saul uel sociorum eius; uel Assiriorum.*

Ps 47 — heading: *Vox Dauid accepto regno. Vox Ezechiae* ... Expository gloss: *"quoniam ecce reges (congregati sunt)"* (v. 5) *id est Assiriorum satrapae; uel reges terrae Israel aduersus Dauid: "conuenerunt in unum"* (v. 5) *id est aduersus Dauid uel Ezechiam.*

The explanation of this phenomenon seems to lie in the desire to bring together two distinct modes of historical exegesis, the one understanding the Psalms as speaking of David and his times, the other looking on them as referring to events of later Jewish history. The latter form of exegesis would be basically that of Theodore.

It was possibly from the convergence of these two traditions that the theoretical presentation of the twofold historical sense of the Psalms (the *first story* and the *second story*), which we find in "Das Bibelwerk" and the *Old Irish Treatise on the Psalter*, emerged[155]. This may have been formed during the course of the eighth century, since the basis for it was already present in the tradition found in the Vatican catena on the Psalms, a work compiled about 700. The theory of the twofold historical sense as put forward in the introduction of *the Old Irish Treatise* proper seems to envisage the subject matter of the second "history" as being later Jewish history (Hezekiah, the people, the Maccabees). Yet the example of the "second story" given both in the *Old Irish Treatise* and in "Das Bibelwerk"[156] is taken from the time of David *(Chusai Archites)*. This may mean no more than that the theory was badly applied with regard to Ps 1.

8. *The* Romani *and Early Irish Psalm Interpretation*

The *Romani* were a well-defined group in seventh-century Ireland especially as proponents of the Roman celebration of Easter during the Paschal controversy from about 630 onwards[157]. They appear to have been a scholarly group, at least in

155 On this see above, p. 364f.
156 Text given above, p. 365.
157 On the *Romani* of the Paschal controversy see L. *Gougaud*, Christianity in Celtic

part. A scholar of the *Romani* is mentioned in connection with computation tables[158]. *Romani* are also mentioned in the Collectio Canonum Hibernensis[159] (made at the beginning of the eighth century) and in the Canons of Adomnán[160].

It is interesting to find *Romani* mentioned with regard to biblical exegesis. Our chief source of evidence for this is the catena of Pal. Lat. 68. The same texts are found in the introductory material in the so-called Psalter of Charlemagne, where, however, it is obvious that the continental scribe was occasionally at a loss to understand the Irish original on which he appears to have depended. The occurrences are as follows:

> (Ps 49). *„Deus deorum Dominus … In finem salmus Dauid." De mirabilibus mundi hic salmus ad Iudeos conponitur qui uirtutem neglegentes solas curarent hostias ligalium iusionum; in priore salmo sermonem ad omnes direxit, in praesenti ad Iudeos tantum. Vox spiritus de aduentu Christi. Hic salmus* secundum Romanos *de iudicio futuro canitur.*

The first part of this heading *De mirabilibus … ad Iudeos tantum* is drawn for the greater part from the Julian Epitome. The mystical heading seems to understand the psalm of the first coming of Christ. The understanding of the *Romani* disagrees with this. Actually, the understanding of the *Romani* has nothing exceptional about it. It is that found in Series I *De aduentu Christi propheta dicit et de iudicio futuro* and is similar to the heading of Series III *Vox apostolica de secundo Christi aduentu*. It is simply impossible, with the little information at our disposal, to determine why the *Romani* understood the psalm in this way. It may have something to do with a theory of interpretation and may be connected with the biblical Psalm heading, which for this psalm in the genuine Gallican and *Romanum* tradition is *Psalmus Asaph,* although Pal. Lat. 68, with other Gallican and *Romanum* texts take it as a Psalm of David — *in finem salmus David*[160a].

> (Ps 52). *„Dixit insipiens … In finem." Salmus David de Saul. Intellegentia Dauid pro Abimelech. id est pro choro. Vox Ezechiae de Rabsace, et de his temporibus quae in illis gesta sunt.* Secundum Romanos *pro insidis Saul et occissione sacerdotum in Nouae (cant)atur. Vox Christi de Iuda traditore.*

Lands, London 1932, p. 185—201; *Kenney,* Sources, p. 216; *Hughes,* CEIS, p. 103—110; *eadem,* Early Christian Ireland, Introduction to the Sources, London 1972, p. 75—80. See also P. Ó *Néill* in the present volume.

158 Thus, for instance, in MS Würzburg M.p.th. f. 61, in an additional folio (fol. 29) added to a Hiberno-Latin biblical commentary; text in Thes. 2, p. 285.

159 Ed. H. *Wasserschleben,* Die irische Kanonensammlung, Leipzig ²1885, p. 62, 159, 163, 183, 211.

160 Cf. L. *Bieler,* ed., The Irish Penitentials, SHL 5, 1963, p. 254.

160a See, e. g., the words of Eucherius, Instructio in Salonium (CSEL 31, 89), cited in the introduction to the Hiberno-Latin work, Eclogae tractatorum in Psalterium (ed. *Sheehy,* as above note 70, p. 286): *Quid sibi uult illud quod frequenter in psalmorum titulis inscribitur: "In finem psalmus Dauid"? Responsio: quod psalmi in finem mundi bonorum repromissionem respiciunt …*

(The Psalter of Charlemagne has: ... *occisione sacerdotum in nouo cantico* — an obvious failure of a continental scribe to make sense out of the Hiberno-Latin spelling in *nouae = in Nobae = in Nobe*, of his original.)

The genuine biblical heading for this psalm in the Gallican and *Romanum* tradition is *In finem pro Melech intellegentiae Dauid*. The tradition represented by Pal. Lat. 68 (and the so-called Psalter of Charlemagne) has read *Salmus Dauid de Saul* into the biblical heading. For *Melech* Pal. Lat. 68 has *Abimelech*, as have many other MSS. We simply cannot say what reading the Psalter of the *Romani* had. Their interpretation, however, does not follow the Theodorean one or the Epitome of Julian which understands the psalm of Hezekiah and the Assyrian general (cf. 2 Kgs 18:17, etc.). They interpret it rather of the slaughter of the priests of Nob (*Nouae*) mentioned in 1 Sam, chapters 21—22. David's visit there and to the priest Achimelech (called Abimelech in Pal. Lat. 68 and other corrupt texts) is the subject of the biblical heading for the preceding psalm (Ps 51). It may well be these two Psalm headings which had the *Romani* opt for the reference to David and his times rather than to later Jewish history. Their interpretation had been read into the very biblical Psalm heading of Ps 52 (*Salmus Dauid de Saul Intellegentia ... pro Abimelech*) and is also found in the explanatory glosses, e.g. vv. 1,3,5,6,7).

> (Ps 54) „*Exaudi Deus orationem ... In finem in carminibus intellectus Dauid."*
> *Vox Honiae sacerdotis expulsi de sacerdotio a regibus Grecorum quod emit*
> *Simon quidam propincius Honiae; inde Honias fugit in Aegiptum et Deum ibi*
> *coluit iuxta mores Hierusolimorum. Hic salmus* secundum Romanos *pro*
> *erumnis Saul cantatur. Vox aeclesiae de Christo.*

In interpreting the psalm as speaking of the persecution of David by Saul, rather than of Onias and Maccabaean times as the Theodorean tradition and the Epitome do, the *Romani* may once again have been guided by the biblical heading of the preceding psalm which connects Ps 53 with the report of the Ziphites to Saul that David was hiding among them. They may even have been influenced by the mention of David in the heading of the present psalm. The glosses, we may note, seek to combine this *Romani* interpretation with the Theodorean one at least as far as v.9. From v. 10 onwards a third form of interpretation enters, understanding the psalm of Ahitophel's counsel and Absalom's revolt — the manner in which the psalm is understood in the glosses of the Montpellier Psalter[161].

It is obvious that the *Romani* referred to in these texts were a clearly identifiable group in the communities in which the catena of Pal. Lat. 68 was compiled, or at least in which the tradition it enshrines was formed, which in the view proposed in the present writer's opinion was in Columban monasteries of either Ireland or Northumbria.

The period of the activity of the *Romani* would be 630 to 670 or so. This would suit admirably other items of evidence concerning the age of the tradition behind

---

161 Ed. *Unterkircher* (as above note 33), p. 226—30.

the catena in Pal. Lat. 68. This, on the evidence of the Old English glosses it contains and of its use of Adomnán's *De locis sanctis,* appears to have been compiled about 700. But even then the non-messianic interpretation of Pss 44 and 109 seems too much for the compiler — an indication that this form of exegesis had come into existence some time previously.

VI. Summary and Conclusions: Psalter Text and Study in Ireland AD 500—800

In conclusion we may bring together considerations arising from the study of the various topics in the course of this essay and examine what light these can shed on the attention paid to the text and interpretation of the Psalter during the early centuries of the Church in Ireland.

1. Psalter Text: Tradition and Creativity AD 500—600

It appears that during the sixth century the *Gallicanum* text of the Psalter was the subject of critical attention in Irish schools. The evidence for this derives from the text of the *Cathach* which was most probably written about AD 630–650. Dom Henri de Sainte-Henri has shown that the critical signs of obelus and asterisk in this Psalter are evidence of a critical collation of the *Gallicanum* text against Jerome's rendering from the Hebrew, and furthermore against the specifically Irish text of the *Hebraicum*. It is hardly presuming too much to maintain that the critical work in question was being carried out during the sixth century. The evidence scarcely permits us to determine how widespread such critical interest in the Psalter text was in Irish schools during the period.

A sixth-century, or early seventh-century revision of the *Gallicanum* text against the Irish family of the *Hebraicum* implies that this latter text must have been brought to Ireland during the sixth century at the latest. We cannot say whether the specifically Irish family of *Hebraicum* texts reached Ireland in the form later transmitted by Irish sources or whether these peculiarites arose in Ireland itself.

2. Irish, *Cathach,* Series of Mystical Psalm Headings: Sixth Century

This series, as we have seen, has roots as far back as the third century. We have no earlier evidence of its existence as a Series, however, before its use in the *Cathach* of St Columba. While we can conclude that it was being used in Ireland in the sixth century at the latest, we cannot as yet say whether it was put together in Ireland or came ready made from outside. Composition in Ireland would imply a rich tradition of Christological Psalm interpretation in the island during the sixth century or earlier.

3. Emphasis on Davidic Interpretation of Psalms — before AD 700

The early Irish schools inherited the Christological interpretation of the Psalms from the generally accepted Christian tradition, and from such commentaries as those of Jerome, Augustine, Hilary and Cassiodorus. This Christian and Christological interpretation has strongly influenced the Columba Series of Psalm headings.

Through the Latin translation of Theodore of Mopsuestia's commentary and the Epitome of this they inherited the historical interpretation of Antioch, in which many of the psalms were interpreted of Jewish history after David's time, especially of the times of Hezekiah, the Babylonian Exile, the restoration and of Maccabean times. However, together with this, and independent of the influence of Theodore or the Epitome, there must have flourished in Ireland a tradition interpreting the Psalms of David and his times. Furthermore, this tradition must have existed well before AD 700 since it is attested to both in the catena on the Psalms of Codex Pal. Lat. 68 and in the headings of the Psalms in the so-called Psalter of Charlemagne, which was written on the Continent about 795—800, but is heavily dependent on tradition that had come from Ireland.

4. Dual Historical Interpretation of the Psalms — before AD 700

Another point that emerges from analysis of the catena on the Psalms in Pal. Lat. 68 and the headings of the Psalter of Charlemagne is that there existed in Irish schools well before 700 a tendency to combine two distinct historical interpretations, and refer them individually either to David's time or to later historical events. It is a dual form of reference as typical of these Irish sources as it appears to have been unknown outside of them.

5. Exegetical Activity of the *Romani*: ca. AD 630—700

The material at our disposal gives little or no information as to places or persons involved in Irish exegetical activity during these early centuries. It is a rare stroke of fortune that we have come across the mention of the exegetical activity of *Romani* and this with regard to the Psalms.

These *Romani* must have been an easily identifiable group in their day, and one may justifiably identify them with the *Romani* of the Paschal controversy, and thus consider the period of their activity as ca. AD 630—700. From the limited evidence provided, their chief interest seems to have been in understanding the Psalms of David and his time. They may have been rather typical of a number of groups in Irish schools at this period. One very interesting aspect of this limited evidence is that it reveals for us a questioning exegetical activity in Irish schools, a preparedness to disagree with accepted positions on the understanding of the Psalms.

6. Literal, 'historical' interpretation of Messianic Psalms before 700

From tradition the early Irish Church would have inherited the Christological interpretation of the entire Psalter. From the Commentary of Theodore and the Epitome of this it would have known of the tradition reducing the number of directly messianic psalms to four. And yet, despite all this we find attested before AD 700 a tradition which interpreted the entire Psalter as non-messianic in the literal, 'historical' sense, that is which refused to admit that any of the Psalms was originally intended as a prophecy of the Messiah in the literal sense. This is an approach to the Psalter of which I know no evidence in Christian tradition outside of Irish sources. The tradition must have been current in the Irish schools in question before AD 700 since in the catena of Codex Pal. Lat. 68 composed about that date, we find the compiler objecting to it. He records this interpretation with regard to psalms 44 and 109 but personally dissociates himself from it and professes his preference for the direct messianic interpretation of these psalms.

7. Origin of Historical interpretation of Psalms found in Irish Sources

All this brings us to the final question: How much of this interpretation of the Psalms not attested in non-Irish sources originated in the Irish schools themselves? In other words: How creative was early Irish Psalm exegesis?

It is, of course, technically possible that the early Irish schools inherited the non-messianic interpretation of the psalms in question and that they also inherited a tradition interpreting the Psalms of David and his times – even the tradition giving a dual historical reference. It seems much more likely, however, that most, if not all, of this exegetical activity originated within the Irish schools themselves during the seventh century, if not earlier. We have seen the positions being adopted by the *Romani* in relation to the meaning of the Psalms. It is legitimate to presume that there was much more of such exegetical activity. Once in possession of two historical interpretative traditions — the Davidic and the Theodorean — it would have been natural to combine them. The interest in interpreting the Psalms of David and his time, which was so obviously a feature of early Irish consideration of the Psalms, could naturally lead to interpretation of even the so-called messianic psalms of David and his time.

This is to suppose that within the early Irish schools there was a self-articulating tradition of Psalm interpretation. The dual historical interpretation, which was a practice during the seventh century, would lead during the eighth to the theoretical presentation of the two-fold historical sense of the Psalms — first story (*cétna stoir*) and second story (*stoir tánaise*), *prima historia, secunda historia* — which we find in the *Old Irish Treatise* and the related „Das Bibelwerk". The theory has not been properly worked through, since its application to Ps 1 is not quite in keeping with the theoretical presentation of it in the introduction.

8. Possible outside influences on Early Irish Psalm Exegesis

Early Irish Psalm exegesis, as other forms of ecclesiastical learning, presumably took place in the monastic schools. In fact, more than any other biblical book the Psalms, by reason of their use in the divine office, were central to the monastic system. It is surprising, then, to see such stress placed on the historical interpretation, attempting to understand the Psalms in a setting of Old Testament history. It was an approach scarcely calculated to aid the use of the Psalms as Christian prayer. One would expect that the early Irish monastic Church inherited rather than created such a system of interpretation. It is one that seems alien to Western monasticism.

We do know a form of monasticism, however, in which precisely this form of approach was at home. It was that lived by Diodorus, Theodore's teacher, in his school at Tarsus — the monastic school or *asketerion*[162]. What little we know of this comes from the Church historians Socrates and Sozomen in the account of the education received by John Chrysostom. Both John and Theodore (to become bishop of Mopsuestia later), ardent aspirants after perfection, entered the *asketerion* under the guidance of Diodorus and Carterius[163]. The former, Socrates continues, wrote many treatises in which he limited his attention to the literal sense of scripture, avoiding all that was mystical[164]. Thus also Sozomen[165]. From the Church historian and theologian Theodoret[166] we learn of Diodorus's special interest in psalmody. He tells us that Diodorus and his companion Flavianus, while not yet priests at Antioch, were the first to divide the choir into two parts and to teach the people to sing the Psalms of David antiphonally; with lovers of the divine word they would spend the night in singing psalms to God.

We can presume that Diodorus would have taken the same love and the same devotional pratice with him to the school or *asketerion*. This *asketerion*, as noted earlier[167], was apparently a religious community directed by Diodorus before he became a bishop in 378. It was probably a monastery in which children and young people were given an intellectual and moral formation before they moved elsewhere, either to enter monasteries of strict observance or become priests devoted to the pastoral ministry.

This information may possibly be supplemented by a passage from the Preface to the Antiochene commentary on the Psalms which its editors believe is from the pen of Diodorus himself. But even if Diodorus is not the author, the text is none the less important as evidence for the use of a commentary like that of Theodore's as an aid to prayer. In the Preface to this Antiochene commentary we read:

> Of this scripture so necessary, I mean the Psalms, I have reckoned it
> fitting to make a succinct exposition, as I myself have received: of the
> arguments proper to each psalm and to give an interpretation that is
> literal. In this manner, the brothers when they chant the Psalms will not
> be dragged away by the words, nor because they do not understand
> them will they occupy their minds with other things. On the contrary,

---

162 See above p. 340.

163 Socrates, Hist. eccl. 6, 3, PG 67, 665B; Sozomen, Hist. eccl. 8, 2, PG 67, 1516A. For John Chrysostom's education in the school of Diodorus see C. *Baur*, transl. Sr M. *Gonzaga*, John Chrysostom and his Time, vol. 1, Antioch, London-Glasgow 1959, p. 89—103.

164 Socrates (as above note 163).

165 Sozomen (as above note 163).

166 Hist. eccl. 2, 19, PG 82, 1060C.

167 Above, p. 340.

because they understand the sequence of what is said they will chant with understanding (cf. Ps 46:8, LXX), as it is written, that is, from the depths of their intelligence and not merely externally — with their lips[168].

These words, introducing a commentary parallel to that of Theodore, tell us that the historical interpretation being presented was intended as an aid to prayer and apparently for monks in choir. This may have been the tradition of the *asketerion* of Diodorus.

The *asketerion* of Diodorus and Antioch in its turn was probably only a reproduction of an institution already in existence in the Syrian Church, notably in that of Edessa, where there existed the strict ascetical life of the anchorites and the freer form of life in the Christian schools of the same kind as in the *asketerion* of Antioch. It may well be that some form of this monasticism also existed in the West and that Irish monastic practice and education was influenced by it.

APPENDIX: Historical Headings of Psalms 1—16 in the Psalter of Rouen, Pseudo-Bede, and the Psalter of Charlemagne.

PSALMUS I

ROUEN PSALTER, Ps 1 (p. 2, top margin, legible only in part)
In .... docet quae merces bona opera et quae ... et de Ioseph posse intelligi qui corpus Domini sepelibit et de his qui ad spectacula ...
PSEUDO-BEDE (PL 93, 483BC)
Omnes generaliter ad studia virtutum incitat, simul adjungens quae merces bona, quae mala gesta sequatur. Tertullianus in libro de Spectaculis asserit hunc psalmum et de Joseph posse intelligi, qui corpus Domini sepelivit, et de his qui ad spectacula gentium non conveniunt.
PSALTER OF CHARLEMAGNE
Illegible for this Psalm.

PSALMUS II

ROUEN PSALTER (p. 1; as heading to the *Gallicanum* text)
Generalem Dauid querimoniam facit in Deum, quod regno suo sibi dato, desuper et gentes et populi Israel inuiderent, commonem ad omnes dirigens coreptionem.

---

168 Ed. *Olivier* (as above note 12), p. 4, 33—42; ed. *Mariès*, Extraits (as above note 11), p. 82—85; English translation by E. *FitzGerald* (as above note 11), p. 77.

PSEUDO-BEDE (PL 93, 489C)

Generalem David querimoniam facit ad Deum, quod regno sibi desuper dato, et gentes et populi Israel inviderint, communem ad omnium correctionem dirigens.

PSALTER OF CHARLEMAGNE

Hic psalmus Dauid. Vox sociorum Dauid iurgentium quod gentes et Absalon persecuti sunt Dauid. Vel uox Ecclesiae (lege: Ezechiae) de Assiris.

PSALMUS III

ROUEN PSALTER (p. 3; on right-hand margin of page with *Gallicanum*)

(Pote)st Ezechiae conuenire qui circumdatus Assir(io) exercitu Dominum inuocau(erit).

PSEUDO-BEDE (PL 93,494C)

Potest Ezechiae conuenire qui circumdatus Assyrio exercitu Dominum invocaverit.

PSALTER OF CHARLEMAGNE

In titulo psalmi istius docetur quae causa Dauid compulserit ita orare quod praedierit Absalon filii sui ... Nec minus temporibus Ezechiae regis conuenit qui circumdatur Aziriorum exercitu Domini.

PSALMUS IV

PSALTER OF ROUEN (p. 5; right-hand margin of page with *Gallicanum*)

Ezechiae .... de auxil(io) .... corrip(iens) ...... (menda)cio confi(dent) .... (only left-hand portion of gloss visible; remainder illegible due to close binding).

PSEUDO-BEDE (PL 93, 501A)

Ezechias contra aemulos suos de auxilio Domini gloriatur, corripiens eosdem, ne in mendacio confidant, sed desinentes a malis cogitationibus, semper Deo serviant.

PSALTER OF CHARLEMAGNE

Psalmus Dauid ex persona Ezechiae contra emulos suos de auxilio Domi gloriantes hoc carmen componitur. Ac deinde hos dicit corripere uidetur ne in mendatio confidunt (2 manu: — ant), sed disinant malis cogitationibus et Domino semper uiuant. Utilariter (interl., 2 manu: Ut Hilarius) dicit: Hic psalmus cantauit Dauid de Abisolon et Acitofel.

PSALMUS V

PSALTER OF ROUEN (p. 5; right-hand margin of page with *Gallicanum*)

Ezechias post (...) tatem gratias a(git ...) et adorat in (templo)

PSEUDO-BEDE (PL 93, 506B)

Ezechias post infirmitatem gratias agit Domino et adorat in templo.

PSALTER OF CHARLEMAGNE

In hoc psalmo ostenditur persona Ezechiae.

PSALMUS VI

PSALTER OF ROUEN (p. 8; left-hand margin)
Ezechias infirmatus inuocat Dominum (....)is fragillitatem naturae humanae.
PSEUDO-BEDE (PL 93, 511B)
Ezechias infirmatus invocat Dominum, causans fragilitatem humanae naturae.
PSALTER OF CHARLEMAGNE
In hoc psalmo formatur oratio Ezechiae in sua infirmitate uocantis Dominum (?) clamantisque infirmitas naturae humanae.

PSALMUS VII

PSALTER OF ROUEN (p. 9; right-hand margin of page with *Gallicanum*)
Ezechi(as) ab hos(tibus) calumniatus (et a suis) proditus Domino su(p)licat inpraecat(us) iudicium eius in eos (qui men)daciter innocen(tiam) accusabant. Vox Dauid uel Christi ...
PSEUDO-BEDE (PL 93, 515B)
Ezechias ab hostibus calumniatus, et a suis proditus, Domini supplicat, imprecatus eius judicium in eos qui mendaciter innocentiam accusabant.
PSALTER OF CHARLEMAGNE
Psalmus istius sensus et titulo praenotatur. Que querellam istam Domino cantauit pro uerbis Chusi filii Iemini quem Ebrei Saulem esse aestimant. Vel in hoc psalmo praedicitur quod Ezechiae hostibus clamantibus et a suis proditus et a nobis rebus defamatus depraecatur Deum loquutus sit de iuditium eos qui mendaciter innocentem accusant.

PSALMUS VIII

PSALTER OF ROUEN (p. 12; left-hand margin, continued interlineary)
Admiratur propheta potentiam Dei per quam gubernat cunctam mundi molem gratiasque agit quod tantus creator hominis memoriam habere dignatus est.
PSEUDO-BEDE (PL 93, 524D)
Admiratur propheta Dei potentiam, per quam gubernat cunctam mundi molem, gratiasque agit quod tantus creator hominis memoriam sit habere dignatus.
PSALTER OF CHARLEMAGNE
Leticia cum inimici conculcamur. Aut Saul in monte Gelboe. In quo admiratus (lege: -atur) profeta Dei potentiam per quam gubernat cunctam mundi molem gratiasque agit qui tantam (corr. in MS from -as) omnis (lege: hominis) memoriam habere (h interl.) dignatus sit.

PSALMUS IX

PSALTER OF ROUEN (p. 15; left-hand margin)
Orat Dauid Dominum pro dolosis cogitationibus filii sui gratias agens quod eas non sequeretur effectus. Vel Ezechias de interritu Assirii exercitus.

PSEUDO-BEDE (PL 93, 529A)

Orat Dominum David pro dolosis cogitationibus filii sui, gratias agens quod eas non sequeretur effectus. Potest et Ezechiae congruere gratias agenti post Assyrii exercitus interitum.

PSALTER OF CHARLEMAGNE

Psalmus istius tituli ita inscribitur: Pro ocultis Abselon. Depraecatus est Deum gratiasque Deo reddidit qui eos affectus potentie Deo proibente non secutus sit. Siue persona Ezechiae ostenditur gratias agentis Deo post excidium Assirii exercitus qui tanta in populum Dei molestus est. Vox Ezechiae dicentis laudes de Christo.

PSALMUS X

PSALTER OF ROUEN (p. 21; left-hand margin)

Conuenit Dauid fugienti Saulem et habitanti in deserto Iudae uel Ezechiae.

PSEUDO-BEDE (PL 93, 544A)

Verba David quando Saulem fugiens in desertis est habitare compulsus.

PSALTER OF CHARLEMAGNE

Hic psalmus sub persona Dauid intellegitur quando fugerit a facie Saulis et in desertis Iudae habitare conpulsus est. Siue et umbra quaedam in tempore Ezechiae deprehenditur quando insistentes (!) Assiriis rogabatur ab amicis suis ut fuga(ret added interl.*) se ipsi liberaretur et populum urbem demitteret. Sic de Ezechia* (corr. from -e) *narrat: Quare inquis me conpellitis ad fugam cum ab eo locum ubi Dominus rogantibus se auxilium adferre solet. Si uero de Dauid intellegatur ipse dicet: Inter me Saul et omnis exercitus eius habitare in patria non sinat. Et (?) errabundus et uagus more auium et bestiarum huc illucque discurrem tunc ab eo praesolem Dominum in quo confidens insidias eorum non timebo.*

PSALMUS XI

PSALTER OF ROUEN (p. 23; left-hand margin above *Salua*)

Ex persona Dauid canitur (interl.) *quod in tempore eius omnis defecerit sanctus, uel querela Ezech(iae) quem quidem principes sui* (continued interl.) *Assiris prodiderunt et consilium cum hostibus habentes (?) sibi dolore loquibantur.*

PSEUDO-BEDE (PL 93, 547A)

Ex persona David canitur quod in tempore eius omnis defecerit sanctus, et diminutae sint veritates a filiis hominum.

PSALTER OF CHARLEMAGNE

In progeniae Dauid. Vel die iudicii. Psalmus Dauid. Iste psalmus ex persona Dauid cantatur qui in templo (lege: *quod in tempore*) *eius omnis defecerit sanctus et deminute ueritatis a filiis hominum. Vel querella Ezechiae quem quidam principes Assirii suo prodiderunt et con(si)lium (??) cum hostibus abentes sibi dolore* (lege: *dolose*) *lo- quebantur.*

PSALMUS XII

PSALTER OF ROUEN (p. 23 *Hebraicum;* left-hand margin above *Usquequo*)
Ezechias depraecatur Dominum ne obliuiscatur illum Dominus.
PSEUDO-BEDE (PL 93, 550C)
Ezechiae preces ab Assyriis obsessi.
PSALTER OF CHARLEMAGNE
Hic psalmus depraecatio Dauid pro erumnis Saul. Inde ait ad Dominum: Usquequo in f(inem). Psalmus Dauid. Ex persona Ezechiae psalmus iste formatur. Quidam depraecatus sit ne diutius obliuiscatur illum Dominus nec permittat manibus inimicorum suorum concludi ne maiorem insultando (— tioni interl. above *— ando) superbis si me agintur* (lege: *agitur).*

PSALMUS XIII

PSALTER OF ROUEN (p. 24; right-hand margin of *Gallicanum* page)
Pro eo quod est insipiens in Ebreo nabal posit(um) est (unde) et Abigal de uiro suo Nabal dixit: Vere secundum nomen suum insipiens est, reliqua.
PSEUDO-BEDE (PL 93, 552BC)
Pro eo quod est insipiens, in Hebraeo Nabal positum est, unde et Abigail de viro suo Nabal dixit: Vere secundum nomen suum insipiens est. Haec Ezechias contra Rapascen loquitur.
PSALTER OF CHARLEMAGNE
Hic psalmus pro erumnis Saul cantauit Dauid. In finem psalmus Dauid. Psalmus iste hoc idem resonat que ueniens Asirius per legatos ad Ezechiam (corr. from *— em) loquutus sit ut non speraret in Dauid (dd;* lege: *Deo) suo uel deos qui dicertarent gentium in nihilum radactos esse commemorat. De Iudeorum et gentium populo quo dicunt de Saluatori nostro non est Deus.*

PSALMUS XIV

PSALTER OF ROUEN (p. 25; right-hand margin of *Hebraicum;* apparently in different hand)
Verba sunt populi in captiuitate Babiloni(ae) optantis reditum ad patriam enumerantisque quibus meritis ad hanc peruenire (.....).
PSEUDO-BEDE (PL 93, 556B)
Verba populi in captivitate Babyloniae optantis reditum ad patriam, enumerantisque quibus meritis ad hanc pervenire queat.
PSALTER OF CHARLEMAGNE
Hic psalmus de portatione arche Domini de Cariatharim et de consumatione tabernaculi Moysi et Aron Dauid cantauit. Vel populi manentes in captiuitate Babilonia obtantisque habitationem reuerti enumeratque quantis bonis quisque merebitur ad ista bona perueniri.

Psalmus XV

PSALTER OF ROUEN (p. 27; left-hand margin and iterlinearly)
Ezechias in egritudine (Domin)um depraecatur et de reparatione uitae gratulatur et quod humanarum rerum non sit egenus exponitur.
PSEUDO-BEDE (PL 93, 557D)
Ezechias in aegritudine Dominum deprecatur, et in vitae suae reparatione gratulatur, et quod humanarum rerum non sit egens, exponitur.
PSALTER OF CHARLEMAGNE
Tituli inscriptio ipsi Dauid. Hoc psalmo de restauratione hereditatis cantauit Dauid. Siue psalmus iste ex persona (-a corr. from -e) Ezechie in egritudine Deum deprecantis canitur.

PSALMUS XVI

PSALTER OF ROUEN (p. 25; left-hand margin)
... deuotum cor hab(entem) (apparently in different hand).
... psalmo Dauid Dominum (de)praecatur et auditu dig(num) faciat quem ini(mici) gratis persecuti sunt.
PSEUDO-BEDE (PL 93, 561D)
Deprecatur Dominum David, ut se devotum cor habentem, auditu dignum faciat, quem inimici gratis impugnabant.
PSALTER OF CHARLEMAGNE
Psalmus Dauid pro erumnis Saul. In hoc psalmo Deum deprecatur ut audire dignetur se faciat quem inimici gratis, non odio, persequentis. Hoc ergo petit ut deuotum cor habentem Dominus adiuuetur.

Irish kings and bishops in the memoria of the German Schottenklöster

By

Dagmar Ó Riain-Raedel

Now preserved in an early seventeenth-century Vatican manuscript (MS Vat.Lat. 10000)[1], the necrology formerly kept at the Irish monastery, or *Schottenkloster*, of St Jakob at Würzburg has already been examined by the Benedictine historian, M. Dilworth, for its late materials of Scottish interest[2]. As P. Breatnach has pointed out, however, the contents of the necrology appear to be of especial interest to Irish medieval studies[3]. Here, therefore, by means of a detailed examination of those entries which concern Irish *episcopi, abbates, reges* and *duces*[4], attention will be drawn to the obviously keen interest evinced by the *Schottenklöster* in Irish affairs, and to the range of contacts which this implies for local and provincial Irish kings and ecclesiastics of the period ca. 1100–1300, many of whom were involved in the movement for reform of the Irish Church.

Quite clearly, the interest of the *Schottenkongregation* at this time focused on Munster. Such literary products of Germano-Irish scriptoria as the *Libellus*[5] and *Visio Tnugdali*[6] already show this. And, as I have argued elsewhere[7], the hagiography cultivated in the *Schottenklöster* of this period reveals a similar bias. It is in the necrology, however, with two hundred or so years covered by its span of liturgical entries, that this concern with Munster is given its most definitive form. Thus, even those few entries which involve natives of other parts of Ireland (5, 10, 14, 28) reveal demonstrable or probable connexions with the southern province. Similarly, the two entries which refer to persons of the period before 1100 concern Brian Bóraimhe (20) and Cormac mac Cuileannáin (26), who were ancestral figures of the Uí Bhriain of Thomond and of the Clann Charthaigh of Desmond respec-

---

1 The MS was copied in 1617 at St Jakob in Würzburg.

2 M. *Dilworth*, Two necrologies of Scottish Benedictine abbeys in Germany, Innes Review 8 (1959), p. 173—203.

3 P. *Breatnach*, Die Regensburger Schottenlegende: Libellus de fundacione ecclesie consecrati Petri, München 1977, p. 61n; *idem*. The origins of the Irish monastic tradition at Ratisbon (Regensburg), Celtica 13 (1980), p. 58—77 (77).

4 I am at present preparing an edition of the complete text of the necrology.

5 See note 3 above.

6 A. *Wagner*, ed., Visio Tnugdali, Erlangen 1882; H. *Spilling*, Die Visio Tnugdali, München 1975.

7 D. *Ó Riain-Raedel*, Aspects of the promotion of Irish Saints' cults in medieval Germany, ZCP 39 (1982), p. 220—34.

tively. These were the Irish families to which the communities of the *Schottenklö-ster* related, and on which, perhaps, they relied for a part of their material support.

The nature of a necrology is such that the privilege of commemoration in it generally had to be bought through some form of endowment[8]. It follows, therefore, that the presence of a Munster king or ecclesiastic in the necrology of a *Schottenkloster* supposes a connexion of this kind. This cannot be substantiated in specific cases, since the records do not survive. On the evidence of such works as the *Vita Mariani* and the *Libellus*, however, it seems certain that Irish support for the upkeep of the *Schottenklöster* was solicited and received[9]. Furthermore, if it can be shown on the evidence of surviving charters that Irishmen distributed largesse to such continental monasteries as Cîteaux (17,18), then it is a fair assumption that the much more closely connected *Schottenklöster* would have benefited in the same way.

Finally, when the evidence of the necrology, which amounts to a register of Irishmen with German connexions, is placed side by side with that of the *vitae* of Flannán and Mochulleus (21), with that of the charter of Holycross (21), or with that of the architecture of Cormac's chapel at Cashel (23), all of which exhibit continental influence, then surely it must be inferred that the dependence of Irish Church practice on German models of this period is far greater than has hitherto been thought.

The text of the necrology is divided into two parts. Of these the first, and very much the shorter, section is limited to monks of Würzburg. The second part is that which concerns us here. Its title, i.e. *Nomina defunctorum monachorum et confratrum ex nostra congregatione Ratisbonensis ex mart[yr]ilogio decerpta*, shows that it was drawn from a source connected with the *Schottenkloster* at Regensburg[10]. It does not confine itself to the Irish community there, however, but, as was to be expected in a text connected with the mother house of these foundations, it takes in representatives of all other *Schottenklöster* as well[11], so that it may be regarded as the official necrology of the *Schottenkongregation*. Furthermore, in addition to a large number of German lay and ecclesiastical benefactors or associates, it includes the Irish patrons and associates of the *Kongregation*, the *episcopi, abbates, reges* and *duces*, who are to be discussed in this paper, and the *monachi, comites* and *nobiles* of whom so many can no longer be identified.

8 K. *Schmid,* J. *Wollasch,* Die Gemeinschaft der Lebenden und Verstorbenen in Zeugnissen des Mittelalters, FMSt. 1 (1967), p. 365—89.

9 P. *Breatnach,* Schottenlegende, p. 58—64;

10 In its preface the necrology claims to cover the period from 1150 to the time of writing.

11 Besides Regensburg and Würzburg there were *Schottenklöster* at Erfurt, Nürnberg, Konstanz, Wien, Eichstätt and Memmingen. See L. *Hammermeyer,* Die irischen Benediktiner Schottenklöster in Deutschland und ihr institutioneller Zusammenschluß vom 12.—16. Jahrhundert, StMGBO 87 (1976), p. 249—338.

The entries taken from the necrology are divided here into two sections, (A) Ecclesiastics and (B) Kings. The order of entry is in each case determined by the calendar day of the obit, which is given in brackets after the text. Identifications are normally given in the Irish form of the name and in Classical Irish spelling. References in the index are to the numbers of the entries, which are consecutive.

A. Ecclesiastics

1. HEULPHUS LUNTICENSIS EPISCOPUS (16.2), i.e. Earolbh, bishop of Limerick († 1151 AFM)? If Earolbh is intended, then the name suggests a Norse background. Three years before his death in 1151, another claimant to the see had taken an oath of profession as suffragan of Canterbury[12].

2. EDANUS EPISCOPUS CATHAGENSIS (8.3), i.e. Aodh Ó Beacháin, bishop of Inis Chathaigh († 1188). While Inis Chathaigh was established at the synod of Kells in 1152 at the expense of Killaloe[13], Aodh's inclusion in the necrology suggests that he may have been an Uí Bhriain appointee[14]. Certainly, by the time of Aodh's death, the alienated diocese was well on its way back to the 'fold' of Killaloe[15].

3. RODERICUS LUENSIS ABBAS (1.4), i.e. Ruaidhrí, abbot of Killaloe (fl. ca. 1175–1200?). Although unrecorded in the annals, Rodericus is no doubt identical with Rudhraighe, comharba Flannáin[16] of the Clann Eochach (i.e. the Uí Maoldúin?), a branch of the Dál Cais[17]. A generation count, using Ruaidhrí's pedigree, points to a floruit in the late twelfth century.

4. NEHEMIAS EPISCOPUS ET MONACHUS HYBERNIAE (7.4), i.e. Giolla na Naomh Ó Muircheartaigh, bishop of Cloyne († 1149)? Nehemias's identity presents some problems. Thus, while we may be sure that he is the same as Nemias episcopus et monachus nostre congregationis who is listed for this day in the so-called Wessobrunn calendar fragments[18], which, as I have shown elsewhere[19],

12 A. Gwynn, M. Hadcock, Medieval religious houses: Ireland, London 1970, p. 90.

13 See D. Gleeson, A history of the diocese of Killaloe, Dublin 1972, p. 15.

14 For a study of the local ecclesiastical policy of the period, see D. Ó Corráin, Dál Cais — church and dynasty, Ériu 24 (1975), p. 52—63.

15 A. O'Sullivan, Limerick, Killaloe and Kells 1194—1250, Éigse 17 (1978—9), p. 451—455.

16 T. Ó Donnchadha, An Leabhar Muimhneach, Dublin 1940, p. 309—10.

17 From the pedigree it appears that Ruaidhrí's grandfather was a contemporary of the battle of Leitreacha which took place in 1117. Again this suggests a floruit in the late twelfth century for Ruaidhrí.

18 A. Dold, Wessobrunner Kalendarblätter irischen Ursprungs, Archivalische

were composed in the *Schottenkloster* at Würzburg, we cannot be as certain as the editor that this is 'Nehemiah O'Moriertach, bishop of Cloyne and Ross [sic.] (1140–1149)'[20], since, for one thing, Cloyne did not officially become a diocese until after the synod of Kells in 1152. Yet, a bishop named Nehemias was very well known in the *Schottenklöster* and elsewhere before 1152. Thus, there is a reference to him in the *vita* of St Malachy (ca. 1140)[21], and in the *Visio Tnugdali* (1148–9)[22] which, significantly, places him in paradise together with Patrick and three contemporary churchmen, Ceallach, Malachy and, his brother, Christian, all well-known reformers, as may have been Nehemias himself. Marcus, the author of the *Visio*, goes on to say that he died in his own see at an advanced age. If he did belong to a *Schottenkloster* (i.e. *nostra congregatio*) then, he did so before becoming bishop.

Bishop Forbes, the presumed author of an anonymous article on the subject[23], surely means this Nehemias when he speaks of *Nehemias Scotus,* a monk of St Jakob's in Würzburg who became bishop of Ross and founded the Benedictine monastery at Rosscarbery, the Irish daughter-house of the *Schottenkloster* at Würzburg. But no sources are cited; so the matter cannot be decided. No such bishop of Ross is recorded, however.

Finally, what do we make of the annal in AFM 1085 which records the death of 'Giolla na Naomh Laighean, noble bishop of Gleann Dá Locha, and afterwards head of the monks of Würzburg ... on the seventh of the Ides of April'? It seems as if the same person is intended, but the *Schottenkloster* at Würzburg was not founded until 1134[24]. There may be confusion with Giolla na Naomh Laighneach, bishop of Glendalough, who attended the synod of Kells in 1152[25].

5. SENIOR ARCHIEPISCOPUS HYBERNIAE (11.4), i.e. Senior mac Maoil Dalua, archbishop of Armagh († 1095). Apparently a non-Munsterman — but note the Dalua (cf. Cill Dalua i.e. Killaloe) of his patronymic — Senior is described as 'primate of Armagh' in the martyrologies for this day. We may ignore Stokes's suggestion that Senach, abbot of Armagh, who died in 611, is intended[26], and safely identify him with 'Senior mac Maoil Molua, chief religious

Zeitschrift 58 (1962), p. 11—33. Cf. R. *Bauerreiss*, Zwei alte Kalendarien aus Wessobrunn, StMGBO 82 (1962), p. 171—192.

19 *Ó Riain-Raedel*, Aspects.

20 Cloyne and Ross were not united until 1429; see F. M. *Powicke*, E. B. *Fryde*, ed., Handbook of British Chronology, London 1961, p. 326.

21 B. *Lawlor*, St Bernard of Clairvaux's Life of St Malachy, London 1920, p. 89.

22 *Wagner*, Visio, p. 53; *Spilling*, Die Visio, p. 14.

23 Edinburgh Review 119 (1864), p. 168—202.

24 For an account of Irish monks at Würzburg before 1134, see A. *Gwynn*, The continuity of the Irish tradition at Würzburg, Herbipolis Jubilans (Würzburger Diözesangeschichtsblätter) 14—15 (1952), p. 37—82.

25 M. *Sheehy*, ed., Pontificia Hibernica I, Dublin 1962, p. 171n.

26 W. *Stokes*, ed., The Martyrology of Gorman, HBS 9, 1895, 394.

counsellor of Ireland', whose death at Dún Dá Leathghlas (Down) is recorded in AU for 1095. This makes him a contemporary of Marianus Scotus († ca. 1085) who founded the first *Schottenkloster* at Regensburg, and who was a native of Ulster[27].

6. MALACHIAS ARCHIEPISCOPUS (11.4), i.e. Maol Íosa Ó hAinmire, bishop of Waterford and archbishop of Cashel († 1135). Molanus's additions to Usuard's martyrology, as quoted by the Bollandists under April 10[28], include a reference to *Malachus, Episcopus Lesmoriensis in Hibernia*. Otherwise known as Malchus, this appears to be Maol Íosa Ó hAinmire. Up to then an Irish Benedictine monk at Winchester, Maol Íosa became the first bishop of the Norse town of Waterford, following a petition addressed by Muircheartach Ó Briain to Anselm, archbishop of Canterbury[29]. Whether he ever relinquished this see is not clear but, at the synod of Ráth Breasail in 1111, he signed himself 'Archbishop of Cashel'[30]. At a later date, however, he was back in Waterford, with his seat at Lismore. Here, he must have exercised considerable influence for Malachy (14) received instruction from him over a period of three years[31]. Also, Cormac Mac Carthaigh, king of Desmond (23), found refuge at Lismore in 1127, and Muircheartach Ó Briain (24) had already assumed the 'pilgrim's staff' there in 1116.

7. ISAAC EPISCOPUS (20.4), i.e. Isaac Ó Cuanáin, bishop of Roscrea († 1161)[32]? Roscrea, like Inis Chathaigh (2), was established as a diocese in 1152, at the expense of Killaloe. Nevertheless, its bishops may always have been Uí Bhriain appointees until it reverted fully to the diocese of Killaloe within fifty years of its institution[33].

Another possibility is that Isaac Ó Cormacáin, bishop of Killaloe from 1253 until his retirement to Holycross in 1267, is intended[34]. His family provided many deans and bishops to Killaloe, and surviving documents show that this Isaac acted as arbitrator of disputes on behalf of the papal see[35].

27 *Breatnach*, Schottenlegende, p. 48.
28 AA SS Aprilis I, p. 857.
29   M. *Rule*, ed., Eadmer, Historia Novorum in Anglia, RS 81, 1884, p. 76.
30 P. S. *Dinneen*, ed., Foras Feasa ar Éirinn le Seathrún Céitinn D. D. 3, ITS 9, 1908, p. 301—07.
31 *Lawlor*, Bernard of Clairvaux's, p. 18—20.
32 In Tig. his *obit* is accompanied by the title *Epscop Ruis* which, in view of the position of the Uí Chuanáin as hereditary coarbs of St Cronán, must refer to Roscrea and not to Ros Ailithir (Rosscarbery), as has been thought.
33 *O'Sullivan*, Limerick, Killaloe and Kells, p. 453.
34 *Gleeson*, History, p. 242; *idem*, The diocese of Killaloe in the thirteenth century, North Munst. Antiq. Journ. 1 (1939), p. 151.
35 *Ó Corráin*, Dál Cais, p. 60.

8. REGINOLDUS EPISCOPUS CORCAIAE (3.5), i.e. Reginald, bishop of Cork (†
ca. 1187–8)[36]. The Normans had been granted the city of Cork in 1176[37]; so we
may assume that Reginald, who succeeded Gregory Ua hAodha ca. 1182, was of
their stock. Like Gregory, Reginald is best known as a witness to a succession of
charters in favour of the canons of St Thomas in Dublin and the monks of St
Nicholas in Exeter[38]. These cover the period 1172–82 which saw him rise from
monk, through archdeacon, to bishop. The annals variously record his death for
1187 or 1188[39].

9. MAURITIUS O BRIEN EPISCOPUS FINNABRENSIS (3.5), i.e. Mauritius Ó
Briain, bishop of Kilfenora. We know for certain of one bishop so called, whose
election to the see in 1303 was contested by a rival — possibly because Mauritius
was an obvious Uí Bhriain choice — but who appears to have occupied it for
sixteen years, if the record of the death of a bishop of Kilfenora in 1319 refers to
him[40].

Another possibility, however, is that *frater Mauritius*, who is named as bishop
in King Henry III's licence to the dean and chapter of Kilfenora, dated March 3,
1265, is intended[41]. Unfortunately, we are not given the (Dominican?) friar's sur-
name, nor is this supplied in the inscription preserved in the Book of the Friars
Preacher of St Saviour in Limerick which reads: *Christian* [1257], *Mauritius, Simon*
[1302] *quoque Fenaborensis*[42].

10. MAURITIUS ARCHIEPISCOPUS UA DUBTAIG (15.5), i.e. Muireadhach Ó
Dubhthaigh, 'archbishop' of Tuam († 16.5.1150). Officially, Tuam became an
archiepiscopal see in 1152, two years after Muireadhach's death; yet, he usually
bears the title. While closely connected through his family with the church of
Cong[43], where he also died, Muireadhach also had an interest in the church of St

36 A second Reginald, bishop of Cork, died on 16.12.1276; see E. *Bolster,* A history of
the diocese of Cork, Shannon 1972, p. 188—9.
37 A. *Gwynn,* The bishops of Cork in the twelfth century 2, IER 74, (1950), p. 104—5.
38 J. *Gilbert,* ed., Register of the Abbey of St Thomas, Dublin RS 94, 1889, p. 209
(CCXLVIII — CCL); E. St J. *Brooks,* Unpublished charters relating to Ireland, 1177—82, from
the archives of the city of Exeter, PRIA 41 C (1936), p. 313—35.
39 *Bolster,* A history, p. 176; M. *Freeman,* ed., The annals in Cotton MS Titus A XXV,
Paris 1929.
40 E.J. *Gwynn,* Fragmentary annals from the West of Ireland, PRIA 37 C (1926), p. 151.
However, in H. *Sweetman,* ed., Calendar of Documents relating to Ireland, London 1877,
17.4.1323 is given as the date of election of the new bishop.
41 *Sweetman,* Calendar, no. 762. He died before 1273, when a new bishop was requested
by the local chapter (ibid., no. 962).
42 M. *Lenihan,* Limerick, its history and antiquities, 1866, repr. Cork 1967, p. 646.
43 M. *Sheehy,* Pontificia Hibernica I, p. 121. The Cross of Cong bears the name of a
member of the Uí Dhubhthaigh, and a later inscription adds: *Or do Muredach U Dubthaig do
senóir Érend* (F. *Henry,* Irish Art in the Romanesque Period 1020—1170 A.D., London 1970,
p. 107).

John, Apostle and Evangelist, at Cork in south Munster whose grant to *Mauritio archiepiscopo et Gregorio [et] successoribus eorum peregrinis de Connacia S. Barri compatriotis*[44] by Cormac Mac Carthaigh (23) is confirmed in a charter drawn up by Diarmuid (27), Cormac's son, in favour of Gill Abbey. The background to this grant is unclear[45] but in 1134 Cormac, who had engaged in a foray into Connacht, is reported to have made peace with Toirdhealbhach Ó Conchobhair 'in honour of the archbishop'[46].

11. KARTHAGUS ABBAS CONSAGENSIS (14[15].6). As far as I know, no Abbot Carthach is on record either for Cork or Cong.

12. GALLUS EPISCOPUS LISINORUM (8.8). No such bishop of Lismore (?) is known to me.

13. BRICCIUS EPISCOPUS ET POSTEA MONACHUS CONFRATER NOSTER (20.8)[47], i.e. Brictius, bishop of Limerick († 1185—7)? If Brictius is intended, then the suggestion that he retired to a *Schottenkloster* may explain why his death is not noticed in the Irish annals. His name is found as a witness to several charters, variously drawn up by Domhnall Mór Ó Briain in favour of Holycross Abbey and St Peter and Paul of Clare (de Forgio)[48], and by Diarmuid Mac Carthaigh in favour of Gill Abbey in Cork[49]. Briccius himself was a beneficiary of the grant made by Domhnall Mór to the cathedral of Limerick[50]. He was also an Irish delegate at the Third Lateran Council in Rome in 1179—80[51].

14. MAELMORHORGIUS EPISCOPUS HIBERNIE (1.11), i.e. Malachy (Maol Maodhóg Ó Morgair), archbishop of Armagh († 2.1.1148). Abbot Congan of the Cistercian monastery of Inislounaght on the river Suir commissioned a Life of St Malachy from St Bernard of Clairvaux, sending him a 'record of deeds' to aid him in its composition[52]. Bernard's aim, however, was to portray an ideal bishop[53], so we cannot be sure that he used all the evidence. Marcus, of the *Schottenkloster* at

44 BL MS Add. 4793, fol. 65.
45 See T.J. *Walsh*, D. *O'Sullivan*, St Malachy, the Gill Abbey of Cork, and the Rule of Arrouaise, JCHAS 54 (1949), p. 41—60 (54). Cf. M. *Blake*, An old rental from Cong Abbey, JRSAI 35 (1905), p. 130—38.
46 S. *Ó hInnse*, ed., Miscellaneous Irish Annals, Dublin 1947, s.a.
47 The MS reads *mon conf nr*.
48 *Gwynn, Hadcock*, p. 162.
49 *Bolster*, A history, p. 95—8.
50 O. *Mac Caffrey*, ed., The Black Book of Limerick, Dublin 1907, p. 34 (XXXII).
51 M.T. *Flanagan*, Hiberno-Papal relations in the late twelfth century, Arch. Hib. 34 (1976—7), p. 55—70.
52 *Lawlor*, Bernard of Clairvaux's, Introduction.
53 B.W. *O'Dwyer*, St Bernard as an historian: the Life of St Malachy of Armagh, Journal of Religious History 10 (1978—9), p. 128—41.

Regensburg and author of *Visio Tnugdali*, visited St Bernard and may also have supplied some of the *uita's* detail[54]. In turn, the *vita* found its way, no doubt through a *Schottenkloster*, into the *Magnum Legendarium Austriacum*[55]. Purely by way of speculation, a fragmentary entry under 2.11 in the Calendar of the *Schottenkloster* at Würzburg, otherwise the Wessobrunn calendar, has been taken to refer to Malachy[56]. Be this as it may, the obviously high regard in which he was held in the *Schottenklöster* shows that the interests of the Irish Cistercians and Benedictines were not irreconcilable.

15. DERMITIUS EPISCOPUS LUENSIS (16.11), i.e. Diarmuid Ó Conaing, bishop of Killaloe († 1195). Diarmuid is included in the seventeenth-century manuscript list of the bishops of Killaloe, with the year 1195 given as his obit[57]. This means that he is the same as Domhnall (sic) Ó Conaing whose death is recorded for this year in AFM[58]. Diarmuid died and was buried at Cork where he had sought refuge following his expulsion from Killaloe by the papal legate, Matha Ua hÉanna, one of whose relatives then succeeded to the see[59].

B. Kings

16. PIE MEMORIAE DONATUS WAGARRIJ ET DONALDUS GLAS WAGARRJ DUCES QUI FUERUNT EX HIBERNIA SCOTORUM ARMATA MANU ET MEDIA AQUILA IN INSIGNIIS GERENTES. (10.2), i.e. Donnchadh and Domhnall Glas Mac Carthaigh. If, as I suspect, *Wagarr(i)j* is a corruption of Mac Carthaigh, then the reference is to two members of the family of Mac Carthaigh, later Mac Carthaigh Riabhach, lords of Carbery in Co.Cork. In that case, Domhnall Glas may refer either to the son of Domhnall Cam[60], who was lord of Carbery between 1320—66 and who rebuilt Timoleague Abbey for the Franciscans[61], or to the son of Domhnall Riabhach, who is attested for 1398[62]. Both of these had a brother named Donnchadh whence, possibly, Donatus of the entry. Furthermore, within Carbery, at Ross, lay the only certain German Benedictine foundation in Ireland, a daugh-

---

54 St John *Seymour*, Studies in the Vision of Tundal, PRIA 37 C (1926), p. 90—1.

55 *Ó Riain-Raedel*, Aspects, p. 232.

56 J. *Hennig* in Dold, Wessobrunner, p. 28.

57 *Gleeson*, A history, p. 156, 160.

58 The confusion probably resulted from the fact that a prior bishop of Killaloe was named Domhnall Ó Conaing († 1131).

59 AI 1195; *Ó Corráin*, Dál Cais, 60; *Gleeson*, A history, p. 170.

60 *Ó Donnchadha*, ed., Leabhar Muimhneach, p. 153.

61 See D. *Mac Carthy* (Glas), A historical pedigree of the Sliochd Feidhlimidh. The Mac Carthys of Gleannacroim, Exeter n. d., p. 49.

62 *Ó Donnchadha*, Leabhar Muimhneach, p. 211. Cf. *Ó hInnse*, Miscellaneous Irish Annals, s. a. 1398. He may have died in 1442, the date wrongly given to the other Domhnall Glas in *Ó Donnchadha*, Leabhar Muimhneach, p. 153n.

ter-house of the *Schottenkloster* at Würzburg, as documents dating from the late fourteenth century show. It is hardly a coincidence, therefore, that the coat of arms of the *Schottenkloster* at Regensburg, a mailed hand and half-eagle[63], should be mentioned in connexion with members of a family which must have had a very special relationship with the *Schottenkongregation*.

17. PIAE MEMORIAE DONATUS KANBRAH REX RAUMINENSIS (7.3), i.e.

Donnchadh Cairbreach Ó Briain († 1242). *Rauminensis* appears to be a corruption of *Mumenensis*, i.e. 'of Munster'. The not always reliable but roughly contemporary Ó Briain text, *Caithréim Toirdhealbhaigh*, agrees with the annals in crediting Donnchadh with the 'erection of many churches and monasteries, as well as with plentiful other benefactions'[64]. Indeed, some extant grants as, for instance, that in favour of the archiepiscopal see of Cashel, are made out in his name. Other monasteries thought to have been founded by him, i.e. Holycross, Co. Tipperary and Kilshane, Co. Limerick, pre-date his period, however[65].

Members of his family figure prominently among the Irish witnesses to charters in favour of the Cistercian monastery at Cîteaux, with dates between 1222—27[66]. Similarly, other entries in the necrology of the *Schottenkongregation* may refer either to members of his family or to close relatives. Thus, *Sabba comitissa soror nostra* (6.4) may represent his wife, Sadhbh. Her family were the Uí Chinnéidigh to whom also belonged *Duncanus Kennedie nobilis Scotus* (6.5) of the necrology, who is no doubt identical with Duncan O Kennedig, a benefactor, together with his wife, Gormlaith, of Cîteaux. Likewise, Donnchadh's son, Conchobhar (19), and father, Domhnall Mór (21), find a place in the necrology.

Donnchadh was buried in the Dominican friary of St Saviour at Limerick which he had founded; the house necrology records his death for May 8, 1241[67].

18. MURCHARTACH REX HIBERNIAE (13.3), i.e. Muircheartach Mór Ó Briain († 13.3.1119).

The outstanding personality of his period, Muircheartach contributed more than any other lay person to the movement for reform of the Irish Church. Not only did he petition Anselm to appoint Maol Íosa Ó hAinmire (6) as the first bishop of Waterford[68], he also presided over two synods, that of Cashel in 1101, which was the first of the reforming synods and which was marked by his spectacular, if not altogether unselfish, donation of the site of Cashel to the religious of

---

63 J. *Hemmerle*, Die Benediktinerklöster in Bayern (= Germania Benedictina 2, 1970), p. 254.

64 S.H. *O'Grady*, ed., Caithréim Thoirdhealbhaigh 2, ITS 26, 1929, p. 1—2.

65 *Gwynn, Hadcock*, p. 134, 138.

66 *D'Arbois de Jubainville*, ed., Chartes données en Irlande en faveur de l'ordre de Cîteaux, RC 7 (1882), p. 81—6.

67 *Lenihan*, Limerick, p. 646.

68 Eadmer (as above note 29), p. 76.

Ireland, and that of Ráth Breasail, ten years later, which implemented the major reform of the Irish diocesan organization. With the assistance of Gilbert, bishop of Limerick and papal legate, Muircheartach pioneered the introduction of continental standards into the practices of the Irish Church[69], thus laying the foundation for many reforms which were later implemented by such continental orders as the Cistercians. The 'common cultural world', with its roots in such centres of imperial Germany as Bamberg, Regensburg and Würzburg, to which Irish and English monks of the pre-Conquest period belonged, according to the late D. Bethell[70], was a realm in which Muircheartach clearly also felt himself at home.

19. CONCHOBUR REX MUMNENSIUM FRATER NOSTER (20.3)[71], i.e. Conchobhar Ó Briain († 1142). Unlike his uncle Muircheartach (18), whose career was of great interest to the native annalists, Conchobhar is well known only through the *literati* of the *Schottenkongregation*, who obviously regarded him as a most deserving benefactor. Thus, in the *Visio Tnugdali*[72] he is numbered among those admitted to the *campus letitie* while in the *Libellus*[73] he is styled *fundator noster* which may be compared with the *frater noster* (written *Fr. nr.*) of the necrology. Likewise in the *Libellus*, he is depicted as the first king to have received the monks of Regensburg on their fund-raising mission to Ireland.

Conchobhar's relations with the Clann Charthaigh appear to have been very good. Thus, he helped to persuade Cormac Mac Carthaigh (23) to return from his place of retirement, and also accompanied him to a meeting at Abhall Cheithearnaigh in Connacht, which Muireadhach Ó Dubhthaigh (10) also attended.

20. BRIAN REX HIBERNIAE MURCHARDUS FILIUS EIUSDEM (23.4), i.e. Brian Bóraimhe and his son, Murchadh († 23.4.1014). Brian's inclusion in the necrology obviously cannot have been merited through contributions to the *Schottenklöster* which did not exist when he together with his son, Murchadh, was slain at the battle of Clontarf. Nor can his contribution to the movement towards reform, which has been somewhat overrated[74], have been the reason. No doubt, he earned a place through his importance in the genealogical scheme of the Uí Bhriain, one of the two Munster families to which the *Schottenkongregation* felt itself most

---

69 J. *Ryan*, The O'Briens in Munster after Clontarf, North Munster Antiquaries Journal 3 (1942), p. 15—16.

70 D. *Bethell*, English monks and Irish reform in the eleventh and twelfth centuries, Historical Studies 8, Dublin 1971, p. 111—35.

71 The MS reads *Conchobur Rex Mumnensium Fr. nr.* P. Breatnach, Schottenlegende, p. 61 wrongly expands as ... *Mummensis fundator noster* and, again wrongly, quotes the necrology under 13.2. as his source.

72 *Wagner*, Visio, p. 72; *Spilling*, Die Visio, p. 125.

73 *Breatnach*, Schottenlegende, p. 58—62.

74 D. *Ó Corráin*, Ireland before the Normans, Dublin 1972, p. 128.

indebted[75]. The ancestral pride of the other family, the Clann Charthaigh, is catered for in the person of Cormac mac Cuileannáin (26).

21. DONALLUS REX HYBERNIAE (3.5), i.e. Domhnall Mór Ó Briain († 1194). The necrology of the *Schottenkongregation* is one of two such continental documents to commemorate Domhnall; the other is the necrology of the monastery of Admont in Austria[76]. This bespeaks a reputation in ecclesiastical circles which, to judge by the sixteen foundations of abbeys accredited to him, was well deserved[77]. All these abbeys were in Munster, and they included several Cistercian houses, i.e. Holycross, Kilcooly, Fermoy, Inishlounaght and Corcomroe, which, as M.T. Flanagan has pointed out, lay outside the limits of the Uí Bhriain diocese of Killaloe[78]. The charter of one of these houses, Holycross, is of particular interest since, while its implications for the actual date of the foundation are a source of controversy[79], it appears to have been written 'by a continental monk or one who had a continental training'[80].

Domhnall Mór built three cathedrals, one at Cashel[81], another at Limerick[82] which had become his place of residence, and a third at Killaloe[83] in whose interest he also succeeded in reversing the alienation of the dioceses of Inis Chathaigh (2) and Roscrea (7)[84]. Interest in the patron of Killaloe, Flannán, also increased around this time as D. Ó Corráin's dating of the *vita* to 1163—8 shows[85]. Significantly, this text and the related *vita* of Mochulleus point to an author who had travelled on the Continent and was well informed about events concerning the imperial court in Germany. Also, the transmission of these *vitae*, which appear to have formed part of a *Schottenkloster* collection before finding their way into the *Magnum Legendarium Austriacum*, implies the existence of contacts between Kil-

---

75 This explanation provides a more specific reason for the inclusion of Brian and his son than that put forward by P. *Breatnach*, The origins (as above note 3, p. 77) who suggests that they 'were remembered by monks aware of their country's history'.

76 MGH Necr. 2, p. 296. This apparently unique mention of an Irish king in a purely German necrology may have come about through the influence of a *Schottenkloster*, Ó Riain-Raedel, Aspects, p. 234.

77 *Gleeson*, History, p. 168.

78 M.T. *Flanagan*, Irish monastic charters 1142—1230, M.A.thesis, UCD Dublin 1973, p. 166.

79 *Henry*, Irish Art, p. 114; *Gwynn, Hadcock*, p. 136—7.

80 *Flanagan*, Irish monastic charters, p. 168.

81 *Henry*, Irish Art, p. 173n.

82 Ibid., p. 29. Domhnall also granted lands to the cathedral at Limerick (*Mac Caffrey*, The Black Book, Nr. XXII p. [IX]).

83 Ibid., p. 166—7.

84 *O'Sullivan*, Limerick, p. 453.

85 D. *Ó Corráin*, Foreign connections and domestic politics: Killaloe and the Uí Briain in twelfth-century hagiography, in: D. *Dumville*, R. *McKitterick*, D. *Whitelock*, ed., Ireland in Early Mediaeval Europe, Cambridge 1982, p. 213—231.

laloe and Germany around the time of their composition[86]. It is unlikely that contacts such as these would have existed without the knowledge and, indeed, the encouragement of Domhnall Mór.

22. CORNELIUS OBRIN REX HIBERNIAE (22.5), i.e. Conchobhar (na Siudáine) Ó Briain († 22. 5. 1268). The only other evidence of Conchobhar's generosity towards the Church, which this entry implies, is provided by a charter in favour of Cîteaux, which pledges him to deliver the funds his father, Donnchadh (17), had already promised[87].

23. CORMACUS REX HIBERNIAE (5.7, 23.8), i.e. Cormac Mac Carthaigh († 1138). One of the two dates in the necrology certainly applies to Cormac Mac Carthaigh, king of Desmond or South Munster, who, up to the time of his murder at the hands of Toirdhealbhach Ó Briain in 1138, was a leading figure in the political and ecclesiastical spheres. His best-known legacy is no doubt Cormac's Chapel on the Rock of Cashel which was built in 1134 and which reputedly exhibits architectural affinities to the church of the *Schottenkloster* in Regensburg. However, the suggestion that German 'carpenters' were actually involved in the building of the chapel is not upheld by the available evidence[88].

Cormac also had an important connexion with Lismore, to which he retired on his temporary removal from the kingship in 1127. Here, the monks made propaganda for his cause in the vernacular[89]. Here also, he met Maol Íosa Ó hAinmire (6) and St Malachy (14), the two men 'on whom he wholly depended' according to St Bernard[90]. It is only fitting, therefore, that he should also have both of these and Conchobhar Ó Briain (19), who came to Lismore to persuade Cormac to return to the kingship, as his companions in the necrology of the *Schottenkongregation*. Similarly sharing a place with him in the necrology is Muireadhach Ó Dubhthaigh (10), whose historic meeting with Cormac at Abhall Cheithearnaigh in Connacht no doubt set those events in motion which culminated in the arrival of a colony of monks from Cong in Connacht at Cork in South Munster. This had the incidental effect of providing the local saint, Fionnbharr, with a Connacht genealogy and with a *vita* which appears to have been composed around this time, partly in order to legitimize the arrival in Cork of the group of Connacht monks[91].

---

86 Ó Riain-Raedel, Aspects, 227.
87 D'Arbois de Jubainville (as above note 66), p. 84.
88 A. Gwynn in Gwynn, Hadcock, p. 104—5. For the views of an art historian and an archaeologist, see F. Henry, Irish Art, p. 170, and L. de Paor, Cormac's Chapel: The beginnings of Irish Romanesque, North Munster Studies, Limerick 1967, p. 133—145.
89 P. Ó Riain, Cath Almaine, Dublin, 1978. For evidence of Cormac's awareness of the value of such propaganda, see D. Ó Corráin, Caithréim Chellacháin Chaisil: history or propaganda? Ériu 25 (1974), p. 1—69 (57).
90 Lawlor, Bernard of Clairvaux's, p. 21—23.
91 P. Ó Riain, St Finnbarr: a study in a cult, JCHAS 82 (1977), p. 63—82.

Cormac's fame in the *Schottenklöster* is also evidenced by his portrayal on the biblical model of King Solomon in *Visio Tnugdali*, whose hero claims to have belonged to the Munster king's household[92].

The second of the two dates refers to a Cormac whom I cannot identify. Thus, while various members of the Clann Charthaigh, i.e. Cormac Liathánach (†1176)[93], his son of the same name († 1244) and Cormac Fionn († 1247) theoretically qualify for consideration, none stood out sufficiently to earn the title *rex Hiberniae*.

24. MUERICHERTACKIUS REX FILIUS CONCHUBER (24.8), i.e. Muircheartach Ó Briain († 1151). Muircheartach, who died at Móin Mór in 1151, was a relatively minor figure, 'lord of Thomond and royal heir of Thomond', as the annalist styles him. However, the place given to his father, Conchobhar *alias* 'Slapar Salach', in the *Libellus* shows that he, at least, was well known in the *Schottenklöster*[94].

25. DONCANUS REX HIBERNENSIUM (2.9). If *Doncanus* represents the Irish Donnchuan[95], then the reference may be to Brian Bóraimhe's brother († 948), who was also an important ancestral figure, his descendants being the Uí Chein-néidigh, Uí Chonaing, Uí Riagáin, and Uí Chéileachair among other families of the Dál Cais. Representatives of the first two families named are listed in the necrology (15, 17).

If *Doncanus* is used of Donnchadh, however, then either of two identifications would be possible. Brian Bóraimhe's son, Donnchadh (*al.* Donatus) († 1064), who figures in the *Libellus*, if P. Breatnach's identification is correct[96], had been entrusted with the churches of Munster, according to the Ó Briain text, *Cogadh Gaedhel re Gallaibh*[97]. If so, this would be a sufficient ground for his commemoration here.

The most likely candidate for identification, however, is Donnchadh Mac Carth-aigh († 1142—3), the brother of Cormac Mac Carthaigh (23) and a man well known to the *Schottenkongregation* in his own right. Thus, he seems to be identical with the king, Donatus, who received the delegation from Regensburg headed by his kinsman, Christianus Mac Carthaigh[98]. Furthermore, as I suggest elsewhere[99], his generosity on this occasion may have prompted the Regensburg author of *Visio*

92 *Wagner*, Visio, p. 42; *Spilling*, Die Visio, p. 7.

93 He is mentioned in a charter as a benefactor of the monastery of Cork (*Bolster*, A history, p. 95).

94 *Breatnach*, Schottenlegende, p. 238, 244.

95 *Gleeson*, History, p. 193 states that Donnchadh Cairbreach (16) was known as 'Duncan'.

96 *Breatnach*, Schottenlegende p. 35—6; *idem*, Medieval traditions from West Munster, Stud. Hib. 17/18 (1977—8), p. 58—70 (67—8).

97 Cited ibid., p. 36.

98 Ibid., p. 62—3, 256.

99 *Ó Riain-Raedel*, Aspects, p. 226.

Tnugdali to justify Donnchadh's place in the *campus letitie* by reference to his treatment of the *pauperes*, i.e. the monks of the *Schottenkloster*, to whom, we are told, 'he had given all'.

26. CORMACUS REX MUMINENSIS (14.9), i.e. Cormac mac Cuileannáin († 14.9.908). Like Brian (20), Cormac, whose day is verified by the martyrologies, may have earned his place in the necrology through his importance as an ancestral figure of the Eoghanachta, from whom the Clann Charthaigh descended.

27. DORMITIUS REX HIBERNIAE (6.11), i.e. Diarmuid Mór Mac Carthaigh († 1185)? Theoretically, the reference could be to Diarmuid Ó Briain († 1118), brother of Muircheartach (18) and father of the notorious Conchobhar 'Slapar Salach'. The likelihood is, however, that Diarmuid Mór, son of Cormac Mac Carthaigh (23) is intended since his record has an otherwise verifiable continental dimension. Thus, in the annals of the Austrian monasteries of Klosterneuburg and Heiligen-kreuz, which appear to have drawn on materials from the *Schottenkloster* at Vienna, his death is noticed under the year 1185 with the words: *Diarmicius rex ab Anglicis dolo occiditur, cui Domnoaldus filius eius succedens*[100]. Also, his generosity towards the Church is confirmed by his endorsement of the grant made by his father, Cormac, to the monks of Gill Abbey in Cork, and by his addition of other lands to the original endowment[101].

28. RODERICUS OLUNKUR REX HIBERNIE (29.11), i.e. Ruaidhrí Ó Conchobhair († 29.11.1198). Like Muireadhach Ó Dubhthaigh (10), Ruaidhrí's connexions were with Connacht, of which he was king, and with Cong, at which he spent the last thirteen years of his life in retirement, possibly in a monastery rebuilt by himself.[102] It seems possible, therefore, that Ruaidhrí's inclusion in the necrology stems from the association between the monasteries of Cong and Cork (23).

---

100 MGH SS 9, 604—46. Cf. D. Ó *Riain-Raedel*, Twelfth- and thirteenth-century Irish Annals in Vienna, Peritia 2 (1983), p. 127—136.
101 *Bolster*, History, p. 95.
102 *Gwynn, Hadcock*, p. 166.

Brian Bóraimhe, king of Ireland, 20.
Brictius (Briccius), bishop of Limerick, 13.
Carthach, abbot of Cork (Cong)?, 11.
Cormac mac Cuileannáin, king of Munster, 26.
Donnchadh mac Briain Bhóraimhe?, king of Ireland, 25.
Donnchuan, brother of Brian Bóraimhe?, 25.
Earolbh, bishop of Limerick, 1.
Gallus, bishop of Lismore (?), 12.
Mac Carthaigh, Cormac, king of South Munster, 23.
        Cormac Fionn?, king of South Munster, 23.
        Cormac Liathánach?, king of South Munster, 23.
        Diarmuid Mór?, king of South Munster, 27.
Mac Carthaigh, Domhnall Glas, lord of Carbery, 16.
        Donnchadh m. Muireadhaigh, 25.
Malachias *see* Ó hAinmire Maol Íosa.
Murchadh mac Briain Bhóraimhe, 20.
Nehemias *see* Ó Muircheartaigh, Giolla na Naomh.
Ó hAinmire, Maol Íosa (Malachias), archbishop of Cashel, 6.
Ó Beacháin, Aodh, bishop of Inis Chathaigh, 2.
Ó Briain, Conchobhar m. Diarmada, king of Thomond, 19.
     Conchobhar na Siudáine, king of Thomond, 22.
     Diarmuid?, king of Thomond, 27.
     Domhnall Mór, king of Thomond, 21.
     Donnchadh Cairbreach, king of Thomond, 17.
     Mauritius, bishop of Kilfenora, 9.
     Muircheartach mac Conchobhair, king of Thomond, 24.
     Muircheartach Mór m. Toirdhealbhaigh, king of Thomond, 18.
Ó Conaing, Diarmuid, bishop of Killaloe, 15.
Ó Conchobhair, Ruaidhrí, king of Ireland, 28.
Ó Cormacáin, Isaac?, bishop of Killaloe, 7.
Ó Cuanáin, Isaac?, bishop of Roscrea, 7.
Ó Dubhthaigh, Muireadhach, archbishop of Tuam, 10.
Ó Maoldúin?, Ruaidhrí, abbot of Killaloe, 3.
Ó Morgair, Maol Maodhóg (Malachy), archbishop of Armagh, 14.
Ó Muircheartaigh, Giolla na Naomh (Nehemias), bishop of Cloyne, 4.
Reginald, bishop of Cork, 8.
Ruaidhrí, abbot of Killaloe, *see* Ó Maoldúin?, Ruaidhrí.
Senior mac Maoil Dalua, archbishop of Armagh, 5.

VI

Zusammenfassung
Results

Irland und Europa: die Kirche im Frühmittelalter

von

Michael Richter

Das erste internationale Kolloquium über „Die Iren und Europa im früheren Mittelalter" (Tübingen 1979) befaßte sich vorrangig mit der Ausstrahlung des irischen Christentums auf Europa. Die kritische Bestandsaufnahme räumte mit einigen lange gehegten Vorstellungen auf; dennoch ist das Gesamtbild der Wirkung irischer Persönlichkeiten auf dem Kontinent eindrucksvoll.

Die Frage, wie es zu der außerordentlich starken Ausstrahlung dieses kleinen Volkes am westlichen Rand Europas in den ersten mittelalterlichen Jahrhunderten kam, in einer Zeit, als auf dem Kontinent große politische Umwälzungen stattfanden, die kulturelle Entwicklungen hemmten, stellt sich nach der Lektüre der Ergebnisse des Tübinger Kolloquiums von 1979 um so dringlicher*. Beiträge zu einer Antwort lieferte das zweite internationale Kolloquium über „Irland und Europa im früheren Mittelalter", das 1981 in Dublin abgehalten wurde. Es war der Ausgestaltung der irischen Kirche gewidmet, denn der große Beitrag Irlands zur Entwicklung der frühmittelalterlichen Kultur Europas manifestierte sich weitgehend im Rahmen der organisierten Christenheit.

Wie gestaltete sich das Christentum in Irland in den ersten fünf Jahrhunderten seines Bestehens? Es ist davon auszugehen, daß zwei wesentliche Kräfte dazu beitrugen, einmal das Christentum, wie es sich im Laufe von drei Jahrhunderten ausgebildet hatte, das Material somit, das nach Irland kam, zum anderen die irische Gesellschaft, die das Christentum rezipierte und im eigenen Land formte. Es ist dabei in Rechnung zu stellen, daß diese beiden wesentlichen Kräfte keine Konstanten waren, sondern sich im Frühmittelalter selbstständig entwickelten. Dadurch wird die Erfassung des irischen Christentums in seiner Eigenheit wesentlich kompliziert. Den Veranstaltern des Kolloquiums in Dublin war von Anfang an bewußt, daß derartig große Themen im Rahmen einer Tagung nicht umfassend behandelt werden können; dazu ist die Forschung in vielen Teilbereichen noch nicht weit genug fortgeschritten. Es ging ihnen vielmehr darum, anhand einiger Probleme die Wechselwirkung von Christentum und irischer Gesellschaft überhaupt klarer herauszuarbeiten, da in diesem Bereich Erkenntnisse für die Eigenart des irischen Christentums und seiner Dynamik deutlich gemacht werden können. Gleichzeitig muß betont werden, daß die Entfaltung der irischen Kirche nur in einem größeren Bezugsfeld richtig eingeschätzt werden kann. Damit ist mehr gemeint als der regionale Vergleich, der indes nicht unter-

---

* Heinz *Löwe*, Hg., Die Iren und Europa im früheren Mittelalter, Stuttgart 1982 (= Veröffentlichungen des Europa Zentrums Tübingen).

schätzt werden soll. Es ist zu zeigen, wie das Christentum in Irland zu allen Zeiten seines Bestehens in engem Kontakt mit dem Christentum in den benachbarten Ländern und in entfernteren Regionen stand. Auch in diesem Bereich gab es laufend gegenseitige Beeinflussung. Deutlicher als bisher wurde zum Beispiel auf diesem Kolloquium die Bedeutung der Bretagne für das Verständnis der frühen irischen Kirche erkennbar. Was an Handschriften irischer Provenienz in der Bretagne oder durch die Bretagne erhalten wurde, wie bestimmte Heiligenkulte in der Bretagne und in Irland Berührungspunkte aufweisen, das sind einige noch erkennbare Überreste und Spuren von Kontakten zwischen beiden Regionen, deren Ausgestaltung im einzelnen kaum mehr faßbar ist. Ähnliches gilt in mancher Weise für andere Gebiete Europas.

Mit der Durchsetzung des Christentums beginnt die Geschichte Irlands, ähnlich wie in den meisten anderen europäischen Ländern, denn durch das Christentum kam es erstmals zur Einführung der Schriftkultur. Die schriftlichen Quellen, die aus dem frühmittelalterlichen Irland erhalten sind, sind in ihrer Fülle und Vielfalt noch keineswegs befriedigend aufgearbeitet worden. Im Unterschied zu den meisten anderen europäischen Ländern außerhalb der Grenzen des ehemaligen römischen Westreiches wurde in Irland schon früh und umfassend die Volkssprache in schriftlichen Aufzeichnungen verwendet. Ein erheblicher Teil der schriftlichen Quellen aus dem irischen Frühmittelalter ist weltlichen Inhaltes. Dennoch kann man in diesen keine bruchlose Fortsetzung der hoch entwickelten frühen oralen Kultur Irlands erkennen. Schriftkultur und orale Kultur waren weitgehend eigenständig. Die orale Kultur, deren Bedeutung in der irischen Gesellschaft zweifellos sehr groß war, läßt sich kaum noch erfassen. Sie bediente sich weitgehend der Versform, während weltliche Texte aus Irland in irischer Sprache überwiegend in Prosa überliefert vorliegen. Darin zeigt sich bereits der Einfluß der christlichen Schriftkultur, die, soweit erkennbar, bis in das 12. Jahrhundert fast ausschließlich von Geistlichen gepflegt wurde.

Wenn man versucht, die weltliche Gesellschaft Irlands aus diesen Quellen zu erfassen, ist diese Tatsache in Rechnung zu stellen. Es gab keine strenge Scheidung in weltliche Literatur in der Volkssprache und geistliche Literatur in lateinischer Sprache; statt dessen gab es fließende Übergänge. Der Ire, der Geistlicher war, entsagte damit nicht selbstverständlich den weltlichen Traditionen seines Volkes. Andererseits darf nicht angenommen werden, daß sich ein Schreiber eines Textes vorbehaltlos mit dem Inhalt identifizierte[1]. Sicher gab es Spannungen zwischen Christentum und irischer weltlicher Gesellschaft, aber es gab auch

---

1 Vgl. Táin Bó Cúalnge from the Book of Leinster, hg. Cecile O'Rahilly, Dublin 1970, S. 136: *Sed ego qui scripsi hanc historiam aut verius fabulam quibusdam fidem in hac historia aut fabula non accomodo. Quaedam enim ibi sunt praestigia demonum, quaedam autem figmenta poetica, quaedam similia vero, quaedam non, quaedam ad delectationem stultorum.* Für ähnliche aufschlußreiche Randglossen aus irischen Handschriften siehe C. Plummer, On the Colophons and Marginalia of Irish Scribes, PBA 12 (1926), S. 11—44.

Harmonie und gegenseitige Beeinflussung. Diese komplizierenden Faktoren sind aufzuzeigen und zu berücksichtigen. In sich über mehrere Jahrhunderte erstreckenden Prozessen entwickelte sich in Irland das Christentum, das die bestehende Gesellschaft recht nachhaltig beeinflußte, aber zugleich von ihr geprägt wurde. Diese Wechselwirkung drängt sich dem Betrachter auf. Sie an einigen Punkten nachzuweisen war ein wichtiges Anliegen des Dubliner Kolloquiums.

Die Anfänge des Christentums in Irland

Schriftliche Quellen aus Irland sind in größerem Umfang erst seit dem ausgehenden sechsten Jahrhundert überliefert. Es gibt aber sichere Anzeichen dafür, daß das Christentum und mit ihm eine Schriftkultur bereits zwei Jahrhunderte zuvor nach Irland gelangt waren. Es ist höchst schwierig, die frühen Spuren der Entwicklung des Christentums dort zu sichern. Die schriftlichen Quellen erfassen die Insel nicht gleichmäßig; sie stammen überwiegend aus dem Nordosten, dem Einflußbereich der Klostergemeinschaft von Iona und meist aus späterer Zeit. Der Historiker ist in diesem Bereich auf die Zusammenarbeit mit Vertretern anderer Disziplinen, besonders der Archäologie, angewiesen. Es sei angemerkt, daß in Irland bisher die vorgeschichtliche Zeit archäologisch umfassender aufgearbeitet wurde als die frühmittelalterlichen Jahrhunderte, die die Periodenbezeichnung „early Christian" tragen[2].

Irland lag am nordwestlichen Rande des römischen Imperiums, vor dessen Grenzen, aber in Kontakt mit ihm. Ein wichtiges Kennzeichen des Imperiums war seine großräumige Organisation mit entsprechender Kommunikation, die die Welt des östlichen Mittelmeerraumes mit der atlantischen Welt Nordwesteuropas verband. Die Ausbreitung des Christentums innerhalb des römischen Reiches wurde seit dem 4. Jahrhundert durch die Universalität des Reiches beträchtlich gefördert. Das Christentum paßte sich recht mühelos dem Raum an, in dem es existierte. Es wurde ebenso universal, wie das Reich universal war; in mancher Beziehung wurde es nachhaltig römisch[3].

Es gilt heute als sicher, daß das Christentum spätestens im 4. Jahrhundert nach Irland gelangte, auch wenn es dafür nur spärliche Belege gibt. Von der geographischen Lage Irlands her ist mit den stärksten Einflüssen auf Irland durch die nächsten Nachbarn zu rechnen, also aus Gallien und Spanien, vor allem aber aus Britannien. Dafür mögen einige Belege angeführt werden. Das irische Wort *bordgal*, eine Entlehnung des lateinischen *Burdigala* (Bordeaux) erscheint als Orts-

---

2 „Early Christian" umfaßt in der irischen Fachliteratur die Zeit zwischen dem 5. und 12. Jh.; „medieval" vom 12. bis zum frühen 16. Jh., vergleichbar mit der in England üblichen Periodisierung „Anglo-Saxon" bis zum 11. Jh. und danach „medieval".

3 Patrick J. *Corish*, The early Irish Church and the Western Patriarchate, in diesem Band, verweist darauf, daß die kirchlichen Feiertage am 22. Februar und 29. Juni auch vorchristliche stadtrömische Festtage waren, oben S. 11.

name im Westen Irlands, aber auch als Bezeichnung für bedeutende Versammlungsplätze (ursprünglich wohl der Treffpunkt von Händlern) und zeigt, welch nachhaltigen Einfluß der Kontakt mit Bordeaux hatte[4]. Jonas, der Biograph Columbans, deutet an, daß die Schiffsverbindung zwischen Nantes und Irland im 6. Jahrhundert selbstverständlich war[5]. Die Kontakte zwischen Spanien und Irland im Frühmittelalter sind seit längerer Zeit bekannt[6]. Die Verbindungen Irlands mit Britannien sind so vielfältig, daß sich eine gezielte Ausführung erübrigt. Schließlich soll erwähnt werden, daß es seit dem 5. Jahrhundert ausgedehnte irische Herrschaften im Westen Britanniens gab[7].

Gleichwohl bot die Universalität des römischen Reiches gute Voraussetzungen für Kontakte Irlands auch mit entfernteren Regionen. Das ist deshalb zu erwähnen, weil in der frühen irischen Kirche manche Eigenheiten aufscheinen, die die deutlichsten Parallelen im östlichen Mittelmeerraum haben. Daraus ergibt sich der Eindruck von Einflüssen aus relativ entfernten Regionen auf die irische Christenheit. Es ist mit der Möglichkeit zu rechnen, daß solche Einflüsse über Mittel- und Westeuropa vermittelt wurden, daß deren Spuren dort aber durch die unruhigen Verhältnisse verwischt wurden. Dennoch ist es nicht unabdingbar, Vermittlung über näher gelegene Regionen zu postulieren. Seit den Arbeiten von Henri Pirenne, somit seit mehr als einem halben Jahrhundert, ist allgemein bekannt, daß auch nach dem politischen Zusammenbruch des römischen Westreiches die Handelswelt der Antike weiter fortbestand und internationale Verbindungen aufrechterhielt. Das bedeutet konkret, daß Einflüsse aus der Welt des östlichen Mittelmeeres auf Irland auch nach dem Ende des römischen Westreiches direkt geltend gemacht werden konnten. Bekannt ist die große Zahl syrischer Kaufleute in Gallien in merowingischer Zeit. Dieses Phänomen muß mit den bereits erwähnten gallisch-irischen Kontakten verknüpft werden. Die Möglichkeit anderer Verbindungen zeigt sich an dem Beispiel des fränkischen Bischofs Arculf, der aus dem Heiligen Land kommend Adomnán in Iona von seinen Erlebnissen berichtete und ihn zur Abfassung seiner Schrift *De locis sanctis* anregte.

Schließlich wurde die Universalität des Christentums, die ihrerseits Kontakte förderte, auch in Irland als selbstverständlich betrachtet. Man vermutet, daß die

---

4 Siehe in diesem Band E. G. *Quin*, The Irish glosses, S. 212 und C. *Doherty*, The use of relics in the early Irish Church, S. 99.

5 MGH SS rer. Merov. 4, S. 97; die letzte zusammenfassende Darstellung findet man bei Edward *James*, Ireland and Western Gaul in the Merovingian period, in: Ireland in early Mediaeval Europe, hg. D. *Whitelock*, R. *McKitterick*, D. *Dumville*, Cambridge 1982, S. 363—386.

6 J. N. *Hillgarth*, The East, Visigothic Spain and the Irish, Stud. Patr. 4, Berlin 1961, 442—56; *idem*, Visigothic Spain and Early Christian Ireland, PRIA 62 C (1961—62), S. 167—94. Zur Kritik vgl. James (wie oben Anm. 5) S. 363. Dagegen nun J. N. *Hillgarth*, Ireland and Spain in the Seventh Century, Peritia 3 (1984).

7 M. *Richter*, Die inselkeltischen Völker im europäischen Rahmen des Mittelalters, Saeculum 32 (1981), S. 274—77.

Bedeutung Bordeauxs für Irland in erster Linie auf dem Weinhandel beruhte, der für die Feier der christlichen Messe unverzichtbar war. Einen ähnlichen Eindruck vermittelt Cogitosus in der *Vita Brigidae*, wenn er beiläufig erwähnt, der Bischof von Kildare beziehe seine Amtskleidung aus Übersee[8]. Diese wenigen Hinweise mögen die internationalen Verbindungen, die in der frühen irischen Kirche immer wieder in Erscheinung treten, verdeutlichen.

In Gallien und Rom wußte man spätestens im Jahr 431, daß es in Irland Christen gab. Da Palladius zu ihnen als erster Bischof, von Papst Coelestin geweiht, geschickt wurde, ist zu vermuten, daß man die Christengemeinde der *Scotti* für recht umfangreich, aber unzureichend organisiert hielt. Die Entsendung des Palladius ist sicher in Verbindung mit der Entsendung des Germanus von Auxerre nach Britannien (429) zu sehen, der dort gegen die Lehren des Pelagius predigte. Die irischen Christen wurden in den folgenden Jahrhunderten verschiedentlich verdächtigt, der pelagianischen Lehre anzuhängen. Man glaubt hierin, die Nachwirkungen eines Eindringens des Christentums nach Irland aus Britannien zu sehen. Auch Palladius kam vermutlich über Britannien nach Irland und scheint vor allem in Leinster tätig gewesen zu sein.

Mit größerer Gewißheit kann man von einer Vermittlung der christlichen Botschaft aus Britannien durch den Briten Patrick sprechen. Wie er waren offenbar viele andere Briten als Gefangene nach Irland gekommen und hatten möglicherweise dort zur Verbreitung des Christentums, vielleicht auch des Pelagianismus, beigetragen. Sollte Patrick ursprünglich als Prediger bei Briten in Irland gewirkt haben[9]? Das muß Vermutung bleiben, ebenso wie die Zeit, in der Patrick in Irland tätig war, weiterhin ungeklärt ist[10]. Den von Patrick verfaßten schriftlichen Zeugnissen, der *Confessio* und dem Brief an die Soldaten des Tyrannen Coroticus, ist freilich zu entnehmen, daß die von ihm bereisten Gebiete bis zu seiner Missionstätigkeit vom Christentum unberührt gewesen waren. Patrick wirkte höchstwahrscheinlich im Nordosten Irlands; ihm wird die Gründung von Armagh (ir. Ard Macha, in unmittelbarer Nähe von Emain Macha, dem politischen Zentrum der Ulaid, gelegen) zugeschrieben, während er in Downpatrick beigesetzt worden sein soll. Patrick gelangte nie auf den Kontinent, obwohl spätere Legenden von einem langjährigen Aufenthalt in Gallien berichten.

Während für den östlichen Teil Irlands das Eindringen des Christentums wenigstens in Umrissen zu erkennen ist, muß auch mit einem Vordringen des Christentums in spätantiker Zeit im Süden und Westen Irlands, in Munster und Connacht, gerechnet werden. Schriftliche Quellen darüber sind sehr spärlich; die vorhandenen Gedenksteine mit Ogham-Inschriften, die in auffälliger Häufung in Munster zwischen dem 4. und 6. Jahrhundert errichtet wurden, harren einer

---

8 Vita S. Brigidae c. 6, AA SS Febr. I, S. 139: *vestimenta transmarina et peregrina.*

9 D. *Dumville*, Some British Aspects of the earliest Irish Christianity, in diesem Band.

10 Vgl. zusammenfassend D. A. *Binchy*, St Patrick and his Biographers, Ancient and Modern, Stud. Hib. 2 (1962), S. 7—173.

neuen Untersuchung. Es wird indes erwogen, in der ungewöhnlich dichten Verbreitung von Gedenksteinen entlang der irischen Westküste, von Cork bis Donegal, mit *alpha-omega* oder *chi-rho* Inschriften die Überreste eines frühen Christentums monastischer Prägung zu sehen, das vielleicht direkt aus Gallien kam, sich aber auf Dauer nicht überall durchsetzen konnte[11].

Zwei Nachbardisziplinen kommen dem Historiker hier zu Hilfe, die Handschriftenkunde und die Ortsnamensforschung. Unabhängig voneinander weisen sie darauf hin, daß sich in Irland in den frühmittelalterlichen Jahrhunderten Römisches aus dem 4. und 5. Jahrhundert niederschlug und fortsetzte, was auf dem Kontinent seit dem 5. Jahrhundert aufgegeben wurde. Der Paläograph zeigt es eindrücklich für die Schriftform und für die physische Ausgestaltung der frühen irischen Handschriften[12]. Der Ortsnamensforscher verweist auf die Bedeutung des Begriffs *dominicum* „Gotteshaus", eine Bezeichnung, die auf dem Kontinent im 5. Jahrhundert außer Gebrauch kam, in Irland aber bis in das 7. Jahrhundert verwendet wurde[13]. Was dem unvoreingenommenen Betrachter als irische Eigenheit erscheint, enthüllt sich bei näherem Zusehen als ungewöhnlich nachhaltiger Niederschlag römischen Einflusses in Irland (und Britannien).

Palladius und Patrick sind in ihren Bestrebungen, in Irland eine Bischofskirche zu errichten, als zweite Stufe der Entfaltung des Christentums auf der Insel zu betrachten. Mochte auch die vor-patricianische und vor-palladische Kirche keine Bischöfe gehabt haben, so wird aus der Verbreitung des Begriffs *domnach* (von lat. *dominicum*) in Ortsnamen geschlossen, daß es bereits vor Patrick und Palladius Kirchen gegeben hatte, die man als frühe Pfarrkirchen betrachten könnte. Manche Ortsnamen zeigen noch deutlich die Zuständigkeit einer solchen Kirche für eine Region (vgl. *Domnach Mór Maig Itha* = „die große Kirche der Ebene von Ithe"). Es spricht einiges für die Vermutung, daß seit dem 7. Jahrhundert *dominicum* als Bezeichnung für eine Kirche außer Gebrauch kam — vermutlich, weil damals *dominicum* in der irischen Ableitung in der Bedeutung „Sonntag" allgemein übernommen wurde. Tírechán bezeichnet *domnach*-Kirchen häufig als *magna ecclesia*. Dennoch läßt sich eine Verbreitung von frühen Kirchen nachweisen, die auch noch im späteren 7. Jahrhundert einen besonderen Status hatten. So wurde im *Liber Angeli*[14] formuliert: *omnis ubique locus, qui dominicus appellatur ... in speciali*

---

11 Ann *Hamlin*, Early Irish Stone Carving: content and context, in: The Early Church in Western Britain and Ireland (= Studies presented to C. A. Ralegh Radford), hg. Susan M. *Pearce*, British Archaeological Reports, British Series 102, 1982, S. 283—96; ähnlich, unabhängig davon, *James* (wie oben Anm. 5) S. 368—70.

12 Julian *Brown*, The oldest Irish manuscripts and their late antique background, in diesem Band S. 321, 324.

13 Deirdre *Flanagan*, The Christian impact on early Ireland: place-names evidence, in diesem Band S. 31.

14 Nach Richard *Sharpe*, Armagh and Rome in the Seventh Century, in diesem Band S. 68ff. stammt der *Liber Angeli* aus dem 7. Jh. *Flanagan* setzt noch die bisher übliche Datierung ins späte 8. Jh. an.

societate Patricii pontificis atque heredis cathedrae eius Aird Machae esse debuerat[15]. Dabei ist die Verbindung dieser Kirchen mit Patrick sicher unhistorisch. Vielmehr sollte sie als Bezeichnung für solche Kirchen verstanden werden, die nicht von Anfang an als Klöster organisiert waren. Interessant ist in dieser Hinsicht die Bezeichnung einer Kirche als *Sendomnach* („alte Kirche").

Die Ortsnamensforschung bestätigt in einer weiteren Hinsicht Aspekte der Entwicklung der irischen Kirche. Vom 8. bis zum 12. Jahrhundert ist das Element *cill* (in Ortsnamen heute als *Kil(l-)*, von lat. *cella*) weit verbreitet. Es bezeichnet ein Kloster, und zwar nicht nur die (ursprünglich vielleicht separat errichteten) Mönchszellen oder das Gebetshaus, sondern die Gesamtheit der zum Kloster gehörenden Gebäude, einschließlich der Wirtschaftsgebäude. Wir berühren damit das umstrittene Thema der Herausbildung der überwiegend monastisch geprägten irischen Kirche. Man könnte hier von einer dritten Entwicklungsstufe reden, wobei aber mit einer langen Übergangsphase zu rechnen ist. Das für das irische Christentum so schwer durchschaubare 5. Jahrhundert hatte sich wahrscheinlich in einer ausgeprägten Bischofskirche manifestiert, stärker, als sie heute noch zu erkennen ist. Daneben gab es ein Mönchtum wohl schon sehr früh, auch vor Patrick[16], der in seinen eigenen Schriften Mönche erwähnt und die Hinwendung zum Mönchtum ausdrücklich förderte. Es spricht manches dafür, daß die Bischofskirche erst im 8. Jahrhundert deutlich an Einfluß verlor.

Freilich, ob Mönchs- oder Bischofskirche, das Christentum war nach Irland auf verschiedenen Wegen gelangt, aber in jedem Fall aus Gebieten, die nachhaltig römisch geprägt waren. Diese Ausprägung zeigt sich am deutlichsten in der Sprache, die von der Christenheit des Abendlandes benutzt wurde. Es war die Umgangssprache des römischen Reiches, die lateinische Sprache. In ihrer Verwendung und im Festhalten an ihr auch nach dem politischen Zusammenbruch des Westreiches zeigt sich am deutlichsten, wie „römisch" die universal konzipierte Religion inzwischen geworden war.

Die Gesellschaft Irlands, in die das Christentum gelangte, unterschied sich in vieler Hinsicht deutlich von der römischen Gesellschaft, aus der das Christentum kam. Politisch war sie kleinräumig organisiert; kulturell war sie selbstbewußt eigenständig. In der irischen Gesellschaftsordnung gab es manche Parallelen zu dem, was Caesar über die keltischen Gallier berichtet hatte. Andere Aspekte der Gesellschaft Irlands sind nicht spezifisch keltisch, sondern waren sehr viel weiter verbreitet. Sie tauchen auch in außereuropäischen Kulturen auf; die Anthropologie ermöglicht durch Vergleiche der irischen Gesellschaft in der Frühzeit mit jenen anderen Kulturen allmählich ein besseres Verständnis des frühen Irland.

Die vorchristliche Gesellschaft Irlands war in vieler Hinsicht nicht einzigartig, nur ist sie durch einige Umstände recht gut bekannt. Es ist davon auszugehen,

15 Zitiert bei *Flanagan* (wie oben Anm. 13) S. 26.
16 Einen möglicherweise beträchtlichen monastischen Einfluß aus Gallien erwägt zuletzt *James* (wie oben Anm. 5), S. 368—70.

daß die vorchristliche irische Gesellschaft so stark entwickelt war, daß sie den Einfluß des Christentums lange Zeit recht unbeschadet absorbieren konnte. Das zeigt sich daran, daß die neue Religion die irische Gesellschaft nur sehr allmählich, im Lauf einiger Jahrhunderte, nachhaltig prägte. Statt dessen wurde das Christentum der in Irland existierenden Gesellschaft weitgehend angepaßt. Damit kam es zur Ausgestaltung einer Variante des Christentums, die unverwechselbare Züge trägt. Das sind die Voraussetzungen dafür, daß man überhaupt von einem Christentum irischer Prägung sprechen kann, während anderes, was lange als typisch irisch galt, nun als in Irland bewahrtes spätrömisches Erbe gelten muß.

Die geistig-kulturelle Vitalität des vorchristlichen Irland muß in ihrer Bedeutung voll zur Kenntnis genommen werden. Sie wird in den Ausführungen des vorliegenden Bandes immer wieder angesprochen. Für die in Irland bedeutende soziale Schicht der Gelehrten, der Priester *(druíd)*, Rechtsgelehrten *(brithemin)* und Dichter oder Seher *(filid)* gibt es Parallelen im gleichfalls keltisch geprägten Britannien und später in abgeschwächter Form in Wales[16a], im keltisch geprägten Gallien, wie es Caesar erlebt und beschrieben hatte, aber auch in anderen indoeuropäischen Gesellschaften. Die Irland benachbarten germanischen Eroberer Britanniens hatten ein heidnisches Priestertum[17] und eine Klasse von Dichtern[18]. Aber in keiner anderen europäischen Gesellschaft blieb diese geistige Elite so einflußreich wie in Irland. Man kann das als ein Zeichen der Schwäche des Christentums deuten; aber es kann auch positiv betrachtet werden, als Zeichen der Stärke einheimischer Traditionen. Die vorchristlichen Traditionen Irlands blieben auch in christlicher Zeit bedeutend und trugen zur Ausprägung des Christentums in diesem Land bei. Oberflächlich betrachtet scheinen die Druiden am stärksten an Einfluß verloren zu haben, aber auch deren Zurücktreten war ein recht allmählicher Vorgang[19]. Die weltlichen Dichter und die Rechtsgelehrten hingegen blieben während des gesamten Mittelalters in Irland höchst einflußreich. Daraus erklärt sich die Diskussion in dem vorliegenden Band um den gegenseitigen Einfluß von Kirchenrecht und weltlichem Recht, von christlicher und vorchristlicher Literatur; daraus erklärt sich letztendlich die eigenartige Beeinflussung von Irischem und Christlichem.

Unter diesen Voraussetzungen hatte das Christentum in Irland keinen leichten Start. Dennoch setzte es sich durch, obwohl es anfangs anscheinend weniger Rückhalt durch die politischen Führungsschichten erhielt als in anderen Ländern. Es scheint außer Frage zu stehen, daß eindrucksvolle Vertreter der neuen Religion, von denen Patrick wohl einer der wichtigsten war, zu diesem Erfolg beitrugen.

16a J. E. Caerwyn *Williams*, Gildas, Maelgwn and the Bards, R. R. *Davies* et al., ed., Welsh Society and Nationhood, Cardiff 1984, p. 19—34.

17 HE II, 13 (über Coifi).

18 Hermann *Moisl*, Anglo-Saxon royal genealogies and Germanic oral tradition, Journal of Medieval History 7 (1981), S. 215—48.

19 Vgl. Proinsias *Mac Cana*, Regnum and Sacerdotium: Notes on Irish Tradition, PBA 65 (1979), S. 443—479.

Dennoch darf man das Ausmaß dieses Erfolges nicht überschätzen. Nichts deutet darauf hin, daß die Iren im Frühmittelalter ein besonders christliches Volk waren. Wie überall gab es auch in Irland erhebliche Unterschiede.

Die Quellen können leicht einen falschen Eindruck erwecken. Information über das Christentum stammt ausschließlich von christlichen Autoren; viele dieser Quellen sind eher Propagandaschriften als Tatsachenberichte. Sicher sind die Erfolge des Christentums in den christlichen Quellen glänzender dargestellt, als sie es tatsächlich waren. Über die Tiefenwirkung der christlichen Religion, vor allem in den sozialen Unterschichten, ist recht wenig bekannt. Es muß jedoch zu denken geben, daß der neuen Religion auch in der Oberschicht erstaunliche Grenzen gesetzt waren. So wurde das Königtum in Irland während des gesamten Mittelalters nicht verchristlicht, sondern blieb älteren Bräuchen verhaftet, und zwar nicht nur in einer Zeit, als sich die einzelnen Könige zum Christentum bekannten, ja nicht selten selbst die Abts- oder Bischofswürde innehatten, sondern auch noch, als das christliche Königtum überall sonst in Europa die Regel geworden war.

Sprache und Literatur

Da wir unsere Kenntnis der irischen Gesellschaft und der Kirche im frühen Mittelalter weitgehend schriftlichen Quellen entnehmen, verdient dieser Themenbereich besondere Beachtung. Er hat verschiedene Aspekte. Vorrangig geht es natürlich um die Information, die durch die schriftlichen Quellen vermittelt wird, aber die Sprache, in der das geschieht, ist ihrerseits eine wichtige Quelle historischer Erkenntnis, die eine eingehende Würdigung verdient.

Es ist davon auszugehen, daß die lateinische Sprache in größerem Umfang mit der christlichen Religion nach Irland gelangte. Sie bereicherte die irische Sprache durch zahlreiche Lehnwörter, die zum Großteil, aber keineswegs ausschließlich, aus dem Bereich der christlichen Religion stammen. Eine erhebliche Zahl von Lehnwörtern scheint bereits während der ersten zwei Jahrhunderte des Christentums rezipiert worden zu sein, aber es gibt auch nachweislich spätere Entlehnungen. Semantische Veränderungen sind dabei von Interesse. Wie bereits erwähnt, war die Einführung der lateinischen Schriftsprache in Irland auch formal bedeutend, nämlich in der relativ frühen Verwendung von Prosa in Quellen irischer Sprache an Stelle der früher weit verbreiteten Versform.

Die frühesten schriftlichen Zeugnisse aus Irland sind die in irischer Sprache verfaßten, in Ogham-Zeichen ausgeführten Inschriften, einer Schriftform, die auf dem lateinischen Alphabet aufbaut. Sie werden verschiedentlich in das ausgehende 4. oder in das 5. Jahrhundert datiert. Ogham-Inschriften wurden etwa zwei Jahrhunderte lang ausgeführt. Abgesehen von diesen Inschriften erscheint generell die lateinische Sprache in führender Position. Die frühesten literarischen Werke in irischer Sprache lassen sich nach sprachwissenschaftlichen Kriterien auf die Zeit seit dem ausgehenden 6. Jahrhundert datieren.

Das Latein, das mit dem Christentum nach Irland kam, erscheint in zwei großen Ausprägungen, nämlich als das Latein Britanniens, das in den Werken des Patrick, des Gildas und in Inschriften für das 5. und 6. Jahrhundert bezeugt ist, und das Latein des Mittelmeerraumes, das vor allem durch die Bibeltexte nach Irland gelangte. Dort war anfangs wohl der altlateinische Bibeltext (Vetus Latina) vorherrschend und wurde erst seit dem 7. Jahrhundert verstärkt von dem Vulgata-Text des Hieronymus verdrängt. Zeugnisse für die Existenz des Vulgata-Texts in Irland beginnen im frühen 7. Jahrhundert[20].

Im europäischen Raum stellt Irland einen Neubeginn der Ausbreitung des Christentums dar: Zum erstenmal kam diese Religion in ein Land, das bis dahin der lateinischen Sprache verschlossen gewesen war. Die irische Kirche übernahm die lateinische Sprache; diese wurde dort erstmals zu einer ausgeprägten Sakralsprache, die der christlichen Gemeinde weitgehend fremd blieb. Latein mußte in Irland von Grund auf gelernt werden, und es blieb Fremdsprache. Die Träger der einheimischen irischen Bildung waren äußerst sprachbewußt; ihr sprachliches Interesse schlug sich auch in der Beschäftigung mit der lateinischen Sprache nieder. Es kam zu einer recht umfassenden Rezeption der lateinischen Sprache im Rahmen der christlichen Religion in Irland. Aber schon früh machten sich Einflüsse der einheimischen Sprachpflege in dem in Irland geschriebenen Latein geltend. Zudem rezipierten die irischen Geistlichen sehr früh die Werke des Isidor von Sevilla und zeigten besonderes Interesse für dessen absonderliche Etymologien. Die einheimische Sprachpflege, die Tatsache, daß Latein Fremdsprache war, und die Vorliebe der Gelehrten für eine außergewöhnliche Sprache trugen dazu bei, daß sich in Irland eine Art von Latein entwickelte, die man als hibernisches Latein bezeichnet[21]. Typische Hibernismen sind lange, kompliziert gebaute Sätze und die Verwendung eines möglichst erlesenen, oft gewollt exzentrischen Vokabulars. In seiner stärksten Ausprägung ist das hibernische Latein weitgehend unverständlich *(Hisperica Famina);* in schwächeren Ausprägungen ist es ein wichtiges Kriterium zur Bestimmung insularer Kontakte in Texten, die außerhalb Irlands überliefert sind.

Die äußerst komplexe Phonologie der irischen Sprache wurde mit Hilfe des lateinischen Alphabets, das dazu recht ungeeignet war, aufgezeichnet. Das geschah vornehmlich durch ungewöhnliche Kombinationen lateinischer Buchstaben (z. B. für Palatalisierung und Nasalisierung) und durch Längezeichen für lange Vokale sowie durch *punctum delens* (über dem Konsonanten geschrieben,

---

20 Z. B. die Wachstafeln aus dem Springmount Moor und der Psalter „Colum Cilles" *(Cathach)*, vgl. Brown (wie oben Anm. 12), S. 312ff.

21 In der englisch-sprachigen Literatur wird der Begriff „insular Latin" benutzt. Für eine Bestandsaufnahme vgl. M. *Herren*, Hg., Insular Latin Studies. Papers on Latin Texts and Manuscripts of the British Isles: 550—1066 (= Papers in Mediaeval Studies 1, Pontifical Institute of Mediaeval Studies), Toronto 1981, und *ders.* dort: Hiberno-Latin philology: The State of the Question, S. 1—22

der stumm bleibt). Es ist festzustellen, daß Spuren dieser schriftlichen Fixierung des Irischen mit lateinischen Buchstaben rückwirkend in der Schreibung des Latein in Irland erkennbar sind. Man kann daraus wichtige Rückschlüsse auf die Aussprache des Latein in Irland sowie auf die Aussprache des Irischen ziehen. Eine derartige wechselseitige Beeinflussung von einheimischer Sprache und Latein gibt es in diesem Ausmaß in keinem anderen Land Europas im früheren Mittelalter. Eigenarten der Orthographie des Latein in Irland blieben im gesamten Frühmittelalter wirksam. Manche sind für den Laien leicht erkennbar, z. B. die unsystematische Verwendung von *s* und *ss (Issidor; obtulisent)*. Das Einfügen eines Gleitvokals *i* zur Palatalisierung des nachfolgenden Konsonanten findet man häufig[22].

Die Deutung anderer Hibernismen erfordert eine Kenntnis der irischen Sprache der Zeit. Irische Präpositionen haben oft eine andere Bedeutungsbreite als das, was in Irland als das lateinische Äquivalent betrachtet wurde. In den Annalen von Ulster, die in ihrer ursprünglichen Fassung bis etwa 800 weitgehend in lateinischer Sprache geschrieben wurden, findet man zu dem Jahr 733:

> *Talorgg mac Congusso a fratre suo victus est, traditur in manus*
> *Pictorum,* et cum *illis in aqua submersus est.*

Hier sieht man die Nachwirkung der irischen Präposition *la*, die sowohl „mit" als auch „durch" bezeichnet[23]. Es läßt sich feststellen, daß die lateinische Sprache in Irland durch die vorgegebene einheimische Sprachtradition nachhaltig geprägt wurde. Sie nahm deutlich regionale und identifizierbar irische Züge an. Mit der geistigen Ausstrahlung Irlands gelangte diese Latinität auch in andere Länder, besonders nach Britannien. Damit ist das hibernische Latein ein wesentlicher Faktor im insularen Latein[24].

Wir müssen noch einmal zur Übernahme der lateinischen Sprache im Rahmen der Einführung des Christentums in Irland zurückkehren. Sie zeigt sich besonders deutlich in den Lehnwörtern im Irischen aus dem Lateinischen, vor allem für

---

22 Z. B. *obtuilit*, S. *Connolly*, Some palaeographical and linguistic features in early Lives of Brigit, in diesem Band, S. 273. *uibi* für *ubi, staitim* für *statim*, vgl. M. *Herren*, Sprachliche Eigentümlichkeiten in den hibernolateinischen Texten des 7. und 8. Jahrhunderts, in *Löwe, Iren*, S. 429.

23 Vgl. auch Annales Cambriae (A), hg. E. *Phillimore*, Y Cymmrodor 9 (1888), S. 141—183: s. a. 453: *Pascha commutatur super diem dominicum* cum *papa leone episcopo rome;* s. a. 778: *Vastatio brittonum dextralium* apud *offa;* s. a. 784: *Vastati* (sic!) *brittonum* cum *offa inestate.* Zu diesen Fragen vgl. Bengt *Löfstedt*, Der hibernolateinische Grammatiker Malsachanus, Uppsala 1965, S. 117 ff.

24 Das hibernische Element wird in England in jüngster Zeit spürbar abgewertet, vgl. Michael *Winterbottom*, Aldhelm's prose style and its origins, Anglo-Saxon England 6 (1977), S. 39—76; Michael *Lapidge*, The present state of Anglo-Latin Studies, in: Insular Latin Studies, hg. M. *Herren* (wie oben Anm. 21), S. 45—82. Die Berechtigung dazu wird sich erst in Zukunft herausstellen.

Begriffe, die aus dem Bereich der neuen Religion stammen. Dieses Thema hat Sprachwissenschaftler seit dem Beginn unseres Jahrhunderts beschäftigt. Es wird in dem vorliegenden Band ausführlich behandelt. Im Gegensatz zu der bisherigen Lehrmeinung, die an zwei Phasen der Entlehnung, im 4. und 5. Jahrhundert, festhielt, in einer Zeit, in der die irische Sprache selbst bedeutende Wandlungen durchmachte, wird hier ein kontinuierlicher Prozeß postuliert. Es wird darauf hingewiesen, daß anfangs die lateinischen Lehnwörter, die wohl überwiegend aus dem britischen Latein nach Irland kamen, stark der irischen Phonologie und Orthographie angepaßt wurden, während eine zunehmende Vertrautheit in Irland mit der lateinischen Sprache diese Tendenz abschwächte. Damit erklärt sich, um ein extremes Beispiel anzuführen, die Übernahme des Namens *Patricius* in Irland als *Cothrige* (früh) und *Pátraic* (spät)[25].

Entlehnungen aus dem Bereich der Sakralsprache in die einheimische Sprache gab es überall im christlichen Raum; sie sind ein Anzeichen der zunehmenden Internationalität der europäischen christlichen Gemeinschaft. In ihrer Mehrzahl behielten diese Lehnwörter im wesentlichen ihre ursprüngliche Bedeutung bei. Semantische Verschiebungen sind aber auch bezeugt. Erwähnt sei der Begriff *ruam*, abgeleitet von „Rom". Er bezeichnet im irischen Frühmittelalter nacheinander bedeutende kirchliche Zentren und später allgemein Friedhöfe. Diese Bedeutungswandlung ist durch die verstärkte Anlehnung der irischen Kirche an Rom zu erklären. Seit dem 7. Jahrhundert wurde es üblich, Reliquien aus Rom zu beschaffen, was für bedeutende Kirchen einfacher war als für kleinere Gemeinschaften; zudem bemühte man sich um Erde aus Rom, die den irischen Friedhöfen den physischen Kontakt mit dem Zentrum der Christenheit verschaffen sollte[26]. Der Begriff *ruam* ist auch deswegen bedeutend, da er die Romverbundenheit der irischen Kirche auf breiter Ebene eindrücklich belegt. Diese Verbundenheit gab es in Irland zu allen Zeiten im früheren Mittelalter; die Ausarbeitung der Aspekte, in denen sich die irische Christengemeinde von Rom unterschied, kann leicht zu falschen Vorstellungen führen.

Am Beginn der in Irland geschriebenen Literatur stehen die lateinischen Werke des Patrick aus dem späten 5. Jahrhundert, die *Confessio* und der Brief an die Soldaten des Coroticus[27]. Danach gibt es eine Lücke von etwa einem Jahrhundert. Seit dem ausgehenden 6. Jahrhundert werden schriftliche Zeugnisse zahlreich. Die Annalistik setzte in dieser Zeit ein, wahrscheinlich in Iona. Sie ist ein beredtes Zeugnis für die anhaltende geistige Verbundenheit der Gründung Colum Cilles und seiner Nachfolger mit dem Heimatland. Heute noch erhaltene Texte der Bibel wurden seit etwa 600 in Irland geschrieben. Die Hagiographie beginnt in der Mitte des 7. Jahrhunderts (Cogitosus, *Vita Brigidae*, um 650; die Werke Muir-

---

25 Damian *McManus*, The so-called *Cothrige* and *Pátraic* strata of Latin loan-words in Early Irish, in diesem Band.

26 Vgl. *Corish* (wie oben Anm. 3), *Doherty* (wie oben Anm. 4).

27 D. A. *Binchy* (wie oben Anm. 10).

chús und Tírecháns über Patrick, 2. Hälfte des 7. Jahrhunderts; Adomnáns Vita Columbae um 700). Die volkssprachlichen Quellen beginnen (nach den Ogham-Inschriften) mit der Elegie auf Colum Cille (um 597). Die irischen Rechtstexte wurden wahrscheinlich seit dem späteren 7. Jahrhundert kompiliert; die Sammlung mit dem Titel *Senchas Már* „Das große Wissen" wird allgemein in die erste Hälfte des 8. Jahrhunderts datiert. Exegetische Schriften sind seit dem 7. Jahrhundert in erheblichem Umfang bezeugt. In dieser Zeit wurden wohl auch die ersten einheimischen literarischen Werke in Prosa geschrieben. Erwähnung verdienen ferner die Schriften des Columbanus aus dem späten 6. und frühen 7. Jahrhundert, die wohl sämtlich auf dem Kontinent verfaßt wurden. In seinem Bußbuch zeigt er sich besonders stark den einheimischen Traditionen verbunden, denn irische Bußbücher wurden seit dem 6. Jahrhundert verfaßt. Allgemein läßt sich feststellen, daß Irland, dieses Neuland schriftlicher Aufzeichnungen, in dieser Zeit sehr produktiv war, daß es im Vergleich mit anderen Ländern, z. B. Gallien und Spanien, positiv auffällt. Hinzu kommt, daß in Irland, anders als in diesen romanischen Ländern, früh eine starke zweisprachige Tradition gepflegt wurde, die im Europa dieser Zeit ohne Parallelen ist.

Die Pflege von Literatur in Latein und Irisch[28] setzte sich in Irland kontinuierlich fort. Besonders starke Anstöße für die Verwendung des Irischen für geistliche Texte kamen aus der kirchlichen Reformbewegung, die im frühen 8. Jahrhundert einsetzte und als Reform der *Céli Dé* bekannt ist. Aus dem Kreis der *Céli Dé* stammt das Bußbuch in irischer Sprache, die umfassende geistliche Lyrik mit ihren weltlichen Ableitungen sowie die Abfassung der Martyrologien[29]. Die Literatur Irlands aus dem Frühmittelalter baut auf breitem Fundament auf. Ihre Zweisprachigkeit ist beeindruckend.

Es wird allgemein angenommen, daß die meisten, wenn nicht sogar alle, literarischen Zeugnisse Irlands im frühen Mittelalter aus geistlichen Skriptorien hervorgingen. Die Übernahme der Schriftlichkeit durch die einheimischen weltlichen Gelehrten ist erst seit dem 12. Jahrhundert in größerem Umfang bezeugt. Man muß demnach annehmen, daß in den geistlichen Zentren sowohl die von außerhalb eingeführte Religon als auch die einheimische Tradition gepflegt und fortgesetzt wurde. Das ist um so leichter zu verstehen, wenn man bedenkt, daß die irische Kirche spätestens seit dem 6. Jahrhundert fest in der Oberschicht verankert war, und daß diese Oberschicht ihrer einheimischen Traditionen nur teilweise entsagte. Hier mag Colum Cille als eindrücklicher Zeuge genannt werden. Als einer der prägenden Geistlichen seiner Zeit war er noch eng mit den weltlichen Ereignissen in Irland verbunden. Die Elegie, die ein irischer *fili* auf ihn in irischer Sprache dichtete, steht ganz in der Tradition der einheimischen weltli-

---

28 Der Begriff „Volkssprache" wäre hier irreführend, denn es handelt sich um eine hoch entwickelte Literatursprache.

29 Peter *O'Dwyer*, The *Céli Dé* Reform; Diarmuid *Ó Laoghaire*, Early Irish Spirituality, beide in diesem Band.

chen Preisdichtung. Ähnliches gilt für die Gebete mit der Bezeichnung *lorica,* die stark von der Tradition vorchristlicher Zaubersprüche geprägt sind. Es zeigt sich deutlich, wie in Irland in dieser Zeit weltliche und christliche Literatur konvergierten.

Ein großer Beitrag der christlichen Religion zur Ausbildung der europäischen Völker vollzog sich sozusagen nebenbei: Die Verschriftlichung der einheimischen Sprachen. Sie geschah in West- und Mitteleuropa mit Hilfe des lateinischen Alphabets. Ursprünglich ging es darum, die in der lateinischen Fremdsprache zelebrierte Religion in wichtigen Punkten auch solchen Personen zugänglicher zu machen, die die lateinische Sprache nicht erlernten oder nur unzureichend beherrschten. Es kann nicht deutlich genug betont werden, daß Latein in den Gebieten des ehemals römischen Westreiches (Romania) noch einige Jahrhunderte lang verstanden, wenn auch nicht unbedingt gesprochen wurde[30], daß in der Romania, mit regionalen Unterschieden, das Latein der christlichen Gemeinden weitaus weniger Sakralsprache war als außerhalb der Romania.

Die Tendenz zur schriftlichen Aufzeichnung der einheimischen Sprache zeigt sich in allen Ländern mehr oder weniger ausgeprägt. Im Lauf von Jahrhunderten führte sie zu einem neuen nationalen Selbstverständnis. Bei den Anfängen der Verschriftlichung stehen meist die Glossen im Vordergrund. Im deutschen Sprachraum scheinen die Glossen tatsächlich am Beginn der Aufzeichnung der einheimischen Sprache zu stehen. Hier fanden die entscheidenden Entwicklungen im 8. Jahrhundert statt, gefördert durch die Missionare aus dem angelsächsischen Raum germanischer Sprache. Die Erfassung der frühesten deutschen Glossen ist noch nicht abgeschlossen[31]. In der Bretagne erkennt man eine ähnliche Entwicklung, mit dem Unterschied, daß die Aufzeichnung längerer volkssprachlicher Texte dort sehr viel später geschah[32].

Die Entwicklung auf den Britischen Inseln verlief anders. Es ist von Bedeutung, daß in Britannien die römische Herrschaft schon vor der Ausbreitung des Christentums eine Schriftsprache eingeführt hatte. Der Übergang zur Verschriftlichung der einheimischen Sprache, des Britischen (später Walisischen) vollzog sich dort sehr viel schneller und umfassender. Recht umfangreiche Dichtungen in walisischer Sprache gibt es seit dem 6. Jahrhundert. Das Corpus der frühen Literatur in walisischer Sprache ist nicht so ausgeprägt christlich wie sein Gegenstück im germanischen Raum.

---

30 Vgl. letztens Roger *Wright,* Late Latin and early Romance in Spain and Carolingian France, Liverpool 1982, passim, sowie Michael *Richter,* A quelle époque a-t-on cessé de parler latin en Gaule? A propos d'une question mal posée, Annales, E. S. C. 38 (1983), S. 439—48.

31 *Rolf Bergmann,* Die althochdeutsche Glossenüberlieferung des achten Jahrhunderts, in diesem Band.

32 Leon *Fleuriot,* The Old Breton Glosses and the cultural Importance of Brittany in the early Middle Ages, in diesem Band.

Das gilt in noch größerem Maß für Irland. Der Beginn der schriftlichen Aufzeichnung des Irischen, nach den heute noch erhaltenen Dokumenten, ist um 600 anzusetzen. Die hagiographischen Werke des 7. Jahrhunderts enthalten wichtiges Namensgut in irischer Sprache. Rechtstexte in irischer Sprache sowie Dichtungen aus dem 7. und 8. Jahrhundert wurden bereits erwähnt. Erst aus dem 8. Jahrhundert stammen die frühesten erhaltenen Glossierungen geistlicher Texte in irischer Sprache, die im 9. Jahrhundert fortgesetzt wurden. Aber die Glossierung war nicht auf lateinische und geistliche Texte beschränkt. Die Grammatik des Priscian, eines der wichtigsten Lehrbücher des Lateinischen in Irland (neben dem einflußreicheren Werk des Donatus) trug zur Schaffung irischer grammatikalischer Begriffe bei, durch Entlehnungen, Lehnsübersetzungen und allgemein den Versuch, grammatikalische Begriffe des Lateinischen in irischer Sprache zu prägen. Die irischen Glossen geistlicher Texte bieten, über das Wortverständnis hinausführend, gewichtige exegetische Ansätze. In späterer Zeit gab es umfangreiche Glossierungen der archaischen irischen Rechtstexte in Form langer Kommentare, die zeigen, wie sehr sich die irische Sprache seit der ersten Aufzeichnung der Rechtstexte entwickelt hatte. Oft dienen die späteren Kommentare der Rechtstexte kaum der Erhellung dieser Texte[33].

Die irische Glossenliteratur zeigt indirekt einen Einfluß des Lateinischen darin, daß sie unübersehbare Anzeichen einer Hochsprache aufweist, deren Regeln in Irland ebenso beachtet wurden wie in den vermutlich in Mitteleuropa aufgezeichneten irischen Glossen. Man vermutet den Einfluß christlicher Zentren[34], eine Entwicklung, die im deutschen Sprachraum in ähnlicher Weise in Erscheinung tritt[35].

Partikulare Aspekte der frühen irischen Kirche

Die am besten bekannte Besonderheit der frühen irischen Kirche ist ihre Organisation als Mönchs- oder Klosterkirche, im Gegensatz zu der römischen Bischofskirche. Es wurde bereits darauf hingewiesen, daß diese Organisationsform nicht von Anfang an bedeutend war, sondern sich erst allmählich in den Vordergrund schob. In diesem Bereich ist die Bedeutung der irischen Kirche derart zu umreißen, daß dort zum erstenmal diese Organisationsform durchdrang, die sich anschließend, teilweise unter direkter Anlehnung an Irland, in den anderen Gebieten außerhalb der Romania durchsetzte[36]. Die römische Kirche hatte sich in

---

33 *Quin* (wie oben Anm. 4).

34 Gearóid *Mac Eóin*, The "standardisation" of Old Irish; eine Druckfassung dieses auf dem Kolloquium gehaltenen Vortrags wurde nicht eingereicht.

35 Stefan *Sonderegger*, Die Bedeutung des religiösen Wortschatzes für die Entfaltung des Althochdeutschen: von früher Vielfalt zu allmählicher Vereinheitlichung, in diesem Band.

36 Denis *Bethell*, The Originality of the early Irish Church, JRSAI 111 (1981), S. 36—49.

ihrer Organisation den einheimischen Strukturen angeglichen, der regionalen Unterteilung des Reiches in Provinzen und Diözesen, die von den *civitates* aus verwaltet wurden. Diese Infrastruktur fehlte außerhalb der Romania. In Irland ist das allmähliche Hineinwachsen der Kirche in die vorgegebene Gesellschaft am deutlichsten zu erkennen, wobei zu beachten ist, daß man in den ersten Jahrhunderten — vergeblich — versucht hatte, das römische Modell, das in den benachbarten Ländern, in Gallien und Britannien, existiert hatte, zu übernehmen.

In Irland ist mit einer Kontinuität von vorchristlichen Kulten und christlicher Religion in erheblichem Ausmaß zu rechnen. Das war durchaus nicht ungewöhnlich; ähnliche Tendenzen lassen sich selbst in Rom nachweisen[37]; im späten 6. Jahrhundert empfahl Papst Gregor der Große seinen Missionaren bei den germanischen Völkern in Britannien ausdrücklich, heidnische Kultstätten in den Dienst der christlichen Kirche zu stellen[38]. Ähnliches vollzog sich, auch ohne päpstliche Empfehlung, in Irland. Als deutlichstes Beispiel dafür gilt das Kloster Kildare, das der heiligen Brigit geweiht war. In Kildare ist der vorchristliche Kult der keltischen Göttin Brigantia bezeugt; das heilige Feuer in Kildare, das auch in christlicher Zeit gewahrt wurde, hat vorchristliche Ursprünge. Ebenso ist das Fest der heiligen Brigit, der 1. Februar, ein bedeutendes Fest im keltischen Kalender *(Imbolc)*. Ferner ist der Name der christlichen Kultstätte wichtig: Kildare, ir. *Cell Dara* „Kirche im Eichenhain". Im alten Irland galt die Eiche (ir. *daur, dair*) als heiliger Baum. Andere Ortsnamen in Irland, die aus kirchlichen Zentren entstanden, enthalten ebenfalls das Wortelement „Eiche", z. B. Derry und Durrow. Auch sie deuten auf ein Fortbestehen vorchristlicher Kultstätten. Desgleichen werden Ortsnamen mit dem Element *tech* („Haus", meist in Verbindung mit Personennamen) als ehemals heidnische Kultstätten gedeutet[39].

Einflüsse der vorchristlichen Gesellschaft zeigen sich auch in anscheinend kleinen Eigentümlichkeiten irischen Christentums. Die typisch irische Unterteilung der 150 Psalmen in drei Gruppen von 50 („die drei Fünfziger") hat in dem in der irischen Literatur häufig zu findenden Zahlenbegriff „dreimal fünfzig" eine deutliche Parallele[40].

In der kirchlichen Architektur aus Holz, die man bis in das 9. Jahrhundert in Irland am häufigsten pflegte, knüpfte man bewußt an einheimische Traditionen an. Die Holzbauweise spiegelt gleichwohl eine fortgeschritttene Entwicklungs-

---

37 *Corish* (wie oben Anm. 3).
38 HE I, 30.
39 *Flanagan* (wie oben Anm. 13), S. 38.
40 Für die Psalmen vgl. *Ó Laoghaire* (wie oben Anm. 29), S. 79, Beispiele aus der irischen Literatur z. B. K. H. *Jackson*, A Celtic Miscellany, Harmondsworth 1971, S. 171, 175, und öfter; auch Martin *McNamara*, Psalter Text and Psalter Study in the early Irish Church (A.D. 600—1200), PRIA 73 C (1973), S. 201—298, hier bes. S. 269f., der darauf verweist, daß diese Unterteilung auch außerhalb Irlands existierte.

stufe wider. Kirchliche Bauten aus bescheidenerem Material, aus Flechtwerk oder sogar aus Torf, werden in den schriftlichen Quellen der Frühzeit erwähnt[41].

Diese Bauten haben nur selten erkennbare Spuren hinterlassen. Selbst für Holzbauten sind die archäologischen Zeugnisse selten, nicht nur wegen der Vergänglichkeit des Materials, sondern auch, weil bedeutendere, ursprünglich aus Holz gebaute, Kirchen später *in situ* durch Steinbauten ersetzt wurden. Die Bezeichnung „Steinhaus", d. h. Steinkirche (ir. *damliag*) taucht in den schriftlichen Quellen erstmals im 7. Jahrhundert auf. Daß man Kirchen aus Stein eigens als solche bezeichnete, drückt die Besonderheit dieser Bauweise deutlich aus[42]. In Ortsnamen ist dieser Begriff sehr selten (vgl. Duleek); das bedeutet, daß in der Regel der Ortsname bereits gebildet war, als eine Steinkirche gebaut wurde.

Es sei ergänzend hinzugefügt, daß sich im Lauf des Frühmittelalters manche kirchlichen Zentren Irlands, das keine Stadtkultur gehabt hatte, zu Siedlungen entwickelten, die man als Frühstädte bezeichnen kann, vor allem Armagh und Kildare. Dort wurden im Lauf der Zeit römische Verhältnisse realisiert. Interessant ist, wie Cogitosus, der erste Hagiograph Brigits von Kildare, der dieses Phänomen in Ansätzen erkannte, die christlich-lateinischen Normvorstellungen mit der Wirklichkeit konfrontierte, als er erörterte, ob Kildare überhaupt eine *civitas* sei, da es dort nicht einmal eine Mauer gäbe[43].

Die Klosterkirche, die sich in Irland allmählich als dominante Organisationsform herausbildete, entsprach am besten der einheimischen Sozialordnung. Die frühe irische Gesellschaft war durch die überragende Rolle der Sippe gekennzeichnet; die Klostergemeinschaft wurde dessen christliche Entsprechung. Bezeichnenderweise wurde der lateinische Begriff *monasterium*[44] ins Irische als *muinter* übernommen; er steht für den Personenverband der Klostergemeinschaft, ursprünglich für alle Menschen, die zu dem Kloster gehörten, später vorrangig für diejenigen Angehörigen des Klosters, die nicht Nonnen oder Mönche waren, mithin für die wachsende Zahl der Abhängigen.

Eine weitere Eigenart der frühen irischen Kirche ist die organisatorische Zusammenfassung mehrerer Klöster zu Verbänden, die als *paruchiae* bezeichnet werden. Anfangs bestand eine *paruchia* aus den Klöstern, die auf einen Gründer zurückgingen, z. B. Durrow, Derry und Iona, die wichtigsten Gründungen Colum Cilles. Sein Nachfolger (ir. *comarba*, „Erbe") behielt die organisatorische Leitung dieser Klöster. Einige bedeutende Klöster waren spätestens seit dem ausgehenden

41 Vgl. C. A. *Ralegh Radford*, The earliest Irish Churches, Ulster Journal of Archaeology 40 (1977), S. 1—11.

42 Ann *Hamlin*, The Study of early Irish Churches, in diesem Band, S. 118.

43 AA SS Febr. c. 8, S. 141: *Si fas est dici civitas dum nullo murorum ambitu circumdatur*.

44 Dieser Begriff taucht in der Frühzeit nur einmal in einer Bezeichnung für ein Kloster auf: Monasterboice, ir. *Mainistir Buithe*. Die geographische Lage in der Nähe der Ostküste Irlands macht hier einen Einfluß aus dem benachbarten Britannien sehr wahrscheinlich.

6. Jahrhundert in den Händen wichtiger Adelsfamilien; die Äbte von Iona z. B. stammten im 7. Jahrhundert mit einer Ausnahme alle aus der Familie Colum Cilles, die ihrerseits mit dem Königsgeschlecht der Uí Néill verwandt war. Die Unterstützung durch die Uí Néill stärkte die Bedeutung der *paruchia* von Iona. Im Lauf der Zeit unterstellten sich auch Kirchen, die nicht von Colum Cille gegründet worden waren, dem Abt von Iona und schlossen sich der *paruchia* an. Es gab mehrere derartige *paruchiae* im frühmittelalterlichen Irland. Sie griffen über die Einflußbereiche der irischen Königreiche hinaus und schufen überregionale Verbindungen, die später auch politische Bedeutung haben sollten.

Besonderheiten der irischen Kirche zeigen sich ferner in dem beträchtlichen Einfluß des weltlichen irischen Rechts auf die Kirche. Es wird noch Jahrzehnte dauern, bis dieser Einfluß voll ausgelotet werden kann. Erst 1978 publizierte D. A. Binchy die diplomatische Edition des Corpus Iuris Hibernici. Seine Auswertung steckt noch in den Anfängen. Die irischen Rechtstexte sind größtenteils in archaischer Sprache verfaßt und waren wohl schon zur Zeit ihrer Niederschrift weitgehend antiquiert. Doch die Tatsache, daß das irische Recht als „heilig" galt, daß die irischen Rechtsgelehrten eine geachtete soziale Stellung innehatten, die während des gesamten Mittelalters ungeschmälert blieb, zeigt das fortdauernde Prestige des irischen weltlichen Rechts.

Es wird erwogen, ob die Aufzeichnung des irischen weltlichen Rechts im ausgehenden 7. und beginnenden 8. Jahrhundert unter kirchlichem Einfluß geschah. Formal schlägt sich dieser Einfluß in der Benutzung von Prosa nieder; Rechtstexte mit längeren Passagen in Versform gelten als besonders archaisch. Inhaltlich ist der Einfluß des Christentums im irischen Recht als gering zu veranschlagen[45].

Anders steht es um den Einfluß des irischen weltlichen Rechts auf die irische Christenheit. Es manifestiert sich besonders deutlich in der extremen Systematisierung der irischen Bußbücher. Es ist auch im irischen Kirchenrecht als hoch zu veranschlagen[46]. Eine eingehende Würdigung dessen kann allerdings noch nicht vorgenommen werden, solange die geplante Neuedition der Collectio Canonum Hibernensis nicht vorliegt. Ihre Fertigstellung wird vor allem dadurch verzögert, daß die Erforschung des irischen weltlichen Rechts noch in den Anfängen steckt. In der Hib. interessieren vor allem die Abschnitte, die spezifisch irische Probleme behandeln. Wenn die Hib., wie allgemein angenommen wird, im frühen 8. Jahrhundert zusammengestellt wurde, bieten die Aussagen über irische Verhältnisse, vornehmlich unter den Rubriken *Sinodus Patricii, Sinodus Romanorum* und *Sinodus Hibernensis* den besten Zugang zu den Problemen, die in der irischen Kirche zwischen dem 5. und frühen 8. Jahrhundert akut waren. Vorläufig muß man sich mit solchen Impressionen zufrieden geben. Vielleicht können sie eines Tages in einen chronologischen Rahmen gesetzt werden; dann würde unser Wissen um die frühe irische Kirche beträchtlich vertieft werden.

---

45 Gearóid *Mac Niocaill*, Christian Influences in early Irish Law, in diesem Band.
46 Donnchadh *Ó Corráin*, Irish Law and Canon Law, in diesem Band.

Universale Aspekte der frühen irischen Kirche

Wenn den Eigenheiten der frühen irischen Kirche großes Interesse entgegengebracht wird, wie auf dem Kolloquium, aber auch generell in der Forschung[46a], so dürfen die universalen Aspekte doch nicht völlig in den Hintergrund gedrängt werden. Damit ist gemeint, daß die frühe irische Kirche trotz einiger regionaler oder nationaler Eigenheiten als Teil der allgemeinen Kirche verstanden wurde, und zwar in Irland und außerhalb, und daß sie auch dem modernen Betrachter als solche erscheint. Am deutlichsten wird diese Tatsache von Columban ausgesprochen:

> De caetero, patres, orate pro nobis sicut et nos facimus, viles licet, pro vobis, et nolite nos a vobis alienos reputare; unius enim sumus corporis commembra, sive Galli, sive Britanni, sive Iberi, sive quaeque gentes[47].

In diesem Satz scheinen vor allem zwei Elemente auf: die Vermutung einiger Christen außerhalb Irlands, daß die irischen Christen teilweise eigene Wege gegangen seien, und die Auffassung Columbans, das einigende Band der christlichen Religion überwölbe nationale Grenzen.

Daß es zu Besonderheiten in der irischen Kirche gekommen war, haben wir bereits angeschnitten. Sie sind teilweise durch die politische Entwicklung Europas in jener Zeit zu erklären, als mit dem Zusammenbruch des römischen Westreiches die Kontakte Irlands mit Rom vorübergehend schwächer wurden. Vor allem Britannien und Gallien waren von germanischen Völkern in Besitz genommen worden, teilweise zwar nur, aber doch mit für Irland spürbaren Auswirkungen. Seit dem ausgehenden 6. Jahrhundert wurden die Kontakte Irlands mit Rom wieder stärker. Columban ist ein Zeuge dafür. Andere Hinweise darauf, auch wenn sie sich nicht personalisieren lassen, wurden an anderer Stelle erwähnt, die weitere Verbreitung des Vulgata-Texts der Bibel sowie die größere Verbreitung von Schriften lateinischer Kirchenväter, die sich in Neuerungen in der Exegese niederschlugen[48].

Besondere Bedeutung wird im allgemeinen den unterschiedlichen Traditonen bei der Berechnung des Osterfestes in Irland und auf dem Kontinent beigemessen. In dieser Frage üben bis heute die Schriften Bedas einen unverhältnismäßig großen Einfluß aus; vor allem die Historia Ecclesiastica Gentis Anglorum wird weitgehend von der römisch-irischen Kontroverse in der Osterfrage beherrscht. Viel weniger wird zur Kenntnis genommen, wie bereitwillig große Teile der irischen

---

46a Vg. dazu neuestens Monastic Studies 14 (1983), mit dem Thema „Celtic Monasticism". In diesem Band werden einige Themen weitergeführt, die auf dem Dubliner Kolloquium 1981 angeschnitten wurden.

47 Sancti Columbani Opera, ed. G. S. M. Walker, SLH 2 (1970), Ep. 2, S. 22.

48 Pádraig Ó Néill, Romani Influences on Seventh-Century Hiberno-Latin Literature; Martin McNamara, Tradition and literary creativity in early Irish psalm-exegesis, beide in diesem Band.

Kirche die römische Osterfestberechnung übernahmen, sobald sich die Gelegenheit dazu bot. Um 630 geschah das in der südlichen Hälfte Irlands (*Leth Moga*), scheint aber auch weiter in den Norden vorgedrungen zu sein[49]. Von besonderer Bedeutung in dieser Frage ist der Brief Cummeans *De controversia Paschali* (um 632), in dem er die Annahme des römischen Ostertermins verkündet. Zudem bringt er in diesem Schreiben seine besondere Hochschätzung für Papst Gregor I. ungewöhnlich klar zum Ausdruck, zu einer Zeit, als in der englischen Kirche noch keine Rede von einer Gregor-Verehrung war:

> *Ad Gregorii papae, urbis Romae episcopi (a nobis in commune suscepti, et oris aurei appellatione donati) verba me converti; qui etsi post omnes scripsit, tamen est merito omnibus praeferendus*[50].

Die Anlehnung vieler irischer Christen an Rom wurde so stark, daß diese von einigen Zeitgenossen geradezu als *Romani* bezeichnet wurden. Sie waren weitgehend für die Modernisierung der irischen Kirche im 7. Jahrhundert verantwortlich; ihre Gegenspieler, Traditionalisten, wenn man so will, werden in der Collectio Canonum Hibernensis als *Hibernenses* bezeichnet. Deutlich ist römischer Einfluß auch in Armagh zu erkennen, als im ausgehenden 7. Jahrhundert der Bischof von Armagh versuchte, seinen Bischofssitz als „Rom Irlands" zu etablieren, als das Zentrum einer bischöflich organisierten Kirche. Dieses im *Liber Angeli*, einem im Book of Armagh erhaltenen Traktat ausgedrückte Bestreben stützte sich in erster Linie auf Patrick als Bischof. Das Book of Armagh stammt aus dem frühen 9. Jahrhundert, aber der *Liber Angeli* ist älter. Eine Voraussetzung für die dort aufgeführten Ansprüche war eine gute Kenntnis römischer Verhältnisse und die Annahme, daß sie auf Irland übertragbar seien. Diese Annahme erwies sich als verfehlt, aber im *Liber Angeli* zeigt sich sehr deutlich eine Orientierung einflußreicher Kreise in der irischen Kirche am römischen Vorbild[51]. Als in Iona schließlich um 716 der römische Ostertermin angenommen wurde, offenbar unter maßgeblichem Einfluß des Engländers Ecgbert, war in dieser Frage die gesamte irische Kirche „römisch" geworden.

„Römisch" wurde die irische Kirche auch zunehmend in ihrer Hochschätzung von Reliquien, wobei denen aus Rom besondere Verehrung entgegengebracht wurde. Kontinentalen Einfluß erkennt man ferner in der Übernahme des Begriffs *basilica*. In der Collectio Canonum Hibernensis wird dieser Begriff irrtümlich als Kirche eines *basileus* gedeutet (Hib. XLIV, 20); hier erkennt man den Einfluß der in Irland beliebten Etymologien des Isidor von Sevilla. *Basilica* erscheint gelegentlich, freilich selten, in Ortsnamen (Baslick, Co. Roscommon). Es wird in Erwägung gezogen, ob dieser Begriff generell in Irland nach römischem Vorbild für solch

---

49 *Sharpe* (wie oben Anm. 14).
50 PL 87, 975. Um 630 scheint auch Gregors *Cura Pastoralis* nach Irland gelangt zu sein, vgl. *Brown* (wie oben Anm. 12), S. 313.
51 *Sharpe* (wie oben Anm. 14).

bedeutende Kirchen (Kildare, Armagh) benutzt wurde, die kontinentale Reliquien, vornehmlich aus Rom, erhalten hatten[52].

Zusammenfassend läßt sich sagen, daß die Initiative für eine verstärkte Anlehnung an Rom und an andere kontinentale Kirchen in Irland im 7. und 8. Jahrhundert aus Irland selbst kam. Römische Einflüsse wurden auf längere Sicht wirksam; das verdient, eigens unterstrichen zu werden, gerade angesichts der Tatsache, daß diese römischen Einflüsse nicht in allen Bereichen durchsetzbar waren. Man darf die frühe irische Kirche nicht als monolithisch betrachten; man muß zur Kenntnis nehmen, daß eine spürbare Orientierung an Rom auch in nachpatricianischer Zeit erkennbar ist. Die frühe irische Kirche war nicht wesentlich romfremd eingestellt, nur erwies sich das römische Modell in mancher Hinsicht als für Irland ungeeignet.

Universale Aspekte der frühen irischen Kirche zeigen sich auch in ihrer Ausstrahlung auf die benachbarten Gebiete. Bekannt, wenn auch bis heute in Einzelheiten umstritten, ist der Einfluß irischer Missionare bei den Angelsachsen seit 635, der wirksam wurde, wo die römischen Missionare gescheitert waren. Die irische Mission in Northumbrien hat eine lange Vorgeschichte und eine recht lange Nachwirkung, die beide nicht genügend in das allgemeine Bewußtsein eingedrungen sind.

Die Vorgeschichte bildet die militärische Expansion der Iren (der *Scoti* bei Gildas) nach Britannien, in das Land der Pikten im Norden sowie in das Land der Briten (Waliser) im Westen. Aus militärischen Eingriffen wurden allmählich dauerhafte Siedlungen, wurde die Errichtung irischer Herrschaften, in Wales und im Land der Pikten, das durch diese Herrschaften zum Land der *Scoti*, zu Schottland, wurde. Die militärischen Auseinandersetzungen der *Scoti* in Britannien mit Briten und Angelsachsen sind quellenmäßig noch schlechter faßbar als das gleichzeitige Vordringen germanischer Stämme nach Britannien vom Osten her. Diese Auseinandersetzungen harren einer ausführlichen neuen Untersuchung. Aber so viel ist schon jetzt klar, daß diese Kontakte die kulturellen Austauschbeziehungen zwischen Irland und Britannien erheblich förderten. Man erkennt das deutlich zu Beginn des nachhaltigen Einflusses irischer Christen in England seit 635. Die Einladung Oswalds von Northumbrien an Bischof Aidan von Iona kam zustande, weil Oswald vor seiner Herrschaftsübernahme längere Zeit in Iona im Exil gelebt hatte[52a]. Der Erfolg der irischen Mission in England beruhte hauptsächlich darauf, daß die Gesellschaftsstruktur der Angelsachsen der Gesellschaftsstruktur der Iren so ähnlich war, daß das in Irland inzwischen bewährte Kirchenmodell ohne größere Änderungen nach England übertragen werden konnte. So viel zur Vorgeschichte.

52 *Doherty* (wie oben Anm. 4), S. 92.
52a Vgl. Hermann *Moisl*, The Bernician royal dynasty and the Irish in the seventh century, Peritia 2 (1983), S. 103—126.

Die Langzeitwirkung irischen Einflusses in England zeigt sich daran, daß es inzwischen Allgemeingut in der wissenschaftlichen Literatur geworden ist, Irland und Northumbrien im 7. und 8. Jahrhundert als *eine* Kulturprovinz zu betrachten. Bei vielen Handschriften aus jener Zeit läßt sich nicht entscheiden, ob sie in Irland oder in Northumbrien ausgeführt wurden. Schriftform und Illumination waren in beiden Gebieten gleich. Hinzuweisen ist ferner auf die Sprache, das insulare Latein. Zwar werden die irischen Einflüsse auf die Ausgestaltung insularer Latinität bis heute unterschiedlich beurteilt[53], aber die northumbrische „Blütezeit" ist damit nicht in Frage gestellt. Es sei hinzugefügt, daß diese „Blütezeit", zweifelsohne unter beträchtlichem irischem Einfluß zustande gekommen, von Irland aus betrachtet weniger prachtvoll erscheint als vom kontinentalen Standpunkt. Es gilt ferner daran zu erinnern, daß in der Zeit, als Beda in seinem Brief an Bischof Egbert von York den Niedergang der christlichen Religion in seinem Land beklagte, in Irland die Reformbewegung der *Céli Dé* im Gang war und in den folgenden Jahrzehnten große Fortschritte machte, eine Reform, die sich besonders in geistlicher Literatur in der Volkssprache niederschlug[54], etwas, was auch Beda gegen Ende seines Lebens nachhaltig gefördert hatte. Wieder war Irland dem englischen Nachbarn um einige Schritte voraus.

Noch etwas anderes verdient Erwägung. Die frühe englische Kirche ist bekannt für ihre enge Anlehnung an Rom, eine Haltung, die durch das Wirken des heiligen Bonifatius auf dem Festland in der ersten Hälfte des 8. Jahrhunderts zur christlichen Grundlegung Europas erheblich beitragen sollte. Es ist denkbar, daß diese Romverbundenheit der englischen Kirche letztlich durch irische Christen in England verstärkt, wenn nicht gar initiiert, wurde. In England ist die Hochschätzung für Gregor den Großen, der in Rom während des 7. Jahrhunderts offenbar wenig Achtung gefunden hatte[55], erst seit dem frühen 8. Jahrhundert bezeugt. Dort erscheint sie in der ältesten bekannten Biographie Gregors, die wahrscheinlich in Whitby im frühen 8. Jahrhundert geschrieben wurde[56], und danach vor allem in der Kirchengeschichte Bedas. Man erinnere sich an die große Verehrung für Gregor in Irland, wie Cummean sie bezeugt[57]. Der irische Einfluß in Northumbrien im allgemeinen und in Whitby im besonderen wird von Beda eindrucksvoll geschildert. Es ist nun sehr wahrscheinlich, daß Northumbrien auch nach der Synode von Whitby irischem Einfluß ausgesetzt blieb; die letzten Schwierigkei-

53 *Lapidge, Winterbottom* (wie oben Anm. 24), sowie J.-M. *Picard,* Une préfiguration du latin carolingien: la syntaxe de la *Vita Columbae* d'Adomnán, auteur irlandais du VIIe siècle, Romanobarbarica 6 (1981—82), S. 235—83, sowie *ders.,* The metrical prose of Adomnán's *Vita Columbae:* an unusual system, in diesem Band.

54 *O'Dwyer* (wie oben Anm. 29).

55 Vgl. etwa P. B. A. *Llewellyn,* The Roman Church in the Seventh Century: the Legacy of Gregory I, Journal of Ecclesiastical History 25 (1974), S. 363—380.

56 The earliest Life of Gregory the Great. By an anonymous Monk of Whitby, ed. Bertram *Colgrave,* Laurence, Kansas 1968.

57 Vgl. oben bei Anm. 50.

ten waren beseitigt, als schließlich auch Iona zur römischen Osterfestberechnung überging[58]. So hat es ganz den Anschein, als ob nicht der Osterstreit, sondern erst die Wikingereinfälle im ausgehenden 8. Jahrhundert die irisch-northumbrischen Verbindungen entscheidend schwächten.

Northumbrien und Rom waren zwei augenfällige Kontaktstellen für die irischen Christen jener Zeit. Wie stark Gallien einbezogen war, ist noch keineswegs endgültig geklärt. Aber Irlands Verbindungen reichten über Westeuropa hinaus. In Erzeugnissen irischer Kunst aus der Zeit zwischen dem 7. und dem 9. Jahrhundert machen sich Einflüsse auch aus dem östlichen Mittelmeerraum bemerkbar, in den prächtigen Kelchen von Ardagh und Derrynavlan vor allem aus dem byzantinischen Raum[59], in der frühen Dekoration der Handschriften aus Ägypten[60], in den Hochkreuzen aus den Ländern um das Kaspische Meer[61]. Hier zeigt sich deutlich die internationale Komponente des Christentums, die, wie bereits erwähnt, von Iren seit dem ausgehenden 6. Jahrhundert empfunden worden war. Die irische Kirche war in mancher Beziehung provinziell, vielleicht sogar antiquiert, aber in anderen Beziehungen war sie überraschend aufgeschlossen und dynamisch. Eine gerechte Beurteilung der Rolle der frühen irischen Kirche im europäischen Rahmen muß alle diese Eigenschaften würdigen, denn alle sind symptomatisch.

Ergebnis

Nach diesen Ausführungen ist es deutlich geworden, daß eine abschließende Würdigung der frühen irischen Kirche noch nicht möglich ist. Im Gegenteil, die Forschung scheint an einem Zwischenziel angekommen zu sein. Es gilt, die schwerpunktmäßige Arbeit fortzusetzen[62], den interdisziplinären Arbeitsansatz weiter zu fördern und Forschungsvorhaben auf internationaler Ebene zu koordinieren. Die Bedeutung der frühen irischen Kirche, und damit auch die Bedeutung der frühen irischen Gesellschaft für die Ausgestaltung der europäischen Zivilisation im Mittelalter rechtfertigt solch ehrgeizige Vorhaben.

58 Michael *Richter*, Der irische Hintergrund der angelsächsischen Mission, in *Löwe*, Iren, bes. S. 135 f.

59 Michael *Ryan*, The Derrynaflan and other early Irish Ecclesiastical Chalices: Some Speculations, in diesem Band. Die Herausgeber des vorliegenden Bandes befürworten die Schreibung Derrynavlan, vgl. Próinséas *Ní Chatháin*, Éigse 18 (1981), S. 210.

60 Man denke besonders an den *Cathach* Colum Cilles; zu beachten sind aber die von *Brown* (wie oben Anm. 12) S. 326 angedeuteten Modifikationen dieser Deutung. Weniger gewichtig scheinen die Einwände von *James* (wie oben Anm. 5), S. 385 zu sein.

61 Hilary *Richardson*, The Concept of the High Cross, in diesem Band, besonders in den Abbildungen.

62 Geplant ist ein weiteres internationales Kolloquium über Irland und Europa im früheren Mittelalter für 1984 mit dem Generalthema: Glaubensinhalte und Glaubensvermittlung in den nicht-romanischen Ländern zwischen 550 und 800.

Sie haben freilich letztlich nur dann Aussicht auf Erfolg, sie versprechen nur dann Fortschritt in wissenschaftlicher Arbeit, wenn das Thema genügend Interesse findet. In dieser Hinsicht braucht man wohl aber für Irland im früheren Mittelalter wenig Bedenken zu haben. Denn die Persönlichkeiten, die zur Entwicklung der frühen irischen Kirche beigetragen haben, treten auch noch nach Jahrhunderten und durch das enge Filter der schriftlichen Quellen als lebendige und vielschichtige Gestalten hervor. Patrick, Colum Cille, Columbanus, Máelrúain und andere faszinieren noch heute. Sie verkörpern zeitlose Wünsche und Ziele des Menschen. Die irische Spiritualität, die in Predigten, Briefen, Regeln, Gebeten und Gedichten in Erscheinung tritt, ist vielseitig und anregend. Irische geistliche Dichter mögen früher oder stärker als anderswo persönliche, manchmal sogar vertraute Zwiesprache mit Gott gehalten haben[63], die im internationalen Vergleich ihrer Zeit voraus war, die aber deutlich den engen zwischenmenschlichen Beziehungen in einem Land entsprang; sie mögen früh und stark eine Verehrung für Rom an den Tag gelegt haben, die vielleicht teilweise durch die Unkenntnis der lokalen Verhältnisse geprägt war; sie mögen früher als andere den Europagedanken artikuliert haben, was immer darunter zu verstehen ist. Sie waren die ersten Förderer des Marienkultes in Westeuropa. In den Hochkreuzen erstellten sie die ersten Monumentalskulpturen im nachantiken Europa[64].

Das sind in der Rückschau beträchtliche Leistungen im internationalen Vergleich. Für die Zeitgenossen mochten sie als Ausdruck der Tiefe des Christentums gelten, die sich vielerorts in Irland zeigte. Wie es zu solchen Leistungen kam, wird sich letztendlich wohl nicht voll erfassen lassen. Es ist möglich, daß das irische Christentum so dynamisch wurde, weil es sich in Irland gegen eine bereits bestehende geistige Elite bewähren mußte, und es ist möglich, daß der Nachhall des Christentums in Irland begrenzt blieb[65]. Aber dem Außenstehenden erschienen damals und erscheinen heute irische Christen im Vergleich zu anderen äußerst gewinnend. Sie entbehren in vieler Hinsicht die strenge Disziplin Roms, sind dadurch schwieriger zu erfassen. Aber dieses Fehlen von Disziplin und Konformität machte es für irische Christen wahrscheinlich leichter, komplexe Persönlichkeiten zu bleiben.

63 Vgl. die Bemerkungen von *Ó Laoghaire* (wie oben Anm. 29) über Gott als König im irischen Gesellschaftssystem, S. 80, sowie das Gedicht über das „Jesulein" (*Ísucán*), hg. E. G. *Quin*, Cambridge Medieval Celtic Studies 1 (1981), S. 39—52.

64 *Richardson* (wie oben Anm. 61).

65 Michael *Richter*, Irland im Mittelalter — Kultur und Geschichte, Stuttgart 1983, passim.

Verzeichnis der Tafeln / List of Plates

1 Clonmacnois from the South Cross, looking north-west to the Round Tower. The Cross of the Scriptures stands in line with the Round Tower

2a Monasterboice, Louth: cap of Muiredach's Cross

2b Durrow, Offaly: high cross cap

2c Clones, Monaghan: 'sarcophagus' from south-east

3a White Island, Fermanagh: excavation in south-east corner of church showing steeper trenches for timber structure of several phases

3b Derry churches, Down: excavation in south-east corner of south church showing south wall of standing ruin (right) separated by earth from earlier stone wall, with ranging pole in socket for wooden post

4a St John's Point, Down: church from south-west

4b St John's Point, Down: excavation under north wall of church showing stone-built grave running under wall

5a Tullaherin, Kilkenny: *anta* at north-east corner of original church (right) with added chancel (left)

5b Clonmacnois, Offaly: Temple Doolin, original east wall built into later stonework

5c Inishmacsaint, Fermanagh: west wall of early church. Position of original west door marked by change in masonry and break in foundation offset

6 Devenish, Fermanagh: imaginary reconstruction of the early, all-wood monastery

7 Cross of Muiredach, Monasterboice, Co.Louth. East face

8a Cross of Muiredach, cross head, east side

8b Bottom panel of east side of shaft. The Fall; Cain and Abel

9 North Cross, Ahenny, Co. Tipperary

10a Detail of apse mosaic, S. Pudenziana, Rome, ca. 400

10b Mosaic cross, apse, S. Apollinaire in Classe, Ravenna. 6th century

11 The Rupert Cross. Dom Museum, Salzburg

12a Map of Jerusalem from the Madaba mosaic, Jordan. 6th century

12b Lid of small wooden reliquary box from Palestine, ca. 600. Top left, The Holy Women at the Tomb. Museo Cristiano, Vatican

13a Sketch of the Church of the Holy Sepulchre and its surroundings. Adomnán's *De Locis Sanctis*

13b Ivory Book-cover, Narbonne Cathedral Treasury. Early 9th century

14a Presentation in the Temple, Armenian Gospels of 1655. Chester Beatty 578

14b Gravestone from Georgia, near Uplis Tsikhe

14c Marginal detail of the Temple of Jerusalem, Four Gospels of 1262, fol. 362r, Walters 539

15 Mtskheta, Sveti-Tskhoveli Cathedral, 1010—1029. From the north-west, showing miniature domed buildings

16   Crosses at Kilkieran, Co. Kilkenny. Lithograph

17a Edsani Sion, relief in east wall, mid-6th century

17b Brdadzor, tall stele

18a Decorated cross, Kilkieran

18b The Descent of the Holy Ghost, Four Gospels of 1262, illustrated by T'oros Roslin. Walters 539, fol. 379r

18c The Forty Martyrs of Sebastia, Armenian Hymnal of 1635, marginal drawing fol. 77r. Chester Beatty 593 (with inset outline drawing of detail)

19   Khandisi, 6th cent. stele, west, south, east and north faces

20a Brdadzor, detail of shaft

20b Khandisi, detail of top, west face. Christ enthroned

21   Kachagani cross, first half of 7th century

22   Pantiani, Base, 6th century, with Exaltation of the Cross

23a Sveti-Tskhoveli from N.W. with Djvari on the height above, on the far side of the Aragvi river

23b Djvari, south façade

24a Djvari, south doorway

24b Djvari, lintel with Christ in a medallion

25   North Cross, Ahenny, Co. Tipperary, east side

26a The Derrynaflan chalice (before cleaning)

26b The Derrynaflan chalice (before cleaning), side view showing handle and handle escutcheons

27a The Ardagh silver chalice (height 17.8 cm., diameter of bowl 23.1 cm.)

27b The Ardagh bronze chalice (height now 10 cm., diameter of bowl 13 cm.)

28a The Trewhiddle chalice (after Wilson and Blunt) (height 12.7 cm., diameter of bowl 11.4 cm.)

28b The Hexham chalice (after Wilson and Blunt) (height 6.5 cm., diameter of bowl 6.2 cm.)

Plate 1: Clonmacnois from the South Cross, looking north-west to the Round Tower. The Cross of the Scriptures stands in line with the Round Tower

Plate 2a: Monasterboice, Louth: cap of Muiredach's Cross. Photo by Seán Goddard

Plate 2b: Durrow, Offaly: high cross cap. Photo by Seán Goddard

Plate 2c: Clones, Monaghan: 'sarcophagus' from south-east. Photo by A. E. P. Collins (Crown Copyright)

Plate 3a: White Island, Fermanagh: excavation in south-east corner of church showing steeper trenches for timber structure of several phases. Photo by A. E. P. Collins (Crown Copyright)

Plate 3b: Derry churches, Down: excavation in south-east corner of south church showing south wall of standing ruin (right) separated by earth from earlier stone wall, with ranging pole in socket for wooden post. Photo by A. E. P. Collins (Crown Copyright)

Plate 4a: St John's Point, Down: church from south-west. Photo by Ann Hamlin

Plate 4b: St John's Point, Down: excavation under north wall of church showing stone-built grave running under wall. Photo by N. F. Brannon (Crown Copyright)

Plate 5a: Tullaherin, Kilkenny: *anta* at northeast corner of original church (right) with added chancel (left). Photo by Seán Goddard

Plate 5b: Clonmacnois, Offaly: Temple Doolin, original east wall built into later stonework. Photo by Seán Goddard

Plate 5c: Inishmacsaint, Fermanagh: west wall of early church. Position of original west door marked by change in masonry and break in foundation offset. Photo by Ann Hamlin

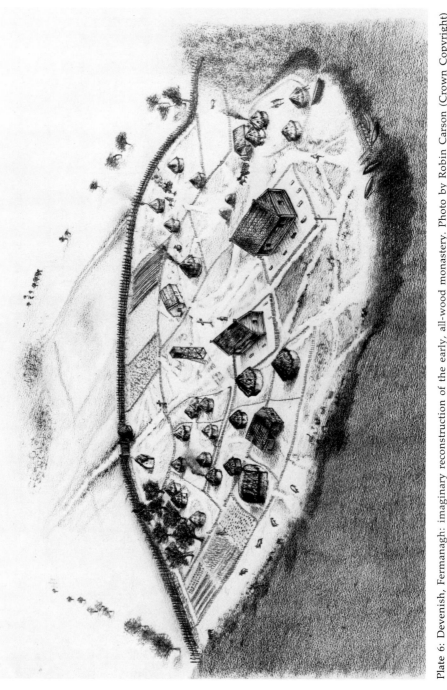

Plate 6: Devenish, Fermanagh: imaginary reconstruction of the early, all-wood monastery. Photo by Robin Carson (Crown Copyright)

Plate 7: Cross of Muiredach, Monasterboice, Co. Louth. East face. Photo Arch.

Plate 8a (left): Cross of Muiredach, cross head, east side
Plate 8b (below): Bottom panel of east side of shaft. The Fall; Cain and Abel. Photo Arch.

Plate 9: North Cross, Ahenny, Co.Tipperary. Photo N.M.

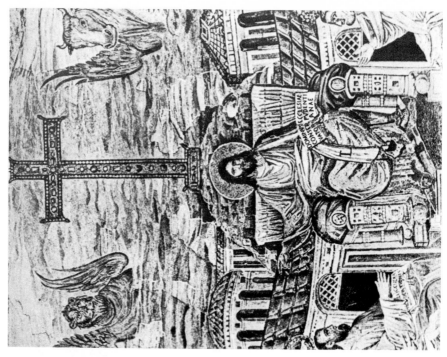

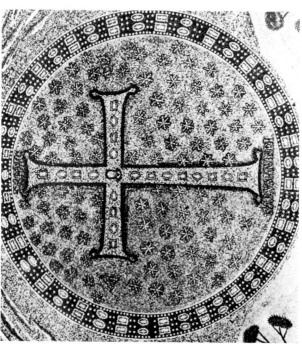

Plate 10a (right): Detail of apse mosaic, S. Pudenziana, Rome, ca. 400
Plate 10b (above): Mosaic cross, apse, S. Apollinaire in Classe, Ravenna. 6th cent. From Van der Meer and Mohrmann

Plate 11: The Rupert Cross. Dom Museum, Salzburg. Photo Bundesdenkmalamt

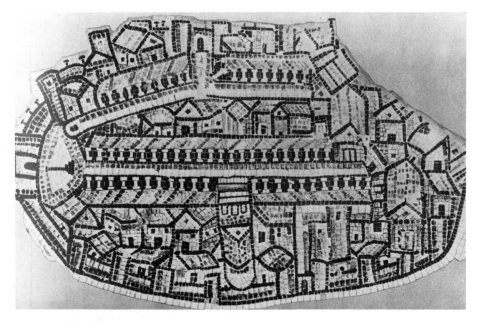

Plate 12a (above): Map of Jerusalem from the Madaba mosaic, Jordan. 6th cent.

Plate 12b (left): Lid of small wooden reliquary box from Palestine, ca. 600. Top left, The Holy Women at the Tomb. Museo Cristiano, Vatican. From Van der Meer and Mohrmann

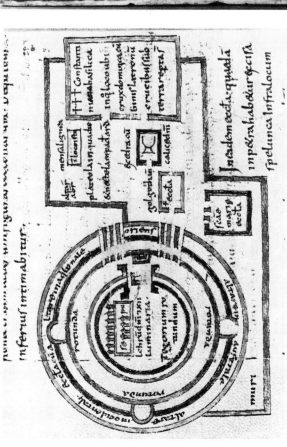

Plate 13a (above): Sketch of the Church of the Holy Sepulchre and its surroundings.
Adomnán's De Locis Sanctis. Vienna Cod.458, fol.4v. Photo National Library, Vienna
Plate 13b (right): Ivory Book-cover, Narbonne Cathedral Treasury. Early 9th cent.
From Treasures of the Churches of France

Plate 14c: Marginal detail of the Temple of Jerusalem, Four Gospels of 1262, fol.362r, Walters 539. Photo Walters Art Gallery, Baltimore

Plate 14b: Gravestone from Georgia, near Uplis Tsikhe. Photo Arch.

Plate 14a: Presentation in the Temple, Armenian Gospels of 1655. Chester Beatty 578

Plate 15: Mtskheta, Sveti-Tskhoveli Cathedral, 1010–1029. From the north-west, showing miniature domed buildings. Photo Arch.

Plate 16: Crosses at Kilkieran, Co.Kilkenny. Lithograph by Henry O'Neill

Plate 17a: Edsani Sion, relief in east wall, mid 6th cent. From Chubinashvili

Plate 17b: Brdadzor, tall stele. Photo State Mus. of Georgian Art, Tbilisi

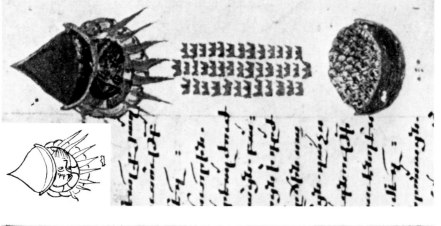

Plate 18c: The Forty Martyrs of Sebastia, Armenian Hymnal of 1635, marginal drawing fol.77r. Chester Beatty 593 (with inset outline drawing of detail)

Plate 18b: The Descent of the Holy Ghost, Four Gospels of 1262, illustrated by T'oros Roslin. Walters 539, fol.379r. Photo Walters Art Gallery, Baltimore

Plate 18a: Decorated cross, Kilkieran. Photo N.M.

Plate 19: Khandisi, 6th cent. stele, west, south, east and north faces. From Chubinashvili

Plate 20b: Khandisi, detail of top, west face. Christ enthroned. From Chubinashvili

Plate 20a: Brdadzor, detail of shaft. Photo Arch.

Plate 21: Kachagani cross, first half of 7th cent. From Aladashvili

Plate 22: Pantiani, Base, 6th cent., with Exaltation of the Cross. From Chubinashvili

Plate 23a: Sveti-Tskhoveli from the N.W. with Djvari on the height above, on the far side of the Aragvi river. From Mepishashvili and Tsintsadze

Plate 23b: Djvari, south façade. From Aladashvili

Plate 24a: Djvari, south doorway. Photo Arch.

Plate 24b: Djvari, lintel with Christ in a medallion. From Aladashvili

Plate 25: North Cross, Ahenny, Co.Tipperary, east side. Photo Arch.

Plate 26a: The Derrynaflan chalice (before cleaning)

Plate 26b: The Derrynaflan chalice (before cleaning), side view showing handle and handle escutcheons

Plate 27a: The Ardagh silver chalice (height 17.8 cm., diameter of bowl 23.1 cm.)

Plate 27b: The Ardagh bronze chalice (height now 10 cm., diameter of bowl 13 cm.)

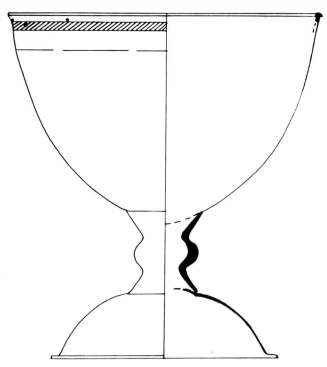

Plate 28a: The Trewhiddle chalice (after Wilson and Blunt) (height 12.7 cm., diameter of bowl 11.4 cm.)

Plate 28b: The Hexham chalice (after Wilson and Blunt) (height 6.5 cm., diameter of bowl 6.2 cm.)

Abkürzungen und Siglen / Abbreviations and Sigla

AA SS	Acta Sanctorum
AB	Analecta Bollandiana
Abh.	Abhandlungen der … Akademie der Wissenschaften, philosophisch-historische Klasse
AFM	Annals of the Four Masters
ags.	angelsächsisch
ahdt.	althochdeutsch
AI	Annals of Inisfallen
ALI	Ancient Laws of Ireland
Arch. Hib.	Archivium Hibernicum
as.	altsächsisch
AU	Annals of Ulster
Aug.	Augustinianum
BBCS	Bulletin of the Board of Celtic Studies
BL	British Library, London
BN	Bibliothèque Nationale, Paris
BP	Bethu Phátraic
ca.	circa
CCSG	Corpus Christianorum, Series Graeca, Turnhout-Leuven
CCSL	Corpus Christianorum, Series Latina, Turnhout-Leuven
CEIS	The Church in early Irish Society, K. *Hughes*
cf.	confer (compare)
CHB	The Cambridge History of the Bible
CIH	Corpus Iuris Hibernici, ed. D. A. *Binchy*, Dublin 1978
CLA	Codices Latini Antiquiores, ed. *Lowe*
Co.	County
CS	Chronicon Scotorum
CSEL	Corpus Scriptorum Ecclesiasticorum Latinorum, Wien
DA	Deutsches Archiv
DIL	Dictionary of the Irish Language, Dublin 1913—1976
EC	Êtudes Celtiques
ed.	editor(s), edited
EHR	English Historical Review
EIHM	Early Irish History and Mythology, *O'Rahilly*
fig.	figure(s)
FMSt.	Frühmittelalterliche Studien
fol.	folio(s)
germ.	germanisch
got.	gotisch
HBS	Henry Bradshaw Society, London

HE	Historia Ecclesiastica Gentis Anglorum, Beda
Hg., hg.	Herausgeber, herausgegeben von
Hib.	Collectio Canonum Hibernensis
HThR	Harvard Theological Review
HZ	Historische Zeitschrift
IER	Irish Ecclesiastical Record
Ir./ir.	Irish, irisch
ITS	Irish Texts Society, Dublin
JCHAS	Journal of the Cork Historical and Archaeological Society
JL	Jaffé-Löwenfeld, Regesta Ponificum Romanorum
JRSAI	Journal of the Royal Society of Antiquaries of Ireland
Kenney, Sources	The Sources for the early History of Ireland. I. Ecclesiastical. An Introduction and Guide, J. F. *Kenney*, rev. ed. Dublin 1961
leg.	lege
LHEB	Language and History in Early Britain, *Jackson*
Löwe, Iren	H. *Löwe*, ed., Die Iren und Europa im früheren Mittelalter, 2 Bände, Stuttgart 1982
LU	Lebor na hUidre
MGH	Monumenta Germaniae Historica
AA	— Auctores Antiquissimi
Epp.	— Epistolae
Necr.	— Necrologiae
SS rer. Germ.	— Scriptores rerum Germanicarum in usum scholarum separatim editi
SS rer. Merov.	— Scriptores rerum Merovingicarum
Ml.	Milan (glosses)
MS, MSS	manuscript(s)
OIr.	Old Irish
OS	Ordnance Survey
PBA	Proceedings of the British Academy
PG	Patrologia Graeca, *Migne*
PL	Patrologia Latina, *Migne*
Pl.	Plate(s)
PRIA	Proceedings of the Royal Irish Academy
Ps(s)	psalm(s)
RBen.	Revue Rénédictine
RC	Revue Celtique
Reg. Pont.	Regesta Pontificum Romanorum
RS	Rolls Series (Rerum Britannicarum Medii Aevi Scriptores), London
RSR	Revue de Sciences Religieuses
RThAM	Recherches de Théologie ancienne et médiévale
SC	Sources Chrétiennes, Paris

SEIL	Studies in Early Irish Law, Dublin 1936
Sg.	St. Gallen, St Gall (glosses)
SHR	Scottish Historical Review
SILH	Studies in Irish Literature and History, *Carney*
SLH	Scriptores Latini Hiberniae, Dublin
St	Saint
StMGBO	Studien und Mitteilungen zur Geschichte des Benediktiner-Ordens und seiner Zweige
Stud. Celt.	Studia Celtica
Stud. Hib.	Studia Hibernica
Stud. Patr.	Studia Patristica, Berlin
Thes.	Thesaurus Palaeohibernicus, *Stokes, Strachan*
Tig.	Annals of Tigernach
Tír.	Tírechán
VL	Vetus Latina
VSH	Vitae Sanctorum Hiberniae, *Plummer*
Wb.	Würzburg (glosses)
ZCP	Zeitschrift für celtische Philologie
ZfdA	Zeitschrift für deutsches Altertum

Verzeichnis der zitierten Handschriften / List of Manuscripts Cited

Angers, MS 14: 354n; 447: 221, 223
Baltimore, Walters 539: 132
Basel, F III 15a: 230
Brussels, Bibliothèque Royale
  2324—40: 87
Cambridge, Corpus Christi College MS
  279: 224
  St John's College MS 9: 350
Dublin, Chester Beatty Library 593: 132
  Royal Irish Academy D II. 3: 86, 128;
  67: 88, 293, 295n; 12 N 22: 107; 23 P
  16: 212
  Trinity College A 1.6: 137; A 4.5: 137;
  H 2.18: 86 ff., 295n; H 3.18: 344, 350;
  50: 352
Edinburgh, University Library MS 56:
  351
Florence, Biblioteca Laurenziana
  Amiatino I: 352
Karlsruhe, Cod. Augiensis 38: 352; 107:
  355; 132: 254n; 167: 254n; 195: 254n
Killiney, Co. Dublin, Franciscan Libra-
  ry 2 A: 61n16; A 1: 344
Laon, Bibliothèque de la Ville MS 261:
  360n
London, British Library, Additional
  MS 4793: 396n; 34124: 274, 277;
  36929: 350
  Cotton MS Galba A V: 350; Tiberius
  A XV: 344; Vespasian A I: 354n;
  Vitellius A XII: 65n37; F XI: 350
  Harley 5280: 304

Royal 5 E 13: 22
Milan, Biblioteca Ambrosiana inf. 301:
  214, 243; inf. C 5: 285
Monte Cassino, MS 57: 345
Montpellier, Faculté de Médicine 409:
  344
München, Staatsbiblithek Clm 14276:
  365n; 14387: 357; 14846: 224
Oxford, Bodleian Library, Bodl. 826:
  343; Laud misc. 610: 61n16; Rawlin-
  son B 458: 278; 502: 295n; 512: 272
Paris, Bibliothèque Nationale, MS Fr.
  2452: 352; MS lat. 4389: 220; 10290:
  221 ff.; 11561: 365n; 12021: 224;
  12273: 357; 13029: 224; 13159: 344 ff.
Rome, Biblioteca Apostolica Vaticana,
  Pal. Lat. 65: 350; 68: 282, 343 ff.; Reg.
  Lat. 11: 351; Vat. Lat. 10000: 390;
  12910: 350
Rouen, Bibliothèque Publique MS 24:
  344, 350
St. Gallen, Stiftsbibliothek 20: 352; 261:
  361n; 904: 213, 247; 908: 344; 911:
  229; 913: 231; 916: 247
Tours, MS 268: 319
Turin, Univ. Libr. MS F IV 1: 343
Vercelli, Codex LXII: 344
Wien, Nationalbibliothek lat. 997:
  366n; Med. Gr. 1: 326
Würzburg, Codex M. th. f. 12: 214
Zürich, Zentralbibliothek Rheinau 81:
  274 ff.

The manuscripted referred to by Brown are listed below according to their
numbers in CLA (cf. above, p. 311).

1, 1a	: 315		1, 69	: 323
1, 12	: 311, 317, 323		1, 78	: 325
1, 35	: 312		1, 87	: 314

1, 110	: 319	3, 394	: 314
1, 115	: 323	3, 397a	: 317, 323
1, 174	: 323	3, 397b	: 314
2, 147	: 313	3, 398	: 317
2, 149	: 327	3, 400	: 314
2, 157	: 326	3, 403	: 314
2, 159	: 326	4, 462	: 317, 319
2, 187	: 323	4, 465	: 324
2, 208	: 315	4, 488	: 319
2, 210	: 319	5, 573	: 315
2, 231	: 326	5, 578	: 323
2, 257	: 314	5, 584	: 314
2, 260	: 323	5, 588	: 314
2, 266	: 313	5, 635	: 319
2, 267	: 326	5, 654	: 318
2, 270	: 314	6, 737	: 319
2, 271	: 312	6, 838	: 313
2, 273	: 326	7, 998	: 320
2, 274	: 326	8, 1196	: 314
2, 275	: 326	8, 1198	: 326
2, 276	: 314	9, 1298	: 313
2, 277	: 326	9, 1324	: 326
3, 280	: 312, 317, 323	10, 472	: 312
3, 292	: 319	11, 1618	: 314
3, 295	: 315		
3, 296	: 312, 319	Suppl.:	
3, 304	: 317, 323	1684	: 312
3, 311	: 314	1705	: 317
3, 328	: 312	1740	: 318
3, 350	: 326	1776	: 319
3, 391	: 314, 315	1782	: 317

Verzeichnis irischer Glossen / List of Irish Glosses

Ml.

3a15	: 191
14d7	: 366
14d10	: 366
16a17	: 367
16b5	: 367
22d21	: 241
30c3	: 85n11
37a15	: 347, 354
38a3	: 369
38b4	: 369
38c5	: 369
44b1	: 371
44b4	: 371
44b6	: 371
55a1	: 214
55c1	: 214
56b39	: 214
68b9	: 214
74a8	: 214
111a9	: 277

Sg.

9a22	: 213

24b5	: 213
31a6	: 213
55b5	: 214
66a23	: 213
68a7	: 191
96b5	: 213
148b7	: 213

Wb.

1c2	: 215
4a27	: 215
5a5	: 193
5b11	: 215
12b28	: 215
12d37	: 193
12c41	: 215
13a22	: 193
13b19	: 215
13d7	: 215
14d17	: 215
16d8	: 215
19d24	: 215
24a17	: 216
26d9	: 363n

Verzeichnis der zitierten Rechtstexte / List of References to Legal Material

Corpus Iuris Hibernici (ed. *Binchy*)

I	1	: 167
	2	: 167
	3	: 167
	40	: 97
	47	: 172n
	64	: 170
	73	: 169
	220	: 172n, 173n
II	351	: 172n
	433	: 173n
	440	: 173n
	444	: 170
	447	: 170
	455	: 173n
	457	: 170
	460—1	: 170
	483	: 173n
	486	: 173n
	488	: 173n
	502—4	: 163
	503	: 172n
	507	: 162
	525	: 174n
	527—8	: 173n
	530	: 173n, 174n
	532	: 170
	532—4	: 167
	536	: 172n
	577	: 167
	588	: 165
	592	: 172n
	593	: 172n
	598	: 152

	634—55	: 157n
III	748	: 153
V	1566	: 153
	1590—1618	: 157n
	1819	: 174n
	1820	: 162
VI	1929	: 162
	2105	: 163
	2129—30	: 171n
	2143	: 153
	2255—7	: 157n
	2261—82	: 157n

Ancient Laws of Ireland

III	48	: 153
	52	: 154
	65—79	: 117

Collectio Canonum Hibernensis (ed. *Wasserschleben*)

XX, 2	: 67 n44
XX, 3	: 67 n43, n44
XX, 5	: 13, 58, 67 n45
XXXII, 14	: 154
XXXII, 20	: 160
XXXIII, 13	: 154
XLIII, 6	: 161
XLIV, 20	: 161—162, 428
XLIV, 30	: 97
XLIV, 31	: 97
XLVIII, 1	: 154
XLIX, 8	: 96 n43
XLIX, 11	: 89 n3a
LII, 3—4	: 285

Register / Index

Abba-Glossar 247

Abbán moccu Cormaic 95

Aberlemno slab 137

abgitir 206

Abrogans 229, 230, 231, 234, 237, 239, 241, 243, 245, 246, 247, 250, 254

Abrogansglossar 238

adaltrach 151, 154

Adelphus Adelpha Meter 205

adgládathar 214

adiecht 213

Admonitio generalis 241

Adomnán 33, 52, 55, 60, 74, 96, 97, 98, 108, 109, 112, 129, 131, 132, 144, 155, 167, 169, 199, 201, 202, 258—265, 287, 288, 320, 349, 412, 421

—, law of 152, 156

—, reliquary of 98

—, De locis sanctis 131, 287, 380, 412

—, see also *Cáin Adomnáin*, Canons of Adomnán, Schaffhausen Adomnán

Aed Dub 95

Aed of Sleaty/Aed of Sletty 64, 168

Ägypten 431

Aethelstan 91, 205, 219

Aethelwulf 207

Aethicus Ister 234

Africa 314, 321

Ahenny 127, 129—133

Ahenny cross 108

Aidan 81

Aidan, Bischof 429

aidbriud 165

Ailbe, law of 155

Ailbhe, St, rule of 77

Aillenn 13

airchinnech (cf. also *erenagh*) 167, 171, 172

aire désa 170

Airgialla 155

Airmed 304

Aislinge Oengusa 279

Alcuin 202, 351

Aldhelm 234, 283, 285, 344

Alexander III, pope 9, 283, 338, 362

Alexandria, school of exegesis of 340

Alither 108

Allen, battle of 297

Alphabet of Piety 84, 86, 88

Altaripa 331, 332

—, vgl. Venerandus v. A.

Altbairische Beichte 230

Ambrose 158, 342, 365

Ammianus Marcellinus 261

Amra Choluim[b] Chille 33, 211, 212

Amra Con Roí 210

Amra Senáin 212

anamchara 76

anchorite 80, 84

Anglo-Saxons / Angelsachsen 10, 12, 53, 64, 81, 119, 122, 125, 158, 429

anmchara 209

Anselm, archbishop of Canterbury 394

antae 122, 123, 124

Antioch 9, 265, 283, 339, 340, 342, 345, 346, 348, 362, 373, 381, 383

—, cf. Rufinus of A.

Antiochene exegesis 341, 344, 347, 354

Aodh Ó Beacháin' bishop of Inis Chathaigh 392

ap 171, 172

Apollinaris of Laodicea 342

Appendix Probi 275

Arbeo von Freising 238

Arculf 129, 131, 132, 144, 412

Ard Oileán 107, 109, 112

Ardagh 123, 431

Ardagh Chalice 135, 137, 138, 141, 143—145

Ardagh chalices 140
Ardagh hoard 136, 139
Ardmore 111, 112, 124
Ardstraw 118, 125
Argentocoxos 306
Arianism 79, 283
Armagh 13, 26, 59, 60, 64, 66, 68, 69, 70,
    71, 72, 74, 92, 93, 95, 99, 100, 101, 105,
    110, 117, 125, 155, 168, 413, 425, 428,
    429
—, Book of 25, 27, 28, 29, 58, 72, 93, 98,
    100, 137, 167, 169, 170, 314, 315, 320,
    321, 428
— — —, see also Liber Angeli
Armenia 131
Armenian 214
Armenian Gospel 132
Armenian hymnal 132
Armenian manuscripts 131
Arnobius 260, 261, 262, 263, 357
arreum 200
Ars Malsachani 206
Ars Sergilii 206
asceterium 340
asketerion 383, 384
Assicus, metalworker 142
astoídi 215
Athanasius 128, 341, 342
auctoritas 10
audacht 171
Augustine of Canterbury 348
Augustine St / Augustinus 83, 92, 158,
    233, 234, 242, 260—262, 287, 317, 342,
    354, 363, 370, 380
— —, Enarrationes in Psalmos 342, 355,
    360
Augustus 10
Auraicept na nÉces 199, 206
Auvergne, council of (535) 158
Auxerre, council of (585) 158
Auxilius 33

Baile In Scáil 299

Bairre 52
Bairre, St 99
Bairrfind 55
Banagher 122
banchomarbai 153
Bangor 125, 280
—, Antiphonary of 277, 285, 314, 323
barae 200
bard 200
bardicatio 200
bardigium 200
Bardsey island 15
Barrock 57
Basel 232
Basil, St 90, 143, 342, 354
basilica 92, 93, 94, 428
Basler Rezepte 230
Baslick 92, 428
—, cf. basilica
Becán mac Luigdech 33
Beccán 65
Beda 254, 427, 430
—, De orthographia 234
Bede 12, 65, 75, 78, 81, 91, 109, 203, 204,
    282, 283, 285, 357
—, see also Pseudo-Bede
Beichte, Altbairische 230
Beichten 242
bél 208
Benedict of Aniane 171
Benedict, St 22
— —, cf. Regula Sancti Benedicti
Benedikt, Hl 330
Benediktbeuern 231, 233, 235
Benediktinerregel 245, 247, 250
beneficia 91
Bérla na Filed 205
besu 206
Bethu Brigte 272
Bethu Phátraic 27, 28, 29, 30, 34, 37,
    38
Bibelwerk 344, 346, 354, 359, 361, 363,
    364, 365, 376, 382

Blathmhac 81
Bobbio 145, 311, 312, 313, 314, 317, 320,
    321, 323, 324, 333, 343
bocetum 169
Boethius 317
Boho 111
Bologna 9, 10, 14
Boniface, pope 15
Boniface, St / Bonifatius 236, 238, 314,
    320, 430
bordgal (cf. also *burdgal*) 212, 411
brandea 91
Brdadzor 132
Brehon Laws 210
Brendan 99
—, law of 155
Bretagne (vgl. auch Brittany) 410, 422
Bretha Comaithchesa 169
Bretha Déin Chécht 164, 165
Breton 21, 55, 204, 222
Breton, Old 224
Bretons 20, 219
Brian Bóraimhe 390, 399
Brian Boruma 100
bríathar 213
Brictius, bishop of Limerick 396
Brigid 13
Brigit, St 63, 94, 95, 98, 272, 424
— —, cf. also *Bethu Brigte*, Cogitosus
Britain 17, 30, 73
Britannien 411, 412, 413, 424, 427, 429
brithemin 416
British 19, 55
British Church 53
British language 311
Britons 18, 20, 219
Brittany 20, 21, 22, 23, 53, 54, 56, 218,
    223, 225, 316
Brittonic 55, 57, 222, 225
Brittonic Latin 223
Brón 94
bronn-arcat 165
bronn-ór 165

Bruscus 94
Brutus 262
Brythonic (cf. Brittonic) 204
buinne 215
Buithe 39
Burdgal 99
Burdigala 99, 212, 411
—, vgl. auch *bordgal*
Bußbuch (vgl. auch penitential) 421,
    426
Byzantine vessels 145

Cadmug Gospels 326
Cadog 56
Caesar 415, 416
Caesarius von Arles 330, 331
Caeticus 92
caillech 274
Caimín, see Psalter of C.
cáin 97
Cáin Adomnáin 61, 155
— —, see also Lex Innocentium
Cáin Domnaig 61
Cáin Lánamna 162, 163
Cáin Phátraic 61
Caincomhrac 84
caingeal 277
Cainnech 99
cainseal 277
Calmanus 281
calvus (cf. also Maol, Mael) 208
Cambrai Homily 290
cána 61, 155
—, see also *cáin*
Canon in Ebreica 22
canon law 9
Canones Hibernenses 164, 165, 220
Canons of Adomnán 378
Canterbury 392
Canu Aneirin 222
capalbia 200
Carmen ad Deum 242
Carnsore 123, 125

444

Carterius 383
cartularies 224
Cashel 87, 111, 112, 391, 400
—, Psalter of 87
—, synod of (1101) 398
Cassian, John 77
Cassiodorus 262, 317, 348, 354, 357, 360,
    363, 364, 380
—, Expositio Psalmorum 342
catacombs 90
Cath Almaine 297
Cath Maige Tuired 299, 301, 303, 304, 305
Cathach 313, 315, 318, 323, 349, 350, 351,
    352, 353, 355, 363, 380, 418, 431
Caucasus 133
celam 277
Ceallach 393
cearcal 277
céile 172, 173, 174
Céilí Dé, cf. Céli Dé 75
ceist 277
Celestine I, pope (cf. also Coelestin I.)
    16, 17, 19
Céli Dé 13, 35, 421, 430
Cell Fine 91
Cell tarsna 119
Cenfrith 205
Cenn Faelad 199
Ceolfrith 285
Cerne, Book of 78
césad 213
Charles the Bald 144
Chindaswind, laws of 158
Christian 393
Christianus Mac Carthaigh 402
Chrodegang of Metz 90
Chrysostom, see John C.
Church, British 23
Church Island 97, 123
Church, Roman, see Rome
Cianán, St 107, 118
Ciarán 208
Ciaran, law of 155

Cicero 260, 261, 262, 263, 264, 275, 311
cill 415
ciombal 277
cís 168
Cistercians 40, 112
Citeaux 391
Claudius Sacerdos 317
cloc, clocca 201, 202, 206, 256
clochán 106, 107, 130
Clonard 52, 53, 54, 56
Clonenagh 88
—, annals of 87
—, book of 87
Clones 111, 122
Clonfertmulloe 282
Clonmacnois 88, 98, 105, 107—112, 118,
    124, 169, 170, 209
Clonmore 98
Clontarf 101
cnet 161
Codex Amiatinus 352, 353, 363
Codex Usserianus Primus 312
— — —, see also Ussher Gospels
Coelestin I. (vgl. Celestine I, pope) 413
Cogitosus 94, 119, 264, 272, 276, 290,
    413, 420, 425
cóiced 209
Cóir Anmann 205
Coire Goriath 210
Coleraine 109, 112, 167
Collectio Canonum Hibernensis 4, 12,
    21, 23, 58, 67, 84, 154, 285, 288, 289,
    378, 426, 428
Colmán 95
Colmán mac Crimthain 99
colonus 174, 175
Colum Cille (Colum, Columba) 12, 33,
    36, 73, 74, 75, 81, 109, 119, 151, 211,
    420, 421, 425, 426, 432
— —, law of 155
— —, Psalter of, see Cathach
— —, see also Columba
Colum's House 120

445

Columba 169, 264, 313, 349, 350, 355
—, tunic of 96
Columban / Columbanus 14, 15, 20, 21, 28, 52, 53, 54, 64, 75,76, 77, 80, 199, 225, 258, 282, 285, 287, 312, 324, 326, 328, 330, 331, 332, 336, 338, 412, 421, 427, 432
Columbanus, rule of 23
comarba 425
Comgall of Bangor 151
Commentary on the Catholic Epistles 283, 284, 286, 287, 288
commotatio 96
comparit 213
comsuidigud 213
Conall, bishop 109, 112
Conchobhar Ó Briain 399, 401
Confessio (Patrick's) 17, 18, 19, 25, 69, 70, 71, 73, 77, 413, 420
Cong 395, 401
—, Cross of 111
Conlaed 97
Conlaeth, bishop 94
Connacht 413
Connachta 307
Connor 168
Constantine 128, 129, 130
Constantinople 10
—, Second Council of (553) 369, 370
Corbie 314
corgus 277
Cormac Mac Carthaigh, king of Desmond 111, 394, 396, 399, 401, 402, 403
Cormac's Chapel, Cashel 391, 401
Cormac mac Cuilleáin 87, 390, 400, 403
Cornish 222
Cornwall 21, 54, 56, 57, 75, 224
Coroticus 73, 413, 420
Corpus Iuris Civilis 4
Corpus Iuris Hibernici 4
Córus Béscna 153, 170, 173
Cothirbe 94
Coupar Angus Psalter 350

cretair 95
Críth Gablach 152
Crúachu 92
Cú Chulainn 296
cúairt 97
cucann 277
Cucuimne 84
Cudda 109
Cúil Dremne, battle of 349
cumal 153, 165
cumdach 313
Cummean 280, 282, 283, 287, 288, 289, 428, 430
Cumméne 93
Cummian 12, 65, 66, 68
Cunpald chalice 142
curucus 201
Cuthbert, St 109, 112
Cyprian 89, 287

Dagán 64
Dagobert I. 332
dair (cf. also *dairthech, daur*) 424
Daire Eidnech
Daire na bhFlann (cf. also Derrynavlan) 84
dairthech 118
Dál Cormaic 95
Dál nAraide 155
Dallán Forgaill 212
damliac (cf. also Duleek) 118, 425
Darinis 82, 84
daur 424
De duodecim abusivis saeculi 258, 288, 289
De Mirabilibus sacrae Scripturae 258, 282, 284, 285, 286, 290
Declan, St 98
Decretum 9, 10
Decretum Gelasianum 286
déorad Dé 167
derbfhine 159, 201
Derry 74, 119, 125, 424, 425

Derry near Portaferry 123
Derrynaflan 135
Derrynavlan 431
Deusdedit, archbishop 70
Deusdona 90
Devenish 125
Devon 122, 224
Dían Cécht 303, 304, 306, 307
Diarmait of Dísert Diarmata 84
Diarmuid Mac Carthaigh 396
Diarmuid Mór Mac Carthaigh 403
Diarmuid Ó Conaing, bishop of Killa-
    loe 397
Dimma Gospels 326
Din Techtugud 159
Diodorus 345, 346, 354, 370, 383, 384
Diodorus of Tarsus 340, 341
Dionysius Exiguus 280, 281, 283
Dionysius of Halicarnassus 264, 265
Díre 173
Dísert Diarmata 84
dobríathar 213
dochenél 174
Domhnall Glas Mac Carthaigh 397
Domhall Mór Ó Briain 400, 401
dominicum 414
—, vgl. auch domnach
domnach 25—31, 414
Domongart, St 98
Donat(us) 234, 423
Donatus, Bischof v. Besançon 330, 331
Donnán, St 99
Donnchadh Cairbreach Ó Briain 398
Donnchadh Mac Carthaigh 397, 402
Dorbbéne 320
Downpatrick 92, 413
Dromiskin 97
druíd 173, 174, 416
Druimmcete 109
Drumacoo 124
Drumcliff 111
Dublin 72, 87, 105
Duleek 118

Dún Sobairche 93
Dunfallandy 137
Durham A. II. 10 Gospel 313, 314, 315,
    321, 323, 326
Durrow 109, 122, 424, 425
—, Book of 137, 326
Duvillaun 105
Dysert O Dea 112

Earolbh, bishop of Limerick 392
Easter reckoning 12, 14, 60, 64, 65, 68,
    313
Easter controversy (see also Paschal
    controversy) 151, 283, 311
Ecgbert 428
Echternach 231, 232, 233, 235, 237, 314,
    320
Echternach glossary 205
Echternach Gospels 323
eclais 172
Eclogae tractatorum in Psalterium 344,
    363, 365, 371
Edessa 131, 384
Edinburgh Psalter 351, 352
Edsani 133
Egbert von York 430
Egypt 317
Eichstätt 232, 233, 391
Einsiedeln 231
Ekerö crozier 138
Ekkehardt IV. 240, 246, 249
Eligius chalice 142
Emain Macha 13, 413
Enda of Aran 98
England 72, 91, 92, 235, 236
English 70
Ennius 275
Epitome of Julian 345, 346, 348, 356,
    357, 358, 361, 363, 367, 371, 372, 373,
    374, 375, 378, 379, 381
Erc, St 111
erdam 119
Erembert von Freising 238

erenagh (cf. also *airchinnech*) 120, 167
Erfurt 391
Eriugena 2, 5, 203
érlam 95
Ermoldus Nigellus 22
Esnada Tige Buchet 299
Ethiopia 324
Eucherius of Lyons 360
euripus 203
Eusebius of Caesarea 71, 129, 340, 341,
    348
Eusebius of Vercelli 340, 342
Eusebius, Chronicle of 281
Eustasius v. Luxeuil 332
Exhortatio ad plebem christianam 242,
    245

familia 172
family law 153
Farne 109, 112
Fearghal 75
Fedelmid mac Lóiguiri 170
Félire 86
Félire Óengusso 13, 15, 98, 212
Felix 200
Fenian Cycle 298
Feradach (?Feradad) 281
Ferdacrich 84
ferta (cf. Na Ferta) 94
Fiacc of Sléibte 98
fiacha 156
Fiachra 75
Fiachrae 170
fiadu 152
fid 169
fili, filid 301, 302, 416, 421
Fínán Camm 98
Findbarr 52, 55
fine 153, 174
Fingal Ronain 298
Finglas 85, 87
Finnian of Clonard 52, 53, 57
Finnian of Moville 52

Finnian, penitential of 77
Finnio 57
fintiu 153
flaith gelfhine 159
Flann, son of Duibthuinne 84
Flann, son of Faircheallach 84
Flannán 391
Flavius Abinnaeus 315
Fleury-sur-Loire 219
fogrigedar 215
fogurred 161
Fomoiri 303
Fothad 86
Fothad, rule of 88
France 121
Francia 21
Franks 10, 155
Fredegar 234
Freising 231, 233, 236, 237, 238
frithorcuin 214
fuidir 172
Fulda 231, 232, 233, 234, 235, 236, 237,
    248, 311
Fursa 75

Gall 75
Gallien 411, 413, 414, 421, 424, 427, 431
Gaul 64, 90, 197, 314
Gauls 181, 182
Gauzelin chalice 142
Gelasius I, pope 10
———, see also Decretum Gelasianum
gelfhine 159, 161
genitiu 213
Georgia 131, 133, 134
Geraint 283
Germania 21
Germans 10
Germanus of / von Auxerre 91, 92, 413
Germany 90, 122
Gilbert, bishop of Limerick 399
Gildas 20, 23, 52, 201, 219, 259, 260, 262,
    285, 316, 418, 429

giolla 81
Giolla na Naomh Ó Muircheartaigh,
   bishop of Cloyne 392
Giolla Riabhach Ó Cléirigh 304
glandella 200
Glendalough 13, 15, 36, 99, 105, 111,
   112, 118, 119, 393
Glossen 422
goire 173
Gorgon, St 90
Gorman, martyrology of 118
Gospel books 219, 220
Gospels of Mac Regol 326
Gothic 214
Goths 19
Gourdon chalice 142
grammar books 220
Gratian 9, 10
Greek 198, 199, 205, 208, 279
Gregor der Große 234, 328, 329, 330,
   331, 333, 334, 336, 338, 424, 428,
   430
— — —, vgl. auch Gregory I., pope
Gregor von Tours, Gregory of Tours 90,
   275, 334
Gregory I, pope 10, 11, 14, 52, 64, 92,
   158, 282, 287, 289, 290, 360
— —, Cura pastoralis 313, 428
— —, Homilies on Ezechiel 286
— —, Moralia in Iob 287, 288
— —, Regula Pastoralis 288
— —, see also Gregor der Große
Gregory III, pope 21
Gregory of Tours, see Gregor von Tours
Gregory Ua hAodha, bishop of Cork
   395
Gregory VII, pope 9
Griffelglossen 227, 237
Grimfridus chalice 141

Hama 142
Handel 412
—, vgl. auch trade

heathenism 291
—, see also paganism
Hebrew 198, 199, 205, 208
Hegesippus 234
Heidenheim 232
Heinrichskelch 144
Helena poem 130
Heliand 248
Hereford Gospels 326
Herefrid 109, 112
hermit 119
hermitage 105, 106
Hermogenes 264, 265
Heroic Age 296, 297
Hexham vessel 141
Hibernenses 68, 428
Hiberno-Latin literature 5
Hieronymus 234
High Cross (see also Hochkreuz) 78, 80,
   108, 109, 111, 122
High Island 105
Hilary 341, 354, 360, 364, 365, 380
Hincmar of Laon 198, 199
Hincmar of Reims 198
Hisperica Famina 22, 119, 197, 198, 202,
   204, 205, 206, 207, 418
Historia Brittonum 299
—, see also *Lebor Bretnach*
Hochkreuz 431, 432
—, vgl. auch High Cross
Holycross 391
Honorius I., pope 280
Honorius, pope 65
Hrabanus Maurus 248
hypocoristic forms 19, 20, 55, 81

iaras 204
iarfine 159
iarmbrethemnas 165
Ide 81
Ignatius of Antioch 11
Illaunlogham 107
Imacallam in da Thúaraid 210

Inchcleraun 124
indoth 162, 163
inducbál 215
Ine, king 12
ingen 172
Ingomar 223
inindraig 165
Inishc(e)altra 105, 123
Inishmacsaint 124
Inishmore 119
Inishmurray 107—110
Inlongad bandtaig banchora 159
Innocent, I, pope 66, 281
Iona 12, 65, 66, 73, 74, 84, 93, 96, 109,
    110, 120, 131, 169, 170, 259, 263, 264,
    280, 323, 411, 412, 420, 425, 426, 428,
    429, 431
—, abbot of, cf. also Adomnán, Colum
    Cille, Dorbbéne, Ségéne
Iordanes 234
Irenaeus of Lyons 10
Isaac Ó Cormacáin, bishop of Killaloe
    394
Isaac Ó Cuanáin, bishop of Roscrea 394
Isidor von Sevilla / Isidore of Serville 4,
    158, 203, 221, 234, 235, 245, 250, 288,
    354, 360, 418, 428
— — —, Allegoriae 287
— — —, De ecclesiasticis officiis 281,
    287, 289
— — —, De fide catholica contra Juda-
    eos 242
— — —, De ortu et obitu Patrum 287,
    289
— — —, Differentiae 287
— — —, Etymologiae 287, 313
— — —, Quaestiones in Vetere Testa-
    mento 287
Isidor, ahd. 230
Isidore fragment 313, 314, 318, 320, 321,
    323, 325
— —, cf. also Pseudo-Isidore
Isle of Man 123

Ísucán 81, 212
Italians 181, 182
Italy 122, 314, 323
Iudicael, life of 223
Iveragh peninsula 105, 106

Jarrow 122
Jerome 14, 260, 261, 262, 281, 288, 317,
    339, 342, 345, 347, 348, 350, 351, 353,
    354, 357, 363, 364, 365, 366, 371, 380
—, Commentarioli 360, 367, 372
—, De Viris Illustribus 286
—, Tractatus sive Homiliae in Psalmos
    360
—, see also Pseudo-Jerome 360
Jerusalem 9, 76, 130, 131, 132, 145, 283
John Chrysostom 340, 341, 370, 383
John IV, pope 65, 283
John Scottus 2
John, St 90
Jonas von Bobbio 21, 330, 412
Julian of Eclanum 343, 359
— — —, see also Epitome of J.
Junilius Africanus 342, 344, 354, 361,
    370
Justin 355
Justinian, code of 319

Kachagani 133
Kartli 133
Keeill Woirrey 123
Kells 109, 110, 119, 120
—, Book of 78, 122, 128, 137, 140, 326
—, synod of (1152) 392, 393
Kent 64
Kevin, St 15, 36, 111
Khandisi 133
Kildare 72, 94, 95, 119, 168, 290, 413,
    424, 425, 429
Kilfenora 111, 122
Kilkieran 131
Killabuonia 106, 107, 111, 112
Killaloe 112, 392, 400

Killamery brooch 137, 138
Killevy 118
Kilranelagh 111
Kirkdale 122
Kirkdale Church 122
Kochel 231
Köln 231, 232, 233
Konstanz 232, 391

Labbamolaga 107
Lactantius 261, 262
Laidcend 287
Laidcenn 204
Laidcenn mac Ercaid 165
Laigin 297
lánamnas comthinchuir 162, 163
Landevennec 22
Laon 221
Laurence 91
Laurence, St 99
Laurentius 237
law, Roman 4, 10, 90, 157
law schools 211
Lawrence, archbishop 64
laws, Irish 4, 302
— —, see also *audacht, cáin, Bretha
    Comaithchesa, Bretha Déin
    Chécht, Córus Béscna, Críth
    Gablach, Din Techtugud,*
    law schools, lex, marriage,
    Senchas Már, Uraicecht Becc
Lebor Brecc (Leabhar Breac) 144, 212
Lebor Bretnach (Historia Brittonum) 299
Lebor na hUidre 88
Lebuinus 141
Lebuinus chalice 144
ledones 203
Leinster 92
—, Book of 86, 87, 88
lénae 169
léni 169
Leo I, pope 10, 15, 311, 335
Lérins 334

less 169
Lex Innocentium 155
Lex Patricii 61, 63, 64
Liber Angeli 13, 26, 39, 58, 60, 61, 62, 63,
    64, 66, 67, 68, 69, 70, 72, 93, 117, 414, 428
Liber Cuanach 63
Liber de Ordine Creaturarum 258, 283,
    284, 287, 288
Liber ex lege Moysi 22
Liber Hymnorum 350
Liber Pontificalis 71
Ligo 206
Limerick 99, 400
Lindisfarne 207, 323
Lindisfarne Gospels 323
Lios Mór, Book of 75
Lismore 82, 84, 282, 394, 401
literacy 302
Livy 262, 264, 265, 311
Llancarfan 56, 57, 181
Llandaff 23
locum tenens 162
Lóegaire 173, 174
Loher 105, 107
lorica 79, 204, 205, 422
Lorrha 124
Lorsch 231, 232, 233
Lough Ree 124
Louis the Pious 22
lubgort 169
Lucian 340
Luxeuil 236, 315, 326, 330, 332, 333, 336,
    338
—, vgl. auch Eustasius, Waldebert
Lyons 312

Mac Uige 84
macc 172
Madaba 131
Madaba map 131
Maedóc of Ferns 36
Mael (see also Maol) 208
Maelbrighde 208

Maelrúain 84, 87, 88, 432
Maeltuile of Dísert Maeltuile 84
mag 169
Mag Ailbe, synod of 68
Mag Léna, synod of 68, 280
Mag Line 168
Mag nEilni 168
Mag Réin 94
Mag Tuired 303
Maghnus Ua Domhnaill 73
maigen dígona 155
Maihinger Evangeliar 236, 237, 238
mainche 174
Mainz 231, 232, 233
Malachy 118
Malachy, St, archbishop of Armagh
    393, 396, 401
Malmesbury 205
Malsachanus 277
manach (pl. *manaig*) 167, 170, 171, 172,
    173, 174, 273
Manegold von Lautenbach 356
Maol, see also Mael
Maol 81
Maol Bhrighde 81
Maol Choluim 81
Maol Domhnaigh 81
Maol Ghiric 81
Maol Íosa 81
Maol Íosa Ó hAinmire, bishop of
    Waterford 394, 398, 401
Maol Íosa Ua Brolcháin 74
Maol Maodhóg Ó Morgair,
    see Malachy, St
Maol Mharthain 81
Maol Mhichíl 81
Maol Mhuire 81
Maol Phádraig 81
Maol Pheadair 81
Maol Phóil 81
Maol Ruain 75
Marcellinus 71
Marianus Scotus 394

Marienkult 432
—, vgl. auch Mary
marriage 4, 157
martar 60
Martin, St 98
martre 60
martyria 105
Martyrologien 421
martyrology 86, 88
—, see also *Félire*
Mary, St 98, 99, 317
Mauritius Ó Briain, bishop of Kilfenora
    395
Meath 99
mebuil 215
Mellifont 40, 112
Mellitus 91
Memmingen 391
Menevia 181
metropolitan position 72
metropolitan rank 70
metropolitan see 69
Metten 232
Míach 303, 304, 305, 306
mind 100
Mo-Chuaróc moccu Neth Semon 280
Mocháemóg, St 99
Mochaoi 118
Mochóe, St 99
Mocholmóc Ua Liatháin 84
Mochonna 74
Mochua 118
Mochuda, St 99
Mochulleus 391
móin 169
Molaise, St 107
— —, house of 125
Molua, St 76, 81
Molua's island 98
monach (see also *manach*) 273
Monasterboice 39, 105, 112, 122, 127,
    128, 129, 425
monastic schools 220

Monenna, St 118
Monseer Fragmente 245, 248, 250, 251, 254
Monte Cassino 231, 330, 333, 343
Montpellier, see Psalter of M.
Montreuil-sur-Mer 219
moralus 364
Moville 52, 56
Mtskheta 131, 133
mug 172, 174
muinter, muintir 80, 172, 425
Muircheartach Mór Ó Briain 398
Muircheartach Ó Briain 394, 402
Muirchú 63, 71, 92, 200, 201, 264, 420
Muireadhach Ó Dubhthaigh 399, 401
Muireadhach Ó Dubhthaigh, archbishop of Tuam 395
Muiredach, Cross of 127, 128
Mulling, Book of 314, 315, 320, 321, 326
Munnu, St 68
Munster 390, 413
Murbach 232
Murbacher Hymnen 245, 247, 250, 253
Murchadh 399

Na Ferta 110
Nabor, St 90
naidm 161
Nazarius, St 90
Nechtan 285
Nemed 165
Nendrum 105, 118, 120, 123
neumatic notation 219
Niederaltaich 232
Nino, St 133, 134
Nisibis 344
Normannen 233
Norse 90
Northumbria / Northumbrien 110, 122, 125, 128, 235, 236, 283, 285, 311, 313, 314, 315, 320, 358, 379, 430, 431
notae juris 318, 319, 320
Notker 243, 253

Notker der Deutsche 240, 244, 249
— — —, Psalter von 242
Notker von St. Gallen 245
Notkers Psalter 240, 246, 249, 250, 256
Novatianism 283
Núada (Airgetlam) 303, 305

oath helpers 153
Óengus 74, 81, 95, 98, 99
Óengus Céle Dé 36
ogham 153, 413, 417, 421
Olcanus 93
Old Irish Treatise on the Psalter 350, 354, 361, 363, 364, 365, 376, 377, 382
Onchú 98
oral tradition / orale Kultur 4, 165, 294—296, 302, 305, 307, 410
orgid 206
orgo 206
Origen 339, 340, 341, 348, 351, 355, 376
Orleans, council of (538) 158
Osterfestberechnung 427, 431
—, vgl. auch Paschal/Easter controversy
Oswald, König von Northumbrien 429
Oswiu, king 70
Oswy 12
Otfrid von Weissenburg 241, 242, 244, 249, 250, 252, 253
othrus 165

pagan survivals 38, 81, 89, 95, 292, 299, 301
Palestine 339, 342
Palladius 16, 17, 18, 19, 27, 30, 33, 37, 71, 72, 91, 181, 182, 413, 414
palliola 91
Pancras 91
Pantiani 133
Papil cross-slab 137
papyrus 324, 325, 326
Paris 10

paruchia 62, 68, 72, 76, 93, 168, 169, 170, 193, 207, 425

Paschal controversy 15, 66, 68, 70, 280, 281, 285, 377, 381

— —, see also Easter controversy

Passau 232

Paterius, Liber testimoniorum Veteris Testamenti 360

Paternus 158

Patrician material 167

Patrick, St 9, 13, 14, 16—19, 26, 27, 31, 34, 37, 57—59, 61, 63, 67—73, 75—79, 91—96, 98, 99, 118, 122, 142, 155, 173, 181, 182, 183, 188, 220, 316, 413—416, 418, 420, 428, 432

— —, Cross of 110

— —, law of 155

— —, Rule of 117

— —, synod of 280

— —, works of, see Confessio, Coroticus

— —, see also Bethu Phátraic, Cáin Phátraic, Lex Patricii

Paul I, pope 90

Paul, St 11, 15, 60, 78, 89, 90, 91, 92, 96, 99, 216

Paul the Persian 344

peace of God 100

Pelagianism 16, 18, 65, 283, 284

Pelagius 16, 23, 24, 92, 215, 284, 413

penitentials 20, 22, 52, 53, 54, 56, 198, 199

penitential, Bigotian 200

— —, cf. also Bussbuch

Peregrinus 236, 238

Periphysion 5

Perrona Scottorum 3

Peter, St 11, 12, 13, 15, 60, 76, 89, 91, 92, 96, 99

Peter the Lombard 10, 14

Physiologus 245, 250, 253

Pictish slabs 137

Picts 81, 201

pignora 91

Pikten 429

pilgrims 11, 12, 15, 75, 91, 112

platea 109

plateola 109, 112

Plautus 275, 279

polygamy 154

Pompeius Messalinus 265

prayer 77, 78

primacy, papal 68

prímchell na túaithe 167

Priscian 213, 216, 217, 234, 423

Probus 317

Prosa 410

Prosper of Aquitaine 16, 17, 19, 71

Psalter 85, 214, 216

Psalter of Caimín 344, 350, 361, 363

Psalter of Charlemagne 346, 369, 371, 372, 373, 374, 375, 377, 378, 379, 381

Psalter of Cormac 350

Psalter of Montpellier 343, 344, 345, 361, 371, 375, 379

Psalter of Ricemarch 352

Psalter of Rouen 344, 346, 350, 369, 371, 372, 377

Psalter of Vercelli 343, 344, 345, 361, 371, 375

Pseudo-Bede, De Titulis Psalmorum 343, 346, 353, 355, 356, 357, 358, 359, 360, 362, 363, 367, 369, 371, 372

Pseudo-Isidore, see Liber de Ordine Creaturarum

Pseudo-Jerome, Commentary on St Mark's Gospel 289, 290

Pseudo-Longinus 264, 265

Quartodecimans 65, 289, 290

Quintilian 263, 275

Quodvultdeus 261, 262

Ragyndrudis-Codex 236, 237

Rahan 282

rangabál 213

Raphoe 155

ráth (legal) 161
ráth 201
Ráth Breasail, synod of (1111) 394, 399
Ravenna 129, 143, 315
Reask 97, 107, 109, 123
Recht, irisches (vgl. laws, Irish) 423, 426
rechtaire 170
Regensburg 231, 233, 235, 391, 394, 397, 398, 399
Reginald, bishop of Cork 395
Regula Magistri 312
Regula Sancti Benedicti 242, 289, 328—337
Reichenau 231, 232, 233, 237, 254,
Reichenauer Glossar 229
reilic 94
reilig 13
relic 94
relics (cf. reilig, *relic*) 59, 60, 63, 64, 69, 70, 72, 219
reliquary 122
Reliquien (vgl. auch relics) 420, 429
Remigius of Auxerre 343, 346
rí 80
Ríagail Phátraic 171
Roland Bandinelli 9
Rom (vgl. auch Rome) 413, 424, 432
Romani 13, 14, 68, 158, 280, 281, 282, 283, 284, 285, 286, 287, 288, 290, 377, 378, 379, 381, 382, 428
—, works by, see Commentary on the Catholic Epistles, De Mirabilibus Sacrae Scripturae, Liber de Ordine Creaturarum, Pseudo-Bede
Romanus, I, emperor 143
Romanus, II, emperor 143
Rome 9—15, 59, 71, 76, 80, 90, 93, 99, 284
—, cf. law, Roman; *rómh, rúam*
rómh (see also *rúam*) 76
Romulus 11
Rónán, son of Berach 97
roscada 295

Roscrea 112
Roscrea brooches 138
Rosscarbery 393
Rouen, Psalter of 343, 361, 372
Roumania 19
Round Tower 108, 110, 111, 125
Ruaidhrí Ó Conchobhair 403
Ruaidhrí, abbot of Killaloe 392
rúam 13, 14, 15, 99, 420
Ruben 84
Rubisca 205
Rufinus 354
Rufinus of Antioch 265
Rupert Cross 129
Rusafa 143

Sachellus 92
Saint Gildas-en-Berry 219
Sallust 262, 263, 264, 265
Salzburg 129, 231, 232, 233
Samson, St 53, 56, 57
Samthann 118
Samthann of Clonbroney 84
sanctuaria 91
Sanskrit 279
Santa Pudenziana 131
Saul 119
scamán 205
scamna 206
scamnae 205
Sceilg Mhichíl 106, 107, 112
Scéla Cano Meic Gartnáin 300
Scéla Mucce Meic Dathó 307
Schaffhausen Adomnán 323
schools, monastic 4
schools, lay 295
Schottenkloster 390, 391, 393, 394, 396
Scotland / Schottland 28, 33, 56, 74, 118, 123, 127, 135, 429, 135
Scotti 16, 17, 18
Secundinus 277
—, hymn of 285
Sedulius, Carmen Paschale 281

Ségéne, abbot of Iona 65, 66, 93, 280, 281, 283, 289
selam 277
selb 169
Senach, St 98
Senchas Már 153, 172, 421
senior (cf. also *senóir*) 159, 274
Senior mac Maoil Dalua, archbishop of Armagh 393
senóir 274
séns 364
senscríbenn deoda 153
Sergius 207
Severinus, pope 65, 66
síans 364
síens 364
Sigibert III. 332
Silos 141
Simon Magus 285
Sinlan, abbot of Bangor 280
siombail 277
siorcal 277
Slane 111
Sléibte 98
Sletty 168
slíab 169
Snedgus 87
Socrates 340, 383
Solnhofen 232
Solomon's Temple 98, 128
soscéle 251, 254
soulscot 153
Sozomen 340, 383
Spain 101, 287, 323
Spanien 411, 421
Speyer 232
spirut 215
Springmount Bog tablets 312, 314, 315, 316, 320, 321, 350
St Germain finials 138
St John's Point 123
St Kew 56, 57
St Nicholas, Exeter 395

St Thomas, Dublin 395
St. Gallen 22, 231—234, 254
St. Galler Glossar 244
St. Galler Glossator 246
Statius 200
Steeple Bumpstead boss 137
Stephen, St 99
stoir 364
Stonyhurst Gospel of St John 323
Stowe Missal 86, 128
Straßburg 232
Suibhne Geilt 80
Sulpicius Severus 265
surety 152
Symmachus 260—263, 317

Tablettes Albertini 321
Tacitus 200, 263
Táin Bó Cúailnge 294, 296, 305, 307
Tallaght 84—88
—, Rule of 119
Tara 173
Tara Brooch 135, 137, 138
Tassilo Chalice 141, 142
Tatian 241—245, 248, 250, 251, 253, 254
tech 36 ff., 424
Tegernsee 231, 233
teist 152
Terence 311
Terentianus Maurus 265
Terenz 234
terminus 68, 155
termonn 155
Terryglass 84, 88, 124
tertia Deo 153
testis 151, 152
Theodora, empress 143
Theodore, archbishop 70, 72
Theodore, pope 90
Theodore of Mopsuestia 266, 340—346, 348, 354, 356, 358—360, 366, 368—371, 373, 377, 381, 383, 384

Theodore of Mopsuestia, exegesis of
344—347, 361, 362, 372
Theodoret of Cyr 341, 370, 383
Theodosius 158
—, code of 319
Three Chapters' controversy 14, 283
Thucydides 264
tigernus 201
Tighernán, St 98
tinfeth 213
Tírechán 25, 26, 28, 30, 33, 34, 37, 39, 61,
62, 63, 68, 71, 72, 92, 93, 94, 95, 118,
168, 421
Toirrdelbach Ua Conchobair 101
tólae 203
Toledo, XI Council of (675) 287
tollus 202, 203, 204
tolo (Brythonic) 203
Tomméne 64, 66, 92
tona 205, 206
tonsure 285, 286
Tours, council of (567) 158
trade (cf. also Handel) 17, 21, 90, 99,
138, 225, 412
Trevet 119
Trewhiddle vessel 141
Trier 233, 312
Trierer Kapitulare 245
Tristan 300
Tuam 102, 112
túath 80
Tuatha Dé Danann 303
Tullaherin 124

Ua Suanaigh, law of 155
Uí Bairrche 168
Uí Choelbad 168
Uí Dúnlainge 95, 168
Uí Néill 297, 426
Uinniau 20
—, penitential of 22
Ulaid 155, 307, 413
Ulster Cycle 296, 300, 306

Ungarn 233
Uraicecht Becc 157
urbs 70
Ursus chalice 142
Ussher Gospels 315, 320, 321, 323, 325
Ussher, James 9

vallum 110
Venerandus von Altaripa 331
Versform 410
Victorius of Aquitaine 282, 283, 311
— — —, Cursus Paschalis 290
Victricius of Rouen 66
Vigilius, pope 369, 370
Vikings 82, 87, 111, 118, 135, 138, 139,
219
Virgil 220, 276, 311
Virgil, St 129
Virgil von Salzburg 234, 238, 239
Virgilius Maro Grammaticus 198, 199,
206, 207
Visigoths 94, 101, 155
Visio Tnugdali 390, 393, 397, 399, 401
Vita Mariani 391
Vitalian, pope 70, 91
Vocabularius Sti. Galli 229, 231, 234,
237

Walahfrid Strabo 75
Waldebert von Luxueil 332
Wales 55, 122, 123, 223, 224
Wales, south 53, 56, 57, 122, 181
Waliser 429
Walisisch 422
Waterford 99
Weissenburg 232
Weissenburger Katechismus 245
Welsh 55, 222
Welsh, Old, computus 222
Wessex 12
Wessobrunner Glauben 245
Wessobrunner Schöpfungsgedicht 230
Wharram Percy 123

Whitby 12, 70, 430
White Island Church 123
Wien 391
Wigheard 70
Wikinger (vgl. Vikings) 431
Wilfrid 283
William the Conqueror 219
Willibald 202
Willibrord 236, 237
Willibrords Calendarium 237

Williram von Ebersberg 240, 242
Winnavius 57
Winniau 53, 54
Winwaloe, St 22, 225
Worms 232
Würzburg 215, 231, 232, 233, 235, 237,
   311, 390, 391, 393
Wulfila 253
Wynnebald 202